PETERBOROUGH UNITED FOOTBALL CLUB

The Official History of:

The Posh

By: Andy Groom & Mick Robinson

Published by:

YORE PUBLICATIONS

12 The Furrows,
Harefield, Middx.
UB9 6AT.

Printed by:
THE BATH PRESS

ISBN 1 874427 15 1

Published by:
Yore Publications
12 The Furrows, Harefield,
Middx. UB9 6AT.

© Andy Groom 1992

....

British Library Cataloguing-in-Publication Data.
A catalogue record for this book
is available from the British Library.

ISBN 1 874427 15 1

'YORE PUBLICATIONS' specialise in Football Books, generally of an
Historic theme relating to both League and non-League Football.

Current titles include Club histories (*Cardiff City and Southend United*), histories
of the ex-Football League Clubs (*Rejected F.C. Vols. 1 & 2*), histories of defunct
non-League Clubs (*More Defunct F.C. and Gone But Not Forgotten*), 'Who's
Who' books (*Newport County and Brentford*), plus such titles as *Football League
Grounds For A Change* (Histories of former Grounds) and *Through The Turnstiles*
(history of Football related to attendances, including extensive statistical section).

Please send a S.A.E. to the above address for full details of these
and other books (plus Football Videos).

Free Newsletters are circulated three times per year.

Acknowledgements:

There have been very little Bibliographical works relating directly to the Club, but reference has been made to the two booklets; *" Never So Posh "* (1960), and *"Posh –The success story of Peterborough United Football Club"* (1974) – both works written by Paul Mowforth. In addition the Supporters Club Handbooks and Football League application brochures have been utilised.

Particular thanks are given to:

The Peterborough Evening Telegraph (with special thanks to Bob French), and *The Peterborough Herald and Post* (with special thanks to Nick Crockford). And for their permission to reproduce the majority of the photographs contained within the book. Note: In a number of cases original photographs were unobtainable, and in order to include these items it was necessary to reproduce them from newspaper cuttings, therefore the quality of reproduction is not up to the high standard of the originals.

The cartoon reproductions were taken from:
The Northamptonshire Evening Telegraph, *'The Pink 'Un'*,
and the *The Daily Express*.

The Authors would also like to thank the following for their help in the research, and for the provision of other illustrative items used in the book:

Pat Groom, Francis Devine, Mark Papworth, Richard Hastings,
Pat Wildman, Chris Lowndes, Viv Tabner, and Louis Burgess.
Plus the facilities provided by, and the staff of:
Peterborough Library, and Peterborough United Football Club.

FOREWORD

It is most unusual, in fact it may even be unique, for the publisher of a book to also write the foreword! However, the Authors felt that I was a suitable contributor, and, as many readers will know, I am more than just a football book publisher, as I am also – most importantly – a football supporter first and foremost.

Often a supporter of the 'underdog' I watched the progress of 'The Posh' from the late 1950's with great interest, and was very pleased when they were deservedly elected into the Football League. However, my first personal experience of the Club was on the 30th of September 1961, when – together with my girlfriend (later wife) Fay – we drove to Peterborough on my Vespa scooter, to see our own team – Brentford – play. Since the Bees lost by 6–0 (and incidentally became the last Brentford match that Fay watched for over 20 years!), the result could have put me off the Posh for life.

Apart from another visit in December 1988 (this time a more respectable scoreless draw in the F.A.Cup), the next trip to London Road was to become a momentous one. The date of course was the 2nd of May 1992. Brentford won the game and became the 3rd Division Champions, and despite their defeat, Peterborough qualified for a play–off place. The mutual scenes of congratulations from both sets of supporters helped to restore the balance with football violence that has become more newsworthy in recent years – although notably there were no mentions of this camaraderie in the Daily Newspapers! Nine days later I saw Posh struggle to obtain a draw with Huddersfield in the first leg of the play–off semi–final, and honestly thought that it would be Huddersfield that would go on to the final. But victory at Leeds Road silenced the critics, and on the 24th of May, Peterborough United made their first Wembley appearance – together with most of you readers no doubt – and myself.

A neutral observer can appreciate a football match, although there is no doubt that to have a personal interest in one of the teams can add to the enjoyment. Sitting in that vast Stadium with the Posh supporters I found myself, in spirit, being drawn in amongst you. I was pleased when Charlery scored his first goal, was distressed when Stockport scored a late equaliser, and leapt to my feet and cheered with the best of them when the 'fairytale' last gasp winner went in. Brentford are my team, and it was unthinkable that I should become so enthusiastic for any other team. But I did, and so I suppose I have to admit that I am now another Posh man – except of course when the Bees are in opposition!

Dave Twydell
(Yore Publications)

- CONTENTS -

Introduction

The history of Peterborough United starts in 1934, and has happily carried on to the present day despite a few occasions when it did not look as though it would! Peterborough United have a proud history that has for some reason been rarely chronicled over the past 58 years, and in writing this book we have tried to capture the highs and lows during that period.

The main aim, at the outset, of this book was to try and produce a more complete, more accurate, history of the 'Posh' than ever before. Every effort has been made in trying to ensure the accuracy of information contained herein, but in order to improve the quality of the history of the Club, any errors or serious omissions will be gratefully accepted, via the Publisher.

Finally the research and background for the book has been gathered over a number of years. At the outset we have talked to numerous Posh supporters for background information and details.

One person provided more information than any other as we tried to assemble the contents for the book – Dr. John 'Rupert' Smith. Just weeks after Peterborough United's greatest triumph, at Wembley, 'Rupert' died in Hospital in Sheffield. One of his greatest wishes was to see a detailed written history of Peterborough United F.C., and due to his assistance it appears here. His untimely death meant that his unique knowledge of the Club could not be tapped during the final months of preparation for the book.

'Peterborough United F.C. – The Official History of The Posh'

is dedicated to the memory of

John 'Rupert' Smith

Andy Groom, Mick Robinson.

## CHAPTER 1

A NEW UNITED EMERGE

'THE POSH'

Peterborough United's history started in 1934, one legacy of previous Peterborough football sides appears to be the now universally used nickname –'The Posh'. Over the years many attempts have been made to establish the origins of the nickname, and during the course of research for this book, the earliest recorded mention of the Posh has been located.

Back in the 1920/21 season, Mr. Pat Tirrel was player/manager of Fletton United – who also played at the Council owned London Road Ground – and up to this time were nicknamed 'The Brickies'. It was a poor season, and at its conclusion, Mr.Tirrel set about rebuilding the Fletton side to try to win the Northamptonshire (later United Counties) League. During the close season Mr.Tirrel was attributed with the quote that he was looking for *'Posh players for a Posh new team'*.

Despite detailed searches of the local newspapers of that time, the actual phrase does not appear to have appeared in print. However, by the time of Fletton United's first match – at Wellingborough on the 27th of August 1921 – this new nickname appeared in Press reports. On the 21st of September the 'Posh' tag was used again, together with the more familiar 'Brickies' name, in reporting the match versus Kettering: *'.... another large crowd assembled on the Rockingham Road enclosure to see another great display. They saw one, but it wasn't exactly to their liking, for the 'Posh' boys were responsible for it'* (Peterborough Standard).

Curiously, further investigation has revealed that Fletton's followers were not entirely happy with the 'Posh' references, which they felt were being used in a derogatory manner:
(Peterborough Standard 22nd October 1921 – 'Fletton Flashes') *'I notice down Kettering way the Scribes are very anxious not to let anyone forget that Fletton United were nicknamed by some nefarious dealer in slang the 'Posh' team. References to Fletton as such appear on every page of one production in various notes and comments. The term would probably have died 'ere now but for the envious record the club has enjoyed this year, and the victors can afford to let others do the shouting.'*

Further research has uncovered additional references to Fletton as 'Posh', and after this club's demise, and subsequent resurfacing as 'Peterborough and Fletton United', in 1923, the by now famous nickname had stuck, and was used by the new club. It seems that after this club folded in 1932, the 'Posh' nickname was resurrected once again, and was used for the new 'Peterborough United', and so it has up to the present day.

First known references to 'The Posh' in print.

(Left) Cartoon regarding Fletton United v. Higham.
(2nd March 1923)
(Below) Report of Fletton United v. Wellingborough.
(2nd September 1921)

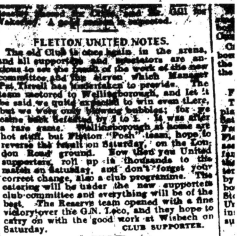

PETERBOROUGH UNITED FOOTBALL CLUB

At a meeting in the Angel Hotel, Peterborough, on May 17th 1934, a group of men gathered. They had decided that it was time for Peterborough to have a new Football Club to replace the now defunct Peterborough & Fletton United Football Club, which, finding itself in financial difficulties, had folded in 1932.

The original proposition for a new Club was made by Mr. A.S.Nicholls, and was seconded by Mr.A.Prior. Messrs. Swain, George, Sharpe, Warrington, Chapman, Cooper, Kelly and Porter were elected to arrange the details of forming a new Company. Mr.George was elected as the Secretary and Mr.Poulter was his assistant. A new name for the Club was decided by Mr.J.W.Cooper, who suggested the name *Peterborough United*. At that very first meeting in 1934, Jack Swain (who had been elected to try and form the new Company), was recorded as saying:

"I think that with the revival of the old enthusiasm in the City, Peterborough will ultimately find a place in the Football League."

The first problem the new Committee encountered was the liabilities of the previous Club, Peterborough & Fletton United, who had outstanding debts of £248.1.11d. Both the Northants. F.A. and the F.A. in London were consulted, and by the end of the month the news had arrived from the F.A. that there were: *"No Liabilities to anyone – Splendid reception – Advise carry on."*

Peterborough United were to hire the ground at London Road, which was owned by the City Council. On June 9th 1934, Peterborough United were elected to the Midland League. As a new Club Peterborough United had no financial backing and when they were required to pay sums of £20 security, £10.10.0d. entry fee, and £5.5.0d subscription, Grantham F.C. had to lend the Club the money! Meanwhile the new officials of the Club appealed to supporters in Peterborough to raise the necessary financial support for the Club.

Mr. W. 'Jock' Porter, the former Peterborough and Fletton United player, was appointed as the first trainer and groundsman for the new Club. The first player to be signed was goalkeeper John Kendall from Sheffield United, followed by another former Peterborough & Fletton United player – Harry Willis. Others signed were; M. Purcell from Exeter, W.Harris of Halifax, J.Staniland (Scunthorpe), Len Hargreaves who came from Luton, W. Rigby of Rochdale, J Cowen an Aldershot player, G.Camidge from Gainsborough and J.Doyle – who was previously with Middlesbrough.

The Club issued 5/0d. (25p) shares and about 150 people turned up for the first shareholders meeting on the 31st July 1934, where they elected the following Directors; Messrs. Swain, Cooper, George, Poulter, Warrington, Sharpe, Chapman, Dillingham, Neaverson and Fisher.

The registered capital of the Company was £1,000 (4,000 25p shares). A Directors' qualification was five shares each. The admission charges to watch Peterborough at London Road were fixed at one shilling (5p), 2½p for women and the unemployed, and 5p extra to the stand. The Club had 11 full time professionals signed on and a weekly wage bill of around £38.0.0d. Mr.A.J.Dillingham was appointed as the Club's first Chairman, and Mr. Poulter became the permanent paid Secretary, a position which required him to resign from the Board. As the start of the season neared, several amateurs were taken on by the Club: F.Briggs from Nassington, A.Keech and J.Taylor (Walton Amateurs), F Towers (Municipal Sports), C.Hart (Co-op Butchers), A.Mason (Deeping Amateurs), J.Reed (Central Sugar Sports), V.Vernon and L.Rippon (Eastern Counties Bus Co.), J.Youles (Wisbech), and P.Smith (Farcet).

The Club were presented with several gifts at the start of the new season including their new playing strip which consisted of a green shirt with lace up collar and a white 'V' and white cuffs, plus white shorts. These were given by Mr.E.Jackson of Midgate. A new ball was presented to the Club by Mr.G.Stokes of Church Street, and a set of towels were presented by Messrs. Hoyles of Westgate.

On September 1st 1934 Peterborough United played their first competitive game in the Midland League, at London Road, against Gainsborough Trinity. Peterborough won 4-0 in front of an attendance of 4,035. The line up for this inaugural match consisted of:

Jackson (in goal), Harris, Purcell, Staniland, Doyle, Hargreaves, Rigby, Cowen, Thompson, Camidge and Roberts.

The first goal for Peterborough United was scored by Hargreaves, the others coming from Rigby, Thompson and Roberts.

Two days later Peterborough drew 0-0 in their first away game, at Scunthorpe & Lindsey, in front of 2,000 people, Goodacre coming into the side for this match. Kendall, the trainer, took over in goal from Jackson for most of the remainder of the season. After a 2-2 draw away with Chesterfield Reserves, they lost their first game in the Midland League, by 4-3 at Bradford Park Avenue Reserves. Thompson and Hargreaves (2) were the scorers.

The first statutory meeting of the Club took place in November. The Club was reported to be in a good financial position and Mr Cooper said that the time was ripe for the Club to think about trying to gain admission to the Football League!

The last game of 1934 was at home to Grantham Town on Boxing Day, and the biggest crowd at London Road for a Midland League match of 4,340, watched Posh win 3–1 with goals from Rigby, Roberts and Willis. It was the start of a good run for Posh as they entered 1935, since they went on unbeaten for seven league games. They were also playing many friendly games at the time against reserve teams, of the likes of Chelsea, Norwich and Crystal Palace. The fans complained that they were playing too many friendlies and by March, the attendances were dwindling to around the 1,500 mark.

The only other incident of note took place at the match at London Road against Lincoln City Reserves on 6th April 1935. Rigby became the first Posh player to be sent off – much to the displeasure of the crowd of 1,777 – and police reinforcements were called to the game.

When the match finished the referee had to be smuggled from the ground in the car of Manager 'Jock' Porter with a plain clothes policeman on the running board!

At the end of the season the Club held their first A.G.M., and despite finishing 10th in the final table, much to the displeasure of the shareholders a loss on the season of £510.12.6d. was shown.

After the season had finished, an attempt was made by Mr.Reg Tee to start a Supporters' Club, but it had to disband because the parent Club refused to allow the use of a dressing room one night a week for Committee meetings.

During the first season, the Supporters raised £60 in six months and bought some new kit for the Club.

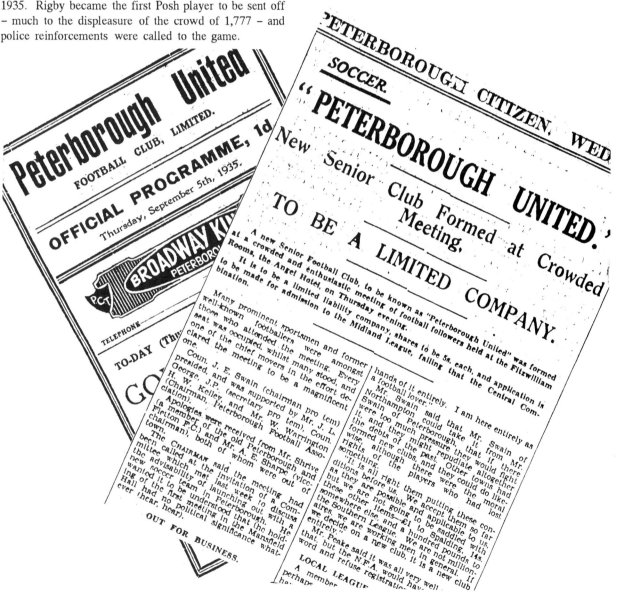

The earliest known Posh programme
..... And how it all started

## CHAPTER 2

PRE-WAR STRUGGLES

1935/36 SEASON

Four new players were signed and made their debut in the first Midland League match of the season, namely: Jefferson, Mitchell, Warren and Collins. Collins scoring in his first match along with Barraclough in a 2–1 victory away at Scarborough. It was not to be a good season however, and Posh started to suffer some heavy defeats, losing 7–0 away to Chesterfield Reserves, 5–0 at Bradford Park Avenue Reserves and 7–0 at Gainsborough Trinity – all before the end of October.

They also made their first appearance in the F.A. Cup on October 5th at home against Rushden, when a crowd of 4,254 saw the Russians run out as 3–0 winners. Attendances started to slump, and on the 7th November a crowd of just 876 came to watch Posh beat Hull City Reserves 4–1. Shortly before Christmas, Club Chairman Jack Swain had to publicly deny rumours that the Club was to close down because of financial difficulties.

Just three wins in the 12 Midland League matches leading up to the end of 1935, saw the club lying 7th from bottom of the table. A special meeting of the shareholders was called – particularly to discuss the serious financial position of the Club – where it was reported that the Club's weekly expenses were running at £78. At the meeting, Mr Dillingham and Mr Gollings resigned from the Board of Directors.

For the league match at Denaby, in order to save the Club the expense, Messrs. Canham, Tee and Porter took the players by car, and some of the financial burden was relieved with the transfer of Jefferson to Queens Park Rangers for £50.0.0d. At Easter, less than two years since the Club was formed, Manager 'Jock' Porter resigned, alleging that he had never been given a free hand in running the Club.

Posh finally finished the season 16th (of 21 clubs) in the league, although some measure of revenge for the early F.A. Cup exit against Rushden was gained when they beat them in the Maunsell Cup final, to win their very first silverware. The victory did not impress the shareholders, however, and a campaign waged in the local press called for the resignation of the Board. At the A.G.M., five new Directors were elected to the Board and five left, including Tommy Peake who was to go on and make a valuable contribution to the Club in other areas. For the second year running the Club made a loss, this time totalling £253.7.11d. Fred Taylor was appointed as the new Manager stepping up from his role as player/coach.

1936/37 SEASON

Posh started the season by beating Scarborough at Seamer Road 1–0 before a crowd of 3,361, with a goal from Chiverton, who was one of eight new players in the side in Taylor's reshaped side. But it was to be another infuriatingly inconsistent season with heavy defeats again, including, Notts County Reserves by 6–3 at home, and at the grounds of Lincoln City Reserves (5–0), and Nottingham Forest Reserves 7–0. However, there were also some notable victories, for Mansfield Town Reserves were beaten 7–0 and Doncaster Rover Reserves by a 5–0 scoreline.

The attendances at least started brightly enough at London Road, with around 2,500 average. For the first time since the Club's formation they had a successful F.A. Cup run. This started with an away victory against Kettering, 2–0, with goals from Chiverton and Wilson in front of 3,250. Wolverton were then beaten 3–0 at London Road before Rushden were disposed of by 4–2 at home, in front of a crowd of 3,572. The next victims were Biggleswade on their own ground by 2–1, before Posh finally bowed out to Dartford 3–0 in front of 4,000 fans.

At the Angel Hotel, on the 27th January, Tommy Peake was elected Chairman of the newly formed Supporters Club. It was a timely move for during the same week Peterborough United's Directors met and held a special meeting to decide that despite crippling debts and financial problems the Club would still carry on. One month later the Supporters Club handed over the first cheque to the parent Club, for £22.10.0d., which helped pay for the rent at London Road. A month later and a further £30.0.0d. was presented, and by the close season the Supporters Club had raised over £100.0.0d. for the Football Club in just a few months. At the end of the season, the club once again finished 16th in the league, Manager Fred Taylor left the Club and former Director Bert Poulter took over. Despite the activities of the Supporters Club, the Club showed their third consecutive loss, this time of £265.0.0d over the season.

1937/38 SEASON

Before the season started a significant change was made when the playing colours were changed from the green and white they had used since their formation, to royal blue and white. In these new colours, for the third consecutive season, Posh started their Midland League campaign away at Scarborough, this time losing 5–2.

John Kendall, the goalkeeper, was by now the only player left from the inaugural season, but the changes that Poulter made showed little or no difference in the early part of the season, for it wasn't until the 11th game that Posh recorded their first victory, at London Road, by 4-0 over Rotherham United Reserves, with Savage scoring a hat trick.

The dismal results continued after this long awaited victory, and a win came just once more in the following ten games. On December 11th 1937 Posh were involved in their first ever abandoned game, at Shrewsbury Town. Despite the appalling form of the team the attendances were still quite buoyant and a further financial boost came when Cecil Wilde was transferred to Everton for £350.0.0d; the Club also played the Toffeemen in a friendly as part of the deal.

In the F.A.Cup, Wellingborough were beaten 5-0 away before Posh went out to Kettering by 1-0. A stronger end to the season came with some convincing victories (in the home matches over Denaby by 8-2, and Lincoln City Reserves 5-2). The brighter finish was sufficient for Posh to just escape a re-election application to the Midland League, with a final placing fourth from bottom.

At the end of the season Bert Poulter was replaced as Manager by Sam Hayden from Notts County, and he became Posh's fourth Manager in only four years. Hayden joined the Club as player/manager and was the first big name to join the Club, having prior to his County days played in the First Division for Arsenal. It was to herald a new style of management with Hayden bringing good professional players to the Club. A further boost was given by the announcement at the A.G.M. of a profit of £242.4.10d. The first time in the Club's history that they had finished a season in the 'black'. With John Kendall now having left the Club none of the original side from 1934 were left.

1938/39 SEASON

Hayden made the worst possible start as Manager, with the side losing their first five games. The attendances for the first two home games however, were up on the previous season, 3,321 watching the 2-1 home defeat to Grimsby Reserves, and 3,299 watching Bradford Park Avenue Reserves winning 3-1. Posh at last started their winning ways, and by the time the F.A.Cup campaign commenced, in October, Hayden's side were beginning to look good. They beat Kettering at home 2-1 in the F.A. Cup, in front of 5,266 – the largest crowd to gather at London Road to watch Posh. They then drew 4-4 at Rushden (again!), and beat them 3-1 at home in the replay. In the next round they travelled to Spalding and won 3-2, with two goals from McCartney, who took his total to eight goals in the four F.A.Cup games. The next tie was at home to St. Neots and a crowd of 5,422 were present, where McCartney scored yet again and gave Posh

a 1-0 victory, earning Posh the right to travel to Bristol Rovers in the first round proper.

It was the first time that Posh had the opportunity to take on a Football League side in competitive football. A crowd of 7,342 at Eastville saw Rovers run out 4-1 winners, McCartney scoring the goal for Posh. The consolation for this defeat came in the league, with a fantastic end to the year with the beating of Denaby at London Road by 7-0 followed by neighbours Boston, who were crushed 12-0 in front of 2,238 at London Road. It was the Club's biggest ever victory with five goals from McCartney, three from Hayden, and the others from Fielding, Warnes, Sharp and Bowaters.

As the side started to climb the table in the New Year, it drew the crowds to London Road and by the time they played Shrewsbury on April 7th, a crowd of 6,144 turn up, the largest at that time, at London Road to watch the Posh.

The side finished the season in 10th place in the league of 22 teams, their best showing to date. McCartney finished as the season's highest scorer with 29 goals in the league and 9 in the F.A.Cup, beating the previous record held by Briggs (with 32 goals). Posh's most successful season paved the way for Sam Hayden to be appointed the Club's first ever full time Manager.

1939/40 SEASON

It was somewhat ironic that at the start of the 1939/1940 season Posh seemed on the verge of their greatest season since their formation. In their opening game they beat Notts County Reserves 8-0, and then went on to beat Lincoln City Reserves by 4-0 and Shrewsbury by 4-2. But as the Second World War started, the Midland League was suspended, and this meant that Posh could only play friendlies until the announcement that a wartime league was to start.

THE WAR YEARS
(And the mysterious case of half a Championship!)

After the suspension of the normal Midland League programme, Posh, along with Scunthorpe, Newark, Denaby, Grantham, Boston, Frickley and Gainsborough, formed a War-time league. The 'mini' League ended in February and despite Posh finishing this short 'season' with one unplayed fixture – due to the bad weather at this time – they none the less attained a very commendable second place in the table. Scunthorpe and Lindsey United finished top. Posh's 13th, and last match, was belatedly played on the 23rd of March, the same day as the game against Grantham – in the second competition!

The second League programme, containing the same eight clubs, commenced immediately after the first, and for this second 'season' Posh finished in top spot.

The league ruled that a 'decider' should be played between Scunthorpe and Peterborough on the 18th of May at London Road, although somewhat inexplicably the Officials stated that the winning team would not be declared as the League Champions! Posh duly beat Scunthorpe 3-2 (with gate takings of just under £62) in what was in effect a meaningless match. However, since at the Midlands League A.G.M. it had been decided that no trophy or medals would be awarded for the season, this would explain the reason for having no official League Champions, but does not justify the playing of the 'decider' in the first place! As far as the Press and the public were concerned, it was accepted that Scunthorpe were the first half Champions, and Peterborough the second, and hence this became the only occasion when Posh 'won' half a Championship!

A move to disband the Club prior to the start of the 1940/41 season was fortunately heavily defeated by the Shareholders, and Posh, with a limited number of available players, were able to continue. However, the Midland League by now had disbanded, and Posh were left to play only the occasional Friendly match, and in front of only a few hundred spectators at each game. Despite the limited 'exposure', Tommy Rudkin soon became a favourite with the (depleted) London Road fans.

However, of particular concern were the events off the pitch. Posh once again found themselves in trouble with their Landlords - the City Council - for non-payment of rent, and there was speculation that the Club's lease on the London Road ground could be terminated. During the 1941/42 season, this fear nearly became a reality, for Newalls Sports Club offered to take on a ten year lease at £80 per annum, and at this time Posh were £50 in arrears. The situation required prompt action from the brothers Messrs. W. and A. Tebbs, who paid off the outstanding amount, and so ensured the Club's continued tenure at London Road.

Matches were few and far between, but of note during the 1942/43 season was the visit of a Czech Army X1, whom Posh beat. One year later, in a very restricted playing season at London Road, a crowd of 1,700 was present to see a match between two Anti-aircraft Command teams. In one of the teams George Swindin made his first appearance at the London Road ground.

The 1944/45 season once again saw only a few Posh matches played, but of particular note was the opening game at London Road, when an exceptional crowd numbering 3,200 saw the locals lose 5-2 to a Nottingham Forest X1. The visitors included in their team a guest player, the renowned Everton star Dixie Dean.

An unnamed team group, believed to be from the 1939/40 season,
but what were the trophies ?

## CHAPTER 3

POST-WAR POSH PROGRESS

1945/46 SEASON

With the War over, normality – to a degree – returned to the Country, and with it came the reintroduction of regularised football matches. Posh kicked off, once again in the Midland League, at home against Notts County Reserves on the 25th August, and won 4–2 with two goals from Fairchild and two from Livingstone. Due to the difficulties of finding players with so many still serving in the Armed Forces, Posh used no less than 54 players during the season. Many of these were local players and despite the inconsistency of the side that they could actually field they managed to finish in a creditable 9th position in the Midland League.

The highlights of the season came with a 3–1 home victory over Grantham that was played in front of 5,000 people at London Road, and the 9–1 thrashing at Rushden Town in the F.A. Cup, when Laxton scored six of the Posh goals. The Supporters Club had raised £310 during the season, which was to be used on the building of a catering hut at London Road. At the end of the season it was announced that for the first time since Posh's formation, in 1934, the admission price would be increased from 1/0d. (5p) to 1/3d. (7p). There was also good news for the Football Club, for the accounts showed a profit of £307.0.0d. for the year.

1946/47 SEASON

In a busy close season the Supporters Club installed loudspeaker equipment at the ground and the City Council gave permission for floodlights to be erected in order for the players to train. Support came from afar, when the people of Peterborough, Ontario (Canada), donated a complete set of new kit to the Club – at a time when such items of clothing were a luxury in post-war Britain.

The actual season started well enough as the team were unbeaten in their first five matches in the Midland League, however it was in the F.A.Cup that Posh were to make their mark. It started on the 5th October with a home tie against Wellingborough Town which Posh won 6–0, Warnes scoring four times. This was followed two weeks later with a 3–0 home win over Westwood Works. Another home tie brought Kettering Town to London Road and they were beaten 4–1 in front of 8,135, the biggest attendance to that date for a match at London Road. The final qualifying round was at home to Hitchin and Posh won 4–1 with Rudkin scoring three goals.

Posh had to travel to Yeovil in the first round proper of the Cup. At 2–1 up, with goals from Rudkin and Bayliss, and with about 20 minutes to go, Silcocks the goalkeeper picked up the ball, tucked it under his arms and then blatantly fouled the Yeovil left winger! Yeovil equalised from the penalty and hung on for a replay at London Road. A crowd of 8,691 turned up to watch Rudkin score the only goal of the game. Posh's reward for beating Yeovil was a home match against Northampton Town. They gained a 1–1 draw in front of 7,793 and then went on to draw 1–1 in the replay after extra time. A third game was therefore required, and this was played at the Coventry City ground, but this time the League side ran out 8–1 winners, being far too strong for Posh.

Following Posh's Cup exit, and two days before Christmas, Rudkin was sold to Arsenal for £1,800. The good Cup run led to Posh hitting a rich vein of form in the League, but this was abruptly ended with an 8–0 defeat away to Bradford Park Avenue Reserves. In the end Posh enjoyed a moderately successful season finishing 9th in the league, and hence equalling their best ever position which they had gained the year previously.

It was announced at the A.G.M. at the end of the season that a profit of £3,162 had been made by the Football Club.

1947/48 SEASON

Another good player was lost, when Wilson was transferred to Luton for £500. But as some compensation Hayden signed one of the first characters to appear at London Road, "Dizzie" Burton from Frickley. The team side made a good start to the new season winning four and drawing three of their opening seven games, and the attendances at London Road were well up on the previous season, all being around the 6,000 mark.

In the F.A. Cup, Posh did well in the early qualifying rounds defeating Westwood Works, Desborough and Kettering before they were beaten 2–1 at Vauxhall Motors. On 1st January Eddie Frieman. a Latvian International forward made his debut for Posh and scored a hat trick in a 3–0 win away at Mansfield Town Reserves. He scored a total of eight goals in his next five games and very quickly became a firm favourite of the London Road fans. Around the same time Manager

Hayden announced that he would resign from the Manager's job at the end of the season. The Posh supporters were upset that he was leaving, after a 10 year association with the Club, and handed him a petition asking him to reconsider his decision. But none the less he left the Club on April 14th, shortly before the end of the season. Ironically Hayden's final year was to be Posh's most successful to date, for they finished 6th in the Midland League.

The new Manager was to be Exeter City full back Jack Blood. Goals had been plentiful during the season at London Road, with Brookbanks being Posh's leading scorer, and Frieman – who had become a huge favourite in his short time at Peterborough – who scored 22 goals in only 21 appearances. Blood's appointment was far from being a popular choice and the mood was not improved when Eddie Frieman was allowed to go, and joined neighbours Northampton Town. Osmond who arrived at the Club at the same time as Frieman, was also sold, to Southend for £500.

The Club announced that there were plans to build a new 4,000 seat Grandstand at London Road, which would raise the total ground capacity to 25,000, and for the second consecutive year the Club showed a profit this time of £1,489.

1948/49 SEASON

Blood brought in several new players, some with Football League experience including Jim Fallon from Exeter City (a Republic of Ireland International with nine caps), and William Guest who played a few games for Walsall after starting his career at Birmingham.

Posh made an indifferent start to the new campaign, with some good wins – 3–0 over Doncaster Rovers Reserves, 3–1 against Hull City Reserves and a 5–0 thrashing of Scarborough – but they also suffered some heavy defeats, the worst by 10–0 at home to Bradford Park Avenue Reserves in front of a crowd of 6,800; also 3–0 against Notts County Reserves plus 4–1 versus Scunthorpe and Lindsey United. In the F.A. Cup Posh again qualified for the first round proper, overcoming works team Symingtons by 4–0, Wellingborough 3–2, (almost inevitably) Kettering and Ransome & Marles, before bowing out with a 1–0 defeat at home to Torquay United in front of 8,769. The match against Kettering Town produced a new best attendance at London Road of 9,370.

Manager Blood had played a few games for Posh in the Midland League, but towards the end of the season it was reported that a leg injury made it doubtful as to whether he would be able to play again. He therefore switched to solely the Club Manager role. The season ended with Posh in 16th place, and therefore another disappointing season in the Midland League. However at the A.G.M., the Club yet again announced a profit, although this time only £476, a big reduction on the previous two seasons.

1949/50 SEASON

Blood again brought in some new faces with Football League experience, including George Moulson from Lincoln City (who had won three International Caps for the Republic of Ireland), Freddie Martin who had played five times the previous season for Nottingham Forest, and Alec Wands who had League experience with both Crewe and Doncaster.

Posh again started indifferently, although their form at London Road was very good, and the forward partnership of Martin, Widdowfield and Robinson produced many goals, but away from home they struggled.

The F.A. Cup run finished in the third qualifying round, when they went out 1–0 to Corby Town, after beating Desborough 5–1 at home and Kettering 5–0 away. The Kettering game at Rockingham Road attracted another new record crowd, of 9,799. As the team went into the New Year lying half way down the Midland League table, Blood announced that after his contract expired in May he would not be staying on as Manager of Peterborough United, blaming lack of confidence from the Board. On February 21st, Peterborough United announced that former England and Sunderland centre forward Bob Gurney would be the new Manager of the Club on a three year contract. Gurney's arrival at London Road coincided with a big improvement in the form of the team, for they lost only three times in their final 13 matches.

By the end of the season Widdowfield was the Club's top scorer with 30 league and cup goals, and he was closely followed by Martin on 24, and Robinson with 23 in total. Posh finished the season in fourth place, by far their best ever showing in the Midland League. They also managed to accumulate five votes in support of their (first) application for a place in the Football League.

1950/51 SEASON

Before the new season started Bob Gurney signed Frank Bee from Blackburn Rovers, and he scored on his debut as Posh beat Boston United 4-1 away in their opening Midland League fixture. The crowds at London Road were by now most encouraging, with 7,246 fans coming to watch the first home game (when they beat Mansfield Town Reserves 3-0), and continuing in excess of 6,500 for their next four home encounters. As the season progressed Gurney went into the transfer market again to bring in Vic Walker from Stockport County, Alan Daley - ex-Doncaster Rovers - and Johnny Dowson from Manchester City.

But it was destined to be another unsuccessful season for Posh though. In the F.A. Cup, after beating Symington's again - in the first qualifying round - they then went out to Kettering 2-1 (before a crowd numbering 9,577), after drawing 2-2 at Rockingham Road. As the season tailed off, attendances dwindled from the early days of over 6,500 down to final numbers of around 3,500. But in April Posh entertained Hull City, and a record attendance of 10,380 came along to watch the teams play a benefit match for Bernie Bryan, Cyril Parrot and Cliff Woods. Raich Carter was in the Hull side that day, who ran out 4-3 winners. It was the only highlight of an otherwise dull season, and at the end of the year a loss of £894 was reported.

1951/52 SEASON

As Posh started the new season Gurney started to sign some of the faces that were to become permanent fixtures at London Road over the next 10 to 15 years, in one of the most successful periods for the Club. Norman Rigby joined the side and was appointed the Captain in his first game, which Posh lost 4-2 to Notts County Reserves in front of 7,325. But they immediately recovered from this setback, and went unbeaten in their next four matches, the last of which was a 1-0 win over Hull City Reserves. Making his debut that day was Andy Donaldson who had been signed from Middlesbrough, it caused a great deal of interest in the football world and was quite a coup for Peterborough United. Donaldson scored in his second game, when Posh lost at home 2-1 to Worksop Town, but he was soon knocking in goals regularly and becoming a big favourite at London Road.

In the F.A. Cup, Posh went out to Hereford United. After drawing 1-1 at London Road, in front 10,061, they lost by 1-0 at Edgar Street in the replay.

On the field the nucleus of a great team was being forged. Donaldson was a firm favourite with the crowds, scoring 17 goals in 28 appearances in his first season. Dowson was the top scorer for the Club with 28 Midland League goals in 40 appearances, and Rigby had also become established as a firm favourite with the London

Road faithful. The season overall was moderately successful, with Posh finishing 5th in the Midland League. Before the end of the season Gurney announced that he was going to leave Posh to become Manager of Darlington, leaving Posh to find their 7th Manager in 16 seasons. On the 4th June 1952 it was announced that Newcastle goalkeeper Jack Fairbrother was to be Gurney's replacement.

1952/53 SEASON

Fairbrother soon started to bring in new and experienced faces, including Al Woollard from Northampton, Johnny Anderson - formerly with Nottingham Forest and Manchester United - plus Paddy Sloan another ex-Republic of Ireland International, with two caps. All three made their debuts in the opening game which ended in a 0-0 draw at home to Rotherham United Reserves, and which drew an impressive attendance of 9,101. Fairbrother had captured the imagination of the fans in Peterborough and large attendances became a feature of the early games at London Road.

Posh made a good start to their league campaign, but the great success of the season yet again would come in the F.A. Cup. They started by beating Symingtons 5-2 away in Market Harborough, before a record attendance for the 'Corsetmen' of 2,700. Two pulsating cup ties followed, drawing away to Spalding United 2-2 with a last minute equaliser from Donaldson, before winning 3-0 at London Road in front of 8,211. They then drew at Corby Town before 10,239 (another new record crowd), before winning at London Road 5-3 after extra time, after a scoreline of 3-3 at the end of 90 minutes. Posh's goals came from Rigby, Campbell, Donaldson, Martin and Hair, in front of 9,845.

Bedford Town were then entertained, and beaten 2-1 in front of by far the biggest ever London Road crowd of 15,327, with Donaldson and Martin scoring the goals. This final victory ensured that they qualified again for the first round proper, and were matched against Torquay United again, this time at home, and gained ample revenge over the League club by beating them 2-1 before 12,938 excited fans. Sloan and Martin scored the goals that provided Posh with this famous victory.

The final game in Peterborough's marvellous cup run came at home to Bristol Rovers, who were riding high in Division III South. A near record crowd of 15,286 packed London Road to watch Bristol Rovers just edge out Posh 1-0. Fairbrother had injected some excitement and some purpose into both the team and the fans, and the crowds continued to flock to London Road.

Following Posh's brilliant cup run Woollard was sold to Newcastle for £4,000, easily the Club's biggest transfer to that date. Shortly after Woollard's departure, it was decided by the Club that they would make an all out effort to gain Football League status, and their first move was to prepare an illustrated brochure outlining the Club's ambitions in this direction. The enthusiasm for the club was sweeping the City, and a new Share Issue was made early in 1953. Additionally a development fund was launched in a joint venture between the Football Club and the Supporters' Club, where fans were asked to buy a brick for 2/6d (12½p) towards the building of a new wall at the Moys End of the ground.

On the pitch Posh were still doing well and they gained some impressive victories, the highlight being an 8-1 home win over Gainsborough Trinity, with Adcock's hat trick amongst the goals. Earlier, on the 30th March, Fairbrother had become the first goalkeeper to score a goal for Posh, when he converted a penalty in the sides 4-0 victory over Bradford City Reserves at London Road.

Peterborough finished the season in 8th place in the Midland League, but the expected improvement in their search for an elusive Football League place was some- what dampened with the news that they had received only six votes.

1953/54 SEASON

Fairbrother moved into the transfer market again capturing the signature of Doug Taft who had played for Derby County in the Football League. The newcomer came in to replace Donaldson who had joined Exeter City, after firmly establishing himself as one of the all time great players and crowd favourites to have appeared at London Road.

Posh started the new season in fine style beating Gran- tham at London Road 2-1 in front of 9,806, with goals from Taft and Sloan. This was followed up by a 9-2 hammering of Gainsborough Trinity before 8,208, Taft scoring an amazing five goals in the rout. An excellent start to the season was ended after five games by Don- caster Rovers Reserves, but they bounced straight back with five straight wins, including a 4-1 victory over York City Reserves in front of 10,053, Posh's best league attendance. This number was soon improved upon, for in the next game – at home against Boston United (whom they also beat 4-1) - was played before 10,399.

Posh also tasted success again in the F.A. Cup, beating Grays Athletic 4-1 at home before overcoming Hitchin away 3-1 in the first round proper. They then entertained Aldershot at London Road on December 12th, and attracted a staggering record crowd of 16,717. Goals from Martin and Taft were enough to see Posh through to a 2-1 victory. Shortly afterwards Fairbrother announced that he was going to leave Posh to take up the appoint- ment as Manager of Coventry City, but he promised that he would not leave Posh while they were still in the cup.

Posh take a surprise lead in the F.A.Cup at Cardiff. After a pass from Matthews (in the background),
Hair - challenged by Montgomery and Rutter - rams the ball goalwards, for Martin (not in picture) to net.

16

His final game for the club was away at Cardiff City, in the third round on 9th January, and what a finale it was. In front of 38,000 fans at Ninian Park, Posh went down 3-1 to the Welshmen after Martin had given Posh a shock lead early in the game. Fairbrother's departure had been a severe blow, but nobody could deny what he had done for Peterborough United in the short space of time that he had been there.

Success on the pitch still continued with some good results including the tight 5-4 victory over Corby Town and a 6-1 demolition of Lincoln City Reserves at London Road, the latter before 9,035 keen fans. By this time it had been announced that George Swindin, the former Arsenal goalkeeper, was to become player/manager of Peterborough United, and he made his debut in the Lincoln match. Swindin took over where Fairbrother had left off, with an impressive string of results towards the end of the season, however Posh just failed to overhaul Nottingham Forest Reserves in the race for their first ever Midland League title. They actually beat Forest Reserves 3-1 at London Road, five games from the end of the season, in front of a crowd of 12,665 - Posh's then record attendance for a Midland League match. Taft finished the season with an incredible 42 league goals and a further three in the cup, to become Posh's most prolific scorer in the Club's history. Once again Posh went to the meeting of the Football League full of hope, and although they substantially increased their votes for entry to the Football League to 18, it was still woefully short of the number required to gain the place they coveted.

GEORGE SWINDIN
(Manager 1954 to 1958)

1954/55 SEASON

Swindin started to put together a squad capable of winning the Midland League, and in came Ellis Stafford, Denis Emery and Jim McCabe - a Northern Ireland International with six caps - although Paddy Sloan was released. At the Club's A.G.M., Posh announced that they had made another profit this time of £2,063. Admission charges were increased again at London Road, now up to 1/9d (9p). The scene was all set for a successful season on the pitch.

Posh opened their league campaign at home to Rotherham United Reserves before a crowd of 9,258, Campbell scoring Posh's only goal in a 1-1 draw. It was boom time for the Club both on and off the pitch with even the reserves incredibly attracting attendances in excess of 6,000 on more than one occasion! It was the 25th September before Posh tasted their first defeat of the season, losing 1-0 away to Gainsborough Trinity. By now the interest in Peterborough United was phenomenal and when they entertained King's Lynn at home on October 2nd in the league, the match attracted a crowd of 13,217 who saw a scoreless draw.

They went out of the F.A. Cup at the first hurdle - in the fourth qualifying round - losing 2-1 to Boston United at London Road in front of a massive 16,558 crowd. Despite Swindin's optimism and enthusiasm, and quite obviously the formation of a great Midland League team, Posh could only finish 3rd, three points behind eventual champions Notts County Reserves. Posh again went to the Football League at the end of the season, but this time only received 6 votes in their search for that elusive Football League place, and at the A.G.M., the Club announced a reduced profit of £542.

1955/56 SEASON

The biggest news at the Club was the return of Andy Donaldson from Exeter City who linked up with Hair, Emery and Billy Hails in the forward line. Posh started the season with a 5-1 away victory over Mansfield Town Reserves, Hails scoring a hat trick on his debut, with Donaldson scoring the other two. In the next match they lost 4-3 at York City Reserves, but were then not to taste defeat in the league for another 30 matches, when they lost away to Nottingham Forest Reserves 1-0. In the interim, the Posh forward line was unstoppable, and regularly rattled in big scores including such London Road victories as; Scarborough 6-0, Doncaster Reserves 7-0 and Lincoln City Reserves by 6-1. During this time Donaldson, Emery, Hails, Gibson and Hair were scoring goals at will.

The F.A. Cup started with a fourth qualifying round match at Ilkeston Town, who Posh beat 3-1 with goals from Hails 2, and Emery.

In the first round proper they took on Ipswich Town at London Road in front of 20,671 by far their biggest gate. Emery scored twice and Hair once to give Posh a memorable 3-1 victory.

Emery puts Posh ahead with a left foot shot which Ipswich goalkeeper Myles fails to block.

Their reward for the Ipswich victory was an away trip to Swindon that saw 8,000 Posh fans make the trip to the West Country to see their team draw 1-1, thanks to a goal from Emery, in front of 23,983. Swindon came back to London Road and 16,672 saw Posh hold Swindon to 1-1 after 90 minutes, with Emery again scoring the goal for Posh, before losing out in extra time.

Back in the league nobody could touch Peterborough, for following the defeat away at Nottingham Forest Reserves Posh won eleven and drew two of their final 13 games, to clinch their first Midland League title, by 5 points. In the process they scored an incredible 137 goals in 46 games. Leading scorers at the end of the season were Emery with 33 league and cup goals, Gibson with 31 in the league, and Donaldson's total of 29. Another highlight of the season was the signing of Tessie Balogun, Posh's first coloured player, and he became a big favourite with the fans. He had been a prolific goalscorer for the Posh Reserve side, teaming up with Martin in the forward line for the second string, who became the Eastern Counties League Champions.

By the end of the season work had started on Posh's long awaited new Grandstand, but the enthusiasm of the fans was dampened somewhat, when once again they were rejected at the Football League Meeting, receiving this time only 8 votes in their quest for league membership.

These were heady days for both the Football and Supporters' Clubs, and by the close season of 1956, the latter had a staggering membership totalling 45,484.

1956/57 SEASON

Swindin moved into the transfer market and brought in former England International – with 13 caps – Henry Cockburn, plus Jack Walls, Ray Smith, Jimmy Crawford and Jack Hogg. They started the season unbeaten in their first eight games and after defeating Boston United at home in the first match in front of 13,431, they then hammered Hull City Reserves at London Road 7-0, with goals coming from Emery 3, Gibson 2, Hogg and Shaw. Their first defeat of the season was at home against Nottingham Forest Reserves on 17th September 1956. This defeat was to become a notable day in Peterborough United's history, for it was the last time they were ever to lose at home in the Midland League, remaining unbeaten at home in these fixtures for the next four years!

Posh again had another fantastic run in the F.A. Cup, which started with the beating of Corby Town 5-1 away from home, and was followed with victory at Yeovil, by 3-1, in the first round proper. They then entertained Bradford Park Avenue, winning 3-0 with goals from Hails, Emery and Donaldson, and in front of 18,618. That set Posh up for a third round tie, again at home, against local rivals Lincoln City of the Second Division.

A new record attendance at London Road was set, with 22,000 cramming into the ground to see Posh share four goals, with both coming from Emery. But if that first game was memorable then the replay game at Sincil Bank will remain in the memories of some Posh fans for a long time. The first game had ended acrimoniously with Lincoln scoring a last minute penalty, it being adjudged that there had been a handball infringement in the final moments of the game.

The replay meant that thousands of Peterborough fans made the journey north to Lincoln to help make up the crowd of 18,216. The team that day was:

Walls, Douglass, Barr, Shaw, Rigby, Coven, Hails, Emery, Donaldson, Smith and Hogg.

The game started with Donaldson giving Posh the lead after just eight minutes, 10 minutes later and Lincoln were on terms, but after 22 minutes it was that man Donaldson again who popped up to give the lead to Posh again. That's the way it remained until just two minutes from time when history seemed to be repeating itself, for Lincoln snatched a dramatic equaliser again, and took the tie into extra time. The crowd was at fever pitch, and one minute before half-time during the extended period, Donaldson centred for Emery who smartly took the ball under control and whipped it into the net to give Posh the lead 3-2. Just minutes into the second half of extra time, Smith latched onto a free kick from Shaw and then calmly picked his spot to make it 4-2 to Posh. The Posh fans were ecstatic, and just minutes later Donaldson completed his hat trick to put Posh in a seemingly impregnable 5-2 lead. But in a grandstand finish, two goals from Lincoln brought the scores back to 5-4 with only two minutes remaining. Posh hung on to gain a deserved victory, but in true Boys Own style the newspaper reported that Donaldson, the hat trick hero, had been taken ill on the way to the game, and just an hour before the kick off trainer Anderson had to rush him out for a brandy and port pick-me-up!

The result earned Posh the right to visit Huddersfield Town, this occasion being the fourth that they had played in the fourth round of the Cup. It was an incredible day out for the Posh fans, and as it was estimated that more than 10,000 travelled to Yorkshire to see Posh take on First Division Huddersfield. They helped make up a crowd of 48,735 and despite a brave performance Posh went out 3-1 to the First Division giants. Emery failed to score for the Posh, and thereby ended a sequence of 10 consecutive F.A. Cup ties in which he had scored.

In the league, Posh were still picking up bumper attendances and excellent results. The week following the defeat of Lincoln City's first team, they hammered their Reserves at London Road by 6-1. They also easily overcame Denaby (7-0), plus Gainsborough and King's Lynn by 5-0, and by Easter the Midland League title was already wrapped up for Posh, for the second consecutive time. Eventually they scored 148 goals in 46 games and won the League by 9 points. Emery was the Club's top scorer with 43 league and 8 Cup goals, ably supported by Donaldson's 20 league successes (and four in the Cup), whilst Gibson managed 20 plus 2.

1957/58 SEASON

Posh started their defence of the Championship with a 4-0 away victory at Corby Town, with goals from Shaw, Emery, Donaldson and O'Donnel. They then went on a fantastic run winning their first 11 matches and scoring 46 goals in the process whilst conceding just eight, before they were beaten away at Sincil Bank by Lincoln City Reserves. The highlight of the 11 match run was a 4-0 victory at Wisbech, in front of 8,844, where Donaldson and an Emery hat-trick were responsible for the Posh goals. Two matches later Posh played Wisbech in the return at London Road in front of 10,500, running out 4-1 winners. By the end of the season Wisbech were to be Posh's closest rivals in the race for the Championship.

In the F.A. Cup Posh started their first match away to Wolverton Town in the fourth qualifying round in front of no less than 13,200, and ran out magnificent 7-0 winners including two own goals and a Longworth hat-trick. The reward for this victory was a match at home to Torquay, yet again, in the first round proper. Posh gave away a 3-0 lead to end up drawing 3-3 in front of 17,800. Unfortunately in the replay the West Country side were too strong and ran out 1-0 winners.

Back in the Midland League it was to be another season of records on and off the pitch, with the Supporters Club now donating a regular £1,500 a month to the Parent Club. Manager George Swindin was much sought after and turned down the offer to manage Leyton Orient, in order to redouble his efforts on behalf of Posh and take them into the Football League. He could do little more than he was actually achieving with the Club at that time, for they won their first 20 home games in the Midland League, and notched up some mammoth scores. Bradford City Reserves were thrashed 7-0, Doncaster Rovers Reserves 8-2, Corby Town 8-1, Frickley Colliery 6-0 and Gainsborough were easily beaten 5-1. In their 21st home game of the season they dropped their first point at London Road, drawing 1-1 with Bradford Park Avenue Reserves in front of 6,675. This slight abrasion was more than made up for with their final home game of the season two weeks later, when Posh dispatched Denaby United 9-0, with goals from Emery 4, Smith 2, Donaldson, McNamee and Hails.

Posh lost just six games all season, one surprisingly 7-3 at Grantham after being 4-0 down at half time, but other results were easily enough to ensure Posh their third consecutive Midland League Championship. They finished the season 7 points ahead of local rivals Wisbech, scoring an incredible 163 goals and conceding only 46.

Posh were desperate after this latest attempt to get into the Football League, especially after the news in February that seven of the strongest Clubs in the Midland League were to quit the competition, and thus devalue its status. Posh redoubled their efforts to gain Football League membership. They also applied to join the Southern League, but as many clubs tried to follow in Posh's footsteps, they abandoned the idea and decided to remain with the Midland League should their Football League bid fail. At the League's A.G.M., Posh managed only 15 votes in their latest bid to gain League membership.

1958/59 SEASON

Just a few weeks after the news that Posh had missed out yet again with their Football League bid, came the news that George Swindin, after declining the job as Manager at Doncaster, had gone back to his former Club, Arsenal, as Manager. It was too tempting an offer for Swindin – who had previously played 297 League and Cup matches for the Gunners. By August Posh fans knew who their new Manager would be – Jimmy Hagan a former England and Sheffield United star.

Posh started in a much reduced Midland League where they were to play only 36 fixtures as opposed to the 46 from previous seasons. Hagan's line up was starting to take on a familiar form for Posh fans. The first team, at home to Ashington, consisted of:

> Walls, Stafford, Walker, Shaw, Rigby,
> Chadwick, Hails, Emery, Donaldson,
> Smith and McNamee.

Donaldson was destined to play only three games in his final season for the Club, before being replaced by Jim Rayner.

Posh won their opening fixture 6–1 with goals from Chadwick, Emery, two from Smith, McNamee and an own goal. Home attendances were again between the 7,000 to 10,000 mark and the home form again became irresistible; this time they went one better than the previous season winning all 18 of their home fixtures and not dropping a single point.

It was almost now an annual event for Posh to have a fairytale F.A. Cup run. The 1958/59 season was no exception, starting with a fourth qualifying round tie against Walthamstow Avenue at London Road. A crowd of 14,700 saw Emery hit a hat trick to dispatch the London side. Kettering Town came to London Road next, and a crowd of 17,800 saw goals from Emery and Donaldson earn a 2–2 draw with the Poppies.

In the replay five days later at Rockingham Road Posh were 2–0 down after 19 minutes, but they pulled one back with a goal from Emery. Then in spectacular fashion, five minutes before the end, ex–Posh defender and Northants. batsman Reynolds headed past his own goalkeeper to take the tie into extra time. Nine minutes into the extra time, Hails wrapped things up for Posh to give them a 3–2 victory and earned them the right to play Headington United at London Road in the next round. 16,855 turned up to watch Posh win 4–2 with 2 goals from Emery and a goal apiece from Hails and Rayner. The reward for winning this game was an away tie with Fulham, who at that time lay second in the Second Division table.

Posh had a following of around 10,000 fans at Craven Cottage as part of the 31,908 crowd that watched the non–Leaguers battle out a 0–0 draw, with an outstanding performance from Emery, to earn a deserved replay at London Road. The Fulham side included George Cohen, Jimmy Hill and Johnny Haynes. The replay saw a gate of 21,600, and the Londoners edged through 1–0, but not without another fine display from Posh generally, and especially Emery again.

On February 8th 1958 Posh entertained Arsenal at London Road to mark the opening of their new floodlighting system. A run of 11 consecutive league victories between 20th September and 20th December put Posh in control, indeed they did not lose another game in the competition all season, and once again took the Championship, for the fourth time, six points clear of second placed Ashington. During this campaign they scored 137 goals and conceded just 26. Jim Rayner finished as top scorer with 42 league and cup goals from 34 appearances. Everybody was again geared up for Posh's bid to try and get an elusive Football League place, and this time they received 26 votes, but it was frustratingly still not enough. The Club called for all Supporters to rally round for yet another all out effort to gain a place in the Football League.

Local rivals Kettering were met in the F.A.Cup. (Right) In the replay the two captains, Norman Rigby and Jack Froggatt, toss the coin. (Above) Emery scores yet again, Posh's first goal.

Action from the Cup matches with Fulham. (Above) Goalkeeper Walls is too quick for Fulham's Leggat. (Right) In the London Road replay Emery's free kick clips the bar, much to Macedo's relief.

1959/60 SEASON

The Midland League was depleted even further, to 17 Clubs, which left Posh with just 32 fixtures. Just as the new season was due to start tragedy struck with the death of the Posh Chairman since 1954, Mr Frank Stimpson, and Stuart Palmer took over in that position.

The season opened at home to Stockton in front of 6,515, and Posh ran out 7–0 winners, with braces of goals from Rayner and West, plus singles from Hails, Emery and Smith. They were then surprisingly beaten away 2–1 by Ashington, the previous season's runners up. After disposing of North Shields at London Road by 3–0 on the 5th of September, Posh then went five matches without a win, but drawing four of them. They pulled out of this 'mini slump' with a 7–1 thumping of Worksop Town at London Road, it was to be the start of 14 consecutive League and Cup victories that swept Posh back to the top of the Midland League table and start yet another stirring Cup run.

Posh played Bury Town at London Road in the fourth qualifying round of the F.A. Cup, and a crowd of 9,922 watched Posh run out 7–1 winners. The good form continued with league victories over South Shields (4–3), 7–0 over Spennymoor and 6–0 at home to Denaby. Sandwiched between those last two results was a 4–3 win over Shrewsbury Town in the F.A. Cup at London Road. A crowd of 16,321 watched as Emery grabbed two with further goals from Rayner and Smith, for the team to take another League scalp. This latest victory required them to travel, and play Walsall at Fellows Park, where a crowd of 20,600 watched a classic Cup tie which Posh won 3–2 with a battling performance, goals coming from Rayner, Smith and McNamee.

An army of supporters travelled to watch Posh in their next Cup game, at Ipswich Town on January 9th 1960. A crowd of 26,000 came to see non-League Posh take on Second Division Ipswich Town. It was a game that was later hailed by the newspapers as **Posh's greatest ever F.A. Cup-tie. It started with Ipswich taking the lead after just 20 minutes, but three minutes before half-time McNamee sent Smith away on the wing, and he whipped in a low cross for Rayner to steer it wide of the Ipswich keeper. By the start of the second half, Walker was a passenger for he sustained an injury shortly before half-time. It seemed this slice of bad luck would be decisive as Ipswich restored their lead early in the second half. After 51 minutes McNamee was again the architect behind Posh's second equaliser, this time drawing two defenders and letting Emery away to stroke the ball past the stranded Ipswich keeper. The drama was completed with just three minutes left to play, and with snow starting to fall. Posh won a throw-in near the Ipswich penalty area, Rayner lobbed the ball to Smith, who feinted past his man, and crossed the ball into the path of Emery whose marker mis-kicked letting in the Posh idol to score the winner. The large travelling contingent of Peterborough fans stormed onto the pitch to carry their heroes shoulder high back to the changing room.**

It was a truly magnificent performance that captured the imagination of the people of Peterborough, with their reward a fourth round visit to Hillsborough to take on Sheffield Wednesday. A following of over 15,000 Posh fans made the trip to the steel town to watch Posh in part of a crowd of 51,144, it was here however that Posh met their match despite a fine battling display in front of the mammoth crowd. They bowed out with two late goals, in the 75th and 78th minutes, to lose by 2–0. They received praise from all quarters for their fighting performance and indeed were honoured later in the season by being awarded the *Sunday Pictorial Giantkiller Cup*, a culmination of Posh's proud giantkilling reputation.

This now meant that Posh were free again to concentrate on the league and try once more to attain their elusive Football League place.

Due to the appalling weather only five games were possible in February and March, but eventually Posh again won the Midland League title, their fifth consecutive, by virtue of winning five and drawing one of their final six matches, and finishing three points clear of North Shields. The Champions finished the season having scored 108 goals and conceding 37. It was, at last, to be their final season as a non-League club, and in this phenomenal run of five consecutive Championships Posh played 103 matches at London Road, winning 94, drawing eight and losing just one. In the process they scored 428 goals. It is little wonder that those Posh fans who witnessed the side during this period claim it was the greatest Peterborough United side to ever take the field.

Jimmy Hagan in action in a Friendly versus the South Africans - his only playing appearance for the Posh.

Denis Emery scores Posh's winner in the F.A.Cup at Ipswich

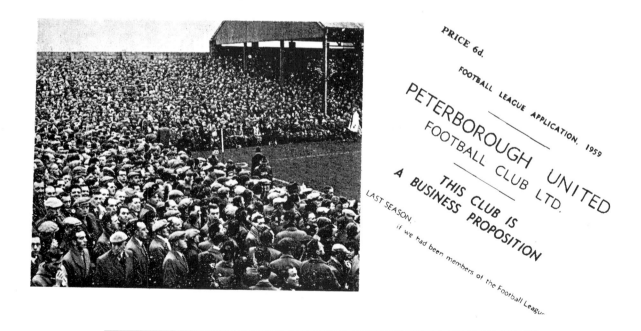

PRICE 6d.

FOOTBALL LEAGUE APPLICATION, 1959

PETERBOROUGH UNITED
FOOTBALL CLUB LTD.

THIS CLUB IS
A BUSINESS PROPOSITION

LAST SEASON... if we had been members of the Football League...

After years of campaigning, and by now regularly attracting five figure gates, the Posh were about to get their just reward.

CHAPTER 4

THE FOOTBALL LEAGUE AT LAST !

1960/61 SEASON

It was May 28th 1960, the time was 11.41 a.m. when the Football League announced to their Annual General Meeting that Peterborough United had been elected to the Football League. The normal staid atmosphere of a Football League Meeting was shattered with cheers and applause as the result of the vote was announced.

Re-elected was Oldham with 39 votes, elected was Peterborough with 35 votes, re-elected was Hartlepool 34 and Southport 29 votes. The Club who was to go out of the League was Gateshead who massed only 18 votes. It was ironic that the initials of the four elected Clubs spelt out the initials *POSH*! Other local Clubs up for election to the Football League were Cambridge City, Kettering Town and King's Lynn who polled just three votes between them.

It was a tremendous boost to the City generally as well as to the Football Club and it's fans. Crowds of supporters gathered to read the good news that was displayed in a bookshop on Broadway. The talk in the pubs, clubs and around the City was all of Posh's election to the Football League. Congratulations came from all over the Country. Former Posh Manager and then Manager of Arsenal George Swindin said; *"Posh certainly deserved to get in, I am delighted"*. Once the initial jubilation surrounding Posh's new status had died down, Manager Jimmy Hagan found himself with some real problems during the pre season as he now had to build a squad which could survive in the Football League.

Billy Hails, Peter McNamee, Roy Banham and Derek Chadwick all refused to accept new terms in July 1960. Hagan managed to resolve the dispute and three of the players signed new contracts. Chadwick, however, left for Cambridge City on a free transfer. Hagan retained 17 players from the previous season and then brought in a total of 8 new players. Three in particular were to become regular members of, arguably, Posh's greatest side. They were Dick Whittaker from Chelsea, Keith Ripley from Mansfield and Terry Bly from Norwich. The manager also signed goalkeeper Johnny Anderson from Leicester, Derek Norris from Gainsborough Trinity, plus Chris Coates who came from Wisbech, John Taylor and Ray Hogg from Mansfield and finally Gerald Graham from Blackpool.

When the big day finally arrived, Posh lined up at home on Saturday August 20th 1960 to play their first ever Football League match, against Wrexham, a side that had just been relegated from Division 3. The line up for Posh that day saw the following players:

> *Walls, Stafford, Walker, Rayner, Rigby,*
> *Norris, Hails, Emery, Bly, Smith and*
> *McNamee.*

A crowd of 17,294 was present to see Posh attack from the start, and after 24 minutes Emery scored Peterborough's first ever League goal, at the Moyes end of the Ground. McNamee added a second after 75 minutes and Bly scored five minutes later to give Peterborough a 3-0 win in this, their first League match.

The sight that thousands of Posh fans had waited years to see - the first Football League goal.
(Emery, out of the picture, was the marksman)

Just two days later Posh played at Hartlepool, who had maintained their League status, despite finishing two places lower than near neighbours Gateshead who had been voted out. Posh fielded the same 11 players and won 2–0 to claim their first away victory in the Football League, with both goals from Bly. The following Saturday the first League point was dropped, at Carlisle. Posh's goals came from Hails, Emery and Bly which gave them a 3–1 lead, only to see the Cumbrians score two late goals with the game finishing as a 3–3 draw.

On Monday 29th August 1960, just nine days into the season, Posh recorded their first League double, in front of 15,245 at London Road, when they beat Hartlepool 3–2, with goals from Smith, Hails and Bly, the latter having scored in every game.

The winning run continued at home by 4–3 over Rochdale, and 2–0 at Crystal Palace. The game at Crystal Palace attracted 36,478 spectators, to date the largest crowd to watch Posh in a league game, a match in which Ripley made his debut. The phenomenal start to the season came to an end on Saturday 10th September when Posh were beaten for the first time in the League, 1–0 at Field Mill, Mansfield. Two days later Posh bounced back completing the double over Crystal Palace, winning 4–1 in front of 21,171 London Road fans. Bly scored the first ever hat–trick by a Posh player in the Football League, with Hails getting the other goal. This was tempered somewhat in the next game as 14,610 fans watched Posh slip to their first League defeat at London Road with a 1–0 defeat to Stockport County. This victory was followed by a 2–1 away win over Doncaster, with two Bly goals, and a 4–3 away victory at Exeter, when Bly recorded another hat–trick.

Bly's incredible run had now seen him score 13 goals in just 11 games. The next match was at home to Doncaster, and Posh recorded their third double of the season after they thrashed the Yorkshiremen 6–2. Jimmy Dunne made his debut for Posh and scored, along with Bly, Hails and McNamee, the latter grabbing his first League hat–trick; Sansby and Hogg made their League debuts for Posh.

The next match was a tremendous game at Gillingham. It saw Posh take the lead with a Hails goal, although Gillingham centre–half Hughes helped the ball into his own net. Eleven minutes later Rayner put through his own net to put Gillingham back on terms. Just before half time the Gills took a 2–1 lead through Gordon Pulley. Five minutes after the break, Hails scored his second goal, after some enterprising play from Emery, and two minutes later Hails completed his first League hat–trick for Posh, to put them ahead for the first time in the game. The lead lasted until the 67th minute when Farralls' shot hit the post and bounced back into keeper Walls's arms, but after consulting a linesman the referee ruled that it had crossed the line and gave the goal. Five minutes later Gillingham went ahead again when the ball

slipped from Walls' grasp and centre forward Terry tapped home the fourth goal.

From then on Posh went flat out for their equaliser and with just 10 minutes left to play Hails blasted home his fourth goal of the game to ensure a point for Posh. The following Monday evening 17,096 saw Posh beaten at home again, 4–3 by Southport. The match ended in controversy, for when Posh were trailing 3–2 they were awarded an indirect free kick virtually on the penalty spot, Smith side footed the ball to Emery who blasted the ball home only for the referee to award a goal kick claiming that Emery had taken the kick directly himself, and the goal was disallowed. After many protests from the Posh players referee Aston finally commented that he had not given a goal kick but a free kick to Southport due to a United player being offside. Either way it was Posh's third defeat of the season and the outcome left them second in the League, one point behind leaders Stockport and one point ahead of local rivals Northampton, the team they were to entertain next at London Road.

This fixture had been built up in the Press for some time and 22,959 fans came to watch the match. It was not only Posh's best crowd of the season so far but it was also a League attendance that was to be later bettered only once in 32 years at London Road. In a season where nothing was surprising to Posh's growing army of supporters, the team fell 3–0 down to Northampton with the Cobblers scoring a goal after just 50 seconds through Leck; three minutes later and Posh were 2–0 down through Deakin. It looked as if it was going to be a sad day for the Posh supporters, when, after 24 minutes Fowler made it 3–0 to the Cobblers, who by now looked well in charge of the game. Posh came out for the second half a different side however, and just 50 seconds after they kicked off Bly centered to McNamee to head the ball home. After 61 minutes McNamee scored again, this time chipping over a static defence and goalkeeper from the edge of the box; two minutes later and the crowd were roaring as Emery hit Posh's equaliser. That was the end of the scoring but the excitement lasted right to the final minutes of the game, even though Northampton finished the match with 10 men after Fowler had to leave the pitch injured. It was Posh's first local derby in the League and has become one of the most memorable.

For their first ever Football League Cup–tie Posh visited Preston, and they crashed out 4–1, with a goal from Hails. Debuts were made by Anderson in goal, Whittaker at full back and Graham in mid–field. Whittaker and Graham retained their places in the side for the visit to Aldershot but Walls returned between the posts, Emery scoring to give Posh a 1–1 draw, to leave them second in the table on goal difference from Crystal Palace. A home game against Oldham resulted in a 2–2 draw before they visited Workington on October 29th, winning 3–0 with goals from Smith, Bly and Emery.

Posh made a 'tour' of the South Coast in the F.A.Cup. The first stop was back into non-League circles, at Dover. This first half shot from Smith was unsuccessful.

On November 6th, Posh started on the F.A. Cup trail with a 4–1 away win over Dover. A week later they were soundly beaten 3–1 at Gresty Road by Crewe, before entertaining York at London Road and drawing 1–1 thanks to a goal from Ripley. Posh visited Torquay in the next round of the F.A.Cup, coming away as 3–1 winners, with two goals from McNamee and one from Bly, before they played Millwall at home on December 3rd. Smith became the fourth individual Posh player that season to score a hat–trick, in a 4–2 win.

A week later Posh lost at Barrow 2–1 and then embarked on a remarkable sequence of 17 games unbeaten in the League, winning 15 games and drawing just 2. Even in this remarkable season it was just too good to be true for most Posh fans.

The run started with a 1–0 away victory over Wrexham with a goal from McNamee. On December 24th Posh beat Darlington at London Road and Bly hit four goals to take his tally for the season to 22 before Christmas. On Boxing Day Posh travelled to Darlington and Bly notched two more in a 2–2 draw. The last game of 1960 was at home to Carlisle, Bly notched another hat–trick with Emery scoring two in a 5–0 win which took Bly's scoring run to an incredible nine goals in the last three games.

On January 7th Posh travelled to Fratton Park to take on 2nd Division Portsmouth in the F.A. Cup. True to their giantkilling tradition Posh won 2–1 with goals from Ripley and Hails. This set up Posh with a glamorous home tie against 1st Division Aston Villa in the next round. Back in the League they beat Mansfield 2–1 with goals from Emery and Bly.

Terry Bly notches up his fiftieth goal of the season
in the last match, at London Road.

The next game was at home to Aston Villa in the F.A. Cup, with a crowd of 28,266 (the largest at that time to attend a game at London Road). Newly promoted Aston Villa were matched stride for stride and blow for blow throughout the game, Hails scoring Posh's all important goal in a 1-1 draw that took them back to Villa Park for the fourth round replay four days later. This was played in front of a staggering 64,500 people with many Posh fans to this day recounting stories of the huge build up of traffic on the A47 trying to get to Birmingham that evening to watch the match. Many thousands of fans were also locked out of the ground on a night when the biggest crowd ever, came to watch Posh play. They went down 2-1 in a memorable Cup-tie with McNamee scoring the Posh goal. This ended their interest in the F.A. Cup in their first ever League season, but the players went out with their heads held high having only been beaten finally by First Division opponents.

Back in the League the phenomenal run was picking up at an alarming pace, and was frightening many of their 4th Division rivals. On February 4th Posh visited Stockport and came away with their largest ever away win in the league, 6-0; two goals from Bly, two from Emery and one apiece from Hails and McNamee. They went one better than that a week later as they thrashed Exeter at London Road by 7-1, Bly this time scoring a hat-trick, incredibly his fifth of the season, Hails scoring two plus – two own goals – in front of a crowd of 11,518. Two more own goals gave Posh a 2-0 victory over Gillingham the following week before they travelled to Northampton on February 25th, and much to the delight of the large travelling Posh support, won 3-0 with goals from McNamee, Smith and Bly.

Posh entertained Aldershot at London Road, and for the second time during the season smashed in seven goals, Smith getting a hat-trick, as did Emery, with Bly scoring the other, in a 7-1 victory. On March 11th Posh visited Oldham and in front of a 27,886 crowd came back with a 1-1 draw thanks to a goal from Ripley. At home though Posh were irresistible and they followed up their recent 7-1 thrashings of Aldershot and Exeter with a 6-0 hammering of Chester, Bly scoring four, plus another own goal and with Hails grabbing the other. This was performed in front of an attendance of 13,000.

The incredible Cup run finally ended at Villa Park. At London Road (above), McFarland beats Posh goal-keeper Jack, however the 'goal' was ruled offside. In the replay (below), Bly challenges the Villa goal-keeper, but it was McNamee who was to score for Posh.

Posh were capable of romping away with the league title at this early stage as they then beat Workington at home 2-1, Chester away 2-1, before coming back and beating Crewe 4-1 at London Road. This astounding run in the League concluded with victories of 3-1 at home to Bradford City and 1-0 at York with a goal from Bly.

It is hard even now to describe just how complete Posh's mastery was of the other teams in the 4th Division. The 1-0 win at York on April 8th actually clinched promotion for Posh with seven games remaining in the League, and they had already scored 115 goals in the process. The run came to an end on April 11th as Posh were beaten 3-2 at Accrington Stanley.

George Hudson scored a hat-trick for Accrington that day and it proved to be the last ever hat-trick scored in the League by an Accrington Stanley player. Posh gained revenge four days later as they won 3-1 with two goals from Bly and one from McNamee. Peterborough were now on the trail of the 4th Division Championship and came away from Rochdale with a 2-2 draw before losing 1-0 at Bradford on April 20th. Two days later they went down 4-3 at the Den to Millwall, with Bly scoring another two goals. It only took a 3-3 draw away at Southport on April 25th to clinch the 4th Division title for Posh, Bly claiming two goals and Hails the other.

It was announced that the Championship Trophy was to be presented by Mr Len Shipman on Saturday April 29th in the final game of the season at London Road, against Barrow. Posh celebrated in style winning 6-2 with a hat-trick from Bly, and one goal apiece from Ripley, Emery and Smith to complete the rout. This final six goal showing took Posh to a new League goal scoring record of 134 goals, that looks unlikely to be ever bettered. Bly finished the season by scoring 52 goals in the league and two in the Cup to set a new individual scoring record in Division 4.

It was a phenomenal first season for Peterborough in the Fourth Division, and the sheer volume of goals and margins of victory that were secured during their debut season did scant justice to the overwhelming superiority they had over every other side in the 4th Division. Whilst Terry Bly led the goalscoring chart, Billy Hails supported him with 22 League goals plus three in the cup, Ray Smith with 17 League goals, Peter McNamee with 16 League goals and three in the cup, and Dennis Emery with 15 League goals and two in the cup.

It is hard for those Posh fans who did not witness Posh's complete domination of their Fourth Division rivals to put into perspective just how great the achievements of this side were. For those Posh fans who did witness, it the side of......

Walls, Whittaker, Walker, Rayner, Rig-by, Ripley, Hails, Emery, Bly, Smith and McNamee

......was arguably the greatest Posh side ever to run on to a football pitch, and the mark that the side made in Peterborough United's history will live on for ever.

Manager Jimmy Hagan had provided the Club with an unforgetable debut season in the Football League............ .... And the fans were happy too!

1961/62 SEASON

The 1961/62 season started with Posh proudly placed in the Third Division in what was only their second League season. Manager Jimmy Hagan was busy in the transfer market bringing in six new players before the season started, whilst retaining all the regular squad who had so stylishly won the Fourth Division Championship the previous season; Derek Norris and Ray Hogg were in fact the only players from that side to have been released. Trevor Atkins, John Taylor, Chris Coates and George Pearce were the other players that were not retained. Johnny Anderson, having made just one appearance in goal in Posh's first ever League Cup tie, was not kept as a player but remained at London Road as trainer, and he was to figure prominently in Posh's future. In came goalkeeper Brian Ronson from Norwich and defender Ken Hawkes (Luton), the latter for a £2,000 fee. The most costly signings were John Turley – a forward from Sheffield United for what was reported at the time as *"a four figure fee"* – and Ollie Hopkins a big strong centre half from Barnsley (again at a time when accurate transfer figures were seldom quoted), for a *"substantial sum"*. Between these signings came forward Barry Tait from York and Roy Senior a winger from Doncaster Rovers. The new players however had few chances to prove themselves as Hagan opened the league season with the same side that finished the 1960/61 season.

Posh opened the Third Division campaign with a Peter McNamee goal after just three minutes at home to Hull – the fastest goal of the new season – and they went on to record a 3–2 victory. An unchanged side then recorded three straight victories in August, at Watford 3–2 and at Port Vale 1–0, before beating Watford again – to complete their first double of the season – at London Road in front of 18,078 spectators, their third largest home gate since joining the League. Bristol City ended the sequence with a 4–3 victory at London Road just four days later. Posh next visited Notts County and despite a brace from Terry Bly, a last minute equaliser from Loxley gave Notts a point. That night the result was shown on television as *Notts Co. 6 Peterborough 2*, giving a fright to more than a few Posh fans, but it proved to be more than prophetic however when two days later Posh slumped 6–2 in an away defeat at Bradford Park Avenue! Posh's biggest League defeat to that date.

The League Cup saw changes in the side, with Ronson replacing Jack Walls, Ellis Stafford for Rigby and Jimmy Sheavills replacing McNamee. The changes caused uproar amongst the fans and unfortunately the changes made no difference to their form as Posh lost 3–1 to First Division Blackburn Rovers at London Road. Hagan reacted to this latest defeat by making one further change, replacing Stafford with debutante Hopkins, the big money signing from Barnsley. Emery and Bly scored as Posh hit the winning trail again with a 2–1 home victory over a Grimsby side destined for promotion later in the season.

On September 20th Posh travelled to Gay Meadow where opponents Shrewsbury took a 3–1 lead. They battled back to make it 3–3 with the help of two Emery goals, the match finally decided by Senior – who was in the side in place of Sheavills – scoring on his debut to make it 4–3 to Posh. A third consecutive win was gained in a convincing 3–1 win at Coventry which kept Posh in the hunt at the top of the table, before they entertained Shrewsbury in the return League match at London Road. The Shrews player Jimmy McLaughlin arrived with the news of his call up that week to the Irish squad to play Scotland, and he celebrated by scoring a hat trick as Posh went down to their second home League defeat. Hagan again rang the changes and brought back Walls, Banham and McNamee to replace Ronson, Rayner and Sheavills, against struggling Brentford. Posh's Lowest league gate of the season – 12,533 – saw Brentford taken apart, with Bly 2, Emery 2, Hails and Smith the scorers in the 6–0 win.

The next big news to break was the signing of George Hudson from Accrington Stanley for £6,000. He was drafted straight into the team in place of Smith and scored in a 3–2 win at Newport on October 2nd. This win took Posh to second in the League. The inconsistency of the team continued with another home defeat, this time by 2–1 to Bournemouth. This was followed by a 2–1 victory at London Road over Newport, who were adrift at the foot of the League. A 28,886 crowd turned up at Selhurst Park for the next League game, the second highest away crowd to watch Posh in the League (the largest was a year earlier at the same venue). The result was a crushing 5–2 defeat, and the supporters' discontent grew at the number of goals the defence was letting in – it had kept only two clean sheets all season.

The first of two local derbies saw Posh beat Lincoln 5–4 in a thriller at London Road, Hudson scored two to make it five goals in five games, and at the County Ground Northampton which finished 2–2. At this time Posh played in the first of a number of friendlies at Norwich City, where they used substitutes for the first time. November saw them starting out in the F.A. Cup, a 3–3 home draw with Colchester, and the replay at Layer Road two days later also ending all square. The second replay was set for Norwich on 13th November 1962, and it proved to be a fateful day. Denis Emery was travelling towards the ground, on the Yaxley road at around 8.30 a.m. He pulled out to overtake a lorry at Nobby Gates, a notorious accident blackspot, and was involved in a collision with another vehicle. He sustained severe injuries including a dislocated thigh and a broken leg. It was feared that one of Posh's most colourful characters and popular players would not play again. The Cup-tie at Norwich went ahead with Smith taking Emery's place, and Posh won 3–0 with Hudson scoring a hat trick. This victory earned the right to play at Torquay in the second round, for the second year running.

Posh first had to entertain Swindon at London Road, they won the encounter 3-2 with goals from Senior, Hails and Hudson. The match at Torquay was easy enough for Posh against a side struggling at the wrong end of the Third Division. The 4-1 victory earned them a glamour trip to Second Division Newcastle. Before that Posh had a busy December programme, starting with the League leaders Portsmouth, who inflicted a 1-0 defeat at London Road, Jimmy Dunne making only his second appearance for the club in place of Bly. Hopkins made a happy return to Oakwell when Posh claimed two points in a 3-0 win, Bly scoring two on his return to the side. A draw at Hull was followed by another home defeat, to Port Vale, leading to speculation that Posh were not good enough to go up to the Second Division. Boxing Day saw Posh's lowest League crowd to that date – 8,237 – but a convincing 4-1 victory over Southend.

A great through ball from Keith Ripley, and Terry Bly scores the only goal of the match at Newcastle, which puts Posh through to the 4th round of the F.A. Cup.

The Newcastle Cup-tie at St. James Park was the first match in 1962, and over three thousand Posh fans made the journey to the North East, in a total crowd of over 42,000. Ivor Allchurch, the inspirational Welsh International and Newcastle skipper, had the ball in the Peterborough net after just five minutes, but surprisingly the referee disallowed the 'goal' for offside despite no signal from the linesman. Posh gradually gained the upper hand but had to wait until the 74th minute before Keith Ripley put Bly through to score. The drama was not quite over as Newcastle's John McGuigan missed a sitter five minutes from time, but Posh held firm to record another giantkilling.

Posh followed up the cup victory with a 2-1 win at Ashton Gate thanks to two Bly goals, which took his scoring to five consecutive games. Another 28,000 crowd came to watch the cup tie with First Division Sheffield United at London Road, as they did for Aston Villa a year earlier. Sheffield however all but won the tie in the first 21 minutes, Billy Russell scoring in the 13th and 18th minutes and Derek Pace robbing Hopkins to make it 3-0. Posh settled after this start, and missed a succession of good chances, but in the end only had a Hudson goal as reward for a final result of 3-1.

This loss sparked off another indifferent spell as Posh crashed to three more defeats, at Grimsby and at struggling Brentford, plus in the home match with Coventry. The newspapers reported that manager Hagan was happy and that, *"he could not get any better players than he already had"*. Chairman Cyril Palmer disagreed and stated:

"We are concerned about our weaknesses in defence, we are also perturbed about our long term policy. We are well up the table but, in the opinion of the Directors, still not good enough for our public." Mr Palmer also added that Hagan had well over £10,000 to spend on players.

For the next game against fellow promotion hopefuls Q.P.R., Ronson was retained in goal after returning to the side at Brentford, and McNamee replaced Senior on the wing. Just under 12,000 people saw Posh return to winning ways with a 5-1 hammering of Rangers. After Hudson and Hails had given Posh a lead, three goals in a three minute second half spell made it 4-1 to Posh, including inside forward Smith's 100th goal for the Club. Hails goal in that match was his 99th for Posh. Gerald Graham returned to the side for a draw at Bournemouth and then came a revenge 4-1 home win over Crystal Palace, to put Posh back into the top six and challenging for promotion once more.

Wins against Lincoln away and Bradford at home, sandwiched the Club's seventh home defeat of the season, to local rivals Northampton. A 17 year old winger marked his debut for the Cobblers with a goal, his name was Tommy Robson.

A friendly against Danish Champions F.C. Odense at London Road was poorly attended, but the stay away fans missed a cracking match as Posh came from 2-0 down to draw 2-2, with Hopkins getting Posh's second from a 25 yard free kick. Posh also played against First Division Huddersfield in Roy Jacobs Testimonial Match, losing 4-1, and then lost at home 6-0 to Norwich in the return match of the friendly that had been played earlier in the season.

Back in the League, Posh came from 3-1 down to draw 3-3 at Loftus Road which left both Posh and Q.P.R. still in the top six. A week later Posh triumphed 5-1 at home to Halifax on Grand National day, and three days later returned from Torquay with a 3-1 victory, to go 4th in the table, just one point behind second placed Bournemouth. The recent good run ended in controversy at Swindon and a 3-2 defeat.

Mike Summerbee scored the Wiltshire club's first goal, but Posh claimed Atkins later goal for Swindon was offside. The fourth straight win over Torquay, 2-1 at London Road, came via a McNamee winner in the 89th minute. In between these games Posh had retained the Northants. Senior Cup at London Road with a 3-1 win. Skipper Norman Rigby commented: *"Without this needle, it wouldn't have been a cup tie, would it?"*. This remark came after a match which was played in a "tough atmosphere" on and off the pitch, the Northampton players being booed and slow handclapped at the end of the game.

The 42nd League match of the season was to be Posh's last defeat of the season, 3-2 at Reading. Turley was brought in at centre forward but without success. Despite Posh leading 2-1, Reading scored two goals in the last eight minutes to win 3-2. Posh then reeled off four straight wins including a 3-0 victory at Champions-elect Portsmouth, but only finished 5th, four points behind second placed Grimsby. Posh had completed their second League season still without having been 'doubled' by another side, and for the second season running had scored 100 League goals.

1962/63 SEASON

Posh had successfully consolidated within the Third Division in the 1961/62 season, and great expectations had grown amongst the supporters for the new campaign. The main worries had previously been the insistence of Posh to throw caution to the wind and play only two defenders and eight attackers. This style had been modified somewhat by the end of April 1962, and fans looked forward to Hagan's team building plans with eagerness.

The changes made by Hagan certainly caused some shocks, of the players released probably the biggest bombshell was the decision to sell Terry Bly to Division Three rivals Coventry for £10,000. It was reported that Bly had been unsettled at London Road for some time and wanted to get away. In his stay at London Road he had become Posh's most prolific League marksman, scoring 81 goals in 88 League appearances, a comparable record unlikely to be ever beaten. Free transfers had been given to Norman Rigby, a stalwart of some 11 season at London Road, who went to Boston . Also Ken Hawkes – signed the previous season – went to Bedford, along with Roy Banham and Jimmy Dunne. Jack Walls, who played in four Midland League Championship sides and was ever-present in the 1960/61 season, also went on a 'free', to King's Lynn. Cliff Sansby who made just one League appearance went to Spalding.

Dick Beattie came in as a replacement, a Scottish U-23 Player who had played against Posh for the previous year's Division Three Champions Portsmouth. Fees of £2,000 were paid for full back Tommy Singleton from

Blackpool, and Port Vale's winger Brian Jackson. Roy Horobin, a forward, came from Notts County for £5,000. Earlier in the close season Hagan had taken Colin Brookes of West Bromwich Albion, a schoolboy International of some promise, and the biggest signing, Terry Simpson came for a record four figure sum. Posh lined up in their first League match of the season, at Dean Court against Bournemouth, who had finished 3rd the previous season, with four players making their Posh debuts. Beattie, Singleton, Simpson and Horobin helped to earn Posh a 3-3 draw. The same team then beat Carlisle 4-1 and Barnsley 4-2, to set the early pace in the Division, Hudson netting two in each game to take his tally to five goals in three games. John Turley came into the side in place of Horobin, when McNamee scored two in a 2-2 draw at Carlisle. Posh then travelled to Northampton for the local derby and won 3-2, with goals from Turley and two from McNamee, to preserve their unbeaten League record at the County Ground.

Horobin returned to the side for the team's first defeat of the season, by 3-1 at Eastville to Bristol Rovers, followed by defeat at home to Q.P.R. Ronson was recalled for the return with Rovers in place of Beattie, and he kept a clean sheet for the 1-0 victory, thanks to a Hudson goal. The same side lost at Hull five days later and that signalled widespread changes. Out went Rayner, Horobin, Hails and Smith – in came Gerald Graham, Jimmy Sheavills, Roy Senior and local lad Alan Morton, the latter for his League debut. Posh won 3-0 and then held Crystal Palace to a 0-0 draw at London Road, Ronson keeping his third clean sheet in four games.

On September 24th Posh travelled to Villa Park to face a second round League Cup tie. Derek Dougan was the thorn in Posh's side that night scoring a hat-trick, as Villa ran out 6-1 winners. Hagan brought back Horobin and Senior for the 4-4 draw at Wrexham, Morton getting his first goal for the club. After drawing with struggling Halifax, Morton made way for Billy Hails's return to the side. Colin Brookes was placed on the transfer list along with Ray Smith who had been with the club since 1956. Bradford P.A. were beaten at London Road in front of the ITV television cameras, with Smith scoring, and it proved to be Smith's last game for Posh. He went to join big rivals Northampton, who were riding high with Posh at the top of the table. Then came a dreadful performance with a 2-0 defeat at the Shay, and this became Hails's last game for Posh as he also joined the Cobblers, for an undisclosed fee. Between them Smith and Hails had scored many goals for Peterborough; Hails having netted 28 goals in 94 League appearances, and Smith 33 in 92 League games. Both players had been great servants to the Club. Brian Jackson made his Posh debut in the 3-2 victory at Watford, the winner from McNamee coming just four minutes from time. The double was completed over Brighton at London Road, leaving Posh second in the table on goal difference from Northampton.

On Tuesday 18th October 1962 the dramatic news of Jimmy Hagan's sacking broke. It was reported that he was *"sacked on the spot"*, allegedly for incidents involving players. Johnny Anderson took over team affairs along with the Directors for a period of nine games that saw Posh beaten only twice. Two days after Hagan's dismissal, Posh beat Bristol City 3-1 at London Road to stay second, and after the game the Directors were applauded by the crowd.

That same Saturday also saw the reserves win 7-1 at Notts County, with Posh favourite Denis Emery scoring his first goal since making a comeback from his car crash injuries. To complete a most successful day, the "A" side won 8-0, beating Mitchells in the Northants. Senior Cup.

Turley was called into the side for the next match at Reading and scored the only goal of the game, he stepped down again for the next match, to allow Hudson to return for the F.A. Cup tie against Notts County. It took Hudson just four minutes to get onto the score sheet as Posh went on to record a 3-0 victory, despite goalkeeper Ronson finishing the match with a painful back injury. The following week Posh were back in League action, at Gay Meadow, Shrewsbury coming out as 5-4 winners, a reversal of the previous season's 4-3 victory! Shrewsbury finally halted Posh's recovery from a 4-3 deficit with minutes left.

They bounced back from this setback with a 6-0 hammering of Millwall at London Road, Jim Rayner – then playing as an inside right – scored a hat trick, the only one scored by a Posh player that season. One week later they returned to Cup action, entertaining non-League Enfield at London Road. Ronson kept a second consecutive clean sheet as Hudson scored the only goal. The 16,000 crowd, was around 5,000 up on earlier attendances. Beattie returned in goal and retained his place a week later when Posh lost at Notts County for only their second defeat since Hagan was sacked. Tony Moulden became the Directors and Anderson's first signing, from Rochdale, which was quickly followed by Graham Sissons arrival from Birmingham City. The two appeared at home to Bournemouth, with Moulden becoming the seventh player to score on his League debut.

George Hudson scores in the 3-0 F.A.Cup win at Meadow Lane.

It was announced on December 19th that Jack Fairbrother was, for the second time, to be the new Manager of Peterborough United. He made just one change in his first side, bringing in Senior for Sheavills, in the 2–0 win at Barnsley. Senior laid on Horobin's 11th minute opener, and McNamee scored the second just a minute later, which kept Posh in the top three. Fairbrother's first home game was on Boxing Day against Coventry City, the club he used to manage. A 13,000 crowd saw Posh well beaten 3–0, by a Coventry side who although lower in the table had been beaten only five times in the League, and had games in hand over others. Three days later Posh went to Highfield Road and came back with a point from a 3–3 draw.

That was to be the last competitive match for some time as the big freeze of 1963 set in, and the F.A. Cup tie against Derby was postponed six times in all. The weather totally decimated the League and Cup programme and the 'Pools Panel' was inaugurated to assess the results of postponed games. Posh did actually get one match under way in January, when Leicester City won a friendly game, in Peterborough – by 2–1 – on the snow covered Brotherhoods Sports Ground. The weather did not stop Posh off the field either, since before the next League match winger Jack Overfield arrived from Sunderland for £5,000 and Dick Beattie went to St. Mirren for *"several thousand pounds"*. Beattie was later to become one of the players found guilty in the match fixing scandal that saw Peter Swan and Tony Kay, both Internationals, banned from playing for life. One of the matches alleged to have been "thrown" by Beattie was the 2–1 home defeat by Q.P.R. in September 1962.

On Saturday February 2nd 1963 an incident occurred that caused a major split in the community and resulted in Posh making their own little piece of history. Due to the big freeze the scheduled home match against Hull City was postponed, however, visitors to the ground that day were a group of Cambridge United players who had come to watch the match. The two sets of players decided to play a friendly game in the absence of their normal fixtures. The result was duly given out on television and there was a match report. Unfortunately when asked for details, neither the local Press nor some of the club Directors knew of the game. The following reports in the local Press criticised Posh for their lack of communication over the affair, with Manager Fairbrother trying to play down the issue. In a bitter dispute that was to last for several months, the club's anger at the report led them withdraw the Press facilities. This in turn led to Posh launching on Wednesday March 13th the *"Posh Post"*, the club's own newspaper, the first in the Football League to publish a newspaper for it's fans.

The next serious action was with First Division Derby in the F.A. Cup, and on a frozen pitch Derby seized on defensive errors to win 2–0. An outstanding player was Posh's Denis Emery, who made his return for the first time since his car crash. The first home game since Boxing Day was played on February 16th, and on a mud

bath of a pitch. Wrexham were the visitors, and they adapted much better to the conditions, winning 3–1, although Overfield made an impressive debut in this match. Despite this latest home defeat Posh were top of the Third Division and they looked a good bet for promotion after the return home match with 4th placed Watford. Overfield was dropped, and Fairbrother's call for tighter defending was answered. A collision between Jim Rayner and Watford defender Nicholas, resulted in the ball spinning free and past Linton in the Watford goal. His lunge at the ball was successful but his momentum only succeeded in carrying the ball over the line. Things became easier after that, although the hapless Nicholas completed his miserable day by handling and giving away a penalty which gave Posh their fourth goal.

The next two games saw a contrast in fortunes, but the same result in both matches – draws. A two goal lead after half an hour at Bradford was squandered, whilst at Bristol City Brian Jackson scored in injury time to get a point, although Stafford had been lucky not to concede a penalty. He pushed John Atyeo face first into the mud in the area, but the referee signalled a fair charge! Stafford lost his place in the side when Singleton returned for a 1–1 draw at Reading, which was followed by a 3–1 home win over Port Vale. This extended Posh's unbeaten League run to five games, and by now they sat on top of the Third Division, three points clear of nearest rivals Swindon.

Posh then embarked on an alarming slide. They first lost 3–2 at Port Vale – despite leading twice before conceding the winner with seconds remaining. Then at London Road, they were 'doubled' for the first time in their League history, by Hull City, who ran out easy 3–1 winners. Denis Emery made a disappointing return in what proved to be his last home appearance. This miserable run then saw Shrewsbury quickly inflict on them their second League double, and Posh's 5th home defeat of the season.

After the two home defeats came another blow for Posh fans, Hudson being sold to fellow Division III rivals Coventry who were managed by Jimmy Hill, just nine months after another star forward, Terry Bly, had been sold to the same club. Jack Fairbrother explained that Hudson was not happy at the club and would not stand in his way if he wished to leave. He left after 65 League appearances, and proceeded to score a hat trick in his first game for Coventry.

The visit to Millwall on 6th April (a 1–0 victory), saw several changes, with Turley and Moulden recalled, and new signing Billy Day (from Newcastle), making his League debut, with Jackson, Sheavills and Hudson making way for them. A Good Friday visit to Swindon was watched by the Wiltshire team's highest League gate of the season, 23,239. It was a match that Posh won 3–2, and a result that knocked Swindon off the top of the Division. It took Swindon only 45 seconds to take the lead through Ernie Hunt, but Posh hit back through Mc-

Namee and Horobin. Despite a second from Hunt after 54 minutes, Turley popped up again for the second consecutive match to head the winner.

The revival was short lived as just 24 hours later another disastrous home defeat followed, this time 3–1 to mid-table Southend. To complete a topsy turvy four days Posh played host to second placed Swindon, who had shaken off their Friday defeat to Posh, when they beat Colchester 6–1. It was to be Posh's day again, for they gave Manager Fairbrother, ill with pneumonia, a boost by winning 3–1 in front of 13,216 fans. Posh outplayed their promotion rivals, and Turley scored his fourth goal in four games since returning to the side.

That was to be the last high point of another good season for Posh gained only one more win from their last six games, finishing sixth, and seven points off the second promotion spot occupied by Swindon.

Probably the biggest blow came in the penultimate match when neighbours Northampton romped to a 4–0 victory at London Road. To make matters worse the large crowd watched Posh old boys Hails and Smith score, along with a Rayner own goal. The final game of the season was played at White City in London, Q.P.R's temporary home. A dull 0–0 draw was played out with mid-table Rangers, in front of a restless Q.P.R. crowd who slow handclapped and booed their side as they clung on to a point, thanks to some good goalkeeping from debutante Peter Springett and some goal line clearances. It proved to be Denis Emery's last game for Posh.

The final statistic saw Posh, with 93, fall just short of the 100 League goal mark. Northampton were in fact the only Division Three side to reach the century that season, with 109. It left many Posh fans pondering Hagan's sacking and Hudson's sale to Coventry which eventually seemed to turn Posh's season.

1963/64 SEASON

Jack Fairbrother started in his first full League season as Manager of Posh. Inevitably the summer saw a great number of comings and goings on the transfer market as Fairbrother strived to build a team capable of winning promotion to Division Two.

Fairbrother disappeared on a 'secret mission' to Germany in May 1963 with the signings of Willie Duff and Brian Wright already complete. Upon his return it was announced that Aston Villa's talented forward Derek Dougan had signed for the Posh. Despite a posse of clubs chasing Dougan's signature the Irish International opted for Posh thanks to the tenacity of Fairbrother in tracking his man down. Aston Villa boss Joe Mercer accepted the transfer bid, but added that Dougan was on holiday abroad and upon his return the highest offer would then be accepted.

Fairbrother had to move quickly, for he knew Dougan was in Germany but nobody, including Mercer, would say where. In hope more than expectation he contacted the German Embassy, gave the particulars of the man he wanted to trace, who was somewhere in the Munich area. Surprisingly Fairbrother was rewarded with an address, and he duly sent a cablegram, asking – tongue in cheek – for Dougan to: *Ring me at 11 a.m. the following day'.*

Dougan phoned the following day telling Jack Fairbrother: *"If you can go to this much trouble finding me, I am coming home immediately to have a real talk to you."* Mercer was shocked when he discovered that Dougan was on his way back from Germany, but stood by Posh's offer, and within five days Dougan had signed for Peterborough. The shocks in the transfer market did not end with the Dougan signing, for popular wing half Terry Simpson went in a straight swap with West Brom.

inside forward Keith Smith, in a deal with former Posh boss Jimmy Hagan. Not surprisingly both sets of supporters and Managers argued as to who had the best of the deal. In July, Denis Emery left Posh for just £1,500 to join Bedford. It was a day that most Posh fans would never have predicted, for despite not having the best of starts to his career at London Road in the Midland League days, he grew into possibly the biggest star seen at London Road.

Of particular note was his run of 10 consecutive F.A. Cup ties in which he scored a goal. In spite of several attempted come–backs in the previous season he struggled to find his old form and slipped into the reserves. The Directors offered Denis a new contract, but he rejected the terms and finally ended his eight year association with the Club.

Several minor signings were made in the shape of Maurice Emmerson – a goalkeeper from Middlesbrough – Reg Pearce and Mike Pickup both from Cambridge City and Peter Thompson from Grantham. Leaving London Road were Brian Ronson to Spalding (as player/coach), Jim Rayner – a veteran from the Midland League – to Grantham as player/manager, Jimmy Sheavills and Colin Brookes to Barnsley, plus Alan Morton to Lincoln. The final signing was the Welsh U–23 International Frank Rankmore from Second Division Cardiff City, who were managed by ex Posh boss George Swindin.

Not for the first time the expectations of the fans had been lifted with the news of the close season signings. It seemed as though Fairbrother had won back many of the stay away supporters who stopped attending matches when George Hudson was sold the previous season.

Posh started with a 5-2 home victory over Wrexham in front of 14,784, fielding a side giving Peterborough United debuts to Duff, Wright, Rankmore, Pearce, Smith and Dougan. Posh came from 2-1 down to gain the win thanks to a Peter McNamee hat trick and debut goals for Smith and Dougan. Following a goalless draw at Hull Posh slipped to their first defeat of the season at Q.P.R. A friendly at London Road drew 5,514 fans to see a Posh side beat Israeli side Hapoel of Tel Aviv 4-0, goals coming from John Turley (2), an own goal, and a Pearce penalty. The gate receipts went towards Jim Walker's and Ron Cooper's Testimonial Fund. Two home games saw Posh pick up three points with a 2-2 draw against Bristol Rovers and a 5-1 thrashing of Hull City. Dougan followed up his goal against Rovers with a hat trick against a Hull defence that had conceded only one goal in their opening four games.

Dougan's booking - for smiling at the Referee - in the match versus Southend is captured by this cartoon!

Two defeats then followed to early pacesetters Oldham and Bournemouth, before rock bottom club Notts County felt the backlash in another five goal performance at London Road, Dougan netting twice. Posh continued their dismal run in the League Cup, losing 3-2 away to Millwall - in four seasons of trying they still had not won a tie. Meanwhile, away from home, they had not won in five matches. At London Road though Posh were still boasting a proud unbeaten record, and victory over Southend was followed by a 2-1 win over top club Bournemouth, following which they moved into 7th spot. Posh's winner in the latter game delighted the 15,138 crowd in the last minute, when Dougan forced Tom Standley to put through his own net.

In the space of three days in October, Posh managed to get rid of two records, by beating Watford 'away', and then promptly surrendering their home record in a 3-2 defeat to Millwall; a young goalkeeper called Pat Jennings played in the Watford side. Hopkins, Walker and Moulden were all drafted into the team for the visit to Ashton Gate, but despite Moulden scoring, they slipped to another away defeat. Moulden then starred in the victory at Millwall, to move Posh into 6th place in the table. Posh next entertained a Walsall side at London Road, who were unbeaten in nine League games. Things looked to be going Posh's way however when Walsall were reduced to 10 men early in the second half due to an injury. It was Posh though that were to be disappointed as Walsall cancelled out a 17th minute Dougan goal to win 2-1.

More changes were made for the visit of Colchester, Singleton and Sissons returning and Ron Cooper making his debut in a 4-0 win. The infuriating inconsistency of the side continued as Posh then embarked on a run of eight games without a win.

Two defeats - at Reading and Colchester - were followed by a scoreless draw at Luton. Gerald Graham came in to the team for the Luton match, but was dropped with Mc-Namee to allow Senior and Smith to return for the 3-2 reverse at Coventry (after leading at one stage by 2-0). The Coventry side contained John Sillett and George Curtis, and one of the Coventry goals came from George Hudson. The 29,633 attendance was City's biggest of the season.

The F.A. Cup tie at home to Watford restored the dwindling crowds briefly when 15,163 watched Posh draw 1-1, but a 2-1 replay defeat, which was settled four minutes from the end of extra time, gave Watford their first victory in seven attempts since Posh joined the League. Just before the replay Jack Overfield was advised to give up playing due to repeated problems with an old knee injury. Back in the League things did not improve, with a 2-0 defeat at Brentford. The next home match was against Shrewsbury in front of a crowd of 8,010, Posh's smallest League attendance since joining. Many of the fans were leaving the ground long before the end of the game as Shrewsbury held a 2-0 lead for most of the match. However two goals in the last three minutes, from a diving Turley header and a back heel by Smith secured a point. This was achieved without Dougan, who was out of the side due to illness.

Dougan returned for the next match at Wrexham, and took just 11 minutes to get on the score sheet, going on to add another. Posh ran out 3-2 winners, leaving Wrexham bottom of the League with 10 points from 23 games. Posh's winning form continued, but the attendance figures plummeted to another all time low of 6,419 for the next home game. The Christmas games saw 14th placed Posh take on 19th placed Crewe - home and away - the first ended scoreless, but the second was a more rousing affair which resulted in a 3-2 Posh victory, in front of a more encouraging crowd of 9,015.

The New year started with another dismal run of results, just as many of the Posh faithful thought a revival was forthcoming. After losing at home to Mansfield, Hopkins was recalled for the visit to Bristol Rovers, a game in which Posh led, and indeed looked the more likely winners, until a late equaliser saved Rovers a point. A scoreless draw with Oldham at London Road was followed with a 1–0 defeat at second placed Crystal Palace.

The fans grew restless, and Fairbrother searched for new names to improve the results. One of these was Peter Deakin of Bolton, however a fee of £18,000 ensured that this became no more than interest! The gloom continued as Posh slipped to defeats at Southend and at home to Watford – 2–0 and 1–0 respectively – after a goalless draw at home to Notts County. Posh had now gone five games without scoring and seven games without a win.

On February 15th, almost exactly one year to the day after he joined Posh, Jack Fairbrother announced his resignation as Manager. Both the *"Posh Post"* and local media maintained that Fairbrother's resignation was not just linked to the poor results on the pitch, although no more information was forthcoming at the time. Just one week later however, Fairbrother told his story in a two part *"People"* newspaper article. He gave his reasons as a series of incidents that had built up into a crisis over a two week period. The main problem it appeared was interference with team selection. In the wake of this resignation a vote of no confidence in the Directors was given by the players. Johnny Anderson, who along with the Directors had temporarily managed the team in 1962 (losing only twice), again took control of team affairs. He started his second stint with Dougan suffering from an injury, and recalling Moulden to replace Billy Day.

In his first match in charge in 1962 Posh beat Bristol City 3–1 at Peterborough, this time Bristol City were dispatched 4–2 at London Road, to break the long run without a victory. Dougan's deputy Turley scored along with McNamee 2 and Smith. This left Posh 13th in the table but an unchanged side made it three out of three for Anderson, with wins at Port Vale and at home to 5th placed Reading.

Dougan returned for the visit to Luton, and Emmerson came on for his debut. Posh won 3–2 and the following week drew 1–1 at home to Port Vale. Anderson's record, since taking over as Manager, had produced 4 victories and 1 draw in the 5 games played. They were beaten in their next match at Mansfield (4–1), but bounced straight back with a 3–2 home win against Barnsley – Dougan scoring twice and Smith getting the other. Twenty four hours later Barnsley reversed the scoreline at Oakwell, but again Posh then replied in the best possible fashion, winning 3–0 at home to Brentford. The following day Gordon Clark of Sheffield Wednesday accepted the job as Manager of Peterborough United, officially taking charge from April 2nd, just before the final game of the season at Walsall.

The season drifted to an uneventful close, with the final home game of the season bringing Coventry City to London Road, the Third Division Champions–elect. Posh had not read the script though and a crowd of 26,307, Posh's record home League gate, saw Thompson on his debut and Dougan, score to give Posh a memorable 2–0 win. The final game of the season at Walsall was lost 2–0 and Posh finished 10th in the table.

Clark went to work immediately, naming Norman Rigby as Assistant Trainer and Johnny Anderson as Trainer, ready for a new campaign in the hope of building a successful side at London Road.

The all time record Football League attendance, over 26,000, at London Road. Coventry are beaten 2–0. Colin Thompson scores his first goal for Posh

1964/1965 SEASON

After the struggle of the previous season Posh started another League campaign in the Third Division, and yet again with a new Manager. Clark went about rebuilding the team by bringing in nine new players in the close season and releasing eleven. The first of the new arrivals came in May with the signing of Tony Reed, a goalkeeper, and Graham Birks – both from Sheffield Wednesday. At the same time Ollie Conmy, an inside forward, came in from Huddersfield. Outgoing were Roy Horobin to Crystal Palace, Brian Jackson to Lincoln, Gerald Graham who moved to Mansfield. John Turley went to Rochdale and Jack Overfield to Bradford City.

The longest serving player to leave was Ellis Stafford who moved to Corby Town. Ellis had been with the club since 1957 and had collected three Midland League Championship medals as well as playing in Posh's first League match. He was renowned for his work off the pitch, being a great organiser of social activities centred around the football club. Although severing a seven year association with the club this was to be renewed in later years.

Completing the new signings were Peter Deakin from Bolton, Ken Maloy from Plymouth, Scunthorpe's Ian Crawford, Harry Orr and Dennis Shiels both from Sheffield United and Clark's biggest signing – Vic Crowe from Aston Villa. Crowe was an experienced 1st Division player and Welsh International, and was joining Posh as a 32 year old.

The first match was at Exeter, and the Posh line up saw five players making their League debuts; Birks, Crowe, Barnes, Conmy and Crawford were the newcomers, but Posh went down to an opening day defeat for the first time since joining the League. After leading, thanks to a 17th minute Smith goal, they went 2–1 behind before half time. Smith scored again, but newly promoted Exeter sealed Posh's fate with two more goals to run out as 4–2 winners. Things soon looked brighter however in front of 13,483 fans at London Road, with a side changed to accommodate Peter McNamee, which saw Crawford switch wings and Barnes dropped. Two more Keith Smith goals led the way led the way as Posh hammered a poor Oldham side. Five days later and Smith took his tally to six goals in three games after Posh beat Bournemouth 4–3 at home in a thrilling game. Posh went into an early 2–0 lead from Smith and Crawford, his first for the Club, before allowing Bournemouth to draw back to 2–2. Just one minute after the equaliser, Smith got his second to make it 3–2 to Posh at half time. Shortly after the break both Dougan and Birks went off injured leaving Posh with only nine men on the pitch for some 15 minutes. As soon as Dougan returned he scored, and Posh hung on to take the points, despite the gap being narrowed six minutes from time. Posh's form was still erratic though, and a 3–1 defeat at Oldham – where Deakin scored on his debut – was followed by a third

straight home win, this time over Southend. Smith again bagged two goals, and got another on the Monday when Posh beat Bristol Rovers 3–1. Rovers had come into the match as unbeaten leaders of the division and finished it with Posh one point behind them in second place. 14,420 fans watched the game that saw Posh become the leading scorers in the League with 19 in six games.

The dismal away showings had not improved though, and a poor display and two bad mistakes by keeper Willie Duff cost the points when Grimsby won 2–0 at Blundell Park. Duff lost his place in the side as Reed replaced him for the visit to Eastville. That game also gave Deakin a recall and Maloy his debut, but all to no avail as a 4–0 defeat saw Posh slip to the bottom half of the table, and Rovers go top.

The first defeat at London Road followed with Posh dropping down to 15th in the table. Reed played his second and final game for Peterborough United in another entertaining game. Things started well enough, McNamee scoring after 22 minutes, but Mansfield hit back with two goals, before Dougan squared it at 2–2 by half time. Dougan made it 3–2 to give Posh a lead that they held until the 73rd minute, after Mansfield's keeper Humphreys was carried off in the 50th minute, being replaced by Gill. Things then started to go wrong for Posh, with Scanlon, Wagstaffe and Chapman all scoring for Mansfield, in a four minute spell to make it an unbelievable 5–3. Dougan completed his hat trick but could not find the equaliser as Mansfield hung on for the two points.

Some respite came with a League Cup match at Filbert Street against the holders of the Cup, when Posh attempted to get past the first match in the competition for the first time. The initial product of Jack Fairbrother's youth policy was given a debut in the shape of 18 year old goalkeeper Brian Robinson, and back came veteran Jim Walker, who had returned from Grantham. Other changes included recalls for Barnes, Shiels (his debut), plus Moulden and Deakin. The revamped side earned a hard fought 0–0 draw to earn a replay. Included in the Leicester line up were Gordon Banks and Frank McLintock.

Before the replay Clark moved to solve his goalkeeping problem by signing ex-Villa star Nigel Sims from Toronto. He made his debut at Luton in an otherwise unchanged side, where a Moulden goal earned a point. Clark changed things again for the visit of top of the table Brentford, Conmy came in on the right wing and McNamee on the left, whilst Smith returned at inside forward. A 13,331 crowd saw Posh lift themselves to 9th with a 3–1 win. McNamee was in irresistible form scoring two goals, with Smith getting the other, and taking his tally to 10 in 10 games. Crowe was the only absentee from the side to play Carlisle at home on the Saturday with Cooper coming in, but a 2–1 defeat resulted.

Clark rang the changes for the return match at Brentford three days later, bringing back Hopkins, Sissons, Shiels and Crawford, but two late goals saw the Bees gain a 3–1 revenge victory.

The Leicester replay was something of an anticlimax as a 10,562 crowd saw Leicester's Colin Appleton and Jimmy Goodfellow get their side through with a 2–0 win. Robinson returned for that game and retained his place for the League match at Scunthorpe, where goals from Deakin, Crawford and Shiels took Posh to a 3–2 victory, their first away win of the season. It was the start of a good run for Posh. They came back from 2–0 to get a draw at home to Port Vale, and then nearly did the reverse letting a 3–0 lead at home to Walsall slip to 3–2, before final victory.

Clark went into the transfer market again signing ex-Wolves and England star, 30 year old Eddie Clamp. He made his debut at Port Vale, where Posh took a 16th minute lead, and did well to hold it after losing Hopkins after 36 minutes. A draw at Watford was followed by another win at London Road, raising Posh to 6th in the table, just four points behind leaders Brentford. Smith made his last appearance for Posh at Workington in a 4–0 hammering, before going to Crystal Palace for £12,000, having during scored during the season 14 goals in 18 League games.

Posh made the trip to Hull fielding a side that was now lacking the transferred top scorer Smith, and Derek Dougan. Even the most ardent Posh fans doubted the team's ability of getting a good result. The new look side, gave Harry Orr his debut, and surprisingly produced a thoroughly deserved 2–0 win. Shiels made way for the fit again 'Doog' when Salisbury were the opposition in the 1st round of the F.A. Cup at London Road. After 28 minutes it looked as though Posh's wretched inconsistency would give them some unwanted headlines in the following day's newspapers, with Salisbury putting Posh under some pressure and initially taking a 1–0 lead. This finally seemed to spur Posh into action and Deakin and Crowe scored before half time. It was then down to the recalled Dougan to finish the contest by grabbing his second hat trick of the season in a 15 minute period after half time.

After losing at Bristol City, Posh prepared to do battle with Q.P.R. over the next three fixtures. The first game, in the League, saw Posh hammer Rangers 6–1, the biggest win for three years, but in front of the lowest crowd of the season at London Road of 8,337. When interviewed after the game Q.P.R. Manager Alec Stock promised that the Londoners would beat Posh in the Cup the following week with *"no trouble at all"*. In reality Q.P.R. rescued the match with two goals in the last 10 minutes after Peterborough had taken a 3–1 lead with goals from Barnes, Deakin and McNamee.

It was Deakin grabbing his 4th and 5th goals in three games against Q.P.R. that made sure it was to be Posh

that earned a trip to Chesterfield in the next round, although he left it very late! Posh trailed 1–0 two minutes into injury time, when Birks crossed the ball for Dougan to head down and Deakin to sweep home, to send the tie to extra time. Just two minutes into extra time McNamee beat three men and then released a through ball to Deakin who was left to slot home the winner. The victory was tinged with some sadness however, as four Chesterfield players who travelled to watch the tie were involved in a car accident at Colsterworth near Grantham. One of them, Ralph Hunt, tragically died later from the injuries he sustained.

Over the Christmas period Clark continued to experiment with his team line-ups in order to find a winning formula but the same inconsistency in results continued – a draw at home to Exeter, victory at Bournemouth, and a 4–1 thrashing of struggling Barnsley on Boxing Day at London Road. 48 hours later, ex-Posh man Sheavills was the main provider of Barnsley's goals in the 3–1 result.

Much to the fans' annoyance Dougan was again dropped for the trip to Southend, which ended in defeat, and dropped Posh to 9th in the table. It was something of a dilemma for Clark who had frequently dropped "Doog", but who was arguably the biggest star to appear at London Road, and was rated very highly by both the Posh fans and other clubs in the Third Division.

The Doog was back for the cup match at Saltergate however, and let everyone know it, notching up a hat trick of headers in a somewhat flattering victory. The Posh side showed only one change – Moulden for Conmy – that took on and beat Grimsby 3–1 at London Road with Dougan again finding the net in front of 13,413, the biggest crowd at London Road since September.

January 30th saw a record attendance for Posh as 30,056 came and packed into London Road to see an Arsenal side, that included Joe Baker, George Eastham, Frank McLintock, John Radford and Don Howe in their F.A.Cup line-up. The game looked to be going predictably the way of the First Division giants when Eastham put 18 year old Radford away to score Arsenal's first after 44 minutes. It stayed that way until the 73rd minute when Conmy passed to Dougan on the edge of the box, and he rifled home the equaliser past the advancing Arsenal keeper Burns. In a frenzied finish to the match, Posh outside right Barnes started a move on the left wing five minutes from time. He rounded full back Howe and slipped a pass into the path of McNamee who tapped the ball into an open Moys End goal. The crowd erupted and a pitch invasion saw mass celebrations. Arsenal launched nine men forward in an attempt to save the match, but Posh hung on to clinch a memorable 2–1 victory. The team for this famous win consisted of:
> *Duff, Cooper, Birks, Crowe, Rankmore, Orr, Barnes, Conmy, Dougan, Deakin and McNamee.*

'Posh's Greatest Day'. Before a crowd of over 30,000 the mighty Arsenal are beaten in the F.A.Cup.
Looking at his goalbound shot, McNamee scores the winner........

............But in the next round Peterborough come down to Earth.
Posh captain Crowe, scores the consolation goal at Stamford bridge.

Both in the City, and nationally, Posh were hailed for their giantkilling acts, but it was back to the bread and butter of Division 3 football one week later, and a home victory over Luton Town. A 2-1 defeat, without Dougan, at top of the table Carlisle followed, as Maloy made his debut for Posh for the missing Conmy.

The 5th round F.A.Cup game against Swansea at London Road saw the ground attendance record broken again when 30,096 watched Posh play out a 0-0 draw, that saw Manager Clark fuming at Swansea's clogging tactics. Clark fielded the same side for the replay that had played in the previous three cup ties and this time the second division Swans went down 2-0, as Posh powered their way into the quarter finals of the F.A. Cup - with two goals from Deakin - for the first time in their history.

An F.A.Cup-tie crowd of 63,635 came to watch Posh do battle with a Chelsea side that boasted the likes of Bonetti, Harris, Hollins, Venables and Tambling. But it was a relatively unknown player, Bert Murray, who was to play a major part in the match and, at a later date, in Posh's history. Murray's challenge with Crowe after just two minutes saw Posh down to 10 men as one of their most influential players was carried from the pitch on a stretcher. 15 minutes into the match and it was all over as Chelsea went 3-0 up, from Tambling (2) and Hollins. A 4th was added by Bridges before half time. Despite a limping returned Crowe scoring Posh's only goal after his return in the second half, Chelsea notched a 5th one minute from time to go into the semi-finals. A sad end to a romantic cup run.

Back in the League Posh were robbed of a home win over Scunthorpe by an injury time equaliser, and then beaten 1–0 at struggling Workington. Deakin helped himself to a hat trick and Doog got one as Shrewsbury were beaten 4–1, followed by another home win, against second in the table Hull. This victory lifted Posh to 8th in the table, just 6 points off a promotion spot and with two games in hand. Unfortunately the next five games brought just two points in a slide down to 10th place with three defeats and two draws.

Long serving Peter McNamee celebrated 10 years at London Road with a benefit game against St. Mirren.

It was a night of ceremony as Vic Crowe received the Sunday Mirror giantkillers cup before the game. Posh lost 2–1 with Mac scoring the goal for Posh before he went on to receive a gold watch from St. Mirren at a benefit dinner.

A mini recovery was staged as Posh won five of the last six games, but it was only good enough to leave them 8th in the table. Robinson was drafted into the side for the 1–0 win at Colchester and Maloy got his first goal for Posh in the 2–1 win at home to Watford, as did Thompson (2) at home to Colchester. The season finished with a 1–0 win over Gillingham, from a Deakin penalty.

1965/66 SEASON

The summer period inevitably saw transfer activity, and it came as no surprise when Derek Dougan was transferred, to Leicester City for £25,000. His record at Posh consisted of 77 League games with 38 goals, but more important was the passing of a larger than life character who had captured the hearts of the Posh faithful. Other departures were Tony Moulden to Notts County, Ollie Hopkins to Chelmsford, Nigel Sims went back to Canada and Eddie Clamp and Dennis Shiels were also handed free transfers.

On the rebuilding side, Clark brought in a clutch of minor signings for little or no financial outlay. Tommy Ross and Jim Rooney – both forwards – came from Scottish side Lochee Harp. Tommy Watson came from Stevenage, John Fairbrother arrived from Worcester City and Johnny Byrne from Barnsley. Clark's next captures were Peter Johnson from Sheffield Wednesday, Mike Beesley (Southend), Mike Hollow (Leyton Orient) and Barry Gould arrived from Chelsea, bringing Clark's total new signings to nine. But he still had to convince the Peterborough public that the right men to win promotion had been made, for too many Posh fans there was nobody of the calibre of Bly, Hudson or Dougan to lead the attack.

Posh played their first matches on the Continent as part of their pre-season build up with a 3–2 victory over T.S.V. Bremerhaven, with goals from Deakin, Fairbrother and Watson, followed by a 4–2 victory over Bremen with those goals coming from a Fairbrother hat trick and Beesley.

The new season began for Posh as the old one had finished, with a 1–0 home win over Gillingham, the goal coming from debutante Mike Hollow just one minute before half time. The line up saw six players making their League debuts for Posh; Johnson, Hollow, Watson, Beesley, Gould and Byrne. It also saw a new strip for Posh, which consisted of shirts of all blue, with two white bands across the chest, and for the first time substitutes appeared in a League match at London Road. Although Gillingham were forced to use their sub for an injured

Pulley, Clark did not make use of the option. Posh then continued to make the indifferent start that fans had come to expect in recent years by losing at home to Millwall 2–0 in front of 10,702 fans.

This was followed by a visit to Oldham, and a win by 4–2, with goals from Barnes, McNamee, Fairbrother and Deakin; Beesley became the first Posh player to come on as a substitute in a League match replacing the injured Orr. McNamee grabbed a late equaliser at home to Watford to save a point after Deakin had initially given Posh a 6th minute lead. It was a Deakin penalty at Scunthorpe in the first half that earned a point, for Scunthorpe came back with an 81st minute equaliser.

Defeat at Walsall was followed by another 2–2 draw at London Road, against Brighton, this time after Posh lead 2–0 at half time. The game had been watched by 7,588 people, and in the match programme the club had declared that 14,000 gates were required just to break even, which allowing nothing for transfer fees. Morale amongst the fans was low as Posh embarked on another League Cup campaign, a tournament in which Posh had still not won a game!

The draw took them to First Division Newcastle where in front of 16,110 fans Posh played out their latest giantkilling role against a side that had previously experienced such heroics from Peterborough. After 36 minutes it was 3–1 to Posh who were playing some inspired football. Beesley gave Posh a 7th minute lead before Newcastle squared things on 25 minutes, a minute later Conmy put Peterborough back in front. The lead was extended by Watson after 36 minutes, but was then pegged back to 3–2 nine minutes into the second half. But Posh once again took a two goal lead through Conmy's second strike on 69 minutes. Eleven minutes from time Hilley brought the deficit back to a single goal, but the Geordies rarely threatened to steal a draw and Posh controlled the rest of the game to record another famous giantkilling act.

It was as well that things were progressing well on the pitch, since at the A.G.M. of Shareholders, Chairman Tommy Peake was voted off the board and new Chairman Vic Grange was installed.

The team came back down to earth with a bump going down at Q.P.R. to a last minute penalty. Barry Gould returned for the home match against Mansfield and Posh started a run of five straight wins to bring back the crowds and increase confidence. Gould scored on his return in the 3-1 win over the Stags, along with Barnes and Byrne. Two days later Walsall were beaten 3-1 at home, which was followed by a visit to Bournemouth. Posh edged out their hosts in a 3-2 thriller, coming back from 2-1 down.

A Home match with Charlton Athletic was the reward for beating Newcastle, and 10,929 watched another pulsating Cup-tie at London Road. The Second Division outfit was aware of their task as early as the first minute when Deakin took a long ball from Gould to go past centre half Haydock to put Posh 1-0 up. Just seven minutes later Charlton were given some hope as Kenning unleashed a 25 yard drive to level the score. The crowd were on their feet just two minutes later though as Byrne picked up another long ball, this time from Crowe, to make it 2-1. Charlton came back again and caused a constant threat from the flanks, and after 16 minutes equalised again, through Ron Saunders. They then took the lead for the first time on 28 minutes from the penalty spot after Rankmore handled the ball. The second half saw Charlton under siege for much of the time and eventually a knock down from Crowe left Byrne to hit the equaliser. With 10 minutes remaining Posh continued to press and a Watson corner was met by Byrne to make it seven goals in four games, and his first hat trick for Posh.

A weak Southend side were the visitors to London Road three days later and Posh duly disposed of them 4-0, goals coming from Barnes, Deakin, Gould and inevitably Byrne. The winning run ended at Swindon with defeat. Byrne took his tally to 10 goals in six games with a second October hat-trick against Shrewsbury (in a 4-1 win) and then incredibly repeated the feat four days later at Millwall in the 4-1 League Cup victory. Clark went into the transfer market again and brought in a player he was linked with earlier in the year, Tom McAnearney from Sheffield Wednesday. McAnearney made his debut in a 3-0 defeat at Grimsby.

The Cup giantkillers then very nearly had a taste of their own medicine when non-League Kidderminster Harriers came to London Road in the F.A.Cup 1st round. Posh won 2-1 but only thanks to another inspired display in goal from Duff, one of many during the season; two Deakin goals won the game.

Four days later a crowd of 14,796 came to watch Posh play the leaders of the First Division, Burnley, in the 4th round of the League Cup.

It was a game that resulted in a resounding 4-0 victory, and had some of the local media heralding the feat as the greatest cup win ever by Posh. After a goalless first half Posh struck four times in a 15 minute spell to leave the First Division side in disarray. Fairbrother opened the scoring after 57 minutes when Byrnes' cross was powerfully headed home. The second came 10 minutes later after Crawford touched a short free kick to Byrne who worked an opening for Conmy to shoot home. The crowd were going wild at this stage and when Fairbrother crossed from the left wing three minutes later, Buxton bundled it into his own net, provoking cries of "easy easy" around London Road. Two minutes later and the impressive Fairbrother dribbled past the hapless Buxton and Merrington at the edge of the Burnley box before shooting into the roof of the net. It was Burnley's biggest defeat of the season, their first for eight games, and it also fully vindicated Clark's decision to drop Gould for Fairbrother as a tactical change. The match became Posh's fourth four goal performance in four League Cup matches, and set up a semi-final clash over two legs with West Bromwich Albion.

Fairbrother retained his place in the side for the match at Bristol Rovers when Posh drew 1-1, a Johnson goal cancelling out Ray Mabbutt's opener for Rovers. John Kirkham was signed from Wolves and made his debut at the Den, with Millwall taking full revenge for their League Cup defeat earlier in the year – a 4-1 victory. A goal one minute into the second half by Fairbrother was enough to secure two points, in a poor match in front of a disappointing attendance of 6,199 against York.

The first leg of the semi-final had been eagerly awaited by most Posh fans. A large Peterborough contingent made up the 20,000 crowd at the Hawthorns, that saw Posh tackling another First Division side, and one that boasted an impressive front line including Brown, Kay, Hope and Astle. It looked as though another incredible Cup performance could be on the cards as Crowe, playing up front, gave Posh a 17th minute lead. Unfortunately it lasted only three minutes as Brown equalised with a deft header. Nine minutes before half time Lovett's lob was met by Astle to give Albion a lead that they kept until the end. The second half brought considerable Posh pressure but no reward, and in fact it was Albion who had the best chance to score, but Duff saved well from Lovett. Clark praised his team's efforts, with most fans and the media considering that Posh were favourites now to reach the final, despite the Albion's First Division status.

A few days later and Shrewsbury ended any further interest in the F.A. Cup for the season with a 3-2 win at Gay Meadow. This match had Clark fuming over the players' attitude and prompted him to remark: "It will be a long time before I forgive the team for this and I will certainly never forget it." In the League, Posh got back to winning ways with a 5-2 drubbing of Swansea, Pulley was named as sub but failed to come on for his debut.

The game that everyone in the City had been waiting for saw a crowd of 18,288 to watch the 2nd leg of the League Cup semi-final. Glory was not to be though, the result being summarised in the following day's paper:

"Posh were out-thought, outfought and outplayed by West Brom".

Albion controlled the game and took a 3-0 lead before Posh mounted a comeback, with goals from Rankmore and Crowe which raised the Posh fans' hopes. But Brown's third of the night killed off Peterborough, and gave Albion a passage to Wembley for the final. The other worrying note on the night was goalkeeper Duff's shoulder injury that left him out of the next three League matches.

Robinson took over in goal for the defeats at Southend and Reading (Pulley finally making his debut), and Posh slid into the bottom half of the table. The unusual step was taken in January when the Management team was split, with Clark appointed as General Manager and Vic Crowe as Player Coach. Clark also signed a five year Management contract.

A crowd of 7,125 saw Fairbrother's goal claim the points in a 1-0 home win over Bournemouth to claim their first double of the season, before going on a run of five games without a win. Defeat at Brentford started the rot, and this was followed with a 3-2 home defeat to Swindon in front of 5,065 fans, the smallest League gate at London Road. A Byrne goal at Gillingham earned a point but another two defeats followed, at Watford and at home to Oldham, leaving Posh 15th in the table.

A change of fortune started with a 3-1 home win over a Scunthorpe, the goals coming from Fairbrother, Watson and Conmy. Clark then made a double swoop to capture ex-England star Derek Kevan and Welsh International goalkeeper Tony Millington, with a £15,000 fee to Crystal Palace.

Kevan made his debut against a very poor Exeter side, who already looked a good bet for relegation – and scored after four minutes. Exeter fought back with goals in the 6th and 9th minutes, but then Posh controlled the proceedings and scored goals through Deakin (2), Kirkham and Rooney, the last two getting their first goals for Posh. A 1-0 defeat came in the next match at Brighton, thanks to an own goal from Kirkham, when at least a share of the points had looked likely.

Posh played hosts to Q.P.R. in a match that was only notable for the outstanding display from Peter Springett in the Rangers goal, and the debut of the Rangers new signing Rodney Marsh. Posh then achieved a stunning result with their record away victory, by 7-1, at Mansfield. A dull 0-0 draw at home to Reading provoked a local paper leader to state: *"United fans deserve better than this"*, berating the Posh team's lacklustre performance. Similar performances were dished up in the home draw with Grimsby and the defeat at Oxford, with Posh's League season falling apart. At last a home win came in style with the 5-2 drubbing of Bristol Rover, Fairbrother scoring twice, along with Kevan, Watson and Byrne. Two 1-1 draws were recorded before Posh entertained League leaders and Champions-elect Hull, sending them crashing to a surprising but comprehensive 4-1 defeat, with goals from Fairbrother, Byrne, Conmy and Pulley.

Posh's infuriating form had by now resulted in attendances dropping to an alarming level, and the fourth home defeat of the season, to Oxford, followed. The end of the season was now all that most Posh fans wanted, and this eventually came with a home 3-0 win over already relegated Brentford. The attendance of just 3,935 fans, was far and away the lowest ever League gate, up to then, at London Road. Posh fans were looking for changes, and so were the Board, for the team finished 13th in Division Three, the lowest position since promotion five years earlier.

Posh were rapidly approaching the end of an era, of dreams fulfilled. Influential in this period (1963-68) was Frank Rankmore, seen here before a Friendly match with Spandauer Sport Club.

CHAPTER 5

DEPRESSING YEARS

1966/67 SEASON

The close season started busily for everybody concerned with the Club. Frank Rankmore and Tony Millington were both taken on tour by Wales to South America where they both earned full International caps. Another new Chairman was elected, John Thornley, and Colin Pinder became the new Club Secretary. Gordon Clark also moved to bring new faces to London Road, the first being Colin Garwood and Phillip Praine who joined the club as apprentices. They were shortly followed by George Adams from Chelsea and John Mason from Alvechurch. On the departure side Barry Gould and Mike Hollow were the only close season transfers.

For the first time Posh therefore started a new season without a debut player. A crowd of 7,313 came to see them play out a 3–3 draw with Doncaster. Posh came from 1–0 and 3–1 down to rescue a point, and even squandered a penalty when Ian Crawford missed, with the score at 2–1. The League Cup campaign opened with a 2–1 home win over Oxford, which secured a 2nd round "derby" clash at Northampton. A League trip to Field Mill saw a tough scoreless draw as the only reward, with Mansfield's star of the show being Peter Morris. Two consecutive home matches brought two wins over Grimsby and Gillingham, leaving Posh sitting on top of Division Three. They then faced two away trips and drew both 1–1, at Walsall and Leyton Orient.

Between the two draws, Posh played the League Cup match with Northampton, and came away sharing four goals. Byrne gave Posh an early lead but it took a Fairbrother goal 16 minutes from time to bring the Second Division side back to London Road. The bright start to the season started to fade with defeat at Torquay, before the League Cup replay two days later. Adams came in for his Posh debut in the week of his 19th birthday and was one of the few good points that came out of the game. Things were all square at half time but just one minute into the second half Duff made a rare mistake and let a soft header in at the near post. Five minutes later and the goalkeeper had no chance as Martin put Cobblers two up, a lead they never looked like losing. The match was disrupted for a short time as a bottle was hurled at the referee from the London Road terrace.

A week later Brighton handed out a 5–2 thrashing, John Mason scoring his first goal for Posh, after making his debut against Torquay. It was also Millington's first League game for the club despite the fact he had already been capped by his Country.

Clark lived up to his reputation, by making more team changes – for the match at Gillingham – some of which were enforced. Adams remained in the side for his League debut, and Fairbrother returned in attack as did Cooper in defence. Fairbrother and Mason scored against the Kentish men, Posh sweeping into the lead after just 30 seconds. But this was cancelled out after 20 minutes, and although the lead was regained early in the second half, Posh were eventually denied their victory. A home match against Workington saw Fairbrother continue his scoring, on his return, by grabbing a hat trick in a 3–0 win. The first away win still eluded Posh however, and a disputed penalty for an alleged Rankmore push five minutes from time saw Scunthorpe win 1–0. Fairbrother was on target again when Posh were involved in their 7th draw in 14 games – 2–2 against Watford.

The following match, against Oldham, saw a one minute silence observed before the game in memory of Posh's long serving groundsman Ben Poole and announcer Harry Porter who had both died the previous week. The silence was also in memory of those who had died in the Aberfan disaster, and this tragedy saw a half time collection to raise funds for the families of the victims.

The game itself was a comprehensive 3–1 win for Posh, and a week later Posh recorded the first away win of the season, at Oxford, with a resounding 3–0 victory to keep them in the top six. A top of the table clash against a strong Bristol Rovers side yielded a point thanks to a Fairbrother goal and an even more emphatic victory came at fellow promotion challengers Colchester, when a brace from both Fairbrother and Mason ensured a 4–1 win. The impressive run came to an end at Watford as a Posh side without Millington (International duty) and Conmy (injury) slipped to a 3–1 defeat. A home defeat to Shrewsbury, by 2–0, saw the Shrews climb to 5th position, and Posh fall to 10th in the League, as the competition at the top of the table hotted up.

The F.A. Cup campaign started with a game against Southern League Hereford, that saw Jock Wallace in goal and ex-Middlesborough star Holliday playing for the opposition. But the pair could not prevent a 4-1 drubbing as Fairbrother, Conmy, Byrne and an own goal from Vale eased Posh home.

It was with some relief that rock bottom Swansea, some nine point adrift at the bottom of the League, were the next visitors to London Road. The game itself did not go to plan though, and produced a classic for the 6,053 fans who came to watch. Despite Posh holding territorial advantage for much of the game Swansea were at home with their quick counter attacks and scored the first after nine minutes when Todd struck. Nine minutes later and Jimmy McLaughlin, the scourge of Posh whilst at Shrewsbury, made it 2-0. Byrne pulled one back for Posh, but an Ivor Allchurch goal after 28 minutes made it 3-1. Peterborough cast aside all defensive notions and went out to try and rescue the game. Two Fairbrother goals before half time gave them an opportunity and left the crowd to reflect on one of the most entertaining 45 minutes of football they were every likely to witness. The second half continued at a frantic pace but with no more goals to show for it, until McLaughlin popped up to put the Welshmen back in front with just eight minutes remaining. However, it was ironically a Welshman who came to the rescue for Posh as Rankmore crashed a shot in off the bar on 86 minutes, to produce a final draw, and a fair result from a remarkable game.

The period up to the Christmas holiday was to prove disastrous for Posh in the League, as a drab draw at Bournemouth was followed by a drubbing at Doncaster, and defeat at home to Swindon – Posh were hardly allowed a shot at goal by the Wiltshire side. Boxing Day provided a daunting trip to Swindon where 14,619 saw Posh comprehensively beaten 4-1 to go slithering further down the table. The slump of seven League matches without a win was finally ended with a 3-1 victory over Mansfield on New Year's Eve at London Road, Ross coming on for half an hour for his Posh debut.

The second round of the F.A.Cup brought a trip to Layer Road to face Colchester where they had won earlier in the season. Goals from Watson (2) and Fairbrother, helped them to another convincing win, this time by 3-0. In the League, Posh won 2-1 at home to Walsall, losing Rankmore with a broken collarbone, and then one week later lost at home to Leyton Orient.

The F.A. Cup Third round saw Posh travel to Bedford. Orr returned to the side and a bumper crowd of 14,053 turned out to see the match, with former Posh idol Denis Emery in the Bedford side. Orr scored on his return to the team and at half time a fine game was in the balance with the score at 1-1. The second half was a different story and Posh scored through Watson (3), Byrne and Conmy to win 6-2. The reward was a trip to the North East to face First Division Sunderland.

Back in the League, Posh's generally indifferent form continued, with defeat at Torquay and victory at home to Brighton. At London Road, the scorers were Fairbrother and Adams, the latter his first for the Club. Posh yet again travelled to the Norbreck Hydro in Blackpool, which had become their traditional base for cup-tie preparations, to get in readiness for the Sunderland match. The injury problems for the team had not subsided with Fairbrother joining Rankmore and Orr as long term casualties. Beesley was drafted into the attack to partner Watson and Mason, and Wright retained his place in the side since replacing Orr in the Brighton match.

A star studded Sunderland line up included Jim Montgomery, John O'Hare, Colin Todd, Bobby Kerr and the great Jim Baxter. A crowd of 43,998 then watched Sunderland's talented team rip Posh apart. After 18 minutes had gone Posh were already 3-0 down, with goals from O'Hare, Martin and Kerr. By half time Martin had added his second to make it 4-0. In the second half it took Sunderland two minutes to get back on the scoresheet with a goal from Martin to complete his hat trick. Three minutes later Kerr made it 6-0 before Watson pulled one back for Posh with a thumping drive. The rout was completed when Baxter scored from the penalty spot to make it 7-1.

This comprehensively ended Posh's interest in the F.A. Cup and now had the fans nursing very real fears over the Club's chances of relegation, as they nestled just four points above a relegation place in the table. Those fears became well founded as Posh commenced a nightmare sequence of results that saw them flirting with a place in the bottom four. A 2-0 defeat at home to Q.P.R. was followed by a 1-0 defeat at Workington, but a Beesley goal at home to fellow strugglers, Scunthorpe, was enough to produce a 1-0 win. That welcome result was followed three days later, on March the 7th, with the news that the Football League had reported the Club to the F.A. for a breach of rules, that had been revealed in the Club's books.

Back on the pitch, a draw at Q.P.R. was followed by another defeat, 1-0 at Oldham, where two new signings made their debut for the Club – Dave Metchick (from Orient) and Jimmy McLaughlin signed from Swansea. McLaughlin had tormented Posh's defence so many times in the past. After defeat at home to Oxford United, two days later McLaughlin scored twice, his first goals for the Club, in a 2-2 draw at Reading. Metchick scored his first goal for Posh in a 2-1 win at home to Reading in the next match, and the unbeaten run was stretched to four games, with a draw at Bristol Rovers and a home victory over Colchester.

Posh lost a vital game to fellow strugglers Darlington 5-0 at Feethams, before facing top of the League opponents. A 1-1 draw was achieved at Shrewsbury followed by defeat at home to Middlesborough.

Posh secured their place in Division Three by taking points off teams in the relegation battle in the next four games. Darlington were beaten 2-0 at home, with draws at Swansea and Grimsby. They then came back to London Road and overcame Bournemouth 2-0, with goals from Watson and Mason, in front of 5,047 relieved fans. Posh's season finished at Ayresome Park where a crowd of 32,503 saw Middlesbrough win 2-1 to finish second in the League and gain promotion to the Second Division. It had been another disappointing season but at least Posh had preserved their Third Division status after it had looked for so long that they may lose it.

1967/68 SEASON

The 1967/68 season was to be one of the most momentous in the Club's history but unfortunately not for the right reasons. It started quietly enough with new Secretary Arnold Blades joining the Club in succession to Colin Pinder who moved on to the F.A. Things began to get busier as Clark tried to rebuild his side for the promotion push. Out went Tommy Ross to York City and Mike Beesley went back to Southend, the club from where he had been signed. Newcomers included John Linnell from Northampton, half-backs Vince Radcliffe from Portsmouth, Mike Maynard from Crystal Palace and two defenders, John Wile a youngster from Sunderland, and Frank Noble from Sheffield Wednesday. Also added to the playing staff were Colin Garwood, Mick Drewery and Dick Kwiatkowski, through Posh's Youth Scheme.

The season opened with the threat of the F.A. investigation uppermost in the minds. Posh started the campaign when they entertained and beat an Italian Olympic XI at London Road 3-0, before losing to 1st Division West Ham. The opening League fixture was a 1-1 draw at home to Scunthorpe, with the only newcomer being sub Frank Noble making his debut for Posh, in front of a 6,985 attendance. Noble started, as did former Cobbler John Linnell, in the home 3-2 defeat at the hands of Northampton in the League Cup five days later. The tie, which was scheduled for the County Ground, was played in Peterborough due to the continued use of Northampton's pitch by the County Cricket Club. Posh then made amends by recording a succession of wins in the League. Three victories were first gained by 2-0 at Oldham, 4-1 at home to Bristol Rovers and 5-1 against Watford. In front of 9,460 Posh fans at the Watford game, Linnell and Noble scored their first goals for the club. An own goal, and one from Fairbrother, saw Posh top of the League after their 2-1 win at Barrow. Further into September however things started to turn sour for Posh, when Derek Vernum resigned as Honorary Youth Team Manager after an argument with Chairman John Thornley over policy, although he did return later.

Meanwhile the team drew 1-1 at Oxford, lost 4-0 at Bury and won 4-1 at Watford. Peter Deakin came back in the side for his second spell at London Road whilst Jimmy McLauglin left the club to go back to Shrewsbury, and Tommy Watson was released to Walsall. Mike Maynard was the substitute, and he became the first black player to appear for Posh in the Football League, although he did not actually come on. Two days after the Watford result Manager, and largest shareholder, Gordon

Clark resigned after a 2¾ hours Board Meeting. In a farcical situation Chairman John Thornley said:
"After careful consideration the Board were unable to accept it (his resignation)", and recalled Clark.

The meeting was originally called to discuss offers for two players but after the meeting Clark said *"I have resigned and that's it, my mind is made up. I can't carry on and that's the end of it."* Clark was not prepared to give his reason for resigning but stressed he may disclose an explanation at a later date. He also said that he had the interests of the club at heart.

Norman Rigby the Midland League stalwart and trainer, took over as Caretaker Manager and Posh won 2-0 at home to Bournemouth on September 30th, Mason and Metchick scoring. He followed his first success with an identical result at home to Mansfield two days later – Thompson and Metchick on target this time – and Conmy grabbed two as Posh kept their unbeaten home record with another 2-0 win over Stockport. After a 1-1 draw at Brighton, the team's first defeat under Rigby came at home to fellow promotion pushers Shrewsbury 1-0. Posh bounced back though as Fairbrother scored twice in a 3-2 win away at Mansfield after being recalled to the side, and Deakin got his first goal (since being re-signed) – the winner. A 0-0 draw at Swindon was then followed by a 3-2 home defeat to fellow promotion hopefuls Reading.

But more serious thoughts were now on the minds of Posh fans with the news that the club's alleged irregularities were to be discussed by a joint F.A. and Football League commission on the 8th November.

Meanwhile Posh continued to slip down the Table with two away defeats, 3-1 at Torquay and 2-1 at Bristol Rovers.

On Friday the 18th of November, the results of the Commission's Meeting were announced, the most ominous being those that were to be imposed by the Football League. Posh played at home to Grimsby the following day and 7,243 saw Fairbrother score a hat trick as Posh beat Grimsby 3-2, with winger Stuart Brace from Mansfield making his debut, the result leaving Posh in 5th place in the table.

On Tuesday 21 November 1967, the League Management Committee informed Peterborough United officials that they were to be demoted to the 4th Division at the end of the current season. The newspapers commented the following day that Posh supporters were unsure whether the punishment was comparably more, or less, severe than they had expected. Leeds City in the 1919–20 season were expelled from the League, whilst in 1957 Sunderland were fined £5,000; both clubs were found guilty of similar charges to those that had been levelled at Peterborough.

The Club and Supporters were devastated, but rallied around the team. Norman Rigby was confirmed as the new Manager and Posh's biggest crowd of the season, 9,457, came to watch as Posh beat League leaders Walsall 2–1 with first half goals from Brace and Metchick. The team were roared on by the crowd in a Cup-tie atmosphere, and were given a rousing ovation at both half time and at the end of the game.

Posh started the F.A. Cup campaign against non–League Falmouth with a 5–2 win that brought Fairbrother his second hat trick of the season, before travelling to Scunthorpe in the League and losing 2–1. Fairbrother was again the Posh scorer.

The next match was at home to Oldham who had the much lauded forward Lawrie Sheffield in their side. Frank Rankmore kept him quiet though as Posh won 2–1 with goals from Thompson and Fairbrother taking the tally of the latter to nine in six games. John Wile was named as substitute but did not come on. Posh then faced Orient at home on Boxing Day, winning 3–2 thanks to Fairbrother, Brace and a Goddard own goal. Four days later Posh lost to struggling Orient by 3–0. Terry Mancini scoring for Orient in both games. The Boxing Day fixture turned out to be Johnny Byrnes last game for Posh as he went to local rivals Northampton in exchange for Jim Hall with a small cash adjustment, Hall making his debut in the 3–0 defeat.

Back in the F.A. Cup Posh faced another non–league side as they travelled to Kent to face Southern League Margate. Peter Deakin came in for the cup-tied Jim Hall and scored Posh's 4th as they ran riot in the second half. Margate held Posh to 0–0 at half time, but the goals came soon afterwards from Thompson, Brace and Conmy in the 4–0 win. Margate missed several good chances and complained that they should have been awarded a penalty when the score stood at 1–0.

The next match at London Road was played against a lowly Barrow side on a snow covered pitch. The Barrow players actually came out to inspect the surface before the game wearing overcoats over their kit! The incident amused a number of the Posh fans in the 6,888 crowd, but a 65th minute goal from Field clinching a 1–0 Barrow victory, did not! Posh's League form continued to suffer with another defeat, 3–1 at Oxford. In the line–up, the home team had Ron Atkinson and his brother Graham – who scored – and Jim Barron in goal.

A crowd of 16,907 came to watch Posh play 2nd Division Portsmouth in the F.A. Cup 3rd round at London Road. In the 5th minute Brace missed a one–to–one with the keeper, although with Posh more than holding their own against Pompey it did not seem important. The match was 75 minutes old when Brace had the chance to redeem his earlier miss when Fairbrother drew the keeper and two defenders to the left of the Moys End goal. He squared for the unmarked Brace in front of an open goal, just a few yards out, but incredibly Brace hooked the ball wide of the gaping goal. A few minutes later, Hiron scored the only goal of the game for Portsmouth to effectively end Posh's season. Manager Norman Rigby was now aware that he had to guide his team through 19 more games knowing that regardless of results they were to be relegated. One player remarked to a newspaper after the game: *"That's it then, back to those friendly games next week."*

The next match was a 2–0 reverse at home to Bury. It looked as if Posh's fortune may change though as they visited Bournemouth and were outplayed by their hosts but still claimed a point in a 3–3 draw. Dick Kwiatkowski made his Posh debut as did Colin Garwood who scored. The other goal came from Jim Hall, one in injury time, his first for Posh. Fairbrother came on to replace Garwood in what turned out to be his last game for Posh, the striker going to Northampton for £7,000, having scored 37 goals in 69 League appearances for Posh. At his departure he was the Club's leading scorer.

Not having won for 5 games Posh faced Colchester, at home, in front of only 5,066 fans. Hall back in the side scored along with Thompson (2) to grab a 3–1 win. A trip to Stockport saw Hall make it four in four full appearances as he gave Posh an early lead, but it took an Adams goal three minutes from time to grab a point from a 2–2 draw.

Two more home matches brought mixed fortunes as 4,580 saw Posh beaten 3–2 by Brighton after conceding a goal in the 89th minute, and only 4,460 came to watch Posh beat Southport 1–0, with a Rankmore header in the 58th minute. Graham Ricketts, signed from Doncaster for £2,500, making his debut in front of the lowest League attendance since May 1966, and the 2nd lowest since Posh joined the League. John Wile also came into the side for his first full appearance. Ricketts scored on his second appearance for Posh to equalise an early Brodie goal to earn a draw with high flying Shrewsbury.

The next match produced a 1–1 draw at home to Swindon, before a Thompson goal made Posh only the second 3rd Division side to win at high flying Reading, a week later. 18 year old Bobby Downes, who had joined the club from West Bromwich Albion in September, made his debut in the Swindon game and retained his place for the trip to Reading. Reports from both games provided glowing reports of Downes, hailing him as Posh's new star. He built up his reputation by scoring in his next game, although Posh lost to Southport 2–1. Wright and

Conmy scored in a 2-0 home win over Torquay, and whatever Norman Rigby was doing to motivate Posh, it was obviously working. A lucky 1-0 win at Tranmere followed, thanks to a Jim Hall goal 12 minutes from time, after Tranmere had a 'goal' disallowed and missed several good chances. A visit to Grimsby brought a 1-1 draw thanks to a Thompson equaliser, and Hall earned a point in the Tranmere visit to London Road. Gillingham were next, when Posh won 3-0 at home, before Posh went to visit struggling rivals Northampton on St. George's Day.

Northampton's side contained ex-Posh players John Byrne and John Fairbrother, and indeed Fairbrother scored as Cobblers won 3-1, beating Posh at the County Ground at the 4th time of asking. Peterborough lost 3-2 at Walsall four days later, with Hall scoring both, before visiting Northampton again, this time in the final of the Senior Cup.

Both teams fielded full sides and Posh won 2-0 with goals from Thompson and Hall in front of 2,560 fans. Two nights later Derby came to London Road to play Ron Cooper's Posh XI in his Benefit game. Ritchie Norman and Derek Dougan played for Posh as did Manager Norman Rigby. Derby's stars shone when Alan Durban, Kevin Hector and Alan Hinton scored, as did one other star guest – Brian Clough the Derby Manager – and the Rams won 4-2. Derek Dougan was mobbed by Posh fans and given a rousing reception at the final whistle. The final two League games of Posh's blackest season saw resounding victories, 4-0 over Northampton at London Road - with a Garwood hat-trick and a Hall single, and finally a visit to relegated Colchester where goals from Hall 2, Conmy, Garwood and Thompson wrapped up a 5-1 win. This left the media to drool over the Posh performance and add weight to Rigby's argument that they would bounce straight back into the 3rd.

This was to eventually become a traumatic season which started in the summer with the threat of the F.A. investigation still hanging over proceedings. The full extent of the 'crime' will probably never be revealed, nor the full list of 'guilty' parties, suffice to record here the irrefutable facts as reported at the time:

On the 8th November 1967 it was reported that a joint Football Association and Football League Commission would meet to discuss the charges levelled against Peterborough United F.C., on Thursday 16th November 1967. The Committee was to consist of Dr. A Stephen and Prof. H Thompson of the F.A. and Mr. L Shipman and Mr. A Would of the Football League. The charges made against the Club were detailed by the Association:

1.   That Peterborough, having failed to produce vouchers for season 1965-66, had contravened Rule 44 (d).

2.   That vouchers in respect of certain players omitted details of amounts received as required by F.A. Rule 25 (a).

3.   That extra bonuses were offered to players, in contravention of League Regulation 41, to beat Sunderland in the 4th Round of the F.A. Cup in season 1966/67, which was recorded in the Minutes at a Board Meeting.

4.   That Signing On bonuses were paid to players in contravention of League Rule 42, from funds made available by their Supporters' Club, which was recorded in the Statement of Accounts of the Company for the year ended 31st May 1966.

....

New Secretary Arnold Blades who had inherited the situation stated that Posh... *"are not the first club to face this sort of trouble"*. John Thornley, the Club Chairman, also announced that no appointment of a Team Manager would be made until after the meeting.

On Friday 17th November the results of the F.A. and Football League Commission's Meeting was announced. The Club was fined £500 on two counts, for failing to produce vouchers under F.A. Rules 44(d) and 25(a). The Commission also concluded that there had been gross negligence by the management of the Club and that the members of the Board, the Manager and the Secretaries who held office during the seasons 1965-66 and 1966-67 would be severely censured.

The Commission also recommended on the other two charges that the Football League should impose the severest penalties provided for in League regulations for the breach of the League rules. Mr Alan Hardaker, the Football League Secretary, said that the findings of the Joint Commission would be reported to the League Management Committee at a meeting on Thursday 23rd November 1967.

Posh did not have to wait until Thursday, as on the preceding Tuesday the League Management Committee informed Peterborough United officials that under regulation 15 (a) they were to be demoted to the 4th Division at the end of the current season.

It was announced by the new Board of Directors that Posh would not fight the League's decision to relegate them at the end of the season but Eric Nicholls said: *"We are not going to lie down and die. We are going to be a footballing phoenix and rise from the ashes of our troubles."*

The summer of 1968 saw Posh back in the Fourth Division, having to start all over again. It inevitably meant losing some players and after much speculation, Frank Rankmore went to Northampton for a fee of £12,000 having made a record 201 league appearances and scoring seven goals for Posh. Posh also released John Kirkham and Peter Deakin to Exeter and Brentford respectively. July became a busy month for transfers; Vince Radcliffe went to Rochdale before Rigby brought in Peter Price and John Pyatt from Liverpool, Ritchie Norman – the veteran of two F.A. Cup Finals – from Leicester and Roger Wosahlo from Ipswich.

The City and the fans were behind Posh and confident of a quick return to Division 3. They started the League campaign at home to Exeter in front of a crowd of 8,532. Norman and Pyatt made their debuts and young John Wile came in to replace Rankmore. Hall equalised an early goal by Exeter to earn a point in a game they could have won in a canter. In midweek Posh travelled to Doncaster for a League Cup tie and drew 0-0 in another game where chances went begging but Posh could not find the net to finish the game. No such excuse could be found at Port Vale in the League though as Posh's hero

was Tony Millington who ensured Vale only won by a single goal in a one sided match. The elusive first win came at home, in the replay of the Doncaster Cup Tie, came when Hall scored after 68 minutes to send Posh into the second round. It was Hall again who saved a point for Posh against Bradford City at London Road in the League. Brace put Posh 1-0 up after 18 minutes only to see Bradford come back to lead 2-1. Three minutes from the end Hall shot Posh level to the relief of the crowd.

Posh were finding the realities of 4th Division life harder than they expected though with consecutive away defeats. It left Posh with just two points and no wins from the first five League matches. In the League Cup Posh had no problems, in front of 11,408 fans at London Road, Posh recovered from a 20th minute goal by 1st Division Q.P.R., to go 4-1 up thanks to a Hall hat-trick and a goal from Thompson. Rangers only reply was a goal in the last minute. With the score at 4-1 referee J.R. Osborne sent off Q.P.R's Bob Finch, for a foul on Garwood, the first player dismissed against Posh in the League Cup. Ironically it was Osborne who dismissed Darlington's Ray Yeoman in 1967 the first ever player to be sent off against Posh since they joined the League.

In a generally bleak period, the fine Football League Cup run brought a welcome relief to the fans and the Club.
Thompson heads the decisive goal in the West Brom victory.

Back in the League it was Hall again with his seventh goal, earning a point at Rochdale and cancelling out their first half effort. Posh finally broke their duck in the League by beating Brentford 2-1 at London Road, with goals from Garwood and Hall, and it was the same two forwards who combined to give Posh a 3-2 win over Scunthorpe, a match in which 18 year old Kevin Keegan made his debut. It took 'Big' Jim Hall, as he was by now christened, to 10 League and cup goals in 10 appearances. It was not the start of a League revival that everybody hoped for, as Posh then lost 1-0 at 2nd placed Doncaster – the 4th Divisions' leading scorers. It was hardly the best preparation for facing First Division League Cup holders West Brom.

The Albion side boasting Brown, Kaye and Astle were not only beaten by an enthusiastic Posh side but, in front of 16,510 fans, were outfought and outplayed. Posh gave 19 year old Peter Price his debut and after just 3 minutes West Brom. keeper Osborne scrambled his shot clear in front of the London Road end. Four minutes later Price found the net and put Posh 1-0 up. Thompson made it 2-0 before half-time and Posh looked comfortably in control, although 8 minutes from time Brown pulled one back from a penalty. It was one of Albion's only threatening moments in the game and Posh's success starved fans duly celebrated on the pitch after the final whistle, with Posh going into the 4th round of the cup.

Price retained his place in the side for the Chester match, but infuriatingly Posh lost 2-1, the first defeat at London Road in 13 games. Rigby switched things around in October, in a bid to haul the team up the table. Pyatt came back into the side in defence and Ricketts, who had been so impressive in that area, was moved into midfield. Brace came in for Wosahlo and Price was dropped. Posh beat Southend 1-0 but the Essex men had their keeper Leslie carried off injured just before half-time. The following match against Chesterfield saw a much improved performance, although it may have been due to the fact that players were aiming for a place in the side to face Spurs nine days later in the League Cup. Ricketts and Pyatt reverted to their 'normal' roles, but with Conmy injured 19 year old Downes returned to the side. Downes laid on two goals as Thompson, Hall and Brace scored in a 3-0 win. An unchanged side failed to repeat the feat against high flying Halifax as their young centre half Chris Nichol scored in Halifax's 2-1 win.

Norman and Conmy returned to the side to face First Division Spurs at White Hart Lane against an impressive Tottenham team containing Jennings, Kinnear, Mullery, Beal, Greaves, Venables and Gilzean. The crowd of 28,378 had plenty to entertain them as Posh did well to contain their hosts with fine displays from Wile, Pyatt, Ricketts and Crawford, and it was Thompson who so nearly became the Posh hero. But Jimmy Greaves scored a rare headed goal – his 16th success of the season – to put Spurs ahead. Six minutes later Thompson had what he thought was an equaliser as he rifled the ball past

Jennings and into the net. The referee disallowed the goal, apparently for offside although the local press reported it as hand ball. Thompson then skyed a good chance over the bar minutes later. It was a creditable Posh performance that won praise and sympathy from the media.

Three days later and Posh's supporters were now their detractors as they drew 1-1 against Grimsby at home in a drab game. Two more draws, at Wrexham and at home to Newport, saw the crowd dip to only 4,553 by the time Notts County came to London Road. A more lively Posh, led by excellent showings from Wright and Conmy (both returning after being dropped for two games), won 1-0 through a Price goal after just six minutes. Price then netted two more in a thrilling game against the Division leaders Darlington. Hall scored after 9 minutes before the Quakers went 3-1 up, the third coming a minute after half-time. Price scored in the 54th and 56th minutes to level the scores and salvage a point.

The opportunity of another cup run to generate interest in Posh's fast fading season began and ended at Eastville. Posh lost 3-1 and Rigby fumed: *"I am not going to tolerate people going out there and only giving 50%. There are certainly going to be some changes next week – as many as possible."* In fact he made only one, signing Tommy Robson from Newcastle for £20,000, who made his debut in a 1-0 defeat at Workington. Rigby was not happy at his team's treatment of Robson, complaining they ignored him on the wing and demanded improvement from his players. Whatever he said in the week before the home match with Bradford P.A. obviously worked as an unchanged side, except for substitute Garwood, won 6-1. Hall got his first League hat-trick for Posh taking his tally to 16 in the competition. Other goals came from Wosahlo, Downes and Robson, their first League goals for Posh.

Rigby went into the transfer market again signing Mike Hellawell from Huddersfield. Hellawell and reserve keeper Mick Drewery both played in a friendly with 3rd Division Orient that ended 0-0, Drewery replacing the injured Millington, an ever present for some 77 League and cup matches. After patiently understudying the Welsh International Millington, Drewery finally made his debut on December 14th at London Road against Halifax and then promptly saw the match, on an ice bound pitch, abandoned at 0-0 after 45 minutes, and therefore not counting in official records! This was certainly the first time a match at London Road had been abandoned since Posh joined the League, and – from available records – the first ever.

Drewery and Hellawell only had to wait seven days for their 'official' debut at Grimsby where Brace, released by Posh in October, played for the home team, in a 2-2 draw. 1968 ended as it had begun, with a defeat, at Southend, extending Posh's record of never winning away on a Boxing Day fixture. Ex-Posh men Birks and Beesley were both in the Southend line up.

Posh faced Wrexham at home on 4th January, 16th in the table and 11 points behind leaders Aldershot. Rumours were rife that Posh were about to sign the Newcastle and former Spurs defender Jim Iley for a reported £80 per week. A figure that led to speculation that 33 year old Iley would be coming as more than a player. Posh lost 3-2 to Wrexham after leading 2-0 through goals from Robson. It was an unhappy return for goalkeeper Millington.

The following week Norman Rigby tendered his resignation from the Club after serving Posh as a player, captain of the side, trainer and finally manager. Rigby played in the five Midland League Championship sides as well as the 1960/61 4th Division Championship side, He made 328 Midland League appearances plus 55 in the Football League, and played in 42 F.A. and League cup matches. In addition with his time as trainer and manager, he was truly one of Posh's greatest servants.

Jim Iley duly joined Posh, to much acclaim, on January 8th 1969 as Player/Manager. He was the first Player/Manager at Posh in the League, and the first since George Swindin in 1954. His first game in charge came at Newport, where he also made his playing debut, Ricketts as substitute making way for him. Posh lost 4-2 after taking a 2-1 lead, with goals from Conmy and Hall coming after the break . Newport adapted to the very heavy conditions much better than Posh and finished the far stronger side.

Iley then experimented with several members of his new squad but with little success, as Posh's dismal run continued with a defeat at Notts County and a home draw with Darlington, after leading in both games. This was followed with goalless matches at Swansea and at home to Halifax before a third draw, at home to Workington, in front of only 4,063 fans. The equaliser in the Workington match came from Hall in the 93rd minute of the game! Posh by now had not won for 10 games – the last victory way back in November.

The three month period without a win was broken at Exeter on the 1st of March, thanks mainly to Iley and Crawford who both had outstanding games. The rest of the side were again in indifferent form and the winning goal came in the 11th minute, as Robson's shot was deflected by Smyth into his own goal. For those who thought it heralded a return to form it was not to be, a Robson goal earned a point at Lincoln, but they were then beaten for the third time at home in the season. Two days later Posh entertained Swansea, with Hall opening the scoring after just 26 seconds and after 14 minutes Price adding a second via a Williams deflection. Most Posh fans thought that the home win that had eluded them for 4 months had arrived, but unfortunately Swansea scored three minutes later and 10 minutes from time to snatch a point. After a victory at Aldershot, Posh at last won at London Road, when Iley scored his first goal for the Club to hit the winner against York.

Just 24 hours before Posh played Rochdale at London Road, Iley was 'officially' named as Manager at Posh, despite holding the reins for three months with a record of 3 victories and 3 defeats plus 7 drawn matches. Rochdale won the game 1-0, scoring after 52 minutes and Melledew was sent off with 2 minutes left to play for allegedly striking Wile.

Posh recorded a second consecutive away win by beating rock bottom Bradford 2-0 at Park Avenue and thus moving themselves clear of the re-election zone. Hall got the first after three minutes, with Robson making sure three minutes from time. Two more victories – at Chester and Scunthorpe – made it seven away games without defeat. At Chester, Posh scored twice in the last four minutes to steal the victory, Wile scoring his first goal for the club after 86 minutes. The Scunthorpe visit, saw Robson and Hall score in the 2-1 victory, over a side fielding 18 year old Kevin Keegan. These four straight away wins set a new club record. It raised the fans hopes for a respectable end to the season, but in the end if was fortunate that Posh had pulled clear of re-election over Easter, as they then lost twice at home.

After drawing at Colchester, Posh visited Brentford and lost 2-0, their 5th successive defeat at Griffin Park in five visits. It was no surprise when Posh entertained Aldershot, themselves near the bottom of the Division, that a crowd of only 3,758 came to watch the 2-0 home win. Robson and Conmy scored in front of Posh's lowest League gate. The end of the season was a relief for players, officials and supporters alike, and it came with a 2-0 defeat at Bradford City in front of 9,171 fans, as City still chased promotion. Posh finished 7th from bottom of Division 4 their lowest League position, in a season that had started with Posh as favourites for promotion. It ended with their lowest League attendance and morale at an all time low.

New Player/Manager Jim Iley
leads out the team for the first time.

Behind the scenes, in June, Gordon Taylor resigned and Geoffrey Woodcock took over as Posh's new Chairman. On the departure side free transfers were given to John Pyatt, Mike Hellawell, Ritchie Norman and Derek Wasahlo, all 1968 signings. Ian Crawford, Ron Cooper and Peter Thompson also left on free transfers, all having been good servants to the Club. Crawford made 172 appearances scoring 6 goals, Cooper 132 League appearances (plus 1 goal) and Thompson scored 15 times in his 79 (plus 6 as a sub) appearances.

Bobby Downes whose arrival had been heralded by the local Press as the unearthing of a new London Road star, went to Rochdale, going on to make over 400 League appearances at Rochdale, Watford and Barnsley. The biggest name to leave London Road however was Welsh International Goalkeeper Tony Millington who joined Swansea for £5,000. It was a move that gave the 20 year old Mick Drewery a chance to establish himself in goal after some good performances towards the end of the 68/69 season. Iley brought in some new faces by signing the diminutive Bobby Moss, a winger from Fulham, and Brian Potts from Leicester City. Ivan Hampton came from Halifax, Dick Dighton from Coventry and Iley's biggest signing – 30 year old ex-England International Eddie Holliday – from Workington. Of the apprentices, 18 year old centre-half Chris Turner was a notable signing.

Posh went to Ireland for their pre-season matches and were undefeated in the five games played. Ballymena were beaten (6–1) – with Moss getting a hat trick, Hall getting two and Price the other – as were Finn Harps (at Ballybofey), Derry City and Dundalk. Coleraine held Posh to a 2–2 draw on the final game of the tour, Posh's equaliser coming from Robson in the final seconds of the match.

The 1969/70 season started with Player/Manager Jim Iley creating history, by becoming the first Posh player to be sent off, when Posh drew 0–0 at Port Vale. As it was reported, what made it all the more remarkable was that Iley's dismissal, for kicking a Vale player when the ball was at the other end of the pitch, was the first in his career and he had only been booked once before in 15 years as a professional! Four Posh players made their debuts at Vale Park – Potts, Hampton, Moss and Holliday. Five consecutive draws on the opening day of each season had now been recorded, and Posh had still only been beaten once on this fixture since joining the Football League.

Peterborough entertained 3rd Division Luton Town in the first round of the League Cup and took an early lead through Price after 11 minutes. The crowd of 10,249, the biggest at London Road since September 1968, watched a memorable Cup Tie against a Hatters side that fielded Alan Slough and Laurie Sheffield, the latter scoring the equaliser after 22 minutes. Hall struck twice as Posh got off to a winning home start in the League, before travelling to Kenilworth Road for the Cup replay. The game followed the same pattern of open attacking play as the first match, and 13,105 fans were treated to an all action Cup Tie. Posh Manager Jim Iley took on a crossfield ball after seven minutes and gave the large contingent of travelling fans plenty to cheer as he hammered the ball into the top corner of the net from fully 20 yards. At this stage Posh looked comfortable, and Hall had good chances both before and after Iley's goal. But the 3rd Division side gradually came back into the game, and it was no surprise when Malcolm MacDonald equalised for Luton on 22 minutes. Seven minutes later Branston put Luton 2–1 up, and 5 minutes from half time Lewis saw Drewery save his penalty but followed up to score with the rebound. Posh came back again in the second half as a fierce Robson shot made it 3–2, however the fightback ended shortly afterwards when Lewis scored his 2nd spot kick of the night.

In the League Posh suffered the first defeat of the season, at the Old Showgrounds, when Scunthorpe won 2–1 with two first half goals, Robson scoring for Posh after 82 minutes, with Kevin Keegan again playing for Scunthorpe. Posh also returned from Layer Road pointless, Moss equalised with just seven minutes remaining – against the run of play – but an injury time winner from Gibbs gave Colchester both points. A drab game at home to Notts County brought a 1–0 win after Garwood came on as substitute and scored after 57 minutes. This was followed by an outstanding performance from Drewery, who stopped Posh being overwhelmed at Crewe when they lost 2–0. Back at London Road Posh entertained two local rivals and gained maximum points inside four days. Lincoln were beaten 2–1, Iley scoring first and Robson grabbing the winner with 18 minutes left. The visit of the Cobblers to London Road brought in a crowd of 8,553 for the first League clash since the 4–0 victory in May 1968, against the 'Old Enemy' at London Road . Phil Neal was in the Northampton side along with ex-Posh men Rankmore and Fairbrother. Posh fielded ex-Cobbler's players Robson and Hall. The match was not the stalemate that some 'Derby' matches can turn into and Hall fired a shot just wide after five minutes. In the 19th minute Rankmore's 'goal' from the edge of the box was disallowed, a Cobbler straying offside. It was Hall who eventually broke the deadlock before half time blasting home Price's low cross.

Posh then visited Darlington and recorded their first away victory of the season, the winner coming four minutes from time, when Iley shot at goal from 25 yards straight from an indirect free kick. Darlington's goalkeeper Crampton, in his first season in the Football League, palmed the ball into the net to give Posh the winner.

Posh made it five home wins from five matches as they hammered Hartlepool 4-0, with four consecutive wins they moved to 5th in the table. Hopes were high for the visit of bottom of the League Workington in midweek, but the Cumbrians held out for a 1-1 draw in front of an excellent 8,064 attendance. Posh were then jolted by a 4-1 defeat at Swansea, who were themselves recovering from a 6-0 hammering at Exeter in midweek. Millington played in goal for the victorious Swans.

Posh shrugged off the disappointment of the two results by completing their first 'Double' of the season, winning 3-2 at Bradford P.A. with two goals from Price and one from Robson. The unbeaten run at home continued with a 4-0 win over Newport. A 0-0 draw at Grimsby was followed by yet another home win, 3-1 against York. 5th placed Posh drew 7,756 spectators for the York visit, and the local papers proclaimed *"No doubts now - Posh can make it"*. The first real test of Posh's promotion credentials came away to Brentford, themselves pushing at the top of the table, and the ground where Posh had never succeeded in the league. The Bees won 5-2 and once again Posh were left wondering if their team was good enough. At home the crowds were still good, and 7,068 saw Posh beat Aldershot 4-1 even though the actual performance left much to be desired.

The F.A. Cup trail began the following week, and Posh were drawn away to South Western League side Falmouth. Hill scored after 4 minutes to silence the 4,000 crowd, but it was not until the 62nd minute that he scored his second and eased the anxiety of the Posh fans who had made the 700 mile round trip. Robson put Posh 3-0 up two minutes later before Falmouth pulled one back five minutes from time. Price restored the 3 goal advantage with two minutes left. Jim Iley suffered an ankle injury, and many Posh fans feared that with Iley missing they could not maintain their fine start to the season. This fear was realised when they lost at home for the first time in 10 matches, to Chesterfield. Iley started the game, but it was obvious that he was not fully fit and he came off after 35 minutes. The score was 1-1 at half time and it was just 9 minutes from time that Randall scored a penalty to seal the win for Chesterfield.

In the next match Posh played Oldham at home on Wednesday November 26th. Fans were still worried as Iley named Eddie Holliday in his place. But before a crowd of only 4,796, the season's lowest home attendance, their fears were soon allayed. Big Jim Hall score after 44 seconds and after 3 minutes it was 2-0, Price scoring from a Moss cross. Six minutes gone and Price had his second goal from a Conmy centre. The crowd were buzzing with anticipation and only had to wait another seven minutes before Hall notched his second from a cross by Robson, who had made a 40 yard run down the wing. Oldham then came more into the game but already at 4-0 down they knew it was a hopeless task. Hall completed his hat trick after 35 minutes by heading home another Moss pass to produce a 5-0 half time lead.

If Oldham were hoping for a reprieve in the second half it lasted only two minutes, before Hall scored his 4th goal. Oldham managed to break the monopoly when Shaw pounced on Wiles's mistake after 54 minutes, but a raking drive by Moss seven minutes later and a left footed shot from Price meant that it was a record breaking 8 goals for Posh, with 21 minutes left to play. Oldham hung on to finish the game without conceding any further goals to give Posh their biggest ever League victory, beating the 7-1 mauling of Mansfield in the 1965/66 season. Another record tumbled on the night as Brian Wright made his 202nd appearance for the Club, the most appearances for a Posh player in the Football League.

Following the euphoria of the Oldham game, Posh played Exeter away on the Saturday. Things started quietly enough but a match full of incidents ended with Posh taking just a point in a 1-1 draw. Eddie Holliday broke his leg and was carried off shortly after half time, but Moss gave Posh a 1-0 lead and they looked well in control to take both points. Thanks to injuries the match dragged on for an extra 15 minutes, and in injury time Exeter snatched the equaliser after Drewery had made a rare error of judgement from Wingate's shot.

The second round of the F.A. Cup paired Posh with another West Country team for 2nd Division Plymouth Argyle were to play Posh, for the first time, at London Road. On a snow covered pitch Peterborough added to their giantkilling reputation in front of a 8,553 crowd. In the 75th minute Conmy converted a penalty, and as Argyle pushed forward for the equaliser, Posh secured the game when Plymouth's goalkeeper Clamp, making his First Team debut, failed to gather Robson's cross and Price tapped home on the line.

In the League Posh's promotion form deserted them and even with Iley as substitute they were well beaten 3-0 at Lincoln. Another point was dropped at home to Scunthorpe on Boxing Day, although even that was a last gasp effort as Conmy equalised in the last minute.

With Jim Hall out with flu', for the second successive game, Iley returned and re-arranged the team for the match at Notts County. Chris Turner made his debut at centre half alongside Wile. Garwood was the lone striker and Posh played defensively. After two minutes Robson put Posh into a surprising 1-0 lead, but eight minutes later County levelled when Ritchie Barker headed home. Just eight minutes from time County finally took the lead that they had threatened for so long, when Turner was judged to have tripped Les Bradd, Don Masson converting the spot kick. When all seemed lost Garwood cracked home Posh's equaliser in the 89th minute and with a depleted team a valuable point was won.

Hall and Price returned for the F.A. Cup game at Rotherham and the former scored the only goal of the game one minute before half time to earn a 4th round trip to Gillingham.

Posh got back to winning ways in the League, with a 3-2 victory over Darlington at London Road – the first win since the Oldham victory. Two matches in the North of England produced only a single point, Posh drawing at Workington and losing 4-2 to Hartlepool.

Both the management and the fans were confident when a large contingent of travelling supporters descended on Gillingham for the 4th round F.A. Cup Tie, but despite scoring first – through Price after 17 minutes – Posh were truly outclassed. The 13,746 crowd watched Gillingham equalise within two minutes, and then romp to a 5-1 victory to end any Peterborough Cup hopes. The result prompted a group of Posh fans to voice their frustration by chanting, *"Jim Iley Out"*, as players and fans waited to return home after the game.

Tony Millington returned to London Road and ensured a point for Swansea with an outstanding performance in a 1-1 draw. A visit to Newport produced a more welcome return with a 1-0 win from a disputed Price goal. Price ran on to a Brian Potts chip over the Newport defensive wall, and lobbed the ball into the net after 23 minutes, with Newport claiming that Price was offside.

Ian Crawford was honoured for his services to Posh with a Benefit Match between Posh and Crawford's XI. Dick Dighton in goal was the only change from Posh's normal League XI, although Kwiatkowski played rather than Iley. Crawford's XI was like a 'Who's Who' of British Football. The Line-up consisting of:

Ron Springett, Maurice Setters, Ian Crawford, Martin Peters, Frank Rankmore, Bobby Moore, Johnny Haynes, Rodney Marsh, Derek Dougan, Geoff Hurst and Terry Venables.

A crowd of over 7,000 saw Posh lose 7-4. Wile, Hall, Garwood and Moss scoring for Posh. Marsh scored 4 and Geoff Hurst 3 for the guests.

Posh now needed to capitalise on the game with fellow promotion hopefuls Aldershot at the Recreation Ground. It was Aldershot who prevailed, a single goal scored by Jimmy Melia after 47 minutes settling the issue in front of 7,601 fans. It could have been more, and there was one incredible incident in the second half when Howarth hit the bar, the rebound was touched by Brown to Melia who drove the ball onto one post, watched it roll along the line, and hit the other post before bouncing into Drewery's arms! A 3-0 home win over Crewe was followed by a 0-0 draw at home to another side hoping for promotion, Brentford. The fans last lingering hopes of promotion finally faded as Posh won only one of their next six games.

The Easter programme started with a 1-0 win over Grimsby at London Road from a Hall goal and it was Hall who scored again in a 1-1 draw at Colchester. Big Jim got two more when Oldham took revenge for the 8-1 hammering, by winning 4-2 at Boundary Park. With the visit of 2nd placed Wrexham, Hall's hat-trick took his tally to 8 goals from 5 matches, as Posh swept the Welshmen aside with a 5-2 victory, Price and Robson scoring the other goals for Peterborough. The 'Derby' match at Northampton produced a 2-2 draw with ex-Posh striker Fairbrother scoring the 'Cobblers' goals and ex-Cobblers striker Hall scoring both of Posh's. Hall, by now having scored in six consecutive League matches, created a new Club record. It now looked like ensuring Posh a place in the Watney Cup for the following season which was given to the leading scorers in the League, only Wrexham had scored more goals in the division, with three games left.

Posh played Chester and drew 0-0 in front of 3,286, a new record low attendance at London Road in the League, and then achieved the same result against 4th placed Port Vale the following Wednesday, before a crowd of 3,844. The disappointing season ended at Saltergate where Posh lost 3-1, to finish 9th in the League, whilst Chesterfield clinched the Championship in front of a 14,250 attendance. Chesterfield's first goal was scored by Moss.

The only positive outcome from the season was the continued good form of Hall, Price and Robson, with 27, 20 and 15 goals each respectively (in League and cup games), and the club's qualification for the new Watney Cup competition the following August.

Three players who between them made over 120 League appearances in the League during the season.

(Top) Olly Conmy
(Middle) Jim Hall
(Bottom) Tommy Robson

1970/71 SEASON

Before the new season started, Posh Reserves were voted out of the Football Combination and opted to join the weaker London Midweek League. Jim Iley signed a three year contract with the Club and moved into the transfer market signing John Duncliffe from Grimsby, Bob Turpie from Queen's Park Rangers, David Pleat from Exeter City and Lawrie Sheffield from Doncaster Rovers. The Club still had severe financial problems and the Supporters Club had earlier handed over a cheque for £2,500 to ensure the Club could pay the player's wages during the summer months.

The season started with the Watney Cup Competition, Posh entertaining Second Division Hull City at London Road, and going down 4-0 in front of 9,353 fans. In an initiative to bring new supporters to the ground, the Club joined forces with the Development Corporation, to attract the ever increasing number of newcomers to the City to become Posh fans, by giving them a free ticket for one game. It certainly seemed to have some success, for after the opening draw at Stockport (and then continuing their dreadful record in the League Cup - losing 2-0 at Watford), Posh beat Aldershot at London Road in front of 5,953, which was considerably up on their gates from the previous season. Making their debuts for Posh in the Stockport game were Duncliffe, Sheffield, Pleat and Turpie at substitute.

Posh then lost their first League match of the season by 3-2 at Exeter, continuing on the following week with defeat at Bournemouth. But this poor start was succeeded with a six match unbeaten run. It started with a 2-1 victory over Newport at London Road, Sheffield scoring his first goal for the Club, before successive 1-1 draws at Brentford and at home to Grimsby. Posh then recorded three straight victories - 2-1 at home to York, 3-2 at Barrow and a London Road victory over Oldham. Sheffield scored in all three games, and at Barrow, Turpie netted his first goal for Posh. After a 2-1 home reverse to Colchester, Posh played their first ever Football League game against newly elected Cambridge United at the Abbey Stadium. The match finished 1-1, Posh's goal coming from Peter Price.

The next two games brought widely differing fortunes, for Posh hammered Stockport 5-1 at London Road - with two goals from Garwood and one apiece from Price, Robson and Moss in front of 5,207 - and then went down 5-2 at Scunthorpe just three days later. After a 2-1 reverse at Lincoln, Posh beat Chester at home and Hartlepool away, before facing their third local derby of the season, at Northampton, where they lost. After another home defeat (1-0 to Darlington) in the following game, the fans again showed their discontent.

The first round of the F.A.Cup was a welcome diversion for Iley when Posh entertained Southern League Wimbledon.

Posh ran out 3-1 winners, with goals coming from Garwood, Hall and Moss in front of 5,919. Back in the League a bumper attendance of 7,119 came to watch Posh entertain Notts County in another game against local opposition, and they drew 1-1 thanks to a goal from Garwood. Crewe were beaten at Gresty Road, 3-1, after which Joe Ryall was transferred to West Bromwich Albion for a Club record fee of £35,000. Posh then turned their attentions once again to the F.A.Cup, when they were again drawn against non-League opposition, this time away to Wigan Athletic. The Posh side that included Iley, Turner, Pleat, Hall and Robson added to the Club's - unwanted - history when they became the first Posh side since joining the League to lose to non-League opponents, going down 2-1.

Posh now had no option but to turn their attentions to the League where results continued in inconsistent form. They drew at Aldershot 2-2 one week before Christmas, and on Boxing Day hammered Southend 4-0 at London Road, with Garwood and Moss both scoring two apiece. The first game of 1971 was at Oldham and Posh were well beaten 3-0. One week later they lost at home again, this time to Scunthorpe, and by now the team were slipping well out of contention in the promotion race. The first home game of the year was won versus Southport, thanks to a goal from Hall, with Jack Carmichael - a signing from Arsenal - making his debut for Posh. In the next game, at Notts County, Posh made their second piece of unwanted history of the season, for they crashed to a 6-0 defeat - their biggest since joining the Football League. Posh completed the double over Crewe with a 3-1 home victory, and were then promptly beaten 3-2 by Southport in the next away game. Posh entertained Northampton looking for revenge for the earlier defeat at the County ground, and they got it in front of 8,068 fans (the biggest crowd of the season), with Moss scoring the only goal of the game.

A dismal run followed with defeats at Chester, York and Darlington, and a 1-1 draw with Lincoln between the trio of losses. By now, and well into March, Posh's next game was at home to Workington, and just 2,771 fans came to watch them win 3-1 with two goals from Robson and one from Garwood. This number was the lowest League attendance at London Road up to that date. Posh claimed their biggest victory of the season in the next game beating Hartlepool 5-0 at London Road, with two goals each from Moss and Garwood and one from Robson, which saw them cruise home. The season was quickly becoming a mere formality for Posh, and they lost their next three matches (at Newport and Workington and by 3-1 at home to Exeter). The Exeter match was played at London Road on a Saturday night for the first time, which was arranged to avoid clashing with the Grand National. Posh got back to winning ways with a 2-1 victory over struggling Southend United, with Garwood and Wright scoring the Peterborough goals.

Posh had a disastrous Easter programme when they lost 3-0 at Colchester on Good Friday, and at home to Brentford on Easter Monday. These two reverses were followed by another pair of defeats - 3-2 at Cambridge in front of 5,067 - and at Grimsby. Posh had by now slid dramatically down the table, and it was with some relief that they faced the final two games of the season at home. Bournemouth were beaten 3-1 (goals from Hall, Conmy and Robson), and finally Barrow by 4-0.

In a dismal season Posh finished ninth from the bottom of the Fourth Division table with 43 points, and had made no real progress in any of the three Cup competitions. The final notable items from this dismal and uninspiring season were the retirement from the game of Lawrie Sheffield due to ankle troubles, and David Pleat's move from Peterborough to become the Manager of Nuneaton.

1971/72 SEASON

The season got off to a farcical start, when 15 players and officials flew out to Spain for a three match tour, but in the end didn't play a game, due to the reluctance of the Spaniards to meet them! In the transfer market Iley looked for new blood and bought in Denis Oakes from Notts County, Micky Darrell from Birmingham and Eric Brookes from Northampton. Colin Garwood left the Club for £12,000, to Oldham, whilst Jack Carmichael was appointed the Club Captain with Billy Hales the trainer.

The League programme commenced at home to Southend and Posh won 2-0 in front of 4,500 fans, Price scoring both Posh goals. Oakes, Brookes and sub Darrell all made their debuts for Posh. A predictable first round exit from the League Cup was made, this time at the hands of Second Division Charlton Athletic by 5-1 at the Valley. But in the League things were going quite nicely, for after a 1-1 draw at Newport, Posh beat Stockport at home 4-2, with two goals apiece from Conmy and Robson. This victory was followed by another at London Road, over Bury in front of 6,800. Posh's first League defeat came at Exeter on September 4th when they were beaten 3-2, and was then followed up with two more defeats - at home to Scunthorpe and by 5-1 at Brentford.

But the team got back to winning ways when they entertained Gillingham and won 2-1, with both goals scored by Price, which took his tally to eight goals in eight League games. Richie Barker who had signed that week from Notts County came in to make his debut. Another two defeats followed, at Hartlepool and at Workington, but then Posh won with some style when they entertained Barrow on October 9th. Hall and Price both scored hat-tricks along with a single goal from Conmy, to record a 7-0 victory in front of 4,681 fans; this was Posh's biggest victory since 1969, when they overcame Oldham by 8-1. Inconsistency again followed with a defeat at Southend, then a return to winning ways with a 3-1 victory over Darlington, in which Price scored his second hat-trick. Barker scored his first goal for the Club in the 3-2 defeat at Lincoln. Posh then embarked on a six match unbeaten run, which started with a 2-0 home victory over Crewe, when Oakes scored his first goal for the Club. The points were shared at Aldershot, before another 2-0 victory at London Road, this time against Chester.

The following week Posh started on the F.A. Cup trail, and were again paired against non-League opposition, this time with Redditch. Posh drew 1-1 in a close affair, with Price scoring his 17th goal of the season, but any thoughts of an upset were quickly dispelled in the replay two days later when Posh ran out 6-0 winners; with two goals from Barker, two from Hall and one each from Robson and Price. The reward for this victory was a home tie, against yet another non-League Club, in the shape of Enfield. Back in the League Posh beat Southport at London Road 2-0, but their gradual climb up the table was halted with the defeat at Doncaster by 3-2. A bumper crowd of 7,702 came to watch Posh take on Enfield in the second round of the F.A. Cup, and a brace of goals from both Price and Hall, saw Posh home to a comfortable 4-0 victory, which set them up with an attractive home tie against First Division Ipswich Town. However before this attraction Posh entered a busy Christmas period which finished with four consecutive draws; 3-3 at home to Exeter, scoreless at Colchester, 2-2 at home to Brentford and another no scoring game, at Stockport.

On January 14th 1972 Posh entertained Ipswich, and the cup match attracted an attendance of 16,970 for a game which captured the attention of soccer fans in the City who were looking for Posh to add another scalp to their great giantkilling tradition. This time they were to be disappointed as Ipswich ran out 2-0 winners and Posh were left to try and improve their form and salvage something in the League. Incredibly with four more single points, Posh made it eight consecutive draws in the League - at home to Hartlepool, at Darlington plus Northampton, and finally 4-4 at home to Lincoln on February 12th in front of 6,601.

Posh's season was again heading nowhere, and discontent amongst the fans was spreading with much talk on the terraces about the removal of Jim Iley as Manager. After a 2-0 defeat at Crewe, followed by yet another two drawn games - at home to Aldershot and at Chester - Posh were left without a win in 12 matches. It was now March, and the last victory had been on November the 27th. But the dismal run was ended when Posh entertained Cambridge, before 4,947. For the first time at London Road, home and away fans were segregated, by being kept in separate sections in the ground.

Oakes and Barker were Posh's scorers in a 2–0 victory. This was immediately followed by another two points, with the same scoreline, at Barrow. Despite a 2–1 defeat at Reading, Posh won in their next home match, this time recording a 3–1 victory over Newport. Two days later Polish Club Gwardia of Warsaw were entertained, and beaten, in a friendly encounter. Posh were goalless for the next two League games, returning with a point from Scunthorpe, followed by a 2–0 home defeat by Grimsby.

Posh entered their final 10 games of the season and were destined to lose only one more game as they found their best run of form to date under Iley. Colchester were easily overcome, by 4–0 at London Road, and successive draws were recorded at Gillingham and at home to Workington. On April 8th Posh faced their old rivals Northampton at London Road, and in front of 5,480 they won 1–0 with a goal from Price. Price then notched four in the following game when Southport were beaten 4–2 on their own soil. Travelling Posh fans were then treated to another goal feast, when they travelled to the Abbey

Stadium to take on Cambridge on April 19th. They ran out 5–2 winners over their near neighbours, with two goals apiece from Robson and Barker plus a single from Hall. These two notable victories were followed by a 2–0 win over Doncaster at London Road, and a 1–1 draw at Bury. The only defeat of the period came at Grimsby, when the Cleethorpes based club secured the Fourth Division Championship with a 3–2 victory. The Club's good run in April was rewarded, with Iley deservedly being named being named *Manager of the Month*.

The final game of the season was at home to Reading and Posh won 3–2 in front of 5,749 fans. The team finished eighth in the table, and gave the Posh fans much more to cheer about for their sparkling finish to the end of, what had become, another overall unsuccessful season. The total of 83 goals scored by Posh during the campaign was the highest since the 1964/65 season, and was enough to qualify them for the following season's Watney Cup competition again.

1972/73 SEASON

During the pre–season period another row started between the Parent Club and the Supporters' Club, on this occasion it concerned the Club's decision to bring in a firm of outside caterers to run the tea bars. In the transfer market Jim Iley bought Ray Smith from Wrexham for £5,000, along with Bobby Park from the same club – on a free transfer – in what proved to be a relatively quiet build up to the new season.

Posh started the new campaign by entertaining Second Division Blackpool in the Watney Cup. 7,651 came to watch the visitors beaten 7–6 on penalties after no goals in normal time. Bob Stokoe put in an official complaint to the Football League as one of the Posh penalty takers was Don Heath, who had earlier been substituted in the game. The appeal was thrown out and Posh went on to meet Sheffield United in the semi–finals. The first Division side were a different proposition however, and despite Tony Currie being sent off in the 26th minute of the game, the Blades went on to win 4–0. One of the goalscorers was Yorkshire cricketer Ted Hemsley. The last major pre–season game was a 2–0 victory at London Road over Scottish First Division club Motherwell, goals coming from Smith and Robson.

The opening game of the season was at Stockport and a 3–2 defeat, Posh coming twice from behind, with Robson and Hall scoring the goals. Making their debuts on the day were Heath, Park and Smith. Posh crashed to their second defeat of the season when they visited Oxford in the League Cup and lost 4–0. Greater problems were on the horizon after the first game of the season at London Road, a defeat to Southport by a single goal.

Posh then travelled to Chester City and came back humiliated after crashing to their biggest ever League defeat, losing 8–2. At half time the score was 2–1, after Hall had equalised an earlier goal from Chester. In the second half Chester ran riot scoring a further six goals without reply until Turner grabbed a last minute consolation. There was no chance of a respite in the local derby against Northampton at London Road, for the Cobblers triumphed 2–1 in front of 3,627. This left Posh with five consecutive defeats at the start of the season, having scored five goals and conceding a staggering eighteen.

Just 2,457, Posh's lowest ever League gate, watched as Posh recorded their first victory of the season – 3–0 at home to Bradford – and this lifted them to 5th from bottom of the table. But the dismal run continued with a 2–0 defeat at Reading and eventually cost Manager Jim Iley his job. Following a crisis Board Meeting Iley resigned and Jim Walker was appointed Caretaker Manager. His First game was at home to Torquay and it resulted in another defeat, this time by 1–0, Alcock scoring after 68 minutes. A Hall goal earned Posh a point at Newport, before their second local derby of the season, when Posh succumbed to Cambridge by 3–1, Oakes scoring the only goal for Posh. After 10 games of the season Posh had only recorded one victory. The next encounter, at home to Bury, saw Bobby Moss back in the side after a six month absence due to a knee injury. The game produced another record low attendance of 2,345, who watched Hall put Posh ahead after 15 minutes only for Bury's Connolly to equalise with 27 minutes remaining. It was Hall again, this time with both goals, that then earned a 2–2 draw with Lincoln City.

John Anderson, Ellis Stafford, Noel Cantwell

Two more defeats followed, at Barnsley and Mansfield, before it was announced that the new Manager of Peterborough United would be Noel Cantwell, the former Manchester United skipper and Coventry Manager. A crowd of 4,134 was present as Posh swept aside Doncaster 3–1, with two goals from Smith and one from Robson. New Manager Cantwell celebrated in style as he cracked open the champagne in the dressing room after the victory.

The new Manager's confidence was sweeping through the City and he was quoted after the match as saying:
"I thought there would be a bigger crowd, particularly as I told them we were going to win." Whatever he was saying to his players was obviously working as a side unchanged from Iley's management then won 2–0 at Crewe. The next game was at home to Colchester and an attendance of 5,648 watched Posh draw, coming back from two goals down, with goals from Oakes and then Heath who snatched a point seven minutes from time. Another home game produced another increase in the attendance, when Posh drew with Hereford 1–1. Smith grabbed the goal after 20 minutes and it was Hereford goalkeeper David Icke who stole the glory with an outstanding display to save the Bulls a point.

Cantwell's first defeat as a Manager came at Bury, by 3–1, with Terry McDermott scoring one of the Shakers goals. But this setback was quickly rectified for Posh then beat Newport at home 1–0. The following week John Barnwell, the former Nottingham Forest, Sheffield United and Arsenal player, was appointed Peterborough United's Trainer/Coach. His arrival, unfortunately, prompted the dismissal of former Posh player and loyal club servant Jim Walker who ended his 15 year association with the Club. Cantwell was full of enthusiasm for the F.A. Cup match, at home against local rivals Northampton. Before the game former Cobblers striker Hall said: *"Nothing would give me more pleasure than to score the winning goal against my old side"*. A crowd of 7,815 came to London Road and in true fairytale fashion Hall

snatched the winner just seconds from full time. The only disappointment for Posh was Bobby Moss, who was stretchered off during the game, and it proved to be his last match for the club.

A week later Posh entertained Hartlepool at London Road and goals from Oakes, Hall and Brookes saw them home to a 3–0 victory. The following week Cantwell moved into the transfer market for the first time, capturing the signature of Notts County striker John Cozens for £8,000, and then taking Manchester United midfield player Eric Young on a three month loan period. The next day Aston Villa defender Keith Bradley arrived at the Club, on a one month loan. Cozens made his debut in the visit to Darlington, along with Young who came on as a second half substitute for Heath. Robson gave Posh a 22nd minute lead, but the Quakers came back with two goals shortly before half time. However, Heath equalised after 58 minutes to give Posh a point.

The next round of the F.A. Cup brought a tricky away tie at non–League Bishop's Stortford. It was a stirring cup-tie, and despite Posh taking an early lead – with Cozens scoring his first goal for the Club – followed by a second from Robson, Bishop's Stortford stormed back with two late goals to make it a cliffhanging finish. Posh held on to take the tie back to London Road for a replay. Two days later and Posh made no mistakes, goals from Robson, Hall and Heath, in front of an attendance of 8,966, saw them safely through to the third round and a glamour tie, at home, to current First Division Champions Derby County.

Back in League action Bradley came in to make his debut in a 2–1 home victory over Workington, and this was followed two days before Christmas with defeat at Gillingham. The Boxing Day fixture saw Posh at home to local rivals Cambridge, and Cozens' goal 23 seconds from the end of the game saw Posh salvage a point. The last game of 1972 was at Southport where Cozens scored again, but Posh went down 2–1.

One week later and Posh entertained Chester, with memories of the 8-2 mauling earlier in the season. Cozens scored his third goal in three games, with Turner adding a second, to give Posh a 2-0 lead. But Chester hit back with two goals in three minutes midway through the second half to leave Posh with a creditable 2-2 draw.

The match that the whole City were waiting for attracted a crowd of 22,000 to London Road as Posh took on Derby, who boasted amongst their players the likes of David Nish, Alan Durban, Roy McFarland, Colin Todd, John McGovern, Archie Gemill, Kevin Hector and John O'Hare. Posh turned in a brave display though and it was only a goal by Roger Davies after 36 minutes that separated the two sides on the day. The sorry side of the occasion, however, was the tide of violence that swept the City before and after the game.

The showing against Derby obviously gave Posh a new lease of life for they then won at Bradford by 4-1, with a Cozens hat trick and a single goal from Hall. This was followed by a home won over Reading (4-2), with Smith (2), Hall and Young scoring, the latter player's first for the Club. Trevor Freestone was called up for the first time, although he was an unused substitute on the day. Posh then secured three consecutive wins, beating Mansfield at London Road 1-0 in front of 7,224. The next two matches were down in the West Country, Posh succumbing 1-0 at Torquay, before Russell scored his first goal for the Club – coming on as substitute – and earning Posh a point at Exeter. Stockport completed a double over Posh with a 3-2 victory at London Road, and this was followed by a visit to Workington where they drew 2-2.

In early March, Posh secured their biggest victory of the season with a 6-3 mauling of Barnsley. It was a highly entertaining game that saw Posh storm into a three goal lead after 17 minutes with a goal from Cozens, and two from Hall.

However, Barnsley fought back with three goals in the 36th, 39th and 41st minute. Posh weren't finished though, for Turner made it 4-3 two minutes before time, and just one minute later Hall gained his hat trick to produce an incredible 5-3 scoreline at half-time, before Robson completed the scoring early in the second half.

Cozens earned Posh a point at Doncaster with Oakes named as substitute but not being called upon to come on and make his League debut. A St. Patrick's Day fixture, home against Crewe, was watched by 4,875, the large majority of whom must have feared the worst as Alexandra went into a 3-0 lead by early in the second half. A Heath penalty put Posh back on track and then an inspired display from Robson laid the foundations for Hall to grab a hat-trick and secure a victory for Posh. Substitute Burton, on loan from Sheffield Wednesday, was not called upon to make his debut for the Club, having to wait for two days, when Posh entertained Aldershot, and he replaced Keith Oakes. Freestone came in to make his full Posh debut and scored the only goal of the game after 13 minutes to give the home side victory. The following Saturday Posh travelled to Hereford and were well beaten 3-0, in front of 9,515 at Edgar Street. A Hall goal at Hartlepool earned Posh a 1-0 victory, which was followed by a home draw with Darlington.

Although Posh were now safe from re-election, they entered on another dismal run, losing the next three matches, with Oakes making his first full appearance for the Club in the defeat at Lincoln. A 1-1 draw at home to Exeter, was followed by a 1-0 reverse to Gillingham, before the final game of the season. Posh finished with a pleasing victory, beating neighbours Northampton 3-1 away from home. An own goal, plus Cozens and ex-Cobbler Robson scored the goals. This brought to an end a season that had started with so much disappointment, one that was rescued by the appointment of Noel Cantwell as Manager.

Jim Hall (centre) had been an ever-present in an unremarkable League season. Freddie Hill (left) and Paul Walker (right) joined Posh during the Summer, and the trio were to make their contribution to a memorable season.

CHAPTER 6

BACK TO THE THIRD

1973/74 SEASON

On the playing side, Cantwell cleared out some of his staff, giving free transfers to Micky Darrell, Richie Barker, Clive Reedman, Alan Russell, Eric Brooke, Ray Smith, John Duncan and Dennis Oakes. He was quick to move for replacements and his first signing in the close season was Paul Walker from Wolves. Dugald McLachlan arrived from Preston but the major signing came at the end of May when former England International Freddie Hill joined the club from Manchester City for £5,000. Secretary Colin Benson resigned from the Club and was replaced by Arnold Blades, who made his second return to the Club. Back in the transfer market Cantwell captured Jeff Lee from Halifax for £6,000, Dave Llewellyn from West Ham and Brendan Phillips from Leicester City, both on free transfers. He also moved into the local non-League market and offered amateur forms to Malcolm Hird and David Gregory, as well as giving a trial to Whittlesey teenager Steve Fallon.

In friendly matches, Third Division Plymouth were beaten before Posh lost to First Division West Ham 2-1. The Watney Cup, started and finished on August 11th as Posh lost to Bristol City at home 2-1 in front of 9,137, the club having qualified (for the third year in succession) to play in the Competition. The League season got under-way at London Road when Posh beat Mansfield 2-1 with goals from Cozens and Lee, the latter's first for the Club on his debut. Other players making their first appearance for Posh that day in front of an attendance of 7,045 were Mick Jones, a late signing from Notts County, Llewellyn, Walker and Hill.

Four days later Posh entertained Scunthorpe, Lee again scoring along with Robson, in a 2-2 draw in the first round of the League Cup. Keith Oakes came into the side in place of Llewellyn, and Gregory made his debut for Posh 16 minutes before the end. In the League a Cozens goal earned an away point at Stockport, before Posh then played Scunthorpe twice in the space of four days. The first match was at the Old Showground, where a Jones goal could not prevent Posh going out of the League Cup. Four days later Scunthorpe came back to London Road and Hill scored his first goal for the club in front of 6,399 to maintain Posh's unbeaten start in the League. Bert Murray had made his debut in the first of the Scunthorpe matches, on loan from Brighton, and retained his place in the side.

Posh then earned a point away at Lincoln thanks to a Hall goal. It was a performance that Manager Cantwell described as one of Posh's best away games since he had arrived at the Club. This match was followed up by another away point, this time at Bradford City, where Cozens scored the only goal for Posh. Posh then hammered Doncaster at London Road 5-1, Hall scoring four times, and Robson getting the other goal. Posh also gained points at home to Torquay and at Reading before tasting defeat in the League for the first time that season, when they lost at Doncaster 3-1, Gregory making his first full League appearance for the Club. The team bounced back in the very next game to move to 5th in the table, after they beat Workington 2-0 at London Road in front of 6,161.

The following week Keith Bradley signed permanently for Posh from Brighton for £6,000. An away trip to Brentford saw Robson score the only goal of the game to give Posh a 1-0 victory, with Stuart Houston in the defeated Bees side. Posh were now in the middle of a magnificent run of seven consecutive wins. The following week they beat Swansea at London Road by 3-0, followed by a 1-0 victory at home to Lincoln City, Lee scoring the only goal with a twice taken penalty in front of 9,125 fans. Cozens scored the only goal of the game at Newport, and repeated this success, along with Robson, when 9,641 watched Posh beat Exeter at home 2-0. The last of the seven consecutive victories came at Gigg Lane when Posh beat Bury 2-0, Cozens scoring (in his third consecutive match) together with Turner. It was enough to see Posh rise to top of the League, and Manager Noel Cantwell named as *'Manager of the Month'* for the Fourth Division during October. The successful run ended at Crewe with a 2-1 defeat at Gresty Road.

Three days later Posh were back on the winning trail again when they entertained Northampton at London Road. An attendance 10,351 saw Hall score yet again against his old Club, in the 14th minute. He added another with a belting goal from fully 25 yards, before completing his hat-trick, to put the final nail in the Cobblers coffin, when he hammered home from 10 yards. The next game was in the F.A. Cup at Colchester, when, in a televised game, Posh came from 1-0 down to win 3-2. TV expert Jimmy Hill pronounced: *"This win for Posh will probably spell the end of their Championship hopes"*.

Posh got back to League action on a snow covered pitch against Hartlepool at London Road, and goals from Turner and Cozens gave Posh a 2-0 victory in front of 7,537. Cozens scored two more in a 2-2 draw at Darlington before the team travelled to Wycombe in the second round of the F.A. Cup. Cozens made it seven goals in four games as they ran out 3-1 winners, Hall scoring Posh's other goal. It took Cozens's tally to 15 for the season to that date, and the victory presented Posh with a home tie against Southend.

Back in the League Posh beat Reading at home 2-0 before travelling to Colchester on Boxing Day when they returned with a point. They ended the year with a 2-1 defeat at Scunthorpe, but bounced straight back again on New Year's Day with a 3-2 home victory over Stockport; Hall, Cozens and Jones got the goals at London Road in front of a crowd of 8,272. Posh started the New Year in second place in the League, one point behind Colchester with one game in hand. Third Division Southend came to London Road in the third round of the Cup and were torn apart by a brilliant display from Posh, who went ahead after 27 minutes with a goal from Cozens. On the stroke of half time Hill made it 2-0 and it looked as though Posh had got the match wrapped up. For a brief period Southend made a comeback as they reduced the deficit after 53 minutes, but after 70 minutes Robson hit Posh's third and sent them through for a glamour tie against Leeds United in the fourth round.

Back in the League Posh's challenge faltered slightly as they drew at home to Bradford City 1-1, in front of a staggering attendance of 15,461. The large number was due in no small part to the fact that tickets were on sale for the Leeds United cup-tie! This match was followed by a 2-1 defeat at Mansfield, their last game before tackling Leeds at London Road.

The attendance was set at 28,000 and if the club and fans were expecting an upset they were disappointed. The impressive Leeds United team romped to a 4-1 victory, with goals from Jordan (2), Lorimer and Yorath, Posh's consolation goal came from Cozens. The Leeds four goals came in an early first half blitz and Posh did well to not completely succumb to the power of the First Division outfit. The Leeds side that day consisted of: Harvey, Reaney, Cooper, Bremner, Ellam, Hunter, Lorrimer, Yorath, Jordan, Cherry, Madeley with substitute Frank Gray, and it was no disgrace that Posh had gone out to one of English Football's great sides.

Placed at third in the table, the next game for Posh finished as a scoreless League drew at London Road, versus Chester. This match saw Steele make his debut, in goal, and he went on to make a record setting 148 consecutive appearances which stretched until the 12th of October 1976. A goal from Hill earned Posh victory over Brentford at London Road, before travelling to Workington eight days later and getting hammered 4-1. It was hardly the preparation they needed as they prepared to face possibly their biggest game of the season, the visit of

Fourth Division leaders Colchester. A crowd of 10,714 watched Posh win 2-0 with goals from Hall and Cozens. This result closed the gap on the leaders, to five points, with Posh having four games in hand. It was the tonic Posh needed and they continued on the winning trail with a 2-0 home victory over Newport before travelling to Swansea and winning again by the same margin. But a setback came with defeat at Chester four days later.

Cantwell moved into the transfer market again bringing Alan Lewis on loan from First Division Derby. Posh drew 2-2 at home with Bury – Robson and Murray scoring the goals in front of 8,145 – before Lewis made his debut two days later in the home match with Rotherham. Cantwell was looking for improvement after two poor results, and he got just that as Robson and Murray again got on the scoresheet and gave Posh another 2-0 victory. Goals from Walker and Cozens ensured a 2-1 win at Exeter before Posh travelled to Gillingham, who were also challenging for promotion at the top of the table. Posh were defeated 1-0 and lost vital ground on the leading pack. They gained ample revenge for their defeat at Crewe earlier in the season when they ran out 4-0 winners at London Road in front of 7,250. The situation prompted Cantwell to say that they needed seven points from their final eight games to secure promotion to the Third Division.

The first of the games was a crunch game at Northampton, the Cobblers themselves on the fringe of the promotion race, and Posh beat them 1-0 with a goal from Murray. This was followed up by a 3-0 home victory against Barnsley in front of an attendance of 10,000, when Lewis scored his first goal for the club. With six games left Posh were 3rd in the Fourth Division, four points behind 56 point leaders Colchester, with four games in hand. Gillingham were in second place, a point ahead of Posh, but Posh had two games in hand on the Gills. The next day, they travelled to Oakwell and came back with a 0-0 draw, before entertaining Darlington four days later. A goal from Hill two minutes before half time sent the 9,207 crowd wild, for the 1-0 victory signalled Peterborough United's return to the Third Division. It also saw them return to the top of the Fourth Division table.

The next prize on the horizon now was the Championship. Posh travelled to the North East to play Hartlepool, and a goal from Robson after 85 minutes left them second in the table with three games remaining. They were one point behind Gillingham who only had one match to play and that against Posh the following Wednesday. Victory in that game would confirm Posh as Fourth Division Champions.

On Wednesday May 1st 1974 an attendance of 17,569 came to London Road and the Posh team that night consisted of:

Steele, Lee, Lewis, Walker, Turner, Jones, Murray, Cozens, Hall, Hill, Robson, substitute Gregory.

The game itself was a fitting climax to the season, with an electric atmosphere at London Road. After just nine minutes Murray was adjudged by a linesman to have handled the ball, and Lindsey put Gillingham 1–0 up from the penalty spot. Six minutes later Posh fans had a smile back on their faces as Lindsey brought down Robson in the box, this time it was Lee who came up, and scored the equaliser from the spot. Fourteen minutes later an intricate move from Lee, Robson and Walker set up the goal for Cozens to put Posh 2–1 up, with no further scoring before the half time break. Fifteen minutes after half time Turner headed home a Cozens corner and Posh were 3–1 in front. But the fans' jubilation was cut short 13 minutes later as Gillingham came back into the game with a goal from Wilkes who scored from Tydeman's deflected shot. The game reached a frantic climax, when, with eight minutes remaining Cozens sealed the issue beyond all doubt as he rose above the Gillingham goalkeeper to head home Lewis's cross. The crowd was ecstatic and as the full time whistle sounded the celebrations began, with thousands of excited supporters swarming onto the pitch, with the chant of *"We are the Champions"* echoing around the ground.

Cantwell had succeeded in taking the Club from bottom of the Fourth Division the previous season to Fourth Division Champions, within a space of 15 months.

The Posh promotion challenge slipped in the New Year, and the mid-February victory over Brentford was the first win since January the 1st...........

...........But it all came out right in the end!

Peterborough U. v Brentford
OFFICIAL MATCH MAGAZINE

FOOTBALL LEAGUE DIVISION 4

Nº 000916

POSH
(blue)

1 Eric STEELE
2 Keith BRADLEY
3 Jeff LEE
4 Paul WALKER
5 Chris TURNER
6 Mick JONES
7 Bert MURRAY
8 John COZENS
9 Jim HALL
10 Freddie HILL
11 Tommy ROBSON
Sub: David LLEWELYN

BEES
(red/white stripes)

1 Paul PRIDDY
2 Paul BENCE
3 Terry SCALES
4 Gordon RIDDOCK
5 Peter GELSON
6 Alan NELMES
7 John GRAHAM
8 Roger CROSS
9 Andy WOON
10 Mike ALLEN
11 Barry SALVAGE
Sub:

Referee:
T. D. SPENCER
(Wootton Basset, Wilts)

Linesmen:
H. Dempsey (red flag)
M. C. Dixon (orange flag)

POSH skipper John Cozens is outnumbered here by three Chester players in an attack during the last home match. Big John was beaten, and it was not the only time he was foiled in the 0-0 draw.

'Robbo' speaks for the Champions

Posh still had two matches to play and they beat Torquay away 2–1 six days later before losing their final game of the season 3–1 at Rotherham. It mattered little, as for the second time in Posh's history, they had finished as Division 4 Champions. The Championship Trophy was presented at London Road on Monday May 14th, when Posh played a game against the All Stars, a match to boost the testimonial funds of Frank Noble and Bobby Moss, who were both forced to quit the game through injuries. The All Stars side included players of the calibre of Brian Hornsby, Ted McDougall, Kevin Keelan and the old Posh favourite Derek Dougan. In the same week Manager Noel Cantwell predictably heard that he had won the Fourth Division's *'Manager of the Year'* award. It proved a fitting end to a successful season.

POSH player of the year, Tommy Robson, in spectacular pre-season form. Paul Walker is in the background.

As the euphoria of Posh's successful season continued to sweep the City, Cantwell quickly moved into the transfer market and by the end of May he had made a new signing in the shape of John Winfield from Nottingham Forest. Within days he also moved to secure the permanent signing, for £10,000, of Eric Steele who had been on loan from Newcastle for most of the previous season, plus Jeff Lissaman a defender from Leicester City who joined the Club as an apprentice. Cantwell's next signing was local player Stuart Hodson who was offered a three month trial at the Club, followed by another move into the transfer market – and something of a surprise – as he went to Portsmouth to bring back former Posh player Peter Price on a three month loan.

Posh kicked off the pre-season in the newly formed Texaco Cup with a visit to Norwich City, that ended in a 2–1 defeat. Ted McDougall scored both of Norwich's goals, with Mick Jones getting the goal for Posh. This was followed by a home match against Birmingham City that saw Posh force a 1–1 draw, John Cozens putting Posh into the lead and Gordon Taylor scoring the equaliser. The final match in the three team group was at home against West Bromwich Albion. Cozens put Posh into the lead after 10 minutes with David Shaw equalising for the Baggies five minutes later. Freddie Hill then scored with a magnificent free kick 15 minutes from time to clinch the win for Posh. It was not enough to progress through to the last eight as Posh finished third in their Group.

The first match back in the Third Division since 1968 was at Huddersfield, and, unusually, Posh started the season without giving a debut to a new player. Following a goalless first half, Huddersfield took the lead five minutes after the break, only for Jim Hall to equalise within two minutes, and then Cozens hit the winner seven

minutes from time to give them the two points on their return to Division 3. It was a different story just three days later as Posh were hammered 4–0 at the Valley against Charlton Athletic in the first round of the League Cup. It did not affect their League form though as Posh played their first Third Division game at London Road for six years and beat Brighton 2–0, the goals coming from Hall after 56 minutes and Turner after 13 minutes later. The performance was, however, far more convincing than the scoreline suggests and goalkeeper Peter Grummitt saved Brighton on more than one occasion as Posh piled on the pressure.

In mid–week Posh travelled to face Hereford United and surrendered their short unbeaten League record, as they lost by 2–0. The goals came from Dixie McNeil, his 100th in the League. Back at London Road Posh fared better again, this time beating Wrexham 2–1, Tommy Robson giving Posh a 16th minute lead which was equalised by Arfon Griffiths for the Welshmen just on the half hour. Hall popped up 14 minutes from time to claim both points for Posh. The price of the victory was the injury to Cozens who was carried off, and it was later discovered that he had broken his knee cap and was to be sidelined for at least six weeks. This injury gave David Gregory his chance in the first team. Posh won 2–1 at Grimsby thanks to two headers from Turner, both from set pieces.

The next match saw one of football's legends arrive at London Road, as Bobby Charlton arrived as player/manager for Preston North End. The game attracted an attendance of 13,120, plus the 'Match of the Day' cameras. Unfortunately it could not produce any goals, but the point left Posh lying fourth in the table. Cantwell moved in to sign a new player in the shape of Jon Nixon from Notts County for £15,000, and he made his debut at home to Halifax coming on as a substitute after 50 minutes. The game itself produced a 1–1 draw, Posh's goal coming directly from a corner in the third minute by Robson. The next game was at Gillingham where Price made his debut for Posh in the Third Division, on the last day of his loan signing from Portsmouth. Paul Walker put Posh ahead just before the hour but Gillingham equalised through Damien Richardson seven minutes later.

Back at London Road things were still going well, Posh beating Southend with Gregory scoring his first League goal for Posh, in front of 8,460. The match was watched by Frank Worthington who had come to see both of his brothers, Dave and Bob, who were in the defeated Southend side. Cantwell again moved into the transfer market and this time signed John Galley a 30 year old striker from Nottingham Forest. Posh returned to the Valley, and Charlton repeated their earlier Cup victory, this time beating Posh 3–0. Galley made his debut at the Valley, and he retained his place in the side two days later when Posh completed the double over Southend. Robson put Posh ahead after 11 minutes, only for Southend to equalise two minutes before the break, and it took a Lee penalty 20 minutes after half time to secure both points for Posh. This sent them to third in the table, equal on points with Preston and one point behind leaders Blackburn. Posh improved that position by one when they beat Watford at London Road in their next game thanks to an own goal four minutes from time.

Posh went top of the Third Division by winning their next game, at home to Bury, but their joy was shortlived as three days later a trip to Plymouth resulted in a 2–0 defeat. A draw at home to Aldershot left Posh third in the table, with Lee scoring from the penalty spot a minute before half time. At Selhurst Park, a crowd of 18,226 watched Galley score his first goal for Posh to give them the lead after 37 minutes, before Taylor equalised for Palace 17 minutes after half time. But the following Wednesday Posh were in the doldrums again as Bury handed out a 3–0 drubbing at Gigg Lane. There then followed an intriguing fixture at London Road, for the match against League leaders Blackburn. A crowd of 11,670 turned out to see Posh win 1–0 with a goal from Hill after just six minutes. It pushed Posh back into second place in the League, but it was not really a reflection of the way the game had gone with Rovers hitting the woodwork on more than one occasion.

Posh lost at Chesterfield before entertaining non-League Weymouth at London Road in the first round of the F.A. Cup. A crowd of 8,984 saw a scoreless draw, much to the frustration of the home crowd who booed and jeered throughout the game. Two points were dropped, to Port Vale, for the first home defeat of the season. Posh had now gone three games without a goal, which saw them slip to ninth place in the League. In the replay of the F.A. Cup-tie, it took the Southern League side just six minutes to go ahead, with a shot that cannoned in the goal off Oakes.

Gregory put Posh level 12 minutes later and that was the way the scores remained at half time. But 17 minutes into the second half Weymouth went ahead again with a well taken shot and it looked as though it would be enough to take Weymouth into the next round and record a memorable giantkilling. But with time running out Turner popped up to snatch an equaliser with just one minute of normal time remaining. With the tie going into extra time Weymouth took only five minutes to go ahead yet again, and just when it looked like Posh were out of luck and heading for an early Cup exit, David Llewellyn snatched a second equaliser in the dying seconds of extra time. The final 3–3 draw surely broke the Southern League team's hearts. The venue for the next match was decided by the toss of a coin that Posh won, and hence brought the second replay back to London Road the following Monday.

Between times Posh travelled to Walsall and won thanks to a moment of brilliance from young striker Gregory who scored a classic solo goal after 62 minutes. The replayed Cup match at London Road drew a crowd of 9,077 and this time they left nothing to chance, as Posh romped home 3–0 winners. It earned Posh a home tie against, by now familiar, Charlton Athletic. This time Posh got their revenge in front of 9,642, running out as 3–0 winners. This success was followed by another victory, this time at Swindon. The Christmas period however brought little luck as Posh went down 3–1 at home to Grimsby, their second home defeat of the season in front of a 10,165 crowd. Two days later they suffered a crushing 4–1 defeat at Colchester.

The New Year brought Tranmere to London Road for the third round of the F.A. Cup, and Keith Bradley chose a good time to get off the mark scoring his first goal for Posh in his two year's stay, and earned the team a fourth round trip to non-League Stafford Rangers.

A week later Posh entertained Walsall in a scoreless draw at London Road before travelling to Vale Park and gaining ample revenge for their earlier defeat at London Road by winning 3–1; it was Vale's first home defeat of the season. David Price, the young Arsenal midfield player arrived on loan and made his debut for Posh Reserves in a Capital Midweek League match along with young Derby loanee, goalkeeper John Turner.

The interest generated for the Stafford Rangers game was phenomenal and the match was played at Stoke's Victoria Ground, attracting a crowd of 31,160. Posh ran out 2–1 winners eventually, but not before the non-Leaguers had given Posh a good run for their money. They took the lead after 10 minutes and it looked as though an upset could be on the cards. But Posh equalised 11 minutes later through Nixon, and a minute before half time Gregory put them into the lead with a spectacular goal, dummying two defenders in the penalty area and slamming home an unstoppable drive into the back of the net. Stafford had their moments in the second half and indeed at one stage actually hit the bar, but Posh hung on and showed just enough character to earn themselves their glamorous 5th round tie at home to First Division Middlesbrough.

The recent improved form continued with the visit to Blackburn Rovers. David Price made his debut for the Club and a penalty from Lee after 37 minutes clinched the points for Posh and completed a double over the League leaders. It left Posh in 6th place with their next game at home against 5th placed Crystal Palace, with whom they were level on points. Alan Whittle gave Palace the lead after 24 minutes and things looked bleak as Posh created few chances, but the 11,698 crowd had something to cheer when Turner rose above the Palace defence to head home his 9th goal of the season and earn Posh a point. Hall at this stage was out on loan with neighbours Northampton.

The Middlesbrough game was played in front of a crowd of 25,750 at London Road, and Jack Charlton's Middlesbrough side were relieved to leave London Road with a draw. Gregory was Posh's star on the day receiving acclaim in all the popular newspapers and tormenting Middlesbrough at every opportunity. He had a hand in the Posh goal, for as Robson's cross came over he jumped with Boam, Foggon and Madden, but the ball ran wide to Nixon who scored from close range to give the home team the lead after just 16 minutes. This sent the crowd wild with joy, and for much of the game it looked as though it would be enough to earn Posh another famous giantkilling. But in the 57th minute David Moles equalised, stabbing the ball home inside the six yard box and past the stranded Steele.

Posh had to return to Ayresome Park for the replay three days later. A crowd of 34,303 saw Middlesborough ease their way through to the quarter finals with two goals from Alan Foggon. Graham Souness was in the 'Boro side for the replay and he seemed to make the difference as they looked a far more composed and confident side than they had at London Road a few days earlier.

The reaction from the defeat at Middlesbrough in the Cup was a truly awful performance at home to Chesterfield in the next game, the Spireites beating Peterborough 2-0 for the second time that season. Posh's next match was at home to Hereford and Galley who had played for Posh earlier in the season put the Bulls 1-0 up after eighteen minutes. Lee scored again from the penalty spot after 68 minutes to earn a point before a crowd numbering 7,108. Defeat at Halifax saw Posh's promotion hopes taking a dive at a vital time, and the next game – at home to Gillingham – finished goalless. Winfield eventually made his debut for the Club 11 months after joining them, having been plagued with knee troubles. Posh had now gone seven games without a win in League and Cup matches, but this was rectified in the very next home game against Huddersfield. Robson gave Posh the lead after 49 minutes, and, when 10 minutes later Huddersfield equalised, it looked as though Posh fans were in for

another frustrating night. However 15 minutes from time Hall, who had returned from his loan spell at Northampton a few games earlier, flicked on a left wing corner from Robson for Nixon to score the winner. It was the boost in confidence that Posh needed, and the following Saturday they visited Wrexham and came back with a 2-1 victory. Posh made it three consecutive wins when they entertained Colchester at London Road. Once more it was all down to another piece of Gregory magic, he weaved past Colchester defenders during a 30 yard run which culminated in a thundering shot from some 15 yards, for the only goal of the game. The win hoisted Posh back to 8th position in the table, six points behind a promotion spot with three games in hand.

Two draws followed, scoreless at home to Swindon, and 1-1 three days later at Preston, this time with no Bobby Charlton. Turner became Posh's saviour again with a goal four minutes from time. The promotion push all but evaporated over the next two games with a 5-0 thrashing at Aldershot and a single goal defeat at Tranmere. This was followed by a 1-1 draw at London Road with third placed Charlton Athletic, who along with Blackburn and Plymouth were virtually assured of promotion to the Second Division. Gregory gave Posh an 18 minute lead but just a minute later Horsfield equalised for Charlton. Two goals from Nixon and one from Hall, his first since returning to the side, gave Posh a 3-0 victory over Bournemouth at London Road, followed by the same score at Watford, who were struggling near the foot of the table. These results kept Posh's slim promotion hopes alive, but things were finally ended after Brighton beat them 2-0 at the Goldstone Ground in front of 11,509.

Posh's next game was at home to Plymouth Argyle, who were assured of promotion but were trying to pip Blackburn for the Third Division Championship. A crowd of 11,176 saw Posh win the game with a goal from Robson. The game, unfortunately, will probably be remembered for some of the worst scenes of football violence in Peterborough, with many of the 5,000 strong Plymouth following causing trouble in the town centre both before and after the game. Problems also occurred during the match, and the referee had to receive treatment after he was struck by a bottle thrown from the Moys End. At the final whistle Argyle fans stormed onto the pitch and fought a pitched battle with police. It was by far and away the worst outbreak of violence that had ever been seen at London Road.

The final home game of the season was with Tranmere Rovers, and the visitors finished as the victors. The curtain finally closing after every other team had finished playing, with a 2-1 defeat at Dean Court against Bournemouth. Posh finished the season in 7th place five points away from a promotion spot.

Sadly with the end of the season came the inevitable break up of the side, several of the older players who had figured in Cantwell's Championship team were to retire or to be sold to other clubs during the coming months.

1975/76 SEASON

Within a week of the season's end Posh were off to Tunisia to play in a four team Tournament which they duly won, beating Oxford in the final. Cantwell moved into the transfer market capturing the signatures of Lyndon Hughes on a free transfer from West Bromwich Albion and Peter Eustace from Sheffield Wednesday. Moving away from London Road was Paul Walker who had signed for former Posh Manager Jim Iley at Barnsley, and striker Jim Hall. Hall had played 298 League games for Posh, plus four as a substitute, and scored 122 goals. Only three players in the Club's League history had made more appearances and his record number of goals for Posh still stands to date. He joined neighbours Northampton for £4,500.

As Posh started their pre-season warm up games in the Shipp Cup, the only other signing Cantwell had made was that of Andy Rogers from Chatteris who signed professional forms with the Club. Posh completed these matches with a 3-3 draw at the Abbey Stadium, and finished third in their group of four teams, before losing 3-2 at home to First Division Norwich City.

The season proper began with a scoreless home draw with Walsall. Dave McCormick who had been on trial from Biggleswade made his debut for the Club as did Lyndon Hughes and Peter Eustace. The only highlight of an otherwise drab game was the appearance of a female streaker at half time! The League Cup started with a visit to Southend and the Shrimpers ran out 2-0 winners in the first leg, leaving Posh a sizable task to progress to the next round. Posh made it three games without a win when they visited Shrewsbury, coming away with a 3-1 defeat. However, it was a much improved performance in the second leg of the League Cup clash at London Road, where Posh won 3-0, with the goals coming from Chris Turner, Tommy Robson and John Cozens, after 22, 37 and 51 minutes respectively.

Posh were still struggling to find their form in the League, and a 0-0 draw at home to Port Vale was followed by another draw – at Chesterfield – Alan Merrick (on loan from West Bromwich) making his debut against the Spireites. He retained his place in the side when Posh beat Blackpool at home 2-0, with David Gregory scoring after 70 minutes and Robson ten minutes later. Three days later Posh entertained Aldershot in the League. Billy Telford came on at half time to replace Merrick and with his second touch of the ball shot Posh into the lead. But it was the only highlight of an otherwise dull game as Aldershot equalised half way through the second half to earn themselves a point. After drawing 1-1 at Chester, Posh made it five draws from their opening six League games. They got their first League win of the season with a 2-0 victory over Wrexham. Robson put Posh ahead after 27 minutes but it was Gregory's goal four minutes into the second half which provided the main talking point, and it will arguably go

down as one of the most spectacular goals scored by a Posh player. Gregory went on a run covering half the length of the pitch beating four players before rifling the ball into the net.

Posh were rocked by a 3-1 home defeat at the hands of Rotherham, Telford scoring the only goal for Posh. They then visited Hillsborough to take on Sheffield Wednesday and returned with a 2-2 draw thanks to goals from Gregory and Jones. Posh then claimed another Cup giantkilling when they travelled to Second Division Fulham and beat them 1-0, with another goal from Gregory. It was a memorable match against a strong Fulham line up containing former England players including Alan Mullery and Bobby Moore. Back in the League Posh could not get out of the drawing habit (their seventh draw in ten League games), after a 1-1 scoreline at Mansfield, thanks to a Turner goal.

The next game at home to Bury was the third anniversary of Cantwell's arrival at London Road, and in front of 7,271 the team celebrated with a 4-0 victory, Robson claiming a hat trick along with a single goal from Turner. In a topsy-turvy week Posh then visited Preston and lost 2-1, before going on to Hereford where they won 4-2, to put them ninth in the table. Cantwell had continued with his experiment of playing Turner at centre forward (since his return from injury), and he scored two goals, along with singles from Gregory and Nixon. It was also a game that saw Hereford's Terry Payne making a record breaking 765th League appearance.

Cantwell brought Jim Walker on loan from Brighton, who were the next visitors to London Road, and he came on as a second half substitute. Posh were 1-0 winners, thanks to a Gregory goal after 34 minutes. The season started to gather momentum as Posh moved into 5th place courtesy of a 4-2 home win over Grimsby three days later. Gregory grabbed a hat trick with Nixon scoring the other goal in front of 7,646 fans. The team then travelled to Crystal Palace where a crowd of 19,000 witnessed a 1-1 draw, Robson scoring Posh's equaliser after Chatterton had earlier given Palace the lead.

The fourth round of the League Cup gave Posh a daunting trip to Ayresome Park where goals from Boam, Hickton and Armstrong gave Middlesboro' a comfortable 3-0 win to end Posh's interest in the League Cup. A convincing 3-1 victory over Swindon, with two goals from Robson and a penalty from Eustace, kept Posh in the promotion picture at 5th place in the table. The following week they entertained non-League Winsford in the first round of the F.A. Cup, but after a goalless first half, the prospects of an upset were all but extinguished as goals from Nixon (61 minutes) and Cozens (67 minutes) put Posh in control. The Cheshire side pulled a goal back but further goals from Gregory and Turner saw Posh safely through to the second round.

A 3–2 home victory over Southend was followed by a victory at Halifax, which put Posh third in the table. The second round of the F.A. Cup brought more non–League opposition, this time in the shape of Coventry Sporting. The game was played at Coventry City's Highfield Road in front of 8,556. Once again Cantwell's side left no room for giantkilling with goals from Hughes, Nixon, Jones plus an own goal, earning Posh a visit to Second Division Nottingham Forest in the third round. Posh extended their unbeaten League run to nine games with two draws, at Gillingham and at home to Millwall. These results left Posh second in the 3rd Division, when they

travelled to Cardiff, who were two places below them. A crowd of 16,094 watched Posh take an early lead before they were taken apart by a talented Cardiff side who went on to beat them 5–2.

A large support followed Posh to the City ground to take on Brian Clough's Nottingham Forest on New Year's Day. On a heavy pitch Posh held the Second Division club to a 0–0 draw to bring them back to Peterborough for a replay. 17,866 packed into London Road on a cold January evening to watch Posh add another prize name to their list of giantkillings.

Jon Nixon fires in the only goal against Forest at London Road.

In a frantic and untidy game one goal always looked enough to settle it, and this came after 23 minutes when Jim Walker burst down the left wing and sent across the ball hard and low to Nixon who met his cross at the near post and buried the ball firmly past the stranded Forest goalkeeper Wells. Posh hung on in determined fashion, and Forest created few chances until the final 15 minutes when goalkeeper Steele made several good saves from Butlin, Chapman and Bowyer. The result itself was enough to send the Posh crowd into wild celebrations, but the news of their reward was even better. Posh now faced a trip to play Manchester United at Old Trafford on January 24th.

Before the Cup highlight, Posh came down to earth with a bang, losing 2–0 at Port Vale. Cantwell made changes for the next game, at home to Colchester, when 19 year old Andy Rogers made his debut in a 3–1 win, the goals coming from Gregory, Turner and Hughes. The Manager then moved at last to sign the big forward he had been looking for since he first came to London Road, with Ernie Moss arriving from Chesterfield. He made his debut in the 3–0 home win over Chester where Cozens scored his first goal (after 3 minutes, since returning from injury, an own goal was added after 62 minutes with a final effort from Robson 3 minutes later.

The following week an army of 10,000 travelling Posh supporters followed their team to Old Trafford. It was a nostalgic return for Cantwell who had skippered Manchester United when they won the F.A. Cup at Wembley in 1963.

A crowd of 56,352 watched as the Reds roared into a 2 goal lead, after just 10 minutes – with goals from Forsyth and McIlroy – before a Cozens goal 10 minutes before half time rekindled the Posh challenge and brought the massive travelling support roaring back into life. For 15 glorious second half minutes Posh put the First Division giants under tremendous pressure without being able to break down the defence, and in the end it took a magnificent strike from Hill after 68 minutes to finally kill off the Peterborough challenge as the Red Devils won 3–1. Posh's performance brought glowing praise from many neutrals after the game, and in the end they contented themselves with a bumper pay day from the massive attendance which tempered their exit from the Cup. Ernie Moss scored twice in the 2–0 home victory over Preston that kept Posh riding high in fourth position in the League, before they travelled to Grimsby where they gained a 1–1 draw.

In the next match Posh took on second placed Crystal Palace who were three points above them in the League but with Posh having two games in hand. 13,308 came to London Road to cheer Posh on to a vital 2–0 victory that saw them close the gap at the top of the table. Robson put Posh ahead after 27 minutes and just three minutes into the second half, after Cannon had upended Gregory, Eustace hammered in the penalty to secure the points. Another vital two points were secured with a 3–0 away win at Swindon with goals from Moss, Eustace and Gregory.

As Posh entered a crucial phase of the season they went on an eight game run that left them without a win and saw them slide out of the promotion race. It started with a beating at Wrexham and was followed four days later by another 3–0 defeat, this time at home to top of the table Hereford, in front of 14,100. A trip to second placed Brighton resulted in a 5–0 defeat, and Posh slipped to eighth. They steadied slightly with a 2–2 draw at home to Sheffield Wednesday before a 8,209 crowd.

But the following home match, with Mansfield, resulted in another 3–0 loss in front of the *'Match of the Day'* cameras. Three consecutive away matches produced just one point as Posh lost to fellow promotion contenders Bury and Aldershot and drew at Southend. By the time Posh got back to winning ways, by defeating bottom of the table Halifax at London Road, crowds had dipped below 5,000. By this time they were 9th in the League and six points off a promotion spot, with just eight games remaining. The next three games were all drawn, and the final death knell on Posh's promotion chances came with a 1–0 home defeat by Chesterfield. Posh's only win in their final eight fixtures was in the last game, at home to Shrewsbury, where Mark Heeley made his debut for Posh when he came on as a substitute with 20 minutes to play.

The following Monday night 4,241 Posh fans came to pay tribute to Tommy Robson in his Benefit Match against First Division Leicester City, as the curtain came down on another season at London Road.

1976/77 SEASON

With the 1975/76 season barely finished Noel Cantwell immediately moved into the transfer market to strengthen his squad for the following campaign. First to arrive was 31 year old defender Peter Hindley on a free transfer from Nottingham Forest, and one week later Tommy Parkin came on loan from Ipswich, followed by Keith Waugh a 19 year old goalkeeper from Sunderland; all three captures being effected before the end of May. Those leaving the Club included centre half Mick Jones (who went on to play in North America), with Peter Eustace, Keith Bradley and Billy Telford departing on free transfers. Cantwell's biggest signing of the close season was Bob Doyle from Barnsley for £20,000.

Posh started their pre season warm-up, in the Shipp Cup, which was initially played on a group basis. The first opponents were Sheffield Wednesday at Hillsborough where Posh lost 3–2. In the second game Posh entertained Cambridge United and won 1–0, with a headed goal from Ernie Moss. The final game in the group saw Posh beat Lincoln 2–1 at London Road with goals from Parkin and Turner. It left Posh second in the group and just behind the unbeaten Sheffield Wednesday. Other pre-season matches consisted of Posh's normal diet of local non-League opposition.

The season proper was opened in the League Cup, with a visit to Elm Park to face Reading, where Cantwell gave debuts to Hindley, Doyle and Parkin. After falling two goals behind early on Posh hit back through Lee, and Cozens – who equalised with seven minutes left – then the same player grabbed Posh's winner in the final minute of the game. Reading gained some revenge however as the following Wednesday night they won 1–0 at London

Road with a goal from Robin Friday, in front of 6,286. The following Saturday Posh entertained Rotherham in the League and lost at home 2–0, before they played Reading at London Road in the League Cup 1st round replay. Robson put Posh ahead eight minutes before half time only to see the Royals equalise with nine minutes of the match remaining. The tie went to extra time where two goals from Moss ensured a glamour game against Fulham in the next round.

Posh travelled to Grimsby, drawing 2–2 with goals from Gregory and Robson, before travelling to Craven Cottage. The Fulham line up included Bobby Moore and Rodney Marsh, as well as Alan Slough who would later play for the Posh. An attendance of 10,222 watched Posh obtain a notable draw after Doyle had cancelled out an early Fulham lead. Posh played York at London Road in their next match and ran out comfortable 3–0 winners. For the League Cup replay, it was announced that George Best was to play at London Road, and his presence attracted a crowd of 16,476, with those who had come just to see the Irish genius play not leaving disappointed. Five minutes before half time Best received the ball outside the box, stepped on it, flicked it in the air and volleyed it into the net to give the Londoners a lead. Slough made it 2–0 after 77 minutes and in a late fight back Robson made the score 2–1, but good saves by Mellor and the crossbar denied Posh another crack at the London outfit.

After losing 2–0 at Tranmere, Posh faced Reading for the fourth time already that season, and won 2–1 with goals from Robson and Doyle. The next game was one of Posh's biggest of the season for they entertained Crystal Palace in front of 8,489, and the TV cameras.

Unfortunately it resulted in a drab scoreless draw, and despite many chances at both ends, neither side looked like breaking the deadlock. Posh's poor away form continued with a 4–1 loss at Bury and a 2–1 defeat at Chester, which came either side of the home success against Swindon, when Turner scored the only goal. The next game was at home to Chesterfield, who were struggling near the foot of the table, and they ran out shock 3–0 winners.

This defeat prompted Cantwell to announce that every player in the side was up for sale and that he was on the look out for new players. He did this immediately by signing David Bradford on loan from Sheffield United, and he made his debut at home to Mansfield in a 2–1 win. Bradford retained his place in the side for the next game at Preston, but Posh were annihilated 6–2. Cantwell brought in goalkeeper Keith Rockford for his debut away to Brighton, who were top of the League, but all to no avail for Posh lost 1–0 in front of 10,267. The team's next game, their 750th League match, was at home to Oxford United and they went into it lying 10th from bottom of the Third Division. But their worries were eased with a 2–0 victory; Derek Jefferies who had signed on loan from Crystal Palace made his debut.

Two away games followed, the first a 0–0 draw with bottom club Portsmouth, followed by four goals shared at the County ground in the first local derby of the season, against Northampton, in front of 7,483. As Posh entered November they were again struggling, and this continued when they lost at home to Gillingham, followed by a 2–0 defeat at Wrexham. They got some welcome relief from the League, with a visit to Tranmere in the F.A. Cup first round, where they turned their recent league form on its head, running out 4–0 winners, with goals coming from Cozens, Moss, Robson and Carmichael. This was Carmichael's first goal for the Club, after playing 247 League and cup matches, and not surprisingly there were great celebrations after he had scored. Back in the League Posh lost at home by 2–1 to Sheffield Wednesday in front of 8,683, and incredibly Carmichael scored his second goal in two matches! This defeat was followed by a 1–1 draw at Walsall.

The reward for beating Tranmere in the first round of the F.A. Cup was an away tie at non-League Northwich Victoria. Posh travelled to Northwich on Saturday December 11th, and were leading the game 1–0 with a Nixon goal when the match was completely enveloped in fog. The match couldn't continue and was abandoned after 24 minutes.

Posh had to travel back to Cheshire on the Tuesday night, and they probably wished they hadn't, as they lost 4–0 to the Northern Premier League side. From Posh's showing just three days earlier, this was a quite unbelievable result. It was only the second time that a non-League side had beaten Peterborough United in the F.A.Cup since they had joined the League. Around this time Ernie Moss left London Road for Mansfield for a fee of £20,000.

Posh ended the year with defeat at Reading, with Ian Ross who had come on loan from Aston Villa making his debut.

Cantwell and Posh entered the New Year looking for a change of fortunes. The Manager started by adding new faces to his squad and Posh's season started to take off. The first player to come in was Mark Heeley, and at the age of 16 he became Posh's youngest player to appear in a League match. Heeley scored on his debut as Posh beat Portsmouth 4–2, with Cozens grabbing a hat trick. It was just the pick-me-up that Posh fans needed and Heeley contributed with an outstanding performance. Posh's next match was a friendly at London Road against Mansfield, in front of 1,854 fans. Moss made a quick return to London Road – playing for the Stags – but it was Robbie Cooke who scored the only goal of the game to give Mansfield the win. The next League match ended scoreless at home to Preston, and was followed up by another affair devoid of goals, at Rotherham. Ian Nimmo, a striker that Cantwell had signed on loan from Sheffield Wednesday, made his debut for Posh in the latter match. Then two important victories which lifted the team up the table followed, when Shrewsbury were beaten at London Road 2–1 – in front of 5,541. Grimsby were then entertained and overcome by 3–1; Nimmo scored his first goal for the Club and Dave Booth appeared in the Grimsby side.

A 2–1 defeat at York, where Carmichael scored his fourth goal of the season, was followed by another 0–0 draw, at home to Tranmere, which left Posh 9th from the bottom of the table. The next game, at Crystal Palace, was played in front of 16,623 fans, and it produced another valuable point for Posh, from a further scoreless draw. Posh then lost 1–0 at Bury, when Cantwell introduced another new player to the side, Billy Woof, who came on loan from Middlesborough. A 1–1 draw at Port Vale made it five games without a win for Posh but they ended the run with a 3–2 home victory over Chester. Two goals came from Turner, who Cantwell had pushed into the forward line in order to give a bit more punch to the attack. Two 1–1 draws followed – at Mansfield and Gillingham – with Cooke equalising for the Stags four minutes from time after Gregory had given Posh the lead, and even more dramatically Gillingham grabbing a last minute equaliser from a penalty after Posh had led through an early Nixon goal.

Posh's next match was at home to top of the table Brighton and 6,852 fans turned up to see Gregory score twice to give Posh a memorable victory, and left them five points clear of the relegation zone. Eric Steele returned to London Road as the goalkeeper for Brighton, and whose miserable day was compounded with the sending off of Tiler. Posh then visited Oxford, where they played the game in an all white strip borrowed from their hosts, and also helped themselves to both points. Posh made it seven games undefeated with a 4–0 trouncing of Swindon at the County ground, with goals coming from Carmichael, Mee, Healey and Doyle.

The recent good run of results and the visit of neighbours Northampton brought out a bumper crowd of 8,944 for Posh's next match, and an impressive display from Posh pushed their neighbours closer to relegation and lifted Posh to a comfortable mid-table place. A 0-0 draw at Chesterfield extended Posh's unbeaten run to nine games, but this was ended in the following encounter, at Shrewsbury, with a 2-1 defeat.

The dismal end to the season was almost as spectacular as their climb away from the relegation zone. They lost their next three matches, at home to Wrexham and Lincoln plus a 4-0 reverse at Sheffield Wednesday. All three opposition teams were promotion candidates, and Posh slid to 10th from bottom. The run of defeats was halted by a 1-1 draw at home to Port Vale, with goal-keeper Stuart Garnham coming in to make his debut.

Posh's last home game of the season ended in a 5-3 defeat at the hands of Walsall, in front of 3,933. Another big shock came for Posh fans just two days before the final game of the season, when Noel Cantwell announced that he was quitting the Club, his Number Two, John Barnwell, stepping up as the new Manager. Cantwell had become something of a folk hero in his stay at London Road, rescuing Posh from near the bottom of the Fourth Division, then taking them to the Championship and up into the Third Division.

Posh's season finally finished with a 1-1 draw at Sincil Banks against Lincoln, which left them 9th from the bottom of the League and six points clear of a re-election spot. It was a particularly sad end to Cantwell's career at London Road after all the good work he had produced since his arrival just three years earlier.

1977/78 SEASON

The initial transfer activity at London Road related to John Nixon, who was given a free transfer and eventually went to join Shrewsbury, and Stuart Hodson who drifted into local non-League football. The next to leave was David Gregory who joined Second Division Stoke City for £55,000, a record fee received for a Posh player. The first of new Manager Barnwell's arrivals at London Road was Gary Sargent front non-League Bedford. His next two signings were also from the bargain basement, 19 year old Nicky Evans a forward from Queens Park Rangers, and Steve Camp from Fulham. Barnwell then moved to sign former Nottingham Forest, Wolves, Chelsea and Oxford keeper Jim Baron on a free transfer before splashing out £20,000 to capture Alan Slough from Fulham.

Posh started their pre-season warm up in the Shipp Cup again, and, in a departure from tradition started at home to Sheffield Wednesday in a strip of light blue and white stripes, light blue shorts and navy socks. It was the first time since 1937 that Posh had deserted their royal blue and white which had been adopted in their fourth season. They lost 2-0 to the Owls at London Road and were then annihilated 5-1 by Huddersfield in their second match. Posh only had their pride to play for in the third and final match of the series, when they beat local rivals Cambridge United at London Road by 2-1, with goals from Sargent and Doyle. Posh drew 0-0 at home with Second Division Sunderland in their final major pre-season match.

The season proper got underway at home to Bradford City in the League Cup first round. Barnwell gave Posh debuts to Slough, Camp and Sargent and the new look side hammered the recently promoted Bradford 4-1, with two goals apiece from Sargent and Camp. Four days later, in the second leg, Posh went through the formality with a 1-1 draw, to qualify for the second round. They attracted a crowd of 6,099 to London Road for the first

League match of the season against Portsmouth, and it ended scoreless. The only headlines made in the local press that day were those regarding the level of violence on the terraces at the match.

On the eve of Posh's away match at Swindon it was announced that teenage wonder boy Mark Heeley had been suspended by Manager Barnwell over an incident when the player had been dropped from the team for the Portsmouth game. Barnwell announced that it was very unlikely that Heeley would play for the Club again. On the pitch Posh suffered two consecutive 2-0 defeats, at Swindon and Chesterfield; Steve Ogrozovic was the Spireites keeper. Posh's next match was at home to Fourth Division Scunthorpe in the second round of the League Cup, a match that everybody hoped would see a change in Posh's form, but in the end, due to poor finishing they were lucky to escape with a 1-1 draw. The following day Barnwell moved into the transfer market to secure the signing of Barry Butlin from Nottingham Forest for £20,000, and then stated that his search for new players was now over. Just a couple of days later Arsenal Boss Terry Neil signed the troubled Heeley on a month's loan from Posh.

Butlin came into the side for Posh at home against Wrexham, but it was two of the older faces at London Road – Robson and Turner – who scored the goals to earn a 2-2 draw, leaving Posh without a League win after the first four matches. In the League Cup Posh triumphed at Scunthorpe 1-0 with a 25 yard thunderbolt from Slough. The following Saturday Posh travelled to Sincil Bank and earned their first League victory of the season thanks to a fortuitous goal from Butlin. An enormous clearance from keeper Keith Waugh, with the wind behind him, allowed the ball to bounce once and find Butlin in position to nod the ball over the stranded keeper just four minutes from the final whistle. Posh consolidated this victory with a 2-1 win at home against

Carlisle, Butlin scoring both, as they started to claw themselves back up the table. They could have made it four consecutive wins in the next game against Exeter, but after Robson had equalised an early Exeter goal, Lee missed a penalty in the 76th minute and Posh had to be satisfied with a 1-1 draw.

Posh's season was now starting to take shape for they overcame Sheffield Wednesday at Hillsborough with a goal from Cozens, and Jim Baron made his debut in goal. The seven match unbeaten run came to an end against Bradford City, when they lost 2-1 at Valley Parade, and even that possessed a large amount of bad luck on Posh's part, as a clearance from Ross was deflected into the path of a Bradford forward who calmly slipped the ball to team mate Joe Cooke and settled the issue.

On the Monday after a point was earned at home to Walsall, the staggering news was announced that Mark Heeley, who had been on trial at Arsenal, was to sign for the Gunners in a £100,000 deal. It was an incredible end to a six week saga that had started with a 17 year old refusing to play for Posh at an hour's notice.

A midweek home match saw Posh beat Oxford with a goal from Robson, before the team travelled to Bury where they gained a draw. Their improved form boosted the crowd to 5,563 with Shrewsbury's visit. Posh got away with another Lee penalty miss, and with Robson scoring twice, a 2-1 victory was obtained. A midweek match in the Maunsell Cup final against Northampton gave Barnwell the chance to try out a few youngsters. Cliss, Evans and Quow were brought in, and Slough scored two in a 3-1 win. After a scoreless draw at Vale Park, Posh travelled to Second Division Bolton Wanderers for the third round of the League Cup. In front of 14,990 Posh were outclassed and beaten 3-1 by a slick Bolton side that contained Sam Allardyce, Willie Morgan and Peter Reid.

Posh visited Colchester in their next League match, looking to bounce back from defeat in the knowledge that if they won they would go top of the Third Division, but they crashed by 3-0, hence giving 18 year old Tony Cliss an unhappy League debut. He had a much better time in his second game, at London Road against Cambridge, where Posh came back in the best possible style, beating their local rivals 2-0 in front of 7,307, the biggest home gate of the season. Cliss opened the scoring after 55 minutes with a well struck shot from the edge of the box, and this was added to by Sargent with just eight minutes remaining. On a lighter 'note', most Posh fans were relieved that an old superstition had been well and truly buried - that Posh had never won when a pre-match marching band had been present at the ground! It was an old story that dated back to the 60's and was regarded by many Posh fans as indisputable fact. The victory left Posh eighth in the table, three points behind leaders Wrexham, and as Posh entered November they embarked on a winning streak that would take them into the New Year.

In their next match they won 1-0 at Rotherham. Meanwhile Barnwell again moved into the transfer market bringing in Billy McEwan from Mansfield and Steve Earle on loan from Leicester City. They both made their debuts in the match at home to Plymouth, Posh winning with a goal from Robson after 24 minutes. It moved Posh to third in the Third Division before they started another F.A.Cup campaign. In this competition they were drawn away to non-League Barnet, and the tie was given greater media attention than normal with the inclusion of ex-England star Jimmy Greaves and ex-Posh man John Fairbrother in the Barnet line up. 4,000 fans packed in to Underhill and Barnet grabbed the lead after just 10 minutes, but goals from Slough - five minutes before half time - and Robson half way through the second half gave Posh victory, and a trip to Gillingham in the second round. Victory at Tranmere made it three consecutive wins in League and Cup, thanks to goals from Doyle and Turner.

It was announced that John Barnwell had won the *'Manager of the Month'* for the Third Division, after Posh had won all four of their fixtures during the month. The same week saw the departure of a former Posh hero John Cozens, who moved to neighbours Cambridge United for £2,000. Stuart Garnham, Andy Rogers and Lyndon Hughes were also released on free transfers from the Club.

● JOHN BARNWELL with the Manager of the Month award he collected from Bells Whisky in the first half of the season.

A 0-0 draw at home to Chester in front of 5,844 kept Posh in the hunt among the promotion pack in the Third

Division, and it also meant that Posh had now gone 476 minutes without conceding a League goal. In the F.A. Cup second round Posh travelled to Kent to take on Gillingham. In a highly entertaining cup-tie, a crowd of 10,181 finally saw the Gills take the lead 10 minutes from time and seemingly put Posh out, but Slough grabbed the equaliser with seven minutes remaining, and so to took the tie back to London Road the following week. The replay brought victory by 2-0 with goals from Carmichael and Sargent in front of 8,540. Posh's reward for this victory was a home draw against Northeast giants Newcastle United in January.

A Boxing Day visit to Hereford finished goalless, before Posh entertained Gillingham (again) in front of the season's best crowd of 10,156. Gillingham went ahead after 49 minutes and thus brought to an end a run, which had lasted 605 minutes, without conceding a League goal. Posh salvaged a point thanks to that man Robson again, who popped up with an equaliser with one minute left to play. Trevor Anderson, the Northern Ireland International, who had signed from Swindon for £20,000, retained his place in the side after making his debut at Hereford.

1977 ended with a home match against Preston before 7,134 fans. Posh left it late but salvaged both points with a Slough penalty in the final minute of the game.

Their first match of 1978 was at the Abbey in a local derby with Cambridge, who were lying fourth in the table, one point behind third placed Posh. Cambridge's record League crowd of 10,998 saw a goal from Alan Biley 17 minutes from time secure the points for Cambridge; former Posh player John Cozens was included in their line up.

Four days later Posh travelled to St. James's Park, and in gale force winds were well and truly blown out of the Cup. Posh's fate was sealed by a penalty four minutes after half time, and a 25 yard drive with four minutes remaining, in front of a crowd of 25,770. Posh again gave a brave performance but never got to grips with their illustrious opponents or the awful weather conditions.

Back to the League, the team travelled to Portsmouth, who were second from bottom of Division Three, and came back with a 2-2 draw. Anderson, with his first goal for the Club, and Turner were the marksmen. Posh were now 7th in the Third Division six points behind leaders Tranmere, and with four games in hand. Their promotion push suffered a set back in their next two games as they lost – what later proved to be – their only home game of the season, to Lincoln City, in atrocious conditions in front of 5,316. The match was played for long periods of time in heavy rain on a quagmire of a pitch, with the goal being scored after 19 minutes. A week later Posh travelled to Exeter and were defeated, the sole Exeter goal coming after Baron was penalised for taking too many steps, and the Grecians scoring from the resulting free kick. Barnwell was furious with his team and threatened to wield the axe for the next game at home to Sheffield Wednesday.

Omitted from this game were keeper Baron, plus Lee and Carmichael, and into the side came Waugh, Hindley and Sargent. It produced the right result as Posh won 2-1, the winner coming just six minutes from time. The overall dismal run in February culminated with Posh's third defeat in four games, at Walsall. Following the game full back Lee – who had made 170 League appearances for Posh – and young winger Rogers, both signed for Kettering, who were managed by former Posh centre half Mick Jones.

17,621 were present when Posh entertained Newcastle in the F.A. Cup third round. They did their best to ensure another upset after the Geordies had taken the lead in the 21st minutes, for Sargent equalised seven minutes later and then proceeded to give Newcastle a footballing lesson for the remainder of the game. Indeed at one stage Posh fans thought that a replay would be unnecessary as Carmichael headed home a Sargent cross, but the goal was disallowed for a foul by Robson. It was a relieved Newcastle side at the end of 90 minutes who at least had the chance to take on Posh back on their own ground.

Barnwell demanded better from the rest of his squad than their recent form and got it as Posh embarked on an 11 match unbeaten run. It started with a 2-1 victory over Bury at London Road. Two goalless draws followed at Carlisle and Shrewsbury before Posh came back to Peterborough and entertained Colchester. Camp, who had recently been returned to the side, stole the points for Posh with a goal seven minutes from time, his first Football League goal. Posh were further boosted by the news that skipper Chris Turner had announced that he would stay with the Club, after being linked with a big money transfer to Wolves. Posh drew 1-1 with Port Vale at London Road in their next game, the highlight being a superb 30 yard strike from Hughes after 22 minutes.

Meanwhile Posh's Youth side had progressed to the quarter-finals of the F.A.Youth Cup, with a side that contained the likes of Micky Gynn, Steve Collins, Trevor Quow, John Winters, Phil Chard, Tony Cliss and Dominic Genovese.

A goalless draw at Gillingham was followed by a home match with Hereford in front of 5,036 fans, where a strike in the 35th minute from the visitors Kevin Sheedy was cancelled out by two goals from Butlin. This result moved Posh to 6th in the table, now 11 points behind leaders Wrexham, but just two points off a promotion spot. Posh featured on 'Match of the Day' when they visited fellow promotion hopefuls Preston. A goal from Robson silenced the 9,695 Deepdale crowd and put Posh right back in the promotion picture. The next game was at home to struggling Bradford City, and the 6,314 who turned up to witness the game were treated to a rare goal spree from the Posh team. Goals from McEwan, Turner, Anderson and a brace from Robson secured Posh a 5-0 victory, their biggest win for five years. It was followed by two more home games. 7,098 turned up to watch Posh complete the double over Rotherham, and 200 more were present when Chesterfield were beaten 2-0.

These two victories was just the boost that everybody at the Club had needed, and led to the front page of the 'Evening Telegraph' proclaiming: "Division Two Here We Come". Posh were now fourth in the Third Division with 50 points, a point behind Preston and Cambridge, with games in hand over both of them and six points behind top of the table Wrexham. Then, just when it seemed that the charge towards Division Two was a mere formality, they visited Home Park and were defeated 1-0 by Plymouth. Barnwell's side repaired the damage in the following game at home to Swindon and saw Posh close on their rivals at the top of the table.

With four games remaining Posh's destiny was in their own hands, if they won all of their remaining games they would be promoted. The first was at home to Tranmere, and a single goal from Robson after 35 minutes secured the points. The position now stood at: Wrexham - top with 59 points from 42 games, Preston - 55 points from 44 games, Cambridge - 54 points from 44 games, with Posh also on 54 points on 43 games.

Their next match was away to lowly Oxford, when a huge Posh contingent travelled to the Manor ground for a midweek fixture, and were stunned as the match started in the worst possible style for Posh. They fell behind to a Turner own goal after four minutes, and were 3-0 down after half an hour and seemingly out of the game. Robson pulled a goal back a minute before half time and in a sensational second half display should have claimed both points. But they had to be happy with a 3-3 draw, after Turner scored in the 59th minute, and a minute later Slough had levelled matters from the penalty spot. It was one of Posh's truly memorable League matches, and will remain fresh in the memory for the many fans who witnessed it.

The result still left Posh a point behind Cambridge, and on level points with Preston, with two games remaining. The penultimate game was at Chester City. Posh's season had been built on a rock solid defence and their ability to poach the occasional goal. All of this had gone by the board at Oxford and most Posh fans thought it was a freak result, but at Chester the whole scenario seemed to be unfolding again, although this time with a more damaging end result. Chester went into a 1-0 lead after 10 minutes, which was cancelled out by Slough from the penalty spot 20 minutes later. After 14 minutes of the second half Chester were 3-1 in front, but Slough reduced the arrears from the penalty spot again. With time fast running out Chester snatched a fourth six minutes from the end. But incredibly Slough completed his unique hat-trick with a third penalty with just a minute of the game to go. As at Oxford, Posh ran out of time but this time they got no reward at all from the game. A side that had only conceded 26 goals in 43 League matches up to that point, had now let in seven goals in their last two games. It was all now crystal clear that Posh had to win their final League match at Wrexham to earn promotion.

Wrexham had already been crowned Champions and a crowd of 20,000 turned up at the Racecourse ground to watch the final game of the season. In a memorable match Wrexham keeper Dai Davies had an outstanding match to keep Posh at bay and break the hearts of the thousand or so visiting supporters. Time and time again Davies denied a succession of efforts from Posh players and at the death when Robson thought he had scored Davies pulled off the best of his saves to keep the score at 0-0. It was not enough and Posh missed out on promotion by goal difference from Preston North End, from whom a large number of fans had made the trip to Wales to see the outcome of the important final game. Barnwell's side had come so close to clinching the elusive place in the Second Division for the first time in the Club's history, when the foundation of success had been a tight defence and the ability to poach vital goals. Eventually Posh were denied, as they seemingly threw caution to the wind by scoring more goals, but also conceding more, for a quarter of the season's tally in the last three games. It was a case of so near but yet so far.

Alan Slough (above) was an ever present – bar one game – in all League and Cup games.

At Chester he scored a hat trick of goals, incredibly the trio from penalties – and was still on the losing side!

PENALTY ONE...

PENALTY TWO...

PENALTY THREE...

Tommy Robson, with the *Player of the Year* award, presented to him at the last home match of the season.

CHAPTER 7

BASEMENT FOOTBALL AGAIN

1978/79 SEASON

Barnwell followed in the footsteps of his predecessor Noel Cantwell by moving into the transfer market after the season had barely been over for more than a few days. His first capture was former Everton and Birmingham full back Archie Styles on a free transfer. By the end of the month Dennis Byatt had arrived from Fulham on a free transfer and speculation was rife that Posh skipper Chris Turner would be leaving London Road in a big money transfer. It transpired that Luton were the interested Club, and they signed Turner for £115,000, a record fee received by Peterborough. His replacement was West Ham centre half Bill Green who himself became Posh's record transfer buy, for £60,000. It was just the sort of transfer activity that had the Posh fans hopeful of another successful season, after missing out so narrowly the previous year on promotion to Division 2. Although skipper Turner had left, Bill Green was seen as an ideal replacement having played all his football in the First Division.

Posh started their pre season friendlies with a home match against Second Division Charlton and lost 3-1. The only other friendly of note was a 1-0 victory over First Division Coventry City at London Road, Robson scoring Posh's goal. Just days before the season opened Barnwell made his last move in the transfer market signing Lammie Robertson from Leicester City.

Posh's first competitive match of the season was away to Hull City in the League Cup, and they returned as 1-0 winners from a Slough penalty. Making their debuts on the day were Green and Styles, whilst Robertson was named as sub but did not make an appearance. In the second leg three days later Posh lost at home 2-1 and for the second year running faced a first round replay. But first Posh had to take on Sheffield Wednesday at London Road, and the match attracted a crowd of 7,468. Green and Styles both made their League debuts for Posh, and 17 year old Trevor Quow came on as substitute to make his first appearance 10 minutes from the end of the game. Posh won 2-0 with a professional and entertaining display, with Slough and Robson grabbing the Posh goals. The League Cup replay was played at Boothferry Park, and Posh again won 1-0, Butlin scoring just two minutes from time.

In the League, Posh travelled to Watford and in front of 12,291 won 2-1. Posh again turned in an excellent performance and Slough cracked in two goals to give Posh the points. They travelled to Ayresome Park four nights later to take on Middlesbrough in the League Cup second round. They drew 0-0 in a lacklustre match where neither side looked likely to grab the initiative. Posh's third League match of the season was at home to Tranmere and a goal from Butlin eight minutes after half time saw Posh sitting third in the table after three games with maximum points.

The following Tuesday night Posh entertained Middlesbrough at London Road in the League Cup second leg, and added another chapter to their glorious giantkilling history. The Middlesbrough side containing Craggs, Boam, Mills and Armstrong was beaten 1-0 after extra time in front of 8,093. The only goal of the game came 11 minutes into extra time from a free kick. Slough floated the ball to the far post where Posh veteran Robson flashed in to guide a header past the stranded Middlesborough keeper. It extended Posh's unbeaten run to six games and in the eight games they had played so far during the season they had conceded just three goals. Centre half Keith Oakes was sold to Fourth Division Newport County for £15,000 the following day.

Posh travelled to Chester next in the Third Division and drew 1-1, Slough putting Posh ahead with 12 minutes to go from the penalty spot, although Chester grabbed an equaliser four minutes later. Two home League games followed, a scoreless draw with Carlisle followed by a 3-1 victory over Brentford. Posh were now fourth in the Third Division table, two points behind leaders Swansea, with a game in hand. Slough was now on the long term injury list and the team's fortunes in the League changed dramatically. Their next game was at Chesterfield and they lost 3-1, Andy Kowalski scoring two of the Spireites goals. This was followed by a 4-1 hammering at Walsall. A home game followed, against Exeter, which ended as a 1-1 draw, before Posh entertained Swindon in the third round of the League Cup. Swindon took the lead 3 minutes after half time, however Styles scored his first goal for Posh eight minutes later to square the tie. This player also had a chance to put the tie beyond the reach of the West Countrymen, but blasted over the gaping goal in the last minute of the game.

Posh played at Boothferry Park for the third time that season, gaining a point from a draw, with Styles again scoring the Posh goal. The following Tuesday Posh travelled to Swindon for the League Cup third round replay, and they looked a much improved side as they swept past Swindon with a convincing 2-0 victory. Styles scored his third goal in three games, Doyle added a second 14 minutes from time, and the reward was a visit to Brighton in the fourth round. Back in the League Posh's form was still dire, and after drawing at home to Oxford, they travelled again to Swindon just one week after their Cup win and lost 3-1. They then entertained Gillingham and in front of 5,001 fans earned their third consecutive 1-1 draw at London Road.

By now Posh had slipped to 13th in the League, and as they prepared for a visit to Swansea, rumours regarding John Barnwell's future as Manager of the Club appeared in the local Press. Blackburn had been given permission to approach Barnwell regarding their vacant Manager's job, and at the same time he had been refused a cash injection from the Board of Directors to enable him to purchase new players. The following day Posh went down 4-1 at the Vetch as they were totally outclassed by a Swansea side containing Tommy Smith, Ian Callaghan, Robbie James, John Toshack and Alan Waddle. In a break from the League action Posh retained the Maunsell Cup against Northampton at the County Ground with a 4-1 victory. Butlin with two, Styles and Doyle were the scorers. The next game was at home to Bury with former Peterborough favourite Dave Gregory playing for the visiting team, Posh raced into a 2-0 lead after 26 minutes and looked set to end their recent long run without a League victory, only to see Bury reduce the arrears after 83 minutes and equalise with five minutes remaining. Dave Cunningham who had been signed on loan from Swindon made his debut.

A crowd of 21,421 packed into Brighton's Goldstone Ground to watch the fourth round League Cup tie, but it was not to be another famous Peterborough giantkilling however, as the South Coast side exerted pressure right from the kick off and throughout the game. But the Sussex team had to be content with a single goal which came from defender Mark Lawrenson after 36 minutes.

Two days later and Posh were without a Manager again after John Barnwell resigned. Talking to a local newspaper after his departure he was quoted as saying: *"I know what needs to be done at this Club, but the Board are not prepared to help me. It appears that I have more ambition and desire than they have."* Barnwell had repeatedly asked for more money to fund a push towards promotion to the Second Division, but this had continually been refused by the Board. Barnwell's right hand man Billy Hales was appointed as Caretaker Manager while the Club sought a successor to Barnwell. Hales' first match was on the same day as Barnwell's resignation, at Tranmere, where Posh lost 1-0. This loss was followed next Saturday by a 3-2 defeat to Plymouth, in Devon, with Cunningham scoring his first Posh goal.

Posh found no respite at London Road when they entertained Watford, and lost 1-0 in front of 8,048 fans. This result left Watford clear at the top of the Third Division

with Posh still well and truly in the relegation zone at seventh from bottom . They had to travel to Southend the following week in the first round of the F.A. Cup, where they went down 3-2, to record their fifth consecutive defeat. This was the first time that Posh had been knocked out in the first round since 1968. Hales went into the transfer market and signed former England Under-23 International Harry Holman for a reported £10,000. He made his debut at home to Shrewsbury, but Posh went down again 2-0, and the club had now not won for 11 matches. As the Christmas programme approached Posh's form didn't improve, with draws at Blackpool and Mansfield before being defeated at London Road by Lincoln on Boxing Day. In the final game of 1978 they lost at home to Southend by a single goal.

In the early New Year, Joe Cooke arrived from Bradford City in a part exchange deal that took Lammie Robertson to Valley Parade, with Posh having to find £20,000 to complete the deal. Cooke made his debut in the home match with Chester and impressed the home fans as he starred in a long awaited victory, the Posh goals coming from Robson and Butlin. They drew away 0-0 to Brentford in their next game, and then lost 3-0 in a vital match at home to Walsall who were struggling with Posh at the foot of the Division. Yet another defeat came at Exeter, by which time they were fourth from bottom of the table with 20 points from 27 games. This position prompted Caretaker-Manager Hales to offer his resignation which was accepted by the Board. He cited amongst his reasons that, as with John Barnwell, he could not get the money that he knew he required to buy new players. During his 13 matches in charge Posh had won just once. The local Press speculated that Geoff Hurst was the latest favourite to take over as the new Manager.

Posh travelled to Oxford for their next game, without a Manager, yet surprisingly won 2-0, with Cooke scoring his first goal for the Club. Despite the rumours, Peter Morris was announced as the new Manager the following week, and his first game in charge was at Gillingham who were lying third in the table. Posh lost 1-0 but turned in a much improved performance. This result dropped Posh back down into the relegation zone, at fourth from bottom with 22 points from 29 matches. The following week Morris swooped in the transfer market to bring in two new signings from Newcastle, Alan Guy and Tony Smith. Both players made their debuts, at home to Swansea, the following Saturday, and in front of 5,550 Posh won 2-0. Both goals were scored by Guy, and they were also his first in the Football League.

Morris signed Pat Sharkey who made his debut in a midweek visit to Carlisle, were Posh were hammered 4-1. They put in another much improved performance at London Road in their next game against Plymouth, winning 2-1. The scorers were Cooke and Smith (his first goal for the Club), but with the other sides near the bottom of the table also winning, Posh were still two points adrift from safety.

After a 3-0 hammering at Sheffield Wednesday Posh were again defeated, at home to Colchester, with Anderson missing a penalty. Another defeat, at Shrewsbury a week later, saw Posh now perched at third from bottom of the table, and three points away from safety, although with two games in hand.

In the local derby at Lincoln they surprisingly won 1-0, where the Imps had Mick Harford and Glen Cockerill in their side. The only goal of the game came a minute after half time from Sergeant, who had been restored to the side. Things started to look brighter as they followed this up with a draw at home with Rotherham, Cliss scoring Posh's goal.

But things again started to look serious for the side as they took on Mansfield at London Road, in a game they had to win to pull clear of the relegation zone. They lost 2-1 and the result saw the Stags leapfrog Posh in the table, and with just eight matches remaining Posh were once again third from bottom.

A goalless draw at Southend was followed by a great win at home over promotion candidates Swindon. Ross put Posh ahead from the penalty spot after just six minutes, but the Wiltshire men equalised early in the second half. However, with four minutes remaining Cooke popped up to head Posh's winner.

It now needed a concerted effort from Posh to avoid the dreaded drop to the Fourth Division, but those hopes were virtually extinguished in the following two games. They first lost at home to Blackpool 2-1, Micky Gynn scoring his first League goal for Posh, and Steve Collins making his debut for the Club. They then drew at Rotherham 1-1 with a goal from Guy six minutes before time. With just four matches remaining Posh were only two points from safety but had played two games more than Mansfield who were just above them.

The match at Colchester saw Posh leading after an hour of the game by 2-1, but they eventually went down 4-2, and by virtue of a scoreless draw in the next game, they found themselves relegated to the Fourth Division for the first time in their history, apart from the enforced demotion in 1968. Almost inevitably Posh won their last home game of the season in style with goals from Chard, Cliss and Gynn, as Morris blooded his teenagers in front of the Club's smallest ever League crowd of 1,875. In the final game Posh lost at Bury by 1-0 with a goal two minutes from time.

It had been a dismal end to a season that had started with so much promise under John Barnwell, and had seen Posh use three Managers during the campaign. In the final result they were back in the Fourth Division, and the support and morale at the Club were at their lowest ebb ever.

1979/80 SEASON

It was apparent from the start of the season that Peter Morris's style was totally different from that of Cantwell and Barnwell before him, for although he was working on a number of transfer deals, he was staying tight lipped over who he would be bringing in. Bill Green (to Chesterfield), plus Gary Sargeant and Dennis Byatt (to Northampton), left the Club, and speculation was rife that Bob Doyle could also be departing. Additionally Morris had already released several players on free transfers, including Ian Ross, Archie Styles, Peter Hindley and Harry Holman. By early July Trevor Anderson had also left the Club, at the age of 28 he announced that he was going to quit League football.

The following week the transfer activity started for real with Mick Lambert joining the Club from Ipswich for £40,000, and Billy McEwan leaving for Rotherham in a £30,000 deal; Colin Foster also joined Peterborough from Mansfield. By the end of July, Morris had bought in another four new faces – Ian Phillips from Mansfield, Andy Parkinson ex-Newcastle, Paul Overton a goalkeeper from Ipswich and Dave McVay the former Notts County player.

At the start of August, the Manager was putting the finishing touches to his squad, with the signing of Billy Kellock for £25,000 from local non-League neighbours Kettering, and Ricky Heppolette for £30,000 from Chesterfield. The final departure was terrace favourite Bob Doyle, who left the Club for a reported £110,000 fee, to Blackpool.

● Peter Hindley   ● Bob Doyle

Two players who together had made over 240 League appearances for the Posh since the 1976/77 season.

Posh started their preparation for the season quietly against a variety of local non–League opponents, but the week before the season started they entertained Luton at London Road and drew 1–1, Kellock scoring the Posh goal. The season proper started with a League Cup–tie at home to Second Division Charlton Athletic, and a crowd of 4,140 turned up to see Morris's new look side back in their traditional royal blue and white colours hammer the Second Division side 3–1. Kellock scored two goals on his debut for the Club, with Guy scoring the other. Other players making their debuts for Posh were Heppolette, McVay, Foster, Parkinson and Lambert. At the end of the game Posh were given a rousing ovation by the home fans who were now full of expectation after the trials and tribulations of the previous season.

In the second leg of the League Cup tie, three days later, Posh drew 1–1 at the Valley. Chard equalised an earlier Derek Hales goal to see Posh comfortably through to the second round.

The League season started with a visit to Lincoln and in front of a crowd of 4,725 Kellock was again the Posh hero, scoring after five minutes. This was to be the only goal of the game and gave the side a winning start. The first home game also brought the first defeat, for Posh went down 2–1 to Tranmere, with Lambert scoring the consolation goal and his first for the Club. Posh took the chance to make amends just three days later as they entertained Halifax, and goals from Kellock and Chard gave Posh a 2–1 victory in front of 4,014; it was Kellock's fourth goal in five games. Dave Syrett, who was signed from Walsall at the start of the season, made his debut but was taken off with a bad ankle injury. The second round of the League Cup saw Posh take on Blackpool in a two legged tie, first drawing 0–0 at London Road. They then travelled to Port Vale and secured a 1–0 League victory before taking on Blackpool at Bloomfield Road in the second leg of the Cup–tie. They were given little chance of winning against Blackpool, but despite Posh having severe injury problems they pulled off a shock 1–0 victory with a second half penalty from Kellock, Phillips coming in to make his debut for the Club. This victory gave Posh a home tie against First Division Bristol City in the third round.

Posh extended their unbeaten run to six games with two victories, the first at York by 2–0, with Robson scoring both goals, and the second at home to Crewe where Posh won 3–0 with goals from Quow, Kellock and Robson in front of 4,525. This result saw Posh go to third in the table, a point behind leaders Bradford City. They were brought firmly down to earth in their next game, at home to Aldershot. Kellock put Posh into the lead after 21 minutes but the Shots hit back with three second half goals to run out easy winners. A bigger blow came in the next game as Posh lost 1–0 to Northampton in the local derby. Morris blasted his players for lack of effort during the latter game and called for greater effort as Posh prepared to take on Bristol City in the League Cup.

The game against the First Division side attracted an attendance of 7,067 and saw Parkinson score his first goal for the Club in the dying seconds of the first half. Posh put on a dominating display and looked better than their First Division rivals for much of the game, but 15 minutes from time a goal from Gerry Gower squared the tie which ensured a replay at Ashton Gate the following week. Sandwiched between the two games was a 2–0 victory over Hereford at London Road, with Kellock and Chard scoring for Posh. Despite the size of their task at Ashton Gate in the replay, the hopes of the Posh supporters were optimistic that they could earn a victory against Bristol City. But these hopes were dashed within the first minute, for after 55 seconds Finnish International Jantunen, put the home team ahead. The tie was finally put out of Posh's range by two goals from ex-Everton favourite Joe Royal and one from Kevin Mabbutt, to give a final 4–0 scoreline.

In the next League match Syrett returned to the side but Posh were given a footballing lesson by visiting Huddersfield, who ran out 3–1 winners. It left Huddersfield second in the table and saw Posh slip to 11th. This was followed by a 3–0 defeat at Tranmere the following week. Posh did have some excuse with the ever growing injury list that forced Manager Morris to come in and make his one and only appearance for the Club at Rochdale, in a scoreless draw. Following this game Lambert was put on the transfer list and was left out of the side that took on Hartlepool at London Road the following Saturday. Posh won 2–0 and Parkinson turned in a good display, capping it with two fine goals. He added another in the next home match against Torquay, who along with Cliss cancelled out an earlier Les Lawrence goal. Parkinson made it four goals in three games when he scored the equaliser at Darlington in a 1–1 draw. In the last game of October Aldershot were met again, and for the second time in the season Posh were well beaten, this time by 2–0. Posh then completed their first double of the season by beating Lincoln at London Road 3–1 in front of a 4,681 crowd.

A dismal nine match run without a win then commenced. It started with four consecutive defeats – at Torquay and Doncaster before losing 3–1 at home to Walsall. In the week prior to the Walsall game Posh drew 1–1 with Northampton in the Maunsell Cup Final but actually lost the Cup on the toss of a coin at the end of 90 minutes. Bournemouth were then taken on in the first round of the F.A.Cup at London Road, when Posh lost by 2–1. The lead was taken after four minutes through Kellock, but within half an hour Bournemouth had won the match. In fact for much of the game Bournemouth were surprised at just how easy it was as they controlled the rest of the game at a leisurely pace. The following week Posh travelled to Bournemouth in the League and secured a 0–0 draw. Despite the dismal run Posh were still 10th in the table after 21 matches. They drew 0–0 at home to Portsmouth before visiting Newport four days before Christmas and gained another draw, at Somerton Park.

Just a few days before the game South African striker Andy Parkinson had walked out on the Club, after scoring six goals in 19 games. It was believed that he had returned home to South Africa and while the Club released him from his contract they still retained his registration. On Boxing Day Posh entertained Wigan and lost 2-1, and this was followed by a visit to Halifax for the last game of the decade where Posh drew 0-0.

As they started the New Year Posh were in 12th position, and their first game of 1980 was at home against Scunthorpe. They ran out comfortable 3-1 winners with Syrett scoring twice and Carmichael once in front of 3,014. Two away games followed which produced a point at Bradford City, and a 1-0 defeat at Stockport, where striker Keith Cassells, on loan from Second Division Watford, made his debut for Posh. At home the form continued to improve when Port Vale were beaten 3-0 with goals from Kellock, Cliss and Syrett.

After the game the Club were in the news for off the field events as the Supporters' Club, not for the first time in their history, were removed from the Posh Club at London Road.

Posh went one better in their next game slamming four goals past Crewe keeper Bruce Grobbelaar in a 4-1 victory, with Syrett, Cliss and Kellock (two) scoring the goals. The two victories moved Posh to 8th in the 4th Division. The next game was another derby game against Northampton, this time at London Road, and attracted a crowd of 4,960 who watched a scoreless draw.

Posh then entered a run of five consecutive victories which gave rise to a march up the table. It started with a 1-0 victory at Hereford – Syrett grabbing the only goal of the game after 29 minutes – and was followed by a 2-0 victory over Rochdale at London Road where Kellock and Phillips scored the goals. Posh by now had risen to sixth place in the table. Two consecutive 2-1 victories, at Hartlepool and at home to York, were followed by a 3-0 victory at London Road over struggling Darlington. Syrett's purple patch continued in the latter match with two more goals. The winning streak ended with a 0-0 draw at second placed Huddersfield, but then continued apace with 3-2 victories over Doncaster and Walsall.

In the Doncaster game an early goal from Cliss was cancelled out, and Doncaster took the lead after 37 minutes. But goals from Kellock and Syrett in the 65th and 67th minutes gave Posh the win. In the victory at Walsall it was two goals from Kellock and one from Gynn that gave Posh the points. Posh were still in 6th position but had now narrowed the gap between themselves and second place Huddersfield to just four points.

The eleven match unbeaten run came to an end with a 2-1 reverse at Wigan. Posh's next game was at home to Stockport on Bank Holiday Monday, and before the game Peter Morris was presented with the *'Bowles Manager of the Month'* for March, award, following the run in which Posh had won five and drawn one of their six matches. The Stockport game brought one of the more humorous controversies that had been seen at London Road in modern times. After just 12 minutes Lambert laid on a ball for Cliss who ran into the left hand side of the box in front of the London Road end and shot low into the side netting of the goal, and the ball somehow lodged in the back of the net. Despite heated protests from the Stockport players and the referee having long deliberations with his linesmen plus an inspection of the net, the "goal" was allowed to stand! County, however, grabbed an equaliser early in the second half and Posh had to be content with a 1-1 draw. The following night Posh were beaten 1-0 at home by Newport and four days later by the same score at Scunthorpe.

They had now taken just one point from their last four games. After the meteoric rise up the table they were now starting to lost ground at an alarming rate, and at a critical time in the season. With three games left Posh were seventh in the table, but seven points behind the promotion spot. They won 2-0 at home to Bournemouth but were then crushed 4-0 at Fratton Park by Portsmouth, before taking on and beating Bradford 1-0 at London Road in the final game of the season.

It left Posh in eighth position in the Fourth Division, eight points behind the promotion spot. But Peter Morris's first season in charge had been an encouraging one and his rebuilt side had won many fans, with the average attendance rising steadily throughout the season.

1980/81 SEASON

Morris quickly moved into the transfer market, and earlier, the season had barely been over a week before he signed Robbie Cooke from Northern Premier League side Grantham for a reported £12,000 fee. The only player not retained from the squad was reserve goalkeeper Paul Overton. At the same time, after 12 years as Chairman, Geoffrey Woodcock stepped down and was succeeded by fellow Board member Hugh Wright.

Cooke became the only pre-season signing for Morris as Posh entered August to start their friendlies with a 2-1 victory over 3rd Division Barnsley. Posh's second match was at the Abbey Stadium in the Cambridgeshire Professional Cup Final against Cambridge United, and Posh ran out 4-2 winners. Morris then made his only other signing before the season proper started when Jackie Gallagher was signed from Wisbech.

Posh's first 'proper' game of the season was at home to Fulham in the League Cup. Trevor Slack and Robbie Cooke made their first senior appearances for the Club, and in front of 3,662 Posh won 3-2, with a debut goal from Cooke, along with singles from Kellock and Syrett seeing Posh home; John Beck was in the beaten Fulham side. The second leg at Craven Cottage saw Posh 1-0 down after 90 minutes, and this was the final score, leaving the tie squared at 3-3. With the game into extra time, the match erupted when Quow was carried from the pitch after a tackle by Strong, with Kellock meting out his own justice to the perpetrator just moments later. The situation ended in a mass brawl with Fulham's Mahoney being sent off. Ten minutes later Cooke scored Posh's equaliser on the night to send them through to the second round. It was some comfort for Posh and gave them a happy end to an ill-tempered match. The following day Gordon Hodgson signed for Posh from Oxford and made his debut in the 1-1 draw at Lincoln. Cooke gave Posh the lead, but Mick Harford cancelled out the goal just three minutes later. Keith Waugh was Posh's saviour on the day saving a second half penalty from Cunningham.

Posh opened their League season at London Road against Halifax and drew 2-2, with Cooke scoring the first home goal and Kellock equalising from the penalty spot, with just two minutes left to play. The first League win of the season came in the next match at Doncaster, goals from Slack, Syrett, Kellock and McVay guided Posh to a 4-0 win and lifted them to sixth place in the table. The next match was a different proposition however, as they travelled to the City ground to play European Champions Nottingham Forest, where they were beaten 3-0 with goals from Robertson, Birtles and Gray, and faced an uphill task in the home leg if they were to make any further progress in the League Cup. They drew 2-2 at home to Bradford in the next League match before Nottingham Forest returned for the second leg.

The cup-tie produced a bumper crowd at London Road of 11,503. Mills put Forest into the lead after 28 minutes, but Cooke levelled matters for Posh five minutes later. From then on it looked as if it would be another Posh 'glory' night as they turned in a dazzling display against their illustrious opponents, but a succession of missed chances meant that Posh had to be happy with a draw on the night and a second round exit from the League Cup.

A 2-1 victory at Tranmere in a Friday night fixture, thanks to goals from Slack and Cooke, saw Posh go to third in the table after five games. This was consolidated with a draw at home to Rochdale, but the team eventually tasted defeat in the League for the first time when they lost at Southend. They got back on to winning tracks with a 1-0 victory at London Road over Bournemouth, with Cooke almost inevitably grabbing the winner – his ninth goal of the season. Posh lost at Torquay by 2-0 in a Saturday night fixture, but came back strongly with a run of three consecutive victories, the first being a 5-2 thumping of Southend at London Road in front of 4,228.

This was followed three days later with a 2-0 victory over Bury at London Road and lifted Posh to fourth in the table, before they travelled to Stockport where they ran out 4-3 winners; John Winters scored his first goal for the Club along with Kellock, Hodgson and Cooke. Posh then grabbed a 1-1 draw at Wigan – Gallagher scoring his first goal for the Club – before getting back into the winning habit by beating Darlington at London Road.

The first home defeat of the season came with the visit of Scunthorpe United. Posh lost 2-0 before 4,262, and lost their heads completely in an ill-tempered second half that saw three home players booked. They could count themselves lucky that they still had 11 men on the pitch at the end of the game! They made it three defeats in a row when they lost 2-1 at Mansfield, and by the same score at Plough Lane against Wimbledon; the Dons goals came in the 87th and 90th minutes of the game, the winner scored by Alan Cork. The poor run continued with a 1-1 draw at home to Port Vale. Goalkeeper Waugh was the villain when he dropped the ball into his own net eight minutes from time to give Vale a point. Posh lost at home by 2-1 to Stockport in front of just 2,776 fans, after drawing at Aldershot. The losing streak was finally arrested with an away victory over Halifax, in front of only 1,151 fans, with goals from Cooke, Gynn and Kellock seeing Posh home 3-2.

The next two games brought Posh two local derbies and two victories. The first was at home to Lincoln in front of Posh's best League crowd of the season of 5,817. The visiting Imps were top of the League, but were none the less beaten 1-0 with a goal from Kellock after 40 minutes, despite the fact that he had earlier missed his third penalty of the season. The next game was away to Northampton in the F.A.Cup, and Posh were given tremendous vocal support by the 1,500 travelling fans who cheered them on to a 4-1 win in front of 5,542. Phillips gave Northampton the lead after five minutes which Robson cancelled out after 39 minutes. Barely had the Posh fans finished celebrating before Quow scored Posh's second, and they went into the half-time break 2-1 up. In the second half Posh looked a different side and added further goals from Slack and Robson to run out easy winners and progressed on to the second round.

Posh disposed of Hereford 3-0 in the League, before they travelled to Barnet in the next round of the F.A. Cup. The tie finished 1-0 to Posh with Robson scoring his fifth goal in three games, but the score did not do justice to Posh's superiority in the match, in which they dominated for long periods but were just unable to make the break-through that would have eased their passage to the third round. After a 1-1 draw at Hartlepool Posh went fourth in the table by beating Northampton for the second time in the season, this time by 3-0 at London Road on Boxing Day, in front of 6,265 – the best League crowd of the season. The following day Posh lost at Crewe in the final game of the year.

The first game of the New Year was a third round F.A.Cup tie against Chesterfield at London Road, and it attracted a crowd of 8,631. In a scrappy game it looked as if the Spireites had done enough to win a passage through to the fourth round when they took a 1–0 lead 11 minutes from time, but Cooke popped up with his 18th goal of the season to earn a Posh a replay the following week. Against all the odds on a cold, wet, misty night two goals from Cooke helped Posh to a 2–1 win and a place in the fourth round of the Cup, which required a visit to Notts County. Posh had two League games to play before that, and in the first, at Scunthorpe, they gained a point. The second match was a 3–0 drubbing of York at London Road, with Hodgson, Slack and Kellock scoring the goals. It was the ideal preparation for the visit to Second Division Notts County in the Cup, where nearly 5,000 Posh fans made the trip and watched Posh claim a memorable victory. In an exciting tie Posh pressured their more illustrious hosts from the start, closing them down and not giving them time to play. The winner came after 57 minutes when Cooke played a 'one-two' with Kellock and rifled the ball into the net in front of the massed Posh fans. It was another historic Cup win for the Posh and set them up for a plum draw in the fifth round, at home to First Division Manchester City.

Back in the League, Posh drew at Bradford 1–1, before losing at home to fellow promotion candidates Doncaster. But they consolidated their sixth place in the table with an exciting win at Rochdale, when they came from 2–0 down to win 3–2, with two goals from Gynn and one from Quow; Gynn's winner came just two minutes from time.

Meanwhile the City was buzzing with anticipation for the visit of Manchester City in the F.A.Cup fifth round. It was guaranteed to be a full house and the week before the match, fences were erected around London Road to combat the ever increasing threat of hooliganism at games. The match itself attracted a crowd of 27,780, and the Posh fans very nearly had something to cheer as early as the first minute, with Gynn – in front of the beckoning goal – just failing to get a final touch in the six yard box. Posh had chances a plenty throughout the game but all were spurned, and then three minutes before half time Tommy Booth – Manchester City's veteran midfield player – shot City into the lead. The lead was not relinquished, and as the game progressed City finished the stronger side. It was the end of Posh's F.A.Cup dreams for another year, but along the way the fans had been provided with some memorable victories and the Club had a large cash bonus for their troubles.

Robbie Cooke secures another F.A.Cup Giantkilling, against Notts. County

It was back to League action against Torquay at London Road in the next game and Posh failed to do themselves justice against lesser opposition, getting hammered 3-1, and so slipped to seventh in the table. The slide continued, for after a 4-1 drubbing at Bournemouth, they could only draw at home to Wimbledon and at Bury by the same score, followed by just one point from the home match against Wigan. They finally got back to winning ways with a 4-1 win over struggling Tranmere in front of just 3,034 at London Road. Although Posh were within three points of a promotion spot, a 2-0 defeat at Darlington severely dented their hopes. But they bounced back immediately from a 2-1 victory against York City at Bootham Crescent against York, with Cooke grabbing both of Posh's goals, his first in five matches. A 1-0 defeat of Mansfield at London Road came courtesy of a Gynn goal and a Robb penalty save, and it was a victory that put Posh into the top four (a promotion position), with just six games remaining.

Posh started to lose ground after they drew 1-1 at Port Vale in their next game, and followed this with a scoreless draw at home to fellow promotion chasers Aldershot. A week later a 2-1 victory over Crewe, with goals from Cooke and Gynn, kept them in touch with the leaders.

With every game becoming vital Posh lost valuable ground in the final derby match of the season, at Northampton, having to come from 2-0 down, to draw 2-2. With two games remaining Posh's promotion hopes were now out of their hands, for they were lying in fifth place – three points behind Wimbledon and Doncaster – with Wimbledon having played one game fewer. Their final home game sealed their fate as they could only draw against Hartlepool, and even that was thanks to a Foster equaliser five minutes from time.

The final game of the season took Posh to Hereford where they again drew 1-1, Cooke scoring Posh's goal, and his 29th of the season. Cooke became the first striker to score 20 goals for Posh since Jim Hall accomplished the feat in 1973. Posh finished the season in fifth place, three points behind Wimbledon who occupied the fourth promotion spot, and yet again it was case of 'so near and yet so far' for Peterborough. The last game of consequence of the season was a Testimonial match for Tommy Robson, against First Division Ipswich at London Road, the visitors winning 1-0 in front of over 4,000 fans.

Posh manager Peter Morris (left) drinks a toast to Tommy Robson.

Morris had guided his team to yet another successful season, in both the Cup and League, but still the elusive Third Division place seemed just beyond Posh's grasp.

1981/82 SEASON

Posh started the build up to the new season by releasing five players, but struggled to keep others. Pat Sharkey was released along with Alan Guy, Dave McVay, Colin Foster, and 37 year old Tommy Robson – which ended an association with the Club that had started in November 1968. Tommy made 440 appearances in the League, 42 as substitute, plus a further 16 as an unused substitute and scored 111 goals. In the Cup he made 74 appearances netting 18 goals. He had made a record number of appearances for the Club, and was the second highest goalscorer. McVay signed for Lincoln and Foster moved to Grantham.

In a hectic pre-season programme, Geoff Butler came in to replace Jim Barron as first team coach and Posh signed a sponsorship deal with city firm *Sodastream*; for the first time Posh would carry the name of a sponsor on the front of their playing shirts, and this was one of the first deals of its kind in the country. Of note was Trevor Slack – from the Posh Youth Team – who won three caps for England in the European Youth Championships in West Germany, and speculation was rife over the departure of keeper Keith Waugh from the club. Manager Peter Morris signed young Northern Ireland born striker Colin Clarke from 1st Division Ipswich, plus Billy Rodaway from Burnley (on free transfers) and forward – Steve Massey – signed from Bournemouth. Ollie Kearns, from Reading, was approached, but would not sign for Posh.

The pre-season games centred around a new competition, the "Group Cup", and the first match was drawn 2-2 at 2nd Division Norwich, against a side that had Chris Woods in goal and Justin Fashanu and Greg Shepherd (the latter scoring), in attack.

Robbie Cooke and Trevor Quow got the Posh goals. A 1st Division side, Notts County, came to London Road for the second of their 3 qualifying Group matches, but two goals from Cooke and one from Gynn saw Posh home to a 3-1 victory. The final Group match ended in a 3-1 home win over 3rd Division Lincoln, with goals coming from Gynn, Massey and Kellock. It was Keith Waugh's last game for Posh as he ended the speculation by signing for, recently relegated, 4th Division rivals Sheffield United, for £90,000. Lee Smelt replaced him, on loan from Nottingham Forest.

Smelt made his League debut for Posh along with Billy Rodaway and Steve Massey when Posh beat Mansfield 1-0 at London Road, with a goal 10 minutes from time; Billy Kellock's penalty was first saved by Rod Arnold, and Kellock headed home the rebound. Second Division Barnsley visited London Road in midweek for a League Cup 1st round 1st leg match and a crowd of 4,608 was treated to a pulsating game that ended 3-2 to Barnsley. Ex-Celtic player Ronnie Glavin put Barnsley 2-0 up inside 11 minutes with the Yorkshiremen looking in irresistible form, but goals by Slack before, and Cooke after, half time levelled the scores. Barnsley won the game with a Joe Joyce strike after 65 minutes.

Jackie Gallagher left the club after playing just 8 games the previous season, the signing of Clarke and Massey prompted the decision. Colin Clarke, who made his Posh debut against Barnsley, made his League debut at Halifax 3 days later when Posh drew 1-1. A week later Posh won again in the League, with a 5-1 thrashing of Rochdale. Cooke scored his first ever League hat trick and Quow and Slack added the other goals. Goalkeeper Lee Smelt finished his spell at Posh, having to pick the ball out of the back of the net on no fewer than 10 occasions during his final 3 games at the club. The reverses started with a 6-0 thrashing at Oakwell against Barnsley in the League Cup 2nd leg – ironically Smelt was Posh's best player – the match was watched by 11,198, with goals coming from Glavin (2), Parker (2), plus Aylott and Barraclough one a piece. The Barnsley side, which included Mick McCarthy, tore Posh apart and had it not been for Smelt it could have been double figures. Stockport were also in goal scoring mood at Edgeley Park when Posh lost their first League match 3-0, and Smelt's final game was a 1-1 draw at Hull, where Morris picked coach Butler in preference to Winters and Smith instead of Slack. Cooke scored the Posh goal, his 6th in 7 games.

Neil Freeman arrived from Birmingham City to replace Lee Smelt and made his debut at home to Crewe. Posh won 3-0 with goals from Cooke, Hodgson and Kellock. Freeman in fact managed to keep a clean sheet in his first 4 matches, with a scoreless draw at Darlington, a 1-0 win at Hartlepool – thanks to a Billy Kellock goal after 75 minutes – and then a home victory over Bournemouth by 1-0. Unusually both Hartlepool and Bournemouth had players sent off, the first time players had received their marching orders in consecutive Posh games.

This was Bournemouth's first defeat of the season. Posh's impressive run took them to 4th in the League after they beat Port Vale away on the following Monday evening. Port Vale's early lead was cancelled out by Steve Massey's first goal for the club, with Chard and Cooke grabbing the others. The down side of the result was the injury to Quow, who had been so inspirational in Posh's start to the season, who broke his leg for the second time in his career.

The following Saturday two records were ended – the Posh 100% home successes and the victory by York City, their first in 9 visits to London Road. In a scrappy game Keith Walwyn scored the only goal after 70 minutes in front of a crowd of 4,220. Posh bounced back with a 3-1 win over Hereford in a re-arranged match from September, and Steve Collins scored a spectacular first goal for the Club, with Syrett and Kellock netting Posh's other goals.

The story broke in both local newspapers that Peterborough was the possible site for a new multi-million pound all-seater super stadium. A row broke out as General Manager Arnold Blades denied knowledge of the plans in 'The Standard', but was quoted in 'The Evening Telegraph', the newspaper which broke the news. Phil Chard handed Manager Peter Morris a transfer request in the same week after being dropped from the team after the York City game.

Syrett grabbed his second goal in 4 days, at Scunthorpe, after a 1-0 win eased them back into the promotion picture. Those who doubted Peterborough's promotion credentials were given food for thought when Aldershot, after taking an early lead, were thrashed 7-1 at London Road. With 41 minutes gone Posh were still trailing 1-0 but in a remarkable 4 minute period goals by Cooke and Gynn turned the match around. One minute after half time Smith made it 3-1, and Massey and Syrett claimed two goals apiece, in a half when it looked as though every Peterborough attack would result in a goal. It was Posh's biggest win since the 7-0 demolition of Barrow in the 1971/72 season. An ironic memory for Colin Garwood in the Aldershot side, who was the substitute for Posh the night they won 8-1 at London Road against Oldham.

Predictably the biggest attendance of the season came to watch Posh play Blackpool 3 days later, and they were not disappointed with Posh's performance. Syrett scored his 5th goal in 4 games, with the other goals from Hodgson and Kellock, in a 3-1 win which sent the team into 3rd place in the table, two points behind Sheffield United. A visit to 4th placed Bury in the next match saw Posh take the lead after 25 minutes from a superb Kellock free kick that he curled around the defensive wall and into the net. The Fourth Division's top scorers soon fought back with 2 goals, including a Kellock own goal, before half time, and went on to win 3-1. Posh started the season's F.A. Cup trail at Halifax, where Lee Smelt was in goal for the home side.

Cooke got back to his scoring ways again with 2 goals to take his tally to 12 for the season and Syrett added a third – all in a 7 minute spell near the end of the game – giving Posh a 3–0 victory.

Steve Phillips and Wakeley Gage were in the Northampton side to face Posh at London Road in the next League match. Billy Kellock the ex-Kettering player took a lot of 'stick' handed out by the visiting Cobblers fans, but got his own back by firing home the only goal after 28 minutes, and in front of the Northampton supporters at the Moyes End. Phil Chard, back in the side since Trevor Quow broke his leg, made his peace with Peter Morris and asked to come off the transfer list in the same week that General Manager Arnold Blades announced Posh would not play in the newly formed Associate Members Cup. Posh played only two games in December due to the cold weather, the first a 2–0 league defeat at Bradford.

Trevor Slack, lying in the penalty box, scores in the early season 5–1 victory over Rochdale.

Peter Morris desperate to strengthen his small squad hit out at the newspapers who criticised the Posh Board's apparent lack of financial support for a promotion bid. But the team aided the financial cause by booking their passage to the 3rd round of the F.A. Cup with a 2–1 home win over 3rd Division Walsall.

Posh Chairman, Mr Hugh Wright, sadly died in Hospital after a short illness before the end of the year. Mr Wright had been Chairman since May 1980. Prior to that date he had served the club as Director for 14 years, when a new Board was elected following the demotion to Division 4. Mr Bill Wilde, the Vice–Chairman became the new Chairman, whilst Cyril Duddington took over his vacated position. Both men were long time servants of the Club, Bill Wilde having first joined the Board in 1969.

The next Posh match was on January 6th when they missed the chance of a glamour 4th round tie against League champions Aston Villa, by losing 1–0 to 3rd Division Bristol City in the F.A. Cup in front of 6,811 fans. A midweek visit to Wigan brought more misery when Posh were hammered 5–0, on a cold misty evening, and manager Morris blasted his team for their lack of commitment. Steve Massey came in for Phil Chard, for the 2–1 victory over Mansfield, the first double of the season for Posh. It was the start of an 11 match unbeaten run in the League that established Posh at the top of the table, and back in the hunt for promotion.

Colin Clarke scored his first ever goal in the win over Stockport, although aside from the League, Posh lost 1–0 at home to 3rd Division Wimbledon in the League Group Cup Quarter Finals. Kevin Gage scored the Dons winner, with Dave Beasant and Glynn Hodges also in their side that night. Back in the 4th Division, Cooke's goal earned a 1–1 draw at Rochdale. He scored again in the home match with Hull after just 5 minutes.

With the score still at 1–0, Hodgson became the 6th Posh player to be sent off after an off the ball scuffle with Hull's Billy Whitehurst, who also received his marching orders. Posh secured the points with 2 late goals from Clarke and Chard. The impressive home run continued with Posh's 11th win in 13 League games at London Road, over a Darlington side that took a 7th minute lead but, despite players of the calibre of David Speedie and Alan Walsh in their side, still lost 3–1.

Posh were now starting to look like a promotion side and two away trips yielded maximum points gained in some style. A fine flowing move led to Phil Chard scoring the only goal at Crewe, and it was goal machine Cooke that fired Posh into 2nd place in the table with his 19th and 20th goals of the season in a 2–1 win at Tranmere.

Steve Massey left Posh for local rivals Northampton, and Morris moved to strengthen his squad with loan signing Bobby Smith (formerly of Hibernian) from 2nd Division Leicester City.

Smith made his debut in place of the suspended Gordon Hodgson at home to Hartlepool, as Posh looked for their 5th consecutive win. It was something of a baptism by fire for the Scot as goals flew in from every angle! Robbie Cooke put Posh ahead after 6 minutes, but a minute later Keith Houchen levelled the scores and then put Hartlepool 2–1 up six minutes on, from the penalty spot after Steve Collins handled the ball in the area. Nine minutes later Paul Staff beat 3 Posh players on a 40 yard run at goal and scored from 10 yards out. Before the 4,610 crowd could catch their breath Cooke converted a 24th penalty, and then, incredibly for the second time in the game, Hartlepool caught Posh asleep straight from the kick off as Houchen completed his hat trick with a header from Linacres' cross to make it 4–2.

Gynn kept the Posh fans interested in the game that looked to be eluding them when he rocketed in Posh's 3rd, 4 minutes before half time. The second half looked as though it may be a repeat of the first, when Cooke completed his hat trick in the first minute, with Colin Clarke for the second being time the provider. The scoring ended there despite a linesman flagging for a penalty to Posh in the 80th minute, which Referee Colin Downey turned down. The disappointment of the two dropped points was increased when a booking for Billy Kellock later resulted in a 2 match ban.

Kellock, leads the protest taken up with Referee Downey, over the penalty dispute. (Photo. supplied by Colin Downey)

Charlie George made his debut for Bournemouth in the draw at Dean Court, the Cherries also having Nigel Spackman in their side. Off the field General Manager Arnold Blades and Director David Ringham announced that the club would soon get the 'go ahead' to build a new VIP Suite in a two storey extension on the main stand, that would be self financing.

Anglia T.V. cameras recorded Posh's 1–0 victory over promotion rivals Bury at London Road, and 4,931 fans came to watch two of the League's most prolific marksmen in confrontation – Cooke with 27 goals behind the Country's leading scorer Madden, with 34. But it was defender Ian Phillips who scored the winner after 40 minutes! Posh were now 3rd, level on points and games played with 2nd placed Sheffield United, and 2 points behind Wigan, with 2 games in hand. After Posh completed their 6th League double of the season, by beating Torquay at Plainmoor, the local press and many fans speculated on winning the Championship rather than just promotion. Leigh Barnard played his first game for the club at Torquay coming on as sub for Phil Chard.

Of the final 9 games, 5 were at London Road, and the next three were against teams in the top 6 in the table, the run starting with a 2–2 draw against Colchester. In a hectic 4 minute period after half time Smith put Posh 1–0 ahead only for Ian Allinson to equalise 2 minutes later. After a further 2 minutes Billy Kellock thundered Posh ahead with a 20 yard shot from a well worked set piece with Micky Gynn. Posh looked comfortably in control until Geoff Butler's ineffective clearance enabled Steve Leslie to lay on Roy McDonagh's 78th minute equaliser.

Fifth placed Bradford were next at London Road and a crowd of 6,765 came to watch as Ian Phillips shot Posh ahead from a Billy Kellock corner. In a predictably tight game the lead was consolidated 12 minutes from time, when Robbie Cooke – playing his 100th League game for Posh – scored his 57th goal and 28th of the season. The result left Posh unmoved in 2nd place, behind Wigan, with a game in hand and 1 point ahead of Sheffield United, who came to London Road 4 days later. Ian Porterfield brought his Sheffield United side to Peterborough with former Posh custodian Keith Waugh in goal, and the top of the table match produced a crowd of 13,439, the biggest League gate at London Road since Gillingham were entertained in 1974. The game started badly for Posh and finished up even worse.

The Blades were in irresistible form and Keith Edwards made it 1–0 after 11 minutes converting Colin Morris's through ball. After 21 minutes Mike Trusson's stinging drive was only parried by Freeman and Jeff King pounced to make it 2–0 from the rebound. By the time Colin Morris punished Smith's sloppy back pass to make it 3–0 (after 34 minutes), the game was all but over. Posh created just two first half chances, both of which were dealt with superbly by Waugh who was in top form. Despite Posh stepping up their efforts in the 2nd half they had nothing to show for it, indeed Edwards made it 4–0 when Sheffield converted their only real chance of the half.

Peter Morris hoped that a local derby against Northampton, who were struggling to avoid re-election, would boost Posh's promotion bid. Instead they missed a string of relatively straightforward chances, until the 77th minute when Gynn was blatantly tripped in the penalty area, but no spot kick was given. In the 84th minute Cooke finally struck, only to have his 'goal' disallowed, as the ball was ruled out of play when it was crossed by Syrett. This compounded the frustrations of Posh's woeful finishing and condemned them to their second straight defeat. The frustration was also felt on the terraces where major crowd trouble occurred throughout the match.

The return visit to Colchester produced the second draw between the sides that season. Kevin Bremner scored for Colchester in the first half, but in a bad tempered game Tony Smith and Steve Wright were sent off in separate incidents and 6 players were booked. With 15 minutes to go Gynn was gifted a ball by Tony Adcock, and he supplied a cross for Syrett to drill home the equaliser. Posh's lingering hopes of promotion seemed even more remote after Wigan demolished Posh 3-0 at London Road, but the final twists in Posh's eventful season came

with a 2-1 defeat at Hereford and another 4-0 drubbing at the hands of Sheffield United, at Bramhall Lane. No fewer than 23,923 came to watch the Blades clinch promotion and condemn Posh to another season in Division 4. Paddy Rayment's debut became one to remember, but for the wrong reasons!

The final match of the season saw Posh beaten 2-1 at home by Tranmere in front of 1,897, the second lowest ever League gate at London Road. In the circumstances it came as no surprise when Robbie Cooke missed an 83rd minute penalty – it would have made him only the second Posh player to score 30 League goals in a season. The final run in produced a solitary point from a possible 21, and a final placing of 5th in the League, 6 points from promotion. The dismal end to the season was a massive blow to everyone involved with the club, and more distressing was this failure which was to lead to the break up of a promising side.

1982/83 SEASON

The gloom around the club after the failed promotion was affecting Manager, Players and Supporters alike. Peter Morris was unhappy at the lack of financial support for his final promotion push and the proposed disbanding of the Youth and Reserve teams to save cash.

On the playing front Billy Kellock refused a new contract and on his decision commented: *"I want to play for a club that really wants success"*. Robbie Cooke then announced that he was asking for a transfer remarking: *"I'm disheartened with the way things are going at the club but I don't blame the Manager, his hands are tied."* As events gathered momentum Chairman Bill Wilde announced that *"It is unlikely that Peter (Morris) will be Manager of Peterborough United next season."*

The second week of June finally brought confirmation that Morris was leaving Posh. He left the Club as one of its most successful Managers but made it clear to the press that even promotion would not have altered his decision. The crucial factor had been the disbanding of the support teams, around which Morris had built his side, and his criticism of the Directors of the club for doing so.

Dave Syrett left the club to join Northampton and then surprisingly on June 22nd the club announced their decision not to scrap the Reserve Team! Ex-Manager Morris would only comment: *"I'm flabbergasted, that says it all."* Interviews had started for the vacant Manager's job and on June 30th, Martin Wilkinson – Alan Clarke's deputy at Leeds United – joined Posh. With Wilkinson's arrival the transfer activity was stepped up. In came Ivor Linton from Aston Villa, who played in Villa's European Cup Winning campaign. Out went Billy Kellock to Luton for £30,000 and Ian Phillips to Northampton on a free transfer.

Ian Benjamin signed for Posh, after it was reported that he had turned down a contract to go to Manchester United, for £5,000. Mike Imlach also signed for Posh after Alan Clarke had arrived for a few weeks at London Road to act as a Consultant to assist Wilkinson. As Posh started the pre-season friendlies against local opponents, two Leeds players – centre half Neil Firm and 18 year old goalkeeper David Seaman – joined the club for small fees, but Tony Smith left to join Halifax. Wilkinson described the signing of Seaman as: *"A pinch ... if Leeds had not been in financial difficulty there is no way I would have been able to sign him."*

Worries grew at the increase in crowd violence at games, and following the previous season's scenes at Northampton, The Maunsell Cup match that Posh won 6-0 at Wellingborough, was marred by fighting throughout the game.

Posh's opening game in the League Trophy was at home to Mansfield. Ivor Linton scored the first goal for Posh after 6 minutes and Posh stretched the lead to 2-0 with a Phil Chard goal before half time. The small 1,873 attendance at London Road also had plenty to smile about in the second half for Benjamin hit two more goals. They came back down to earth with a bump though when 1st Division Norwich hammered them 6-2 in the next game, Clarke and Benjamin scoring for Posh. During the same week, Reserve team player Richard Sutton was named for the England Youth Squad.

The last group game of the League Trophy saw Posh slaughter local rivals Northampton, with four former Posh players in the side, 5-2. Benjamin 2, Cooke, Slack and Chard were the Posh scorers.

The League campaign opened at Stockport where Seaman, Firm, Benjamin and Linton made their debuts for Posh. They made history for all the wrong reasons, as for the first time since joining the League two Posh players were sent off during the game – Neil Firm, in the 64th minute, and Trevor Slack; it was also the first time in the League that a Posh player had been sent off on his debut. Amazingly the nine men held out for a 1-1 draw, thanks to Benjamin who scored – in his first game for Posh. In midweek Posh travelled to Darlington for a Milk Cup tie, and won 2-0 with goals from Micky Gynn and Robbie Cooke, but the real star of Posh's win was keeper David Seaman who made several outstanding saves.

The first League game of the season at London Road saw Posh scrape home in a 2-1 win over Hartlepool. Linton put Posh ahead on 26 minutes, Stimpson equalised before half time, and John Winters was the unlikely match winner. With four minutes left to play he scored his first ever League goal at London Road. It was a fortunate result considering an inept display, and five days later Wimbledon capitalised on a similar display to win 3-0 at London Road. For the 4th consecutive game Posh had players booked, which caused early concern over their mounting disciplinary record.

Posh faced Aldershot at the Recreation Ground without the suspended centre half pairing of Neil Firm and Trevor Slack. Wilkinson, who had been trying to sign a player on loan to cover their suspensions, pitched 17 year old Richard Sutton into his first League match. This turned out to be a bad decision for he was substituted after only 28 minutes, giving Mike Imlach his Posh debut. Sutton was obviously not match fit and very much out of his depth, whilst the team were outplayed and lost 2-0. Firm returned for the 2nd leg tie against Darlington at London Road and Imlach retained his place in the side, as Posh won comfortably by 4-2, with Imlach grabbing his first goal for the club.

Against Bury at home, it was another tale of missed chances as Posh dominated but scored only once through Gynn in a 1-1 draw, Robbie Cooke missing an earlier penalty. Two successive away games brought two more draws, with penalty saves by Seaman in both games. Posh then faced Bristol City at London Road, placed 8th from bottom of the table. Quow returned after a 12 month absence due to a broken leg, and starred along with Micky Gynn, when Posh took full advantage of John Economous's dismissal after 41 minutes. By that time Posh were already two goals up. Gynn scored again with 6 minutes left, but this success was shortlived for Posh then lost 1-0 at home to Scunthorpe.

A crowd of 3,798 saw a classy Crystal Place win the first leg of the Milk Cup 2nd round tie with two goals from Ian Edwards and in the League Posh slid further into a dismal run, losing at Tranmere and drawing at Chester. Seaman, again, saved a penalty, at Sealand Road. Robbie Cooke by now had eventually left the Club to join Billy

Kellock at Luton, although only on one months loan. Mike Small came to London Road in a similar arrangement and made his debut in the Tranmere defeat.

Posh suffered their 4th defeat in 5 games, at home to Torquay, and within the Torquay side were Steve Bould and ex-Posh forward Jackie Gallagher. It was then back to Cup action where Posh made a spirited exit from the Milk Cup when they lost 2-1, to go out 4-1 to Crystal Palace on aggregate.

Posh went to Northampton for the next League game, but could not reproduce their League Trophy form from earlier in the season. Steve Collins missed a penalty, and the Cobblers again included Neil Freeman, Ian Phillips, Mark Heeley Dave Syrett plus Dave Buchanan in their line-up. Freeman's save from Collins spot kick ensured a scoreless draw, but it was now 7 games since Posh's last victory. Halifax, together with former Posh players Lee Smelt and Tony Smith, visited London Road. After Firm headed Posh into a 5th minute lead, Nobbs equalised, but Small came off the subs bench and smashed the winner in the 68th minute.

Bill Harvey was caretaker Manager for the next match, at Hull, since Martin Wilkinson went into Hospital for a fortnight with suspected appendicitis. The in-form Tigers hammered Posh 4-1, with former on loan Billy Woof scoring for Hull, leaving Posh 6th from bottom of the division. Cooke returned for the home game with Rochdale (scoring the only goal of the game), when Posh gained a much needed win to cheer caretaker boss Harvey.

London Road was the venue for the first round of the F.A. Cup on November 20th, but not for Posh who played at Chesterfield. It was United Counties League side Holbeach who entertained Wrexham, whilst Posh were denied a deserved victory with a last gasp equaliser from the Spireites.

Four days later at London Road Posh came from behind to beat the Third Division side in front of a crowd of 3,185. Robbie Cooke scored his second goal in 3 games since his return from Luton.

Two goalless displays followed the Cup victory, drawing at home to Port Vale and losing 1-0 at Swindon, to a controversial penalty that 18 year old Paul Rideout converted. It was rumoured at this time that Jim Iley could return as Manager at London Road. But the fans gave their verdict at Swindon by chanting *"We hate Jim Iley"* during the game, illustrating to Chairman Bill Wilde the supporters reaction to such a proposal. Better news was that from Robbie Cooke who asked to come off the transfer list, and he celebrated this decision by grabbing two goals in the 5-2 F.A. Cup win over Doncaster.

Off the field the club served notice on the Supporters Club to quit the Posh Social Club at the ground, the Football Club preferring to run the facility themselves.

This action started a bitter row between the Supporters' and the Football Clubs. Posh were offered John Fashanu on loan by Norwich Manager Ken Brown but Martin Wilkinson spoke in a local paper saying he felt the move was unnecessary unless an injury crisis loomed.

Posh's next game was on December 27th against Colchester. A 6th minute goal from John Winters was cancelled out on half time, but 20 minutes into the second half Firm clinched the 3 points for Posh with a header. The game produced 7 bookings and 2 Colchester players were sent off. The following day Posh demolished Peter Morris's Crewe side, that included recently transferred Tony Cliss, by 3-0 at Gresty Road, and then went one better at home to Hereford on New Year's Day with goals from Gynn 2, Cooke and Firm. An excellent holiday programme was completed with a 3-0 victory over Blackpool. The four victories lifted Posh to 12th in the League table.

As Posh prepared to face First Division Luton at Kenilworth Road in the F.A.Cup, the poor disciplinary record was to take its toll, for Winters and Rodaway were both suspended from the League matches following the tie. After much speculation regarding the eventual outcome, the game ended up being a one sided affair. The Hatters took control and never looked in danger of losing, and so ended any F.A. Cup aspirations for another year.

Back in the League, Posh's improved form continued with a 0-0 draw at Hartlepool, followed by victory over Stockport - courtesy of a 12th minute Benjamin goal. It was hardly surprising that it was Posh's bogey side, Wimbledon, that ended the recent run of form in the League, for the Dons won 2-1 at Plough Lane with Steve Leslie grabbing their winner with 4 minutes left to play. The following game against Aldershot ended as a frustrating scoreless draw, Gynn missing a last minute penalty. Posh entered February in 10th spot and were doing well enough in the game against York, until they were hit by tragedy. Trevor Quow suffered a broken leg for the 3rd time in his career, and although Posh battled on to take a 2-1 lead, York equalised with a penalty in the 88th minute. Malcolm Crosby was one of the two York players who were booked in the match.

Off the field events during the following week made all the headlines. Steve Kendrick was named as a new Director, but behind the scenes rumours were causing much annoyance at the club, concerning a group of - "disillusioned but prominent" - supporters who were putting together a revival plan to bring Noel Cantwell back to London Road.

Posh lost 1-0 at Ashton Gate to another penalty, before going down by the same score at home to Chester, before their lowest ever League attendance of 1,661. As *The Evening Telegraph* reported, the half time announcement that Coronation Street's Deidre Barlow had not left her husband Ken got the loudest cheer of the frosty evening!

To add to Posh's problems David Seaman sustained a cracked collar bone in the 2nd half of the game. It was all change for Posh's next fixture as Robbie Cooke signed for Cambridge United for £20,000. Mario Ippolito came in for his Posh debut along with on loan goalkeeper Stuart Naylor as Posh faced Tranmere at home.

It proved to be a dream debut for both players as Naylor kept a clean sheet and 18 year old non-contract player Mario Ippolito scored Posh's second goal in the 3-0 win. But a few days later Posh faced another shock when Martin Wilkinson resigned as Manager. In interviews with the media his main reason appeared to be the lack of cash for players due to strict budget controls. The final straw for Wilkinson came when he was forced to transfer Robbie Cooke. This left Bill Harvey in charge as caretaker boss again, but it did not take long for rumours to start since former Posh boss Noel Cantwell made it clear that he wished to return to London Road. John Wile and John Duncan were also linked with the position.

Meanwhile back on the pitch, Ippolito's fairytale start in League football continued when he scored both goals in his second game, at the Shay, where Posh beat Halifax 2-1, after losing 2-1 at Torquay where former Posh Player Jackie Gallagher impressed for the home side. Northampton were the next visitors to London Road, and Caretaker boss Harvey turned back the clock with Jack Carmichael returning to the side at right back. It was 'Jolly' Jack's first full game in the League for the club since 1979. Former player John Wile was interviewed for the Manager's job, and just two days before the Northampton game Wile accepted the offer from Posh Chairman Bill Wilde. But exactly when he would take over in the position was left undecided. The general feeling was that it would be at the end of the season, and Wile was still negotiating with his club, West Bromwich, for a release date. The 'derby' match resulted in victory for Posh and it completed a good week, reviving flagging support and lifting the spirits of everyone connected with the club. There was a buzz of anticipation regarding John Wile's arrival, for it seemed to be a universally popular appointment, but with West Bromwich Albion still in the hunt for a place in Europe, Wile eventually had to wait until the end of the season before taking up his post.

Posh drew their next match at home to top of the table Hull, who had a player sent off after only 17 minutes, and continued in the League with a draw at Rochdale followed by a 1-0 defeat at Colchester.

The row between the Supporters' and the Football Clubs came to a head as the Chairman of the former, Gordon Meade, announced that they would not move out of the Posh Club at the end of May, but if they were forced to, they would file for £300,000 in compensation.

Posh returned to winning ways with a home victory over Crewe before Bill Harvey was forced to make changes to the side the for the home match against 8th placed Swindon.

Seaman returned in goal and 17 year old Stephen Mercer came in at full back, since Firm was again suspended, for the 3rd time during the season. The game itself was a cracker with Trevor Slack heading Posh in front after 14 minutes before Paul Rideout equalised 5 minutes later. Slack was in commanding form and drove the team on from the back. After 27 minutes Chard's penalty was saved, but he followed up and netted the rebound. Two goals in the 32nd and 33rd minutes, from Clarke and Gynn, seemed to have sealed Posh's victory but a spirited fightback saw Town just lose out by the odd goal in 7 in an entertaining game.

Promotion chasing Bury beat Posh 1-0 at Gigg Lane from a penalty by Tommy Gore, and this was followed by a home draw with Darlington. After a 3-0 drubbing at Scunthorpe (with Neil Pointon amongst the Irons' goal-scorers), a 2-1 defeat at Vale Park followed. It came as no real surprise when only 1,636 fans, another new record low League attendance, came to London Road to see Posh beat Blackpool 3-1. Paul Stewart gave Blackpool a 3rd minute lead, Gynn equalised within a minute, followed by Chard and Benjamin goals, all before half an hour had gone.

New manager - John Wile

John Wile was in the stand for the game and was full of optimism for his new side, and he announced that his first signing – Martin Pike – would be coming with him from West Bromwich in the summer. Posh beat Mansfield at London Road and moved to 9th in the table, before completing the season with two away fixtures. They won 1-0 at Hereford and lost 4-3 at Darlington, the latter match in front of a crowd of 1,002. Fred Barber played in goal for Darlington and goals from Ivor Linton and Ian Benjamin (2) completed Posh's scoring for the season.

1983/84 SEASON

John Wile started as Manager of Posh with severe limitations on the money he could spend to strengthen his squad. His team building started with Martin Pike coming with him from West Brom. Steve Mercer and Jack Carmichael were not retained from the previous season. Dave Buchanan then arrived from Leicester City after Billy Rodaway rejected a contract on reduced terms and left to join Blackpool. Within 24 hours Wile had captured the signature of Kenny Beech from Walsall, but he made it clear that there would be no more newcomers until he could assess the strength of the team. Wile had the early opportunity to do so in a friendly at Aston Villa, which Posh lost 4-3, in an entertaining game in which Villa paraded their new signings Steve McMahon and Paul Rideout. Steve Collins left the club, which upset Wile since neither his new Club – Southend – or the player himself, had notified Posh of the move. Collins was the first to leave London Road, from a talented quintet of players who came through from the same Youth Squad. Southend paid a reported £7,500 for his services. There were only two friendlies of note. The first against a Malaysian National side on a pitch near Ipswich, where Posh took a first half lead through Ian Benjamin, Malaysia equalised on 50 minutes, and Mario Ippolito won Posh the match with a header in the dying seconds.

The other game was a 2-0 success over First Division Coventry. Just as the team for the opening fixture (versus Hartlepool) seemed settled, Micky Gynn became the second home grown talented player to leave the Club when he joined First Division Coventry City for £60,000.

It was the only damper at the start of a new season that saw fans again in an optimistic mood after the set backs of the previous 15 months. A crowd of 3,213 turned out to see them start in style with Beech, Pike, and Buchanan all making their League debuts. John Wile skippered the side in his first appearance for Posh since 1970. Clarke opened the scoring after 36 minutes and Buchanan scored on his debut to make it 2-0 a minute before half time. Benjamin added a third after 64 minutes shortly after Robinson had pulled a goal back which had given 'Pool some brief hope. It was just the start Posh needed as they prepared to face a difficult trip, for the second successive season, to Crystal Palace in the Milk Cup.

In the same week Posh announced their intention to build four VIP boxes and a TV camera and commentary box on the Glebe Road, and that they were attempting to sign former 1st Division star Ray Hankin. Posh's League Cup run looked to have ended when they lost 3-0 at Selhurst Park in the first leg of the opening round.

Posh then faced two away trips, drawing 2–2 at Wrexham – in which David Gregory played – and losing 2–0 at York – who scored in the 57th and 58th minutes. But within a space of five days Wile's side triumphed in two remarkable games. Ray Hankin had finally signed and made his debut for Posh at London Road against Torquay. Posh opened the scoring after 8 minutes when Quow, back on form after recovering from his (third) broken leg, centred and watched Torquay keeper John Turner palm the ball into his own net. Hankin captured the hearts of the crowd in the period up to half–time with a stirring display full of the skill and power that had been lacking up front at Posh for so long. On the 15th minute Chard floated in a free kick which Hankin headed with ferocious power past a motionless Turner to open his account for Posh. One minute before half time Pike saw his shot beaten away by Turner but picked up by Hankin just outside the box. Hankin thundered home a 20 yard drive in front of the London Road end and turned to salute his delirious new fan club. Goals from Chard and Clarke completed the demolition, and Impey capped a miserable day, getting himself sent off in the 87th minute.

Posh's Cup exploits made no impression on Hereford who won 2–1 at Edgar Street in the next game, before Posh faced two more home matches. They started the first game without Beech who had cracked a rib and punctured a lung in the Hereford defeat. Posh swept aside Mansfield by 3–0, in a victory only marred by Hankin's sending off after 78 minutes.

Benjamin scored after two minutes as Posh went on to make it four straight home victories in the League, scoring twelve and conceding just one goal in those matches. It also saw Seaman save his 6th penalty since joining the Club. Posh travelled to 1st Division Stoke in the Milk Cup and against a side which included George Berry and Sammy McIlroy, drew 0–0 to bring the Potters back to London Road.

Against this optimistic background it was reported that at the forthcoming A.G.M. Peterborough United would announce that the Club had lost £100,000 during the previous season, their biggest ever deficit.

In the League, Posh drew with Doncaster 1–1 at London Road before losing their next two away games 2–1, against Halifax and Rochdale. The 'Dales winner came in the last minute of a rainsoaked game at Spotland. Two days later Wile signed 32 year old midfield player Dick Tydeman from Gillingham, who made his debut at home to Tranmere, where goals from Pike and crowd favourite Hankin secured a 2–0 win. A bumper crowd of 9,898 watched Posh take on Stoke at London Road in the Milk Cup, and the Potteries side showed their First Division class with goals from O'Callaghan and James to win 2–1. Ray Hankin became the first player to be sent off twice for the Club, when he received his marching orders, after 56 minutes, for fouling Micky Thomas; he had already been booked after just 12 seconds for fouling Dyson.

Hankin's fairytale start with the Club started to assume larger than life proportions on the following Wednesday when Posh entertained Crystal Palace, in their second leg Milk Cup tie. Hankin's arrogance on the ball had a positive effect on his team mates who played with a new found confidence. After 42 minutes he put Posh 1–0 up, and six minutes later Clarke latched on to Imlach's long through ball to slot home Posh's second. Within four minutes of the second half re–starting Quow put Posh 3–0 up on the night with a spectacular 18 yard shot to send the home crowd wild. But despite making the chances the final killer goal just seem to elude them. Extra time came, and with it more chances for Posh to win, but George Wood and poor finishing denied them. It all came down to a penalty shoot–out to decide the winners of a storming Cup–tie; it was the first time that Posh had been involved in such a shoot–out in the Cup. Chard scored with the first kick before Seaman – who had saved three spot kicks the previous season – saved Jerry Murphy's kick for Palace. Buchanan's effort was saved by Wood, and Seaman repeated his feat, this time from Stan Cummins. Pike and Brooks were successful with their efforts, as were Beech (for Posh) and Palace's Billy Giles. Benjamin, who had come on with only two minutes of extra time remaining, stepped up, and as Wood dived to his left he calmly drove the ball into the opposite corner to send Posh through 7–5 on aggregate, and provide yet another memorable giantkilling performance.

Another giantkilling is completed!
Benjamin nets the all important penalty in the shoot–out versus Crystal Palace.

6'2" Hankin had a new partner for the visit of top of the League Bristol City in the shape of new signing, and one inch taller, Alan Waddle, the former Liverpool player. The only goal of the game was scored by Buchanan with a spectacular diving header after 75 minutes to secure a hard fought victory. The Country's top goal ace, Trevor Senior, added two to his total in a thrilling game with Reading. Posh battled from 2-0 down to 2-2 before half time. The Royals went 3-2 up with nine minutes to play, only for Imlach to make it 3-3 four minutes later.

A visit to Aldershot brought more goals in another exciting game, but unfortunately no points. Waddle and Quow made amends and got Posh back on the winning track in the next game with two goals in a home victory over Chesterfield.

Oxford United in the first round of the F.A. Cup were the next opponents, but the Third Division Club proved too strong for Posh. But they got back to winning ways again in the League with another 2-0 win, at home over Stockport County. Jimmy Holmes, the ex-Tottenham player made his debut in this game, in a week that also saw Ivor Linton leave the Club. Posh then travelled to Gigg Lane to face Bury. After Wayne Entwhistle had given Bury a 25th minute lead, Chard pulled back the deficit from the penalty spot just six minutes later. It was Bury's turn to have a penalty in the second half which Joe Jakub confidently converted and just when all seemed lost, Waddle popped up just two minutes from the end to head home Posh's valuable equaliser.

The team entered December lying 5th in the table and five points behind leaders York City. The next game, at Blackpool, left John Wile with selection problems. At the last minute Wile found himself without the impressive goalkeeper Seaman, and he drafted into goal Zenchuk, a 17 year old on the Manpower Service Scheme. In a remarkable match Posh's defence was outstanding as they protected the novice Zenchuk, but when Blackpool did break through, the keeper was up to the task. Posh took the lead in the 13th minute, but Blackpool recovered from this blow and started to mount an assault on the Posh goal.

However, Zenchuk, Slack and Wile were up to everything that the 'Pool could throw at them. In the second half Benjamin put Posh further ahead after 58 minutes, and Blackpool stepped up their efforts to reduce the arrears. Zenchuk made his only mistake of the game after 71 minutes when Deary fired in a shot from fully 30 yards and although the youngster got to the ball he could only watch as it slipped under his arms and entered the net. It made for an exciting 19 minutes with Zenchuk being called in again to make several good saves before the end of the game. The youngster was rightly hailed as the hero of the match, that lifted Posh to third place in the table, now just one point behind Blackpool. As it transpired this was to be Zenchuk's only game for the Club, but he became the youngest ever goalkeeper to appear for Posh in the Football League.

In the week following, Kenny Allen joined Posh as their reserve goalkeeper. The second away game, at Chester City, was watched by only 1,191 fans. Posh dominated the game, making several chances, but were unable to capitalise, until Chard scored to equalise Chester's 7th minute goal.

The Christmas period started with Colchester at London Road on Boxing Day. Ian Phillips, Perry Groves and Tony Adcock were all in the visitors line-up that lost 2-0 thanks to two late goals from Beach in the 75th and Waddle in the 89th minute. The following day the Posh's good run ended with defeat at nearby Northampton. To make matters worse Hankin suffered his third sending off of the season. Posh ended the year with a home game against Swindon Town on New Year's Eve, when Slack put Posh into the lead after 20 minutes only for Swindon's Jimmy Quinn to equalise with 11 minutes remaining of the game.

As Posh started 1984 they were 7th in the table, with 36 points, five points behind the leading bunch and some 13 points behind Division leaders York City. The first game of the year was at Darlington, and in atrocious conditions Posh slithered to a 1-0 defeat in the mud at Feetham's. Hankin was banned for three matches after his latest sending off, and to complete a dismal holiday period Posh slipped to yet another defeat – the first of the season at London Road – when 'old boy' David Gregory of Wrexham scored after 67 minutes. Two weeks later Hereford United were entertained, and in a another lacklustre performance Posh went behind to an Ollie Kearns goal after 14 minutes. Posh's lowest League gate of the season (2,559) must have thought that they were finished as they trailed, with two minutes left. But not for the first time in the season Benjamin popped up to crash home the Posh equaliser. The long trip to play down in Devon resulted in another crushing blow to Posh's promotion dreams when Torquay stole the three points with an injury time winner from John Sims.

This prompted Manager John Wile to tell the critics to get off the team's backs and ask his players to rally round with an improved performance in their next match, a home game against Bury. It brought instant results for Posh claimed their first victory in the League since December 3rd.

Before their following game, at Field Mill to face Mansfield, Wile moved into the transfer market again to sign Manchester United player Gary Worrall on a month's loan. The newcomer made his debut coming on as a substitute in the 0-0 draw and did enough to persuade Wile to name him in the starting line-up for the away game at Reading four days later. Goal machine Senior (the Fourth Division's leading goalscorer) made his mark again by scoring in the 16th minute of the game, but Waddle equalised for Posh in the 38th and they held on to claim a draw. After this confidence boosting point against the 4th placed team, Posh entertained 3rd placed Bristol City at London Road.

It resulted in one of the best wins of the season, and included Worrall's first goal for the Club, in a 4-1 victory. Posh made their bow in the new Associate Members' Cup at Wrexham in mid-week. John Wile who declared that he was no fan of the tournament named a side with no less than seven team changes from his normal League line-up, one of which was Allen in the Posh goal. Despite Wile's stated opposition to the tournament Posh were leading 2-1 with 17 minutes left to play. But Wrexham staged a comeback with their winner finally coming – again – from ex-Posh man Gregory, in the last minute. A Friday night visit to Tranmere saw Posh lose further ground in the League with a scoreless draw. At home to Rochdale, Wile scored his first goal for Posh since August 1970, it came three minutes after an own goal that gave Posh victory.

Posh then had a chance to make further ground on the leaders with another home match, this time against 4th placed Aldershot. Yet again it all went wrong, for after McDonald had given Aldershot the lead after 59 minutes, and Wile had replied with the equaliser, Mazzon score the winner for the visitors in the 73rd minute. To make matters worse Posh's Hankin found himself sent off for the fourth time that season. As he went down the players' tunnel he clashed with Aldershot defender Don Suiter after the match. Any further hopes that Posh had of promotion seemed to be extinguished after the trip to Chesterfield and defeat by 1-0. Wile moved to sign 20 year old Ipswich goalkeeper Gary Westwood on loan as Allen returned to Torquay after his loan stint as cover for Seaman. Westwood arrived in the same week as skipper Hankin was rapped by Posh Boss Wile, and fined two weeks wages for his latest disciplinary misdemeanours.

A visit to Doncaster only yielded one more point. As Hankin started his third ban of the season, Wile moved into the transfer market yet again, this time signing Coventry forward Errington Kelly. He made an explosive start to his Posh career when Halifax were brushed aside 4-0 at London Road. Both newcomers were impressive as they did the damage to Halifax down both wings.

It also saw another fine display in goal from Seaman who made four good stops to keep Halifax at bay. This was a result that prompted Wile to say that Posh were still not out of the promotion hunt. Posh made a little piece of history by playing their first ever Sunday game, home against the 4th Division's runaway leaders York City. York were 12 points clear at the head of the table having lost only six games in the season, and they were also the division's leading scorers with 76 goals from their 36 games. Even a resurgent Posh could not hold City as goals from McPhail and Byrne gave York a 2-0 win to consolidate their position. The season's biggest League gate of the season, 5,216, turned out.

As Posh resigned themselves to another season in Division 4, they went on another predictable run of good form starting with an away victory at Crewe and followed this up with an impressive 4-0 home victory over Blackpool, who were 6th in the table. After a draw at Colchester United, Posh then made amends for the Christmas defeat by Northampton Town, when they slaughtered their local rivals 6-0 at London Road. It was the perfect way for the Posh goalkeeper to celebrate his call up to the England Under-21 Squad, and Kelly's goal took his total to six in seven games since he joined Posh. It was Posh's biggest ever Football League victory against the Cobblers. It was down to earth with a bump the following week when Stockport County slammed four goals past Posh in a 4-1 defeat. With nothing to play for the attendance at London Road was down to 1,925 when they drew 2-2 with Darlington. As the season drifted hopelessly to its conclusion Posh lost 2-0 at Swindon before facing their final game on May 12th at home to Chester. This was played in front of only 1,679 fans (only 18 more than their lowest every League crowd), who watched a 1-0 victory with a single goal from Kelly after 83 minutes.

It was hardly a fitting end to Posh's 50th year as a football club, although few of the men who formed the Club at that time could have envisaged Posh finishing the season in the top 10 of Division 4 of the Football League.

Local lad makes good. Trevor Slack comes close to scoring in the home game versus York City.

1984/85 SEASON

Posh were busy in the pre-season, following another disappointing year in the 4th Division. They finally announced plans to develop the Executive Suite that had been mooted for so long, at a cost of £65,000. This was to form an extension at the back of the main stand and would also compliment the four Executive Boxes already under construction on the Glebe Road side of the ground.

Wile named five players to be released from the squad, viz. Mario Ippolito, who had started his career in such fine style at London Road, Ian Benjamin, Dick Tydeman, Dave Buchanan and Mike Imlach. Doubts surrounded the future of Colin Clarke – who was currently on loan at Gillingham – and the permanence at London Road of Errington Kelly, the scorer of 7 goals in 11 League games at the end of the previous season. John Wile moved quickly though to secure Kelly's signature and also added the signing of Watford midfield player Francis Cassidy.

Wile moved again and signed 21 year old striker David Johnson – also from Watford – on a free transfer, but was then told that as his squad was so large he would have to get rid of some of his players. It was good news for Posh when Trevor Slack signed a new contract to stay at Posh, and Brian Klug – a midfield player from Chesterfield – arrived during the Summer. Phil Chard was persuaded to stay, as was Trevor Quow who eventually re-signed at the end of July.

Posh commenced their normal round of pre-season friendlies against non-League opposition with the usual success, but a visit to Kettering to contest the Maunsell Cup ended in defeat. After drawing 1–1 in normal time, they were beaten 5–4 on penalties by the Poppies. In the first of the major public friendlies Posh beat Derby 5–1 at London Road, and Wile announced that he was happy with his pre-season preparations as Posh faced another season in Division 4.

The opening fixture was a home game against Tranmere Rovers, a crowd of 3,045 turned up to watch Posh win 1–0 with a penalty from Jimmy Holmes after 86 minutes. It was a win that they deserved, but yet again the old Posh trait of creating many chances and converting few was evident for all to see. The game saw Johnson and Klug making their debuts for the side, Cassidy who was named as substitute was unused. The game saw a swift return to London Road of former Posh players Clarke and Rodaway in the Tranmere side.

Three days later Posh travelled to 2nd Division Sheffield United in a 1st round 1st leg game in the Milk Cup where they lost 1–0 in front of 7,451 fans. Cassidy came in for his debut in an away match against Hereford where Posh's bogeyman Ollie Kearns scored the only goal of the game. Posh returned to London Road to compete in the 2nd leg Cup match against Sheffield.

In an exciting match they took an early lead after five minutes. Kelly built on this success after 36 minutes to give Posh a real hope of going through at the expense of their 2nd Division rivals. In the second half things were different though as Morris pulled one back for the Blades after 65 minutes from the penalty spot. It was the goal that Sheffield needed for Posh's heads dropped and their rhythm and superiority trailed off after their performance in the first hour. The tie went into extra time when Edwards, the man who destroyed Posh 2 years earlier in the 4th Division, scored a goal after 114 minutes to ensure Sheffield went through to the next round of the Cup.

Meanwhile the injury worries piled up for John Wile as it was announced that Jimmy Holmes would be out for 6 weeks after breaking his breastbone in the cup match. In addition striker Ray Hankin announced that he would have to go into hospital for an operation on a groin injury. Slack came into the side to replace Holmes as Posh gained their second League victory at London Road, with a 1–0 win over Mansfield thanks to a Kelly goal. They then travelled to Wrexham and ran out 3–1 winners. Goals came from Wile after 29 minutes, Kelly (two minutes before half time), and after Jim Steel had pulled one back for the Welshmen, Quow made it 3–1 just one minute later. A second away match during the week resulted in a 0–0 draw at Aldershot's Recreation Ground.

Posh came back to London Road to play Hartlepool and maintained their 100% record against a side that had never won at London Road. David Robinson was in the Hartlepool side that lost 3–1, with goals from Beach plus Johnson and Klug who both got their firsts for the Club. After a goalless visit to Torquay, Posh entertained Scunthorpe. Brolley gave Scunthorpe an 8th minute lead, but Posh took only four minutes to get back on terms with a goal from Worrall. Nine minutes later they went ahead after Kelly bundled in Slack's nod across goal. Kelly grabbed his second of the game to put Posh 3–1 up, and they could even afford the luxury of Chard's second penalty miss of the season after Neil Pointon had brought down Johnson. Scunthorpe keeper Joe Neenan dived well to his right to save the shot.

With Posh sitting 4th in the League, it was no surprise when it was announced that David Seaman was set to leave the Club after his outstanding form over the previous two seasons. The Club had agreed a £100,000 fee with Birmingham and it was only left for Seaman to agree terms before he left London Road. Since his call-up for the England Under-21 Squad great things were predicted for the goalkeeper, who had made 106 appearances at London Road, and it was only a matter of time before he moved on to better things. Wile moved quickly to bring the experienced goalkeeper, John Turner, to London Road, making his debut in the away game at Swindon on October 7th. Lou Macari was in the Swindon side, with Mayes opening the scoring after 19 minutes.

In a bad tempered match Slack earned Posh a point with a 35th minute goal, before Ramsey was sent off for an horrific tackle on Worrall. Posh returned to London Road and made it 5 wins from 5 games with a 3–1 victory over Stockport. Johnson put Posh 1–0 ahead after 37 minutes but within a minute Sword had levelled matters for Stockport. In the second half Worrall put Posh 2–1 up after 58 minutes, and 10 minutes later Klug scored to secure the 3 points. Paddy Rayment was released to Cambridge on loan, before Posh travelled to Rochdale and proved that away from London Road they still had their problems as they lost 2–1. Another home game yielded 3 more points with a 2–0 win over Halifax. Posh suffered another defeat when they travelled to Port Vale, and despite Cassidy equalising an early goal after 22 minutes, Vale went on to win 3–1.

Posh Boss Wile left his defensive role in the home match against Crewe

November started with two home victories, over Crewe 2–1, followed 4 days later by a win versus Blackpool, taking Posh's run at London Road to 8 consecutive wins. It left them 5th in the table on 27 points, 4 points behind League leaders Bury. Trevor Parr, after his recent signing from Yorkshire non–League side Thackley, was named as substitute in the Blackpool game, but didn't come on to play. Posh travelled to Roots Hall to take on Southend, with the Essex side fielding Steve Collins, Steve Phillips, Billy Kellock, Greg Shepherd, Lil Fucillo and Trevor Whymark. Lucillo scored both Southend goals as they beat Posh 2–1.

Posh also travelled on the following Saturday as a start was made on the F.A. Cup trail, and a game at the Abbey Stadium against local rivals Cambridge United. A large following of Posh supporters travelled to Cambridge, and saw Kelly score both goals for the advance to the second round.

Paddy Rayment and Robbie Cooke were in the beaten Cambridge side. It was a result that pleased manager John Wile and had him beaming over the support that Posh got from their band of supporters, who urged Posh on throughout the game. The same weekend Trevor Parr, who had made his debut at Southend, was injured in a bottle attack in Bradford, and had doctors fearing for his sight as he was nearly blinded in the incident.

In the League, Posh dropped their first points of the season at London Road in a 1–1 draw with Darlington. Worrall gave Posh a 1–0 lead on 41 minutes, but the 5,341 crowd – the largest at London Road that season – saw MacLean snatch an equaliser for the Quakers 15 minutes from time. An away trip to Colchester resulted in a 3–1 defeat and left Posh still 5th in the table. Irving, Groves and Adcock put Colchester 3–0 up before Kelly pulled a goal back three minutes before half time. It left manager Wile puzzled, for their excellent home form was matched with an abysmal away record that kept them from the top of the table.

The next game was a tricky looking away tie to non–League Dagenham, who had in their side Richard Sutton, who made just one appearance for Posh two years earlier. The day was a disaster all round, not only the result – a 1–0 defeat – but also for a game marred with fighting throughout the match and the collapse of a wall that saw many fans injured. Posh demanded an F.A. enquiry into the game as the referee David Letts was alleged to have ended the match early. Neither the trouble nor the early end of the match could make up for Posh's dismal showing and poor finishing on the day. It was only the second time since Posh had joined the League that they had been defeated in the F.A. Cup by a non–League side.

The following week Wile moved to sign Southend United's striker Greg Shepherd, that he had been searching for for so many weeks. Shepherd made his debut in the match at Exeter, where Posh recorded only their second away League win, thanks to a Beech goal. Unfortunately in a reversal of form Posh took on top of the table Bury at home and lost 4–1, but despite the setback still sat at 6th position in the table 7 points behind their conquerors. Boxing Day saw them travel to the County Ground to play Northampton and a crowd of 4,350 saw Shepherd score his first goal for the Club, which was then added to by goals from Kelly, after 75 minutes, and Worrall 2 minutes from time, to put a smile back on the faces of the Posh supporters. The defeated Northampton side included Bobby Barnes, Ian Benjamin and Phil Cavener. Posh were disappointed though when three days later they visited Saltergate, an unsuccessful venue in the past, and lost 2–0. Ernie Moss scored the first goal for the 'Spireites'. New Year's Day saw Posh at home to Chester City and despite going a goal down in the 33rd minute they fought back to win 3–1 to keep in touch with the leaders at the top of the table. For Wile it was all change again with his squad, with Trevor Parr going to Irish League club Cork City, and Kelly plus Cassidy being placed on the transfer list.

Into the Club came Everald La Ronde on loan from Bournemouth, and Shawn Lowther a Canadian International who had been playing for Blyth Spartans in the Northern League. La Ronde made his debut in the home match with Hereford United at London Road. Kearns did the damage for Hereford again, giving them a six minute lead, but Johnson earned Posh a point with a 56th minute equaliser.

Lowther made his debut for the side in a Freight Rover Trophy game against Cambridge at London Road. Posh won 2-0 with goals from Slack and Quow. Ray Hankin returned to the side and Wile announced that he was to sign former Eire International Mick Martin from Cardiff City. The third consecutive home match was marked with victory versus Wrexham, Martin making his debut and Shepherd scoring both of Posh's goals. A week later Torquay were the 4th visitors to London Road in the space of three weeks, and Posh won again, this time 1-0 with another goal from Shepherd.

It was a series of results that lifted Posh back into contention at the top of the table as they were now 5th, six points behind leaders Bury, and just three points behind second placed Chesterfield. Posh went out of the Freight Rover Trophy losing the second leg of their tie by 2-0 to Cambridge. Steve Wilkins, the brother of England International Ray, made his debut for Posh, in what was to be his only appearance for the Club. Four days later Posh got back to League business when they visited Hartlepool. Alan Waddle, who had been released from Posh just a few weeks earlier, was playing for 'Pool. Two goals from Kelly and one from Hankin sunk the North Eastern Side and sent Posh to 3rd in the Table. The next match, at the Old Showgrounds, saw Posh take on Scunthorpe with England cricketer Ian Botham turning out for the home side, coming on as a sub nine minutes from time. By then Posh were already 2-0 down although Worrall pulled a late goal back. Posh then played away yet again, this time visiting Crewe. Tony Cliss scored the second goal for Crewe as they beat Posh 2-1 and Posh slipped down to 6th place in the table.

Ray Hankin announced that he wanted to leave the club and put in a transfer request to John Wile. Following a 0-0 draw at home to Port Vale, Hankin was sent off for the fifth time since he joined Posh, and his plea for a transfer request was deemed unnecessary as the following week Posh Manager Wile sacked him: *"Because of the persistent indiscipline on the field and despite previous verbal and written warnings as to his conduct, the Board of Directors has instructed me to terminate his contract forthwith"*. In his short but explosive career at London Road Hankin had become a firm favourite with the fans, but his nickname of Yosser from the terraces indicated his uncompromising style of play on the pitch. He left the club possessing the worst disciplinary record of any Posh player in their League history, but also one of the terrace fans' biggest idols.

Three consecutive draws then followed, and as the run up to the end of the season started, Posh's form took a real nose dive. They lost at home to Swindon, before travelling to Mansfield where they earned another point

in a goalless draw. Three days later they travelled to Blackpool where 17 year old Danny Reilly made his debut, coming on as a substitute to replace Wile. Posh were 3-1 down by then, and went on to lose the game 4-2. A home match against Northampton saw another goalless draw and the crowd slumped to alarming proportions, with only 2,482 present at the game.

Posh were now 10th in the table and with no hope of gaining promotion, but they recorded their first win in 11 matches when they won away at Chester. Worrall, Shepherd and Pike scoring the Posh goals. The overall dismal run continued with a home defeat by 4-1 to Southend, where Steve Phillips was among the scorers. The next home game, against Aldershot, produced a 2-1 defeat and also saw the lowest League crowd at London Road, when only 1,467 fans turned up to watch Posh's spineless end to the season. They made it four consecutive defeats when they lost at home to Colchester 1-0, Rudi Hedman scoring the goal after 30 minutes. The following game saw another record low crowd, with an attendance of just 1,464, turning up to watch Posh draw 0-0 with Exeter. They laid siege to the Exeter goal for most of the time but a combination of good goalkeeping from former Posh keeper Lee Smelt and some woeful finishing ensured a run of five games without victory. The last home game of the season came with another 0-0 draw, against Chesterfield. The point was enough for Chesterfield to clinch the 4th Division Championship. The events of the day however were overshadowed by the tragic events at Bradford, where the Main Stand burnt down at the Valley Parade Ground.

The season ended with Wile giving a Posh debut to Pat O'Keefe who came on as a substitute with 15 minutes to go, replacing Cassidy, in a 1-1 draw with Bury who finished 4th and were promoted to the 3rd Division. The point ensured that Posh finished 11th in the table, but the result was marred by another Posh player being sent off, when Slack was dismissed for violent conduct in the second half of the game. It was the end of yet another season that had started with so much promise and finished in disappointment for the expectant Posh faithful.

Big Ray Hankin in action against Torquay
A few weeks later he was sacked.

1985/86 SEASON

10 players were released during the close season, free transfers being given to Kenny Beech, Brian Klug, Mick Martin, Danny Reilly, Stuart Hicks, Simon Haigh and Paul Whittington. The club was also looking for offers for Neil Firm, Francis Cassidy and David Johnson. Other events off the pitch however were overshadowing Wile's attempts to rebuild his squad. Chairman Bill Wilde announced that Posh were up for sale if the bid was right. He was quoted in local newspapers as saying: *"If a Robert Maxwell or Elton John came along today and wanted to buy us out fair enough, the Directors would only be too glad to get out of it."*

Meanwhile close circuit television cameras were installed at London Road and the ban on alcohol being sold at Football Grounds was imposed. Mark Heeley, the one time teenage wonderboy from London Road, returned to start pre-season training again with the club, but after less than a week he quit. Posh fielded several trialists in the pre-season friendlies, including Len Cantello, Jackie Gallagher and Lil Fucillo in the home defeat at the hands of West Bromwich Albion. Following the game Jackie Gallagher signed for the second time for Peterborough. Meanwhile Posh's Assistant Manager Jimmy Holmes enjoyed a Testimonial Match in Dublin with his Eire side beating a Glen Hoddle X1 2-1 in front of 10,500 supporters. On the eve of the season Phil Chard signed on for Northampton, and Gallagher remained Wile's only signing, although he still had Kowalski, Cantello and Fucillo with the Club on trial. The first game was away at Preston and Posh made an explosive start to the season, Gallagher getting on the score sheet after just 2 minutes. Brazil equalised for Preston after 15 minutes, only for Worrall to restore Posh's lead one minute before half time. Thomas equalised eight minutes into the second half for Preston, but one more goal apiece from Worrall and Gallagher gave Posh an opening day 4-2 victory. In the side, last minute signing Alan Paris made his debut for Posh, along with Andy Kowalski and Lil Fucillo.

A postponement of the first round first leg Milk Cup Tie with Northampton was requested due to an injury crisis, but the match went ahead and Peterborough drew 0-0 at London Road. On the same day Wile announced that to boost his squad he was signing former England and Ipswich striker Trevor Whymark, on a week to week contract. Whymark made his debut in the second League match, at home to Chester, and two goals from Pike and one from Kowalski – his first for the Club – gave Posh their second victory. A mid week away trip to Orient resulted in a 2-2 draw before Posh came back to London Road to entertain Scunthorpe. In front of 2,928 Posh won 1-0 with a goal from Fucillo after just nine minutes.

Posh then went to visit Northampton in the second leg of the Milk Cup. Former Posh players Benjamin and Chard both played in a Cobblers side which won 2-0, thus ending Posh's cup progress. The following day Whymark was released from the club having played four games in his two week spell at London Road. Four days later Posh visited Rochdale and lost 2-1 before they came back to London Road to entertain Swindon Town, and an impressive display brought a 3-0 victory with 2 goals from Gallagher and one from Holmes from the penalty spot. This was followed with a home win over Torquay, leaving Posh in second place in the League, one point behind Southend, after seven games.

Following the Torquay victory, John Wile announced that he was to quit playing and had made his last appearance for Posh in the Swindon match. Posh visited Hereford and found themselves two goals down after 19 minutes, but despite Holmes pulling a goal back for Posh from the penalty spot, they spurned some late opportunities and lost their chance of points. A crowd of 3,700 was present for the Burnley game, and the Lancashire side became the first club to take a point at London Road. Off the pitch speculation was rife that the vacant Manager's job at West Bromwich Albion could be filled by John Wile.

Fuccillo scores his first goal for Posh against Scunthorpe which for a brief period took the team to the top of the table.

Posh Chairman Bill Wilde even went as far as having talks with his West Bromwich counterpart Sid Lucas after the game at Tranmere Rovers. The match at Prenton Park saw Posh leading 1-0 after 57 minutes, when a floodlight failure caused the match to be abandoned. The long saga of the future of Len Cantello also came to a conclusion during the week when he announced that his playing days were over, and he now wanted to go into management with a non-League club. Posh visited Hartlepool next where Gallagher gave them a 35th minute lead.

Borthwick levelled matters for Hartlepool four minutes later and a Hogan penalty two minutes from time gave the North East side a 2-1 win.

The following Monday John Wile announced that he would not be joining West Bromwich Albion, which prompted Chairman Bill Wilde to offer him an extension to his contract, which was accepted. Meanwhile Wile was scouring the non-League and reserve circuit to find a striker, hopefully to end Posh's scoring problems. Their run of three games without a win was extended when they entertained Northampton at London Road in front of a crowd of 3,866. It proved to be one of the most controversial of derbies between the two local rivals. Posh were one goal down after just two minutes, Chard scoring for the Cobblers. To make matters worse, only four minutes later, Turner fouled Morley inside the box and was sent off for the professional foul. Jimmy Holmes donned the goalkeeper's shirt but after nine minutes of the game a tame header from Mann was flicked through Holmes's arms and trickled over the line to make it 2-0. For a time it looked as if Posh would lie down and fold completely, but they showed great character in battling back. However as the game wore on 10 man Posh were overrun by the Cobblers, who scored three more times with goals from Mann (72 minutes), Cavener 3 minutes later, and Benjamin 5 minutes from time, to complete a 5-0 scoreline.

The poor run continued with drawn matches at Stockport and at home to Crewe. Wile made his 100th League appearance for Posh in the Crewe game, despite his earlier statement that he had retired from playing!

The next game was another local derby, this time against Cambridge United. The Manager brought in three new players for the game - Peter Corder (in goal), Doug McClure at midfield, and Tony Rees a striker on loan from Birmingham City. It made no difference however as Posh slumped to another disastrous performance with a 3-1 defeat. The situation worsened with the rearranged game against Tranmere Rovers, for this time it resulted in a 7-0 thrashing, Ian Muir scoring 4 goals, Manager Frank Worthington twice and Johnny Morissey netting the seventh. It was a result that left Manager John Wile speechless. Turner returned for the game at home against Exeter City and despite a goal from on loan striker Rees in the first minute, Posh could only manage a 1-1 draw. It was almost a repeat performance in the following game when Tony Rees gave posh a 1-0 lead after 19 minutes, only for a Slack own goal to level matters for Wrexham. This result now saw Peterborough lying 9th from bottom in the 4th Division. The frustrations continued with the third consecutive 1-1 draw when Posh visited Halifax. Worrall gave Posh the lead, but they threw it away again, when Gallagher grabbed an equaliser for Halifax after 21 minutes.

The following week Assistant Manager Jimmy Holmes announced that he was to leave the club, and hence giving Manager John Wile even more problems. It left Posh going into a tricky looking F.A. Cup tie away at Bishop's Stortford, which the club needed to win to keep some interest in the season alive.

Posh made their customary start after 17 minutes and went 1-0 ahead (through an own goal), but Duncan Hardy became the Bishop's Stortford hero when he equalised after 25 minutes. Worrall restored Posh's lead 10 minutes later but it was Hardy again who popped up with 20 minutes to play, and so ensured Bishops Stortford a replay at London Road. Posh's 13 match run without a win was finally ended against the non-Leaguers, in the replay. Cassidy put Posh 1-0 ahead up after 24 minutes and it looked as if it was going to be a case of 'dejavu' when Flynn equalised for the visitors on the hour, but two later goals, from Gallager in the 85th and Kowalski in the 87th minute, put Posh through to the second round of the Cup.

The following week Wile moved to sign Wakely Gage from Northampton, and he went straight into the team for their game at home to Port Vale on the Saturday. Vale had not lost for 12 matches and Posh had failed to win in the League for 11 games, but the odds were turned on their heads when Posh won 1-0 with a goal from Worrall after 6 minutes. The dismal away form continued (without a victory since the opening day), with defeat at Aldershot, the only goal being scored in the first minute. The following week saw Posh back in F.A. Cup action, and again paired with non-League opponents – Bath City this time – at London Road. In a drab game Posh just edged out the West Country men with a goal from Gallagher after 53 minutes. The prize that it brought however could set Peterborough's dismal season alight, for they were drawn at home against 2nd Division Leeds United.

The news that the Yorkshiremen were coming to play at London Road seemed to bring some interest back into the team and the supporters. They entertained Mansfield in the League the following week and ran out 4-2 winners with a much improved performance.

Another away defeat was suffered at Chester, then back at London Road Posh took on Orient on an icy pitch which saw a surprisingly entertaining game end as a 2-2 draw. John Wile again moved into the transfer market to strengthen his squad by bringing back Steve Collins, who had played for the club some two and a half years earlier. Collins was named as substitute when they faced Southend on New Year's Day, but he was not used in the 1-1 draw. Kelly put Peterborough ahead before Caddette levelled matters after 72 minutes.

The City was buzzing in anticipation with the visit of Leeds United in the next game, and a crowd of 10,137 turned up for the all ticket match, a restriction placed on them because of the violent reputation of Leeds United's travelling fans. The crowd that attended were to witness another one of Posh's great giantkilling acts. On an icy pitch things started badly for Posh as early as the 26th minute when Errington Kelly limped out of the game to be replaced by Greg Shepherd, who was unknowingly to become the Posh hero. The team started well in the second half, after a fairly evenly matched first period, when both teams battled to come to grips with the conditions. In the 67th minute Worrall sent across a corner that was only partially cleared, Cassidy played the ball back, leaving an unmarked Shepherd to send in a fine header from 18

yards. The home fans were obviously delighted, but three minutes later another disaster hit Posh when John Turner collided with Andy Ritchie on the edge of the box, at the London Road end. Turner was stretchered off with a broken leg, and Martin Pike took over in goal, with Posh left facing the 2nd Division side with only 10 men. In a storming end to the game Leeds came forward in search of the equaliser. As time ran out for the Yorkshire side they became increasingly frustrated, and in the 86th minute Scott Sellars had the ball in the net only to see it disallowed by the linesman for offside. Sellars was so incensed that he went to argue with the linesman's decision, and after an initial booking his continued arguing left the referee with no option but to give him his marching orders. As the snow swirled around the London Road pitch Leeds last effort was a Ritchie drive from a full 20 yards that rattled the top of the crossbar. It was to be Posh's day though and another famous victory was chalked up, with joyous scenes from the home fans at the end of the game.

The reward for beating Leeds was another home tie, against 2nd Division Carlisle or 1st Division Queen's Park Rangers. But Manager John Wile was in desperate need of a goalkeeper for the next fixture, at Scunthorpe, a week later. It looked as though Pat Jennings would be coming to London Road but he turned down John Wiles's offer, preferring to remain in Tottenham's Reserve team. In a farcical situation John Wile actually signed three goalkeepers the following week. The first to come on loan was Eric McManus but no sooner had he arrived at Peterborough, than he discovered that his side Bradford City did not want him Cup-tied, and he had to return to Yorkshire. Wile then moved to sign Jake Findlay, as well as bringing in 21 year old Mike Astbury on loan from York City. It was Astbury who was to make his debut for Posh in the following game. Unfortunately for him it was a losing start as Posh went down 2-0 at the Old Showground. They dropped more home points, drawing 1-1 with Preston, before Findlay announced that after 12 days at London Road he was leaving to join Portsmouth in the 2nd Division.

The Freight Rover Trophy tie away at Colchester resulted in a 4-1 hammering for Posh, and it was hardly the right preparation for their 4th round home tie four days later with 2nd Division Carlisle United. Despite their appalling League form, 8,311 fans turned up for the match and witnessed another Posh giantkilling. Shepherd the hero from the Leeds victory was again the danger man as he slotted Posh ahead after just five minutes. Instead of the rousing cup-tie that had been witnessed in the previous rounds, the match resulted in a fairly tedious game between the two sides, with most of the play in the middle of the field, and hence leaving the two goal-keepers with very little work to do. Posh's only moment of worry came in the last minute when a free kick from the edge of the box was fired in by Carlisle's Mick Halsall, but Astbury made a good save, and so Posh went through to the 5th round of the Cup.

Shepherd heads the 67th minute winner against Second Division Leeds in the F.A.Cup match.

Posh's nightmare continued in the League with a 1-1 draw away at Crewe along with the shock news that Errington Kelly had handed in a transfer request, and that defender Wakely Gage could be out for at least 3 weeks with a hamstring injury. The next round of the F.A. Cup was played at London Road against 2nd Division Brighton on a snow covered pitch. A crowd of 15,812 came to watch the match, and what a game it turned out to be!

In appalling conditions both sides contributed to an excellent contest, with all the goals coming in the last 17 minutes. It looked likely that Shepherd would again be the hero when he headed Posh in front after 73 minutes from Worall's free kick, but within two minutes Brighton struck back with a Dean Saunders goal. Posh then received a large slice of good luck when they took the lead in the 78th minute. Kelly, after beating defender Eric Young, shot more in hope than expectation from at least 25 yards. As the shot sped across the ground, Digweed seemed to have it well covered, only for the ball to hit an icy divot and cannon into the net to give Posh a 2-1 lead. It was really no more than Brighton deserved, although with 7 minutes left Jacobs grabbed the equaliser for the Seagulls to force a replay.

The bad weather resulted in no matches until the 1st of March, and a 1-1 draw at Burnley. Two days later Posh travelled to the Goldstone Ground and were cheered on by nearly 2,000 of their supporters. 19,010 watched the match, Brightons biggest crowd for over 2 years, but Saunders goal ended Posh's F.A. Cup dreams for another season. Goalkeeper Mike Astbury returned to York City, and John Wile finally signed Eric McManus on loan, who made his debut at home against Tranmere. The Mersey-siders achieved a double over Posh when a 19th minute goal gave them victory.

Three days later Posh entertained Hartlepool and ran out 3-1 winners in front of a crowd of 2,361, but another defeat followed as Posh lost 2-0 at Torquay. Morley and Hill gave Northampton a 2-0 half time lead in the return derby match, but late goals from Slack and Kelly earned Posh a point, although this left them 5th from bottom, and only on goal difference from the re-election zone. The alarming slide continued with a 1-0 away defeat at Exeter and two goalless games against Cambridge and Hereford, before finally getting back to winning ways with a much needed 1-0 win at Southend. A Bank Holiday Monday defeat at home to Colchester followed, before a Shepherd goal after 4 minutes secured another three valuable points from a visit to Wrexham. The next game was at home to Stockport who were 5th in the table and battling for promotion. Two early goals from Kowalski and Shepherd saw Posh cruise along to their second consecutive win, but the frustrated Stockport side let tempers boil over towards the end of the match, resulting in Chapman being sent off for a wild challenge on Quow, and Kelly and Sword getting their marching orders in the 84th minute, after getting involved in a scuffle on the pitch. Phil Cavener, who signed the previous week on a non-contract basis, made his debut for the Club in this stormy match. He played again in the next game, a 1-1 draw versus Halifax Town at London Road. Posh then travelled to meet a rampant Swindon Town side, who were 12 points clear at the top of the table, and with a game in hand. Goals from Bamber, Wade and Gordon in front of a crowd of 6,426 at the County ground saw Posh slide to a 3-0 defeat.

Posh then lost at Port Vale, before facing their third consecutive away game, at Colchester. Micky Nuttell was given his debut for the Club, but Posh were hammered 5-0 and they remained in the re-election zone and had everybody in the City nursing real doubts about whether the team could pull away from the bottom of the table. The following match was at home to Aldershot, another club in trouble, and a match that Posh had to win. They managed to do it in some style with goals from Fucillo after 42 minutes, Gallagher after 44 and a Paul Shrubb own goal after 75, which completed a 3-0 victory for Posh. Bobby Barnes played in the defeated Aldershot side. With two games left to play Posh were 4th from bottom, but they had a game in hand over their rivals.

It was announced that Peterborough United were to call an emergency Public Meeting the following week to discuss the future of the Club, although the officials were not giving away exactly what the agenda would be. A single goal from Quow after 14 minutes gave Posh the much needed win they desired against Mansfield at Field Mill, coupled with a 1-1 draw at home to Rochdale in the final game of the season, which saw Posh finish the campaign 8th from bottom with 56 points. It had been a close call, Cambridge who finished 3rd from bottom had only two points fewer. It was the end to another disastrous season for Posh that had seen home attendances dip below the 2,000 mark on a regular basis, and despite Posh's fantastic Cup run half way through the season it was going to need a major rebuilding job to get Posh back in the running as a promotion team.

The Public Meeting at the Cresset Centre attracted some 1,000 fans, who heard David Ringham announce a new rescue package for Peterborough United. The Club announced the launch of a scheme to be called 'The Posh Lifeline', with fundraising of up to £140,000 per year. The sole aim was to provide the money for John Wile to produce a successful side on the pitch.

1986/87 SEASON

This was one of the busiest pre-season's in Posh's history. With Peterborough United being voted into the Midland Intermediate League it would ensure that the youth team could compete with clubs of a high calibre. This announcement was followed almost immediately with the list of players that Wile was going to release. The departures included Trevor Slack, who went to Rotherham, and Martin Pike who joined 2nd Division Sheffield United – both for fees of around £20,000; Trevor Quow went to Gillingham, Andy Kowalski returned to Chesterfield, Errington Kelly drifted out of the game, and David Johnson, Francis Cassidy and youngster Patrick O'Keefe all moved on.

Among Wile's incoming signings were David Gregory – a former Posh player from Wrexham – Mark Nightingale (formerly of Norwich City) who came from Bournemouth, Geoff Doyle (a midfielder from Coventry), Derek Christie (Cardiff winger) and Andy Beasley a goalkeeper on loan from Mansfield Town.

With money from the Lifeline Scheme which had been set up the previous season, Wile then went on to sign Noel Luke from West Bromwich Albion, who had been on loan previously to Mansfield, but his biggest captures were Les Lawrence – a proven goal scorer in the lower divisions with Burnley, Aldershot and Torquay United, Paul Price the ex-Spurs player from Swansea, plus Brynn Gunn a man who had won a European Cup Winners Medal with Nottingham Forest.

With nine new players, Wile had virtually changed the squad in the course of the close season.

A crowd of 2,206 turned up at London Road for the pre-season friendly with Seville from Spain. The final result was decided by a penalty from Seville player Francisco after 41 minutes. In goal for Posh was yet another Wile signing, Kevin Shoemake, who was with the Club on a trial basis.

Other items of interest concerned the news that former idol of the London Road fans Tommy Robson had returned to the Club to be the Youth Team Manager, and also that Posh had clinched a new sponsorship deal with Fairview and would sport their name on the front of their new kit in the coming season.

The Club were honoured when they were advised that they would have the opportunity to stage the England Under-21 game against Yugoslavia at London Road. But just before the season started it was announced that John Turner, attempting a comeback from the broken leg that he sustained against Leeds United, had suffered a severe setback after cracking his shin during a training session.

A crowd of 3,548 turned up at London Road for the first game of the season which saw Posh take on Southend United. John Wile awarded debuts to no less than 6 players, namely: Andy Beasley in goal, Brynn Gunn, Paul Price, Mark Nightingale, Les Lawrence, Noel Luke and a seventh player, Derek Christie, who was on the substitutes bench. The new look Posh side started the season in style, Greg Shepherd giving Posh a 20th minute lead and Les Lawrence adding another after 81 minutes.

The former League Cup – and now Littlewoods Cup – started at Colchester United with a 0-0 draw, Derek Christie coming on after 77 minutes to make his debut for Posh. The second League game ended in a 1-0 defeat at Leyton Orient, a blow to the Posh who had done enough in the game to deserve at least a point. Gallagher was recalled to the side as substitute for the second leg of the Littlewoods Cup tie, and Christie also came into the side in place of Nightingale. Gallagher had been on the pitch for no more than three minutes before he scored his first goal of the season, and four minutes before the end of the match Luke scored his opener for the Club. The 2-0 victory took the Posh through to the second round of the Cup, with 1st Division Norwich City in opposition.

A Gregory goal in the 89th minute, gave Posh a point in the home League match with Aldershot, and in the next game (Posh's second on a Sunday), they took on Northampton at the County Ground. The local derby was watched by a crowd of 5,517 and after just 4 minutes Trevor Morley put Northampton ahead. A 41st minute penalty put the Cobblers further ahead, before Gregory managed to pull one back for the Posh after 76 minutes. Despite a grandstand finish from Posh they couldn't salvage the point they deserved from this entertaining game. After the good start to the season the 2-1 defeat to Crewe sent the team to third bottom of the table after 5 matches. To compound matters, Nightingale got himself sent off after 85 minutes, and it prompted the first murmurings of discontent from the London Road crowd who began calling for the resignation of Wile and the Board.

Micky Nuttall was drafted into the side that faced Norwich City in the 1st leg Littlewoods Cup tie at London Road.

It ended 0-0, in front of a crowd of 6,956, with the 1st Division leaders more than matched by a sporting Posh. This was the lift that Posh needed for in the next game they travelled to Colchester United and won 3-1. Lawrence scored after 44 minutes and a minute after half time Gregory added the second. Brynn Gunn provided the third with a penalty after 64 minutes, before Colchester pulled one back six minutes from time. John Wile named himself as substitute although he didn't bring himself on.

Home matches were still causing problems, and when the Posh took on Cardiff City they crashed to another defeat this time by 2-1, leaving the team anchored 5th from bottom of the 4th Division. Goalkeeper Shoemake had made his debut as Beasley had to pull out after a knee injury. The following week Wile released goalkeeper John Turner since after 9 months out of the game he had not been able to regain his fitness.

The next game brought no relief for Posh as the slump continued, this time to a 2-0 defeat at Hereford. It was no surprise, considering their form at that time, when they travelled to Norwich and were beaten 1-0. This brought their Littlewoods Cup run to an end, although the result didn't reflect the superb display that Posh managed to put up at Carrow Road. Despite the difficulties on and off the pitch a large contingent of travelling supporters cheered Posh on throughout the game, and it took a goal from Biggins after 48 minutes, to break the deadlock for the Canaries.

With an ever mounting injury list that was causing Wile selection problems, he moved into the transfer market and signed winger Russell Doig on a month's loan from Leeds United. Doig made his debut in the home game against Rochdale. A dismal 1-1 draw was no more than either side deserved, with Rochdale grabbing their goal from a Taylor penalty after 41 minutes and with Gunn replying, also from the penalty spot, in the 61st. Just 19 minutes later Brynn Gunn became the second Posh player to be sent off in the season, together with Rochdale's Wakenshaw, after what seemed to most onlookers as a minor incident.

A major incident occurred the following week when three Directors quit the Club. Former Chairman Bill Wilde, Cyril Duddington and Eric Nicholas all resigned saying they were not satisfied with the financial running of the Club. A fourth Director, Geoffrey Woodcock, also stated that he would be considering his position on the Board.

Despite their poor position, the midweek match at Wrexham turned out to be another thrilling game and Posh nearly pulled off one of their greatest comebacks, yet again returned home pointless. Jim Steel put Wrexham ahead after 9 minutes with Steve Massey adding a second just one minute later. Steel added his second of the night on 18 minutes and it looked as though Posh were about to suffer a massacre. There was nothing to relieve this position as Steel grabbed

his hat-trick on 31 minutes with Posh reeling from the continued attacks from the Wrexham side. Whatever Wile said at half time obviously did the trick though as Posh came back and grabbed a goal through Gallagher after 46 minutes. Three minutes later and David Gregory, who had formerly played for Wrexham, scored Posh's second to make it 4-2. Nightingale scored his first goal for the Club from a free kick in the 69th minute that set up a thrilling end to the game. Substitute Nuttall saw a header flash wide, and Doyle – one of Posh's better players on the night – produced a shot that was also just wide of the mark. The crowd gave both teams a rousing ovation when the match ended, but for Posh the harsh reality was that they were still anchored 5th bottom of the table with just 8 points from 10 games.

Geoffrey Woodcock finally became the fourth Director to quit the Posh Board when he announced that he would not stand for re-election at the Annual General Meeting later in October. The dissention within the Board became apparent when it was announced that the Club had a debt of almost £400,000. The situation looked very grim, with the team near the foot of the 4th Division table whilst off the field Posh had the biggest debt in their history.

Wile's misery was compounded when Mansfield goalkeeper Beasley returned to his Club. Posh answered back in the best possible way when they visited Hartlepool and won 2-1 after first going a goal down, but coming back through a Nobbs own goal and a Gunn winner 14 minutes from time. The crowd of 2,301 at London Road then saw Posh take on Swansea and Gallagher again salvaged a point for Posh with an equaliser 16 minutes from time. Not for the first time in the season it was a false dawn for Posh. The next game was at London Road against local rivals Lincoln City, and it was the Imps who scored the only goal of this match, through Gary Strodder after 53 minutes. Yet another inept display from Posh prompted the crowd's dissatisfaction to grow louder, with further calls for the removal of manager John Wile.

At the Club's Annual General Meeting which followed the Lincoln game, Shareholders called on John Wile to resign, and in unprecedented scenes they demanded that their views should be heard, with further criticisms of both the running of the Club and the team. Wile admitted a few days later that it had been the worst week of his football career, but that he had no intention of stepping down. Posh next travelled to Burnley and local player Steve Collins made his 200th appearance for the Club when Posh drew 0-0. It turned out to be John Wile's last game in charge of Peterborough United, for despite the manager's determination to stay at the Club the Board of Directors made their own decision and sacked him just hours after the match at Turf Moor. Lil Fucillo the player/coach was appointed as Caretaker Manager, temporarily taking over team affairs. Rumours soon circulated in the City that former Posh Boss Noel Cantwell would be the favourite to come back to London Road as the new Manager.

Fucillo's first game in charge started with a victory at London Road with a 2-1 victory over Tranmere – but in front of 1,812, the lowest crowd of the season – the result lifting them to 7th from bottom. The following day Russell Doig returned to Leeds United after his loan period had ended and Steve Phillips, a proven goal scorer in the lower divisions, signed for Posh on a month's loan from Torquay United.

Rumours were rife as to who would be coming in to the hot seat as the Manager of Posh, the two most likely candidates being Cambridge United boss Chris Turner, and Halifax's Mick Jones. The pair were former Posh players and were both reported to be interested, but Cantwell's name still loomed larger in the background than any of the others.

Steve Phillips made his debut for Posh when they travelled to Exeter and drew 1-1, it was also his 500th Football League appearance which he celebrated by cancelling out Robson's first minute goal for Exeter with an equaliser 7 minutes from time. A diversion for the fans was the next match at London Road, with the England Under-21 International versus Yugoslavia which was drawn 1-1. The England side that night included such names as Stuart Pearce, Tony Adams, David Rocastle and Nigel Clough.

Posh's next match was an F.A. Cup tie at Northampton Town and it proved to be Caretaker Manager Lil Fucillo's first defeat as Posh were well beaten 3-0 in front of a 9,114 crowd. It was a big blow to the Supporters, but they got the perfect tonic when the following Wednesday, the 20th of November, Noel Cantwell was named as Posh Manager – the second time that he had held the position. The acclaim with which the appointment was received says something for the charisma of the man and how important he was to the Peterborough Supporters. The local newspaper heralded his return as that of 'The Messiah'. It was a reaction that was endorsed by the Peterborough Directors, for despite applications from managers of the calibre of Ian Porterfield, Eoin Hand and Chris Catlin, Cantwell was the only man interviewed for the job.

Ironically Cantwell made his debut as Posh Manager for the visit to local rivals Cambridge United. The Cambridge manager, Chris Turner, was one of Cantwell's protege's when he was in charge of Peterborough in the seventies, and Turner was strongly tipped to take over as the Posh Assistant Manager. David Gregory equalised an early John Beck goal to earn Posh a 1-1 draw. After the game Turner announced that he was staying at the Abbey and would not be joining Cantwell as his assistant. Posh travelled to Colchester to meet them for the fourth time that season to play in a Freight Rover Trophy game. Posh lost 2-1, and Cantwell started his search to bring new players to the Club.

Posh entertained Preston North End for Cantwell's home 'debut', and his incredible pulling power in Peterborough was demonstrated with the gate of 3,462, a big increase from previous attendances of less than 2,000. Goals from Luke after 64 minutes and Steve Phillips 5 minutes later put Posh 2-0 up, and despite Preston pulling a goal back with 6 minutes to play, the team hung on to give Cantwell his first win in his first match back at London Road.

Cantwell's first moves into the transfer market saw striker Errington Kelly return to London Road, and the next capture was Steve Phillips who finally put pen to paper when he was signed for a £4,000 fee. A crowd of 3,153 came to London Road for the next match and Posh beat Halifax 2-0. Halifax manager Jones returned to London Road the following week, to become Cantwell's Assistant Manager. Another new arrival was 19 year old Arsenal goalkeeper Nicky Hammond, on loan, as cover for Kevin Shoemake.

Posh next appeared on Boxing Day, at home to Scunthorpe United. Russell gave Scunthorpe a 20th minute lead which Luke equalised 5 minutes later. It was a bruising battle, for neither side could break the deadlock, despite the dismissal of Scunthorpe's David Harle for a 52nd minute foul. The crowd of 4,267, was the highest of the season at that time at London Road. Posh were then beaten 3-1 at Stockport, but then made some amends on New Year's Day when they swamped Wolverhampton Wanderers with a stunning 3-0 victory. Phillips scored after 40 minutes, Gallagher after 78 and Luke got the third in the final minute. Posh's second home game on a Sunday took place the following week against Cambridge United in the local derby. Another good crowd – of 4,713 – watched a bruising encounter, but Posh triumphed. Kimble gave Cambridge the lead, Luke grabbed a goal in the 69th minute and 5 minutes from time Kelly blasted home a close range effort, much to the delight of the London Road crowd.

Cantwell moved to sign yet another goalkeeper on loan when John Smeulders arrived from Torquay United to back up Kevin Shoemake, following the departure of Nicky Hammond. Posh's climb up the table continued after a 2-2 draw with second placed Southend United which lifted them to 10th in the League. As a big freeze struck most matches in the Football League, Peterborough actually managed to get their next home match underway. After a massive pitch clearing operation to clear snow from the surface Posh entertained Orient on a bone hard pitch, and lost 1-0.

John Smeulders came in for his Posh debut, when they travelled to Aldershot and came back with a 1-1 draw. The home clash with Northampton Town attracted a large crowd of 7,911, and it was former Posh player Ian Benjamin who scored the only goal of the game to give the visitors a 1-0 victory. Tragedy almost struck after Steve Collins collided with Peter Gleasure, the Northampton goalkeeper, when he was knocked unconscious, and it was only the prompt action of physio Bill Harvey that saved Steve's life.

The attendance marked a remarkable turnabout in Posh's crowd figures that season, since before Cantwell's arrival the average was 2,546, but this had now risen to nearly 4,500.

Posh won their next game, against Wrexham, followed by a 3-1 victory at Crewe. This was the response to Cantwell's rallying call of one big effort from his players to try and achieve a promotion or play off place. The remarkable reversal in League form had seen Posh come from 4th bottom to 9th in the table. To back up his words Cantwell also launched the start of *"The Cantwell Crusade"*. It was to be a fundraising drive to raise £100,000 to pay for new players to back up the promotion bid.

Posh made it three consecutive wins with a 2-0 home victory over Colchester United, with Phillips and Gallagher the scorers. Within eight days *"Cantwell's Crusade"* had brought in a staggering £15,000 and Posh now stood 6th in the table. When they visited Cardiff, Cantwell called for an all out attack, and it brought its rewards as a goal from Noel Luke seven minutes from time gave Posh their 4th consecutive victory. The next game was at London Road, and a crowd of 4,304 came to watch Posh take on Burnley. Gallagher gave Posh a 29th minute lead and it looked as though they were on their way to victory number five, before the Lancashire club equalised after 62 minutes. Within a minute former Posh player Billy Rodaway upended Gallagher in the box, which gave Steve Phillips the chance for Posh to take their well deserved victory. But despite seeing keeper Needham dive the wrong way the spot kick flew over the bar into the London Road end, and Posh had to be content with a single point. The team soon got back to their winning ways when they visited Lincoln City for another Sunday game. Lund put Lincoln 1-0 up, but Luke and Phillips with two goals within 10 minutes gave Posh the 3 points and put their promotion efforts back on course.

Steve Phillips drives home the
winning goal at Lincoln City.

However, just as things were going so well, a new row blew up that split the supporters down the middle, when the Directors announced that they would sell the present London Road Ground for ten million pounds and move to a new purpose built stadium to the East of Peterborough, just off Fengate.

Cantwell was named as Bell's *"Manager of the Month"*, and in typical Cantwell style he announced that he would be throwing a party after the Hartlepool game. When questioned if it would be regardless of the outcome Cantwell replied that he didn't see the outcome of the game becoming a problem! As usual he was correct, Posh running out 3-1 winners with goals from Phillips, Luke and Kelly, and a climb to 4th in the table. Cantwell as promised held his party. The only minor blemish on the day was a demonstration by a couple of hundred fans at half time and after the match, protesting against the proposed switch to a new ground.

Posh made a mid-week trip to Swansea City and returned with three points, with Luke's 42nd minute goal. For the next game, at Rochdale, Cantwell called upon Posh fans to travel to Spotland and match the Rochdale supporters in number. He very nearly got his wish as almost 700 saw their impressive run come to an end. They recovered from a 2-0 deficit, with two Gregory goals, but just a minute after the equaliser Rochdale fought back to make it 3-2. Cantwell eventually went into the transfer market to sign the cover that had been required all season for Shoemake, and Paul Crichton – a reserve team goalkeeper from Nottingham Forest – was brought to the Club. Young striker Micky Nuttall went to Nottingham Forest to train as part of the loan deal.

With 10 games remaining Posh were in 4th place and still looking good for promotion. A crowd of 4,110 watched them beat Hereford at London Road 2-1, Gunn scoring a penalty after 28 minutes to cancel out Spooner's own spot kick 8 minutes earlier. Wakely Gage was the Posh hero, when he scored his first goal for them in his 300th Football League appearance. It was again one of the lowly clubs that became Posh's undoing when they slipped up with an away defeat at Torquay United. Promotion jitters became more evident when they entertained Exeter City at London Road. The visitors were also on the fringe of the play-off race, and they drew 2-2. The following week Alan Paris was named by his fellow professionals in the P.F.A. 4th Division Select side. But the pressure was now stepping up on Posh, and despite extending their unbeaten run with a 1-1 result at Tranmere, draws were no longer enough, for it was victories that were required.

The crunch game for Posh came with the visit of Wolverhampton Wanderers to London Road. The Wolves were four points ahead of Posh, and with 6 games remaining it was vital for Posh's promotion chances that they did not lose. An excellent crowd of 9,360 attended, and watched Steve Bull give Wolves a lead after just 2 minutes. It proved to be the only goal of the game and

virtually secured the fourth and final promotion spot for the Midlands team. This left only play-off places open to the chasing pack for there was now a 7 point gap between Wolverhampton and Peterborough. The dream finally faded with defeat at Scunthorpe, for with four games remaining Posh were now in 7th position – the final play-off spot – but only on goal difference from Aldershot who had one game in hand, and four points ahead of Wrexham who had two matches in hand.

The next game, at home to Torquay United, ended with the right result, but with some disgraceful scenes on the pitch at the end of the game. Gunn gave Posh the lead on the half hour but the real action was confined to the last few minutes of the game. Derek Dawkins equalised for Torquay with barely a minute left to play and feelings were running high among the Posh fans as they saw their final chances of promotion slipping away. But within 60 seconds of the equaliser Collins handled in the box. As Gunn stepped up to take the penalty, Kenny Allen guessed right and dived low to his right to save the spot kick, but Gunn followed up and slotted home the rebound to give Posh a 2-1 victory. As the players left the pitch Allen was involved in a scuffle with some 'fans' and was punched and thrown to the floor. Paul Crichton made his debut for the Peterborough side, and the game also marked the first change in the team for 14 games, that run being the longest in Posh's history without change; this bettered the record set by a Jimmy Hagan side of the 1960/61 season. After a stirring season Posh's promotion hopes finally petered out with three goalless performances at the end of the season, drawing 0-0 at Preston and at home to Stockport County, before losing to Halifax in the last match. Cantwell used this final game at The Shay to blood some new youngsters, giving debuts to Adrian Fife, Gary Butterworth and Ashley Carr; the average age of the team was just 22.

It left Posh just short of their illusive dream of promotion from the 4th Division, but Cantwell had brought about a remarkable change in fortunes, picking up a Club at the foot of the table when he arrived, and leaving it just short of promotion. An incredible achievement from Peterborough's favourite son.

Noel Cantwell

Cantwell started the season in search of new talent with a £25,000 bid for Clyde defender Paul Flexney but this was rejected by the Scottish Club. Meanwhile he gave free transfers to Lil Fucillo, Wakely Gage, David Gregory and Geoff Doyle, and returned 18 year old goalkeeper Paul Crichton to Nottingham Forest. Derek Christie who had never recovered from a series of injuries had his contract terminated by the Club. Tommy Robson took his Youth Team for a five match tour of West Germany, and included in the squad were Gary Butterworth, Micky Nuttall, Adrian Fife, Jeremy Mould, Lee Philpotts and Ashley Carr. The Team triumphed, beating German side Osnabruck 4-2 in the final, with Steven George being voted the outstanding keeper of the tournament.

Meanwhile Posh's loyal servant Bill Harvey picked up the Football League's top award for Football Club staff. 67 year old Bill was awarded the Football League Executive Staff's Association's award honouring his services to Football. He won the award ahead of people of the calibre of Watford's Bertie Mee, and followed in the footsteps of the likes of Bill Nicholson and Jimmy Cyril.

Cantwell's first pre-season signing was Gary Pollard from Mansfield on a free transfer. Wakely Gage left and joined 4th Division rivals Crewe, whilst Geoff Doyle travelled to Australia to play for Morwell in the Australian Victoria State League. Jackie Gallagher also departed, joining 4th Division rivals Wolverhampton Wanderers. The next signing was goalkeeper Joe Neenan on a free transfer from Burnley, and this was followed by the signing of Grimsby midfielder Mick Halsall. Halsall's move was only possible from funds raised through *"Cantwell's Crusade"* and the Lifeline Appeal. The £25,000 fee was the biggest sum splashed out on a Posh player since 1979. Posh then tied up a deal with a new sponsor, when Charles Wells Breweries agreed to pay for their name on the front of the Club shirts for the coming season. As Posh started their pre-season warm up period David Riley joined the Club on loan from Nottingham Forest. The final piece of Cantwell's team building came with the signing on August 12th of the man that Cantwell described as *'the best midfield player in the 4th Division'*, Micky Gooding from Rotherham, who cost Posh another reported £25,000.

Just three days later Posh got their 4th Division campaign underway, against Carlisle, at London Road. Making their debuts for Posh were Joe Neenan in goal, Micky Gooding, Gary Pollard, David Riley and Mick Halsall. An encouraging crowd of 3,800 turn up and saw Micky Gooding score after 23 minutes to give Posh three points. In mid-week Posh travelled to Chesterfield to start their Littlewoods Cup campaign where they lost 2-1 which left manager Cantwell fuming. Dave Caldwell had given Chesterfield the lead, with what looked like a punch of the ball.

Errington Kelly equalised after half an hour only to see Chesterfield take a 2-1 victory on the night, courtesy of a hotly disputed penalty after Alan Paris was adjudged to have handled the ball.

Posh travelled to Rochdale for their next League match, and David Riley scored his first goal for the Club after 39 minutes. Derek Parlane equalised for Rochdale and Posh returned from Spotland with a 1-1 draw. Cantwell vowed that Chesterfield would pay for their disputed victory over Posh in the 1st leg of the Littlewoods Cup. Posh took the lead through Gunn after 35 minutes – from the penalty spot – and just before the hour Tristan Benjamin put through his own net to give them an aggregate 3-2 victory. Darren Bradshaw was in the beaten Chesterfield side.

Posh's third League game, with Cambridge United, ended in victory, but this was a tempestuous affair marred with bad-tempered fouls, bookings and sendings off. After 22 minutes Errington Kelly was given his marching orders, for alleged retaliation following a foul, and 3 minutes later Peter Butler was dismissed for a late tackle. The following game was also at home, against Darlington, but ended in defeat. Mark Hine was in the Darlington side that was victorious at London Road that day.

At this time, Posh unveiled plans to leave their London Road ground and move to a new one at the edge of town.

The next trip was away to Colchester United, who had introduced an all-members scheme that banned away fans from attending games at Layer Road. The ban didn't stop all the fans however as a sprinkling of Posh fans were among the 1,164 who watched Colchester sweep them aside with a 4-1 win. The game was in stark contrast to Posh's next game which was an all ticket affair against Wolverhampton Wanderers. However the all ticket restriction was placed upon the Black Country club because of the reputation of their travelling fans rather than the large numbers coming to attend. 3,089 watched Posh draw 1-1 after Gooding equalised with a 56th minute penalty following a Steve Bull goal early in the first half. Les Lawrence, who two games earlier had returned from a 10 month period of absence thorough injury, scored his second goal in three games when Posh beat Wrexham at London Road 1-0.

It was just the boost that Posh needed before they took on 2nd Division Plymouth in the 2nd round 1st leg of the Littlewoods Cup. Gerry McElhinney and Steve Cooper were in the Plymouth side that were trounced 4-1 at London Road. The goals came from Lawrence after 18 minutes, Gooding after 26, and Halsall 16 minutes later to put Posh 3-0 up at half time. Tommy Tynan grabbed one back with 21 minutes to play, but Riley later made it 4-1, and sealed their passage to the 3rd round of the Cup.

Meanwhile off the pitch Steve Phillips headed for Exeter City on loan after Cantwell had axed him from the team. Posh lost 2-0 at Orient, a result that left Posh 8th from bottom of the League. A 'tongue-in-cheek' bet by Manager Noel Cantwell cost him £50 in their next match, when Posh won 1-0 at Edgar Street to beat Hereford United. Cantwell pledged £50 for Alan Paris to 'break his duck', Paris having made 100 League appearances for Posh, but never having scored for them. Paris duly received his debut goal to give Posh a much needed win! A spectacular goal from Micky Gooding in Posh's next game at home against Scunthorpe United earned in a 1-1 draw.

David Riley had his loan extended, which was good news for the Club, and not being 'cup-tied', he was able to play in the Littlewoods Cup match at Plymouth. A spirited 1-1 draw saw Posh comfortably go through to the next round on a 5-2 aggregate score. The reward for ousting the Devon side was a home tie against 2nd Division Reading, a tough game but hardly the glamour side that Cantwell had hoped for. Back in the League, Les Lawrence found the back of the net again, giving Posh another win, at Stockport. Three days later in an explosive match at Layer Road, Posh lost to Colchester 3-2 in a Freight Rover Trophy game. The match saw Micky Nuttall score his first 1st team goal for the Club, but Mick Halsall was sent off in the tunnel after leaving the pitch at the end of the game.

The talk off the pitch at this time was of Posh's cash crisis and the fact that the Club were still over £400,000 in debt. They were therefore unable to afford David Riley, and he left to join Port Vale for a reported £15,000. The following day it was announced that the City Council had rejected Peterborough United's package to sell their ground to the ASDA Supermarket chain and move to a new ground in Paston.

On the field Posh entertained Cardiff City at London Road in their next match in what turned out to be the League game of the season. Mike Ford rifled home a 20 yard drive to put Cardiff 1-0 in the lead after 14 minutes, but a spectacular Gooding overhead kick levelled matters with 25 minutes gone. Four minutes before half time Ford struck again for Cardiff to put them ahead, but five minutes after the break Lawrence levelled matters with a header from Halsall's free kick. In a seesaw game, just 5 minutes later, ex-Arsenal player Brian McDermott crashed Cardiff back into the lead with another shot from outside the box. The 3,473 crowd were certainly getting good entertainment, for Luke made it 3 goals in 6 minutes almost straight from the restart and he also turned out to be the match winner. With just 12 minutes remaining he hammered home the rebound from a Mick Halsall shot which had struck the post.

On the 20th October 1987 it was announced that a mystery businessman was heading a rescue package to take over the ailing City Club and clear its debts.

Meanwhile the players continued unaffected, and secured a fine 3-0 win over Newport County. Gooding grabbed his first hat trick for Posh with a header after 12 minutes, a chip over stranded keeper Paul Bradshaw after 37 minutes, and with time running out grabbed his third with just a minute to play, from his second header of the night following Mick Halsall's corner.

Speculation continued about the future of the Club as Chairman Steve Kendrick upped the asking price for Peterborough United to £500,000. He also added that whatever the outcome of the bid it was almost certain that Posh would go to the High Court in London the following Monday to seek permission to appoint an Administrator to run the Club's finances. Posh's improved form in the League continued as they returned from Halifax with a 0-0 draw, and as predicted the following Monday, October the 26th, an administrator was applied for. It ensured that all the Club's debts were immediately frozen and it was then up to the Administrator to put forward a proposal to the Creditors to decide which way the Club should be run. It prompted Peterborough City Council Leader, Charles Swift, to call an extraordinary meeting of the Council to discuss Posh's future and the support it would get from the City.

It was with this backdrop that Posh entertained 2nd Division Reading at London Road in the 3rd round of the Littlewoods Cup. A crowd of 6,285 watched Posh match their rivals in every department and come away with a goalless draw. Off the pitch the Administrators started their work and their first move was to dismiss Secretary Arnold Blades and Youth Team Manager Tommy Robson. Speculation was rife that Noel Cantwell was the next man to be axed by the Administrator (Richard Summerfield), and the dismissals were followed by Chairman Steve Kendrick tendering his resignation. The reasons cited for the moves were lack of communication and a clash of personalities with the Administrators. Tommy Robson announced that he would come back in charge of the Posh Youth Team in a purely voluntary capacity, but Ellis Stafford, from the Commercial Department, and another long serving member of Peterborough United — both as a player and a member of the backroom staff — also resigned.

On Sunday November 1st, Arnold Blades organised a meeting for a movement which was very aptly christened *"SOS POSH"*, in a bid to raise £500,000 to save the Club. In just 48 hours supporters pledged £100,000 to keep the Club going. Blades's movement gained the support of Steve Kendrick, Ellis Stafford and the current Manager Noel Cantwell. In the next match Posh entertained Torquay United at London Road and lost 2-0. The Club had been torn asunder and fans showed their displeasure at half time as several hundred supporters invaded the pitch and sat down in front of the Directors' box. Noel Cantwell came out to address the disgruntled fans and asked the fans to clear the pitch promising that he would return to speak to them after the match.

Cantwell was as good as his word and addressed the fans after the game, stating:

" The heart has been ripped out of the Club. I don't know how we are going to recover, somebody is going to have to try and pick up the pieces and get on with it."

The Club was in the middle of the biggest crisis in its history and the fans were starting to show their displeasure with the situation. The biggest anger being reserved for Cantwell's position, which was under threat. He was still the most prominent personality at Peterborough United, as summed up on a protestor's banner on the pitch at the Torquay game that pronounced:

"You Don't Sack Kings".

The following week 1,000 supporters turned up at London Road for another *"SOS POSH"* meeting. Cantwell was there again, giving the supporters the lead that they needed. Addressing them he called for fans to rally round the Club: *"I believe in Peterborough, there are enough of us to keep this Club going. Everybody has got to work in the same direction and I am sure we can do it together."*

As events off the pitch gathered pace, City businessman Roger Speechley saved the future of Noel Cantwell by agreeing to pay his wages, and it was announced that Steve Kendrick would sever his connections with the Club by resigning from the Board of Directors. People around the City were now joining a rallying call to get behind the Club. The City Council voted unanimously to work out a deal to save the Club as local businessmen tried to get together a package to clear the Club's debts. Peterborough engineering company *Peter Brotherhood's* pledged to pay the wages of Youth Team Boss Tommy Robson for the rest of the season.

Posh got back into action on the pitch by visiting Reading in the replay of their Littlewoods Cup-tie which they lost 1-0 to a goal after 28 minutes, but they went out with their heads held high. Events escalated in the board room, and after pressure from the City Council and the general public, the final three Directors (Mike Lewin, David Ringham and Alf Hand) stepped down and resigned from the Board.

On the field performances continued to slide, Posh losing at home to Hartlepool in front of 3,200 fans. Everyday the local newspaper seemed to bring news of a new package to save Posh, whether it be from the City Council or from local businessmen, but nothing had been decided when Posh made their bow in the F.A. Cup with a home tie against Cardiff City. Two goals from Micky Gooding gave Posh passage through to the 2nd round in a 2-1 victory in front of 3,600 supporters. Unfortunately the match was marred with ugly scenes at the end of the game as fans from both sides spilled onto the pitch and fought running battles which resulted in twelve arrests. The reward for winning the game was to be paired with 1st round giantkillers Sutton United who had beaten 3rd Division Aldershot 3-0. In the League, Posh's slide down the table continued with a 2-1 defeat at Swansea, resulting in 8th position from the foot of the table. As November came to a close Posh took on Burnley and came out with their biggest win of the season, a 5-0 thrashing. Goals came from Gooding (2), Paris, Collins and Kelly. The confidence boosting result was followed a few days later with a home win over Cambridge United 3-0 in the Freight Rover Trophy, to give Posh a place in the knock-out section of the competition.

Posh then made history, and not for the first time for all the wrong reasons. It was Posh's 100th cup-tie, and for the first time they were beaten on their home soil by a non-League side, for Sutton United triumphed 3-1. A crowd of 4,400 watched Les Lawrence score a goal at either end before 7 minutes of the game had passed! But Sutton then went on to claim a famous victory. Cantwell immediately dived into the transfer market and brought in United States International John Kerr on a one month loan from Portsmouth. He was joined by Dale White, who also came in on loan, from top of the 3rd Division Club Sunderland. Both players made their debuts when Posh visited League new boys Scarborough, their first visit to Seamer Road since the two clubs were rivals in the Midland League. Simon Lowe gave Scarborough the lead after 19 minutes, before Luke claimed a point with an equaliser after 66. Cantwell complained bitterly when the referee disallowed another Luke effort after 84 minutes for what seemed a harsh offside decision.

Mick Halsall scores against Cambridge United in the 3-1 victory.

As Christmas approached Posh entertained Crewe on a Friday night at London Road and were hammered 4-0. Posh made it three consecutive home defeats, losing to Orient on Boxing Day, before visiting Tranmere who won 3-1 to bring to a close a torrid end to 1987. The New Year could only see an improvement both on and off the field and it came as Posh beat local rivals Cambridge United 3-1 at the Abbey.

It was just the boost they needed and they then returned to London Road and beat Colchester 2-0, Dale White scoring his first goal in the Football League, with Noel Luke securing the result seven minutes from time.

Cantwell again turned to America in his search for new players, and another United States International, Bruce Murray, joined the Club on trial. Posh's next home match saw them entertain second bottom of the table Rochdale. White scored his second goal for Posh to claim Posh's equaliser, after John Moore had given the visitors a 4th minute lead. Peterborough's first defeat of 1988 came with a visit to the Racecourse Ground where they lost 3-1 to Wrexham. John Kerr scored his first goal in the Football League, but two goals from Kevin Russell and one from Bourne youngster Shaun Cunnington a minute from time gave Wrexham the points.

Posh were hit with another bombshell when it was announced that they had been summoned to appear before the Football League to answer allegations of making irregular payments. It raised the spectre of 1967 all over again as one of the possible disciplinary actions, should they be found guilty, included expulsion from the 4th Division.

Kevin Shoemake returned in goal when Posh progressed to the next round of the Freight Rover Trophy with a 2-1 win at Walsall. Fred Barber was in goal for the Saddlers but he could not stop goals from Ashley Carr and Micky Gooding. Rumours were now rife that Posh would shortly have a new owner, the favourite being multi-millionaire and former Luton Chairman Dennis Mortimer, who was confident of winning the 'race'. Other packages included a rescue bid from the City Council to make them the Club's largest shareholder, and a bid from a Consortium led by John Dollimore the Club's Financial Controller, that involved several other money making schemes. The story took another twist, when, at the end of January, Dollimore left Posh by mutual consent and the former Club Secretary, sacked by the Administrator, returned to help out on a voluntary basis. On Thursday January 28th, The Football League announced that Posh had been fined £2,500 by the Commission of Inquiry having been found guilty of irregular payments to players. It centred around the transfer to the Club of Micky Gooding, and the Football League announced that the matter was now closed.

Promotion chasing Bolton were the next visitors to London Road, and they left as convincing 4-0 winners. A 'flu virus struck the Posh players that prompted Manager Cantwell to ask for a postponement of their Freight Rover Trophy tie away to Wolverhampton Wanderers the following night. The Football League agreed, but Wolves rejected the idea and insisted that the match went ahead. It was no real surprise when the home side – six points clear at the top of the 4th Division – ran out 4-0 winners. Paul Benning came on as a second half substitute to make his debut for Posh.

On Wednesday February 10th, City Councillors voted overwhelmingly in favour of a £1.5m package that would save Peterborough United. Meanwhile on the pitch Posh beat Tranmere at London Road 2-1, the goals coming from White after 11 minutes and Kelly after 66. This was followed by a 2-0 victory at Carlisle. Posh's topsy-turvy form continued when they returned to London Road to take on lowly Hereford, and lost 2-1; Hereford's second goal came with just one minute left to play. Andy Flounders scored a hat-trick for Scunthorpe when Posh were hammered 5-0 away in their next game. It was to be Posh's last visit to the Old Showgrounds, as Scunthorpe announced the following week that they were due to go to a new purpose built ground at Glanford Park on the edge of the town.

Posh travelled to Cardiff City and returned with a 0-0 draw before Cantwell brought in David Corner from Sunderland, another player on loan. Corner made his debut in the 1-0 victory at Exeter City, but White, a man that Cantwell had wanted to sign on a free transfer, turned down the Club to return to Roker Park, unhappy that he had only been offered terms until the end of the season.

On March 11th it was announced that the City Council's plan to save Posh could yet be abandoned following a new Bill enforced by Environment Secretary Nicholas Ridley in Central Government.

A scoreless draw at home to Stockport kept Posh in 14th place in the table before they travelled to Darlington and lost 2-1. Another goalless draw followed at Torquay United, before Posh pulled off their result of the season by beating League leaders Wolves at Molineux. Micky Gooding scored the only goal of the game after 70 minutes in front of a crowd of 8,049. It was Gooding again who was Posh's saviour in their next match, when they beat 6th from bottom Halifax 1-0 at London Road – Gooding's goal coming from a penalty one minute from time.

Rumour had been rife for several few months that Bolton Wanderers were interested in taking away Posh's dynamic midfield pairing Micky Halsall and Micky Gooding. But Halsall killed the speculation by announcing that as soon as Bolton's interest had been declared he had seen Manager Cantwell to confirm that he was happy to stay at London Road.

Posh gained their third consecutive 1-0 victory, this time at Hartlepool, but the run came to an end with defeat at home to Swansea City, with the Welshmen well in the hunt for a play-off spot. The next trip was away to Newport County for their last ever League visit to Somerton Park. The struggling Welsh side could only field a team which included within it four Y.T.S. players. A crowd totalling just 988 was boosted by a couple of hundred visiting Peterborough fans who witnessed Steve Phillips produce the last ever League hat-trick to be scored on Newport's ground.

Mark Nightingale also scored in Posh's 4-0 victory that was all too easy, but it at least guaranteed them another three points in their late bid for a play-off spot. Errington Kelly meanwhile left the Club to play in Sweden, and Cantwell called for maximum points from Posh's last four games to achieve the final play-off place available.

In a break from League matches 1,300 fans turned out to honour Posh's Physio. Bill Harvey. A Posh XI, including Coventry's Micky Gynn and Gillingham's Trevor Quow, played in the Testimonial Match against Leicester City, as a tribute to this popular and much respected 67 year old Club official. Posh took the lead with a goal from youngster Dominic Genovese, Leicester equalised through Nick Cusack and in injury time another local youngster, Gary Butterworth, drove home Posh's winner. Posh grabbed the first of the four wins that Cantwell wanted when they beat Exeter City at London Road 2-1. Paul Benning made his League debut for Posh as did Dominic

Genovese, but Micky Gooding, as on so many occasions during the season saved the team with his goals, grabbing both, the second from the penalty spot. Posh moved to 8th in the table, and an away victory at Burnley - with goals from Halsall and Luke late on in the game - left them with two games remaining and three points away from a play-off spot. Despite a 0-0 draw in their final home game of the season against Scarborough, Posh entered their last match of the season knowing that if they won and Orient or Swansea lost they could still clinch a place in the play-offs.

The final match was at Crewe Alexandra and in a stirring display Posh got the win that they needed with Noel Luke scoring the only goal of the game after 40 minutes. It was enough to overhaul Leyton Orient, but with Swansea also winning, Posh were condemned to 7th spot, and hence missing out on a play-off place. Yet another case of 'so near and yet so far', and so the fans were left with the prospect of yet another season in the 4th Division.

1988/89 SEASON

The season started with a lot more hope and optimism than previous ones for John Devaney became the saviour of Peterborough United, wiping out the Club debts and taking over as the new Club Chairman. His first move was to appoint Noel Cantwell as General Manager plus Mick Jones as Team Manager, and stated that his aim was to see Peterborough United in the First Division within 5 years. As well as putting in £800,000 to clear the Club's debts, Mr Devaney also pledged that a further £400,000 would be available to invest in the team to strengthen it. It was just the boost that Posh needed off the field after several years of insecurity. Arnold Blades also returned to London Road as Secretary.

By the middle of July, Jones moved into the transfer market bringing back former central defender Keith Oakes from Fulham, and striker Nick Cusack, who joined Posh in a swap deal that saw Alan Parris going to Leicester City. The Manager then moved into the local non-League scene to capture the signatures of Dominic Genovese and Craig Goldsmith. The next big money signing was Dave Langan, a 31 year old former Republic of Ireland International, for £25,000 from Second Division Bournemouth. The same week Gary Andrews a 19 year old central defender arrived from Nottingham Forest.

Posh's pre-season 'warm ups' started badly, with a 3-0 defeat to Kettering at Rockingham Road in the Maunsell Cup. This was followed by a 7-0 mauling at London Road to Newcastle United, who included in their side Brazilian star Mirandinha, who helped himself to four goals. The next scheduled big friendly match was against Tottenham Hotspur at London Road. Noel Cantwell had promised that George Best would make an appearance as would Paul Gascoigne, who had just made a £2m transfer move from Newcastle to Tottenham.

9,314 turned up to watch the friendly but were disappointed as, not for the first time, George Best failed to make an appearance, nor did Gascoigne! Posh ran out 2-1 winners against a side that was basically Tottenham's Reserves, and left many fans furious that they had been misled into attending, when neither player was likely to appear.

Posh captured the signature of central defender Gerry McElhinney from Plymouth on the eve of the opening game of the season. Posh travelled to Carlisle and came back with a creditable 2-2 draw, Gooding scoring both of Posh's goals. Making their debuts for Posh were Langan, McElhinney and Cusack. The following week they opened their Littlewoods Cup run with an excellent 3-0 win away against West Bromwich Albion at the Hawthorns, with goals from Oakes, Cusack and Genovese. Posh came down to earth with a bump the following Saturday, when they lost at home to Scarborough 4-1. The second leg of the Littlewoods Cup-tie brought about another defeat, this time by 2-0, but Posh went through to the next round as aggregate 3-2 winners over West Bromwich Albion.

For the next game Posh travelled to Feethams to play Darlington, where they earned a 2-2 draw, with Cusack scoring twice, and Goldsmith coming on as a substitute to make his debut for the Club. A home match against Lincoln attracted an encouraging gate of 4,256, this time Andrews made his debut, along with Carl Madrick who came off the substitutes bench. Genovese scored Posh's goal in a 1-1 draw. Defeats at Tranmere and at home to York preceded the Littlewoods Cup second round first leg tie against Leeds United at London Road. A crowd of 4,979 saw Posh go down 2-1 with their goal coming from Goldsmith.

Goldsmith scores the Posh goal in the home Littlewood's
1st leg Cup-tie against Second Division Leeds United.

Cusack scored in a 1-1 draw at Wrexham which was followed by a 1-0 victory over Stockport at London Road. The following week David Longhurst was signed from Northampton for £55,000, and he made his debut in a goalless draw at Grimsby and retained his place in the side the following week when Posh travelled to Leeds for their second round second leg Cup-tie. They lost 3-1 on the night, Gunn scoring Posh's goal, to go out 5-2 on aggregate. The next game was at home to Burnley (Posh being the Potters bogey side), and on this occasion Posh ran out 3-0 winners in front of 5,023 – the biggest crowd of the season at London Road – with goals from Oakes, Cusack and Goldsmith. The following game saw Posh win again at London Road, against Hereford, when Longhurst scored his first goal for the Club.

However, Posh were having yet another indifferent season and one week later suffered a 5-0 drubbing at Halifax before losing at home to Scunthorpe 2-1. Paul Crichton replaced Neenan in goal for the next game, at Leyton Orient, where Posh won 2-1 thanks to goals from Longhurst and a 25 yard drive from Steve Collins. In the next game Posh slipped to their fourth home League defeat of the season (in eight games), when they lost to Hartlepool 1-0. Langan suffered the indignity of coming on as a substitute for Collins and shortly afterwards being substituted himself. The next match was won, at Doncaster, with two goals from Gunn and one from Cusack.

The F.A.Cup campaign started at Third Division Gillingham, and Posh drew 3-3 in a memorable tie, with a hat trick from Longhurst, and four days later the Gills came to London Road for the replay. Posh were rather fortunate to win 1-0 in front of 4,494.

A goal from Cusack, in a 1-1 draw at Crewe, stretched the unbeaten run to five games. This was followed by a 1-0 win at Rochdale, thanks to an Oakes goal, before taking on Third Division Brentford in the F.A. Cup at London Road. The tie finished goalless, and four days later they travelled to Griffin Park for the replay, Posh just losing out by 3-2, in a thrilling match, with Halsall and Cusack scoring the Posh goals.

Lee Philpott made his League debut for Posh in the home defeat to Exeter City, and the following game was lost, again at London Road. On this latest occasion it was in the Sherpa Van Trophy, with Posh going down 2-0 to local rivals Northampton. Boxing day saw Posh travel to Colchester where a crowd of 2,828 saw Posh win 2-1, Gunn and McElhinney – with his first goal for the Club – scoring the goals and securing the points. New Year's Eve required a trip to Torquay, Dave Swindlehurst coming in to make his debut for Posh. The 1-0 defeat was scant reward for the handful of Posh fans who had managed to beat the 'all members' ban that Torquay had imposed. It seemed that things could not get much worse, but at London Road Posh entertained Cambridge on January 3rd, and they were hammered 5-1 in front of 4,622; Dublin scoring a hat trick for Cambridge.

It was too much for many Posh fans to swallow, but worse was to come with three more defeats (including two at home), before a point was picked up at Lincoln, to complete a miserable January.

By this time Gary Butterworth had come into the side and Swindlehurst was on his way from London Road. Posh were now languishing dangerously near the foot of the table, and the first game in February produced only one point against Tranmere, in a 1-1 draw, in front of 2,744. Jones moved again into the transfer market bringing Colin Walsh, the ex-Nottingham Forest player, from Charlton on loan. He made his debut against Tranmere, and in the following game managed to score, but Posh were drubbed 5-1 by York City at Bootham Crescent. February ended with two goals shared at Burnley's Turf Moor ground.

Halifax were then beaten 2-1 at London Road, but a dire sequence of results then saw Posh spiralling towards the bottom of the table. They lost 4-0 at Hereford, 1-0 at home to Leyton Orient, and 3-0 away to Scunthorpe before finally salvaging a point against fellow strugglers Darlington at London Road. The sequence was completed with another defeat, in the local derby with Cambridge, this time by 2-1. Worrall Sterling had been signed for £70,000, a record transfer fee by the Club, and made his debut at the Abbey Stadium.

The next match was at home to bottom of the table Colchester, David Harle and Steve Osborne making their debuts for Posh. It was a match that Posh needed desperately to win, and they did so by 3-0, with two goals from Longhurst and an own goal. It was hardly a fight back but at least it gave Posh the breathing space they needed as they languished near the bottom of the table.

But they then lost again, this time at Exeter 3-1, before gaining a valuable point at Rotherham 1-1. Posh next entertained Torquay at London Road and a crowd of 2,614 saw Posh win 3-1, with the goals coming from Longhurst (2) and Sterling.

A 1-0 win at London Road the following week against Wrexham saw Posh edge nearer to safety, Cusack scoring the only goal of the game. A battling performance at Edgeley Park produced three points at Stockport, with goals from Luke and Gunn in the 2-1 victory. Defeat at home to Grimsby, was followed up with a 3-2 London Road win over Crewe, in front of 3,546. Defeat followed at Hartlepool, then a goalless draw at Rochdale followed, but it was all pretty meaningless by the time they beat Doncaster 2-0 at London Road in the final game of the season.

Posh finished the season in 17th position – a far more comfortable position than in January, when they were just two places off the bottom. Ironically the desperate battle against relegation towards the end of the season had at least given the fans something to rally around, but it was a far cry from the pre-season promises which had been brought about by the influx of cash and new faces, which followed years of financial struggle.

Record signing Worrall Sterling, who was signed late in the season, is congratulated by Noel Luke, after scoring one of his three League goals at London Road.

108

Mick Jones continued to build his side during the summer, with the arrival of – for the Posh – big money signings. Phil Crosby arrived from Rotherham for £42,500, Dave Robinson from Halifax for a new Club record £100,000, £72,000 was paid to Chester for Milton Graham, and Carl Richards came to Peterborough from Birmingham for £37,500; Tony Godden was also signed on a free transfer from the St.Andrews club. It was an unprecedented spending spree from a Posh Manager, and financed by Chairman John Devaney.

Posh embarked on a pre season tour of Eire, beating Shelbourne 1–0 in Dublin, Limerick 4–3 and drawing with Sligo 2–2. On their return the pick of the friendlies was a 2–2 draw at London Road with Leicester City.

The season started against the League new boys, Maidstone United, at London Road, and drew a crowd of 6,022. Posh were rather fortunate to record a 1–0 win with a last gasp winner from Mick Halsall. No less than five players made their debut for Posh; Godden, Crosby, Robinson, Graham and Richards. Four days later Aldershot were entertained in the Littlewoods Cup 1st round 1st leg, and were beaten 2–0, with Sterling and Richards the scorers. Posh then lost 1–0 at York before disaster struck in the 2nd leg cup-tie at Aldershot. Defending a comfortable 2–0 lead Posh slipped to a dismal 6–2 extra time defeat to crash out of the Cup.

It was a result that cost Manager Mick Jones his job and split the opinion of Posh fans down the middle, many feeling his newly purchased side had been given little chance to gel under his guidance.

The following Saturday Dave Booth, Jones's assistant, took charge when Posh played The Shots at home in the League. Dave Robinson scored his first goal for Posh in a 1–1 draw. One week later, Chairman John Devaney announced to the media that former Liverpool and Republic of Ireland star Mark Lawrenson was to be the new Manager of Peterborough United. It was just the news that the disillusioned Posh faithful needed, a big name Manager at London Road.

New Manager Mark Lawrenson

His first game in charge was at Doncaster, and a larger than normal following from Posh saw the team sweep to a 3–0 victory with goals from Luke, Halsall and Richards. The next two games were drawn, at London Road against Scunthorpe and at Hartlepool. Lawrenson's first defeat came in front of 6,106 fans at Sincil Bank, Lincoln and this was followed by a 1–1 draw at home to Gillingham.

For Posh's next match Lawrenson moved into the transfer market to sign Paul Culpin from Northampton for £40,000. Culpin made his debut in the home match with high flying Exeter.

David Harle was recalled to the side and scored, when Posh won 4–3 in a thrilling game, the winner coming from Milton Graham's spectacular shot late in the game. Graham's first goal for Posh came in the 2–1 win at Spotland against Rochdale, and this victory was followed by a 2–1 win at Burnley, thanks to two Luke goals; Fred Barber, on loan from Walsall, made his debut in this game. Stockport were beaten 2–0 at London Road and then Colchester were beaten by a late goal from substitute Osborne at Layer Road. The unbeaten run was extended with a 1–1 home draw against Grimsby and a goalless draw at Southend, before Posh took on Fulham in the Leyland Daf Cup at London Road, which they won 1–0. Posh drew 1–1 with Hereford at London Road, with Barber making his last appearance as a loanee in this game.

Posh then received Hayes at home in the first round of the F.A. Cup. The non-Leaguers put on a storming display, and Posh were lucky to escape with a 1–1 draw, to enable them to go back to Hayes the following week for the replay. The replay was won with a single goal from Robinson in the first half, and it was freely admitted that Posh were lucky to get through to the next round. Two more draws followed, 1–1 at home to Torquay and 0–0 at Carlisle, which extended the unbeaten run to 14 games. In fact in the 19 games since Lawrenson's arrival Posh had lost only once.

Unfortunately the Christmas period brought a dramatic change of fortune. It started on December 9th, when Posh lost 3–1 at Swansea in the F.A. Cup second round, when Milton Graham sustained a serious knee injury.

After a 2–2 draw at Notts County in the Leyland Daf Cup, Posh lost away to rivals Cambridge the following Sunday, in a League fixture, by 3–2; the scoreline however flattered Posh who were always second best to their neighbours. On Boxing Day Chesterfield were entertained, and a 1–1 draw ensued, thanks to a goal from Osborne. The last game of 1989, at home to Scarborough, saw Posh suffer their first home defeat of the season.

David Longhurst holds off a close challenge. He was transferred to York City mid season, where he tragically died during a match.

Paul Culpin salutes the crowd, after scoring against Rochdale, at London Road.

On New Year's Day a 2-2 draw was gained at Halifax, but the following week Posh lost at Wrexham, when Mark Hine made his debut for the Club. The poor run continued with a home defeat to Hereford followed by two 1-1 draws at home to York and away to Maidstone. This meant that Posh had now gone 10 games without a victory. Try as they might Posh could not regain their early season form. Ronnie Jepson made his debut in the 2-1 victory over Doncaster at London Road, but the following week Posh went down 2-0, at home to Hartlepool, Martin Moore making his debut in this match. After a goalless draw at Scunthorpe, Posh beat Carlisle at London Road 3-0, one of the goalscorers being Jepson, his first for the Club.

Two away games at the end of February brought mixed fortunes, losing at Torquay – traditionally a ground where they had little luck – but beating Aldershot away. David Riley was on loan when Noel Cantwell was in charge, and he returned to the Club to partner Jepson up front. He scored in his first game since his return, when Posh defeated Wrexham. Another goalless draw followed at Gillingham, but Posh gained revenge for losing to Lincoln earlier in the season when they beat them 1-0 at London Road with a goal from Jepson. Top of the table Exeter beat Posh 2-0 at St. James's Park and four days later they suffered a further set back with a 1-0 home defeat to Rochdale.

It would now take a big push by Posh to get into the promotion picture, and it started with a 4-1 hammering of Burnley at home, Halsall, Robinson, Jepson and Riley scoring. A goalless draw at Stockport was followed by a valuable win over Colchester, with Sterling grabbing the only goal. Grimsby were then beaten in Cleethorpes, in a fine display from Posh with Halsall and Riley getting the goals. A 3-0 victory over Halifax at London Road followed by a 1-1 draw at Saltergate against Chesterfield saw Posh lying 7th in the table, the last promotion play-off place, and with four fixtures remaining. The next game was at home to Cambridge and if ever Posh needed to win a local derby this was the game. Unfortunately they lost 2-1, their single goal coming from Luke! It left them with an uphill struggle and despite defeat at Scarborough, a 2-1 win at Edgar Street against Hereford kept Posh in the frame up to the final game.

It was quite simple as Posh entered their last game of the season against Southend at London Road, they needed to win to be sure of a play off place against their promotion rivals. It was another anti-climax for the large crowd as the Shrimpers finished 2-1 winners, and for the second time in three years Posh had got so close to qualifying for a play off place, only to fall at the final hurdle. It was a bitter blow to everybody connected with the Club but particularly for the Chairman after he had invested so much money in the team, and failure was almost unthinkable.

## CHAPTER 8

UPWARDS TO NEW HEIGHTS

1990/91 SEASON

Mark Lawrenson was starting his first full season with the Club, and the pre-season period was remarkably quiet. The only new faces were George Berry – the ex-Wolves and Stoke star and former Welsh International – plus Kevin Bremner a consistent marksman with Colchester and Brighton. Lawrenson's build up to the season was mainly against non-League opposition with the first major fixture against Second Division Ipswich Town at London Road. The Suffolk side ran out 3-0 winners, and Posh then took on Kettering in the Maunsell Cup and drew 2-2, but after extra time won 4-3 on penalties to earn the first silverware of the season. The final two friendly fixtures were both against opposition from London, Tottenham Hotspur came to London Road and won 5-2 with a mixture of First and Reserve team players. Posh were then trounced by Second Division Millwall 5-0, in hardly the most inspiring pre-season warm up they could achieve!

The first game of the season was at Wrexham and a crowd of 2,863 saw Kevin Dearden, a goalkeeper on loan from Tottenham, make his debut along with Berry and Bremner. Dearden kept a clean sheet in the drawn game, which extended since 1976, the undefeated run on the opening game of the season. Third Division Fulham were the opponents in the Rumbelows Cup first round first leg. Posh travelled to Craven Cottage and came back with a well earned 2-1 victory, with goals from Sterling and Bremner. In goal was Eddie Herbert an untried local teenager, who had previously been playing for local non-League sides. Posh extended their good start to the season with a 1-1 home draw against Carlisle, Dale Watkins making his debut for the Club, before completing the formality of progression on to the second round of the Rumbelows Cup, with a 2-0 victory over Fulham at London Road.

The 8th September saw Posh travel to Scunthorpe where Kevin Russell, on loan from Leicester, made his debut for the Club and scored in another draw. The game was tarnished, however, with the tragic news that former Posh striker David Longhurst, who had left the previous season for York City, collapsed and died on the pitch during a game against Lincoln the same day.

A goalless draw at London Road in front of 4,099 was followed by a 2-0 home victory over Halifax, Russell and Culpin being the marksmen. The encouraging start to the season continued after Posh's visit to the County ground for their local derby of the against Northampton.

A crowd of 5,573 watched as Russell and Culpin were again Posh's scorers in a 2-1 victory, much to the delight of former Cobbler Culpin, and it was a result that lifted Posh into the top five in the table. The troublesome goalkeeping position, where Lawrenson had only temporary cover, was resolved with the signing of former Wolves goalkeeper Paul Bradshaw. He made his debut in the second round of the Rumbelows Cup, first leg, against Q.P.R. at Loftus Road. Posh lost 3-1 against a strong Rangers side but could hold their heads up after giving a battling performance right until the end of the game. Defeat at home followed, to Torquay United, with Posh sorely missing Russell who was out injured, but he returned for the following game and Posh beat Darlington away 1-0. Just four days later Posh lost 2-1 at Stockport when Russell made his last appearance, before returning to Leicester at the end of his loan spell. Berry came back into the side in the next game for the 1-1 draw at home to Q.P.R. in the second leg Rumbelows Cup tie. The Posh score came thanks to an own goal by former Arsenal and England International Kenny Samson, in front of 7,454.

Posh's voodoo over Burnley continued with a 3-2 home victory. Luke, Berry and Culpin were the scorers, and the homesters were even afforded the luxury of missing a penalty during the game. Paul Hill came in for his one and only game for the Club at right back in place of the injured Noel Luke at Hartlepool, when the team lost by 2-0. At Cardiff, in the next game, Posh picked up a point in a 1-1 draw that had Berry sent off. Berry's last game before he was suspended was at home against Chesterfield and he scored one of the goals in a 2-1 victory, Mark Hine grabbing the other. They then lost at home 2-0 to Cambridge in the Leyland Daf Trophy in front of 3,279.

This was a dismal performance, and just three days later Lawrenson resigned as Manager. He gave no reason at the time for his resignation but intimated later in the season that it was interference with his team management that made him leave. Dave Booth, his assistant, was appointed Caretaker Manager and was in charge for the next game at home to Doncaster Rovers. Thanks to a goal from Bremner, Posh drew 1-1 in front of 4,691.

Posh's next three fixtures were all against Hereford United, the first in the F.A. Cup first round played at Edgar Street. Posh drew 1-1, and in the replay three days later they ran out 2-1 winners.

The Following Saturday the two teams opposed each other for the third time in seven days, and drew 0-0 in the League fixture. The trip to Wrexham in the Leyland Daf Trophy produced a 3-3 draw and ended Posh's interest in the competition for another season. In the League Posh travelled to play Maidstone and were beaten 2-0 at Watling Street, but despite the general poor run of form they were still 8th in the table at this stage.

The second round of the F.A. Cup paired Posh with non-League opposition in the shape of Wycombe Wanderers. The first game was postponed due to heavy snow, but the following Wednesday night the game was played and Posh hung on for a 1-1 draw, thanks to a spectacular goal from Culpin, and despite the sending off of Mc-Elhinney. The home game against York City brought a welcome return of three points, with goals coming from Culpin and Sterling in front of 3,335.

Posh then entertained Wycombe in the F.A. Cup replay at London Road and this time beat them 2-0 in front of a 5,693 crowd. It was however, a flattering scoreline and goals from Halsall and Culpin secured the win early on in the game, but Posh were lucky to hang on to that lead in the end. The third 2-0 win on the trot came with Scarborough's visit to London Road, Culpin was again on the mark scoring along with Riley.

A Boxing Day visit to Blackpool saw Culpin make it four goals in four games when Posh came away with a 1-1 draw. Disaster was to strike three days later though, when the visit to Aldershot ended in a 5-0 drubbing. After a 1-1 draw at home to Rochdale, Posh visited Second Division Port Vale in the third round of the F.A. Cup. Despite a battling performance Posh bowed out, losing 2-1 in front of 7,490. Watkins came into the side and made a spirited display on the wing, whilst ex-Posh striker Ronnie Jepson was playing in the victorious Vale side. The long trek to Carlisle saw Posh come away pointless, and to make matters worse they threw away a 2-1 lead with just four minutes remaining, to let the points slip.

Rumours were rife after the game that Dave Booth was to become the second Managerial casualty of the season at London Road, rumours that were strenuously denied by the Chairman and the Club. The following week Posh drew 2-2 at home to Wrexham, Sterling again scoring both goals as he had done at Carlisle. The following Monday it was announced that Dave Booth had parted with the Club, despite the denials of his imminent move only the previous week! The new Manager was to be former Posh centre half Chris Turner, and it was probably the most popular appointment of a Manager at London Road for many years. In a change from the norm of new Managers when arriving at London Road, Turner predicted not of the potential and possibilities within the Club, but conversely of the turmoil and the state that it was in at that time, and of the hard work that would have to be done to bring the Club around.

His first game in charge was at Walsall on the 26th January. A large travelling contingent of Posh fans turned up to watch the side in which Turner had drafted in full back Gary Clayton on loan from Cambridge United. Posh won 1-0 with a Peter Skipper own goal at Walsall's brand new Bescot Stadium. His second match in charge was also away, this time at Halifax on a Friday night, where a goal by Riley salvaged Posh a point in front of just 1,333 fans. Four days later Posh entertained Northampton at home in the second local derby of the season. There was great media attention as Northampton were pushing for promotion along with Posh, and indeed at that stage the Cobblers were looking a certainty. Posh won 1-0 with a goal from Halsall in front of a bumper crowd.

Turner's arrival had caused a new wave of optimism to surge though the Club and they then embarked on a series of games that extended their unbeaten run to 13, and put them right back in the promotion picture. Firstly there was a 2-0 Friday night win at Doncaster, goals coming from Osborne and Halsall. Halsall scored again along with Riley (2) in the victory at Gillingham. Another David Robinson, this one from Newcastle United and a striker, made his debut for the Club in Kent. The next game was at home, to Maidstone, and Posh won 2-0, with a 4-0 victory at York following this performance. Robinson (the loanee striker) scored one of the goal in the 4-0 victory. Posh were now 4th in the table and riding high. Darlington were the next London Road visitors, and it was a real top of the table clash. The best crowd of the season by far, 8,632, turned up to watch a stunning encounter between the two sides which ended in a 2-2 draw, with goals from Robinson and Riley. A scoreless draw at Torquay kept Posh in the hunt, and then on March 20th, a following of some 2,500 Posh fans were present in a crowd of 5,524 when Posh beat local rivals Lincoln 2-0 with goals from Riley and Robinson. Another home game brought another bumper crowd, this time of 7,947, against another fellow promotion outfit, and a scoreless draw was played with Stockport.

Turner went into the transfer market the following week and created a Football League record by signing no less than six players on transfer deadline day. For a combined fee of £40,000, in came Gary Cooper and Ken Charley from Maidstone, Pat Gavin joined the club from Leicester for £15,000, Peter Costello from Rochdale for £30,000, and completing the six were Darren Morgan on loan from Millwall and Chris Swailes for a moderate fee from Ipswich.

The following game was at home to another promotion chasing team, Blackpool, and a crowd of 7,721 saw four new Posh players making their debut – Morgan and Gavin starting the game, with Charley and Costello both coming on as substitutes. Posh were ahead after just two minutes with a fantastic free kick from Berry, in front of the Moys end. New boy Gavin then scored on his debut four minutes from time to give Posh the 2-0 victory to keep them second in the table.

The run came to an end after 13 games, at Scarborough, where Posh were outfought, outbattled and outplayed in a 3–1 defeat. Gavin grabbed his second goal in two games, with Cooper coming on as a sub to make his debut for Posh. Posh's next game looked a formality – on paper – against lowly Aldershot, but after just five minutes Posh were stunned as they went 1–0 down to a freak kick from fully 30 yards from Aldershot's Russian sweeper Victor Yanushevsky. It was certainly one of the best goals seen at London Road for many years. Posh got back on terms through Oakes after 13 minutes and Gavin put Posh ahead, his third in three games, nine minutes before half time. Despite holding most of the territorial advantage throughout the match, Aldershot equalised with just 19 minutes remaining, and it was left for another newcomer – Cooper – who came on as substitute, to shoot home the winner with 11 minutes left. Gavin extended his stunning start to his Posh career with goals in the 3–0 victory at Rochdale and the 2–0 home victory over Gillingham, making his total of 5 goals in 5 matches.

Posh's next game was against Burnley, another promotion clash, and a season's best crowd of 10,018. Posh were thrashed 4–1 and were never in the game. Neil Pope came in for his Posh debut, coming on as a substitute to replace Cooper after an hour. Just as promotion had seemed a formality, Posh now entered a jittery stage drawing first at Scunthorpe 0–0, and then at home to Hartlepool. The only Posh goal in the latter match was thanks to a Berry penalty. Posh had now slipped to 6th and were in danger of missing out on an automatic promotion spot, but a 3–0 win over Cardiff was memorable. As Culpin was about to score Posh's third, about 50 Cardiff fans invaded the pitch, but the scorer calmly slotted home the goal which the referee incredibly allowed to stand, despite the chaos being played out on the centre of the pitch. Posh's last home game of the season was against Hereford, which again they comfortably won – 3–0 – with goals from Sterling, Gavin and Berry.

The last game of the season was away at Chesterfield on May 11th, and as they approached the match there were many permutations, but if Posh actually won the game then nobody could stop them getting automatically promoted. Around 5,000 fans made the trip to Saltergate as part of a crowd of 8,937, but the Spireites had not read the script. After just nine minutes of the game Chesterfield had taken a 2–0 lead silencing the large Posh following and the shellshocked team. It seemed again that Posh were destined to miss out right at the death, but Turner's amazing ability to bring success to the team that he had been in charge of for a little over three months, started working again, and ten minutes after half time Luke swung over a corner which was nodded on by Robinson and looped into the net. 2–1 and Posh were back in with a hope. The crowd roared Posh on with news filtering through from other grounds that other promotion candidates were also losing. With 17 minutes remaining Sterling took a throw from the Grandstand side, Berry flicked it on, Culpin mis-kicked and the ball crept inside the far post to make it 2–2. It was a desperate final quarter of an hour, but puzzling for the travelling supporters was the team who, five minutes from time, just seemed to stop playing. By this time news had filtered through from the bench that Blackpool were losing at Walsall and if their score remained at 2–2 Posh were promoted. The final minutes were slowly played out, and as the final whistle blew the crowd were delirious with delight. After 17 years Posh had got themselves back into the Third Division. There were joyful scenes after the game as fans poured onto the pitch to honour their heroes.

Chris Turner had taken a side lying 9th in the Division and in desperate internal turmoil, to promotion in a little over three months. His style as a Manager was very reminiscent of Cantwell, who he cited at the end of the season as one of his greatest influences. He had now emulated his predecessor's success by taking Posh to the Third Division for the third time in their history.

The joy can be seen in the expressions of the Posh players, as Berry nets the all important equaliser at Chesterfield.

The 1991/92 season was to prove to be not only the longest but by far the most eventful and successful that the Club had ever seen it its 58 year history. It was the opportunity for Manager Chris Turner to prove himself over a full season, having some act to follow given the previous season's promotion.

It started with a busy build up of friendlies as Turner lived up to his reputation of wheeling and dealing in an attempt to piece together a successful side. His search even spread as far as the Continent for Stefan Stoenkomps and goalkeeper Peter Sirch came on trial from Germany and played in a match at Kettering, but neither were signed. Outgoing players from the previous season included the scorer of that all important equaliser at Chesterfield – George Berry – to Preston (and soon to move on to Aldershot). Veteran goalkeeper Paul Bradshaw retired, Steve Osborne left for York, Dale Watkins moved into local football, whilst Neil Pope and Chris Swailes went to Boston. The biggest surprise was the fans *"Player of the Season"*, Phil Crosby, who left for York City. Returning from playing elsewhere were Gerry McElhinney and Keith Oakes, both being given jobs at the Club. Oakes replaced Bill Harvey as Physio and McElhinney managed the Youth and Reserve teams.

Bill Harvey's retirement ended a long and happy association with the Club in almost every conceivable position from Caretaker Manager to Physio, from Coach to Assistant Manager, and on one occasion – although well into his fifties – appearing for the Reserves as a player. Bill was still a figure that was regularly consulted and seen frequently at the Club, even after his official retirement.

Incoming personnel included Chris White and Micky Turner from Portsmouth. Marcus Ebdon – a Welsh U-21 International – was picked up on a free transfer from Everton, while Steve Welsh – a centre half from Cambridge – and Garry Kimble, both also came for little or no fees. The one major signing made by Turner was that of flamboyant goalkeeper Fred Barber from Walsall for £25,000, after reports in the local press of pleas from Barber for Turner to sign him, which stemmed from his previously successful loan period at the Club.

Posh opened the season at home against Preston who had former London Road favourites Ronnie Jepson and George Berry in the side. 6,036 people turned up to watch, as Barber made what was to become a familiar entrance, in an old man's face mask and bowing to the Posh fans standing on the London Road terrace. Newly promoted Posh grabbed the points through a late winner from David Riley. In the home side six new players made their League debuts; Barber, White, Welsh, Ebdon and Kimble plus McInerney who came on as sub for Gavin. It was now fifteen years since Posh had lost an opening day fixture.

Fourth Division Aldershot were the next visitors, in the Rumbelows Cup. Only 2,713 attended and Gavin scored a hat trick of headers in the 3–1 first leg victory, with Noel Luke coming into the side for Sterling in his least preferred role as winger. The first away match of the season was at Hull, and McInerney came off the bench to score the winner in the 89th minute after Kimble had earlier given Posh the lead, which was immediately cancelled out by Payton. The second leg of the Rumbelows Cup was watched by 1,601 people as Gavin scored another goal to take his tally to 10 in 14 games, Halsall was the other scorer in the 2–1 win on the night, and 5–2 on aggregate.

August ended with a home match against Stoke City who scored after less than a minute through Biggins. Kimble equalised after 16 minutes though to leave Posh 6th in the table. The next five games however brought little reward as Posh adjusted to life in the Third Division. Defeat at Bury was the trigger for Turner to ring the changes and for the home game with Wigan five were made. Luke switched to right back in place of White, and Sterling came back on the wing. Ebdon, Gavin and Riley made way for Cooper, Charlery and McInerney. It was to no avail as Wigan earned a 0–0 draw. The visit to top of the table Birmingham saw Gavin return for Charlery, but it was defender Dave Robinson who forced Hicks to put through his own goal to give Posh the lead after 74 minutes. It seemed as though Posh had done enough to secure a well earned victory when five minutes into injury time Atkins crossed for Cooper to scramble the ball onto the underside of the bar. Despite Barber's protests the referee gave a goal to deny Posh a win. Even more annoying was the subsequent news that Birmingham were disciplined for fielding an unregistered player in the game – the player being Atkins who had supplied the all important last minute cross! Four days later Posh visited the Hawthorns for a League match, when West Bromwich cruised to a 4–0 win. A Halsall penalty then gave Posh another point in a 1–1 home draw with Exeter.

The reward for beating Aldershot in the Rumbelows Cup was a two legged tie against first Division Wimbledon who were now sharing Crystal Palace's ground for home games. A paltry 2,081, including several hundred Posh fans, turned up to watch the Dons beaten 2–1 as another giantkilling was added to Peterborough's already impressive record. Charlery got his first goal for the Club and Sterling added a second.

A long trek to bottom club Swansea was next in line, and despite Posh having more possession, a dismal game was settled by Swansea's only real opportunity to take the game, and left Posh 18th in the table. Robinson was sent off in the next match, and Leyton Orient became the first side to win at London Road in the League – since August 29th 1990 – when two Nugent goals gave the visitors the victory.

The second leg of the Rumbelows Cup gave some welcome relief from the pressure of League football, when 5,939 came to watch an entertaining game. Posh completed an aggregate victory over Wimbledon with a 2-2 draw, Kimble and Riley getting the Posh goals. Chris White returned to the side for the visit to Brentford along with fans' favourite Paul Culpin. Posh lost 2-1 with Culpin coming on and scoring. The match at Reading was drawn the following week, leaving Posh without a League win for nine games. Lee Howarth came in for his debut in place of the suspended Robinson and 32 year old Peter Johnson was present at left back as a non contract player. Charlery scored his first League goal for Posh, before Reading equalised through a disputed penalty when Howarth was judged to have handled the ball.

Posh got under way in the second cup competition of the season by beating Wrexham 2-0 in the first group match of the Autoglass Trophy, just 1,085 fans came to watch as Charlery and Howarth got the goals. The victory came amidst rumours in the local press that the Club had been put up for sale, with an advert in the Financial Times, the asking price was allegedly £2million. Charlery's scoring run continued as Posh nearly let a 2-0 lead slip, but held on to win 3-2, with Riley scoring the other two goals, against Hartlepool at home.

The following Tuesday saw Second Division Newcastle as the next opponents in the Rumbelows Cup at London Road. 10,382 turned up and Ossie Ardiles's struggling side were added to the list of higher division casualties for the season. Charlery headed the winner five minutes from time, his fourth in four games. The visit to Shrewsbury started well enough, but soon went downhill as Posh, appearing in Shrewsbury's change kit, slumped to another defeat. An appalling display left the Club 4th from the bottom.

Turner persevered with an unchanged side at Chester and a sparkling display from Cooper laid the foundations for a 2-0 victory with both goals coming from Charlery in front of 2,810 fans. Posh were paired in the Rumbelows Cup draw with the mighty Liverpool (if they beat Port Vale in a replay), and the next game – against Bradford City – saw a gate of 9,224, since ticket vouchers were given out for the forthcoming Cup-tie. Riley scored the first goal, although he knew little of it as the ball cannoned off him from a clearance. Posh won 2-1, and the result ultimately lost Bradford Manager John Docherty his job later that week.

The start of the F.A. Cup brought Harlow Town to London Road and Posh's biggest F.A. Cup win since joining the League. A game, but woefully inadequate, Harlow side crumbled as Posh led through Cooper on six minutes, before 12 minutes later a very harsh penalty award resulted in Harlow's Gleeson getting sent off. Cooper duly converted the penalty and one minute later Riley made it 3-0. A stunning Sterling strike made it 4-0 four minutes later, and in the 27th minute it was 5-0 through Halsall. Posh had still not finished though as Charlery got a 6th before the break.

Posh started the second half in a somewhat relaxed style, and despite a couple of close calls only added a 7th through substitute Culpin three minutes from time. It was just the sort of result that was needed and a League visit to lowly Darlington produced a fourth consecutive win. The last game before the now confirmed visit of Liverpool was at home to Torquay, 4,007 came and saw Culpin come on and put Posh ahead after 78 minutes, only to be denied by Elliott's 86th minute equaliser. The result left Torquay bottom and Posh 12th.

December 3rd brought the most successful side in English football to London Road for the Rumbelows Cup 4th round. Liverpool had started the season badly but were now on an eight match unbeaten run and were performing well in Europe. Manager Chris Turner was quoted: *"we'll need to have the referee, the ball and the wind in our favour to claim a draw,"* **and continued** *"and then only if we board the goal up."* **Turner named an unchanged side for the 4th match running and an all ticket crowd of 14,114 turned up to witness an historic evening. Posh took the game to the Reds and played Liverpool off the park. In the 19th minute, Sterling knocked the ball to Luke who put in a swirling cross to the penalty spot, Grobelaar came for the ball but only succeeded in helping it on to an unmarked Kimble who rifled the ball home from eight yards in front of the Moys End. The crowd went berserk and as if to prove it was no fluke Posh kept coming forward – against a side containing no fewer than five internationals – creating but failing to take three or four good chances. As the final whistle approached the noise was deafening, and Liverpool's final chance was a McManaman shot in the last minute that Barber turned away at full stretch. It was testament to Posh's performance that it had been their first chance of the night. Seconds later the final whistle was blown, to emotional scenes of fans and players celebrating undoubtedly Posh's greatest ever Cup victory.**

Reading were the next visitors, in the F.A. Cup, and Posh were lucky to survive a 0-0 draw. The hangover from the Liverpool match continued as Stockport handed out a convincing 3-0 defeat at Edgeley Park where new loan signing Ronnie Robinson came on as a substitute to make his debut for Posh. The Cup replay at Reading also brought another defeat, and another game without a goal. The Friday night game for the Hull City game brought another bumper attendance, this time for vouchers being issued for the quarter-final tie with Middlesbrough. Posh recorded their first double of the season with goals from Robinson, Riley and Charlery in a 3-0 win.

Boxing Day saw a trip to 5th placed Stoke, and a match to warm up the 14,733 present. Kevan put Stoke 1-0 up and at that point it looked like they might run riot, however, Dave Robinson crashed a powerful header home to equalise after 17 minutes as Posh hauled themselves back into the match. After half an hour the impressive Stein made in 2-1 to Stoke, but just three minutes later Halsall score with an unstoppable drive from the edge of the box.

In the Rumbelows (League) Cup, Charlery scores the only goal that beats Newcastle United at London Road

In the next round, it's Kimble who scores the all important goal that knocks out the mighty Liverpool.

The other half of Stoke's lethal strike force put the score at 3–2 when Biggins scored a fortuitous goal, a weak shot somehow squirming under Barber's body and into the net. This goal was by now against the run of play and Sterling finished the simplest of chances from Riley's cross, to produce a deserved equaliser. Two days later and Posh had keeper Barber to thank for a point at Preston. A penalty award after 12 minutes, that had Manager Turner fuming, was taken by Shaw and turned away acrobatically to his left by Barber.

Tony Adcock was signed on loan from Northampton and came on for half an hour for his debut against Bury at London Road. The result was 0–0, and Posh failed dismally to turn 17 corners into any sort of advantage. The following week Second Division high fliers Middlesbrough came to London Road as a near capacity 15,302 watched the Rumbelows Cup quarter final. Posh turned in another polished performance, as they had against Liverpool, but this time found their opponents made of sterner stuff and they drew 0–0, to earn a money spinning replay. The match became Peter Johnson's last game for the Club, for after turning in some solid performances he had lost his place in the team to the younger Ronnie Robinson.

Back in the League Fulham arrived as the next visitors, and in his first full appearance Adcock scored twice when the visitors were hammered 4–1. Sub Ebdon scored his first goal for the Club with a rebound from his missed penalty. The midweek Autoglass group match was abandoned with the score at 2–1 to Mansfield, due to thick fog closing in on an already icy pitch. Posh returned from Leeds Road with a point off Huddersfield, leaving Posh unbeaten in six League matches. The fans then suffered another abandonment, this time at Middlesbrough, when the match was called off, but not before an estimated 2,000 Posh fans had travelled North.

The next action was at home to F.A. Cup conquerors Reading, and this time they were disposed of comfortably. Manchester United's loan keeper Jim Leighton, who had been so impressive for Reading in the previous encounters, picked the ball out of the net on five occasions this time, as Posh won 5–3. The Mansfield game was finally staged the following week and this time Posh made no mistakes as Gavin was recalled, and scored in a 3–0 victory that ensured qualifying for the knockout stages. A Charlery goal at Hartlepool was enough to clinch a win in a close encounter in the first of two trips to the North East in four days. The second was to Middlesbrough for the Cup replay where Turner faced a selection crisis at left back. He plumped for Hamis Curtis who had progressed from the Youth ranks, and he made his Posh debut in front of 21,792 fans at Ayresome Park. The match was another hard fought, close encounter – similar to the one at London Road – and it was only settled 10 minutes from time by a stunning strike from Stuart Ripley.

Back in the League, Posh made it three straight wins, beating 6th placed Stockport in a match packed with incident. Bobby Barnes (who had signed from Northampton), made his debut in place of Kimble. Posh trailed to a 4th minute penalty before Adcock put the score at 2–1. Stockport came back and levelled again after 57 minutes, before Charlery was fouled in the 78th minute. Posh were awarded a penalty but in the resulting melee both Charlery and Todd were send off. Cooper confidently converted the spot kick though, and Posh moved to 9th in the table. Posh were now having to play two games during most weeks, and next were Shrewsbury in the Autoglass Trophy. Turner used Gavin, Ebdon and Costello from his squad, and it was Costello who grabbed the only goal of the game to send Posh through. The team then powered into a fantastic sequence of results that saw three more consecutive single goal victories (at Fulham, at home to Exeter – in the Autoglass Trophy – and Bolton). Riley returned to the side for the Bolton game, replacing the suspended Charlery. This run clinched the *'Manager of the Month'* award for Chris Turner, and also boosted Posh to 8th in the table.

Probably the most impressive League display of the season came with the 2–0 win over Huddersfield at London Road. Huddersfield were swept aside as Posh turned on a memorable display for the 6,257 crowd. Riley opened the scoring on 24 minutes, after Sterling had flicked the ball on to Cooper, who in turn carved through the defence and chipped the ball to a grateful Riley. The second goal came on 77 minutes when Adcock swept a pass out wide to Barnes, who cut inside the defender and buried a shot past the helpless Martin in the Huddersfield goal. Huddersfield's Manager, former Posh player Ian Ross, said it was the best performance he had seen in the Third Division all season. It also extended the run to six consecutive wins.

A tricky trip to Bournemouth, just one place below Posh in the table, was next. In the second minute of the game the large Peterborough following at Dean Court were silenced as Peter Shearer was allowed a free header to put Bournemouth 1–0 up. It took only four minutes for Posh to get back on level terms and Posh created, although failing to take, a number of opportunities as the game went on. But in the 73rd minute Riley scored an almost identical goal to the one that he netted against Huddersfield, glancing in a Cooper cross. The match ended with Barnes tormenting both his former team mates and the Bournemouth fans, with some outrageous ball juggling and time consuming skills in front of the main stand in the final moments of the game. The win equalled a club record of seven consecutive wins that had been previously achieved in the 1960/61 and 1973/74 seasons.

A midweek visit to Macclesfield, where Chester City were sharing a home ground, saw the record beaten as Posh recovered from going a goal behind five minutes before the break, to finally win 4–2. The team were playing right at the top of their form, and Cooper and Halsall in midfield plus Welsh and the two Robinsons at the back were inspirational during this period. The next visitors were Shrewsbury who played five across the back and looked happy enough to try and steal a point, but a Halsall goal in the 79th minute made it nine League wins in a row, and secured 4th place in the, four points off the top, and with two games in hand.

In the Autoglass Trophy 3,929 fans turned up at London Road as the competition now assumed greater importance. A win would provide Posh with only a two legged area final away from a first ever Wembley appearance. Adcock and Barnes were both Cup tied so Costello and Charley – who had been unable to regain his place from Riley – came back into the side. All three of the strikers scored in a 3–1 win over the team who had earlier received national acclaim for putting Arsenal out of the F.A. Cup.

A phenomenal run since December 20th had seen Posh play 21 games, win 15, draw five and lose just one (to Second Division Middlesbrough). The run ended at Valley Parade, with 1,750 Posh fans who travelled to cheer the team on, but who saw them lose 2–1. Posh keeper Barber was banned by the Police from wearing his famous mask, as it may have incited the fans!

It was a similar story at Bolton. After an early Charley lead had been cancelled, the striker put through his own goal for another 2–1 defeat. A home match with bottom of the table Darlington, managed by former Posh favourite Ray Hankin, should have seen a return to winning ways. Turner had strengthened the squad with the signings of forward Steve Cooper (who came on as sub) from Tranmere and defender Danis Salman from Plymouth – both on loan – but a frustrating performance saw Posh escape with only a point.

The following Tuesday saw the visit of 3rd placed Birmingham City and a bumper crowd of 12,081. Things started well enough for Posh when Barnes put Posh into a 1–0 lead after just five minutes. An error of judgement after 28 minutes dramatically changed the course of the game however, when a through ball to the right of the Posh goal appeared to be beyond Mark Cooper's reach and Ronnie Robinson controlled the situation. But Barber raced from his line and felled Cooper giving away a penalty that Frain converted. In the second half a goal from Sturridge after a suicidal back pass from Robinson put Posh behind. Eight minutes later Barnes got the equaliser, but only for two minutes, when Matthewson drove home what proved to be the winner. A Friday night visit to Wigan, where Salman made his first appearance, produced a 3–0 defeat – and now five games without a win – with Posh slipping to 9th in the League. To make matters worse Cooper was sent off early in the game.

The first leg of the Autoglass Trophy Southern Area Final was watched by 14,355 at Stoke who silenced the small band of visiting supporters by scoring twice in the opening five minutes and threatened to overwhelm Peterborough. It was a baptism by fire for debut making goalkeeper Ian Bennett, replacing out of form Barber, and young Matthew Edwards on loan from 'Spurs. However, Posh battled back in some style and scored through Halsall and Charley in the 24th and 51st minutes, before taking the lead through a Vince Overson own goal. It was only a stroke of misfortune in the end that saw Posh miss out on a win. Salman pulled up injured on the touchline, Stoke pressed forward, and an unmarked Sandford headed home the equaliser.

Bournemouth were beaten 2–0 in the League, Bennett retaining his place, Luke coming back in for the injured Salman, and with the return of Barnes and Adcock. A Ken Charley goal after eight minutes and a Gary Cooper penalty – the result of an assault on Adcock that saw Morris sent off – secured the victory. Then came the visit of West Bromwich, and a 9,040 crowd, but no goals in a game that Albion needed to win to stay in the hunt for promotion. Posh were now 7th, just one point behind a play off spot, with a match in hand on the teams above them.

An all ticket match for a crowd of 12,214 to see Posh attempt to clinch a first ever trip to Wembley came next, against Stoke. An ill tempered game was settled by a Stoke goal in the 51st minute from a 20 yard free kick. After the match Chairman John Devaney praised the team and the supporters for their efforts and reminded everyone that promotion was still a real possibility.

Butterworth and Ebdon were recalled for the suspended Halsall and Cooper at Exeter, and both turned in fine displays as Posh missed several good chances and had to be content with a 2–2 draw. The biggest worry for Turner was losing Barnes with a bad looking knee injury after half an hour. The only changes for the visit to Swansea were Kimble on the wing in place of Barnes, and Halsall returning at Butterworth's expense. Kimble made the most of his opportunity by scoring Posh's second goal in the 3–1 win, with Charley and Sterling scoring the other two.

The win put Posh back in a play–off place, with three games left, and the next match at Orient – who were still hopeful of promotion. Lee Howarth came in at centre half for Welsh who, after a brilliant debut season, was looking jaded. A 2–1 victory for Posh against the run of play ended the O's hopes and lifted Posh to 5th. It was now made known that Gary Cooper had not been in contact with the Club since the Exeter match, and was not to play again for Posh that season.

The last scheduled away game of the season was at Torquay, and despite taking the lead twice through Charley (after 33 minutes and 64 minutes), the relegated South coast side came back both times to deny Posh the win that would secure a play–off place. Justin Fashanu got the first Torquay equaliser with Dave Robinson putting through his own goal for the second.

The final match of the season had a number of different permutations hanging on the result. If Brentford won and Birmingham didn't, then the Bees would be Champions. Posh could make the play off's regardless of the result as long as Bournemouth did not win by more than two goals, and in any event a point was sufficient! In a predictably tight game it was Brentford who triumphed 1–0 in front of 14,539, the biggest home League gate since May 1st 1974. It didn't matter as Bournemouth lost at Hartlepool, Birmingham at Stockport, and both Brentford and Posh fans celebrated for different reasons.

The final League placing paired Posh against Huddersfield with the first leg being played at London Road on Monday 11th May. The only change to the side was Edwards coming in for Kimble. Posh started impressively and as early as the second minute when Sterling had a good shooting opportunity, but preferred to pass the ball instead of shoot and the chance went begging. As the match progressed it was the Terriers rather than Posh who looked the more likely to score, and in the 27th minute they did just that. Roberts knocked down a cross for Starbuck to shoot firmly at Barber, who parried the ball. In the melee that followed, Posh failed to clear and Onuora took the simple chance from close in. Although Posh continued to come forward, Huddersfield looked far more comfortable with the lead which they protected until half time. It took only 15 seconds into the second half for Charlery to square things, when Adcock laid on the ball to Charlery on the right hand side of the box, and in front of a packed London Road end he coolly shot home. Huddersfield came again though and put Posh under tremendous pressure for 15 minutes. This culminated in a 67th minute goal, when Starbuck crossed hard and low and Dave Robinson, in an attempt to clear, cracked the ball into his own net. The final 20 minutes or so saw Posh under even more pressure and always vulnerable to the counterattack as they looked for an equaliser. But the fairytale ending Posh were looking for came with a minute left, from Ebdon's throw-in which was picked up by Charlery and crossed into the box. Halsall met the ball on the run on the right side of the box and hit a firm drive into the net to put things level for the second leg and gave Posh a big psychological boost over their rivals who appeared devastated when the final whistle sounded moments later.

A massive 3,500 strong following of Posh fans trekked North for the 2nd leg three days later. Turner changed things again, bringing back Welsh in place of Howarth, Barber in place of Bennett and gambled on the fitness of Barnes instead of Edwards. After two minutes Posh hopes suffered a massive setback when Huddersfield took the lead after Chris Billy sped down the wing and wriggled free of a stumbling Ronnie Robinson to cross for Starbuck, who prodded home – unchallenged – past a startled Posh defence. For the next 30 minutes Posh forced corners but rarely threatened the Huddersfield goal and they looked very shaky whenever Huddersfield's talented front line pushed forward. The half-time whistle came with Posh thankful to be still in the game. The second half was a different story. Posh started to play with the passion that had become a trademark of Turner's sides at London Road. Ebdon, Sterling, Halsall and Barnes in particular were outstanding. Eventually Sterling latched on to Adcock's head-on and bravely lunged out his boot to knock home the deserved equaliser, despite taking a fearful blow from the keeper in the process. There were still 20 minutes to go though and the price was paid by Sterling seven minutes later, when he was replaced by Cooper. The pace of the game picked up considerably and Posh piled on the pressure but always looked under threat from Huddersfield's attack on the break, as chances were missed at both ends. With four minutes remaining a shattered Barnes was fed the ball by Adcock on the right wing, and he somehow summoned the energy to send in a perfect cross for Cooper to head the ball home from the edge of the 6 yard box. The celebrations started in earnest a few minutes later as the final whistle went, and Posh were through to Wembley, to play Stockport for the right to play in the newly named *First Division*. It was over an hour before the pitch was cleared, and the team returned for players and fans to celebrate on and off the pitch, as interviews for T.V. and Newspapers were given.

Cooper ensures a visit to Wembley

The greatest occasion in Posh's short League history came on Sunday 24th May 1992, as nearly 25,000 Posh fans made Wembley their home for the day as part of a 35,087 crowd. It was the 67th game, the record number played in one season by the Club. Turner plumped for an unchanged line up of:

Barber, Luke, R. Robinson, Halsall, D. Robinson, Welsh, Sterling, Ebdon, Charlery, Adcock and Barnes. Steve Cooper and Lee Howarth were again the substitutes.

Barber answered one of the pre—match queries by wearing his now famous mask as he came out with the team on to the Wembley pitch, and after the introduction to the dignitaries came across to the Posh fans and bowed to them, again wearing the mask.

The match began with Barnes relishing the opportunity of a big stage on which to show off his talents again, as he made several penetrating runs that caused havoc in the Stockport defence. It was Barnes who had the first chances in the game as he saw two shots narrowly miss early on, both coming from the impressive Ebdon passes. Charlery also wasted a good opportunity after 15 minutes, just shooting over from Sterling's knock down. Slowly though the balance of play changed as Stockport created chances, but both teams reached half-time goalless. The second half started with tremendous support from the Posh fans, and after 52 minutes Barnes's corner was headed against the underside of the Stockport crossbar by Charlery and bounced just over the line. The Stockport players furiously contested the decision, but the linesman had quickly signalled a goal and the referee after consultation verified the decision. Fifteen minutes later Posh benefitted from another marginal decision as Francis was given offside when he headed home what the Stockport fans thought was an equaliser. Chances again came and went at both ends without a serious threat of a goal until the 71st minute, when Adcock's lunge at a Charlery cross went agonisingly inches wide. None of this seemed to matter as Posh looked to have soaked up the best that Stockport could offer.

But, with two minutes of normal time remaining, the ball was laid wide to Preece who fired a shot which Barber failed to hold, and it squirmed through his hands for the grateful Francis to head home on the line at the far post. A minute later and substitute Howarth cleared off the line as Stockport, now fired up, looked for the winner. Then in the last minute of normal time Ebdon drilled a 30 yard pass into the path of Charlery who nodded the ball on the bounce past his marker, and from just inside the area placed a perfect lob over Stockport's stationary keeper Edwards, to make it 2-1. Charlery wheeled away to take the applause from the ecstatic Posh support, who cheered and celebrated for another four minutes, until the final whistle blew, to a deafening roar from the Peterborough supporters. Posh for the first time in their history had made it to what was to be the renamed First Division.

Mick Halsall (along with Noel Luke) as one of the longest service players in the side, fittingly went up to collect a Commemorative Trophy before the lap of honour to thank the joyful Posh fans. It sparked off mass celebrations in the City with Manager Chris Turner and Skipper Mick Halsall appearing in Cathedral Square around midnight, where about 2,000 fans had gathered to celebrate.

The following day the Club officials and players toured the City before an estimated 60,000 crowd, who had turned out to greet the victorious side, before the Players and Management appeared on the balcony of the Town Hall to acknowledge the supporters.

A truly memorable ending to a remarkable season.

(Above) Was it over the line? The referee said 'yes' .... 1–0 to Posh.
(Below) Charlery lets fly to score the dramatic last minute winner.

## CHAPTER 9

THE LONDON ROAD GROUND

T he ground, which was owned by the City Council, had been used from the early 1900's by each of Peterborough United F.C.'s forerunners, viz. Peterborough City, Fletton United and Peterborough & Fletton United, and since the formation in 1934 of the current Club, it has continued as the Posh's home.

The new Club applied to the City Council in May 1934 to hire the London Road ground, and commenced their Midland League matches there. In 1945, Posh were offered a seven year lease at £45 per annum. Over the previous decades the London Road enclosure had changed little, and for the spectators convenience there was only a small wooden Grandstand, which was sited in front of the current seated stand, and grass banking elsewhere around the ground. In the late 1940's, the City Council agreed that should a new Stand be built, then a 25 year lease would be granted to the Club. In the Summer of 1948, plans were announced that the capacity of the ground would be increased to 25,000, and these developments would include the building of a 4,000 seated Grandstand. When these plans were announced, the fans – as now – were sceptical of any such announcements, but in January 1949 the plan was submitted to the County Planning Committee, but a decision was deferred, pending consultations with the Ministry of Transport. Approval was finally given, although construction work was not started for several years. Meanwhile the active Supporters Club ensured that the lot of the supporter would be improved, and during the 1951/52 season they provided £185 for the steelwork that was used to cover the terrace at the London Road end. Additionally £70 was raised and used for other general ground improvements.

At the start of the 1953/54 season a development fund by the Supporters' and parent Clubs' was launched. Supporters were asked to 'buy a brick' for 2/6d. (10p), which was to be used to build a new retaining wall at the Moyes End, and this scheme was enthusiastically welcomed by the fans. Work immediately commenced on the retaining wall, and through to 1955 other facilities, including the construction of terraces and catering bars, continued at both ends of the ground.

At the start of the 1955/56 season the Mayor came to London Road, and ceremoniously cut the first sod for the foundations of the long awaited 'dream' Grandstand. The Stand, which is 340 feet (104 metres) long, was built immediately behind the former timber structure. On completion of the new Stand, the old one was demolished, and the pitch was moved about 30 metres. By the start of the 1958/59 season the new Stand was ready for occupation, and the terraced paddock had been extended to meet the newly located pitch. With the Club at the height of its non–League success days, work soon included the construction of concrete terracing to the Glebe Road side, and the full covering of both the London Road and Moyes End terraces. By the time that the Club were at last accepted into the Football League, the current four pylon floodlights had been erected.

Work on the Stand didn't really start until 1959.

Below – The Steelwork erection commences.

1955 .... The Mayor cuts the first sod for the foundations of the club's new grandstand.

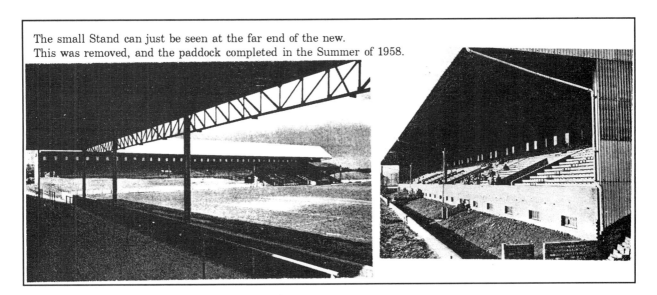

The small Stand can just be seen at the far end of the new.
This was removed, and the paddock completed in the Summer of 1958.

The only significant changes made to the ground since 1960 have consisted of the construction of the Office block adjoining the main Stand (which currently houses the Probation Service), the Bill Harvey Clinic (at the corner of the Stand and the London Road terrace), the addition of the Executive Boxes and T.V. facility above the Glebe Road terrace, and the Executive Suite at the rear of the main Stand.

(Left) After the pitch was moved, new drains were installed, and the playing area was re-seeded, ready for the 1958/59 season (note the half pitch width cover at the Moys End at this time).

(Below) In October 1960, work progressed on concreting and extending the Glebe Road terrace.

## CHAPTER 10

SEQUENCES AND RECORDS

(Complete to end 1991/92 Season):

League record:
1934/35 – 1959/60 Midland League.
1960/61 – Football League Division 4.
1961/62 – 1967/68 Division 3.
1968/69 – 1973/74 Division 4.
1974/75 – 1978/79 Division 3.
1979/80 – 1990/91 Division 4.
1991/92 – Division 3.
1992/93 – Division 1.

Most Appearances – Tommy Robson
(Original line up/Substitute,Unused substitute)

League	F.A.Cup	League Cup
440/42/16	43/2/1	31/1/0

1968 – 1981 Total: 514/45/17

Most Goals – Jim Hall

League	F.A.Cup	League cup
122	11	4

1967 – 1975 Total: 137

Record Transfer Fees:
Received: £110,000 (Blackpool, July 1979) – Doyle
£100,000 (Luton Town, July 1978) – Turner
£55,000 (Stoke City, July 1979) – Gregory
Paid: £100,000 (Halifax Town, July 1989) – Robinson
£72,500 (Chester City, June 1989) – Graham
£70,000 (Watford, March 1989) – Sterling

Longest (Football League) Sequences:
Undefeated matches – 17 (17/12/60 to 15/4/61)
Undefeated home matches – 32 (21/4/73 to 9/11/74)
Undefeated away matches – 8 (28/1/69 to 19/4/69)
Consecutive wins – 9 (1/2/92 to 14/3/92)
Consecutive home wins – 15 (3/12/60 to 28/8/61)
Consecutive away wins – 5 (22/3/88 to 7/5/88)
Consecutive defeats – 5 (26/12/88 to 21/1/89)
Without a win – 17 (28/9/78 to 30/12/78)
Without a home win – 9 (2/2/85 to 24/8/85)
Without an away win – 26 (7/1/76 to 22/3/77)

Major Honours
Football League:
Division 4 Champions: 1960/61 and 1973/74.
Division 3 Promoted : 1991/92.
Division 4 Promoted : 1990/91.

F.A.Cup:
Best Run – 1964/65 season, reached 6th round.

League Cup:
Best Run – 1965/66 season, reached Semi–final

Managers:
1934–36: Jock Porter
1936–37: Fred Taylor
1937–38: Vic Poulter
1938–48: Sam Haden
1948–50: Jack Blood
1950–52: Bob Gurney
1952–54: Jack Fairbrother
1954–58: George Swindin
1958–62: Jimmy Hagan
1962–64: Jack Fairbrother
1964–67: Gordon Clark
1967–69: Norman Rigby
1969–72: Jim Iley
1972–77: Noel Cantwell
1977–78: John Barnwell
1978–79: Billy Hails
1979–82: Peter Morris
1982–83: Martin Wilkinson
1983–86: John Wile
1986–88: Noel Cantwell
1988–89: Mick Jones
1989–90: Mark Lawrenson
1990–91: Dave Booth
1991 – Chris Turner

Oldest (League) Player:
N. Rigby (38 years 333 days) 21/4/62.
Youngest (League) Player:
M. Heeley (16 years 229 days) 24/4/76.
Most Capped Player:
8 – A. Millington (Wales)

Overall Divisional Records:

Division	Played	Won	Drawn	Lost	For	Against	Points
3	598	235	161	202	906	840	651
4	874	349	253	272	1289	1083	1128
Totals	**1472**	**584**	**414**	**474**	**2195**	**1923**	**1779**

Additional Club Records

Most Goals scored in Season (League):
134 (1960/61)

Most Goals conceded in Season (League):
82 (1961/62)

Most League Wins:
28 (1960/61)

Most League Draws:
18 (1975/76 & 1980/81)

Most League Defeats:
21 (1978/79)

Most Points:
82 (1981/82 – 3 points for win)
66 (1960/61 – 2 points for win)

Biggest Victories:
League   – 8–1 v. Oldham Athletic (26/11/69)
                – 7–0 v. Barrow (9/10/71)
F.A.Cup   – 7–0 v. Harlow Town (16/11/91)
League Cup – 4–0 v. Burnley (5th rd. 17/11/65)

Biggest Defeats:
League   – 0–7 v. Tranmere R. (29/10/85)
F.A.Cup   – 1–8 v. Northampton T.(18/12/46)
                (pre–League, played at Coventry City)
League Cup – 0–6 v. Barnsley (18/9/81)

Most First Class Matches In Season:
67 (incl. play–off plus Autoglass Trophy) 1991–92
Season (plus 1 Autoglass abandoned)

Fewest Goals Conceded:
33 (1977/78)

Fewest Goals Scored:
44 (1978/79)

Additional Individual Records:

Most Goals in Match:
6 – J. Laxton (Pre–league F.A.Cup 6/10/45)

Most Goals in Season:
54 – T.Bly (52 League, 2 F.A.C.) 60/61 Season.

Consecutive Appearances:
148 – E. Steele (124 League, 24 Cup)

Consecutive Scoring Games:
6 – J.Hall (28/3/70 – 14/4/70)

Consecutive 'Clean Sheets':
7 – M. Drewery (6/10/73 – 10/11/73)

Top Five Appearances

	League	F.A.Cup	Lge.Cup.	Total
T.Robson	440+42	43+2	31+1	514+45
J.Carmichael	336+22	30+3	28+1	394+26
C.Turner	308+6	33	16+1	357+7
J.Hall	298+4	19+1	12	329+5
B.Wright	291+2	17	12	320+2

Top Five Gaolscorers

J.Hall	122	11	4	137
T.Robson	111	10	7	128
T.Bly	81	6	0	87
P.Price	62	7	2	71
P.McNamee	60	7	1	68

STATISTICAL SECTION:

The statistics pages have been designed for easy reference and are generally self–explanatory. however the following notes explain various specific details.

Players: *Every player who has made appearances for the Club in the Football League, F.A.Cup and/or Football League Cup (and later names) – between the 1960/61 and 1991/92 seasons – have been included. The figures under the 'Years' column relate to the season(s) in which that player made appearances, e.g. 1965/71 refers to the seasons 1965/66 to 1970/71, and 1984/85 refers to season 1984/85. Appearances and goals scored have been separated between the three competitions, and the figures in the four columns under each heading refer as follows:*

        ① = *no. of appearances.*   ② = *no. of used substitute appearances.*
        ③ = *no. of unused substitute 'appearances'.*   ④ = *no.of goals scored.*

In addition to the those scored by Peterborough players, the following number of goals have been attributed to the opposition (i.e. 'own goals'):

        Football League = 54. F.A.Cup = 5. Football League Cup = 4.

General Statistics: *The first page for each season includes a summary of the League matches played, and lists the full details of the Football League (or Midland League) games, complete with match numbers in the left hand column (abandoned matches are unnumbered). The figure in the top box of this column, refers to the accumulative number of Football League (or Midland League – excluding the 1939/40 season) matches played; seasonal totals shown are given to the completion of the preceding season.*

The fixture dates ('Date'), results ('Res'), half time score, where known ('H.T'.), attendances ('Attend.') where known, and Peterborough United goalscorers for each match are self explanatory ('O.G.' refers to an own goal).

The opposition shown in upper case (capital letters) refers to a Peterborough United 'home' match, and lower case team names refer to the opposition in an 'away' match.

All players that have appeared for the Club in League or major Cup matches are shown (listed at right angles to the statistical details), and their appearances are shown by a number entered for the appropriate match. For pre–war matches, players did not wear numbered shirts, and the number refers to the normally accepted position, i.e. Goalkeeper = '1', Right back = '2', Left back = '3', Right half = '4', etc. through to Left winger = '11'. Substitutes are included, when applicable. 'S' refers to an unused substitute. '12' or '14' refers to one (or two) substitutes that have been used in that match. '12' replaced the player suffixed '*' (e.g. 10*), and '14' replaced the player suffixed '''' (e.g. 9'').

The second page refers to major cup matches. Cup matches follow a similar pattern to League matches (as explained above). The left hand column undicates the round number, e.g. 3/Q. = 3rd qualifying, 2nd = 2nd round, 2/R. = 2nd round replay, 1/1L = 1st round, 1st leg, etc.

THE FOOTBALL LEAGUE PLAYERS

Player:	Years	Football League:				F.A.Cup				Football Lge. Cup			
		①	②	③	④	①	②	③	④	①	②	③	④
ADAMS	1966/68	13	3	6	2	1	1	3		1			
ADCOCK	1991/92	23	1		7								
ANDERSON J.	1960/61									1			
ANDERSON T.	1977/79	49		1	6	1			1	8			
ANDREWS	1988/90	42	1	9		4			1	3		3	
ASTBURY	1985/86	4				3							
BANHAM	1960/62	16				4							
BARBER	1989/90+1991/92	45				3				8			
BARKER	1971/72	36			9	4			2				
BARNARD	1981/82	1	3	5									
BARNES B.	1991/92	15			5								
BARNES R.	1964/66	39		1	6	9			1	5			
BARRON	1977/81	21				5				1			
BEASLEY	1986/87	7								3			
BEATTIE	1962/63	10											
BEECH	1983/85	58	2	4	5	3				3			
BEESLEY	1965/67	23	2	2	3	1				1			1
BENJAMIN	1982/84	77	3	4	14	5				7	1		1
BENNETT	1963/65	4											
BENNETT I.	1991/92	7											
BENNING	1987/88	2		2									
BERRY	1990/91	28	4	4	6			3		1			
BIRKS	1964/66	34		2		8			1	1			
BLY	1960/62	88			81	11			6	2			
BRACE	1967/69	22	1	2	6	3			2	2		3	
BRADFORD	1976/77	4											
BRADLEY	1972/76	106	3	3		12	1		1	6			
BRADSHAW	1990/91	39				5				2			
BREMNER	1990/91	13	4		3	3				2			3
BROOKES	1971/73	41	1		1	7				2			
BUCHANAN	1983/84	13	3	1	4		1			4			
BURTON	1972/73	3	1										
BUTLER	1981/82	39				3							
BUTLIN	1977/79	64			12	4			1	9			1
BUTTERWORTH	1986/92	101	22	27	3	8	1	1		8	1	4	
BYATT	1978/79	2	1	1									
BYRNE	1965/68	106	1		28	6			2	10			8
CAMP	1977/78	6	1		1					3			2
CARMICHAEL	1970/83	336	22	20	5	30	3		2	28	1	1	
CARR	1986/89	8	6	9		1	1	2		1	1		
CASSELLS	1979/80	8											
CASSIDY	1984/86	44	2	8	9	7		2	1	2		1	1
CAVENER	1985/86	9	1										
CHARD	1974/85	153	19	12	18	9		1	1	15	2	1	2
CHARLERY	1990/92	35	6	4	16	3			1	6			2
CHRISTIE	1986/87	6	2	1		1				1	1		
CLAMP	1964/65	8											
CLAYTON	1990/91	4		2									
CLARKE	1981/84	76	6	2	18	4			2	7		1	2
CLISS	1977/83	65	20	11	11	1	2	3		4	1	1	
COLLINS	1978/88	196	10	12	3	15				19	1	2	
CONMY	1964/72	251	12	18	34	25			4	16			6
COOKE J.	1978/79	18			5								
COOKE R.	1980/83	115			51	13			10	9			7

Player:	Years	Football League:				F.A.Cup				Football Lge. Cup			
		①	②	③	④	①	②	③	④	①	②	③	④
COOPER S.	1990/91	2	7										
COOPER G.	1990/92	35	4	1	5	3			2	6		1	
COOPER R.	1963/68	132		3	1	16				2		1	
CORDER	1985/86	2											
CORNER	1987/88	9											
COSTELLO	1990/92	3	3	3								1	
COZENS	1973/78	127	5	1	41	12	1		10	8	2		3
CRAWFORD	1964/69	172			6	9				15			
CRICHTON	1986/87+1988/90	47				5							
CROSBY	1989/91	85	2	2		8				6			
CROWE	1964/67	56		2		9			2	9			1
CULPIN	1989/92	30	17	8	14	4	5	2	3	3	2	1	1
CUNNINGHAM	1978/79	4			1								
CURTIS	1991/92					1							
CUSACK	1988/89	44			10	4			1	4			1
DANZEY	1990/91		1										
DARRELL	1971/73	32	10	7	6		1			1		1	
DAY	1962/64	18			2								
DEAKIN	1964/68	90	1	4	35	11			10	7			2
DEARDEN	1990/91	7											
DIGHTON	1970/72	8											
DOIG	1986/87	7											
DOUGAN	1963/65	77			38	10			7	3			1
DOWNES	1967/69	23	3	6	3	1			1			2	
DOYLE J.	1986/87	13	1	2		1				2			
DOYLE B.	1976/79	130			10	8				18			2
DREWERY	1968/74	209				18				7			
DUFF	1963/67	118				9				10			
DUNCLIFFE	1970/73	120				6				3			
DUNNE	1960/62	4			1								
EARLE	1977/78	1				1							
EBDON	1991/92	12	3		2		1			2	1	1	
EMERY	1960/63	68			29	8			3	2			
EMMERSON	1963/64	7											
EUSTACE	1975/76	42	1		5	5				5			
FAIRBROTHER	1965/68	69	3	4	37	7			6	6			5
FIFE	1987/88		1	1									
FIRM	1982/85	71	1	1	3	4				3	1		
FOSTER	1979/81	71			5	1				10			
FREEMAN	1981/82	41				3							
FREESTONE	1972/73	2	1	1	1								
FUCCILLO	1985/87	82			3	7				6			
GAGE	1985/87	73			1	1				4			
GALLAGHER	1979/87	89	6	4	21	4	2	1	2	4	4		
GALLEY	1974/75	7			1								
GARNHAM	1976/77	2											
GARWOOD	1967/71	58	8	9	30	3	3	3		1			
GAVIN	1990/92	18	4	4	6					4	1		4
GENOVESE	1987/88	8	8	17	1					2	1		1
GODDEN	1989/90	24				2				2			
GOLDSMITH	1988/90	39	7	5	6	4				4		2	1
GOODING	1988/89	47			21	1			2	8			2
GOULD	1965/67	18		5	3	1				3			

Player:	Years	Football League:				F.A.Cup				Football Lge. Cup			
		①	②	③	④	①	②	③	④	①	②	③	④
GRAHAM G.	1960/64	17			1					2			
GRAHAM M.	1989/90	10	4		2	2	1			2			
GREEN	1978/79	30								8			
GREGORY	1973/79+1986/87	141	32	16	40	14	1		6	12	2	1	2
GUNN	1987/89	130	1	3	14	7				14			2
GUY	1978/81	42	11	11	4	1				3	2	1	1
GYNN	1978/83	152	4	1	33	13			3	12			1
HAILS	1960/63	94			27	11			3	2			2
HALL	1967/75	298	4		122	19	1		11	12			4
HALSALL	1988/92	223			26	17			4	24			3
HAMPTON	1969/70	3	1	1						2			
HANKIN	1983/85	31	2	1	8					3			1
HARLE	1988/90	21	1	8	2			1					
HAWKES	1961/62	1											
HEATH	1972/73	43	1	1	4	4			1	1			
HEELEY	1975/78	12	5	5	3							1	
HELLAWELL	1968/69	9											
HEPPOLETTE	1979/80	5								3			
HERBERT	1990/91									2			
HILL F.	1973/75	73	2	3	7	10	1		1	3			
HILL P.	1990/91	1		2								1	
HINDLEY	1976/79	112			1	6				11			
HINE	1989/91	55			7	5				3			
HODGSON	1980/82	82	1		5	8				3			
HODSON	1974/77	24	10	5						2	2	2	
HOGG	1960/61	2											
HOLLIDAY	1969/70	12	4	3	1	1				1		1	
HOLLOW	1965/66	14			1					1			
HOLMAN	1978/79	9			1								
HOLMES	1983/86	48	1	2	7	4				4			
HOPKINS	1961/65	104				8				2			
HOROBIN	1962/64	80			20	5				1			
HOWARTH	1991/92	6	1										
HUDSON	1961/63	65			39	9			10	1			1
HUGHES	1975/78	75	2		5	7			1	6			
ILEY	1968/73	64	4		4	5				3			1
IMLACH	1982/84	37	5	2	1	1				6			1
IPPOLITTO	1982/84	8		3	3						1		
JACKSON	1962/64	47			4	3				1			
JEFFERIES	1976/77	7				2							
JEPSON	1989/90	18			5								
JOHNSON D.	1984/86	28	7	10	4	1		2		2			
JOHNSON Peter	1965/67	42		4	1	4		1		6			
JOHNSON Peter	1991/92	11		1		3				3			
JONES	1973/76	82	6	5	4	7	1	2	1	5			1
KELLOCK	1979/82	134			43	10			1	12			4
KELLY	1983/88	95	23	17	28	8	2		3	4	2		2
KERR	1987/88	10			1								
KEVAN	1965/67	16	1	2	2								
KIMBLE	1991/92	30			4	3				8			2
KIRKHAM	1965/68	46		6	2	5				3			
KLUG	1984/85	39			2	2				2			

Player:	Years	Football League:				F.A.Cup				Football Lge. Cup			
		①	②	③	④	①	②	③	④	①	②	③	④
KOWALSKI	1985/86	35			3	7			1	2			
KWIATKOWSKI	1967/72	49	11	12		1				1			
LA RONDE	1984/85	8											
LAMBERT	1979/81	15	6	2	2					3	1		
LANGAN	1988/89	18	1			1				3			
LAWRENCE	1986/88	28	5	4	8	3			1	7		2	1
LEE	1973/78	170	2		12	19				16			2
LEWIS	1973/74	10			1								
LINNELL	1967/68	24	2	4	1	1		1		1			
LINTON	1982/84	24	3	6	3			1		5			
LLEWELYN	1973/75	11	2	2	3	4			1				
LONGHURST	1988/90	51	7	1	7	5	1		3	3			
LOWTHER	1984/85	1											
LUKE	1986/92	248	1	1	27	17				25			1
MADRICK	1988/89	3	5	11				4		1		1	
MALOY	1964/65	6			1								
MARTIN	1984/85	13		1									
MASON	1966/68	37		2	18	3				1		1	
MASSEY	1981/82	13	5	2	3	1	1	1				1	
MAYNARD	1967/68	2	1	6		1							
McANEARNEY	1965/66	12		1		1				3			
McCLURE	1985/86	4											
McCORMICK	1975/76	1											
McELHINNEY	1988/91	87		2	1	12				8		1	
McEWAN	1977/79	62	1		3	6				8			
McINERNEY	1990/92	3	7		1						1	3	
McLAUCHLIN	1966/67	8			2								
McLAUGHLAN	1973/74	1											
McMANUS	1985/86	18											
McNAMEE	1960/66	192		1	60	17			7	3			1
McVAY	1979/81	47	2		1	6				7			
MERCER	1982/83	3											
MERRICK	1975/76	5								1			
METCHICK	1966/68	38			6	2				1			
MILLINGTON	1966/69	118				8				6			
MOORE	1989/90	6	1	2									
MORGAN	1990/91	5											
MORRIS	1979/80	1											
MORTON	1961/63	7			2					1			
MOSS E.	1975/77	34	1	2	9	2			1	5			2
MOSS B.	1969/73	86	18	9	17	5	2	2	2	3			
MOULDEN	1962/65	62			9	3				1			
MOULDS	1986/87											1	
MURRAY	1973/76	123		2	10	17			2	7			
NAYLOR	1982/83	8											
NEENAN	1987/89	55				2				9			
NIGHTINGALE	1986/88	71	7	4	3	3				5		3	
NIMMO	1976/77	4			1								
NIXON	1974/77	104	6		16	12	3		6	5		1	
NOBLE	1967/72	205	2	1	1	10				9			
NORMAN	1968/69	9	1	4				1		3			
NORRIS	1960/61	5											
NUTTALL	1985/88	12	9	19			2				1	3	

Player:	Years	Football League:				F.A.Cup				Football Lge. Cup			
		①	②	③	④	①	②	③	④	①	②	③	④
O'KEEFE	1984/86		1	1								1	
OAKES K.	1972/78+1988/91	143	150	23	11	12	1	5		15	2	2	1
OAKES D.	1971/73	84	1	2	5	8				2			
ORR	1964/67	47	1	8		10			1	1			
OSBORNE	1988/91	18	43	23	7	1	2	1		2	2	1	
OVERFIELD	1963/64	1											
PARIS	1985/88	135	2		2	10				12			
PARK	1972/73	15	3	2	1					1			
PARKIN	1976/77	3								2			
PARKINSON	1979/80	12	1		5	1				4			1
PARR	1984/85		1	1									
PAYNE	1969/70									1			
PEARCE	1963/64	28			2	1				1			
PHILLIPS I.	1979/82	97			3	7				7			
PHILLIPS S.	1986/88	46	2	2	16	2		1		3		1	
PHILLIPS B.	1973/74	1											
PHILPOTT	1987/89	1	3	4			1	1				1	
PIKE	1983/86	119	7	5	8	10				8			
PLEAT	1970/71	28	1		2	1				1			
POLLARD	1987/89	20		2						4			
POPE	1990/91	1	1										
POTTS	1969/70	49	1			3				3			
PRICE D.	1974/75	6			1	2							
PRICE Peter	1968/72+1974/75	116	5	6	62	8			7	3	1	1	2
PRICE Paul	1986/88	86				2				10			
PULLEY	1965/67	16	1	6	4	1				1			
PYATT	1968/69	15	1	4	1					3			
QUOW	1979/86	191	12	5	17	10	1		2	16	1	1	1
RADCLIFFE	1967/68	2		1									
RANKMORE	1963/68	201			7	17				13			1
RAYMENT	1981/85	24	6	9	3					1	1		
RAYNOR	1960/63	119			12	13				2			
READ	1964/65	2											
REES	1985/86	5			2								
REILLY	1984/85		1	1									
RICHARDS	1989/90	16	4	1	5	2	1			2			2
RICKETTS	1967/70	46	3	4	1	1				5			
RIGBY	1960/62	55				2				1			
RILEY	1987/88+1989/92	85	11	1	25	8			3	12	1		2
RIPLEY	1960/62	88			12	11			2	1			
ROBERTSON	1978/79	12	3	3	1	1				1	1	4	
ROBINSON B.	1964/66	8								2			
ROBINSON D.	1989/92	94			9	6			1	11			
ROBINSON D.J.	1990/91	7			3								
ROBINSON R.	1991/92	24	3										
ROBSON	1968/81	440	42	16	111	43	2	1	10	31	1		7
RODAWAY	1981/83	80	1			6				6			
ROGERS	1975/78	25	4	1	1					3			
RONSON	1961/63	50				3				2			
ROONEY	1965/67	7		1	2								
ROSS I.	1976/79	112			1	6				13			
ROSS T.	1965/67	5	2	2	2	1							
RUSSELL A.	1971/73	7	8	9	1	1		2					
RUSSELL K.	1990/91	7			3								
SALMAN	1991/92	1		2									
SANSBY	1960/61	1											
SARGENT	1977/79	27	7	7	5	4	1	1	2	5		1	2
SEAMAN	1982/85	91				5				10			
SENIOR	1961/64	38			11	7			1	1			

Player:	Years	Football League:				F.A.Cup				Football Lge. Cup			
		①	②	③	④	①	②	③	④	①	②	③	④
SHARKEY	1978/80	15				1				1			
SHEAVILLS	1960/63	30			8	3				2			
SHEFFIELD	1970/71	17	1		6			1		1			
SHEPHERD	1984/87	53	2	1	14	5	1		3	2			
SHIELS	1964/65	12			4					1			
SHOEMAKE	1986/88	40				1				2			
SIMPSON	1962/63	45			4	3				1			
SIMS	1964/65	16				3							
SINGLETON	1962/65	85			1	4				3			
SISSONS	1962/65	68				4				2			
SLACK	1977/81	201	1	2	18	20			1	13			1
SLOUGH	1977/81	104	1		10	11			2	12			4
SMALL	1982/83	2	2		1								
SMELT	1981/82	5								2			
SMEULDERS	1986/87	1											
SMITH B.	1981/82	5											
SMITH K.	1963/65	55			28	2				1			
SMITH Ray	1960/63	92			3	9				2			
SMITH Ray.	1972/73	22		1	8		2			1			
SMITH T.	1978/82	68		2	5	4				3			
STAFFORD	1960/63	17								1			
STEELE	1973/77	124				13				11			
STENSON	1971/72	2											
STERLING	1989/92	147	2		19	11			3	12			3
STYLES	1978/79	32			1	1				8			2
SUTTON	1982/83	1											
SWINDLEHURST	1988/89	4			1								
SYRETT	1979/82	75	4	9	23	4	1	2	1	4			1
TAYLOR	1960/61	1											
TELFORD	1975/76	3	1	1	2								
THOMPSON	1963/69	79	6	11	15	3		1	1	6		1	2
TURLEY	1961/64	32			14								
TURNER C.	1969/78	308	6	4	37	33		1	3	16	1	1	3
TURNER J.	1984/86	60				6				2			
TURNER M.	1991/92			1								1	
TURPIE	1970/72	31	6	10	3	1				1			
TYDEMAN	1983/84	29				1							
WADDLE	1983/85	35	1	4	12	1						1	
WALKER J.	1960/65	125				13				5			
WALKER J.	1975/77	20	11	4	1	2				3	1		
WALKER P.	1973/75	75	3	1	3	8	1	1		3			
WALLS	1960/62	78				11							
WALSH	1988/89	5			1								
WATKINS	1989/91	5	5	13		1		1			1	3	
WATSON	1965/68	75			20	5			6	9			1
WAUGH	1976/81	195				10				22			
WELSH	1991/92	42				3				8			
WHITE C.	1991/92	7	1	4						2			
WHITE D.	1987/88	14			4								
WHITTAKER	1960/63	82				12				2			
WHYMARK	1985/86	3								1			
WILE	1967/71+1983/86	202	3	6	10	14				16			
WINFIELD	1974/75	11											
WINTERS	1980/83	60		2	3	4				4	1		
WOOF	1976/77	2	1	1									
WORRALL	1983/86	93	2		16	8		1	1	4			
WOSAHLO	1968/69	13	2	3	1	1				2			
WRIGHT	1963/72	291	2	3	9	17				12		1	
YOUNG	1972/73	24	1		2	3							
ZENCHUK	1983/84	1											
Own Goals					54				5				4

SEASON 1934/35

Midland League

#	Date		Opposition	Res	H.T.	Attend	Goalscorers
1	1	Sep	GAINSBOROUGH TRIN.	4-0	2-0	4033	Hargeaves Rigby Thompson Roberts
2	3		Scunthorpe & L.Utd.	0-0	0-0	2000	
3	10		Chesterfield Res.	2-2	1-2		Rigby Cowen
4	15		Bradford P.A. Res.	3-4	3-2	1000	Hargeaves (2) Thompson
5	17		Lincoln City Res.	1-4	0-1	1000	Hargeaves
6	24		Notts County Res.	1-1	1-0		Camidge
7	4	Oct	GRIMSBY TOWN RES.	4-4	2-1	2406	Cowen (2) Thompson Camidge
8	6		Frickley Colliery	3-2	1-1		Roberts Young (2)
9	11		Hull City Res.	1-0	1-0		Camidge
10	20		MEXBOROUGH TOWN	3-1	0-1	2985	Rigby (2) Camidge
11	27		BARNSLEY RES.	3-2	1-2	4190	Hargeaves Rigby Thompson
12	3	Nov	Barnsley Res.	2-4	1-2		Rigby Cowen
13	10		SCARBOROUGH	9-1	4-0	1655	Rigby(3) Cowan(2) Cam. Roberts Willis O.G.
14	17		Boston Town	1-1	1-1		Cowen
15	24		Norwich City Res.	0-6	0-4		
16	1	Dec	Doncaster Rov. Res.	1-5	0-2		Rigby
17	8		NOTTS. COUNTY RES.	2-4	1-2	3202	Hargeaves Cowen
18	15		CHESTERFIELD RES.	1-3	0-2	2334	Rigby
19	25		Grantham	0-4	0-2		
20	26		GRANTHAM	3-1	1-0	4340	Rigby Roberts Willis
21	5	Jan	HULL CITY RES.	4-1	1-0	2581	Cowen Thompson Camidge (2)
22	12		Scarborough	3-1	1-1	1100	Cowen Thompson (2)
23	2	Feb	FRICKLEY COLLIERY	2-2	0-2	2393	Hargeaves Camidge
24	5		Grimsby Town Res.	1-0	0-0		Mettam
25	9		Gainsborough Trin.	6-2	4-1		Rigby Cowen Thompson(3) O.G.
26	16		Rotherham Utd. Res.	4-4	2-2		Camidge (2) Willis (2)
27	23		NORWICH CITY RES.	0-4	0-1	4060	Cowen
28	14	Mar	BOSTON TOWN	1-2	0-2	1772	Roberts
29	16		Mexborough Town	1-5	1-4		Hargeaves Duthie
30	23		ROTHERHAM UTD. RES.	2-4	1-3	1332	Camidge (2)
31	4	Apr	SCUNTHORPE & L. UTD.	2-0	1-0	1051	
32	6		LINCOLN CITY RES.	0-0	0-0	1777	
33	13		DONCASTER ROV. RES.	1-0	1-0	2719	Roberts
34	19		DENABY UNITED	0-0	0-0	4329	
35	20		Bradford City Res.	3-5	2-2		Rigby Thompson Duthie
36	22		Denaby United	3-3	1-2	1621	Hargeaves Thompson Roberts
37	27		BRADFORD CITY RES.	2-1	2-0		Camidge Roberts
38	4	May	BRADFORD P.A. RES.	2-1	0-0	2036	Thompson (2)

Team selections (shirt numbers)

#	Jackson	Harris	Purcell	Staniland	Doyle	Hargeaves	Rigby	Cowen	Thompson	Camidge	Roberts	Goodacre	Kendall	Willis	Young	Harvey	Lenton	Hart	Trotter	Vernum	Mettam	Mansfield	Duthie	Westwood	Barrowclough
1	1	2	3	4	5	6	7	8	9	10	11														
2	1	3		4	5	6	7	8	9	10	11	2													
3		3		4	5	6	7	8	9	10		2	1	11											
4		3		4	5	6	7	8	9	10	11	2	1												
5		3		4	5	6	7	8	9	10	11	2	1												
6		3		4	5	6	7	8	9	10	11	2	1												
7		3		4	5	6	7	8	9	10	11	2	1												
8		3		4	5	6	7	8		9	11	2	1		10										
9		3		4	5	6	7	8		9	11	2	1		10										
10		3		4	5	6	7	8		9	11	2	1		10										
11		3		4	5	6	7	8	9	10	11	2	1												
12		3		4	5	6	7	8	9	10	11	2	1												
13		3		4	5	6	9	8		10	11	2	1	7											
14		3		4	5	6	7	8	9	10	11	2	1												
15		3		4	5	6	7	8	9	10	11	2	1												
16		3		4	5	6	7	8		10	11	2	1			9									
17		3		4	5	6	7	8		10	11	2	1			9									
18		3		4	5	6	7	8			11	2	1			9			10						
19		3		4	5	6	7	8	9	10	11	2	1												
20		3		4	5	6	7		9		10	2	1	11						8					
21		3		4	5	6		8	9	10	11	2	1	7											
22		3		4	5	6		8	9	10	11	2	1	7											
23		3		4	5	6		9		10	11	2	1	7						8					
24		3		4	5	6		8	9		11	2	1	7							10				
25		3		4	5	6	7	8	9	10	11	2	1												
26		3		4	5	6		8	9	10	11	2	1	7											
27		3		4	5	6		8	9	10	11	2	1	7				3							
28		3		4	5	6		8	9	10	7	2	1	11											
29	1	3		4	5	6	7	8	9			2									4	6	10		
30		3		4	5	6	7	8		9	11	2	1										10		
31		3		4	5	6	7	8	9		11	2	1										10		
32		3		4	5	6	7	8	9		11	2	1										10		
33		3		4	5	6	7		9		11	2	1										10	8	
34		3		4	5	6	7		9		11	2	1										10	8	
35					5	6	7	8	10	9	11	2	1												
36		3		8	5	6	7		9	10	11	2	1										4		
37		3		4	5	6	7			10	11	2	1											8	
38		3		4	5	6	7		9	10		2	1										8		11

	Jackson	Harris	Purcell	Staniland	Doyle	Hargeaves	Rigby	Cowen	Thompson	Camidge	Roberts	Goodacre	Kendall	Willis	Young	Harvey	Lenton	Hart	Trotter	Vernum	Mettam	Mansfield	Duthie	Westwood	Barrowclough
League Appearances	3	36	1	34	38	38	32	33	27	33	31	35	35	14	3	3	1	2	1	2	2	1	9	3	1
League Goals (+ 2 O.G.)						9	14	12	14	13	8			4	2					2	1	1	2	3	1

SEASON 1935/36

Midland League

38	Date	Opposition	Res	H.T.	Attend	Goalscorers
1	31	Scarborough	2-1	2-1	3361	Collins Barraclough
2	5 Sep	DONCASTER ROV. RES.	2-2	0-2	3289	Collins O.G.
3	7	FRICKLEY COLLIERY	1-3	1-0	3268	Fenton
4	12	BRADFORD P.A. RES.	0-1	0-0	2531	
5	14	ROTHERHAM UTD. RES.	2-1	1-1	2311	Hargreaves Rigby
6	19	NOTTS. COUNTY RES.	1-0	1-0	2058	Collins
7	25	Chesterfield Res.	0-7	0-5		
8	12 Oct	BURTON TOWN	2-2	1-2	1992	Barraclough O.G.
9	19	Bradford P.A. Res.	0-5	0-2		
10	23	Gainsborough Trin.	0-7	0-1		
11	7 Nov	HULL CITY RES.	4-1	1-1	876	Hargreaves Collins (3)
12	9	Scunthorpe & L. Utd.	0-1	0-1		
13	16	Frickley Colliery	0-3	0-1		
14	23	Boston United	0-2	0-2		
15	30	Doncaster Rov. Res.	0-1	0-0		
16	14 Dec	BOSTON UNITED	2-0	1-0	1792	Hargreaves Rigby
17	21	Lincoln City Res.	1-2	1-1	1000	Mitchell
18	25	GRANTHAM	3-1	1-0	1479	Collins Barraclough Roberts
19	26	Grantham	1-1	1-1		Barraclough
20	28	GRIMSBY TOWN RES.	3-2	0-2	2391	Collins (2) Roberts
21	4 Jan	SCARBOROUGH	0-2	0-0	2370	
22	25	GAINSBOROUGH TRIN.	1-5	1-3	1500	Collins
23	6 Feb	Hull City Res.	0-0	0-0		
24	15	Denaby United	4-1	2-0	800	Collins Camidge (2) Barraclough
25	20	BRADFORD CITY RES.	1-0	0-0	1066	Camidge
26	26	Bradford City Res.	0-6	0-2		
27	14 Mar	Grimsby Town Res.	0-0	0-0		
28	19	Mexborough Town	1-2	0-1	2090	Collins
29	21	SCUNTHORPE & L. UTD.	3-1	2-0	2090	Collins Camidge Roberts
30	28	CHESTERFIELD RES.	1-4	0-1	2330	Roberts
31	1 Apr	Burton Town	3-3	1-1		Collins (3)
32	4	DENABY UNITED	4-4	1-3	1544	Hargreaves Collins Camidge Rigby
33	10	Norwich City Res.	1-2	0-0	5000	O.G.
34	11	LINCOLN CITY RES.	0-1	0-0	1946	
35	13	NORWICH CITY RES.	1-1	1-1	3032	Wilson
36	14	Notts. County Res.	1-0	0-0		Wilson
37	16	MEXBOROUGH TOWN	6-2	3-0	877	Collins (4) Camidge (2)
38	18	Barnsley Res.	0-5	0-2		
39	25	BARNSLEY RES.	1-0	0-0	1360	Collins
40	2 May	Rotherham Utd. Res.	0-4	0-2		

Player appearances (shirt numbers)

#	Kendall	Jefferson	Mitchell	Warren	Doyle	Hargeaves	Willis	Duthie	Collins	Camidge	Barraclough	Fenton	Rigby	Macaulay	Beach	Marsden	Upton	Barber	Hart	Wilson	Roberts	Wyles	Rippon	Walker	Vernum	Setchfield	Blunt
1	1	2	3	4	5	6	7	8	9	10	11																
2	1	2	3	4	5	6	7	8	9	10	11																
3	1	2	3	4	5	6	7	8	8	10	11	9															
4	1	2	3			6		4	9	10	11		7	8													
5	1	2	3	4		5	11	6	9	10			7	8													
6	1	2	3	4		5	7		9	6	11		8	10													
7	1	2	3	4		5		6	9		11			10	8												
8	1	2	4			5			9	6	11		7		10	3	8										
9	1	2	4			6		10		9	11		7			3	8	5									
10	1					6		10		9	11		8			3	10	5	2								
11	1		4			6	7		9	10	11		7			3		5		2	8						
12	1		4			6		9		10	11		7			3		5		2	8						
13	1		4			6		10	9	9	11		7			3		5		2	8						
14	1		4			6			9	10	11		7			3		5		2	8						
15	1					6		4	9	10	11		7			3				2	8						
16	1					6		4	9	8	11		7			3		5		2	10						
17	1		7			3		4	9	6	11		8			2		5			10						
18	1	2			5	5		4	9	6	11	7	8			3					10						
19	1	2			5	6		7	9	10	11		8							4							
20	1	2				6		4	9	10	11		7			3		5		4	8						
21	1				4	6		4	9	10	11		7					5		2	8						
22	1	2	4		5	6	11	4	9	10	11		8														
23	1				5	6		4	9	10	11		7			3				2	8						
24	1				6	6		4	9	10			7			3		5		2	8	11					
25	1				5	6		4	9	10			7			3		5		2	8						
26	1		11					4	9	10			7			3		5		2	8						
27	1					6		4	9	10			7			3		5		2	8	11					
28	1				6	11	11	6	9	10			7			3		5		2	8						
29	1					6		8	9	10			7			3		5		2	8						
30	1					6		4	9	10			7			3		5		2	8						
31	1		3			11	11	6	9	10			7			2		5			8	11	4				
32	1		3			6		8	9	10			7			2		5				11	4				
33	1		6			11	11	4	9	10			8			3		5		2	8						
34	1		6				11	4	8	10			8			3		5				7					
35			6			5	11	4	8	10			7			3				2	8	11	9	1	8		
36			6			5	11	4	9	10			7			3				2				1			
37			3		5			4	9	10			7			3		5		2			8	1	6		
38			1		5			4	9	10			7			3		5		2	8	11				8	
39	1		6			6		4	9	10		8	7			3		5		2		11	8				
40			6			11	8	8	9	10			7			3		5		2			1	1			4

F.A.Cup

1/Q.	5 Oct	RUSHDEN TOWN	0-3	0-3	4254

	1	2	6	4	5	7	9	11	10	3	8

	1	2	6	4	5	7	9	11	10	3	8													
League Appearances	35	12	27	11	37	11	34	35	36	24	36	4	2	31	3	24	1	26	21	8	4	4	2	1
League Goals (+ 3 O.G.)		1	1	4	4			22	7	5	1	1		1				2	4					
Cup appearances	1	1	1	1	1	1	1	1	1	1	1	1		1	1									
Cup Goals	1																							

Peterborough United Team in 1934

United's team for their first match was H. Jackson; Harris, Purcell; Staniland, Doyle, Hargreaves; Rigby, Cowen, Thompson, Camidge and Roberts.

Season Summary

After the new United are formed from the ashes of the former Club, a reasonable season is followed by a poor one on the pitch. The first F.A.Cup match is played – without success – but of more concern is another financial loss which is shown at the end of the campaign.

SEASON 1936/37

Midland League

78	Date		Opposition	Res	H.T.	Attend	Goalscorer	Kendall	Wilson C.	Bisby	Rowbotham	Froggart	Hargeaves	Rigby	Saunders	Chiverton	Briggs	Wilson J.	Willis	Walker	Vernum	Robson	Mansfield	Roberts	Fenton	Sims	McDonagh	Hart	Wyles	Bickerson
1	29 Aug		Scarborough	1-0	0-0	2548	Chiverton	1	2	3	4	5	6	7	8	9	10	11												
2	31		NOTTS. COUNTY RES.	3-6	1-1	2535	Hargeaves Chiverton Briggs	1	2	3	4	5	6	8	9	9	10	7	11											
3	3 Sep		LINCOLN CITY RES.	0-5	0-0	2416			2	3			6	8		4	10	7	11	1	5	7		6	8	9				
4	5		SCARBOROUGH	4-1	2-1	2402	Briggs (3) Fenton		2		4		3	7		5	10	11	1				6	8	9				
5	7		Lincoln City Res.	1-2	1-1		Briggs		2		4		3			5	10	7	1				6	8	9				
6	12		Grantham	0-2	0-1	1500		1	2		4		3	7		5	10	11					6	8	9				
7	17		Boston United	3-2	2-1		Briggs Fenton (2)	1	2		4		3	8		5	10	7	11					6	8	9				
8	19		GRANTHAM	1-3	1-2	3436	Briggs	1	2		4		3	6		5	10	7	11						8	9				
9	8 Oct		GAINSBOROUGH TRIN.	1-2	1-0	1351	Sims	1	2	3	4	5				9	10	7					6	8		11			
10	10		Chesterfield Res.	0-3	0-1			1	2	3	4	5	6	8		9	10	7								11			
11	14		Bradford City Res.	1-3	0-0				2		4		3			6	10	7		1				8	9	11	6		
12	22		Hull City Res.	0-4	0-0			1	2	3			6			4	10	7						8	9	11	6		
13	24		HULL CITY RES.	4-2	2-1	2386	Rigby Briggs (3)	1	2	3	4	5	6	8		9	10	7								11	6		
14	26		Nottm. Forest Res.	1-7	0-3		Chiverton	1	2	3	4	5	6			9	10	7						8		11	6		
15	21 Nov		Grimsby Town Res.	1-3	1-0		Wilson J.	1	2	3	8	5	6			4	10	7						9		11	6		
16	5 Dec		Bradford P.A. Res.	0-6	0-5	500			2	3	4		3	8		5	10	7			6			9		11	6		
17	12		SCUNTHORPE & L. UTD.	3-5	2-3	1129	Chiverton (2) Sims	1	2	3	4	5	6	8		9	10	7		1						11	6		
18	19		BRADFORD CITY RES.	0-5	0-1	1466		1	2	3	4	5	6	8		9	10	7						8		11	6		
19	26		BRADFORD P.A. RES.	1-1	0-1	2929	Wilson J.	1	2		3		11	8		5	10	7						9			6	2		
20	2 Jan		GRIMSBY TOWN RES.	2-2	1-0	1820	Wilson J. Sims	1	2	3	4			8		5	9	7						10		11	6	2		
21	9		Newark	0-4	0-0			1					10	8		5	9	7								11	6		
22	16		BURTON TOWN	2-0	1-0	1580	Briggs Roberts	1	2	3	4		3	7		5	10	11						8	9		6		
23	23		BOSTON UNITED	3-3	1-0	1417	Wilson C. Briggs Fenton		2	3	4		3			5	10	11			1			8	9		6		
24	28		Notts. County Res.	3-2	2-1		Briggs Roberts Fenton		2	3	4	2		7		5	10	7			1			8	9		6		
25	30		Rotherham Utd. Res.	1-1	0-1		Wilson J.		2	3	4					5	10	7			1			8	9		6		
26	6 Feb		NOTTM. FOREST RES.	2-2	1-2	2563	Wilson J. Fenton	1	2	3	4		3			5	10	7						8	9	11	6		
27	13		Gainsborough Trin.	2-5	2-3		Briggs Fenton	1	2	3	4					5	10	7						8	9	11	6		
28	20		DONCASTER ROV. RES.	5-0	2-0	2241	Briggs (2) Roberts Fenton (2)	1		3	4					5	10	7						8	9	11	6	2	
29	24		Mansfield Town Res.	3-1	1-1		Sims Biggs (2)	1	2	3	4	2				5	10	7						8	9	11	6		
30	27		NEWARK	3-0	2-0	2071	Briggs Roberts (2)	1	2	3	4					5	10	7						8	9	11	6	2	
31	6 Mar		ROTHERHAM UTD. RES.	1-0	1-0	2464	Fenton	1		3	4					5	10	10						8	9	11	6	2	7
32	13		Doncaster Rov. Res.	1-1	1-1	3000	Briggs	1		3	4					5	10	7						8	9	11	6	2	
33	18		FRICKLEY COLLIERY	4-0	2-0	873	Roberts (2) Fenton Sims	1		3	4					5	10	7						8	9	11	6	2	
34	20		MANSFIELD TOWN RES.	7-0	5-0	2748	Briggs(3) WilsonJ. Roberts Fenton Sims	1		3	4					5	10	7						8	9	11	6	2	
35	26		DENABY UNITED	3-0	1-0	3904	Briggs (2) Fenton	1		3	4					5	10	7						8	9	11	6		
36	27		Scunthorpe & L. Utd.	0-4	0-2			1	2	3	4					5	10		7					8	9	11	6	2	11
37	29		Denaby United	0-2	0-1			1	2	3	9	6				5	10							8	9	11	6		7
38	7 Apr		Frickley Colliery	2-1	1-1		Briggs (2)	1	2	3	4	4	11			5	10							8		7	6		
39	10		Burton Town	3-0	2-0	700	Sims (3)	1	3		8	6				5	10	7							9	11	6	2	
40	14		Barnsley Res.	1-3	1-0		O.G.	1	4		8	4				5	10	7			1				9	7	6	2	
41	17		CHESTERFIELD RES.	0-4	0-1	1556		1		3	4		11			5	10	7							9	11	6	2	
42	24		BARNSLEY RES.	2-0	1-0	2860	Briggs Wilson J.	1		3						5	10	7							9	11	6	2	8

F.A.Cup

1/Q	3 Oct	Kettering Town	2-0	1-0	3250	Chiverton Wilson J.
2/Q	17	WOLVERTON TOWN *	3-0	2-0	2427	Briggs (2) Wilson J.
3/Q	31	RUSHDEN TOWN	4-2	3-0	3572	Briggs Wilson J. Roberts (2)
4/Q	14 Nov	Biggleswade Town	2-1	0-0		Briggs Wilson J.
1st	28	Dartford	0-3	0-2	4000	

* Drawn 'away', tie reversed & played at Peterborough.

1	2	3	4	5	6	8	9	10	7									11
1	2	3		5	6	9		10	7							8		11
1	2	3	4	5	8	6		10	7							9		11
1	3	2	5	6		4		10	7							9		11
1	2	3	8	5	6	4		10	7							9		11

League Appearances
League Goals (+ 1 O.G.)
Cup appearances
Cup Goals

33	27	34	40	18	22	16	2	42	41	38	5	9	2	1	5	31	27	29	22	14	3	1
		1			1	1		5	28	7						8	14	9				
5	5	5	3	5	4	4		5	5	5						4		5				
5		5				4		1	4	4						2						

The match programme cover for the game versus Scunthorpe. The two teams were, years later, to meet in the Football League

Season Summary

Four victories in the F.A.Cup take Posh through to the first round of the F.A.Cup. But the financial situation is still desperate, and only the timely formation of the Supporters Club saves the Club from possible closure.

SEASON 1937/38

Midland League

Match results

No.	Date	Opposition	Res	H.T.	Attend	Goalscorer
1	28 Aug	Scarborough	2-5	0-3		Savage (2)
2	30	GRIMSBY TOWN RES.	1-1	0-1	3009	Savage
3	4 Sep	SCUNTHORPE & L. UTD.	3-3	2-2	3086	Atkin Bowaters G. (2)
4	8	Burton Town	0-0	0-0		
5	11	Frickley Colliery	1-2	0-0	1848	Boulton
6	13	MANSFIELD TOWN RES.	0-0	0-0		
7	18	Gainsborough Trin.	0-3	0-2		
8	25	FRICKLEY COLLIERY	3-3	1-2	2781	Bowater G. Compton O.G.
9	27	Scunthorpe & L. Utd.	0-5	0-4		
10	7 Oct	BRADFORD CITY RES.	3-3	2-2		Bowaters G. (2) Foxall
11	9	ROTHERHAM UTD. RES.	4-0	2-0		Savage (3) Roberts
12	14	Hull City Res.	2-5	1-2		Savage Bowaters G.
13	23	NEWARK	1-1	0-1	2384	Sims
14	30	Bradford City Res.	1-3	0-2		Atkin
15	6 Nov	BARNSLEY RES.	1-2	0-1	2656	Roberts
16	13	Rotherham Utd. Res.	0-1	0-0		
17	20	Notts. County Res.	2-2	1-1	2196	Atkins Savage
18	27	BRADFORD P.A. RES.	2-1	0-0	1421	Leary Lancelot
19	4 Dec	DONCASTER ROV. RES.	2-3	0-2	60 min.	Lancelot (2)
—	11	Shrewsbury Town	Aban.	0-0		
20	18	GAINSBOROUGH TRIN.	4-4	2-2	1905	Atkin (2) Bowaters G. Lancelot
21	25	NOTTS. COUNTY RES.	1-3	1-2	3145	Maudsley
22	1 Jan	SCARBOROUGH	1-1	1-1	1863	Atkin
23	8	NOTTM. FOREST RES.	3-2	0-1	2191	Smith J. Roberts Maudsley
24	22	Denaby United	2-2	1-0		Bowaters G. (2)
25	12 Feb	GRANTHAM	0-1	0-1	2825	
26	19	Newark	1-2	1-1		
27	26	BOSTON UNITED	2-2	1-1	2569	Bowaters G.
28	5 Mar	HULL CITY RES.	1-0	0-0	2647	Atkin Roberts
29	12	Grantham	2-3	1-2		Roberts Bowaters E.
30	19	Doncaster Rov. Res.	1-4	0-2		Foxall
31	31	Nottm. Forest Res.	0-5	0-3		
32	2 Apr	Barnsley Res.	1-4	0-3		Rippon
33	7	Boston United	1-3	0-2		Roberts
34	11	BURTON TOWN	3-0	1-0	975	Clarke (2) Roberts
35	15	SHREWSBURY TOWN	1-1	1-0	4460	Foxall
36	16	Grimsby Town Res.	0-4	0-0		
37	19	DENABY UNITED	8-2	4-0	794	Atkin Roberts(3) Foxall Gott(3)
38	20	Bradford P.A. Res.	0-5	0-2		
39	26	Mansfield Town Res.	3-3	2-2		Roberts (2) Foxall
40	30	LINCOLN CITY RES.	5-2	2-2	907	Roberts (2) Bowaters G. Gott (2)
41	2 May	Shrewsbury Town	1-5	0-0		Foxall
42	7	Lincoln City Res.	1-4	1-1		Maudsley

Player appearances (shirt numbers)

Players (in table order): Willis (‡ Holmes), Brooks († Winslow), Brooksbanks, Manterfield, Gott, Bowaters E., Allan, Tolliday, Maudsley, Lancelot, Leary, Wysall, Leek, Rippon, Mellows, Foxhall, Roberts, Sims, Compton, Boulton, Bowaters G., Sleaford, Savage, Wyles, Bickerson, Atkin, McDonagh, Smith H., Rowbotham, Smith J., Clarke, Kendall

No.	Foxhall	Roberts	Sims	Compton	Boulton	Bowaters G.	Sleaford	Savage	Wyles	Bickerson	Atkin	McDonagh	Smith H.	Rowbotham	Smith J.	Clarke	Kendall
1							11	10	9	8	7	6	5	4	3	2	1
2						11	10	9		8	7	6	5	4	3	2	1
3						11	10	9		8	7	6	5	4	3	2	1
4					9	11		10		8	7	6	5	4	3	2	1
5					9	11		10		8	7	6	5	4	3	2	1
6			10	2		11		9		8	7	6	5	4	3		1
7			10	2		11		9		8	7	6	5	4	3		1
8	10	8		2		11		9			7	6	5	4	3		1
9	10	8		2	9	11					7	6	5	4	3		1
10	10	8				11		9			7	6	5	4	3		1
11	10	8				11		9			7	6	5	4	3		1
12	10	8				11		9			7	6	5	4	3		1
13	8		11			10		9			7	6	5	4	3	2	1
14	10	8				11		9			7	6	5	4	3	2	

F.A.Cup

1/Q.	2 Oct	Wellingborough Town	5-0	3-0	4053	Rowbotham Atkin (2) Boulton(2)
2/Q.	16	Kettering Town	2-2	0-2		Bowaters G. Boulton
3/Q.	21	KETTERING TOWN	0-1	0-1	2563	

	1	2	3	4	5	6	7	8	9		11			9			10
	1	2	3	4	5	6	7	8	9		11		10	9			10
	1	2	3	4	5	6	7	8	9		11			9			8
	1	2	3	4	5	6	8	7	11				9				10

	1	2	3	4	5	6	7	8	9	10	11	12	4	41	11	32	15	25	6	19	3	21	1	3	4	16	5	2	2	4	2	1	1	1
League Appearances *	22	19	27	38	37	42	39	8	7	14	4																							
League Goals (+ 1 O.G.)		2	1	3	3	8	8			8	11	1	1	1	1	15		6	1	1				1	4	3		1	1	5				
Cup appearances	3	3	3	3	3	3	3		2	2	3	1				2		2																
Cup Goals			1				2				3					2		2																

League Appearances *

League Goals (+ 1 O.G.)

Cup appearances

Cup Goals

(* + Winslow and Holmes 1 each)

A change in Midland League opposition was provided, by the Club's membership of the London Mid-Week League.

Season Summary

A change in colours from Green and White to Blue and White doesn't change the luck for a poor start to the season sees 'Posh' struggling. But the first big transfer – Cecil Wilde to Everton for £350 – relieves the financial worries. A re-election application is just averted, and for the first time a profit on the season is made.

SEASON 1938/39

Midland League

162	Date	Opposition	Res	H.T.	Attend	Goalscorers
1.	27 Aug	Scarborough	0-1	0-1		
2.	29	GRIMSBY TOWN RES.	1-2	0-2	3321	Fielding
3.	3 Sep	BRADFORD P.A. RES.	1-3	1-1	3299	Warnes
4.	7	Burton Town	1-4	0-4		McCartney
5.	10	Shrewsbury Town	0-3	0-0	1984	
6.	12	MANSFIELD TOWN RES.	2-1	1-1		Fielding McCartney
7.	17	BURTON TOWN	3-0	2-0	2843	Fielding McCartney Bowaters G.
8.	22	Boston United	1-2	0-1		Bott
9.	24	DONCASTER ROV. RES.	2-0	1-0	3056	Fielding McCartney
10.	22 Oct	SCUNTHORPE & L. UTD.	0-3	0-0	3381	
11.	5 Nov	GRANTHAM	2-1	0-1	3169	McCartney (2)
12.	19	SCARBOROUGH	3-2	1-1	2904	Fielding Haden (2)
13.	3 Dec	Barnsley Res.	2-5	0-4		Fielding McCartney
14.	10	Rotherham Utd. Res.	1-2	0-1	1505	Fielding
15.	17	DENABY UNITED	7-0	2-0	2238	Fielding(4) Bott White Cooper
16.	31	BOSTON UNITED	12-0	4-0	1619	†
17.	7 Jan	HULL CITY RES.	4-2	3-2	2705	McCartney(2) Bowaters G. Haden
18.	14	BARNSLEY RES.	2-6	0-5	2229	Bowaters G. O.G.
19.	21	NOTTM. FOREST RES.	2-2	1-0		Sharp Haden
20.	28	Bradford C. Res.	2-1	2-1		White
21.	2 Feb	Hull City Res.	3-4	0-3	2798	McCartney (2) Bowaters G.
22.	4	LINCOLN CITY RES.	1-4	1-3		Fielding
23.	8	Mansfield Town Res.	3-2	2-2	3212	Fielding (2) White
24.	11	FRICKLEY COLLIERY	6-3	4-2	2811	McCartney (2) Sharp Bowaters G.(2) White
25.	18	Lincoln City Res.	2-1	0-1		McCartney Bowaters G.
26.	25	BRADFORD C. RES.	1-0	0-0		McCartney
27.	1 Mar	Gainsborough Trin.	2-4	1-1		McCathey Sharp
28.	4	Frickley Colliery	3-0	1-0		McCartney White (2)
29.	6	Scunthorpe & L. Utd.	1-2	1-1		O.G.
30.	22	Nottm. Forest Res.	3-0	2-0	1123	Sharp McCartney Parr
31.	25	Bradford P.A. Res.	0-1	0-0	2500	
32.	30	GAINSBOROUGH TRIN.	2-1	1-0		Fielding Sharp
33.	1 Apr	Grantham	1-2	1-1	6144	Rowbotham
34.	3	Newark	4-0	3-0		McCartney Parr(2) O.G.
35.	7	SHREWSBURY TOWN	1-1	1-1	4287	White
36.	8	Grimsby Town Res.	1-5	0-3	2626	Fielding
37.	10	ROTHERHAM UTD. RES.	2-1	0-1		Warnes (2)
38.	15	NOTTS. COUNTY RES.	7-1	3-0		Bowaters G. (4) McCartney (3)
39.	22	Doncaster Rov. Res.	0-1	0-1		Fielding
40.	24	Notts. County Res.	1-1	1-0		Parr
41.	29	NEWARK	1-1	0-1	2633	Bowaters G.
42.	6 May	Denaby United	6-2	4-1		Sharp McCartney Parr (3) White

† Fielding McCartney(5) Warnes Sharp Bowaters G. Haden(3)

Player appearances (shirt numbers)

#	Peckett	Black	Parr	Levy	Cooper	White	Tolliday	Compton	Haden	Bott	Dickens	Bowaters G.	Sharp	Warnes	McCartney	Fielding	McDonagh	Smith H.	Rowbotham	Smith J.	Hart	Mellows
1												11	10	9	8	7	6	5	4	3	2	1
2												11	10	9	8	7	6	5	4	3	2	1
3												11	10	9	8	7	6	5	4	3	2	1
4										8	1	11		9		7	6	5	4	3	2	
5										8	1	11			9	7	6	5	4	3		
6									10		1	11	11		9	7	6		4	3		
7									6	10	1	11	8		7		2		4	3		
8									6	10	1	11	8		9	7	2		4	3		
9								3		10	1	11	8	6	9	7	2		4			
10								3		10	1	11	8	6	9	7	2		4			
11			10					3	10	10	1	11	8	5	9	7	2	5	4			
12								3	10	10	1		8	6	9	7	2		4			
13						11			10	10	1	6	8	5	9	7	2	3	4			
14									10	10	1		8	6	9	7	2		4	3		
15					4	8			10	10	1	11		5	9	7	2	5		3		
16					4	11	5		10	10	1			6	9	7	2			3		
17					4	11		2	10	10	1		8	5	9	7	2			3		1
18						11	5	2	10	10		5	8	5	9	7	2			3		1
19					4		5		7	10		5	8	5	9		2			3		1
20					4	11			11	10			8	5	9	7	2		6	3		1
21					4	11			11	10		10	8	5	9	7	2		6	3	4	1
22						11				10		10	8	5	9	7	2		6	3		
23				1	4	11						10	8	5	9	7	2		6	3		
24			10	1	4	11						10	8	5	9	7	2		6	3		
25					4	11						10	8	5	9	7	2		6	3		1
26					4	11						10	8	5	9	7	2		6	3		1
27					4	11	5	2	6			10	8	5	9	7	2		6	3		1
28					4	11						10	8	5	9	7	2		6	3		1
29					4	11						6	8	5	9	7	2		4	3		1
30			10		4	11			6			6	8	5	9	7	2		4	3		1
31		1										10	8	5	9	7	2		6	3		
32		1				11			10			6	8	5	9	7	2		4	3		
33			10			11						6	8	5	9		2		4	3		
34			10			11						6	8	5	9	7	2		4	3		
35		1	10			11						6	8	5	9	7	2		4	3		
36		1	10			7			11			6	8	5	9		2		4	3		
37		1	10	1	4	11						10	8	5	9	7	2		6	3		
38		1	10		4	11						6	8	5	9	7	2		6	3		
39		1	10			7						10	8	5	9		2		6	3		
40		1	10		4	11						10	8	5	9	7	2		6	3		
41		1	10		4	11						6	8	5	9	7	2		6	3		
42	11	1	10		4	11						6	8	5	9	7	2		4	3		

F.A.Cup

						Scorers
1/Q.	1 Oct	KETTERING TOWN	2-1	1-0	5266	McCartney Bott
2/Q.	15	Rushden Town	4-4	0-3	4251	Fielding McCartney (2) Bott
2/QR	20	RUSHDEN TOWN	3-1	1-1	4167	McCartney (3)
3/Q.	29	Spalding United	3-2	0-1	3055	McCartney (2) Bowaters G.
4/Q.	12 Nov	ST. NEOTS TOWN	1-0	1-0	5422	McCartney
1st	26	Bristol Rovers	1-4	1-2	7342	Fielding

Cup match line-ups (shirt numbers):

3	4	5	2	7	9		8	11	1	10	6					13	1
3	4	5	2	7	9		8	11	1	10	6					7	
3	4	5	2	7	9	6	8		1	10	11		8	1			
	4	5	3	7	9	6	8	11	1	10	2		6	1			
3	4	5	2	7	9	6	8	11	1	10			2				
3	4		2	7	9	5	8	6	1	10	11						

Totals:

11	5	39	40	12	42	41	37	40	38	17	6	20	5	4	27	12	1	10	13	1
		1	6	5	17	29	4	7	13	1		8	1		8	1			7	
5		6	5	6	6	6	4	6	5	3		6	1		1					
				2	9	2		1	2											

League Appearances
League Goals (+ 3 O.G.)
Cup appearances
Cup Goals

(Rear Row) Hart, McDonagh, Manterfield, Willis, Rose

(2nd Row) Carmichael (Res.Train.), Poulter (Sec.), Cooper, Black, Smith, Warnes, Leavy, Smith (Train.), Compton, Griggs (Dir.)

(3rd Row) Swain(Dir.), Hall(Dir.), Fielding, Brooksbank, Gollings(Chair.), Haden(P./Man.), Bowater, Warrington(Dir.), Whitelam(Dir.)

(4th Row) Rowbotham, Sharp, MacCartney, Parker, White, Watts

Season Summary

Posh make a poor start under Hayden – the fourth Manager in four years – but the attendances are up. For the first time Posh oppose a Football League club in the F.A.Cup, and weeks later the all–time Club record victory is recorded. The best season to date sees Posh finish 10th in the League.

SEASON 1939/40

Midland League (Abandoned)

#	Date	Opposition	Res	H.T.	Attend	Goalscorer	Black	Perry	Smith J.	Rowbotham	Warnes	Bogg	Fielding	McCartney	Haycox	Johnson	Rudkin	Brooksbanks	Shelton	Wyles	Fletcher	Tasker	Tricker	Morley	Hewitt	Lawson	McNaughton	Sutton	Smith H.	Tolliday	Haden	Parr	Dudds	Attwell
1	26 Aug	NOTTS. COUNTY RES.	8-0	4-0	3594	McCartney 2 Haycox 4 Johnson Rudkin	1	2	3	4	5	6	7	8	9	10	11																
2	28	LINCOLN CITY RES.	4-0	2-0	3051	Johnson Rudkin Brooksbanks 2	1	2	3	4	5	6		8	9	10	11	7																
3	2 Sep	Shrewsbury Town	4-2	3-2		McCartney Haycox Johnson Rudkin	1	2	3	4	5	6	7	8	9	10	11																

† Guest players (from Notts. County)

Midland League – First Competition

#	Date	Opposition	Res	H.T.	Attend	Goalscorer	Black	Perry	Smith J.	Rowbotham	Warnes	Bogg	Fielding	McCartney	Haycox	Johnson	Rudkin	Brooksbanks	Shelton	Wyles	Fletcher	Tasker	Tricker	Morley	Hewitt	Lawson	McNaughton	Sutton	Smith H.	Tolliday	Haden	Parr	Dudds	Attwell
1	28 Oct	Gainsborough Trin.	3-2	2-1		McCartney 2 Fletcher		2	3	6	5		7	9		10	11		1	4	8													
2	4 Nov	NEWARK TOWN	7-1	4-1	1733	Fielding 2 McCartney 2 Rudkin Fletcher O.G.		2	3	6	5		7	9		10	11		1	4	8													
3	11	Grantham	0-2	0-1				2	3	6	5		7	9		10	11		1	4	8													
4	18	FRICKLEY COLLIERY	3-2	1-1	1730	McCartney 2 Fletcher		2	3	4	5		7	9		10	11		1		8	6												
5	25	GRANTHAM	7-1	4-1	1593	McCarty Haycox 3 John'n Rudkin O.G.		2	3	6	5		7	8	9	10	11		1		4													
6	9 Dec	DENABY UNITED	2-2	1-1	1560	Haycox 2		2	3	6	5		7	8	9	10	11		1		4													
7	16	Newark Town	2-5	1-3		Haycox Rudkin		2	3	6	5		7	8	9	10	11		1		4													
8	25	Boston United	1-2	0-1		Rudkin		2	3	6			7		9	10	11		1		4		8											
9	26	BOSTON UNITED	3-1	0-0	1765	Johnson 2 O.G.		2	3	6	5			9		10	11		1		4		8	7										
10	6 Jan	SCUNTHORPE & LUTD.	1-1	1-1	1024	Johnson			3		5		7	8	9	10	11		1		4	2	6											
11	13	Scunthorpe & LUtd.	6-3	1-2		Rowbotham Warnes Fielding2 McCarty Johnson			3	8	5		7	9		10	11		1		4	2	6											
12	20	GAINSBOROUGH TRIN.	4-0	1-0	915	Haycox 2 Johnson Rudkin			3		5		7	8	9	10	11		1		4	2	6											
13	23 Mar	† Denaby United	2-2	1-0		Brooksbanks Dudds									9			7			8		6			1	2	3	4	5	6	10	11

Midland League – Second Competition

#	Date	Opposition	Res	H.T.	Attend	Goalscorer	Black	Perry	Smith J.	Rowbotham	Warnes	Bogg	Fielding	McCartney	Haycox	Johnson	Rudkin	Brooksbanks	Shelton	Wyles	Fletcher	Tasker	Tricker	Morley	Hewitt	Lawson	McNaughton	Sutton	Smith H.	Tolliday	Haden	Parr	Dudds	Attwell
1	10 Feb	DENABY UNITED	3-3	2-2	1116	Haycox 2 Hewitt			3		5		7	8	9	10	11		1		4	2			6									
2	24	FRICKLEY COLLIERY	7-6	4-3	1205	Fielding 2 McCartney Johnson 4			3	8	5		7	9		10	11		1		4	2			6									
3	2 Mar	Frickley Colliery	3-3	2-1		Rowbotham Johnson Rudkin			3	8	5		7	9		10	11		1		4	2			6									
4	9	NEWARK TOWN	4-0	0-0	1509	Fielding Haycox 2 Hewitt			3	8	5		7		9	10	11		1		4	2			6									
5	22	BOSTON UNITED	6-0	2-0	3116	Rowbotham 2 Fielding Johnson Rudkin2			3	8	5		7		9	10	11		1		4	2			6									
6	23	† GRANTHAM	6-2	4-2	2013	Fielding Haycox 3 Rudkin Hewitt			3	8	5		7		9	10	11		1		4	2			6									
7	25	Boston United	2-0	2-0		Rudkin 2			3	8	5		7	9		10	11		1		4	2			6									
8	30	SCUNTHORPE & LUTD.	5-3	2-1	2207	McCartney 3 Johnson 2			3	4	5		7	9		10	11		1			2			6									
9	6 Apr	Scunthorpe & LUtd.	1-4	0-1		Fielding			3	8			7	9		10	11		1	1	4	2			6									8
10	13	GAINSBOROUGH TRIN.	3-1	2-1	1603	McCartney Johnson Hewitt			3	8	5		7	9		10	11		1		4	2			6									
11	20	Denaby United	2-1	0-1		Rudkin 2			3	8	5		7	9		10	11		1		4	2			6									
12	4 May	Grantham *	1-0	0-0	1558	Hewitt			3		5		7		9	10	11		1		8	2			6									4
13	11	Gainsborough Trin. *	11-0	3-0	1453	Rowb'am Fielding 2 McCart 3 Johns'n 3 Rudkin 2			3	8	5		7	9		10	11		1		4	2			6									
14	25	Newark Town	2-1			Johnson 2			3	8	5		7	9		10	11		1		4	2			6									

† Both matches (different competitions) played on same day! * 'Away' games, but played at London Road, Peterborough

Midland League Championship 'Play-off'

	Date	Opposition	Res	H.T.	Goalscorer	Smith J.	Rowbotham	Warnes	Fielding	McCartney	Haycox	Johnson	Rudkin	Shelton	Fletcher	Tasker	Hewitt
	18 May	SCUNTHORPE & LUTD.	3-2		McCartney 2 Fielding	3	8	5	7	9		10	11	1	4	2	6

	Smith J.	Rowbotham	Warnes	Bogg	Fielding	McCartney	Haycox	Johnson	Rudkin	Brooksbanks	Shelton	Wyles	Fletcher	Tasker	Tricker	Morley	Hewitt	Lawson	McNaughton	Sutton	Smith H.	Tolliday	Haden	Parr	Dudds	Attwell
League Appearances	30	25	30	3	28	27	14	30	29	2	27	3	26	19	3	1	18	1	1	1	1	1	1	2	2	1
League Goals (+ 3 O.G.)	5	5	1		14	20	20	23	18	3			3				5									

After the start of the season – abandoned due to the Second World War – The Midland League continued (with a reduced membership). Two separate competitions (in effect two League competitions) were played. Posh finished overall top, although they were not officially recognised as Champions and neither Trophies or Medals were presented. The Midland League then closed down until the 1945/46 season.

The team line-ups from the match programme.
a 3-1 victory in a period of high scoring games.

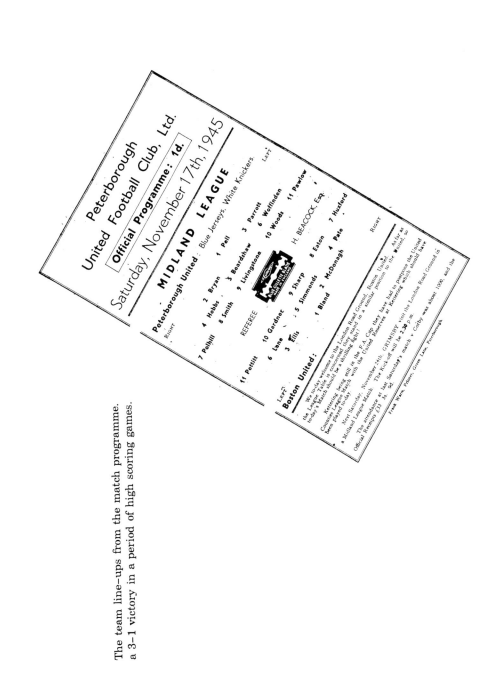

Peterborough
United Football Club, Ltd.
Official Programme: 1d.
Saturday, November 17th, 1945

MIDLAND LEAGUE

Peterborough United: Blue Jerseys, White Knickers.

RIGHT   LEFT

7 Polhill   4 Hobbs   2 Bryan   1 Pell   3 Beardshaw   3 Parrott   6 Wolfinden   10 Woods   11 Pawlow

REFEREE   9 Livingstone

H. BEACOCK, Esq.

11 Pettitt   10 Gardner   6 Lane   5 Ellis   5 Simmonds   9 Sharp   8 Eaton   7 Huxford

3 Ellis   1 Bland   2 McDonagh   4 Pate

LEFT   RIGHT

Boston United:

We to-day welcome to the London Road Ground Boston United. As far as the League Table is concerned they stand in a similar position to the United, so to-day's Match should be a thrilling fight!

Returning being still in the F.A. Cup they have had to postpone the United Counties League Match with the London Road Ground in been played today.

Next Saturday, November 24th, GRIMSBY visit the London Road Ground in a Midland League Match. The Kick-off will be 2.30 p.m. Saturday's match v Corby was about 1000, and the

The attendance at last Saturday's match v Corby was about 1000, and the Official Receipts £33 3s. 5d.

Frank Wren, Printer, Green Lane, Peterborough

Midland League

Match No.	Hilliard	Bryan	Parrott	Smith R.	Hobbs	Warner	Polhill	Fairchild	Livingstone	Woods C.M.	Rudkin	Fielding	Ashman	Laxton	Woffinden	Barraclough	Elliott/! Jones	Smith J./* Pinder	Tasker/$ Haden	Rodgers/† Atkins	Odell/‡ Wilson	Newsom	McClelland	Beardshaw	Firth	Murdoch	Pell	McCartney	Pawlow
1	1	2	3	4	5	6	7	8	9	10	11																		
2	1	2	3	4	5	6	7	8	9	10		11																	
3	1	2	3	4	5		7			6			8	9	10	11													
4		2	3	4	5		7			6				9	10	11	1	8											
5	1	2	3		5	4	7			6			8	9							10	11							
6	1	2	3	8	4									9	6					11				5	7	10			
7		2	3	8	4		7								6							11		5		10	1	9	
8		2	3	8	4		7			10			9		6									5			1		11
9		2	3	8	5							7	9		6											10	1		11
10	1	2	3		4					6		7	9		10				5			8							11
11		2	3		4					6		7	9		10				5										11
12	1	2	3		5	4					11	7	10						6										
13		2	3		5		11			6	10	7	9						4										
14		2	3		4		8			6	11	7	9									10		5					
15		2	3							6		7	9						10	11				5					
16		2	3		4					10		7	9						8					5					
17		2	3		4							7	10	9						11				5					
18		2	3									7	9							11				5					
19		2	3									7	9							11				5					
20		2	3								11	7	10											5					
21		2	3							6	11	7	10																
22		2	3							10	11	7	8											5					
23			3									7												5					
24			3									7					*1							5					
25			3																					5					
26		2																!3						5					
27	1		3							6		7							$8					5					
28		2	3																					5					
29			3																					5					
30			3							6										†11				5					
31			3							6			9											5					
32		2	3							6														5					
33		4	3							6			8											5					
34		4	3				11			6		7									‡2					9			
35		2	3							6																			
36		4	3							6		7									‡2								

Match No.	Walker	Stankowski	Massey	Whitehouse	McGuiness	Whitney	Williams	Smith J.	Smith T.	Louden	Barkham	Lambton	Perry	Hustwaite	Padgett	Gray	Urien	Hindley	Salt	Scobie
1																				
2																				
3																				
4																				
5																				
6																				
7																				
8																				
9	4																			
10																				
11		1	8																	
12			8	9																
13			8		1															
14						1														
15			8			1	4													
16						1		6												
17			8			1		6												
18			8			1		6	4	10										
19			8			1		6	4	10										
20			8			1		6	4		9									
21			8			1		5	4		9									
22						1		6	4		9									
23			8					6	4			1	2	9	10	11				
24			8					6	4				2	9	10	11				
25			8					6	4				2	9	10	11	1	7		
26			8					6	4					9	10	11				7
27									4				2	9	10	11				
28								6	4					9	10	11		8	1	7
29							8	6	4				2	9	10	11		7	1	
30							7		4				2		9	10		8	1	
31							7		4				2		10	11		8	1	
32							7		4		9				10	11		8	1	
33						1	7						2	9	10	11				
34			8					5								10			1	
35			8					5	4					9	10	11			1	7
36			8					5						9	10	11			1	

F.A.Cup

	Hilliard	Bryan	Parrott	Smith R.	Hobbs	Warner	Polhill	Fairchild	Livingstone	Woods C.M.	Rudkin	Fielding	Ashman	Laxton	Woffinden	Barraclough	Elliott/! Jones	Smith J./* Pinder	Tasker/$ Haden	Rodgers/† Atkins	Odell/‡ Wilson	Newsom	McClelland	Beardshaw	Firth	Murdoch	Pell	McCartney	Pawlow
Q1	1	2	3		5	4	7	8		6				9					10	11									
Q2	1	2	3		5	4	7	8		6				9						11			10						
①	8	29	35	8	16	4	11	2	2	22	7	20	19	5	8	2	1	1	6	5	1	4		22	1	4	3	1	4
②				2				2	2		6	3	3	3	3					1					1				3
③	2	2	2		2	2	2	2		2				2					1	2			1						
④							1	1						6					1	1									

	Walker	Stankowski	Massey	Whitehouse	McGuiness	Whitney	Williams	Smith J.	Smith T.	Louden	Barkham	Lambton	Perry	Hustwaite	Padgett	Gray	Urien	Hindley	Salt	Scobie
Q1																				
Q2																				
①	1	1	16	1	1	10	6	16	16	2	4	1	8	10	13	14	1	6	9	3
②			5				1			2	2			12	5	3		1		1
③																				
④																				

① = League appearances ② = League goals (+ 1 O.G.) ③ = Cup appearances ④ = Cup goals Wilson – 2 appearances. Jones, Pinder, Haden, Atkins (+ 1 goal) – 1 League appearance each.

SEASON 1945/46

Midland League

204	Date	Opposition	Res	H.T.	Attend	Goalscorer
1	25 Aug	NOTTS COUNTY RES.	4-2	2-1	2002	Fairchild (2) Livingsone (2)
2	1 Sep	SHREWSBURY TOWN	0-5	0-1	2850	
3	15	Denaby United	3-0	2-0		Laxton (2) Woffinden
4	29	Barnsley Res.	0-4	0-2		
5	13 Oct	DONCASTER ROV. RES.	0-3	0-1	2500	
6	27	MANSFIELD TOWN RES.	4-0	1-0	2450	Smith R.(2) Laxton Firth
7	10 Nov	Frickley Colliery	0-8	0-4		
8	17	BOSTON UNITED	3-1	1-0	2450	Ashman (2) Pawlow
9	24	GRIMSBY TOWN RES.	0-3	0-1	2608	
10	8 Dec	Doncaster Rov. Res.	1-2	0-1		Pawlow
11	15	LINCOLN CITY RES.	5-6	3-3	1950	Woffinden (2) Pawlow Massey (2)
12	25	Gainsborough Trin.	2-6	1-3	3100	Rudkin Massey
13	26	GAINSBOROUGH TRIN.	0-3	0-2	3100	
14	29	BARNSLEY RES.	0-2	0-0	2200	
15	5 Jan	Boston United	1-1	0-0		Fielding
16	12	Scunthorpe & L. Utd.	0-1	0-1		
17	19	RANSOME AND MARLES	0-1	0-1	2100	
18	26	Rotherham Utd. Res.	2-2	1-1		Rodger Louden
19	2 Feb	DENABY UNITED	3-3	2-1	2400	Fielding Ashman Louden
20	9	Mansfield Town Res.	4-0	1-0		Rudkin Barkham (2) O.G.
21	16	SCUNTHORPE & L. UTD.	3-1	2-0	2700	Rudkin (3)
22	23	Ransome and Marles	1-3	1-3		Rudkin
23	9 Mar	Grimsby Town Res.	1-0	0-0	4000	Hustwaite
24	16	ROTHERHAM UTD. RES.	2-1	1-0	2700	Hustwaite (2)
25	23	BRADFORD P.A. RES.	3-2	1-2		Padgett (3)
26	27	Lincoln City Res.	5-2	2-0		Massey (2) Hustwaite (2) Scobie
27	30	Shrewsbury Town	0-3	0-2		
28	6 Apr	FRICKLEY COLLIERY	2-0	2-0	3000	Hustwaite Gray
29	13	OLLERTON COLLIERY	1-0	0-0	3200	Williams
30	15	Bradford P.A. Res.	4-1	2-0		Padgett Gray Hindley Atkins
31	19	Grantham	0-3	0-3		
32	20	NOTTM FOREST. RES.	0-2	0-1	4700	
33	22	GRANTHAM	3-1	2-0	5000	Hustwaite (3)
34	25	Notts. County Res.	2-1	0-1		Fielding Gray
35	27	Ollerton Colliery	3-1	2-1		Hustwaite (2) Padgett
36	4 May	Nottm Forest Res.	1-0	0-0		Hustwaite

F.A.Cup

| 1 Q. | 6 Oct | Rushden Town | 9-1 | 5-1 | | Polmill Laxton(6) Tasker Rodgers |
| 2 Q. | 20 | Kettering Town | 1-2 | 1-2 | 2855 | Fairchild |

Season Summary

A new start after the War sees Posh use no fewer than 54 different players during the season – many of them local men. Continued financial help from the Supporters Club provides money for developments at the Ground, and the Football Club show a profit on the season of over £300.

SEASON 1946/47

Midland League

Player columns (top to bottom): Watson, Kirk, Neal, Hustwaite, Coles, Ellmer, Long, Haddington, Murdoch, Marshall, Newby, Ross, Woods C., Brooksbanks, Bayliss, Osmond, Smith J., Stanyon, Beardshaw, Smith T., Wilson, Rudkin, Padgett, Bramham, Massey/* Whittle, Scobie, Mitchell, Warnes, Rickards, Parrott, Bryan, Silcocks

240	Date	Opposition	Res	H.T.	Attend	Goalscorer
1	31 Aug	BOSTON UNITED	2-2	0-2	4500	Mitchell Rudkin
2	2 Sep	NOTTS. COUNTY RES.	3-2	2-1	3500	Parrott Scobie Rudkin
3	7	Boston United	2-2	0-0	5000	Scobie Padgett
4	11	Mansfield Town Res.	1-1	1-0		Padgett
5	14	SHREWSBURY TOWN	3-2	0-2	5634	Mitchell Scobie Padgett
6	21	Bradford P.A. Res.	0-4	0-1		
7	28	FRICKLEY COLLIERY	6-0	5-0	5626	Warnes 4 Mitchell Padgett
8	3 Oct	ROTHERHAM UTD. RES.	1-1	0-0		Warnes
9	12	Scarborough	0-0	0-0		
10	26	Hull City Res.	1-1	1-1		Warnes
11	9 Nov	HULL CITY RES.	4-0	1-0	3717	Warnes Mitchell Rudkin Brooksbanks
12	23	DENABY UNITED	3-4	3-3	4173	Padgett Rudkin Bayliss
13	7 Dec	NOTTM. FOREST RES.	1-3	1-2	2986	Rudkin
14	21	BARNSLEY RES.	1-3	1-1	2541	Brooksbanks
15	25	Ollerton Colliery	2-3	2-0		Bayliss Brooksbanks
16	26	OLLERTON COLLIERY	6-0	3-0	5053	Rickards Scobie Bramham2 Padgett Brooksbank
17	4 Jan	Ransome and Marles	5-2	4-1		Bramham 3 Bayliss Brooksbanks
18	11	RANSOME AND MARLES	3-1	2-1	3610	Scobie Bramham Brooksbanks
19	18	Bradford City Res.	3-1	1-1		Scobie 2 Bayliss
20	25	BRADFORD P.A. RES.	0-8	0-6	3481	
21	1 Feb	Scunthorpe & L. Utd.	0-3	0-1		
22	22	Shrewsbury Town	0-5	0-2		
23	1 Mar	SCARBOROUGH	2-2	0-1	2744	Rickards Osmond
24	13	DONCASTER ROV. RES.	4-2	1-1	few 100	Brooksbanks Haddington 3
25	15	Grimsby Town Res.	1-2	1-1	6000	Bramham
26	22	BRADFORD CITY RES.	7-2	3-0	3355	Bramham 2 Brooksbanks 2 Haddington 3
27	29	Gainsborough Trin.	2-6	1-2		Brooksbanks 2
28	4 Apr	GRANTHAM	3-2	1-1	5790	Bramham Brooksbanks Haddington
29	5	MANSFIELD TOWN RES.	3-0	1-0	4015	Mitchell Bramham Brooksbanks
30	7	Grantham	1-1	0-0	4000	Mitchell
31	12	GAINSBOROUGH TRIN.	3-0	0-0	4602	Rickards Mitchell Haddington
32	19	Lincoln City Res.	2-2	1-1		Haddington
33	26	Nottm Forest Res.	2-2	1-0		Bramham Osmond
34	3 May	LINCOLN CITY RES.	2-0	1-0	3827	Bramham Haddington
35	10	Denaby United	4-3	4-2		Bramham 2 Brooksbanks Bryan
36	17	SCUNTHORPE & L. UTD.	1-0	1-0	4082	Bramham
37	24	Doncaster Rov. Res.	0-2	0-1		
38	26	Notts. County Res. †	3-0	1-0	4422	Bramham 2 Rickards
39	31	GRIMSBY TOWN RES.	0-1	0-1	3305	
40	7 Jun	Frickley Colliery	0-0	0-0		
41	9	Rotherham Utd. Res.	1-1	0-1		Rickards
42	14	Barnsley Res.	2-1	1-1		Murdock Branham

† Played at London Road, Peterborough

F.A.Cup

	Date	Opponent	Score	HT	Att.	Scorers
1 Q.	5 Oct	WELLINGBOROUGH T.	6-0	3-0	4981	Warnes 4 Scobie Padgett
2 Q.	19	WESTWOOD WORKS	3-0	2-0	4043	Rickards Warnes Scobie
3 Q.	2 Nov	KETTERING TOWN	4-1	1-1	8135	Mitchell Scobie Rudkin Brooksbanks
4 Q.	16	HITCHIN TOWN	4-1	2-1	6897	Mitchell Rudkin 3
1st	30	Yeovil Town	2-2	2-1	8000	Rudkin Bayliss
1 R.	5 Dec	YEOVIL TOWN	1-0	0-0	8691	Rudkin
2nd	14	NORTHAMPTON TOWN	1-1	1-1	7793	Bramham
2 R.	19	Northampton Town	1-1*	1-0	6800	Padgett
2/2R	23	Northampton Town ‡	1-8	1-4	3164	Brooksbanks

‡ Played at Coventry City F.C.   * After Extra Time (F.T. 1-1)

League Appearances	39	21	41	40	39	29	16	‡38	17	8	29	11	1	18	1	7	13	14	29	1	5	4	17	1	1	4	1	3	1	2
League Goals		1	1	5	7	7	7		20	6	5							2	4	14	1		1	10						
Cup appearances	9	9	9	8	9	6	8		6	9	8	1	3	1	1		5	2	5	5										
Cup Goals				1	5	2	3		1	2	6								1	2										

‡ + Whittle – 1 appearance.

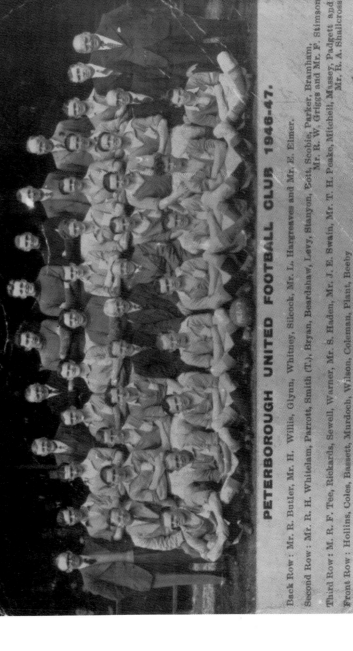

PETERBOROUGH UNITED FOOTBALL CLUB 1946-47.

Back Row: Mr. R. Butler, Mr. H. Willis, Glynn, Whitney, Silcock, Mr. L. Hargreaves and Mr. E. Elmer.

Second Row: Mr. R. H. Whitelam, Parrott, Smith (T.), Bryan, Beardshaw, Levy, Stanyon, Eott, Scobie, Parker, Bramham, Mr. R. W. Griggs and Mr. F. Stimson.

Third Row: M. R. F. Tee, Rickards, Sewell, Warner, Mr. S. Haden, Mr. J. E. Swain, Mr. T. H. Peake, Mitchell, Massey, Padgett and Mr. R. A. Shallcross

Front Row: Hollins, Coles, Bassett, Murdoch, Wilson, Coleman, Plant, Beeby

Season Summary

Floodlights for training purposes are erected. A good start is made in the League followed by progress through to the 2nd round of the F.A.Cup – Posh entertain Northampton Town before a crowd of nearly 8,000. Rudkin leaves to join Arsenal for £1,800. Posh finish 9th in the League, and a highly successful financial season provides a profit in excess of £3,000.

SEASON 1947/48

Midland League

No	Brannan	Bryan	Parrott	Neal	Warnes	Harris	Burton	Rickards	Hustwaite	Jones	Ranshaw	Brookbanks	Squire	Ferguson	Rawson	Ellmer	Bramham	Millington	Dyer	Woods C.	Frieman	Osmond	Winslow	Wood R.	Date	Opposition	Res	H.T.	Attend	Goalscorer
1	1	2	3	4	5	6	7	8	9	10	11														23 Aug	Boston United	1-0	0-0	5234	Hustwaite
2	1	2	3	4	5	6	7			10	11	8	9												25	HULL CITY RES.	4-2	3-1	6093	Harris 2 Ranshaw Brookbanks
3	1	2	3	4	5	6	7	8	9	10	11														30	BOSTON UNITED	1-1	0-0	6080	Rickards
4		2	3	4	5	6	7	8	9	10	11			1											1 Sep	ROTHERHAM UTD. RES.	1-1	0-0	5915	Jones
5		2	3	4	5		7			10	11	8	9	1	6										6	Gainsborough Trin.	3-3	2-0	5915	Ranshaw Brookbanks Squire
6		2	3	4	5		7		9	10	11			1	6	8									8	LINCOLN CITY RES.	1-0	0-0	6064	Ranshaw
7		2	3	4	5		7			10	11	8	9	1	6										13	Scarborough	3-1	3-0		Squire 3
8		2	3	4	5		7			10	11	8	9	1	6										17	Lincoln City Res.	1-4	1-2	5559	Brookbanks
9		2	3	4	5	6	7			10		8	9	1				11							20	BRADFORD P.A. RES.	0-1	0-1		
10		2	3	4	5	6	7	8					9	1			10	11							27	Shrewsbury Town	1-2	0-0		Bramham
11		2	3	4	5		7	10		8	11			1	6		9								11 Oct	SCARBOROUGH	4-2	3-2	5296	Rickards Jones 2 Bramham
12		2	3	4	5		7	10			11	8		1	6		9								25	DONCASTER ROV. RES.	2-0	0-0	4954	Rickards Brookbanks
13		2	3	4	5		7	10			11	8	9	1	6										8 Nov	FRICKLEY COLLIERY	3-1	1-1	4888	Brookbanks Squire 2
14		2	3	4	5		7	10			11	8		1	6		9								22	RANSOME AND MARLES	5-0	2-0	4109	Ranshaw Brookbanks Bramham 3
15		2	3	4	5		7	10			11	8		1	6		9								29	Denaby United	2-3	2-1		Brookbanks 2
16		2	3	4	5		7	10		10	11	8		1	6		9								6 Dec	NOTTS. COUNTY RES.	1-2	1-1	4001	Bramham
17		2	3		5		7	10			11	8		1	6		9		4						13	NOTTM. FOREST RES.	3-1	1-0	3878	Brookbanks Bramham 2
18		2	3		5		7	10			11	8		1	6	4	9								20	Nottm. Forest Res.	0-2	0-0	5000	
19		2	3		5		7	10			11	8		1	6		9		4						25	Ollerton Colliery	4-1	1-0		Brookbanks 2 Bramham 2
20		2	3		5		7	10			11	8		1	6		9		4						26	OLLERTON COLLIERY	2-4	1-1	5111	Brookbanks Bramham
21		2	3		5		7	10			11	8		1		4	9			6					27	Scunthorpe & L. Utd.	1-7	1-3		Bramham
22	1	2	3	4	5		7				11	8			6						9	10			1 Jan	Mansfield Town Res.	3-0	1-0		Frieman 3
23		2	3		5		7	4			11	8		1	6						9	10			3	GRIMSBY TOWN RES.	3-1	3-0	5110	Rickards Frieman 2
24	1	2	3		5		7	4			11	8			6						9	10			10	Doncaster Rov. Res.	2-8	1-2	2000	Burton Frieman
25		2	3		5		7	4			11	8		1	6						9	10			17	Frickley Colliery	3-6	1-3		Brookbanks Frieman Osmond
26		2	3		5		7	4			11	8		1	6						9	10			24	Grimsby Town Res.	1-3	1-0		Frieman
27		2	3		5		7	4			11	8		1	6						9	10			31	Bradford City Res.	2-3	1-2		Brookbanks 2
28		2	3		5		7	4			11	8		1	6						9	10			7 Feb	SCUNTHORPE & L. UTD.	2-1	1-1	4454	Brookbanks 2
29		2	3		5		7	4			11	8		1	6						9	10			14	Notts. County Res.	1-3	1-2		Frieman
30		2	3		5		7	4			11	8		1	6						9	10			21	BRADFORD CITY RES.	3-0	1-0	2650	Bryan Rickards Brookbanks
31		2	3		5		7	4			11	8		1	6						9	10			28	Hull City Res.	1-3	1-3	12000	Brookbanks
32		2	3		5		7	4			11	8		1	6						9	10			6 Mar	GAINSBOROUGH TRIN.	1-1	1-0	4013	Brookbanks
33		2	3		5		7	4			11	8		1							9	10		6	13	YORK CITY RES.	5-0	2-0	4552	Brookbanks 2 Rawson Frieman 2
34		2	3		5		7	4			11	8		1	6						9	10			26	Grantham	2-1	0-1	4900	Frieman 2
35		2	3		5		7	4			11	8		1	6						9	10			27	MANSFIELD TOWN RES.	1-0	0-0	5761	Frieman
36		2	3		5		7	4			11	8		1	6						9	10			29	GRANTHAM	3-0	1-0	8046	Burton Ranshaw Brookbanks
37		2	3		5			4			11	8		1	6	7					9	10			3 Apr	Bradford P.A. Res.	5-2	1-1		Brookbanks Frieman 4
38		2	3		5		7	4			11	8		1	6						9	10			10	SHREWSBURY TOWN	3-0	2-0	7526	Frieman 3
39		2	3		5		7	4			11	8		1	6						9	10			17	Rotherham Utd. Res.	2-1	1-0		Burton Frieman
40		2	3				7	4				11		1	6				5		9	10			22	Ransome and Marles	1-4	0-1		Brookbanks
41		2	3				7	4			11	8		1	6				5		9	10			24	York City Res.	1-0	1-0		Brookbanks
42		2	3		5		7	4				11		1	6						9	10			1 May	DENABY UNITED	0-3	0-1		Brookbanks

F.A.Cup

2	3	5	6	4	8	11	7	37	8	1	10	9
2	3	5	6	4		11	7		6	1	10	8	9
2	3	5	6	7	4	11	8	9		1	10	
2	3	5	6	7	4	11	8	9		1	10	

1 Q.	4 Oct	WESTWOOD WORKS *	5-0	3-0	4083	Jones Ranshaw 2 Brookbanks 2
2 Q.	18	Desborough Town	2-1†	0-0	3400	Rawson Bramham
3 Q.	1 Nov	Kettering Town	4-3	2-2	11526	Brookbanks Squire Rickards 2
4 Q.	15	Vauxhall Motors	1-2	1-1	3148	Squire

* Tie venue reversed (drawn 'away')   † After extra time (after 90 mins. 1-1)

5	42	37	10	40	12	33	37	38	8	37	1	33	4	20	2	1	21	17	5	1	League Appearances
1		4			4	3	5	26	6	1				12			22	1			League Goals
4		4	4	2	4	1	4	4	4	1		4	1	2							Cup appearances
4		4			2	1	2	3	2	1				1							Cup Goals

A prestigious Friendly match was played with Arsenal.

Season Summary

Wilson moves on to Luton Town for £500. Early attendances of around 6,000 at London Road. A Latvian International is signed, but Hayden leaves after 10 years. Plans announced for new 4,000 seater Grandstand to bring Ground capacity to 25,000. Posh finish 6th in League and another large profit is made.

SEASON 1948/49

Midland League

No	Date	Opposition	Res	H.T.	Attend	Goalscorer	Ferguson	Bryan	Parrott	Rickards	Warnes	Cockcroft	McGuinn	Harkin	Fensome	Beaumont	Guest	Blood	Vaughan	Fallon	Huxford	Brookbanks	Sanderson	Tapping	Woods	Boylin	Laxton	Conner	Robertson	Taylor	Robinson	Foreman
1	21 Aug	Boston United	0-3	0-1	7000		1	2	3	4	5	6	7	8	9	10		11														
2	23	DONCASTER ROV. RES.	3-0	0-0	5700	Fensome Guest 2	1	2	3	4	5	6	7	8	9	10		11														
3	28	BOSTON UNITED	2-2	1-1	7300	Fensome Beaumont	1	2	3	4	5	6	7	8	9	10		11														
4	30	HULL CITY RES.	3-1	0-0	6286	Rickards Beaumont Guest	1	2	3	4		6	7		9	8	11	5	10													
5	4 Sep	Gainsborough Trin.	1-4	0-1		Guest	1	2	3	4		6	7		9	8	11		10	5												
6	9	Doncaster Rov. Res.	3-0		5725	Fensome 2 Guest	1	2	3	4		6	7		9	10	11			5		8										
7	11	LINCOLN CITY RES.	1-3	1-2		Beaumont	1	2	3	4		6	7		9	10	11			5		8										
8	16	Ransome and Marles	2-3	1-2		Guest Huxford	1	2	3	8		6		4	9	10	11			5	7											
9	18	Scarborough	2-1	1-1		Rickards McGuinn	1	2	3	8		6	7	4		10	11			5	9											
10	20	SCARBOROUGH	5-0	2-0	4148	McGuinn Fensome Guest Vaughan 2	1	2	3	8		6	7	4	9		11		10	5												
11	9 Oct	Rotherham Utd. Res.	2-1	1-1		Guest O.G.	1	2	3	8		6	7	4			11		10	5	9											
12	23	BRADFORD P.A. RES.	0-10	0-4	6800		1	2	3	8	5	6	7	4			11		10		9											
13	6 Nov	Notts. County Res.	0-3	0-1			1	2		8		6	11	4				3	10	5	7		9									
14	20	GRIMSBY TOWN RES.	1-0	1-0	5092	Guest	1	2		8		6		4			11	3	10	5		7	9									
15	4 Dec	Frickley Colliery	0-1	0-1			1	2				6		4		8	11	3		5		7	9	10								
16	11	Grimsby Town Res.	3-4	2-0		Guest Brookbanks Sanderson	1	2				6		4		8	11	3	10	5		7	9									
17	18	NOTTS. COUNTY RES.	1-2	0-1	4400	Guest	1	2						4		8	11	3	10	5		7	9		6							
18	25	Mansfield Town Res.	2-0	1-0	1500	Guest Vaughan	1	2		8		6		4		3	11		10	5	9					7						
19	27	MANSFIELD TOWN RES.	0-0	0-0	4000		1	2		8				4		3	11		10	5		9			6	7						
20	28	Bradford City Res.	2-1	1-0	751	Brookbanks 2	1	2		8				4		3	11		10	5		9			6	7						
21	1 Jan	GAINSBOROUGH TRIN.	0-1	0-1			1	2		8				4		3	11		10	5		9			6	7						
22	8	Scunthorpe & L. Utd.	1-4	1-2	4000	Guest	1	2		8				4		3	11		10	5		9			6	7						
23	15	SHREWSBURY TOWN	3-1	1-0	2971	Guest 2 Brookbanks	1	2		8				4		3	11		10	5		9			6	7						
24	22	Lincoln City Res.	0-5	0-1	4768		1	2		8				4		3	11		10	5	7				6		9					
25	29	Denaby United	0-2	0-0			1	2		9				4		3	11		10	5					6	7		8				
26	5 Feb	YORK CITY RES.	2-0	1-0	4233	Sanderson Harkin	1	2	3	4				8		7	11		10	5			9		6	7		8				
27	12	Bradford P.A. Res.	0-2	0-1			1	2	3	6				4		7	11		10	5			9						8			
28	19	RANSOME AND MARLES	0-1	0-0			1	2	3	6				4		7	11		10	5		7	9						8			
29	26	Goole Town	0-0	0-0			1	2	3	6				4			11		10	5		7		9					8			
30	5 Mar	SCUNTHORPE & L. UTD.	4-3	2-1	3500	Rickards Guest Tapping 2	1	2	3	8				4			11		10	5		7		9	6							
31	12	Hull City Res.	0-2	0-1	7000			2	3	8				4			11		10			7		9	6					1	5	
32	19	DENABY UNITED	3-0	0-0	3328	Robinson 2 Vaughan		2	3	8				4			11		10	5		7			6					1	9	
33	26	Shrewsbury Town	1-4	0-2	4500	Guest		2	3	8				4		7	11		10	5					6		9			1		
34	28	BRADFORD CITY RES.	2-1	1-0	3000	Robinson Guest	1	2	3	8		4					11		10	5		7			6						9	
35	2 Apr	ROTHERHAM UTD. RES.	0-0	0-3	4300		1	2	3	8		4					11		10	5		7			6						9	
36		NOTTM. FOREST RES.	0-6	0-3	3000		1	2	3	8		4					11		10	5		7			6						9	
37	15	GRANTHAM	1-1	0-1	6000	Robinson	1	2	3	8		4					11		10	5		7			6						9	
38	16	Nottm. Forest Res.	1-4	0-3		Sanderson	1	2	3	8		6							10		7		9		4						5	
39	18	Grantbam	1-1	1-1		Foreman	1	2	3	8		4							10		7		9		6						5	10
40	23	GOOLE TOWN	4-1	3-1	4000	Robinson 3 Tapping	1	2	3			4	11						10	5	7			8	6						9	
41	30	FRICKLEY COLLIERY	1-3	0-2		Robinson	1	2	3			4	11						10	5	7			8	6						9	
42	2 May	York City Res.	1-2	1-0		Robinson	1	2	3	8		4	11						10	5	7				6						9	

F.A.Cup

			1	2	3	8	6	7	4	11	10	5	9					Scorers
1 Q.	2 Oct	SYMINGTONS REC.	4-0	1-0	5000												Rickards McGuinn Guest Huxford
2 Q.	16	Wellingborough Town	3-2	1-1	2888										9		Rickards Vaughan Huxford
3 Q.	30	KETTERING TOWN	2-1	2-0	9370							7	9	10		Guest Sanderson
4 Q.	13 Nov	RANSOME AND	3-1	0-1	8431							7	9			Rickards Brooksbanks
1st	27	TORQUAY UNITED	0-1	0-1	8769												

League Appearances	39	42	29	37	25	13	30	9	21	38	6	35	34	9	24	9	8	22	7	2	1	3	11	1
(1 O.G.) League Goals	5	5	2	3	5	2	1	5	18	4	1	4	3	1	9	1								
Cup appearances	5	2	4	5	5	1	3	3	5	4	5	3	2	2	1									
Cup Goals			3		1		2		2	1		2	2	1										

(Back) Brooksbanks, Bryan, Rickards, Ferguson, "Mr. Posh", Blood (P/Man.), Tapping, Smith (Train.)
(Front) Parrott, Guest, Vaughan, Cockroft, Harkin, Fallon

Season Summary

An indifferent start includes a 10–0 home defeat to Bradford P.A. Reserves, and before an embarrassed crowd of nearly 7,000! Over 9,000 come to London Road for the visit of Kettering in the F.A.Cup, and Torquay United are later met in the 1st round. But in the League a disappointing season sees Posh finish 16th in the League.

SEASON 1949/50

Midland League

366

#	Date	Opposition	Res	H.T.	Attend	Goalscorer	Moulson	Bryan	Wyles	Wands	Fallon	Mills	Houghton	Widdowfield	Martin	Nearney	Jennings	Dally	Taylor	Cockcroft	Robinson	Woods	Grant	Foley	Vaux	Woolley	Lister	Machin	Plant	Parrott	Flowers
1	20 Aug	BOSTON UNITED	2-2	1-1	7619	Houghton Martin	1	2	3	4	5	6	7	8	9	10	11														
2	24	Grimsby Town Res.	1-2	0-1		Martin	1	2	3	4	5	6	7	8	9		11	10													
3	27	Scarborough	3-2	1-1	5737	Mills Houghton Widdowfield	1	2	3	4	5	6	7	8	9		11	10													
4	1 Sep	Doncaster Rov. Res.	1-4	0-1		Houghton	1	2	3	4	5	6	7	8	9		11	10													
5	3	FRICKLEY COLLIERY	6-2	3-1	6020	Houghton Widdowfield 2 Martin 3	1	2	3		5	6	7	8	10		11			4	9										
6	8	Ransome and Marles	0-1	0-1			1	2	3		5	6	7	8	10		11			4	9										
7	10	GOOLE TOWN	3-2	3-1		Houghton Widdowfield Robinson	1	2	3		5	6	7	8	10		11			4	9										
8	12	NOTTS. COUNTY RES.	2-1	0-1	6500	Houghton Robinson	1	2	3		5		7	8	10					6	9	4	11								
9	17	Halifax Town Res.	2-1	1-1		Martin Robinson	1	2	3		5		7	8	10					6	9	4	11								
10	19	BRADFORD CITY RES.	1-0	1-0	6133	Robinson	1	2	3		5		7	8	10					6	9	4	11								
11	24	GAINSBOROUGH TRIN.	4-4	2-1	6032	Wyles Martin Robinson 2	1	2	3		5		7	8	10					6	9	4	11								
12	8 Oct	SCARBOROUGH	5-2	3-1	6900	Mills Widdowfield 2 Martin 2	1	2	3		5	9	7	8	10					6		4		11							
13	12	Bradford City Res.	5-1	2-1	781	Houghton 2 Robinson 2 O.G.	1		3	5	11		7	8	10					6	9	4			2						
14	22	Rotherham Utd. Res.	1-2	0-0	2614	Houghton	1		3	5	11		7	8	10					6	9	4			2						
15	5 Nov	SHREWSBURY TOWN	1-0	†		Martin	1	2		5			11	8	10					6	9	4			3	7					
	19	Bradford P.A. Res.	†			(Robinson) † Aban.35 mins.at 1-0	1	2		5			11	8	10					6	9	4			3	7					
16	26	Lincoln City Res.	3-3	1-2	2797	Martin 3	1	2	3	5			7	8	10		11			6	9	4									
17	3 Dec	York City Res.	1-4	0-2		Martin	1	2	3	5			7	8	10		11			6	9	4									
18	10	RANSOME AND MARLES	1-0	1-0	4000	Jennings	1	2	3	5			7	8	10		11			6	9	4									
19	17	GRIMSBY TOWN RES.	1-4	1-3	2700	Cockcroft	1	2	3	5		10	7	9	8		11			6		4									
20	24	LINCOLN CITY RES.	2-1	1-1	4326	Martin 2	1	2	3	5		10	7	9	8		11			6		4									
21	26	MANSFIELD TOWN RES.	1-1	1-1	5789	Cockcroft	1	2	3	5			7	8	10		11			6	9	4									
22	27	Mansfield Town Res.	1-3	0-1		Robinson	1	2	3	4	5		7	8	10						9	6					11				
23	31	NOTTM. FOREST RES.	1-3	0-2	5005	Widdowfield	1	2	3	4	5		7	8	10						9	6					11				
24	2	Denaby United	1-1	1-0		Martin	1	2	3	4	5		7	8	10						9	6					11				
25	7	Scunthorpe & L. Utd.	0-1	0-0	6000		1	2	3	4	5		7	8	10					6	9						11				
26	14	WORKSOP TOWN	2-0	0-0	4307	Robinson 2	1	2	3	4	5		7	8	10					6	9						11				
27	21	Frickley Colliery	4-2	3-1		Widdowfield 2 Martin Robinson	1	2	3		5			8	10					6	9	4		7			11				
28	28	Nottm. Forest Res.	0-1	0-1			1	2	3		5		7	8	10					6	9	4					11				
29	4 Feb	DONCASTER ROV. RES.	0-0	0-0	800		1	2	3		5		7	8	10					6	9	4					11				
30	9	HALIFAX TOWN RES.	3-0	1-0	4056	Houghton Widdowfield Robinson	1	2	3		5		7	8	10					6	9	4					11				
31	11	YORK CITY RES.	4-4	0-2		Widdowfield Martin Robinson Lister	1	2	3		5		7	8	10					6	9	4					11				
32	16	Notts. County Res.	0-0	0-0			1		3				7	8	10					4	9	6			2		11	5			
33	18	SCUNTHORPE & L. UTD.	3-1	1-0	5519	Robinson Martin 2	1		3					8	10					4	9	6		7	2		11	5			
34	4 Mar	Boston United	1-0	0-0		Robinson	1		3					8	10					4	9	6		7	2		11	5			
35	9	Hull City Res.	2-0	1-0		Widdowfield Robinson	1	2	3					8	10					4	9	6		7			11	5			
36	11	ROTHERHAM UTD. RES.	0-1	0-1	4951	Robinson		2	3				11	8	10				1	4	9	6		7				5			
37	18	Gainsborough Trin.	2-2	1-0		Robinson Martin		2	3				11	8	10				1	4	9	6		7				5			
38	22	Bradford P.A. Res.	1-1	1-0		Martin		2	3				7	8	10		11		1	4	9	6						5			
39	25	HULL CITY RES.	3-1	3-0	5519	Martin Houghton Jennings		2	3				7	8	10		11		1	4	9	6						5			
40	1 Apr	Worksop Town	0-1	0-0			1		3					8	10					4	9	6		7	2		11	5			
41	7	Grantham	2-2	0-2		Widdowfield Robinson	1	2	3					8	10					4	9	6		7			11	5			
42	8	BRADFORD P.A. RES.	3-1	1-0	5118	Widdowfield 2 Robinson	1	2	3				10	8						4	9	6		7			11	5			
43	10	GRANTHAM	5-1	1-0		Widdowfield 4 Robinson	1	2	3				10	8						4	9	6		7			11	5			
44	13	Goole Town	0-2	0-0			1	2	3				11	8	10						9	6		7				5	4		
45	29	Shrewsbury Town	0-5	0-4				2	3					8					1		9	10		7			11	5	6		
46	4 May	DENABY UNITED	2-0	0-0		Woods Foley	1	2						8							9	10		7			11	5	6	3	4

F.A.Cup

	Date	Opponents			Att.	Scorers
1 Q.	1 Oct	DESBOROUGH TOWN	5-1	2-0	7908	Houghton Widdowfield 2 Martin 2
2 Q.	15	Kettering Town	5-0	2-0	9799	Fallon Widdowfield 2 Robinson
3 Q.	29	Corby Town	0-1	0-0	7162	

Cup line-ups:

	1	2	3		5		7	8	10					6	9	4		11
	1													6	9	4	14	11
	1	3	5		10		7	8						6	9	4	14	11	2
	1	3	5	11			7	8	10					6	9	4	14		2

| | | | | | | | | | | | | | | | Martin 2 |
| Fallon Widdowfield 2 Robinson |

	1	2	3	5	7	8	10	17	6	9	4	14	11	18	14	2	1
League Appearances	41	41	43	19	22	12	37	45	42	1	17	3	5	38	38	39	5	14	7	1	18	14	2	1
(1 O.G.) League Goals		1				2	11	20	28	2			2	21	1		1	1			1	
Cup appearances	3	1	3	2	3	1	3	3	2		3			3	3	3	1	2
Cup Goals		1			1		4	2	2					2			1

(Back) Woolley, Cockcroft, Foley, Dalley, Fearney, Robinson, Parrott, Woods, Poole, Martin, Chilman.
(Middle) Smith, Houghton, Jennings, Mills, Wands, Taylor, Machin, Moulson, Vaux, Fallon, Wyles, Widdowfield, Willis.
(Front) Rigby, Head, Warrington, Tee, Palmer, Stimson, Swain, Blood, Peake, Shallcross, Poulter, Grange, Griggs.

Season Summary

Manager Blood signs on several very experienced players. The visit to Kettering in the F.A.Cup sets a new attendance record at Rockingham Road. Widdowfield scores 30 League goals, and Posh attain their best final position – 6th. The first – of many – applications to join the Football League receives 5 votes.

SEASON 1950/51

Midland League

412	Date	Opposition	Res	H.T.	Attend	Goalscorer	Moulson	Bryan	Palethorpe	Flowers	Machin	Woods	Houghton	Bee	Robinson	Martin	Jennings	Parrott	Bell	Walker	Foley	Woolridge	Gunn	Daley	Dowson	Ward	Pycroft	Clarke
1	19 Aug	Boston United	4-1	4-0		Houghton Bee Martin 2	1	2	3	4	5	6	7	8	9	10	11											
2	21	MANSFIELD TOWN RES.	3-0	2-0	7246	Robinson 2 Martin	1	2	3	4	5	6	7	8	9	10	11											
3	26	Frickley Colliery	1-5	1-3	3000	Robinson	1	2	3	4	5	6	7	8	9	10	11											
4	28	HULL CITY RES.	3-0	1-0	6164	Houghton Martin 2	1	2	3	4	5	6	7	8	9	10	11											
5	2 Sep	HALIFAX TOWN RES.	1-1	0-1	6481	Bee	1	2		4	5	6	7	8		10	11	3	9									
6	4	LINCOLN CITY RES.	0-1	0-0	6490		1	2		4	5	6	7	8		10	11	3	9									
7	9	DONCASTER ROV. RES.	3-0	1-1	6596	Robinson 2 Martin	1	2			5	6	7	8	9	10	11	3		4								
8	16	Doncaster Rov. Res.	3-0	0-0		Bee Foley	1	2			5	6		8	9	10	11	3		4	7							
9	28	Notts. County Res.	2-1	2-1		O.G.	1	2			5	6		8	9	10	11	3		4	7							
10	7 Oct	Bradford P.A. Res.	1-1	1-0	4693	Walker	1	2			5	6		8		10	11	3	9	4	7							
11	21	FRICKLEY COLLIERY	1-1	1-1	4463	Bee Robinson Martin	1		3		5	6		8	9	10	11			4	7	2						
12	4 Nov	SCARBOROUGH	3-2	1-0		Martin Bell 2	1	2				6		8	9	10		3		4	7		5	11				
13	11	Denaby United	3-1	2-0		Bell Walker	1	2			5	6		8	9	10		3		4	7			11				
14	18	Mansfield Town Res.	2-2	0-1		Daley Dowson	1	2			5	6		8	9	10		3		4				11	7			
15	25	Scunthorpe & L. Utd.	2-3	1-2	4522		1	2			5	6		8	9	10		3		4				11	7			
16	2 Dec	BRADFORD CITY RES.	0-0	0-0			1	2			5	6		8	9	10		3		4				11	7			
17	7	Hull City Res.	0-0	0-0			1	2			5	6		8	9	10		3		4				11	7			
18	23	NOTTS. COUNTY RES.	2-2	2-1	4100	Bell Walker	1	2			5	6		8	9	10		3		4				11	7			
19	25	GRIMSBY TOWN RES.	3-1	2-0	4723	Robinson Martin Daley	1	2			5	6		8	9	10		3		4				11	7			
20	26	Grimsby Town Res.	5-4	3-1		Robinson 2 Martin Daley 2	1	2			5	6		8	9	10		3		4				11	7			
21	6 Jan	SCUNTHORPE & L. UTD.	1-1	0-0	4210	Dowson	1	2			5	6			9	10		3	8	4				11	7			
22	11	Halifax Town Res.	2-0	1-0		Robinson Martin	1	2			5	6		8	9	10		3		4				11	7			
23	13	Scarborough	0-1	0-1	2400		1	2			5	6		8	9	10		3		4				11	7			
24	27	Bradford City Res.	1-1	0-1		Daley	1	2			5	6		8	9	10		3		4				11	7			
25	3 Feb	NOTTM. FOREST RES.	0-4	0-1	2973		1	2			5	6		8	9	10		3		4				11	7			
26	10	GAINSBOROUGH TRIN.	0-3	0-1	4387		1	2			5	6			9	10		3		4				11	7	8		
27	17	Worksop Town	2-3	0-1		Martin Dowson	1	2			5	6			9	10		3		4				11	7	8		
28	22	Nottm. Forest Res.	1-3	0-3		Robinson	1	2			5	6		8	9	10		3		4				11	7			
29	24	BRADFORD P.A. RES.	3-0	1-0	3488	Robinson Walker Dowson	1	2			5	6		8	9	10		3		4				11	7			
30	3 Mar	York City Res.	3-2	0-2	2319	Martin Bell 2	1	2			5	6		8		10		3	9	4				11	7			
31	10	YORK CITY RES.	2-1	1-0	3449	Dowson 2	1	2			5	6		8		10		3	9	4				11	7			
32	17	BOSTON UNITED	3-1	1-0	3550	Robinson Walker Dowson	1	2			5	6		8	9	10		3		4				11	7			
33	23	GRANTHAM	2-1	1-1	3587	Robinson Martin	1	2			5			8	9	10		3		4				11	7		6	
34	24	WORKSOP TOWN	3-0	2-0	3861	Dowson Bee Foley	1	2			5			8	9	10		3		6	11				7			
35	26	Grantham	0-3	0-2			1	2			5	6		8	9	10		3		4	11				7			
36	2 Apr	Goole Town	1-1	1-0		Martin	1	2			5	6		8	9	10		3		4					11			
37	5	GOOLE TOWN	1-1	1-1		Walker	1	2			5			8	9	10		3		4	7				11		6	
38	7	Lincoln City Res.	1-1	1-0	2741	Dowson	1	2			5	6		8	9	10		3		4	7				11			
39	11	Gainsborough Trin.	0-4	0-2			1	2			5			8	9	10		3		4	7				11		6	
40	14	DENABY UNITED	1-1	0-1	3244	Dowson	1	2			5		11	8	9	10		3		4					7		6	
41	21	ROTHERHAM UTD. RES.	1-1	1-1	3755	Dowson	1	2			5			10	9			3		4					7		6	11
42	5 May	Rotherham Utd. Res.	1-5	0-3		Walker	1	2			5			10		9		3		8					7		6	11

F.A.Cup

1 Q.	30 Sep	SYMINGTON REC.	3-0	1-0	5187	Martin Jennings Foley
2 Q.	14 Oct	Kettering Town	2-2	1-2	10398	Bee Robinson
2Q/R	19	KETTERING TOWN	1-2*	0-1	9577	Foley

* A.E.T. Score 1-1 at 90 minutes.

League Appearances	42	5	6	41	7	39	30	42	11	36	12	33	14	1	22	28	2	6	2
(1 O.G.) League Goals				2		6	14	15		6	7	2		5	11			
Cup appearances	3		3	3		3	3	3	3	3	3		3	3			6	2
Cup Goals						1	1	1	1							2

Posh's exploits in the F.A.Cup (versus Kettering and Symington's), and in the Midland League are captured in cartoons.

Season Summary

Under new Manager Gurney crowds are up at start of season to over 7,000, however by the end are down to 4,000. Benefit match versus Hull City (complete with Raich Carter) attracts a record 10,380. But at the end of an overall disappointing season a loss of nearly £900 is recorded.

SEASON 1951/52

Midland League

No	Date	Opposition	Res	H.T.	Attend	Goalscorer	Moulson	Moody	Rigby	Walker	Machin	Woods	Dowson	Swincoe	Brown	Bee	Hair	Martin	Houghton	Donaldson	Hall	Saxton	Pycroft	Randall	Kay	Storer	Thornley	G. Stafford	Clarke
1	18 Aug	NOTTS. COUNTY RES.	2-4	0-2	7325	Dowson Swincoe	1	2	3	4	5	6	7	8	9	10	11												
2	22	Frickley Colliery	1-1	1-0	2000	Dowson	1	2	3	4	5	6	7	8	9	10	11												
3	25	Lincoln City Res.	3-3	1-0		Dowson Brown 2	1	2	3	4	5	6	7	8	9		11	10											
4	27	FRICKLEY COLLIERY	3-0	2-0	6096	Dowson Swincoe 2	1	2	3	4	5	6	8	9			11	10	7										
5	1 Sep	HULL CITY RES.	1-0	1-0	7587	Swincoe	1	2	3	4	5	6	8	9			11		7	10									
6	3	WORKSOP TOWN	1-2	1-2	7250	Donaldson	1	2	3	4	5	6	8	9			11		7	10									
7	8	Scunthorpe & L.U. Res.	0-2	0-2			1	2	3	4	5	6	8	9			11		7	10									
8	12	Worksop Town	3-1	3-0	5000	Swincoe Donaldson 2	1	2	3	4	5	6	7	8				10	11	9									
9	15	YORK CITY RES.	6-1	3-0	4953	Dowson 2 Martin Donaldson 2 O.G.	1	2	3	4	5	6	7	8				10	11	9									
10	22	Bradford City Res.	1-3	1-0		Dowson	1	2	3	4	5	6	7	8				10	11	9									
11	6 Oct	HALIFAX TOWN RES.	7-0	2-0	5636	Rigby Dowson 2 Swincoe Martin 2 Donaldson	1	2	3	4	5	6	7	8			11	10		9									
12	13	Bradford P.A. Res.	4-3	1-2	5488	Swincoe Martin Donaldson 2	1	2	3	4	5	6	7	8			11	10		9									
13	20	DENABY UNITED	2-2	1-2		Swincoe Martin	1	2	5	4		6	7	8			11	10		9	3								
14	27	Grimsby Town Res.	3-0	1-0	5800	Dowson 2 Swincoe	1	2	5	4		6	7	8			11	10		9	3								
15	3 Nov	GAINSBOROUGH TRIN.	4-0	1-0		Dowson 3 Donaldson	1	2	5	4		6	7	8			11	10		9	3								
16	17	NOTTM. FOREST RES.	1-2	0-1	6261	Dowson	1	2	5	4		6	7	8			11	10		9	3								
17	1 Dec	MANSFIELD TOWN RES.	2-2	1-1	4976	Saxton 2	1	2	5	4		6	7	8			11	10			3	9							
18	8	Rotherham Utd. Res.	0-4	0-1			1	2	5	4	5	6	7	8			11	10			3	9							
19	15	Notts. County Res.	0-6	0-3			1	2		4	5	6	8				11	10	7		3	9							
20	22	LINCOLN CITY RES.	2-2	1-2	3746	Dowson Hair	1	2	5	4		6	8				11	10	7		3	9		4					
21	25	Grantham	2-1	1-1	1791	Martin 2	1	2	5	4		6	8				11	10	7		3	9							
22	26	GRANTHAM	2-1	1-1		Martin Kay	1	2	5	4		6	8				11	10	9		3				7				
23	29	Hull City Res.	1-1	0-1	7000	Hair	1	2	5	6			8				11	10	9		3			4	7				
24	5 Jan	SCUNTHORPE & L.U. RES.	1-0	1-0		Swincoe	1	2	5	4		6	7	8			11	10		9	3					5			
25	12	BRADFORD CITY RES.	2-1	1-0	4660	Donaldson 2	1	2	5	4		6	7	8			11	10		9	3								
26	2 Feb	BOSTON UNITED	4-1	3-1	5066	Dowson 2 Martin Donaldson	1	2	5	4		6	7	8			11	10		9	3								
27	9	Boston United	2-1	2-0	500	Hair Martin	1	2	5	4		6	7	8			11	10		9	3								
28	16	Halifax Town Res.	2-4	0-0	3200	Hair Donaldson	1	2	5	4		6	7	8			11	10		9	3								
29	25	Scarborough	2-2	2-1		Dowson Swincoe Donaldson 2	1	2	5	4		6	7	8			11	10		9	3								
30	1 Mar	BRADFORD P.A. RES.	4-1	1-0	5133	Swincoe 2 Donaldson	1	2	5			6	7	8	4		11	10		9	3								
31	19	York City Res.	3-2	2-1		Dowson	1	2	5			6	7	8	4		11	10		9	3								
32	22	Gainsborough Trin.	1-3	0-0		Dowson	1	2	5	4		6	7	8			11	10		9	3								
33	24	Denaby United	4-2	1-2		Swincoe Hair Martin 2	1	2	5	4		6	7	8			11	10		9	3								
34	3 Apr	Nottm. Forest Res.	1-3	0-2		Martin	1	2	5	4		6	7	8			11	10		9	3								
35	11	Goole Town	2-2	2-1		Dowson 2		2	5	4			7	8		6	11	10		9							1	3	
36	12	SCARBOROUGH	3-0	2-0	5377	Dowson Donaldson Martin		2	5	4			7	8		6	11	10		9							1	3	
37	14	GOOLE TOWN	0-0	0-0	5550			2	5	4			7			6	11	10		9		8					1	3	
38	19	Mansfield Town Res.	0-0	0-0			1	2	5	4			7			6	11	10		9		8						3	
39	21	DONCASTER ROV. RES.	2-1	2-0	4135	Dowson Clarke	1	2	5	4			7	8		6		10		9								3	11
40	26	ROTHERHAM UTD. RES.	1-3	1-3		Martin		2	5			6	9	10		4	7	8									1	3	11
41	28	Doncaster Rov. Res.	3-1	1-1		Dowson 3		2	5			6	8	7		4	10			9							1	3	11
42	3 May	GRIMSBY TOWN RES.	2-3	0-3	3430	Martin 2	1	2	5	4		6	7	8			11	10		9								3	

454

F.A.Cup

4 Q.	10 Nov	HEREFORD UNITED	1-1	1-0	10061	Martin
4Q/R	15	Hereford United	0-1	0-1	6000	

1	2	5	4	6	7	8	14	11	10	9	3
1	2	5	4	6	7	8	14	11	10	9	3

League Appearances	35	41	32	13	38	40	37	4	38	36	9	28	24	6	2	1	5	1	7	6	4
(1 O.G.) League Goals		1				28	14	2	5	18		17	2				2	1			1
Cup appearances	2	2	2	2	2	2	2		2	2	2	2	2			1					1
Cup Goals										1											

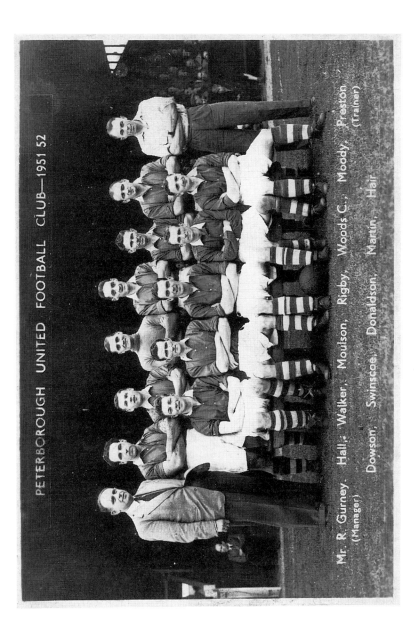

PETERBOROUGH UNITED FOOTBALL CLUB—1951 52

Mr. R. Gurney. Hall.; Walker, Moulson, Rigby, Woods C., Moody, Preston
(Manager)   (Trainer)

Dowson, Swinscoe, Donaldson, Martin, Hair.

Season Summary

Several new signings are made and will eventually become crowd favourites. Over 10,000 attend a London Road F.A.Cup match. Gurney leaves to be replaced by a new Manager – Fairbrother the ex– Newcastle United goalkeeper. A final League position of 5th is attained.

Midland League

#	Date	Opposition	Res	H.T.	Attend	Goalscorer
1	23 Aug	ROTHERHAM UTD. RES.	0-0	0-0	9101	
2	25	GRANTHAM	3-2	3-0	8831	Campbell Martin McCulloch
3	30	Scarborough	3-1	2-0		Bee Martin McCulloch
4	1 Sep	Hull City Res.	1-3	1-0		Martin
5	4	Grantham	1-1		3921	McCulloch
6	6	YORK CITY RES.	0-1	0-1	7875	
7	8	HULL CITY RES.	2-2	0-2	7409	Donaldson Wood
8	10	Frickley Colliery	1-2	1-1	5792	McCulloch
9	13	Grimsby Town Res.	1-2	1-1	6229	Anderson
10	15	FRICKLEY COLLIERY	2-1	1-0	9257	Campbell Martin
11	20	CORBY TOWN	0-0	0-0		
12	23	Denaby United	1-1	0-1	1200	Wood
13	23	DENABY UNITED	3-1	2-0	4328	Martin 3
14	4 Oct	BRADFORD P.A.RES.	3-3	1-3	7157	Sloan Martin 2
15	1 Nov	Scunthorpe & L.U. Res.	2-0	1-0	7328	Martin Hair
16	15	Lincoln City Res.	0-0	0-0	2000	
17	29	Goole Town	0-2	0-2		
18	13 Dec	Worksop Town	2-1	2-1		Donaldson Hair
19	20	Rotherham Utd. Res.	2-2	1-0	5925	Donaldson 2
20	26	WISBECH TOWN	3-0	2-0	5802	Sloan Martin Hair
21	27	Wisbech Town	0-1	0-1	5254	
22	10 Jan	HALIFAX TOWN RES.	3-1	1-1		Campbell Sloan Martin
23	17	York City Res.	3-3		6629	Donaldson Martin 2
24	24	GRIMSBY TOWN RES.	1-0	1-0	4970	Wood
25	31	BOSTON UNITED	2-2	1-1	5584	Sloan Martin
26	7 Feb	Corby Town	1-2	0-2	5056	Martin
27	14	NOTTS. COUNTY RES.	4-2	1-0		Anderson Campbell Donaldson Martin
28	21	Bradford P.A. Res.	0-1	0-0		
29	28	Bradford City Res.	1-2	1-1	7581	Wood
30	7 Mar	NOTTM. FOREST RES.	3-0	1-0	4467	Martin 2 Campbell
31	12	SCARBOROUGH	1-0	1-0	5000	Donaldson
32	14	Boston United	0-0	0-0		
33	19	Nottm. Forest Res.	1-1	1-1	6400	Campbell
34	21	SCUNTHORPE & L.U. RES.	2-0	2-0	5275	Campbell 2
35	23	Halifax Town Res.	0-3	0-1	4512	
36	30	BRADFORD CITY RES.	4-0	2-0		Fairbrother Walker Martin 2
37	3 Apr	Mansfield Town Res.	1-2	1-1	7586	Campbell
38	4	LINCOLN CITY RES.	1-1	1-1	8047	Martin
39	6	MANSFIELD TOWN RES.	3-0	2-0	5275	Martin 2 Campbell
40	11	Gainsborough Trin.	2-3	0-1		Sloan Adcock
41	13	GAINSBOROUGH TRIN.	8-1	3-1	6839	Martin Sloan 2 Hair 2 Adcock 3
42	16	Notts. County Res.	0-0	0-0	6248	
43	18	GOOLE TOWN	1-0	0-0		Martin
44	20	DONCASTER ROV. RES.	2-2	0-1	5259	Wood O.G.
45	25	Doncaster Rov. Res.	0-3	0-0		
46	2 May	WORKSOP TOWN	2-0	0-0		Anderson Adcock

Player appearances (shirt number by match):

#	Fairbrother	Moody	Woolard	Anderson	Rigby	Bee	Campbell	Sloan	Donaldson	Martin	Hair	Wood	Walker	McCulloch	Clarke	Foley	Butler	Mellow	Vardy	Hall	Shaw	Tomlinson	Pycroft	Rudkin	Adcock
1	1	2	3	4	5	6	7	8	9	10	11														
2	1	2	3	4	5	6	7			10	11		8	9											
3	1	2	3	4	5	8	7			10	7	6	8	9	11										
4	1	2	3	4	5	8				10	11	6		9		7	5	8							
5	1	2	3	4						10	11	6		9		7	5								
6	1	2	3	4				8	9	10	11	6		9		7									
7	1	2	3	4				8	10	10	11	6				7	5		7						
8	1		3	4		6	11	8	10		11	6		9			5		7	2					
9	1	2	3	6			7	8	9	10	11		4				5	10	7			1			
10	1	2	3	4	5		7	8	9	10	11	6		9							5	1			
11																									
12	1	2	3		5		7	8	9	10	11	6	4						7	3					
13	1	2	3	4	5		7	8	9	10	11	6	4						7	3					
14	1	2	3	4	5			8	9	10	11	6					6			3					
15	1	2	3	4	5		7	8	9	7	11	10											6		
16		3		4	5		7	8	9	10	11	8								2		1			
17		3		4	5		7	8	9	10	11	6		9						2		1			
18	1		3	6	5		7	8	9	10	11		4												
19	1	2		6	5		7	8	9	10	11		4							3					
20	1	2		6	5		7	8	9	10	11		4						7	3					
21	1	2		6	5	9	7	8	9	7	11	10	4							3					
22	1	2		6	5		7	8	9	10	11		4							3					
23	1	2		6	5		7	8	9	10	11		4						7	3					
24	1	2		6	5		7	9	9	8	11	10	4							3		1			
25	1	2		6	5		7	9	9	8	11	10	4							3	1				
26	1			6	5		7	8	9	10	11		4			7				3					
27	1			6	5		7	8	9	10	11		4							3					
28	1			6	5		7	8	9	10	11	8	4						7	3					
29	1			6	5		11	8	9	10	11	8	4							3					
30	1	2		6	5		7	8		10	11	6	4							3					
31	1	2		6	5		7	8	9	10	11	6	4							3					
32	1	2		6	5		7	8	9	10	11	6	2							3					
33	1			6	5		9	8		10	11	6	4							3				7	
34	1			6	5		9	8		10	11	6	4							3				7	
35	1			6	5		9			10	11		4						7	3					
36	1			2	5		7	8		10	11	6	4			7				3					9
37				2	5		7	8		10	11	6	4							3					9
38				2	5		7	8		10	11	6	4						7	3					9
39				4			7	8		10	11	6	2							3		1			9
40		2		4	5		7	8	9	10	11	6	4						7	3					9
41	1	2		4	5		7	8	9	10	11	6	4						7	3				7	9
42		2		4	5		7	8	9	10	11	6	4						7	3					9
43	1	2		4	5		7	8	9	10	11	6	4						7	3					9
44		2		6	5		7	8	9	9		6	4				5		11	3					9
45	1	2		6			7	7	8	10	11	11	4							3		1			8
46		2		6	5		7	8	8		11	10	4							3					9

F.A.Cup

Round	Date	Opponent	Score	HT	Att.	1	2	3	4	5	7	8	9	10	11	6		Scorers
1 Q.	27 Sep	Symington Rec.	5-2	5-0	2760	1	2	3	4	5	7	8	9	10	11	6		Anderson Sloan Donaldson Martin Hair
2 Q.	11 Oct	Spalding United	2-2	0-2	6228	1	2	3	4	5	7	8	9	10	11	6		Rigby Donaldson
2Q/R	16	SPALDING UNITED	3-0	1-0	8211	1	2		4	5	7	8	9	10	11	6	3	Rigby Campbell Sloan
3 Q.	25	Corby Town	0-0	0-0	10239	1	2	3	4	5	7	8	9	10	11	6		
3Q/R	30	CORBY TOWN	5-3 *	2-0	9845	1	2	3	4	5	7	8	9	10	11	6		Rigby Campbell Donaldson Martin Hair
4 Q.	8 Nov	BEDFORD TOWN	2-1	2-0	15327	1	2	3	4	5	7	8	9	10	11	6		Donaldson Martin
1st	22	TORQUAY UNITED	2-1	0-0	12938	1	2	3	4	5	7	8	9	10	11	6		Sloan Martin
2nd	6 Dec	BRISTOL ROVERS	0-1	0-1	15286	1	2	3	4	5	7	8	9	10	11	6		

* After extra time (90 minutes – 3-3)

League Appearances	40	39	18	43	39	4	33	36	27	42	42	31	29	7	1	4	7	2	11	31	1	6	1	2	10
(1 O.G.) League Goals																									
	8	8		3	1		10	7	7	26	5	5	1	4						1					5
Cup appearances	8	8	7	8	8		8	8	8	8	8	8	8							1					
Cup Goals			1				2	3	4	4	2														

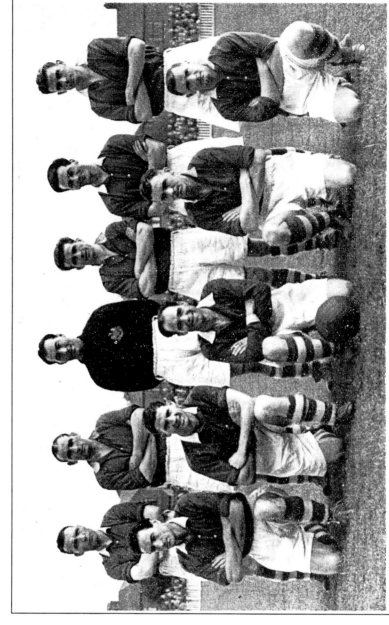

(Back) Anderson, Moody, Fairbrother, Butler, Wood, Woolard.
(Front) Sloan, Bardy, McCulloch, Donaldson, Hair

Season Summary

The first home League game attracts 9,101, and a good F.A.Cup run (which includes a record attendance at nearby Corby Town) ends at home to Bristol Rovers. Woollard is transferred to Newcastle United for £4,000. Big efforts are made to get accepted into the Football League, but only 6 votes received.

SEASON 1953/54

Midland League

542	Date	Opposition	Res	H.T.	Attend	Goalscorer
1	20 Aug	GRANTHAM	2-1	2-1	9806	Taft Sloan
2	22	GAINSBOROUGH TRIN.	9-2	4-1	8208	Walker Campbell Martin Taft 5 Sloan
3	24	Scarborough	3-1	1-0	4500	Campbell Martin Taft
4	26	York City Res.	2-0	2-0	1375	Taft 2
5	29	Doncaster Rov. Res.	0-1	0-1	2400	
6	31	YORK CITY RES.	4-1	1-1	10053	Martin Taft 3
7	5 Sep	Corby Town	1-0	0-0	8086	Sloan
8	8	Denaby United	1-0	0-0		Campbell
9	12	BOSTON UNITED	4-1	3-1	10399	Campbell Martin 2 Taft
10	14	DENABY UNITED	2-1	1-1	9466	Martin Taft
11	19	Lincoln City Res.	1-4	0-3	6300	Taft
12	21	BRADFORD P.A. RES.	6-3	3-2	7277	Taft 2 Sloan 3 Matthews
13	26	SCUNTHORPE & L.U. RES.	3-2	2-0	9237	Campbell Taft 2
14	3 Oct	Notts. County Res.	2-2	2-0	2500	Martin Matthews
15	8	Hull City Res.	1-0	0-0		Campbell
16	10	SCARBOROUGH	2-2	2-0	8984	Campbell Hair
17	17	Bradford City Res.	3-2	1-1	1551	Martin 2 Taft
18	24	ROTHERHAM UTD. RES.	2-2	0-1	9293	Martin Taft
19	31	Frickley Colliery	3-3	1-2	1000	Martin Taft Matthews
20	5 Dec	HALIFAX TOWN RES.	5-1	3-0	7357	Anderson Martin 2 Taft Hair
21	19	Gainsborough Trin.	0-4	0-3		
22	25	MANSFIELD TOWN RES.	2-3	1-2	5030	Martin Taft
23	28	Mansfield Town Res.	1-0	1-1		Hair
24	2 Jan	DONCASTER ROV. RES.	1-1	1-1	8164	Taft
25	16	CORBY TOWN	5-4	2-3	9519	Martin Taft 2 Reynolds 2
26	23	Boston United	2-1	2-1	5990	Martin Hair
27	30	GOOLE TOWN	1-3	0-1	5262	Taft
28	6 Feb	LINCOLN CITY RES.	6-1	3-0	9035	Moody Taft Matthews Hair Foley 2
29	13	Scunthorpe & L.U. Res.	1-2	1-2	2500	Taft
30	20	NOTTS. COUNTY RES.	4-1	1-0	8839	Martin 2 Taft 2
31	27	Wisbech Town	1-2	0-0	7402	Moody
32	6 Mar	BRADFORD CITY RES.	3-1	1-1	8321	Taft Pateman 2
33	13	Rotherham Utd. Res.	1-1	1-1		Wood
34	25	Nottm. Forest Res.	1-2	0-2		Taft
35	27	Grantham	1-3	1-2	4100	Wood
36	29	GRIMSBY TOWN RES.	1-1	1-1		Woodgate
37	1 Apr	Goole Town	1-0	1-0	5799	Martin
38	3	WISBECH TOWN	1-1	0-0	10131	Wood
39	8	FRICKLEY COLLIERY	2-0	0-0	5511	Woodgate Taft
40	10	Grimsby Town Res.	4-1	2-0		Woodgate 2 Martin Butler
41	12	Worksop Town	2-1	1-0	2500	Martin 2 Taft
42	17	NOTTM. FOREST RES.	3-1	2-0	12665	Martin 2 Taft
43	19	HULL CITY RES.	4-3	3-0	10287	Woodgate Taft 2 Hair
44	24	Halifax Town Res.	3-4	0-4		Woodgate Martin Powell
45	28	Bradford P.A. Res.	1-2	0-1		Taft
46	1 May	WORKSOP TOWN	3-1	1-0	8149	Taft 2 Hair

Player appearances (shirt numbers)

#	Fairbrother	Moody	Senior	Walker	Rigby	Anderson	Campbell	Martin	Taft	Sloan	Matthews	Hall	Sanderson	Wood	Vardy	Hair	Reynolds	Swindon	Foley	Butler	Pateman	Woodgate	Stafford G.	Powell
1	1	2	3	4	5	6	7	8	9	10	11													
2	1		3	4	5	6	7	8	9	10	11	2												
3	1		3	4	5	6	7	8	9	10	11	2												
4	1		3	4	5	6	7	8	9	10	11	2												
5	1		3	4	5	6	7	8	9	10	11	2												
6		2	3	4	5	6	7	8	9	10	11		1											
7	1	2	3	4	5	6	7	8	9	10	11													
8	1	2	3	4	5	6	7	8	9	10	11													
9	1	2		4	5	6	7	8	9	10	11	3												
10	1	2		4	5	6	7	8	9	10	11	3												
11	1	2		4	5	6	7	8	9	10	11	3												
12	1	2		4	5		7	8	9	10	11	3		6										
13	1	2		4	5	6	7	8	9	10	11	3												
14	1	2		4	5	6		8	9	10	11	3			7									
15	1	2		4	5	6	7	8	9	10	11	3												
16	1	2		4	5	6	7	8	9	10		3				11								
17	1	2		4	5		7	8	9		10	3		6		11								
18		2			5	4	7	8	9	6	10	3	1				11							
19	1	2			5	4	7	8	9	6	10	3					11							
20	1	2			5	4	7	8	9		10	3		6		11								
21	1	2			5	4	7	8	9	6	10	3				11								
22			5			4	7	8	9	6	10	3	1				11							
23	1				5	4	7	8	9	6	10	3				11								
24		2	5			4		8	9	6	10	3	1			7	11							
25	1	2			5	4		8	9	6	10	3				7	11							
26	1	2			5	4		8	9	6	10	3				7	11							
27	1	2			5	4		8	9	6	10	3				7	11							
28	1	2			5	4		8	9	6	10	3				11			7					
29		2		6	5	4		8	9		10	3					11	1	7					
30		2			5	4		8	9		11	3		10				1	7					
31		2			5	4		8	9		11	3		10				1	7					
32		2			5			8	9		10	3						1		4	7			
33				2				8	9			3		10		11		1				7		
34								8	9			3		10		11		1				7		
35								8	9			3		10		11		1				7		
36		2			5			8	9		10							1		4	7	11	3	
37		2			5			8	10									1		4	7	11	3	
38		2			5			8				3		9		11		1		4		7	3	
39		2						8	9			3		9		11		1			10	7		
40					5			8	9			3				11		1		4		7		10
41				2				8	9		10	3				11		1		4		7		
42		2						8	9							11		1		4		7		10
43				2				8	9							11		1		4		7		10
44								8	9							11		1		4		7		10
45			5			6		8	9	10						11		1		4		7	2	
46			5			6		8	9	10						11		1		4		7	2	

F.A.Cup

4Q.	7 Nov	GRAYS ATHLETIC	4-1	3-0	11200	Martin Matthews O.G.2
1st	21	Hitchin Town	3-1	2-1	6332	Campbell Taft 2
2nd	12 Dec	ALDERSHOT	2-1	0-0	16717	Martin Taft
3rd	9 Jan	Cardiff City	1-3	1-1	38000	Martin

1	2	5	4	7	8	9	10	11	3	6													
1	2	5	4	7	8	9	10	11	3	6													
1	2	5	4	7	8	9	10	3	6													11	
1	2	5	4	7	8	9	6	10	3													11	
1	2	5	4	7	8	9	6	10	3													11	

	20	34	24	19	44	38	23	46	46	44	30	29	8	12	1	26	4	18	4	9	4	14	5	4
League Appearances	20	34	24	19	44	38	23	46	46	44	30	29	8	12	1	26	4	18	4	9	4	14	5	4
League Goals		2		1		1	7	24	42	6	41			3		7	2	2	2	1	2	6		1
Cup appearances	4	4		4	4	4	4	4	4	4	3	4		3		3	2	2						
(2 O.G.) Cup Goals	4	4		4		1	3	3	3	4	1			2		3								

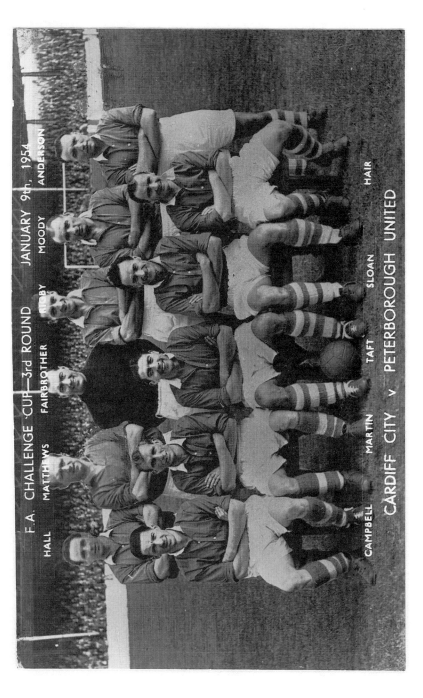

F.A. CHALLENGE CUP—3rd ROUND   JANUARY 9th, 1954

HALL   MATTHEWS   FAIRBROTHER   KIRBY   MOODY   ANDERSON

CAMPBELL   MARTIN   TAFT   SLOAN   HAIR

CARDIFF CITY v PETERBOROUGH UNITED

Season Summary

Nearly 10,000 present for the first game at London Road, and over 16,000 see Aldershot knocked out of the F.A.Cup. The run ends at Cardiff City before a crowd of 38,000. A good season ends with Manager Fairbrother moving on — to be replaced by George Swindin, from Arsenal. The League application vote increases to 18, but still not enough!

Midland League

#	Date	Opposition	Res	H.T.	Attend	Goalscorer
1	21 Aug	ROTHERHAM UTD. RES.	1-1	0-0	9258	Campbell
2	25	Wisbech Town	2-1	1-0	7081	Emery Taft
3	28	Scunthorpe & L.U. Res.	2-2	2-2		Campbell 2
4	30	WISBECH TOWN	3-1	3-0	9982	Stafford E. 2 Taft
5	4 Sep	BRADFORD CITY RES.	2-0	2-0	9616	Woodgate Taft
6	9	Goole Town	2-1	2-1	5875	Martin Taft
7	11	Lincoln City Res.	1-0	1-0		Devlin
8	13	GOOLE TOWN	4-0	2-0	7728	Stafford E. Martin Woodgate Taft
9	18	HULL CITY RES.	1-0	1-0	9502	Woodgate
10	23	Nottm. Forest Res.	1-1	1-0		Devlin
11	25	Gainsborough Trin.	0-1	0-0		
12	2 Oct	KINGS LYNN	0-0	0-0	13217	
13	9	NOTTM. FOREST RES.	1-1	1-1	11256	Emery
14	16	Scarborough	2-2	1-1	2900	Martin Kelly
15	23	GRIMSBY TOWN RES.	3-1	0-1	9282	Kelly 2 Hair
16	30	Frickley Colliery	0-1	0-0		
17	13 Nov	Denaby United	2-2	1-2		Woodgate Emery
18	20	DONCASTER ROV. RES.	3-1	1-0	7605	Moody Emery Kelly
19	27	Worksop Town	0-1	0-1	2276	
20	4 Dec	GAINSBOROUGH TRIN.	2-2	1-1	7279	Emery Taft
21	11	Grantham	1-1	0-1		Tyrer
22	18	Rotherham Utd. Res.	2-3	1-2		Stafford E. Woodgate
23	27	Notts. County Res.	1-1	1-0	600	Tyrer
24	28	NOTTS. COUNTY RES.	0-0	0-0	3000	
25	1 Jan	SCUNTHORPE & L.U. RES.	2-0	1-0	6602	Moody Bull
26	8	YORK CITY RES.	2-0	0-0	6750	Davey Bull
27	29	York City Res.	1-1	1-1	600	Davey
28	5 Feb	Hull City Res.	0-4	0-2	3000	
29	12	BOSTON UNITED	1-0	1-0	5955	Kelly
	19	Kings Lynn	*			Abandoned- score at 35 min. 0-0
30	5 Mar	SCARBOROUGH	5-0	2-0	6706	Woodgate Kelly Hair 2 Davey
31	12	Grimsby Town Res.	1-0	1-0		Kelly
32	16	Bradford City Res.	0-0	0-0		
33	19	FRICKLEY COLLIERY	1-1	1-0	6130	Woodgate
34	28	LINCOLN CITY RES.	2-2	1-0	5186	Kelly Hair
35	2 Apr	DENABY UNITED	2-0	2-0	6366	Woodgate Martin
36	8	Mansfield Town Res.	1-2	0-2		Hair
37	9	Doncaster Rov. Res.	1-0	1-0		Kelly
38	11	MANSFIELD TOWN RES.	2-0	0-0	8032	Martin McCabe
39	14	Boston United	1-0	1-0		Hair
40	16	WORKSOP TOWN	2-0	2-0	6960	Martin O.G.
41	18	BRADFORD P.A. RES.	2-0	1-0	5681	Davey Campbell
42	23	Bradford P.A. Res.	3-2	2-1		Taft Kelly Hair
43	30	GRANTHAM	0-2	0-0	7395	
44	2 May	Corby Town	0-0	0-0		
45	5	CORBY TOWN	3-0	3-0		Woodgate Martin O.G.
46	7	Kings Lynn	1-0	1-0	7591	Martin

Player appearances (shirt numbers)

#	Lowery	Moody	Killin	McCabe	Rigby	Garrett	Campbell	Powell	Stafford E.	Martin	Woodgate	Emery	Taft	Devlin	Tyrer	Butler	Williams	Satfford G.	Kelly	Hair	Anderson	Bickerstaff	Davey	Bull	McNamee
1	1	2	3	4	5	6	7	8	9	10	11														
2	1	2	3	4	5		7		6	10	11	8	9												
3	1	2	3	6	5		7		4			8		10	11										
4	1	2	3	6	5				10		7	8	9	11		4									
5	1	2	3	6	5				10		7	8	9		11	4									
6	1	2	3	6	5				6	10	7	8	9		11	4									
7	1	2	3	6	5				6	8	7			10	11	4									
8	1	2	3	6	5				10	8	7		9		11	4									
9	1	2	3	6	5				10	8	7		9	10	11	4									
10	1	2	3	6	5				10	8	7			11			4								
11	1	2	3	6	5				10	8	7			11			4	3							
12	1	2	3	6	5		7					8		11			4		9	10					
13	1	2	3	6	5				8	10	7	8	8	11			4		9		4				
14	1	2	3	6	5				8	8	7			11					9	11	4				
15	1	2	3	6	5				4	8	7		8	11					9	11	4				
16	1	2	3	6	5				4	8	7		8						9						
17	1	2	3		5				6	7	7	8		11			4		9						
18	1	2	3	5					6	10	7	8		11		4	4	2	9	11					
19	1	2	3	5					6	10	7	8		11			4		9						
20	1	2	3	5	5				6	10	7	8		11			4		9						
21	1	2	3		5				6		7	9	10	11			4		10						
22	1	2	3		5				9		7	10	8	11		4	4								
23		2	3	6	5				6		7	9	8	11		4			9	11		1			
24		2	3	6	5				6		7	9	8	10	11	4						1			
25	1	2	3		5		7				7	8	8	10	11				9				8	9	
26	1	2	3	6	5		7				7		8	10	11				9				8	9	
27	1	2	3	6	5		7				7		8	10	11				9				8	9	
28	1	2	3	6	5		7				7		8	10	11								8		
29	1	2	3	5	5		7		6		7		4	10	11				9				8		
30	1	2	3		5		7		6		7		4	10					9	11			8		
31	1	2	3	6	5		7		6		7		4	10					9	11			8		
32	1	2	3	6	5		7		6		7		4	10					9	11			8		
33	1	2	3	6	5		7		6		7		4						9	11			8		
34	1	2	3		5				6	10	7	8	8				6		9	6			8		
35	1	2	3		5			7	6	10	7								9	11			8		
36	1	2	3	6	5			7		10									9	11			8		
37	1	2	3	4	5			7	10										9	11			8		
38	1		3	6				7	6				4	10		6		2	9	11			8		
39	1		3					7		10				10		6		2	9	11			8		
40	1		3	4	5			7	4	10		9	9					2	9	11			8		
41	1		3	5	3		7	7	6			10	4					2	9	11			8	10	
42	1	2	3	5	5			7	6			10	6					3	9	11			8		
43	1	2	3	5	3			7	6	8	7	8		10				2							
44	1		3	4	5				6	8	7	10	4	11				2	9				8		
45	1		3	5	5				6	8	7	10	6	11				2	9				8		
46	1		3	5	5				4	8	7	10	6					2	9				8		11

F.A.Cup

4 Q.	6 Nov	BOSTON UNITED	1-2	1-1	16558	Emery

	2	3	6	5		4	10	7	8	11		9										1	
League Appearances	44	36	42	30	43	1	12	1	38	26	36	13	37	25	16	9	10	12	29	20	2	2	17
(2 O.G.) League Goals	2		1				4		4	8	9	5	7	2	2				1	7			4
Cup appearances	1	1	1	1			1		1	1	1	1	1	1	1				1	1	1		4
Cup Goals											1												2

Three stars of the Season:

Norman Rigby (Top left)

Jim McCabe (Left)

Jim Kelly (Above)

Season Summary

Admission charges increase to 1/9d. (9p). The popularity of Posh increases – even Reserve games attracting 6,000. 13,217 watch the League game with Kings Lynn. No luck in the F.A.Cup, but best Midland League position of 3rd is reached, but Football League application gets only 6 votes.

Midland League

634	Date	Opposition	Res	H.T.	Attend	Goalscorer
1	20 Aug	Mansfield Town Res.	5-1	2-0		Hails 3 Donaldson 2
2	22	York City Res.	3-4	2-1	3500	Hails Donaldson Ramscar
3	27	NOTTS. COUNTY RES.	2-2	0-1	9841	Emery Martin
4	29	YORK CITY RES.	4-0	2-0	8600	Emery Donaldson Hair 2
5	3 Sep	Bradford City Res.	2-1	1-0	10019	Hails Emery
6	5	ROTHERHAM UTD. RES.	1-1	1-0		Hair
7	10	SCARBOROUGH	6-0	4-0	9224	Hails 2 Emery 3 Donaldson
8	12	Rotherham Utd. Res.	2-2	0-1		Stafford E. 2
9	17	Scunthorpe & L.U. Res.	1-1	0-1		Donaldson
10	20	Denaby United	2-1	1-1	1530	Emery Gibson
11	26	DENABY UNITED	4-0	1-0	7378	Hails 2 Donaldson Gibson
12	1 Oct	Worksop Town	3-3	3-2		Emery Hair Gibson
13	4	Grimsby Town Res.	3-1	1-1	9500	Donaldson 2 Gibson
14	8	Boston United	5-2	4-1	9935	Farrow Emery Donaldson Gibson 2
15	15	DONCASTER ROV. RES.	7-0	3-0	9935	Emery Donaldson Hair 2 Gibson 3
16	29	NOTTM. FOREST RES.	2-2	1-1	10398	Gibson 2
17	12 Nov	HULL CITY RES.	3-1	2-1	9955	Hails Donaldson Gibson
18	26	LINCOLN CITY RES.	6-1	4-0	8745	Hails Donaldson 3 Hair 2
19	3 Dec	Corby Town	2-0	0-0	4500	Emery Gibson
20	17	MANSFIELD TOWN RES.	2-0	1-0	5658	Hails Donaldson Hair
21	24	Notts. County Res.	3-1	2-0	6000	Hails Donaldson Hair
22	26	Grantham	2-0	0-0		Hails Emery
23	27	GRANTHAM	4-1	1-0	11000	Emery Donaldson 2 Hair
24	31	BRADFORD CITY RES.	4-1	3-0	8805	Hails Gibson 3
25	7 Jan	Kings Lynn	2-0	0-0	8110	Emery Donaldson
26	14	Scarborough	2-2	2-0	9200	Gibson 2
27	21	SCUNTHORPE & L.U. RES.	3-0	3-0	9200	Emery 2 Hair
28	28	KINGS LYNN	4-2	1-1	10178	Emery 4
29	11 Feb	WORKSOP TOWN	1-1	0-0	6185	Donaldson
30	18	BOSTON UNITED	1-0	0-0	11412	Emery
31	25	Doncaster Rov. Res.	1-1	1-1		Gibson
32	7 Mar	Bradford P.A. Res.	4-3	2-2		Hair Emery Donaldson Gibson
33	10	Nottm. Forest Res.	0-1	0-0		
34	17	GRIMSBY TOWN RES.	2-1	1-1	8873	Shaw Emery
35	26	Frickley Colliery	2-1	0-0		Donaldson Gibson
36	30	WISBECH TOWN	3-1	1-0	10986	Emery Donaldson Hair
37	31	BRADFORD P.A. RES.	1-0	1-0	8715	Donaldson
38	2 Apr	Wisbech Town	4-2	2-1	6758	Emery Donaldson Gibson Hair
39	5	GAINSBOROUGH TRIN.	1-1	1-1	5535	Donaldson
40	7	Lincoln City Res.	1-1	1-1		Shaw
41	12	Goole Town	7-1			Shaw Gibson 3 Hair Martin 2
42	14	CORBY TOWN	4-0	3-0	7382	Gibson 3 O.G.
43	16	GOOLE TOWN	7-0	2-0	6145	Emery 2 Donaldson Gibson Longworth Martin 2
44	21	Gainsborough Trin.	3-0	1-0		Emery Donaldson Gibson
45	23	Hull City Res.	2-1	2-0	200	Hails Gibson
46	28	FRICKLEY COLLIERY	4-1	1-0	8201	Hair Longworth 2 O.G.

F.A.Cup

4 Q.	5 Nov	Ilkeston Town	3-1	1-0	9000	Hails 2 Emery
1st	19	IPSWICH TOWN	3-1	1-1	20671	Emery 2 Hair
2nd	10 Dec	Swindon Town	1-1	1-0	23983	Emery
2/R.	15	SWINDON TOWN	1-2*	0-1	16672	Emery

* A.E.T. (score at 90 mins. 1-1)

League Appearances	32	15	38	46	41	25	39	46	45	3	42	14	3	3	28	23	30	2	1	13	2	10
(2 O.G.) League Goals					3	1	16	28	29	1	16		5		2		31			3		
Cup appearances	4		4	4	4	4	4	4	4		4				2	4	4					
Cup Goals							2	5			1											

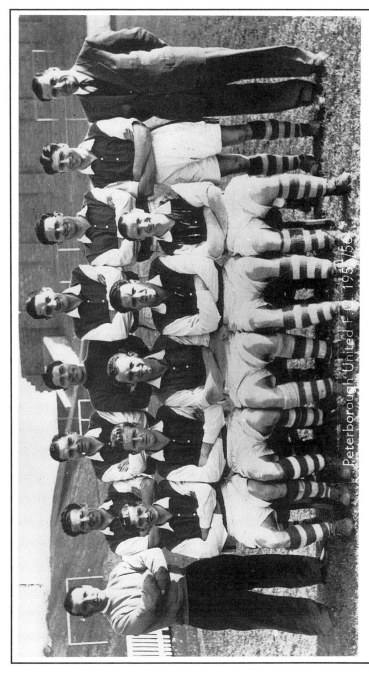

Peterborough United F.C. 1957/58

(Back) Anderson (Trainer), Shaw, Clarke, Lowery, Rigby, Killin, Farrow, Swindin (Manager)
(Front) Hails, Emery, Donaldson, Gibson, Hair.

Season Summary

A formidable forward line produces high scores (137 scored in League). 20,671 are present for home F.A.Cup win over Ipswich Town. Work starts on new Grandstand. Midland League title won at last, but Posh again rejected from entry into the Football league – only 8 votes in favour.

SEASON 1956/57

Midland League

#	Date	Opposition	Res	H.T.	Attend	Goalscorer
1	18 Aug	BOSTON UNITED	1-0	0-0	13431	Gibson
2	20	HULL CITY RES.	7-0	3-0	9161	Shaw Emery 3 Gibson 2 Hogg
3	25	Goole Town	3-1	2-0	2000	Emery Gibson Codd
4	27	Hull City Res.	1-1	1-0	9043	Emery
5	1 Sep	ROTHERHAM UTD. RES.	1-1	0-0	7147	Shaw
6	3	BRADFORD P.A. RES.	5-1	0-0		Emery 2 Gibson 2 Crawford
7	10	Bradford P.A. Res.	4-1	4-0	8387	Emery 2 Gibson Donaldson
8	15	SCUNTHORPE & L.U. RES.	4-0	2-0	7500	Shaw Donaldson 2 O.G.
9	17	NOTTM. FOREST RES.	0-1	0-1		
10	22	Gainsborough Trin.	2-1	2-1		Gibson Stafford
11	24	Lincoln City Res.	0-1	0-0	9131	
12	29	CORBY TOWN	6-1	2-0	7413	Gibson McNamee Longworth 4
13	6 Oct	SCARBOROUGH	2-0	0-0	3500	Hails Gibson
14	13	Bradford City Res.	5-2	1-0	7634	McNamee Longworth 2 O.G. 2
15	20	MANSFIELD TOWN RES.	8-0	3-0	1474	Emery 4 Gibson Longworth 3
16	27	Denaby United	4-2	1-2		Gibson 2 Smith Longworth
17	10 Nov	Doncaster Rov. Res.	2-1	0-1		Shaw Emery
18	24	Grantham	1-1	1-1	8255	Hails
19	1 Dec	YORK CITY RES.	6-0	1-0	1000	Emery Gibson 3 Hogg Donaldson
20	15	Boston United	4-2	2-1	9301	Emery 3 Gibson
21	22	GOOLE TOWN	3-0	1-0	10600	Emery Hogg Donaldson
22	24	Nottm. Forest Res.	2-0	1-0	5000	Donaldson 2
23	26	GRANTHAM	3-0	1-0	4661	Emery Hogg 2
24	29	Rotherham Utd. Res.	1-3	0-0	4919	Gibson
25	12 Jan	LINCOLN CITY RES.	6-1	3-0	9707	Hails Emery 2 Hogg Donaldson Smith
26	19	Scunthorpe & L. U. Res.	1-1	0-0	1000	Gibson
27	2 Feb	GAINSBOROUGH TRIN.	5-0	4-0	9301	Emery 2 Donaldson Smith Middlemass
28	9	Corby Town	4-1	1-0	2800	Shaw Hails Emery Donaldson
29	16	Scarborough	2-0	1-0	4007	Emery Donaldson
30	23	BRADFORD CITY RES.	5-1	2-1	2000	Emery Donaldson Middlemass 2 O.G.
31	2 Mar	Frickley Colliery	1-1	0-0	8248	Donaldson
32	9	DENABY UNITED	7-0	4-0	4800	Hails3 Emery Smith Middlemass Gibson
33	11	FRICKLEY COLLIERY	3-1	0-1	4712	Shaw Smith 2
34	16	Grimsby Town Res.	2-1	1-1	8576	Emery Smith
35	23	DONCASTER ROV. RES.	3-1	1-1	7500	Emery Donaldson Smith
36	30	Mansfield Town Res.	3-0	1-0	2100	Hails Emery Hogg
37	6 Apr	NOTTS. COUNTY RES.	1-1	0-0	9200	Donaldson
38	13	York City Res.	2-0	1-0	9140	Donaldson O.G.
39	19	WISBECH TOWN	4-0	2-0	5342	Shaw Smith McNamee 2
40	20	GRIMSBY TOWN RES.	4-1	1-0	5086	Emery 2 Donaldson Smith
41	22	Wisbech Town	4-1	2-1		Emery 2 Donaldson Smith
42	25	KINGS LYNN	5-0		2000	Hails Emery 2 McNamee 2
43	27	Notts. County Res.	1-2	0-1	5102	Emery
44	30	Worksop Town	3-1	0-1	5328	Shaw Emery Donaldson
45	2 May	WORKSOP TOWN	4-0	0-0		Cockburn Hails Emery 2
46	4	Kings Lynn	3-1	0-0		Emery 2 O.G.

Player appearances (shirt numbers)

#	Walls	Douglass	Barr	Shaw	Rigby	Cockburn	Hails	Emery	Gibson	Crawford	Hogg	Dickson	Orr	Codd	Killin	Donaldson	Sansby	Smith	Stafford	McNamee	Guy	Longworth	Farrow	Jacobs	Middlemass	McJarrow
1	1	2	3	4	5	6	7	8	9	10	11															
2	1	2	3	4	5	6		8	9	10	11			7												
3	1	2	3	4	5	6		8	9	10	11			7												
4	1	2	3	4	5	6	7	8	9	10	11			7												
5		2	3	4	5	6	7	8	9	10	11	1			2											
6			3	4	5	6		8	9	10	11	1			2	9										
7	1		3	4	5	6	7	8	10		11			7	2	9										
8	1		3	4	5	6	7	8	10		11			7	2	9										
9	1	2	3	4	5	6	7	8	10		11					9	2									
10	1	3		4	5	6	7	8	9		11				3				10							
11	1	2	3	4	5	6	7	8	9	10	11	1							10							
12	1	2	3	4	5	6	7	8	9				5							11	2	10				
13	1	2	3	4	5	6	7	8	9				5	7						11	2	10				
14	1	2		4	5	6	7	8	9						3		2			11	2	10				
15	1	2	3	4	5	6	7	8	9					7						11	2	10				
16	1		3	4	5	6	7	8	9							2		11			2	10				
17	1		3	4	5	6	7	8	9									11			2	10				
18	1	2	3	4	5	6	7	8	9									11	9							
19	1	2	3	4	5		7	8	10	10	11					9										
20	1	2	3	4	5	6	7	8	10	10	11					9										
21	1	2	3	4	5	6	7	8	10	10	11					9										
22	1	2	3	4	5	6	7	8		10						9		11	6							
23	1	2	3	4	5	6	7	8	10	10	11					9		11	6							
24	1	2	3	4	5	6	7	8	10	10	11					9	2	11								
25	1	2	3	4	5		7	8		10	11					9		10					6			
26	1	2	3	4	5	6		8	9									10	6		3		6			
27	1	2	3	4	5	6	7	8		10	11					9		10	6						11	
28	1	2	3	4	5	6	7	8		10						9		10								
29	1	2	3	4	5	6	7	8								9				10						
30	1	2	3	4	5		7	8								9		10						3	11	
31	1	2	3	4	5		7	8								9		10						3	11	
32	1	2	3	4	5	6	7	8	9									10						3	11	
33	1	2	3	4	5	6	7	8										10						3	11	
34	1	2	3	4	5	6	7	8								9		10						3	11	
35	1	2	3	4	5	6	7	8			11					9		10						3		
36	1	2	3	4	5		7	8			11					9		10	6					3		
37	1	2	3	4	5		7	8			11					9		10	6					3		
38	1	2	3	4	5	6	7	8			11					9		10						3		
39	1	2	3	4	5	6	10	8								9		7		11				3		
40	1	2	3	4	5		7	8								9		10		11			6	3		
41	1	2	3	4	5		7	8								9		10		11			6	3		
42	1	2	3	4	5		7	8								9		10	6	11				3		
43	1	2	3	4	5		7	8								9		10	6	11				3		
44	1	2	3	4	5	6	7	8							2	9		10	6	11				3		
45	1		3	4	5	6	7	8			11					9		2	2	11				3		10
46	1	2	3	4	5		7	8			11					9		10	6	11				3		10

680

F.A. Cup

	Date	Opponent	Score	HT	Att.	1	2	3	4	5	6	7	8	9			11	Goalscorers
4 Q.	3 Oct	Corby Town	5-1	1-0	8357	1	2	3	4	5	6	7	8	9		10	11	Emery 2 Gibson 2 Smith
1st	17 Nov	Yeovil Town	3-1	2-1	10575	1	2	3	4	5	6	7	8	10	9		11	Hails Emery 2
2nd	8 Dec	BRADFORD P.A.	3-0	2-0	18618	1	2	3	4	5	6	7	8	10	9	9	11	Hails Emery Donaldson
3rd	5 Jan	LINCOLN CITY	2-2	0-0	22000	1	2	3	4	5	6	7	8	10	9		11	Emery 2
3/R.	9	Lincoln City	5-4*	2-1	18216	1	2	3	4	5	6	7	8		9	10		Emery Donaldson 3 Smith
4th	26	Huddersfield Town	1-3	0-1	48735	1	2	3	4	5	6	7	8		9	10	11	Shaw

* After Extra Time (score at 90 mins. 2-2)

League Appearances	42	34	22	46	45	33	38	46	25	8	22	4	1	8	6	27	3	24	14	14	5	6	4	20	7	2
(6 O.G.) League Goals		2	8		1	10	43	20	1	7	1		1		20		10	1	6		10	4				
Cup appearances	6	6	6	6	6	6	6	6	4		4	1	1		4		4	4					4		2	
Cup Goals		1			1	2	8	2			2				4		2						2			

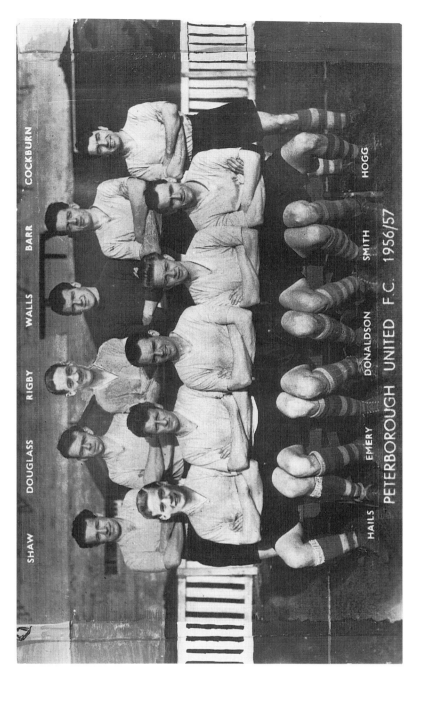

SHAW DOUGLASS RIGBY WALLS BARR COCKBURN

HAILS EMERY DONALDSON SMITH HOGG

PETERBOROUGH UNITED F.C. 1956/57

Season Summary

13,431 attend first Midland League match, to see new signings. Beaten by Nottingham Forest Reserves in September – this becomes the last home defeat in League (4 years)! 22,000 present for home F.A.Cup match versus Lincoln City, and Posh progress through to 4th round. League Championship won – again – by 9 points.

Midland League

Player columns (shirt numbers recorded per match), listed from the chart:
Wright, Smith T., Sansby, Lingberg, Cluroe, Crawford, Walker, Bannister, Smith R., Longworth, Chadwick, Killin, Cresswell, McNamee, O'Donnel, Donaldson, Emery, Hails, Cockburn, Rigby, Shaw, Jacobs, Stafford, Walls

726	Date	Opposition	Res	H.T.	Attend	Goalscorer
1	24 Aug	Corby Town	4-0	1-0	4000	Shaw Emery Donaldson O'Donnel
2	28	Wisbech Town	4-0	1-0	8044	Emery 3 Donaldson
3	31	SCUNTHORPE & L.U. RES.	6-0	2-0	10169	Emery O'Donnel 2 McNamee 3
4	2 Sep	WISBECH TOWN	4-1	1-1	10500	Stafford Hails Emery O'Donnel
5	7	Worksop Town	3-1	2-0		Emery 2 McNamee
6	9	NOTTS. COUNTY RES.	2-0	1-0	9600	Shaw McNamee
7	14	Kings Lynn	5-2	1-1	9765	Hails Donaldson Longworth Smith R. 2
8	19	Notts. County Res.	3-1	3-1		Shaw Longworth Smith R.
9	21	GOOLE TOWN	5-0	2-0	10000	Shaw Emery Donaldson Smith R.2
10	23	LINCOLN CITY RES.	4-2	1-0		Donaldson Smith R. 3
11	28	Mansfield Town Res.	6-1	3-0		Hails 2 Emery 2 Donaldson Smith R.
12	30	Lincoln City Res.	0-1	0-0		
13	5 Oct	BRADFORD CITY RES.	7-0	2-0	8750	Hails 2 Emery 2 Donaldson Longworth2
14	12	GRANTHAM	4-1	2-1	9200	Emery 3 Donaldson
15	19	Nottm. Forest Res.	0-3	0-2		
16	26	GRIMSBY TOWN RES.	5-2	3-1	9100	Donaldson 3 Longworth 2
17	9 Nov	ROTHERHAM UTD. RES.	3-0	0-0	8500	Donaldson 2 Smith R.
18	23	SCARBOROUGH	1-0	0-0		Donaldson
19	30	Bradford P.A. Res.	5-1	1-1		Emery 4 Donaldson
20	7 Dec	DONCASTER ROV. RES.	8-2	5-1	6800	Emery 2 Donaldson 2 McNamee Smith R. 3.
21	14	Denaby United	4-2	2-1		Hails Emery 2 McNamee
22	21	CORBY TOWN	8-1	3-0	8267	Hails Emery 4 Donaldson Longworth 2
23	26	Boston United	1-2	1-2		Emery
24	28	Scunthorpe & L.U. Res.	1-1	0-0		Emery
25	4 Jan	HULL CITY RES.	4-0	0-0	6856	Emery 2 McNamee 2
26	11	WORKSOP TOWN	6-0	1-0	7487	Hails Emery 2 Cluroe 3
27	18	KINGS LYNN	3-1	2-1	8856	Emery 2 Cluroe
28	1 Feb	Goole Town	4-2	2-0	3500	Emery 2 McNamee Smith R.
29	8	MANSFIELD TOWN RES.	3-1	2-0	7382	Hails Emery McNamee
30	15	Bradford City Res.	2-0	1-0		Hails Smith R.
31	22	Grantham	3-7	0-4		Longworth Smith R. 2
32	1 Mar	FRICKLEY COLLIERY	6-0	1-0		Emery Donaldson McNamee Smith R.3
	8	Grimsby Town Res.	*	3-0		Hails Smith R.McNamee2 (Aban.67min.)
33	15	NOTTM. FOREST RES.	4-0	0-0	9388	Donaldson 2 Smith R. 2
34	22	Rotherham Utd. Res.	5-1	2-1		Hails Emery 2 Donaldson 2
35	29	YORK CITY RES.	1-0	0-0		Emery
36	31	BOSTON UNITED	3-2	1-2	8077	Chadwick Hails Smith R.
37	4 Apr	Gainsborough Trin.	0-2	0-2		
38	5	Doncaster Rov. Res.	3-0	0-0		Emery 2 McNamee
39	7	GAINSBOROUGH TRIN.	5-1	3-1	9183	Shaw Emery Smith R. Cluroe 2
40	10	Hull City Res.	1-1	1-1		Smith R.
41	12	BRADFORD P.A. RES.	1-1	1-0	6675	Smith R.
42	17	Frickley Colliery	3-0	0-0		Chadwick 2 McNamee
43	19	Scarborough	0-0	0-0	3800	
44	24	York City Res.	1-1			Emery
45	26	DENABY UNITED	9-0	2-0		Hails Emery 4 Donaldson Smith R.2 McNamee
46	1 May	Grimsby Town Res.	0-2			

F.A.Cup

4.Q.	2 Nov	WOLVERTON T. & B.R.	7-0	2-0	13,200	Emery Longworth 3 Smith R. O.G. 2	1	2		4	5		7	8	9				3	11	10	6
1st	16	TORQUAY UNITED	3-3	3-0	17800	Emery Donaldson 2	1	6	2	4	5		7	8	9				3	11	10	
1/R.	20	Torquay United	0-1	0-1			1	6	2	4	5		7	8	9				3	11	10	

League Appearances	37	46	15	44	20	6	42	46	30	6	33	7	10	42	21	30	1	28	16	11	9	2	2
League Goals		1		5			14	51	24	4	15			3	9	28				6			2
Cup appearances	3	3	2	3	3		3	3	3					3	3	3	1					2	2
(2 O.G.) Cup Goals							2	2							3	1							

(Back) Rigby, Shaw, Jacobs, Chadwick, Walls, Killin, Stafford, Cockburn.
(Front) Hails, Emery, Donaldson, Smith, Longworth.

Season Summary

First eleven Midland League matches won. Supporters Club make regular payments to Parent Club of £1,500 per month. High scoring victories continue as the unstoppable Posh go on to win third successive League title. Yet Club rejected by Football league again, receiving only 15 votes.

SEASON 1958/59

Midland League

772	Date	Opposition	Res	H.T.	Attend	Goalscorer	Cooper	Smith T.	Jacobs	Reilly	Rees	Banham	Rayner	Cresswell	McNamee	Smith R.	Donaldson	Emery	Hails	Chadwick	Rigby	Shaw	Walker	Stafford	Walls
1	23 Aug	ASHINGTON	6-1	3-0	9781	Chadwick Emery Smith R.2 McNamee O.G.									11	10	9	8	7	6	5		3	2	1
2	30	Stockton	5-1	4-1		Hails Emery McNamee Cresswell2								9	11	10		8	7	6	5		3	2	1
3	1 Sep	South Shields	0-0	0-0										9	11	10		8	7	6	5		3	2	1
4	6	SCUNTHORPE & L.U. RES.	5-0	2-0	8895	Emery 2 Smith R. McNamee 2						6			11	10	9	8	7		5		3	2	1
5	13	Scarborough	1-1	0-0		Shaw						6			11	10	9	8	7		5	4	3	2	1
6	20	GOOLE TOWN	5-1	2-0	7883	McNamee Rayner 4							9		11	10		8	7	6	5		3	2	1
7	27	Blyth Spartans	5-1	2-1		Hails 3 Rayner 2							9		11	10		8	7	6	5		3	2	1
8	29	North Shields	3-1	2-0	5000	Hails Rayner 2							9		11	10		8	7	6	5		3	2	1
9	4 Oct	SOUTH SHIELDS	2-0	1-0	9885	Emery Rayner							9		11	10		8	7	6	5		3	2	1
10	11	Gainsborough Trin.	3-1	3-1	2250	Hails Smith R. Rayner							9		11	10		8	7	6	5		3	2	1
11	18	BLYTH SPARTANS	6-1	4-1	7961	Smith R. 2 Rayner 4							9		11	10		8	7	6	5		3	2	1
12	25	Sutton Town	2-0	1-0	4270	Emery Smith R							9		11	10		8	7	6	5		3	2	1
13	22 Nov	SKEGNESS TOWN	5-0	1-0	7307	Emery 2 Rayner 3					11		9			10		8	7	6	5		3	2	1
14	29	Frickley Colliery	5-0	1-0		Hails 2 Emery 2 Rayner					11	5	9			10		8	7	6			3	2	1
15	13 Dec	Worksop Town	5-1	5-1		Hails Emery Rayner 3					11		9			10		8	7	6	5		3	2	1
16	20	Spennymoor United	2-2	1-2		Hails Emery 3 Rayner 3							9		11	10		8	7	6	5	4	3	2	1
17	26	Grantham	2-2	1-1	3026	Hails McNamee							9		11	10		8	7	6	5	4	3	2	1
18	27	GRANTHAM	7-1	1-1	9212	Chadw'k Hails Emery Smith R.McNamee 2 O.G.				9		4			11	10		8	7	6	5		3	2	1
19	3 Jan	SPENNYMOOR UNITED	4-1	0-0	7600	Hails Emery Smith R. Reilly				9		4			11	10		8	7	6	5		3	2	1
20	7 Feb	WORKSOP TOWN	7-0	3-0		Hails Smith R. 3 Rayner 3						4	9		11	10		8	7	6	5		3	2	1
21	14	SUTTON TOWN	6-2	4-1		Emery 2 Smith R. McNamee 2 Rayner			2			4	9		11	10		8	7	6	5		3		1
22	21	Denaby United	4-0	2-0		Emery 2 Smith R. Rayner						4	9		11	10		8	7	6	5		3	2	1
23	28	FRICKLEY COLLIERY	4-2	3-2	6250	Hails Emery McNamee Rayner						4	9		11	10		8	7	6	5		3	2	1
24	14 Mar	GAINSBOROUGH TRIN.	4-1	3-0	5000	Emery McNamee 2 Rayner						4	9		11	10		8	7	6	5		3	2	1
25	19	Scunthorpe & L.U. Res.	0-0	0-0									9		11	10		8	7	6	5		3	2	1
26	27	CONSETT	2-1	0-0		Smith R. 2		2				4	9		11	10		8	7	6	5		3		1
27	28	Ashington	2-0	0-0	8600	Hails O.G.						4	9		11	10		8	7	6	5		3	2	1
28	30	Consett	1-0	1-0		Rayner						4	9		11	10		8	7	6	5		3	2	1
29	4 Apr	Goole Town	3-1	2-0		Emery Smith R. Rayner						4	9		11	10		8	7	6	5		3	2	1
30	6	Hordon Colliery Wel.	5-1	4-1		Hails Rayner 2 Smith R. McNamee						4	9		11	10		8	7	6	5		3	2	1
31	11	SCARBOROUGH	2-1	0-0	1500	Rayner McNamee						4	9		11	10		8	7	6	5		3	2	1
32	18	Skegness Town	2-0	2-0		McNamee Reilly	6			9					11	10		8	7		5	4	3	2	1
33	20	HORDON COLLIERY WEL.	5-1	1-1		Emery 2 Raynor Smith R. McNamee	6						9		11	10		8	7		5		3	2	1
34	25	DENABY UNITED	4-0	1-0		Hails Emery O.G. 2	6						9		11	10		8	7		5		3	2	1
35	1 May	NORTH SHIELDS	5-2	3-1		Emery Rayner Smith R. 3						4	9			10		8	7	6	5		3	2	1
36	9	STOCKTON	3-0	1-0		Rayner 3						4	9			10		8	7	6	5		3	2	1

F.A. Cup

4/Q.	1 Nov	WALTHAMSTOW AVE.	3-0	2-0	14700	Emery 3
1st	15	KETTERING TOWN	2-2	1-1	17800	Emery Hails
1/R.	20	Kettering Town	3-2*	0-2	11246	Emery Hails O.G.
2nd	6 Dec	HEADINGTON UNITED	4-2	2-0	16855	Hails Emery 2 Rayner
3rd	10 Jan	Fulham	0-0	0-0	31908	
3/R.	24	FULHAM	0-1	0-1	21600	

* After Extra Time (2-2 at 90 minutes)

Cup line-ups (by shirt number, each match):

1	2	3	4	5	6	7	8	9	10	11
1	2	3	4	5	6	7	8	9	10	11
1	2	3	4	5	6	7	8	9	10	11
1	2	3	4	5	6	7	8	9	10	11
1	2	3	4	5	6	7	8	9	10	11
1	2	3	5	6	7	8	9	4	11	
1	2	3	5	6	7	8	9	4	11	

	Totals
League Appearances	36 34 21 35 30 36 36 3 36 32 1 28 19 4 4 1 1 3
(5 O.G.) League Goals	1 2 18 27 2 17 2 41 2
Cup appearances	6 6 4 6 6 6 6 6 5 6 2 1
(1 O.G.) Cup Goals	3 7 1

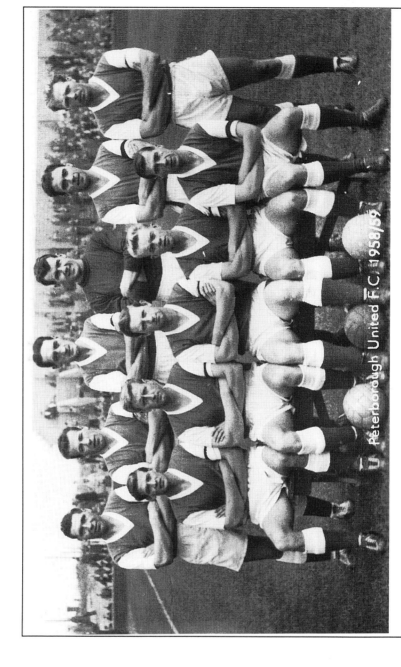

(Back) Stafford, Shaw, Rigby, Walls, Walker, Chadwick,
(Front) Hails, Emery, Rayner, Smith, McNamee

U Peterborough United F.C. 1958/59

Season Summary

George Swindin returns to Arsenal, Jimmy Hagan (ex-Sheffield United) takes his place as Manager. Reserve teams leave League and, despite new Clubs, membership reduced to 19 teams. Every home League match is won, and memorable home F.A.Cup-tie replay with Fulham is watched by 21,600. Another Championship, and although Football League voting is increased to 26, this is still not enough.

SEASON 1959/60

Midland League

808	Date	Opposition	Res	H.T.	Attend	Walls	Haynes	Walker	Banham	Rigby	Chadwick	Hails	Rayner	Emery	Smith	West	Asher	McNamee	Bushby	Daley	Chamberlain	Cooper	Stafford	Dunne	Sansby	Reilly	Jacobs	Fletcher	Sheavils	Goalscorer
1	22 Aug	STOCKTON	7-0	5-0	6515	1	2	3	4	5	6	7	8	9	10	11														Hails Rayner 2 Emery Smith West 2
2	29	Ashington	1-2	1-1	6000	1	2	3	4	5	6	7		9	10	11	8													West
3	31	Spennymoor United	3-1	3-0		1	2	3	4	5	6	7		9	10	11	8													Emery 2 O.G.
4	5 Sep	NORTH SHIELDS	3-0	2-0	7158	1	2	3	4	5	6	7		9	8	11		10												Hails Emery 2
5	12	Blyth Spartans	3-3	2-1		1	2	3		5	6	7		9	8	11		10	4											Hails Smith McNamee
6	19	South Shields	1-1	1-0	7000			3		5	6	7	9	8	10			11		1	2	4								Emery
7	21	North Shields	1-5	0-2	5000			3		5	6	7	9	8	10			11		1	2	4								Hails
8	26	Goole Town	3-3	1-1	2500			3		5	6	7	10	8				11		1		4	2			9				McNamee 2 O.G.
9	10 Oct	Sutton Town	1-1	1-0				3	4	5	6	7	9	8	10			11		1			2							Smith
10	17	WORKSOP TOWN	7-1	3-0				3	4	5	6	7	9	8	10			11		1	2									Hails Rayner 3 Emery McNamee2
11	24	Horden Colliery Wel.	4-2	1-1				3	4	5	6	7	9	8	10			11		1	2									Rayner 3 Smith
12	7 Nov	SOUTH SHIELDS	4-3	2-0				3	4	5	6	7	9	8	10			11		1	2									Rayner 3 O.G.
13	21	SPENNYMOOR UNITED	7-0	4-0	7602			3	4	5	6	7	9	8	10			11		1	2									Hails Rayner Emery Smith McNamee 3
14	28	DENABY UNITED	6-0	2-0	5762			3	4	5	6	7	9	8	10			11		1	2									Hails Rayner 2 Emery Smith McNamee
15	12 Dec	SUTTON TOWN	8-0	5-0	6501			3	4	5	6	7	9	8	10			11		1	2									Hails Rayner 2 Emery 2 Smith McNamee 2
16	19	Stockton	4-3	2-1				3	4	5	6	7	9	8	10			11		1	2									Hails Rayner Smith McNamee
17	26	SKEGNESS TOWN	6-2	1-0				3	4	5	6	7	9	8	10			11		1	2									Hails Rayner Emery 3 Smith
18	2 Jan	ASHINGTON	3-0	1-0	10507			3	4	5	6	7	9	8	10			11		1			2							Rayner Emery 2
19	23	BLYTH SPARTANS	2-1	1-1	7081				4	5	6	7	9	8	10			11		1			2				3			Emery O.G.
20	6 Feb	Skegness Town	1-1	1-0				3	4	5	6	7	9		10			11		1			2	8						Dunne
21	27	HORDON COLLIERY WEL	4-0	2-0	5680	1		3	4	5	6	7	9					10					2	8				11		Rayner McNamee Dunne Fletcher
22	5 Mar	Scarborough	2-0	1-0	2360	1		3	4	5	6	7	9					10					2	8				11		Rayner Fletcher
23	19	Frickley Colliery	3-1	2-1	140	1		3	4	5	6	7	9		10			11					2	8						Hails Smith Dunne
24	26	GOOLE TOWN	3-0	2-0	3626	1		3	4	5	6	7	9		10			11					2	8						Hails Rayner Smith
25	2 Apr	Denaby United	2-1	2-1	1500	1		3		5	6	7	9		10			11				4	2	8						Smith McNamee
26	9	Gainsborough Trin.	1-3	1-3		1		3		5	6	7	9		10			11				4		8			2			McNamee
27	15	GAINSBOROUGH TRIN.	4-0	3-0	6548	1		3		5	6				10			11					2	8	4			9	7	Smith Fletcher Sheavills 2
28	18	Consett	1-1	1-0		1		3		5	6				10			11					2	8	4			9	7	Smith
29	21	Worksop Town	2-0			1		3	4	5	6	7	9		10			11					2	8						Rayner Smith
30	23	SCARBOROUGH	3-0	0-0	5438	1		3	4	5	6	7	9					10					2	8					11	Banham Sheavills 2
31	25	FRICKLEY COLLIERY	3-0	1-0		1		3		5	6	7	9					10					2	8	4				11	Hails McNamee 2
32	30	CONSETT	5-2	4-1		1		3		5	6	7	9					10					2	8	4				11	Hails Rayner McNamee 2 Sheavills

F.A.Cup

4/Q	31 Oct	BURY TOWN	7-1	4-1	9922	Hails2 Rayner Emery Smith2 McNamee
1st	14 Nov	SHREWSBURY TOWN	4-3	0-1	16321	Rayner Emery 2 Smith
2nd	5 Dec	Walsall	3-2	1-1	20600	Rayner Smith McNamee
3rd	9 Jan	Ipswich Town	3-2	1-1	26000	Rayner Emery 2
4th	30	Sheffield Wednesday	0-2	0-0	51144	

	17	5	31	22	31	23	32	26	18	25	5	2	29	1	15	3	9	22	13	11	1	2	4	5
League Appearances																								
(4 O.G.) League Goals		1		14	24	17	15	5	3			19			5		1	3						
Cup appearances		5		5	5	5	5	5	5			5			5		1	3						5
Cup Goals		5		2	4	5	5	4	5			2			5		4	2						5

(Rear) Stafford, Shaw, Rigby, Walls, Walker, Chadwick, Anderson.
(Front) Hails, Emery, Rayner, Smith, Rees.

Season Summary

Midland League depleted even further – now down to 17 teams. Shrewsbury Town, Walsall and Ipswich Town all beaten in F.A.Cup, before going out at Sheffield Wednesday before 51,144 crowd. 5th succesive Midland League title won – but the last in the Midland League!

Football League Division 4

#	Date	Opposition	Res	H.T.	Attend	Goalscorer	Walls	Stafford	Walker	Rayner	Rigby	Norris	Hails	Emery	Bly	Smith	McNamee	Banham	Ripley	Taylor	Sheavills	Hogg	Sansby	Dunne	Anderson	Whittaker	Graham
1	20 Aug	WREXHAM	3-0	1-0	17294	Emery Bly McNamee	1	2	3	4	5	6	7	8	9	10	11										
2	22	Hartlepool United	2-0	2-0	10304	Bly 2	1	2	3	4	5	6	7	8	9	10	11										
3	27	Carlisle United	3-3	2-1	8334	Hails Emery Bly	1	2	3	4	5	6	7	8	9	10	11										
4	29	HARTLEPOOL UNITED	3-2	2-0	15245	Hails Bly Smith	1	2	3		5	6	7	8	9	10	11	4									
5	3 Sep	ROCHDALE	4-3	1-1	14285	Hails Smith 2 McNamee	1	2	3	4	5	6	7	8	9	10	11										
6	7	Crystal Palace	2-0	1-0	36478	Hails McNamee	1	2	3	4	5	6	7	8	9	10	11										
7	10	Mansfield Town	0-1	0-0	11385		1	2	3	4	5		7	8	9	10	11		6								
8	12	CRYSTAL PALACE	4-1	3-0	21171	Hails Bly 3	1	2	3	4	5		7	8	9	10	11		6								
9	17	STOCKPORT COUNTY	0-1	0-0	14610		1	2	3	4	5		7	8	9	10	11		6								
10	20	Doncaster Rovers	2-1	1-0	9644	Bly 2	1	2	3	4	5		7	8	9	10	11		6								
11	24	Exeter City	4-3	2-2	9142	Hails Bly 3	1	2	3	4	5		7	8	9	10			6	11							
12	26	DONCASTER ROVERS	6-2	3-1	16290	Hails Bly McNamee 3 Sansby	1	2		4	5		7	8	9	10	11		6				3				
13	1 Oct	Gillingham	4-4	2-1	11542	Hails 3 O.G.	1			4	5		7	8	9			3	6		11	2		10			
14	3	SOUTHPORT	3-4	2-2	17096	Emery Bly McNamee	1			4	5		7	8	9	10	11	3	6			2					
15	8	NORTHAMPTON TOWN	3-3	0-3	22959	Emery McNamee 2	1	2	3	4	5		7	8	9	10	11	6									
16	15	Aldershot	1-1	0-0	12440	Emery	1		3	4	5		7	8	9	10	11									2	6
17	22	OLDHAM ATHLETIC	2-2	2-0	11934	Hails McNamee	1		3	4	5		7	8	9	10	11		6							2	
18	29	Workington	3-0	0-0	6538	Hails Bly Smith	1		3	4			7	8	9	10	11	5	6							2	
19	12 Nov	Crewe Alexandra	1-3	0-2	11016	Bly	1		3	4			7	8	9	10	11	5	6							2	
20	19	YORK CITY	1-1	0-1	11992	Ripley	1		3	4	5		7	8	9	10	11		6							2	
21	3 Dec	MILLWALL	4-2	4-0	10674	Bly Smith3	1		3	4	5		7	8	9	10	11		6							2	
22	10	Barrow	1-2	0-2	6338	Smith	1		3	4	5		7	8	9	10	11		6							2	
23	17	Wrexham	1-0	0-0	8002	McNamee	1		3	4	5		7	8	9	10	11		6							2	
24	24	DARLINGTON	5-1	2-1	11232	Hails Bly 4	1		3	4	5		7	8	9	10	11		6							2	
25	26	Darlington	2-2	0-1	9325	Bly 2	1		3	4	5		7	8	9	10	11		6							2	
26	31	Carlisle United	5-0	2-0	11539	Emery 2 Bly 3	1		3	4	5		7	8	9	10	11		6							2	
—	14 Jan	Rochdale			5000	Abandoned 33 min. (scored 0-1)	1		3	4	5		7	8	9	10	11		6							2	
27	21	MANSFIELD TOWN	2-1	1-1	10628	Emery Bly	1		3	4	5		7	8	9	10	11		6							2	
28	4 Feb	Stockport County	6-0	2-0	7004	Hails Emery 2 Bly 2 McNamee	1		3	4			7	8	9	10	11	5	6							2	
29	11	EXETER CITY	7-1	3-0	11518	Hails 2 Bly 3 O.G. 2	1		3	4			7	8	9	10	11	5	6							2	
30	18	GILLINGHAM	2-0	1-0	12652	O.G. 2	1		3	4			7	8	9	10	11	5	6							2	
31	25	Northampton Town	3-0	1-0	19516	Bly Smith McNamee	1		3	4	5		7	8	9	10	11		6							2	
32	4 Mar	ALDERSHOT	7-1	4-1	12746	Emery 3 Bly Smith 3	1		3	4	5		7	8	9	10	11		6							2	
33	11	Oldham Athletic	1-1	0-1	27886	Ripley	1		3	4	5		7	8	9	10	11		6							2	
34	13	CHESTER	6-0	4-0	13180	Hails Bly 4 O.G.	1		3	4	5		7	8	9	10	11		6							2	
35	18	WORKINGTON	2-1	0-1	11888	Hails Smith	1		3	4	5		7	8	9	10	11		6							2	
36	25	Chester	2-1	0-1	5493	Hails Bly	1		3	4	5		7	8	9	10	11		6							2	
37	1 Apr	CREWE ALEXANDRA	4-1	1-0	12717	Rayner Ripley 2 Hails	1		3	4	5		7	8	9	10	11		6							2	
38	3	BRADFORD P.A.	3-1	2-0	16549	Bly Smith McNamee	1		3	4	5		7	8	9	10	11		6							2	
39	8	York City	1-0	1-0	12525	Bly	1		3	4	5		7	8	9	10	11		6							2	
40	11	Accrington Stan.	2-3	0-1	5150	Hails Smith	1		3	4	5		7	8	9	10	11		6							2	
41	15	ACCRINGTON STAN.	3-0	2-0	13436	Bly 2 McNamee	1		3	4	5		7	8	9	10	11		6							2	
42	18	Rochdale	2-2	1-1	5434	Bly Smith	1		3	4	5		7	8	9	10	11		6							2	
43	20	Bradford P.A.	0-1	0-0	20461		1		3	4	5		7	8	9	10	11		6							2	
44	22	Millwall	3-4	2-3	18503	Bly 2 McNamee	1		3		5		7	8	9	10	11	4	6							2	
45	25	Southport	3-3	1-1	6104	Hails Bly 2	1		3		5		7	8	9	10	11	4	6							2	
46	29	BARROW	6-2	3-0	15318	Ripley Emery Bly 3 Smith	1		3		5		7	8	9	10	11	4	6							2	

F.A. Cup

Rd	Date	Opponent	1	3	4	5	7	8	9	10	11	5	6			Att	Scorers
1st	5 Nov	Dover	1	3	4		7	8	9	10	11	5	6	4-1	0-1	5205	Emery 2 Bly Ripley
2nd	26	Torquay United	1	3	4	5	7	8	9	10	11	5	6	3-1	3-0	9304	Bly McNamee 2
3rd	7 Jan	Portsmouth	1	3	4	5	7	8	9	10	11	5	6	2-1	1-0	27533	Hails Ripley
4th	28	ASTON VILLA	1	3	4		7	8	9	10	11	5	6	1-1	1-1	28266	Hails
4/R.	1 Feb	Aston Villa	1	3	4		7	8	9	10	11	5	6	1-2	0-0	64531	McNamee

Football League Cup

Rd	Date	Opponent	3	4	5	7	8	9	10	11	1	2	6			Att	Scorers
1st	11 Oct	Preston North End	3	4	5	7	8	9	10	11	1	2	6	1-4	1-2	12958	Hails

	1	3	4	5	7	8	9	10	11	5	6								
League Appearances	46	13	43	43	40	5	46	46	46	45	44	12	39	1	1	2	1	1	31	1
(6 O.G.) League Goals			1		3		21	15	52	17	16	5					1	
Cup appearances	5		6	6	3		6	6	6	6	6	3	5				1	6	1
Cup Goals	5		6	3			3	2	2	3	2		2					1

PETERBOROUGH UNITED

(Back Row) Banham, Sansby, Anderson, Walls, Walker.
(2nd Row) Whittaker, Jacobs, Graham, Emery, Rigby, Norris, Dunne, Ripley.
(3rd Row) Hails, Coates, Bly, Rayner, Smith, McNamee, Atkins, Sheavills.
(Seated) Stafford, Taylor, Cooper.

DIVISION 4

	P	W	D	L	F	A	W	D	L	F	A	Pts
Peterboro' U	46	18	3	2	85	30	10	7	6	49	35	66
Crystal P	46	16	4	3	64	28	13	2	8	46	41	64
Northampton T	46	16	4	3	53	25	9	6	8	37	37	60
Bradford	46	16	5	2	49	22	10	3	10	35	52	60
York C	46	17	3	3	50	14	4	13	6	30	46	51
Millwall	46	13	7	3	56	33	8	5	10	41	53	50
Darlington	46	11	7	5	41	24	7	6	10	37	46	49
Workington	46	14	3	6	38	28	4	7	12	36	48	49
Crewe A	46	11	4	8	40	29	9	5	9	21	38	49
Aldershot	46	16	4	3	55	19	2	5	16	24	50	45
Doncaster R	46	14	3	6	38	28	4	7	12	24	45	45
Oldham A	46	15	0	8	52	23	4	7	12	24	50	45
Stockport Co	46	13	6	4	57	38	6	3	14	22	45	45
Southport	46	14	5	4	47	27	7	0	16	22	40	44
Gillingham	46	12	6	5	31	21	4	6	11	19	32	44
Wrexham	46	12	4	7	38	22	4	6	13	24	34	42
Rochdale	46	13	7	3	43	19	4	1	18	17	47	42
Accrington S	46	12	4	7	44	32	4	4	15	30	56	40
Carlisle U	46	12	7	4	43	37	3	6	14	18	42	39
Mansfield T	46	10	3	10	39	34	6	3	14	32	44	38
Exeter C	46	12	3	8	39	32	2	7	14	27	62	38
Barrow	46	10	6	7	33	28	5	3	15	19	51	37
Hartlepools U	46	10	6	4	46	40	2	4	17	25	63	32
Chester	46	9	7	7	38	35	2	2	19	23	69	31

Season Summary

Elected to the Football League at last! 17,294 present for the first game at London Road, and a new record attendance for a 4th round F.A.Cup match. All season entertainment sees Bly score 52 League goals as Posh take 4th Division by storm, becoming Champions with all-time Football League goalscoring record of 134.

SEASON 1961/62

Football League Division 3

#	Date	Opposition	Res	H.T.	Attend	Goalscorer	Walls	Whittaker	Walker	Rayner	Rigby	Ripley	Hails	Emery	Bly	Smith	McNamee	Ronson	Stafford	Sheavills	Hopkins	Senior	Banham	Hudson	Hawkes	Dunne	Morton	Graham	Turley
1	19 Aug	HULL CITY	3-2	2-1	14730	Bly McNamee O.G.	1	2	3	4	5	6	7	8	9	10	11												
2	22	Watford	3-2	1-1	20433	Emery McNamee O.G.	1	2	3	4	5	6	7	8	9	10	11												
3	26	Port Vale	1-0	0-0	18767	Smith	1	2	3	4	5	6	7	8	9	10	11												
4	28	WATFORD	4-3	2-1	18078	Ripley Emery Bly 2	1	2	3	4	5	6	7	8	9	10	11												
5	2 Sep	BRISTOL CITY	3-4	2-3	14768	Hails Emery McNamee	1	2	3	4	5	6	7	8	9	10	11												
6	7	Notts. County	2-2	1-1	19267	Bly 2	1	2	3	4	5	6	7	8	9	10	11												
7	9	Bradford P.A.	2-6	1-2	11866	Bly Smith	1	2	3	4	5	6	7	8	9	10	11												
8	16	GRIMSBY TOWN	2-1	2-0	14804	Emery Bly		2	3	4		6	7	8	9	10		1		11	5								
9	20	Shrewsbury Town	4-3	1-3	12547	Emery 2 Smith Senior		2	3	4		6	7	8	9	10		1			5	11							
10	23	Coventry City	3-1	2-0	19913	Ripley Smith Senior		2	3	4		6	7	8	9	10		1			5	11							
11	25	SHREWSBURY TOWN	0-3	0-1	17106			2	3	4		6	7	8	9	10		1		11	5								
12	30	BRENTFORD	6-0	3-0	12533	Hails Emery 2 Bly 2 Smith	1	2	3			6	7	8	9	10					5	11	4						
13	2 Oct	Newport County	3-2	2-1	9027	Hails Emery Hudson	1	2	3	4		6	7	8	9						5	11		10					
14	7	BOURNEMOUTH & BOS.	1-2	0-1	17268	Emery	1	2	3			6	7	8	9	10					5	11	4						
15	9	NEWPORT COUNTY	2-1	1-1	13029	Emery Bly	1	2	3			6	7	8	9	10					5	11	4						
16	14	Crystal Palace	2-5	1-2	28886	Hudson 2	1	2	3	4		6	7	8	9						5	11		10					
17	21	LINCOLN CITY	5-4	3-1	13502	Emery 2 Bly Hudson 2	1	2	3	4		6	7	8	9						5	11		10					
18	28	Northampton Town	2-2	1-0	17324	Emery Bly		2	3	4		6	7	8	9	10		1			5	11							
19	11 Nov	Halifax Town	1-2	0-2	5000	Hudson	1	2	3	4		6	7	8	9						5	11		10					
20	18	SWINDON TOWN	3-2	1-2	12509	Hails Senior Hudson	1	2	3	4		6	7	8	9						5	11		10					
21	2 Dec	PORTSMOUTH	0-1	0-1	14289		1	2	3	4		6	7		9	8					5	11				10			
22	9	Barnsley	3-0	3-0	8027	Ripley Bly 2	1	2	3	4		6	7		9	8					5	11		10					
23	16	Hull City	1-1	0-1	6674	Senior	1	2	3	4		6	7		9						5	11		10			8		
24	23	PORT VALE	1-3	1-3	9249	Bly	1	2	3	4		6	7		9	8					5	11		10					
25	26	SOUTHEND UNITED	4-1	3-1	8237	Ripley Bly Senior Hudson	1	2	3	4		6	7		9	8					5	11		10					
26	30	Southend United	1-1	0-0	6687	Bly	1	2	3	4		6	7		9	8					5	11		10					
27	13 Jan	Bristol City	2-1	1-1	16839	Bly 2	1	2	3	4		6	7		9	8					5	11		10					
28	3 Feb	Grimsby Town	1-2	2-0	11465	Ripley	1	2	3	4		6	7		9	8					5	11		10					
29	10	COVENTRY CITY	2-3	2-1	11751	Senior O.G.	1	2	3	4		6	7		9	8					5	11		10					
30	17	Brentford	0-2	0-1	11000			2	3	4		6	7		9	8		1			5	11		10					
31	19	Q. P. RANGERS	5-1	1-0	11922	Hails Smith Hudson 2 McNamee		2	3	4		6	7		9	8	11	1			5			10					
32	24	Bournemouth & Bos.	1-1	0-1	13219	Bly		2	3	4		6	7		9	8		1			5	11		10					
33	3 Mar	CRYSTAL PALACE	4-1	3-1	12095	Smith Bly 2 Hudson		2	3	4		6	7		9	8		1			5	11		10					
34	10	Lincoln City	2-1	2-1	10857	Smith Bly		2	3	4		6	7		9	8		1			5	11		10					
35	17	NOTHAMPTON TOWN	0-2	0-0	17009		1	2	3	4		6	7		9	8					5	11		10					
36	19	BRADFORD P.A.	1-0	1-0	8732	Bly	1	2	3	4		6			9	8			7		5	11		10					
37	24	Q. P. Rangers	3-3	0-1	13430	Bly McNamee Sheavills	1	2	3	4					9	8	11		7		5			10				6	
38	31	HALIFAX TOWN	5-1	1-0	7738	Smith Bly Hudson 2 Ripley	1	2	3	4	5	6			9	8	11		7					10					
39	2 Apr	Torquay United	3-1	3-1	3776	Smith Bly Hudson	1	2	3	4	5	6			9	8	11		7					10					
40	7	Swindon Town	2-3	0-2	8875	Bly Ripley	1	2	3	4	5	6			9	8	11		7					10					
41	14	TORQUAY UNITED	2-1	0-1	8697	McNamee 2	1	2	3	4	5	6			9	8	11		7					10					
42	20	Reading	2-3	0-1	11959	Smith McNamee	1	2	3	4	5	6			9	8	11		7					10					
43	21	Portsmouth	3-0	1-0	21167	Bly Hudson McNamee	1	2	3	4	5	6			9	8	11		7					10					
44	23	READING	1-0	1-0	11320	Sheavills	1	2	3	4		5				8			7	11				10				6	9
45	28	BARNSLEY	4-2	3-0	8000	Rayner Hudson Turley 2		2		4		5					11	1	7					10	3	8		6	9
46	30	NOTTS. COUNTY	2-0	0-0	7873	Hudson Turley		2		4		5					11	1	7					10	3	8		6	9

F.A.Cup

							Scorers
1st	4 Nov	COLCHESTER UNITED	3-3	1-0	16469		Bly McNamee Hudson
1/R.	6	Colchester United	2-2*	0-1	10653		Emery Bly (* After extra time)
1/2R.	13	Colchester United	3-0	3-0	11857		Hudson 3
2nd	25	Torquay United	4-1	1-0	8365		Hails Bly Hudson 2
3rd	6 Jan	Newcastle United	1-0	0-0	42782		Bly
4th	27	SHEFFIELD UNITED	1-3	0-3	28174		Hudson

Football League Cup

							Scorers
1st	11 Sep	BLACKBURN ROVERS	1-3	1-2	15094		Hails

* After extra time (2-2 after 90 minutes)

League Appearances	32 46 46 43 15 43 37 19 42 37 25 14 11 11 26 19 4 33 1 3 1 6 3		
(3 O.G.) League Goals	1 7 5 14 29 11 9 2 6 17		
Cup appearances	6 7 7 7 7 3 7 5 1 1 1 5 5 1 6		
Cup Goals	2 1 4 1 1 7		

DIVISION 3

	P	W	D	L	F	A	W	D	L	F	A	Pts
Portsmouth	46	15	6	2	48	23	12	5	6	39	24	65
Grimsby T	46	18	3	2	49	18	10	3	10	31	38	62
Bournemouth	46	14	8	1	42	18	7	9	7	27	27	59
QPR	46	15	3	5	65	31	9	8	6	46	42	59
Peterboro' U	46	16	0	7	60	38	10	6	7	47	44	58
Bristol C	46	15	3	5	56	27	8	5	10	38	45	54
Reading	46	14	5	4	46	24	8	4	11	31	42	53
Northampton T	46	12	6	5	52	24	8	5	10	33	33	51
Swindon T	46	11	8	4	48	26	6	7	10	30	45	49
Hull C	46	15	5	3	48	20	5	6	12	24	34	48
Bradford	46	13	5	5	47	27	7	2	14	33	51	47
Port Vale	46	12	4	7	41	23	5	7	11	24	35	45
Notts Co	46	14	5	4	44	23	4	4	16	23	51	43
Coventry C	46	11	6	6	38	26	5	5	13	26	45	43
Crystal P	46	8	8	7	50	41	6	6	11	33	39	42
Southend U	46	10	7	6	31	26	3	9	11	26	43	42
Watford	46	10	9	4	37	26	4	4	15	26	48	41
Halifax T	46	9	5	9	34	35	6	5	12	28	49	40
Shrewsbury T	46	8	7	8	46	37	5	5	13	27	47	38
Barnsley	46	9	6	8	45	41	4	6	13	26	54	38
Torquay U	46	9	4	10	48	44	6	2	15	28	56	36
Lincoln C	46	9	10	9	31	43	5	7	11	26	44	35
Brentford	46	11	7	5	34	29	2	1	16	19	64	34
Newport Co	46	6	5	12	29	38	1	3	11	17	64	22

Season Summary

3rd Division football in only the second League season. Another F.A.Cup run through to the 4th round, beating Newcastle United at St. James' Park en route. Last 4 league games won, including 3–0 victory over Champions Portsmouth, and Posh finish in creditable 5th place in the final table, after serious promotion challenge during the season.

(Back) Whittaker, Walker, Rigby, Walls, Ripley, Rayner.
(Front) Hails, Emery, Bly, Smith, McNamee.

Peterborough United F.C. 1961-62

SEASON 1962/63

Football League Division 3

№	Date	Opposition	Res	H.T.	Attend	Goalscorer
1	18 Aug	Bournemouth & Bos.	3-3	1-0	13144	Hudson Smith O.G.
2	21	Carlisle United	4-1	1-1	12238	Rayner Hudson 2 McNamee
3	25	BARNSLEY	4-2	2-1	12944	Hudson 2 Smith McNamee
4	27	CARLISLE UNITED	2-2	1-1	13686	McNamee 2
5	1 Sep	Northampton Town	3-2	2-1	16064	Simpson McNamee 2
6	4	Bristol Rovers	1-3	1-0	11860	Hails
7	8	Q. P. RANGERS	1-2	0-1	14481	Smith
8	10	BRISTOL ROVERS	1-0	1-0	13180	Hudson
9	15	Hull City	2-3	1-1	8158	Hudson Smith
10	18	Brighton & H.A.	3-0	2-0	11238	Hudson 2 Senior
11	22	CRYSTAL PALACE	0-0	0-0	12806	
12	29	Wrexham	4-4	3-2	12388	Hudson 2 Sheavilles Morton
13	1 Oct	HALIFAX TOWN	1-1	0-1	10407	Sheavilles
14	6	BRADFORD P.A.	2-0	0-0	10142	Smith Sheavilles
15	8	Halifax Town	0-2	0-1	4643	
16	13	Watford	3-2	0-2	13627	Simpson McNamee Horobin
17	15	BRIGHTON & H.A.	3-1	3-0	11314	Horobin Turley Morton
18	20	BRISTOL CITY	3-1	1-1	12760	Horobin Hudson 2
19	26	Reading	1-0	0-0	13284	Turley
20	10 Nov	Shrewsbury Town	4-5	4-3	7062	Rayner Hudson Sheavilles Jackson
21	17	MILLWALL	6-0	2-0	11422	Rayner 3 Horobin Hudson 2
22	1 Dec	COLCHESTER UNITED	6-2	3-1	11290	Horobin 2 McNamee Sheavilles 2 O.G.
23	8	Notts. County	0-2	0-0	5640	
24	15	BOURNEMOUTH & BOS.	3-0	2-0	11706	Simpson Hudson Moulden
25	21	Barnsley	2-0	2-0	9540	Horobin McNamee
26	26	COVENTRY CITY	0-3	0-1	13112	
27	29	Coventry City	3-3	2-1	25399	Horobin 2 Moulden
28	16 Feb	WREXHAM	1-3	0-1	10700	McNamee
29	2 Mar	WATFORD	4-0	2-0	12692	Horobin Hudson McNamee
30	6	Bradford P.A.	2-2	2-0	6457	Senior 2
31	9	Bristol City	1-1	0-1	7347	Jackson
32	16	READING	1-1	0-0	10460	Senior
33	18	PORT VALE	3-1	3-1	12608	Hudson 2 Rayner
34	23	Port Vale	2-3	2-1	10260	Simpson Rayner
35	25	HULL CITY	1-3	0-1	10193	Hudson
36	2 Apr	SHREWSBURY TOWN	2-3	1-2	10942	Hudson McNamee
37	6	Millwall	1-0	1-0	13332	Turley
38	12	Swindon Town	3-2	2-1	23239	Horobin McNamee Turley
39	13	SOUTHEND UNITED	1-3	0-2	10632	Rayner
40	15	SWINDON TOWN	3-1	2-1	13216	Senior Turley 2
41	20	Colchester United	0-2	0-1	5143	
42	24	Crystal Palace	2-0	0-0	21777	Horobin Rayner
43	27	NOTTS. COUNTY	0-0	0-0	12781	
44	6 May	Southend United	1-2	1-0	10763	Day
45	11	NORTHAMPTON TOWN	0-4	0-2	17518	
46	18	Q. P. Rangers	0-0	0-0	5959	

Player appearances (shirt numbers)

№	Day	Overfield	Stafford	Emery	Moulden	Sissons	Whittaker	Jackson	Senior	Morton	Sheavilles	Graham	Ronson	Turley	McNamee	Smith	Hudson	Horobin	Hails	Simpson	Hopkins	Rayner	Walker	Singleton	Beattie
1															11	10	9	8	7	6	5	4	3	2	1
2															11	10	9	8	7	6	5	4	3	2	1
3															11	10	9	8	7	6	5	4	3	2	1
4														8	11	10	9		7	6	5	4	3	2	1
5														8	11	10	9		7	6	5	4	3	2	1
6															11	10	9	8	7	6	5	4	3	2	1
7															11	10	9	8	7	6	5	4	3	2	1
8													1		11	10	9	8	7	6	5	4	3	2	
9													1		11	10	9	8	7	6	5	4	3	2	
10									11	8	7	4	1		10		9			6	5		3	2	
11									11	8	7	4	1		10		9			6	5		3	2	
12										8	7		1		11		9	10		6	5	4	3	2	
13										8	7	6	1		11		9	10		5		4	3	2	
14										8	7		1		11	10	9			6	5	4	3	2	
15									11	8	7		1	9				10		6	5	4	3	2	
16								4		8	7		1		11		9	10		6	5		3	2	
17								4		8	7		1	9	11			10		6	5		3	2	
18								4			7		1	10	11		9	8		6	5		3	2	
19								4			7		1	10	11		9			6	5	8	3	2	
20								4			7			10	11		9			6	5	8	3	2	1
21								4			7				11		9	10		6	5	8	3	2	1
22								4			7				11		9	10		6	5	8	3	2	1
23								4			7				11		9	10		6	5	8	3	2	1
24					10		2	4			7		1		11		9	8		6	5		3		
25					10		2	4			7		1		11		9	8		6	5		3		
26					10		2	4			7		1		11		9	8		6	5		3		
27					10		2	4			7		1		11		9	8		6	5		3		
28		11		8				4					1		10		9	7		6	5		3	2	
29								4	7				1		11		9	8		6	5		3	2	
30						3		4	7				1		11		9			6	5	8		2	
31						3		4	7				1		11	10	9			6	5	8		2	
32					10	3		4	7				1		11		9			6	5	8		2	
33			2			3		4	7				1		11		9	8		6	5	10			
34			2			3		4	7				1		11		9	10		6	5	8			
35			2	8		3		4	7				1		11		9	10		6	5				
36					10	3		4				7	1		11		9	8		6	5			2	
37	7				10	3							1	9	11			8		6	5	4		2	
38	7				10	3							1	9	11			8		6	5	4		2	
39	7				8	3							1	10	11			9		6	5	4		2	
40					10	3			7				1	9	11			8		6	5	4		2	
41					10	3							1	9	11			8		6	5	4		2	
42	7				10	3							1	9	11			8		6	5	4		2	
43					10	3			11				1	9				8		6	5	4		2	
44	7				10	3							1	9	11			8		6	5	4		2	
45	7				10	3							1	9	11			8		6	5	4		2	
46	7			8	10	3							1	9	11					6	5	4		2	

1st	3 Nov	Notts. County	3-0	3-0	20473	Hudson 2	McNamee
2nd	24	ENFIELD	1-0	0-0	16761	Hudson	
3rd	4 Feb	Derby County	0-2	0-1	14916		

Football League Cup

2nd	24 Sep	Aston Villa	1-6	0-4	17392	Hudson

League Appearances	10	37	27	33	41	45	11	40	32	10	45	16	36	7	18	6	15	22	5	22	14	4	1
League Goals			10		4	1	12	22	5		13	6			6	2	5	2		3	1	1	
Cup appearances	3	3	2	4	4	3		4	4		4	4	4	1	4	1	1	3	1	1	1	1	
Cup Goals								4			1												

DIVISION 3

	P	W	D	L	F	A	W	D	L	F	A	Pts
Northampton T	46	16	6	1	64	19	10	4	9	45	41	62
Swindon T	46	18	2	3	60	22	4	12	7	27	34	58
Port Vale	46	16	4	3	47	25	7	4	12	25	33	54
Coventry C	46	14	6	3	54	28	4	11	8	29	41	53
Bournemouth	46	11	12	0	39	16	7	4	12	24	30	52
Peterboro U	46	11	5	7	48	33	9	6	8	45	42	51
Notts Co	46	15	5	3	46	29	4	10	9	27	45	51
Southend U	46	11	7	5	38	24	8	5	10	37	53	50
Wrexham	46	14	6	3	54	27	6	3	14	30	56	49
Hull C	46	12	6	5	40	22	7	4	12	34	47	48
Crystal P	46	10	7	6	38	22	7	6	10	30	36	47
Colchester U	46	11	6	6	41	35	7	5	11	32	58	47
QPR	46	9	8	6	44	36	8	5	10	41	40	45
Bristol C	46	10	9	4	54	38	6	4	13	46	54	45
Shrewsbury T	46	13	4	6	57	41	3	8	12	26	40	44
Millwall	46	11	6	6	50	32	4	7	12	32	55	43
Watford	46	12	3	8	55	40	5	5	13	27	45	42
Barnsley	46	12	6	5	39	28	5	3	15	24	46	41
Bristol R	46	11	8	4	45	29	4	3	16	25	59	41
Reading	46	13	4	6	51	30	3	4	16	23	48	40
Bradford	46	10	9	4	43	36	4	3	16	36	61	40
Brighton & HA	46	7	6	10	28	38	5	6	12	30	46	36
Carlisle U	46	12	4	7	41	37	1	5	17	20	52	35
Halifax T	46	8	3	12	41	51	1	9	13	23	55	30

Sheavills, Stafford, Smith, Price, Turley, Haynes, Jacobs, Beattie, Hopkins, Senior, Walker.

Morton, Simpson, Rayner, Jackson.

Mr. A. Preston, Mr. B. Poole, Cooper, Brookes, Thompson, Ronson, Hails, Graham, McNamee, Hudson, Whittaker, Emery, Singleton, Horobin, Mr. H. Willis, Mr. J. Anderson.

Mr. J. Hagan, Mr. G. Taylor, Mr. J. Vernum, Mr. W. Peck, Mr. V. Grange, Mr. T. Peake, Mr. C. Palmer, Mr. W. Head, Mr. H. Trelfa, Mr. F. Terrell, Mr. R. Rigby, Mr. E. Patterson, Mr. H. Pepper.

Season Summary

Team changes include the shock move of Terry Bly. In October Manager Jimmy Hagan sacked, and Fairbrother later takes over the reins. Following dissention with the local Press, Club launch own newspaper – "The Post Post". Promotion is missed again with a final, but respectable, 6th place in the 3rd Division.

SEASON 1963/64

Football League Division 3

138	Date	Opposition	Res	H.T.	Attend	Goalscorer
1	24 Aug	WREXHAM	5-2	2-2	14784	Smith K. Dougan McNamee 3
2	28	Hull City	0-0	0-0	18433	
3	31	Q. P. Rangers	0-3	0-2	10971	
4	7 Sep	BRISTOL ROVERS	2-2	0-1	12256	Dougan McNamee
5	9	HULL CITY	5-1	3-1	12259	Dougan 3 McNamee O.G.
6	14	Oldham Athletic	2-4	0-1	14428	Pearce Smith K.
7	18	Bournemouth & Bos.	0-3	0-1	15015	
8	21	NOTTS. COUNTY	5-1	3-0	11791	Jackson Dougan 2 Horobin 2
9	28	SOUTHEND UNITED	3-0	1-0	11173	Smith K. Dougan Horobin
10	30	BOURNEMOUTH & BOS.	2-1	0-1	15158	Smith K. O.G.
11	5 Oct	Watford	2-1	1-1	10543	Horobin 2
12	7	MILLWALL	2-3	2-1	14002	Pearce Dougan
13	11	Bristol City	1-3	1-1	10770	Moulden
14	14	Millwall	2-0	2-0	8924	Smith K. Dougan
15	19	WALSALL	1-2	1-1	11732	Dougan
16	21	COLCHESTER UNITED	4-0	3-0	11505	Smith K. 2 Dougan 2
17	26	Reading	0-1	0-1	9247	
18	28	Colchester United	1-4	0-2	6966	Smith K.
19	2 Nov	LUTON TOWN	0-0	0-0	10687	
20	9	Coventry City	2-3	2-2	29663	Dougan Cooper
21	23	Brentford	0-2	0-1	15900	
22	30	SHREWSBURY TOWN	2-2	0-1	8010	Wright Turley
23	14 Dec	Wrexham	3-2	2-2	4529	Dougan 2 Turley
24	21	Q. P. RANGERS	2-1	2-0	6418	McNamee Moulden
25	26	Crewe Alexandra	0-0	0-0	6117	
26	28	CREWE ALEXANDRA	3-2	1-2	9015	Rankmore Day Turley
27	4 Jan	MANSFIELD TOWN	1-3	1-3	8806	McNamee
28	11	Bristol Rovers	2-2	2-1	11009	Smith K. Dougan
29	18	OLDHAM ATHLETIC	0-0	0-0	7036	
30	25	Crystal Palace	0-1	0-1	15138	
31	1 Feb	Notts. County	0-0	0-0	7026	
32	8	Southend United	0-2	0-2	8002	
33	15	WATFORD	0-1	0-1	9225	
34	22	BRISTOL CITY	4-2	2-1	7400	Turley Smith K. McNamee 2
35	29	Port Vale	2-1	2-0	6613	Jackson Smith K.
36	7 Mar	READING	1-0	1-0	6567	McNamee
37	14	Luton Town	3-2	2-0	6279	Horobin Smith K. O.G.
38	23	PORT VALE	1-1	1-0	10408	Horobin
39	28	Mansfield Town	1-4	0-2	8639	Turley
40	30	BARNSLEY	3-2	2-2	7220	Smith K. Dougan 2
41	31	Barnsley	2-3	0-1	4479	Horobin Graham
42	4 Apr	BRENTFORD	3-0	2-0	5550	Moulden 2 Smith K.
43	11	Shrewsbury Town	0-0	0-0	4340	
44	18	CRYSTAL PALACE	1-1	1-0	11837	McNamee
45	20	COVENTRY CITY	2-0	1-0	26307	Dougan Thompson
46	25	Walsall	0-2	0-2	5611	

Player appearances (shirt numbers)

No	Duff	Singleton	Sissons	Wright	Rankmore	Pearce	Jackson	Smith K.	Dougan	Horobin	McNamee	Senior	Day	Hopkins	Walker	Moulden	Cooper	Graham	Turley	Emmerson	Bennett	Thompson
1	1	2	3	4	5	6	7	8	9	10	11											
2	1	2	3	4	5	6	7	10	9	8	11											
3	1	2	3	4	5	6	7	10	9	8	11											
4	1	2	3	4	5	6		10	9	8	11	7										
5	1	2	3	4	5	6	7	10	9	8	11											
6	1	2	3	4	5	6	7	10	9	8	11											
7	1	2	3	4	5	6	7	10	9	8	11		7									
8	1	2	3	4	5	6	7	10	9	8	11											
9	1	2	3	4	5	6	7	10	9	8	11											
10	1	2	3	4	5	6	7	10	9	8	11											
11	1	2	3	4	5	6	7	10	9	8	11											
12	1			4	5	6		10	9	8	11			2	3	7						
13	1			4	5	6		10	9	8	11			2	3	7						
14	1			4	5	6		10	9	8	11			2	3	7						
15	1	2	3	4	5	6	7	10	9	8	11											
16	1	2	3		5	6	7	10	9	8	11						4					
17	1	2	3		5	6	7	10	9	8	11						4					
18	1	2	3		5	6	7	10	9	8		11					4					
19	1	2	3		5	6	7	10	9	8	11						4	10				
20	1	2	3		5	6	7	10	9	8		11					4					
21	1	2	3	4	5	6	7	10	9	8		11										
22	1	2	3	4	5	6	7			8	11					10			9			
23	1	2	3	4	5	6	7		9	8	11								10			
24	1	2	3	4	5	6		10	9	8	11					7						
25	1	2	3	4	5	6	7		9	8	11								10			
26	1	2	3	4	5	6	7		9		11		8						10			
27	1	2	3	4	5	6	7	10	9		11		8									
28	1		3	4	5		7	10	9		11		8	2			6					
29	1		3	4	5		7	10	9		11		8	2			6					
30	1		3	4	5		7	10	9		11		8	2			6					
31	1		3		5			10	9		11		7	2		8	6					
32	1		3		5			10	9		11		7	2		8	6					
33	1		3	4	5		7	10	9		11			2		8	6					
34	1		3	4	5			10		8	11			2		7	6		9			
35	1		3	4	5		7	10			11			2		8	6		9			
36	1		3	4	5			10		8	11			2		7	6		9			
37			3	4	5			10	9	8	11		7	2		7	6			1		
38			3	4	5			10	9	8	11		7	2		7	6			1		
39			3	4	5			10	9	8	11			2		7	6		11	1		
40			3	4	5			10	9	8	11			2		7	6			1		
41			3		5			9	9	8	11			2		7	6	10		1	4	
42			3		5			10	9	8	11			2		7	6			1	4	
43			3		5			10	9	8	11			2		7	6			1	4	
44	1	3		4	5	6		10	9		11		7	2		7	6			1		
45	1	3		4	5	6		9	9		11			2		8	6	8	9	1		7
46	1	3		4	5	6	6	9	9		11			2		8						7

Page 183 of 244

F.A.Cup

	Date	Opponent	Score	H/T	Att.	1	2	3	4	5	6	9	10	8	11	7	4
1st	16 Nov	WATFORD	1-1	0-1	15163	O.G.									7		4
1/R.	19	Watford	1-2*	0-1	15081	Senior									7		6

Football League Cup

	Date	Opponent	Score	H/T	Att.	1	2	3	4	5	6	7	10	9	8	11
2nd	25 Sep	Millwall	2-3	0-2	5595	Dougan McNamee										

* After extra time (1-1 score at 90 mins.)

	39	27	40	24	46	28	25	37	38	40	42	4	12	22	3	30	21	3	13	7	3	2
League Appearances	39	27	40	24	46	28	25	37	38	40	42	4	12	22	3	30	21	3	13	7	3	2
(3 O.G.) League Goals		3	1	1	1	2	2	14	20	8	11	1		1		4	1	1	5	7	1	1
Cup appearances	3	3	3	2	3	2	1	3	3	3	1	2				2	2					
(1 O.G.) Cup Goals	3	3	2	3	3	2	1	3	1	3	1	1				1						

DIVISION 3

	P	W	D	L	F	A	W	D	L	F	A	Pts
Coventry C	46	14	7	2	62	32	8	9	6	36	29	60
Crystal P	46	17	4	2	38	14	6	10	7	35	37	60
Watford	46	16	6	1	57	28	7	6	10	22	31	58
Bournemouth	46	17	4	2	47	15	7	4	12	32	43	56
Bristol C	46	13	7	3	52	24	7	8	8	32	40	55
Reading	46	15	5	3	49	26	6	5	12	30	36	52
Mansfield T	46	15	8	0	51	20	5	3	15	25	42	51
Hull C	46	11	9	3	45	27	5	8	10	28	41	49
Oldham A	46	13	6	4	44	35	7	5	11	29	35	48
Peterboro' U	46	13	6	4	52	27	5	5	13	23	43	47
Shrewsbury T	46	13	6	4	43	19	5	5	13	30	61	47
Bristol R	46	9	6	8	52	34	10	2	11	39	45	46
Port Vale	46	13	6	4	35	13	3	8	12	18	36	46
Southend U	46	9	10	4	42	26	6	5	12	35	52	45
QPR	46	13	4	6	47	34	5	5	13	29	44	45
Brentford	46	11	4	8	54	36	4	10	9	33	44	44
Colchester U	46	10	8	5	45	26	2	11	10	25	42	43
Luton T	46	12	2	9	42	41	4	8	11	22	39	42
Walsall	46	7	9	7	34	35	6	5	12	25	41	40
Barnsley	46	9	9	5	34	29	3	6	14	34	65	39
Millwall	46	9	4	10	33	29	5	6	12	20	38	38
Crewe A	46	10	6	7	29	26	1	7	15	21	51	34
Wrexham	46	9	4	10	50	42	4	2	17	25	65	32
Notts Co	46	7	8	8	29	26	2	1	20	16	66	27

Peterborough United

Back Row, L. to R. Sissons Cooper Duff Rankmore Pearce Singleton
Front Row, L. to R. Moulden Horobin Dougan Dougan Graham McNamee

Season Summary

Derek Dougan signs for Posh and Denis Emery ends his eight year association with the Club. Six new players make their debuts in the first League match. A bad run sees Fairbrother resign after only one year as Manager, and Gordon Clark takes over. 26,307 fans see Posh beat Champions Coventry in the last game.

SEASON 1964/65

Football League Division 3

#	Date	Opposition	Res	H.T.	Attend	Goalscorer	Duff	Singleton	Birks	Crowe	Rankmore	Wright	Barnes	Conmy	Dougan	Smith K.	Crawford	McNamee	Hopkins	Deakin	Read	Maloy	Robinson	Walker	Moulden	Sims	Cooper	Sissons	Shiels	Clamp	Orr	Bennett	Thompson
1	22 Aug	Exeter City	2-4	1-2	10218	Smith K. 2	1	2	3	4	5	6	7	8	9	10	11																
2	24	OLDHAM ATHLETIC	5-0	3-0	13483	Wright Conmy Smith K. 2 McNamee	1	2	3	4	5	6		8	9	10	7	11															
3	29	BOURNEMOUTH & BOS.	4-3	3-2	11813	Dougan Smith K. 2 Crawford	1	2	3	4	5	6		8	9	10	7	11															
4	1 Sep	Oldham Athletic	1-3	1-2	11500	Deakin	1		3		5	6		4	9	10	7	11	2	8													
5	5	SOUTHEND UNITED	4-2	2-1	10404	Dougan Smith K. 2 Crawford	1	2	3	4	5	6		8	9	10	7	11															
6	7	BRISTOL ROVERS	3-1	0-1	14420	Conmy Dougan Smith K.	1	2	3	4	5	6		8	9	10	7	11															
7	12	Grimsby Town	0-2	0-2	10469		1	2	3	4	5	6		8	9	10	7	11															
8	15	Bristol Rovers	0-4	0-1	17415		1	2	3	4	5	6		8	9	10	7	11															
9	19	MANSFIELD TOWN	4-5	2-2	10256	Dougan 3 McNamee		2	3	4		6		8	9	10	7	11			1			5									
10	26	Luton Town	1-1	1-0	9339	Moulden		2	3	4	6				9	10	7	11			1			5	8								
11	28	BRENTFORD	3-1	3-1	13311	Smith K. McNamee 2	1	2	3	4	6				9	10	7	11						5	8								
12	3 Oct	CARLISLE UNITED	1-2	1-0	11012	Deakin	1	2	3		6				9	10	7	11		8				5			4						
13	6	Brentford	1-3	1-0	12400	Smith K.	1	2	3	4	5	6			9	10	7	11		8													
14	10	Scunthorpe United	3-2	1-1	5207	Crawford Deakin Shiels	1		3	4		6				10	7	11	2	8				5					9				
15	12	PORT VALE	2-2	0-1	9878	Smith K. Deakin	1		3	4		6				10	7	11	2	8				5					9				
16	17	WALSALL	3-2	3-1	9372	Singleton Wright Deakin	1	2	3	4		6			9	10	7	11		8				5									
17	19	Port Vale	1-0	1-0	6110	Barnes	1	2	3	4		6	7	8	9	10		11										5					
18	24	Watford	1-1	1-1	8159	Crawford	1	2	3	4			7	8	9	10		11										5		6			
19	26	READING	2-1	0-1	11096	Smith K. 2	1	2	3	4			7	8	9	10		11										5		6			
20	31	WORKINGTON	0-4	0-1	9431		1	2	3	4			7		9	10		11	5	8										6			
21	7 Nov	Hull City	2-0	0-0	8056	McNamee Shiels		2	3	4	5		7	8		10		11								1			9		6		
22	21	Bristol City	1-3	0-1	9222	Crawford		2	3		5		7	8	9	10		11								1	4				6		
23	28	Q. P. RANGERS	6-1	2-1	8337	Barnes Dougan McNamee 2 Deakin 2		2	3		5		7	8	9			11		10						1	4				6		
24	12 Dec	EXETER CITY	0-0	0-0	7817			2	3		5		7	8	9			11		10						1	4				6		
25	19	Bournemouth & Bos.	1-0	0-0	6008	Deakin		2	3		5		11	8	9		7			10						1	4				6		
26	26	BARNSLEY	4-1	3-0	8963	Deakin 2 Moulden O.G.		2	3		5		11	8	9					10					7	1	4				6		
27	28	Barnsley	2-3	1-1	3220	Shiels 2		2	3		5			8	11					10					7	1	4		9		6		
28	2 Jan	Southend United	0-2	0-0	6875		1	2	3	4	5			8	9		7	11		10											6		
29	16	GRIMSBY TOWN	3-1	1-0	13414	Dougan Deakin O.G.		2	3	4	5			7	9		11			10					8	1					6		
30	6 Feb	LUTON TOWN	2-0	0-0	12946	Conmy Dougan		2	3	4	5			7	9		11			10					8	1					6		
31	13	Carlisle United	1-2	0-1	9847	Deakin		2	3	4	5			8	9			11		10					7	1					6		
32	27	Walsall	1-0	1-0	8859	Moulden		2	3	4	5			8	9			11		10					7	1					6		
33	8 Mar	SCUNTHORPE UNITED	2-2	1-1	9961	Dougan Deakin		2	3	4	5			7	9			11		10					8	1					6		
34	12	Workington	0-1	0-1	3800		1		3		5	4		7				11		10					8		2		9		6		
35	15	SHREWSBURY TOWN	4-1	2-1	6701	Dougan Deakin 3	1		3		5			8	9			11		10							2		7	4	6		
36	20	HULL CITY	2-1	1-0	9136	Dougan 2	1		3		5			8	9			11		10							2		7	4	6		
37	26	Gillingham	0-2	0-1	15552		1		3	4	5				9			11		10					8		2		7		6		
38	29	Mansfield Town	0-0	0-0	15352		1		3	4			7	8	9			11	5	10							2				6		
39	3 Apr	BRISTOL CITY	0-1	0-1	8156		1		3	4			7	8				11	5	10							2		9		6		
40	7	Shrewsbury Town	1-1	0-1	5118	Deakin			3	4			7	8	9			11	5	10			1				2				6		
41	10	Q. P. Rangers	2-3	0-3	4971	Dougan McNamee	1		3	4			7		9			11	5	10							2				6		8
42	16	Colchester United	1-0	0-0	6074	Dougan	1		3	4					9				5	10		11					2		7		6		8
43	17	WATFORD	2-1	1-0	7294	McNamee Maloy	1		3	4					9			11	5	10		7					2				6		8
44	19	COLCHESTER UNITED	4-1	0-0	6262	Barnes Dougan Thompson 2	1		3	4			7		9			11	5	10							2				6		8
45	24	Reading	2-4	1-1	6062	Dougan 2			3	4			7		9			11	5			10	1				2				6		8
46	28	GILLINGHAM	1-0	0-0	6405	Deakin	1		3	4			7		9			11	5	10							2				6		8

Back row—R. Barnes, P. Deakin, A. Moulden, D. Shiels, H. Orr, M. Robinson, B. Robinson, M. Ennerson, P. Thompson, O. Canny, P. McNamee.

Centre row — Mr. J. Anderson, G. Birks, K. Smith, T. Singleton, B. Wright, F. Rankmore, W. Duff, A. Read, J. Walker, O. Hopkins, D. Dougan, R. Bennett, R. Cooper, Mr. B. Poole, Mr. N. Rigby.

K. Maloy, I. Crawford, G. Sissons, I. Crowe.

Front row — Mr. H. Pepper, Mr. R. Rigby, Mr. E. Patterson, Mr. J. Vernum, Mr. C. Palmer, Mr. T. Peake, Mr. V. Grange, Mr. H. Trelfa, Mr. E. Terrell, Mr. J. Thornley, Mr. A. Preston.

Season Summary

Eleven players released and nine players are signed on, including Vic. Crowe from Aston Villa. The all-time record attendance at London Road see Arsenal beaten in the F.A. Cup, and Posh advance on to the quarter-finals. But promotion is missed again, the team finishing eighth in the 3rd Division.

SEASON 1965/66

Football League Division 3

230

Player appearance grid (player numbers by match; S = substitute, * = as marked):

#	Duff	Johnson	Crawford	Crowe	Rankmore	Hollow	Watson	Beesley	Gould	Byrne	McNamee	Deakin	Barnes	Conmy	Orr	Fairbrother	Thompson	Birks	Wright	McAnearney	Kirkham	Pulley	Robinson	Cooper	Rooney	Kevan	Ross
1	1	2	3	4	5	6	7	8	9	10	11	S															
2	1	2	3	4	5	6		9			11	10	7	8													
3	1	2	3		5	6					11	10	7	8	4*	9											
4	1	2	3		5	6					11	10	7	8		9	4										
5	1	2	3	4	5	6	7			10	11	8		S													
6	1	2	11	4	5	9		8		10	11		7	S				3	6								
7	1	2	3	4	5			8	9	10	S		11	S					6								
8	1	2	3	4	5	2	7	9		10		8	11	7		S	S		6								
9	1	2	3	4	5		7	9	9	10		8	11	S					6								
10	1	2	3	4	5		7		9	10		8	11	S					6								
11	1	2	3	4	5		7		9			8	11	S					6								
12	1	2	3	4	5		7		9	10		8	11	S	S				6								
13	1	2	3	4	5		7		9	10		8	11	S	S				6								
14	1	2	3	4	5		7		9	10		8	11	6													
15	1	2	3	6	5		7		9	10		8	11	S				11		4							
16	1	2	3	4	5		7			10		8				9	10	11		6							
17	1	2	3	4	5		7			10		8	11			9		S		6	8						
18	1	2	3	4	5		7		8	10		8	S	11		9				6	4	S					
19	1		3	4	5	2	7					11		7		9				8	6	S					
20			3	4	5		7	10	S												8	11	1	2			
21		2	3	6	5					10		8	7	8	S	9			6	4	6	11	1				
22	1	2	3		5		7			10		8	7			9				4	6	11					
23	1	S	3	8	5					10		7	7			9				4	6	11					
24	1		3		5	2	7		9	10		8*		12						4	6	11					
25	1		3		5	2	7		9	10				S						4	6	11					
26	1		3		5	2	7	8	9	10				9						4	6	11					
27	1		3	4	5	2	7			10		8		9						S	6	11					
28	1		3	S	5		7					10		8		9			4	6	6			2			
29	1		3	4	5		7					9	S	8		S				6	6			2	11		
30	1		3		5		7					9		8	4	S					6			2	11	10	
31	1		3	4	5		7			9		8	11	11	6	S			4	8	6	11		2	11	10	S
32	1	2	3	4	5		7		12			8	11	11	6	S			4	8	6	11		2		10	
33	1	2	3	4	5		7		10			8	11	11	6	S			4	8	6	11		2		9	
34	1	2*	3	4	5		7		9			10	7	6	6	12			6	4		11			11	9	
35	1	2	3	4	5		7		8			10		2	S				4			11				S	
36	1		3		5		7			8		10*		9		12			6	S	6			2	11	9	
37	1		3		5	7*			8			12		8		9			4	6	6			2	11	10	
38	1		3		5			10		8		9		S	4	S			4		6	11		2	11	10	S
39	1		3		5	5				8		9		6		11			4	9	6			2	11	10	
40	1		3					10		8		8		7	6	9			4			11		2		9	
41	1		3		5					10		8		7	6	9			4			11		2	11	9	
42	1		3					8		8		8		6	6	S			4	S		11		2		S	
43	1		3		5			4		10		8		9	6	9			4	9	9	11		2	9	9	
44	1		3			5	7	4		11		8		6	6				5	S	S	11		2			
45	1		3					4				8	7	6	6	11			5	S	S	S		2	9	10	S
46	1		3			7		4		11		10		11	6	9			5	S		S		2	7	10	S

Match results:

#	Date	Opposition	Res	H.T.	Attend	Goalscorer
1	21 Aug	GILLINGHAM	1-0	1-0	9670	Hollow
2	23	MILLWALL	0-2	0-2	10702	
3	28	Oldham Athletic	4-2	3-0	6535	McNamee Deakin Barnes Fairbrother
4	4 Sep	WATFORD	2-2	1-2	10431	McNamee Deakin
5	11	Scunthorpe United	1-1	1-0	4682	Deakin
6	14	Walsall	0-2	0-1	16643	
7	18	BRIGHTON & H.A.	2-2	2-0	7588	Beesley Conmy
8	25	Q. P. Rangers	1-2	1-1	5094	Watson
9	2 Oct	MANSFIELD TOWN	3-2	0-0	8312	Gould Byrne Barnes
10	4	WALSALL	3-1	2-0	9309	Byrne 2 Deakin
11	9	Bournemouth & Bos.	3-2	1-2	6508	Crawford Watson Byrne
12	16	SOUTHEND UNITED	4-0	1-0	9623	Gould Byrne Deakin Barnes
13	23	Swindon Town	0-3	0-1	12628	
14	30	SHREWSBURY TOWN	4-1	3-0	8105	Gould Byrne 3
15	6 Nov	Grimsby Town	0-3	0-2	9749	
16	20	Bristol Rovers	1-1	0-0	6330	Johnson
17	22	Millwall	1-4	0-3	9218	Fairbrother
18	27	YORK CITY	1-0	0-0	6196	Fairbrother
19	11 Dec	SWANSEA TOWN	5-2	0-1	7280	Byrne 2 Deakin 2 Conmy
20	18	Southend United	0-2	0-2	5364	
21	27	Reading	1-2	0-0	10070	Pulley
22	1 Jan	BOURNEMOUTH & BOS.	1-0	0-0	7125	Fairbrother
23	8	Brentford	0-1	0-1	7380	
24	15	SWINDON TOWN	2-3	1-1	5065	Byrne Deakin
25	29	Gillingham	1-1	1-1	8598	Byrne
26	5 Feb	OLDHAM ATHLETIC	0-1	0-0	6703	
27	19	Watford	0-1	0-0	6429	
28	26	SCUNTHORPE UNITED	3-1	2-0	6696	Watson Conmy Fairbrother
29	5 Mar	Exeter City	5-2	3-2	5362	Kirkham Deakin 2 Kevan Rooney
30	12	Brighton & H.A.	0-1	0-1	12682	
31	19	Q. P. RANGERS	1-1	1-1	7487	Deakin
32	26	Mansfield Town	7-1	2-0	3545	Watson 3 Conmy Deakin Byrne 2
33	28	READING	0-0	0-0	6631	
34	2 Apr	GRIMSBY TOWN	1-1	0-1	5601	Deakin
35	9	Oxford United	0-1	0-1	6145	
36	11	WORKINGTON	1-1	0-1	5456	Watson
37	16	BRISTOL ROVERS	5-2	2-1	4926	Watson Kevan Fairbrother 2 Byrne
38	21	Workington	1-1	1-0	2375	Ross
39	23	York City	1-1	0-1	3101	Byrne
40	25	HULL CITY	4-1	1-0	9547	Conmy Fairbrother Byrne Pulley
41	30	OXFORD UNITED	2-3	1-0	6260	Fairbrother Byrne
42	7 May	Swansea Town	1-1	1-0	7528	Deakin
43	9	EXETER CITY	2-0	1-0	4467	Deakin 2
44	12	Shrewsbury Town	1-3	1-1	2892	Pulley
45	17	Hull City	1-2	0-2	28285	Conmy
46	21	BRENTFORD	3-0	0-0	3935	Conmy Byrne O.G.

F.A.Cup

Round	Date	Opposition	Score	H/T	Att	Scorers
1st	13 Nov	KIDDERMINSTER HAR.	2-1	1-0	11709	Deakin 2
2nd	4 Dec	Shrewsbury Town	2-3	1-1	8980	Deakin Birks

Football League Cup

Round	Date	Opposition	Score	H/T	Att	Scorers
2nd	22 Sep	Newcastle United	4-3	3-1	16110	Watson Beesley Conmy 2
3rd	13 Oct	CHARLTON ATHLETIC	4-3	2-3	10929	Byrne 3 Deakin
4th	3 Nov	Millwall	4-1	3-0	11033	Byrne 3 Deakin
5th	17	BURNLEY	4-0	0-0	14796	Conmy Fairbrother 2 O.G.
S/F/1	1 Dec	West Brom. Albion	1-2	1-2	20933	Crowe
S/F/2	15	WEST BROM. ALBION	2-4	0-2	18288	Rankmore Conmy

Appearances

	Values (across squad)
League Appearances	43 22 46 26 42 14 28 9 18 36 5 33 19 25 14 19 3 2 20 12 18 3 16 5 13 3
League Sub. Appear.	1 1 1 1 1 1 1 3 1
League Sub. non-Appear.	1 1 2 4 3 2 1 3
(1 O.G.) League Goals	1 1 8 6 1 1 1 16 3 1 9 1 2 1 5 4 2 1
Cup Appearances	8 6 8 6 8 1 7 1 3 7 6 5 6 1 4 1 2 4 3 1
Cup Sub. Appear.	1
Cup Sub. non-Appear.	1 1
Cup Goals	6 5 1 1

DIVISION 3

	P	W	D	L	F	A	W	D	L	F	A	Pts
Hull C	46	19	2	2	64	24	12	5	6	45	38	69
Millwall	46	19	4	0	47	13	8	7	8	29	30	65
QPR	46	16	3	4	62	29	8	6	9	33	36	57
Scunthorpe U	46	9	8	6	44	34	12	3	4	38	33	53
Workington	46	13	6	4	38	18	6	8	9	29	39	52
Gillingham	46	14	4	5	33	19	8	4	11	29	35	52
Swindon T	46	11	8	4	34	18	8	5	10	31	30	51
Reading	46	13	5	5	36	19	6	8	9	34	44	51
Walsall	46	13	7	3	48	21	7	3	13	29	43	50
Shrewsbury T	46	13	5	5	48	22	6	4	13	25	42	49
Grimsby T	46	15	6	2	47	25	2	7	14	21	37	47
Watford	46	12	4	7	33	19	9	2	12	32	47	47
Peterboro' U	46	13	6	4	50	26	6	3	14	30	40	46
Oxford U	46	11	3	9	38	33	8	5	10	32	41	46
Brighton & HA	46	13	4	6	48	28	3	7	13	19	37	43
Bristol R	46	11	10	2	38	15	3	4	16	26	49	42
Swansea T	46	14	4	5	61	37	1	7	15	20	59	41
Bournemouth	46	9	8	6	24	19	4	4	15	14	37	38
Mansfield T	46	10	5	8	35	25	3	5	15	28	53	38
Oldham A	46	8	7	8	34	33	4	6	13	21	48	37
Southend U	46	15	1	7	43	28	1	3	19	11	55	36
Exeter C	46	9	6	8	36	28	3	5	15	17	51	35
Brentford	46	9	6	8	36	28	1	7	14	14	39	32
York C	46	5	7	11	30	44	4	2	17	23	62	27

Season Summary

Dougan moves on to Leicester City for £25,000. At last the first League Cup win is recorded – at 1st Division Newcastle. Posh progress on to the semi-final after beating 1st Division leaders Burnley in the 4th round. In the final 3rd Division League table, Posh finish below half-way.

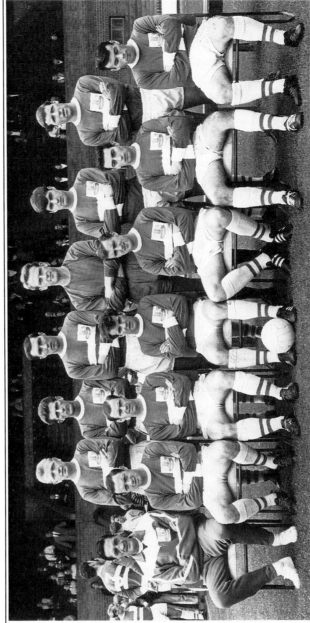

(Back) Cooper, Thompson, Wright, Emmerson, Birks, Orr. Rigby, Barnes, Conmy, Ross, Gould, Crawford, Rooney.

SEASON 1966/67

Football League Division 3

No	Date	Opposition	Res	H.T.	Attend	Goalscorer
1	20 Aug	DONCASTER ROVERS	3-3	1-2	7317	Rankmore Watson Conmy
2	27	Mansfield Town	0-0	0-0	6326	
3	3 Sep	GRIMSBY TOWN	2-1	1-1	6890	Byrne Thompson
4	5	GILLINGHAM	2-0	1-0	7286	Watson Byrne
5	10	Walsall	1-1	0-0	9236	Kirkham
6	17	Leyton Orient	1-1	0-0	5358	Fairbrother
7	24	TORQUAY UNITED	0-1	0-0	7347	
8	1 Oct	Brighton & H.A.	2-5	1-0	8598	Fairbrother Mason
9	5	Gillingham	2-2	1-1	7829	Fairbrother Mason
10	8	WORKINGTON	3-0	2-0	5790	Fairbrother 3
11	14	Scunthorpe United	0-1	0-0	5723	
12	17	WATFORD	2-2	1-0	7402	Watson Fairbrother
13	22	OLDHAM ATHLETIC	3-1	0-1	7637	Watson Mason 2
14	29	Oxford United	3-0	2-0	7317	Watson Fairbrother Conmy
15	5 Nov	BRISTOL ROVERS	1-1	0-0	7226	Fairbrother
16	12	Colchester United	4-1	2-0	6523	Fairbrother 2 Mason 2
17	15	Watford	1-3	0-1	6080	Fairbrother
18	19	SHREWSBURY TOWN	0-2	0-1	7060	
19	3 Dec	SWANSEA TOWN	4-4	3-3	6053	Rankmore Byrne Fairbrother 2
20	10	Bournemouth & Bos.	1-1	0-1	4332	Mason
21	17	Doncaster Rovers	1-3	1-3	7035	Byrne
22	23	SWINDON TOWN	1-2	1-2	5393	Mason
23	26	Swindon Town	1-4	0-1	14619	Fairbrother
24	31	MANSFIELD TOWN	3-1	2-1	6596	Watson Pulley Rooney
25	14 Jan	WASALL	2-1	0-1	7330	Fairbrother Ross
26	21	LEYTON ORIENT	0-2	0-1	6460	
27	4 Feb	Torquay United	0-1	0-1	6209	
28	11	BRIGHTON & H.A.	2-1	2-0	6432	Fairbrother Adams
29	20	Q. P. RANGERS	0-2	0-1	6410	
30	25	Workington	0-1	0-0	1610	
31	4 Mar	SCUNTHORPE UNITED	1-0	0-0	5485	Beesley
32	11	Q. P. Rangers	0-0	0-0	16716	
33	18	Oldham Athletic	0-1	0-1	6594	
34	25	OXFORD UNITED	2-3	1-0	6405	Watson Byrne
35	27	Reading	2-2	1-2	6840	McLaughlin 2
36	28	READING	2-1	1-0	5569	Beesley Metchick
37	1 Apr	Bristol Rovers	1-1	0-1	9202	Watson
38	8	COLCHESTER UNITED	2-1	1-0	5362	Watson Byrne
39	10	Darlington	0-5	0-4	4469	
40	15	Shrewsbury Town	1-1	1-0	3778	Watson
41	22	MIDDLESBROUGH	1-2	1-1	6458	Metchick
42	24	DARLINGTON	2-0	1-0	4631	Mason 2
43	29	Swansea Town	3-3	2-1	5664	Conmy Mason 2
44	2 May	Grimsby Town	1-1	1-0	3456	Mason
45	6	BOURNEMOUTH & BOS.	2-0	0-0	5047	Watson Mason
46	13	Middlesbrough	1-2	0-0	32503	Mason

Appearances (shirt number per match; S = substitute)

Player	1	2	3	4	5	6	7	8	9	10	11	12	13	14	15	16	17	18	19	20	21	22	23	24	25	26	27	28	29	30	31	32	33	34	35	36	37	38	39	40	41	42	43	44	45	46
McLaughlin																																		11	11	11	11	11	11	11	11*					
Metchick																																		10	10	10	10	10	10	10	10	8	8	10	10	10
Ross																								12	12			8	S		7															
Rooney																							8	12	11	11		8	S																	
Kevan								10	10		10								12			S																								
Millington								1	1	1	1	1		1	1	1		1	1	1	1	1		1	1	1	1	1	1		1	1	1	1	1	1	1	1	1	1	1	1	1			1*
Gould										S																																				
Adams								4	4		4	4	S	S									12	4				4	9	12	S	S						S								
Beesley																8							8*							3	9	9	9	3	9	9	9	9	9						
Mason								9	9	7	7	7	7	7	7	7	7	7	7	7	7	8	8					S		9*		7		3							9		9	9	9	9
Pulley						S			S			S				12								11	11*			S	11	11																
Kirkham				6	6	6	6	6	6			6	6	6	6	6	6	6				6	6	6	6	6	S	6			10	10	S					6	6						6	6
Wright				4	4	4		S	6	6	6	6	4	4	4	4	4	4				6	6	4				6	6	6	5		5					5	5	5	6	6	12	8	6	12
Thompson			12	S				2											4	4		12		2						2	2	2	2	2	2	2	2	2	2	2	2	2			S	
Cooper	S	S	4	2	2	2	2	2	2	2	2	2	2	2	2	2	2	2	2	6	6	3*		4	5		4	4	4	4	4		4	4	4	4	4	4	4	4	4	4	4	4	4	4
Conmy	11	11	11	11	11	11	11	11	11	11	11	8	10	8	8*			8	8	8*	8	8		8	8*				11	8	8	11		12	11*		11	S		11	12	11*	11		8	11
Deakin	10	10	10	10	10	10	10																																							
Fairbrother	9	9	9	9	9	9	9	10	10	9	9	9	9	9	9	9	9	9	9	9	9	9	9	9	9	9		9	9																	
Byrne	8	8	8	8	8	8	8		8	8		10	10	10	10	10	10	10	10	10	10	10	10	10	10	10	10	10	10	10	8	8	8	9	8	8	8	8	8	8	8	10	10	11	11	8
Watson	7	7	7	7	7	7	7	7	7			11	11	11	11	11	11	11	11	11	11	7		7	7	7	7	7	7	7	7	7	7	7	7*	7	7*	7	7	7	7	7	10	7	7	7
Orr	6	6	6*															S									4							S	12	S	S									
Rankmore	5	5	5	5	5	5	5	5	5	5	5	5	5	5	5	5	5	5	5	5	5	5	5	5*	5	5																				
Crowe	4	4	4				4	S	4																																					
Crawford	3	3	3	3	3	3	3	3	3	3	3	3	3	3	3	3	3	3	3	3	3	3	6'	3				3	3	3	3		8	3	3			3	3	3	3	3	3	3	3	3
Johnson	2	2	2		S		2																									11	7		8							2	2	2	2	2
Duff	1	1	1	1	1	1	1						1				1						1							1														1	1	

F.A.Cup

	Date	Opponent	Score	HT	Att	Scorers
1st	26 Nov	HEREFORD UNITED	4-1	2-0	12218	Byrne Fairbrother Conmy O.G.
2nd	7 Jan	Colchester United	3-0	1-0	9081	Watson 2 Fairbrother
3rd	28	Bedford Town	6-2	1-1	14053	Orr Watson 3 Fairbrother Conmy
4th	18 Feb	Sunderland	1-7	0-4	43998	Watson

Football League Cup

	Date	Opponent	Score	HT	Att	Scorers
1st	24 Aug	OXFORD UNITED	2-1	2-0	5847	Fairbrother 2
2nd	14 Sep	Northampton Town	2-2	1-1	5778	Byrne Fairbrother
2/R.	26	NORTHAMPTON TOWN	0-2	0-0	9581	

Appearances & Goals

League Appearances	13	20	46	3	38	7	39	46	28	6	32	39	16	32	27	4	27	14	7	33	3	2	14
League Sub. Appear.						1						1	2	2	1		1	1		1	1		2
League Sub. non-Appear.				3		4					1	2	4	3	2	3	1	5	1	1	1		
League Goals					2		11	6	17		3		1		1	1	15	2	1	4		1	2
Cup Appearances	3	4	7	3	5	2	6	7	5	1	7	5	3	5	1	4	1	1					1
Cup Sub. Appear.													1	1				1					
Cup Sub. non-Appear.	1												1	1		2							
(1 O.G.) Cup Goals						1	6	2	6		2				2	1		2					2

DIVISION 3

	P	W	D	L	F	A	W	D	L	F	A	Pts
QPR	46	18	4	1	66	15	8	11	4	37	23	67
Middlesbrough	46	16	3	4	51	20	7	6	10	36	44	55
Watford	46	15	5	3	39	17	5	9	9	22	29	54
Reading	46	13	7	3	45	20	9	2	12	31	37	53
Bristol R	46	13	8	2	47	28	7	5	11	29	39	53
Shrewsbury T	46	15	5	3	48	24	5	7	11	29	38	52
Torquay U	46	17	3	3	57	20	4	6	13	16	34	51
Swindon T	46	14	5	4	53	21	6	5	12	28	38	50
Mansfield T	46	12	4	7	48	37	8	5	10	36	42	49
Oldham A	46	15	4	4	51	16	4	6	13	29	47	48
Gillingham	46	11	9	3	36	18	4	7	12	22	44	46
Walsall	46	12	8	3	37	16	6	2	15	28	56	46
Colchester U	46	14	3	6	52	30	3	7	13	24	43	44
Leyton O	46	10	9	4	36	27	3	9	11	22	41	44
Peterboro' U	46	12	4	7	40	31	2	11	10	26	40	43
Oxford U	46	10	8	5	41	29	5	5	13	20	37	43
Grimsby T	46	13	5	5	46	23	4	4	15	15	45	43
Scunthorpe U	46	13	4	6	39	26	4	6	13	19	47	42
Brighton & HA	46	10	8	5	37	27	3	7	13	24	44	41
Bournemouth	46	8	10	5	24	24	4	7	12	15	33	41
Swansea T	46	9	9	5	50	30	3	6	14	35	59	39
Darlington	46	7	8	8	26	28	5	4	14	21	53	37
Doncaster R	46	11	6	6	40	40	1	2	20	18	77	32
Workington	46	9	3	11	35	35	4	3	16	20	54	31

Peterborough United F.C. 1966/67

Unusually a mid-term group 'photo was taken. A season in which many players were used. Amongst the popular players here, are: (Back row) Millington – 4th from left, Wright – 3rd from right, and Conmy in the front row – third from left.

Season Summary

Rankmore and Millington receive their 'caps' in the Welsh Summer Tour. Posh exit from F.A.Cup in 4th round, with 1-7 defeat at Sunderland – which has later serious repercussions. A disappointing season ends with only a late rally preventing relegation, with a final position of 15th. But a bigger disaster looms ahead!

SEASON 1967/68

Football League Division 3

#	Date	Opposition	Res	H.T.	Attend	Goalscorer
1	19 Aug	SCUNTHORPE UNITED	1-1	0-1	6985	Byrne
2	26	Oldham Athletic	2-0	1-0	7462	Byrne O.G.
3	2 Sep	BRISTOL ROVERS	4-1	1-0	6649	Conmy 2 Rankmore Watson
4	4	WATFORD	5-1	0-1	9460	Conmy Byrne Fairbrother Noble Linnell
5	9	Barrow	2-1	1-0	6714	Fairbrother O.G.
6	16	OXFORD UNITED	1-1	0-1	9254	Rankmore
7	23	Bury	0-4	0-3	6612	
8	26	Watford	1-4	0-2	9930	Metchick
9	30	BOURNEMOUTH & BOS.	2-0	0-0	7041	Metchick Mason
10	2 Oct	MANSFIELD TOWN	2-0	1-0	9045	Metchick Thompson
11	7	STOCKPORT COUNTY	2-0	1-0	8628	Conmy 2
12	14	Brighton & H.A.	1-1	0-0	10905	Mason
13	21	SHREWSBURY TOWN	0-1	0-1	8250	
14	23	Mansfield Town	3-2	2-0	5132	Fairbrother 2 Deakin
15	28	Swindon Town	0-0	0-0	12227	
16	4 Nov	READING	2-3	0-2	6837	Wright Mason
17	11	Torquay United	1-3	0-1	6991	Wright
18	14	Bristol Rovers	1-2	1-0	10742	Thompson
19	18	GRIMSBY TOWN	3-2	1-1	7243	Fairbrother 3
20	25	Gillingham	2-3	1-3	5922	Fairbrother Brace
21	2 Dec.	WALSALL	2-1	2-0	9479	Metchick Brace
22	15	Scunthorpe United	1-2	1-1	3390	Fairbrother
23	23	OLDHAM ATHLETIC	2-1	1-0	6262	Fairbrother Thompson
24	26	ORIENT	3-2	1-1	8314	Fairbrother Brace O.G.
25	30	Orient	0-3	0-1	4826	
26	13 Jan	BARROW	0-1	0-0	6888	
27	20	Oxford United	1-3	0-3	6000	Conmy
28	3 Feb	BURY	0-2	0-2	4902	
29	10	Bournemouth & Bos.	3-3	1-1	6495	Hall 2 Garwood
30	17	COLCHESTER UNITED	3-1	2-1	5066	Thompson 2 Hall
31	23	Stockport County	2-2	2-1	9113	Adams Hall
32	2 Mar	BRIGHTON & H.A.	2-3	0-1	4580	Rankmore Wright
33	9	SOUTHPORT	1-0	0-0	4460	Rankmore
34	16	Shrewsbury Town	1-1	1-1	4549	Ricketts
35	23	SWINDON TOWN	1-1	0-0	4667	Brace
36	30	Reading	1-0	0-0	4889	Thompson
37	1 Apr	Southport	1-2	0-1	4173	Downes
38	6	TORQUAY UNITED	2-0	1-0	5875	Wright Conmy
39	12	Tranmere Rovers	1-0	0-0	8078	Hall
40	13	Grimsby Town	1-1	1-1	3910	Thompson
41	15	TRANMERE ROVERS	1-1	1-1	6402	Hall
42	20	GILLINGHAM	3-0	3-0	5429	Conmy Hall 2
43	23	Northampton Town	1-3	0-1	8934	Downes
44	27	Walsall	2-3	2-3	5620	Hall 2
45	4 May	NORTHAMPTON TOWN	4-0	2-0	6658	Hall Garwood 3
46	11	Colchester United	5-1	3-1	2483	Thompson Conmy Hall 2 Garwood

Player appearances (shirt numbers)

#	Millington	Cooper	Crawford	Conmy	Rankmore	Wright	Watson	Byrne	Fairbrother	Metchick	Kirkham	Noble	Linnell	Mason	Thompson	Deakin	Maynard	Brace	Adams	Wile	Hall	Radcliffe	Kwiatkowski	Garwood	Ricketts	Downes
1	1	2	3	4	5	6	7	8	9	10	11	S														
2	1	6	3	11	5		7	8	9	10	S	2	4													
3	1	6	3	11	5		7	8	9	10	S	2	4													
4	1	6	3	11	5		7	8	9	10		2	4	S												
5	1	6	3	11	5		7	8	9	10		2	4	S												
6	1	6	3	11	5		7	8	9	10		2	4	S												
7	1	6	3	11*	5		7	8	9	10		2	4		12											
8	1	6	3*	7	5			8	9	11		2	4			S	10									
9	1	3		7	5	6	2	8	9	11			4	S												
10	1	3		7	5	6	2	10	9	11			12		8											
11	1	3		8	5	6	2	10	9	11			4		7											
12	1	3		8	5	6	2	10	9	11			4		7											
13	1	3		8	5	6	2	10	9	11			4		7											
14	1	3		7	5	6	2	11	9				4			10										
15	1	3		7	5	6	2	11	10				4			S										
16	1	3		7	5	6	2	8	10				4	9	12	S										
17	1*	3		7	5	6	2	8	9				4		12											
18	1	3		8	5	6	2	10	9	11			4		7											
19	1	3		8	5	6	2	10	9	11			4		S			7								
20	1	6		8	5		2	10	9	11			4*				12	7								
21	1	6*		8	5	4	2	10	9	11			S				3	7								
22	1	3		8*	5	6	2	10	9	11				6	12		3	7								
23	1	3		8	5	6	2	10	9						12			7	4							
24	1	3		8	5	6	2	10	9						11			7	4	12						
25	1	3		8	5	6	2	10	9						11	S		7	4							
26	1	4		8	5	6	2	10	9						11	10		7	4							S
27	1	4		8	5	6	2*	10	9						11	10		7	4							
28	1			8	5	6	2	10	9						11	10		7	S		8					
29	1			8	5	6	2	10	9	11					10			7	S		9			7*		8
30	1	S		8	5	6	2		12	11					10		12	7			9		3	7		8
31	1	2		10	5	6			4			3			8				11		9		3	7		8
32	1	2		8	4	6		4				3			3			10			9		3	7		8
33	1	2		8	5	6						3			11					5	9		S		7	8
34	1	2		8	4	6						3			11*	10				12	9				4	8
35	1	2		8	5	6						3			10	10			11	S	9			11	4	8
36	1	2		7	5	6						3			11	10		7			9		S		4	8
37	1	2		7	5	6						3		S	11	10		7			9				4	8
38	1	2		8	5	6						3			11	10		S			9		3	7	4	8
39	1	2*		7	5	6				11		3	S		11	10			12		9		3	7	4	8
40	1			7	5	6				S		2			11	10			11		9		2	7	4	8
41	1			7	5	6						3			11	10			10		9			7	4	8
42	1	2		7	5	6						3			11	10			9		9		12		4	8
43	1			7	5	6						3			11	10			9	2	9	2			4	8
44	1			8	5	6						2			11	10	S		9	3	9	3			4	8
45	1			8	5	6						3		2	11						9		S	7	4	10
46	1			8	5	6						3		2	11						9		S	7	4	10

F.A. Cup

1st	11 Dec	FALMOUTH TOWN	5-2	1-0	6484	Byrne Fairbrother 3 Brace
2nd	6 Jan	Margate	4-0	0-0	7366	Conmy Deakin Thompson Brace
3rd	27	PORTSMOUTH	0-1	0-0	16907	

Football League Cup

1st	23 Aug	NORTHAMPTON TOWN	2-3	2-1	8157	Conmy Byrne

DIVISION 3

	P	W	D	L	F	A	W	D	L	F	A	Pts
Oxford U	46	18	3	2	49	20	4	10	9	20	27	57
Bury	46	19	3	1	64	24	5	5	13	27	42	56
Shrewsbury T	46	14	6	3	42	17	6	9	8	19	32	55
Torquay U	46	15	6	2	40	17	6	5	12	20	39	53
Reading	46	15	5	3	43	17	6	4	13	27	43	51
Watford	46	15	3	5	59	20	6	5	12	15	30	50
Walsall	46	12	7	4	47	22	7	5	11	27	39	50
Barrow	46	14	4	3	43	13	7	2	14	22	41	50
Peterboro' U	46	14	4	5	46	23	6	6	11	33	44	*50
Swindon T	46	13	8	2	51	16	3	9	11	23	35	49
Brighton & HA	46	11	8	4	31	14	5	8	10	26	41	48
Gillingham	46	13	6	4	35	19	5	6	12	24	44	48
Bournemouth	46	13	7	3	39	17	3	8	12	17	34	47
Stockport Co	46	16	5	2	49	22	3	4	16	21	53	47
Southport	46	13	6	4	35	22	4	6	13	30	43	46
Bristol R	46	14	3	6	42	25	3	6	14	30	53	43
Oldham A	46	11	9	3	37	32	7	4	12	23	33	43
Northampton T	46	11	3	9	37	32	5	4	12	18	47	41
Orient	46	10	8	5	40	25	4	5	14	18	41	41
Tranmere R	46	10	7	6	27	24	2	11	10	19	38	41
Mansfield T	46	10	7	6	39	28	4	5	14	23	46	40
Grimsby T	46	8	7	8	32	31	4	6	13	19	36	37
Colchester U	46	10	7	6	33	21	4	2	17	19	48	37
Scunthorpe U	46	8	6	9	29	40	3	7	13	21	47	33
	46	8	9	6	36	34	2	3	18	20	53	32

Appearances / Goals

League Appearances	46	37	9	41	46	39	8	24	22	24	1	43	24	10	29	16	2	15	6	3	20	2	6	7	14	12
League Sub. Appear.							1						2		3	3	1		1	2	2	1	5		1	
League Sub. non-Appear.		1						3		3	3	1	4	1	8	1		4	1	2	13			5		2
(3 O.G.) League Goals	4	4		9	4	4	1	3	11	4		4	2		2	1	1	3	1							
Cup Appearances	4	4	1	4	4	3	1	2	4			4	2		1	1		3	1							
Cup Sub. Appear.														1	1											
Cup Sub. non-Appear.											1			1		1			1		2					
Cup Goals				2		2		2	3						1	1		1			2					

(Back) Crawford, Wile, Linnell, Millington, Drewery, Byrne, Kirkham, Wright.
(Middle) Radcliffe, Metchick, Conmy, Thompson, Garwood, Fairbrother, Noble, Adams.
(Front) Kwiatkowski, Watson, Maynard, Rankmore, Mason, McLaughlin.

Season Summary

Manager Clark mysteriously resigns, and Trainer Norman Rigby takes over. In November the F.A. announce that following payment irregularities, Posh are to be relegated to the 4th Division. Defeat in January in the F.A.Cup 3rd round, at home to Portsmouth, effectively ends the season for Peterborough.

Football League Division 4

368	Date	Opposition	Res	H.T.	Attend	Goalscorer
1	10 Aug	EXETER CITY	1-1	1-1	8532	Hall
2	17	Port Vale	0-1	0-0	5085	
3	24	BRADFORD CITY	2-2	1-0	6457	Brace Hall
4	28	Chesterfield	0-2	0-1	6493	
5	31	York City	1-2	0-1	4089	Garwood
6	7 Sep	Rochdale	1-1	0-1	4030	Hall
7	14	BRENTFORD	2-1	0-1	6435	Hall Garwood
8	16	SCUNTHORPE UNITED	3-2	1-0	5401	Hall 2 Garwood
9	20	Doncaster Rovers	0-1	0-0	12951	
10	28	CHESTER	1-2	0-1	6897	Hall
11	5 Oct	SOUTHEND UNITED	1-0	0-0	5987	Thompson
12	7	CHESTERFIELD	3-0	0-0	6102	Brace Hall Thompson
13	12	Halifax	1-2	1-0	4075	Pyatt
14	19	GRIMSBY TOWN	1-1	0-0	5783	Thompson
15	26	Wrexham	0-0	0-0	7858	
16	2 Nov	NEWPORT COUNTY	1-1	1-1	4792	Wright
17	4	NOTTS. COUNTY	1-0	1-0	4553	Price
18	9	Darlington	3-3	1-2	5374	Hall Price 2
19	23	Workington	0-1	0-0	2116	
20	30	BRADFORD P.A.	6-1	3-0	5416	Hall 3 Downes Wosahlo Robson
	14 Dec	HALIFAX	*	0-0	4726	* Abandoned after 45 mins.
21	21	Grimsby Town	2-2	1-1	3412	Price Robson
22	26	Southend United	1-2	1-2	10627	Price
23	4 Jan	WREXHAM	2-3	2-2	6312	Robson 2
24	11	Newport County	2-4	0-1	1649	Conmy Hall
25	13	LINCOLN CITY	0-0	0-0	6564	
26	25	Notts. County	1-2	1-1	5740	Hall
27	29	DARLINGTON	1-1	1-0	6463	Robson
28	1 Feb	Swansea Town	0-0	0-0	3447	
29	5	HALIFAX TOWN	0-0	0-0	5118	
30	24	WORKINGTON	1-1	0-1	4064	Hall
31	1 Mar	Exeter City	1-0	1-0	4604	O.G.
32	5	Lincoln City	1-1	1-1	7653	Robson
33	8	PORT VALE	0-1	0-0	5377	
34	10	SWANSEA TOWN	2-2	2-1	4224	Hall Price
35	19	Aldershot	4-1	1-0	5972	Hall Price 2 O.G.
36	22	YORK CITY	2-1	1-1	4668	Iley Conmy
37	29	ROCHDALE	0-1	0-1	4107	
39	2 Apr	Bradford P.A.	2-0	1-0	2471	Hall Robson
39	5	Chester	3-2	0-1	4010	Wile Robson Price
40	7	Scunthorpe United	2-1	2-0	2713	Hall Robson
41	8	COLCHESTER UNITED	0-1	0-1	6548	
4#	12	DONCASTER ROVERS	0-1	0-0	5779	
43	14	Colchester United	2-2	1-1	6564	Hall Price
44	19	Brentford	0-2	0-1	4490	
45	21	ALDERSHOT	2-0	1-0	3758	Conmy Robson
46	29	Bradford City	1-2	0-1	9175	Price

1st	16 Nov	Bristol Rovers	1-3	1-0	7108	Downes

Football League Cup

1/1L	14 Aug	Doncaster Rovers	0-0	0-0	7765	Hall
1/2L	19	DONCASTER ROVERS	1-0	1-0	8627	
2nd	4 Sep	Q. P. RANGERS	4-2	0-1	11408	Hall 3 Thompson
3rd	25	WEST BROMWICH A.	2-1	2-0	16510	Thompson Price
4th	16 Oct	Tottenham Hotspur	0-1	0-0	28378	

Appearances (shirt numbers)

F.A. Cup: 1 2 S 4 5 6 8 9 10 11 7 3

Match	1	2	S	4	5	6	7	8	9	10	11	7	3	
	1	2	3	4	5	6	7	8	9	10	11	7	3	
1/1L	1	2	3	4	5	6	7	8	9	10	11	S		
1/2L	1	2	3	4	5	6	7	8	9	10	11	S		
2nd	1	2		4	5	6	S	8	9	10		11	7	3
3rd	1	2		4	5	6	S	8	9	11		7		3
4th	1	2	3	4	5	6	S	7	9	8	11	10		10

	39	38	9	32	46	46	7	42	46	15	22	11	13	13	37	24	28	7	9	22					

League Appearances	39	38	9	32	46	46	7	42	46	15	22	11	13	13	37	24	28	7	9	22
League Sub. Appear.		2	1	3			1		1	1	1	3	2	3	1	2				
League Sub. non-Appear.		4	2			1			4	4	6	3	3	2	1	3		2		
(2 O.G.) League Goals	6		3	6	6	2	2	6	20	3	6	1	3		4	1	11	10		1
Cup Appearances	6	6	3	6	6	2	2	6	20	3	6	1	3	1	4					
Cup Sub. Appear.							3				2			2	1					
Cup Sub. non-Appear.		1							4											
Cup Goals				1					4						1					

DIVISION 4

	P	W	D	L	F	A	Pts
Doncaster R	46	13	8	2	42	22	59
Halifax T	46	15	5	3	36	18	57
Rochdale	46	14	7	2	47	11	56
Bradford C	46	11	10	2	36	18	56
Darlington	46	11	6	6	40	26	52
Colchester U	46	12	8	3	31	17	52
Southend U	46	15	3	5	51	21	51
Lincoln C	46	13	6	4	38	19	51
Wrexham	46	13	7	3	41	22	50
Swansea T	46	11	8	4	35	20	49
Brentford	46	12	7	4	40	24	48
Workington	46	8	11	4	24	17	47
Port Vale	46	8	8	7	16	26	46
Chester	46	12	4	7	43	24	45
Aldershot	46	13	3	7	42	23	45
Scunthorpe U	46	10	5	8	28	22	44
Exeter C	46	11	8	4	45	24	43
Peterboro' U	46	8	9	6	32	23	43
Notts Co	46	10	8	5	33	22	42
Chesterfield	46	7	7	9	24	22	41
York C	46	12	8	3	36	25	39
Newport Co	46	9	9	5	31	26	39
Grimsby T	46	5	7	11	25	31	36
Bradford	46	5	8	10	19	34	20

(Back) Iley (Manager), Pyatt, Wile, Millington, Wright, Crawford, Walker (Trainer). (Front) Downes, Price, Thompson, Hall, Conmy, Robson.

Season Summary

Rankmore signs for neighbours Northampton Town, before life in the 4th Division – again – starts. Posh reach 4th round of the League Cup, only losing narrowly to Spurs. Jim Iley joins as Player/Manager, but morale is at an all-time low, and re-election is only just avoided, with a final 18th position.

Football League Division 4

414	Date	Opposition	Res	H.T.	Attend	Goalscorer	Drewery	Potts	Noble	Hampton	Wile	Wright	Moss	Price	Iley	Holliday	Robson	Garwood	Hall	Conmy	Kwiatkowski	Turner	Payne	Ricketts
1	9 Aug	Port Vale	0-0	0-0	5453		1	2	3	4	5	6	7	8	9	10	11	S						
2	16	BRADFORD P.A.	2-1	0-1	6304	Hall 2	1	2	3	4	5	6	7*	8	12	10	11		9	10				
3	23	Scunthorpe United	1-2	0-2	2582	Robson	1	2	3	4	5	6	7	9*	4	8	11		12	8	S			
4	25	Colchester United	1-2	0-0	7133	Moss	1	2	3	4	5	6	7			10	11	12	9	8				
5	30	NOTTS. COUNTY	1-0	0-0	5984	Garwood	1	2	3	4*	5	6	7			10	11	12	9	8				
6	6 Sep	Crewe Alexandra	0-2	0-0	2687		1	2	3		5	6	7	8		10	11	8*	9	4	12			
7	13	LINCOLN CITY	2-1	1-0	5858	Iley Robson	1	2	3		5	6	7*	8	10		11		9	4				
8	17	NORTHAMPTON TOWN	1-0	1-0	8553	Hall	1	2	3		5	6	7	8	10	S	11		9	4				
9	20	Darlington	2-1	1-0	3721	Hall O.G.	1	2	3		5	6	7	8	10	S	11		9	4				
10	27	HARTLEPOOL UNITED	4-0	1-0	6872	Price Holliday Robson 2	1	2	3		5	6	7	8	10*	12	11		9	4				
11	1 Oct	WORKINGTON	1-1	1-0	8064	Robson	1	2	3	12	5	6	7	8	10	8	11		9	4*	4			
12	4	Swansea Town	1-4	0-3	6279	Hall	1	2	3	S	5	6	7*	8	10	12	11		9	4	4			
13	6	Bradford P.A.	3-2	0-0	2568	Price 2 Robson	1	2	3		5	6	7	8	10	7	11		9	S	4			
14	11	NEWPORT COUNTY	4-0	3-0	7002	Price Robson Hall 2	1	2	3		5	6	7	8	10		11		9	S	4			
15	18	Grimsby Town	0-0	0-0	3545		1	2	3		5	6	7	8	10	S	11		9	S	4			
16	25	YORK CITY	3-1	2-1	7756	Price Robson Hall	1	2	3		5	6	7	8	10		11		9	S	4			
17	1 Nov	Brentford	2-5	1-3	8650	Wile Iley	1	2	3		5	6	7	8	10	12	11		9*		4			
18	8	ALDERSHOT	4-1	2-1	7068	Price 2 Robson Garwood	1	2	3		5	6	S	9	10	7	11	8		4				
19	22	CHESTERFIELD	1-2	1-1	8111	O.G.	1	2	3		5	6	12	8	10*	7	11		9	4				
20	26	OLDHAM ATHLETIC	8-1	5-1	4796	Moss Price 3 Hall 4	1	2	3		5	6	7	8	10		11	12	9	4*				
21	29	Exeter City	1-1	0-1	5027	Moss	1	2	3		5	6	7	8		10*	11		10	4	12			
22	13 Dec	Lincoln City	0-3	0-1	5407		1	2	3		5	6	7*	8	12		11		10	4	9			
23	26	SCUNTHORPE UNITED	2-2	0-1	7796	Garwood Conmy	1	2	3		5	6	7	8*	10		11	9		4	12			
24	27	Notts. County	2-2	1-1	6924	Robson Garwood	1	2	3		5	6	7		10		11	8	9	4	12	9		
25	10 Jan	DARLINGTON	3-2	2-0	4607	Price Hall 2	1	2	3		5	6	7	8	10		11	7	9	4	S			
26	15	Workington	1-1	0-1	1919	Wile	1	2	3		5	6	7*		10		11	8	9	4		12		
27	17	Hartlepool United	2-4	1-3	2380	Robson Garwood	1	2	3		5	6		8	10		11	7*	9	4	12	12		
28	31	SWANSEA TOWN	1-1	0-0	6890	Iley	1	2	3		5	6	7	8	10		11	8	9	7	4			
29	7 Feb	Newport County	1-0	1-0	1590	Price	1	2	3		5	6	7	8*	10		11	12	9	7	4			
30	21	Aldershot	0-1	0-0	7601		1	2	3		5	6	7	8	10		11	S	9	7	4*	12		
31	25	CREWE ALEXANDRA	3-0	1-0	5300	Moss Price 2	1	2	3		5	6	7	8	10		11	S	9	4	4			
32	28	BRENTFORD	0-0	0-0	7528		1	2	3		5	6	7	8	10*		11	12	9	4	S			
33	9 Mar	Southend United	0-2	0-1	4816		1	2	3		5	6	7	8			11		9	4	10	12		
34	14	EXETER CITY	1-1	0-1	5783	Moss	1	2	3		5	6*	12	8			11	7*	9	4	10	S		
35	16	Wrexham	1-2	1-1	9563	Price	1	2	3		5	4	12	8			11		9	10	10	6		S
36	21	Chester	3-2	1-2	4024	Wile Moss Robson	1	2	3		5	4	7	8	10		11	S	9	S	10	6		
37	27	York City	0-3	0-1	3153		1	2	3		5	6	7	8	10		11	12	9	12	10	6*		
38	28	SOUTHEND UNITED	3-4	2-3	4911	Conmy Wile Hall	1	2	3		5	6	7	8	10		11	8	9	4	10	6		S
39	30	GRIMSBY TOWN	1-0	0-0	4715	Hall	1	2	3		5	6	7	8	10		11	S	9	4	10			
40	4 Apr	COLCHESTER UNITED	1-1	0-1	4168	Hall	1	2	3		5	6	7	8	10	S	11		9	4	S			
41	7	Oldham Athletic	2-4	1-2	4493	Hall 2	1	2	3		5	6*	7	8	10		11	7*	9	4	12	12		
42	10	WREXHAM	5-2	1-0	4280	Price Hall 3 Robson	1	2	3		5	6	7	8*	10		11	8	9	4	6	6		
43	14	Northampton Town	2-2	1-1	6732	Hall 2	1	2	3		5	6	7	8	10*		11		9	4	12	12		
44	18	CHESTER	0-0	0-0	4760		1	2	3		5	6	7	8	10		11	8	9	4	10*	6*		
45	22	PORT VALE	0-0	0-0	3844		1	2	3		5	6	7	8	10		11	S	9	4	2	12		
46	27	Chesterfield	1-3	0-1	14250	Price	1	2	3		5*	6	7	8	10		11	8	9	12	4	10		

F.A.Cup

							Scorers
1st	15 Nov	Falmouth Town	4-1	1-0	4000	Price Robson Hall 2	1 2 3 · 5 6 · 8 10* 7 11 12 9 4
2nd	6 Dec	PLYMOUTH ARGYLE	2-0	0-0	8553	Price Conny	1 2 3 · 5 6 7 8 · 11 12 9 4* 10
3rd	3 Jan	Rotherham United	1-0	1-0	13146	Hall	1 2 3 · 5 6 · 8 10 11 7 9 4 · S
4th	24	Gillingham	1-5	1-2	13746	Price	1 · 3 · 5 6 7* 8 10 11 12 9 4 · 2

Football League Cup

						Scorers	
1st	13 Aug	LUTON TOWN	1-1	1-1	10249	Price	1 2 3 4 5 6 7 8 10 S 11 9
1/R.	19	Luton Town	2-5	1-3	13105	Iley Robson	1 2 3 4 5 6 7 S 8 10 11 9

Appearances

League Appearances	46	45	46	3	46	45		38	38	33	12	46	9	41	35	17	6	
League Sub. Appear.				1				2		2	4		4	1	2	5	6	
League Sub. non-Appear.					1			1	1	3			5		3	2	2	2
(2 O.G.) League Goals					4			6	17	3		13	5	24				
Cup Appearances	6	5	6	2	6	6		4	5	5	2	6	1	6	4	1		
Cup Sub. Appear.											1		3					
Cup Sub. non-Appear.								1		1		2		3	1	1		
Cup Goals								4	1									

DIVISION 4

	P	W	D	L	F	A	W	D	L	F	A	Pts
Chesterfield	46	19	1	3	55	12	8	9	6	22	20	64
Wrexham	46	17	6	0	56	16	9	3	11	28	33	61
Swansea T	46	14	8	1	43	14	7	10	6	23	31	60
Port Vale	46	13	9	1	39	10	7	10	6	22	23	59
Brentford	46	14	8	1	36	11	6	9	8	22	28	56
Aldershot	46	16	5	2	52	22	4	8	11	26	43	53
Notts Co	46	14	4	5	44	21	8	4	11	29	41	52
Lincoln C	46	11	8	4	38	20	6	8	9	28	32	50
Peterboro' U	46	13	8	2	51	21	4	6	13	26	48	48
Colchester U	46	14	5	4	38	22	3	9	11	26	41	48
Chester	46	14	3	6	39	23	7	3	13	19	43	48
Scunthorpe U	46	11	6	6	34	23	7	4	12	33	42	46
York C	46	14	7	2	38	16	2	7	14	17	46	46
Northampton T	46	11	7	5	41	19	5	6	13	14	33	44
Crewe A	46	12	6	5	37	18	4	6	13	14	33	44
Grimsby T	46	9	9	5	33	24	5	6	12	21	34	43
Southend U	46	12	8	3	40	28	3	2	18	19	57	40
Exeter C	46	13	5	5	48	20	1	6	16	9	39	39
Oldham A	46	11	4	8	45	28	2	9	12	15	37	39
Workington	46	9	9	5	31	21	3	5	15	15	43	38
Newport Co	46	12	3	8	39	24	1	8	14	14	50	37
Darlington	46	8	7	8	31	27	5	3	15	22	46	36
Hartlepool	46	7	7	9	31	30	3	3	17	11	52	30
Bradford	46	6	5	12	23	32	0	6	17	18	64	23

(Back) Noble, Wright, Wile, Drewery, Millington, ?, Turner, Hampton, Potts.
(Mid.) Kwiatkowski, Garwood, Moss, Conny, Iley, Hall, Price, Holliday, Robson.
(Sitting) Apprentices.

Season Summary

Long serving players Crawford, Cooper and Thompson leave on free transfers, and goalkeeper Millington joins Swansea. Player/Manager Iley becomes first Posh player to be sent off – in first League match of season! Despite a prolonged challenge for promotion, the team finish in a disappointing 9th in the 4th Division table.

SEASON 1970/71

Football League Division 4

#	Date	Opposition	Res	H.T.	Attend	Goalscorer
1	15 Aug	Stockport County	0-0	0-0	4123	
2	22	ALDERSHOT	1-0	1-0	5956	Wile
3	29	Exeter City	2-3	1-1	4537	Wile Hall
4	31	Bournemouth & Bos.	0-1	0-1	7359	
5	5 Sep	NEWPORT COUNTY	2-1	1-0	4647	Sheffield Moss
6	12	Brentford	1-1	0-0	2707	Sheffield
7	19	GRIMSBY TOWN	1-1	0-0	5478	O.G.
8	23	YORK CITY	2-1	0-0	4854	Hall Sheffield
9	26	Barrow	3-2	1-1	2486	Sheffield Hall Turpie
10	30	OLDHAM ATHLETIC	2-1	0-1	5847	Sheffield Moss
11	3 Oct	COLCHESTER UNITED	1-2	1-1	5935	Robson
12	10	Cambridge United	1-1	0-0	7575	Price
13	17	STOCKPORT COUNTY	5-1	1-1	5207	Price Moss Robson Garwood 2
14	20	Scunthorpe United	2-5	1-2	3801	Price Garwood
15	24	Lincoln City	1-2	1-1	6419	Pleat
16	31	CHESTER	1-0	0-0	5395	Moss
17	7 Nov	Hartlepool	2-1	1-0	2038	Sheffield Garwood
18	10	Northampton Town	0-2	0-1	8190	
19	14	DARLINGTON	0-1	0-0	4614	
20	28	NOTTS. COUNTY	1-1	0-0	7119	Garwood
21	5 Dec	Crewe Alexandra	3-1	1-0	3840	Hall Robson Garwood
22	19	Aldershot	2-2	2-0	5195	Garwood O.G.
23	26	SOUTHEND UNITED	4-0	1-0	4396	Moss 2 Garwood 2
24	9 Jan	Oldham Athletic	0-3	0-1	10805	
25	16	SCUNTHORPE UNITED	1-2	1-1	5209	Garwood
26	23	SOUTHPORT	1-0	1-0	4250	Hall
27	30	Notts. County	0-6	0-1	9440	
28	6 Feb	CREWE ALEXANDRA	3-1	1-1	4102	Price Moss Garwood
29	12	Southport	2-3	0-1	1673	Hall Robson
30	20	NORTHAMPTON TOWN	1-0	0-0	8068	Moss
31	27	Chester	0-2	0-2	4223	
32	6 Mar	LINCOLN CITY	1-1	1-1	4292	Garwood
33	8	York City	1-2	0-2	4957	Hall
34	13	Darlington	0-1	0-0	2622	
35	17	WORKINGTON	3-1	1-0	2771	Garwood Robson 2
36	20	HARTLEPOOL	5-0	2-0	3895	Garwood 2 Robson Moss 2
37	27	Newport County	0-2	0-1	2588	
38	31	Workington	1-2	0-1	1842	Garwood
39	3 Apr	EXETER CITY	1-3	1-2	3880	Pleat
40	5	Southend United	2-1	0-1	5810	Wright Garwood
41	9	Colchester United	0-3	0-0	7650	
42	12	BRENTFORD	1-2	0-0	3821	Turner
43	17	CAMBRIDGE UNITED	2-3	2-3	5067	Hall Robson
44	24	Grimsby Town	1-1	1-1	3012	Hall
45	28	A.F.C. BOURNEMOUTH	3-1	1-1	3014	Conmy Hall Robson
46	1 May	BARROW	4-0	1-0	3552	Robson 2 Price 2

Player appearances (shirt numbers; S = substitute):

#	Drewery	Potts	Duncliffe	Kwiatkowski	Wile	Wright	Price	Sheffield	Hall	Iley	Pleat	Turpie	Noble	Conmy	Robson	Moss	Garwood	Turner	Carmichael	Dighton
1	1	2	3	4	5	6	7	8	9	10	11	S				S				
2	1		3	4	5	6	7	8	9	10	11	S	2			S				
3	1		3	4	5	6	7	8	9	10	7*	10	2		11	S				
4	1	12	3	4	5	6	7	8*	9		7	10	2		11					
5	1		3	4	5	6	12	8	9			10	2		11	7*				
6	1		3	4	5	6	S	8	9			10	2		11	7	S			
7	1		3	4	5	6		8	9			10	2	10	11	7	8			
8	1		3	4	5	6	S	8	9				2	10	11	7	8	6		
9	1		3	4	5	6	9	8	9			7	2	10	11	12	8	6		
10	1		3	4*	5	6	8*	8	9			7	2	10	11	12	8			
11	1		3	4	5	6	9	8*	9	4*	7	7	2	10	11	12	8			
12	1		3		5	6	9		9	4	7	12	2		11	7*	8	6		
13	1		3	4	5	6*	9*	12	9	10	7	11	2	10	11	12	8	6		
14	1		3		5	6	9	8	9	10	7		2	10	11	12	8	6		
15	1		3	4	5	6*	9*	8*	9	10	7	11	2	10	11	12	8	6		
16	1		3	4	5	6		8	9	4*	7		2	10	11	12	7			
17	1		3	12	5	6		8*	9	4*	7		2		11		10			
18	1		3	12	5			8	9	4	7		2		11		10			
19	1		3	4	5		9	8	9			11	2	7	12	7	10			
20	1		3	4	5		9	8*	9			12	2	4	11	7	10			
21	1		3		5	6			9	10	10	4	2	12	11	7	8	5		
22	1		3		5	6	9		9	10*	10	4	2	12	11	7*	8	5		
23	1		3			6	S		9	10	10	4	2	S	11*	7*	8	5		
24	1		3			6	12		9	10	10	4	2		11	7	8	5		
25	1	2	3		5	6	S		9	10	10	4	2*		11	7	8	5	6	
26	1	4	3						9	10	10	4			11	7	8	5		
27	1										7	11		10	12		8	5*		
28		2		4	5	6	9	8	6	10	10	4	3	12	11*	7	8	8		1
29				12	5	9	11	9	9	10*	10*	3	2	4	12	7	8	9	6	
30			3		5	9*	9*		6	12	10	4	2	12	11	7	8	9*		
31			3	S	5	9		8*	9		10	12	2		11	7*	8		4	
32	1		3		4	9	9*		9		10	4	2	12	11	7	8	S	6	
33	1		3	4	4	9			9	7*	10	12	2	12	11	7*	8	5	6	
34	1		3	4		9			9	S	7	7	2	7	11		8	5	6	
35	1		3	4		9			9*	8	10		2	12	11	9	8		6	
36			3	4		9	9*		6	12	9	S	2	10	11	7	8	5	6	
37	1		3	4	4	9			9			S	2	10	11	7	8	5	6	
38			3	10	4	9	9*		9		10		2*	7	11	7	8	5	6	
39	1		3	7*		9		9*	9		10	12	2	12	11		8	5	6	
40			3	S		9			9		10	7	2	12	11		8	5	6	
41			3	8					9	12	10	7*	2	7	11		8	5	6	
42			3	S		9			9		10	8	2	12	11	7	8	5	6	
43			3	12	4				9		10	11	2	10	10	7	8	5*	6	
44			3	11					9*		8	12	2	8	11	7	8	5*	6	
45	1		3	10	5		9				10	8	2	4	11	9	12	5	6	
46	1		3	12	5		9				10	10	2	4	11	8*	6	6	6	1

460

F.A.Cup

1st	21 Nov	WIMBLEDON	3-1	2-1	0-1	5919	Hall Garwood Moss
2nd	12 Dec	Wigan Athletic	1-2	0-1	17300	Moss	

Football League Cup

1st	19 Aug	Watford	0-2	0-2	9757	Moss

	1	2	3	4	5	6	S	8	9	10	4	7*	27	44	19	40	28	29	15	17	7
League Appearances	39	4	44	23	21	44	13	17	39	10	4	28	27	44	19	40	28	29	15	17	7
League Sub. Appear.		1		4			3	1		1	1	1	6	3	5	1	1				
League Sub. non-Appear.			2			3		6			5	2	1	1	2	1	1				
(2 O.G.) League Goals				2	2	1	6		10		2	2	2	2	11	10	17	1	1		
Cup Appearances	3	1	3	1	2	3			3		3	2	2	2	2	1	2	1			
Cup Sub. Appear.																					
Cup Sub. non-Appear.		1					1							1							
Cup Goals							1		1								2	1			

(Back) Walker, Moss, Conny, Turpie, Price, Robson, Kwiatkowski, Hails.
(2nd Row) Wright, Drewery, Dighton, Turner, ?, ?, Duncliffe.
(3rd Row) Preston, Hall, Noble, Wile, Garwood, Pleat, Iley. (Sitting) Apprentices.

DIVISION 4

	P	W	D	L	F	A	W	D	L	F	A	Pts
Notts Co	46	19	4	0	59	12	11	5	7	30	24	69
Bournemouth	46	16	5	2	51	15	8	7	8	31	34	60
Oldham A	46	14	6	3	57	29	10	5	8	31	34	59
York C	46	16	6	1	45	14	7	4	12	33	40	56
Chester	46	17	2	4	42	18	7	5	11	27	37	55
Colchester U	46	14	6	3	44	19	7	6	10	26	35	54
Northampton T	46	15	4	4	39	24	4	9	10	24	35	51
Southport	46	15	2	6	42	24	6	4	13	21	33	48
Exeter C	46	12	7	4	40	23	5	7	11	27	45	48
Workington	46	13	7	3	28	13	5	5	13	20	36	48
Stockport Co	46	12	8	3	28	17	4	6	13	21	48	46
Darlington	46	15	3	5	42	22	2	8	13	16	35	45
Aldershot	46	8	10	5	32	23	6	7	10	34	48	45
Brentford	46	13	7	3	45	27	5	5	13	21	35	44
Crewe A	46	13	1	9	49	35	5	5	11	26	41	44
Peterboro U	46	13	6	4	46	23	4	4	15	24	48	43
Scunthorpe U	46	9	7	7	36	23	6	6	11	20	38	43
Southend U	46	8	11	4	32	24	6	4	13	21	42	43
Grimsby T	46	13	6	4	37	26	5	3	15	20	45	43
Cambridge U	46	9	9	5	31	27	6	4	13	20	39	43
Lincoln C	46	11	4	8	45	33	4	7	11	24	45	41
Newport Co	46	8	3	12	32	36	5	2	16	23	49	28
Hartlepool	46	6	10	7	28	27	2	2	19	6	47	28
Barrow	46	5	5	13	25	38	2	3	18	26	52	22

Season Summary

Manager Iley signs a three year contract with Club. Posh lose in F.A.Cup at Wigan Athletic – their first defeat to a non-League side since joining the League. At the end of the season David Pleat moves on to manage Nuneaton, and a poor playing season finishes with a lowly placing in the 4th division.

SEASON 1971/72

Football League Division 4

Match details

506	Date	Opposition	Res	H.T.	Attend	Goalscorer
1	14 Aug	SOUTHEND UNITED	2-0	0-0	4557	Price 2
2	21	Newport County	1-1	0-1	3963	Hall
3	28	STOCKPORT COUNTY	4-2	1-1	4934	Conmy 2 Robson 2
4	30	BURY	2-0	1-0	6898	Price Conmy
5	4 Sep	Exeter City	2-3	0-0	4125	Price 2
6	11	SCUNTHORPE UNITED	0-1	0-0	6387	
7	18	Brentford	1-5	1-1	8770	Price
8	25	GILLINGHAM	2-1	1-0	4917	Price 2
9	27	Hartlepool	0-1	0-1	3460	
10	2 Oct	Workington	1-4	0-2	2242	Hall
11	9	BARROW	7-0	5-0	4681	Price 3 Hall 3 Conmy
12	15	Southend United	1-2	1-1	10695	Price
13	18	DARLINGTON	1-3	1-1	4350	Price
14	23	Lincoln City	2-3	1-2	6784	Robson Barker
15	30	CREWE ALEXANDRA	2-0	1-0	4516	Oakes Price
16	6 Nov	Aldershot	1-1	0-0	4912	Price
17	13	CHESTER	2-0	1-0	4659	Hall Price
18	27	SOUTHPORT	2-0	1-0	4958	Hall Barker
19	4 Dec	Doncaster Rovers	2-3	1-1	3258	Price Conmy
20	18	EXETER CITY	3-3	0-0	5341	Moss Price Robson
21	27	Colchester United	1-1	0-0	7750	Hall
22	1 Jan	BRENTFORD	2-2	1-2	7013	Price Darrell
23	7	Stockport County	0-0	0-0	2218	
24	22	HARTLEPOOL	2-2	1-0	4516	Turner Barker
25	29	Darlington	1-1	1-0	2065	Price
26	5 Feb	Northampton	1-1	0-1	5186	Hall
27	12	LINCOLN CITY	4-4	1-2	6601	Price Robson Barker O.G.
28	19	Crewe Alexandra	0-2	0-1	1620	
29	26	ALDERSHOT	0-0	0-0	4395	
30	4 Mar	Chester	1-1	0-1	1868	Hall
31	9	CAMBRIDGE UNITED	2-0	1-0	4947	Oakes Barker
32	11	Barrow	2-0	1-0	2658	Turpie O.G.
33	15	Reading	1-2	0-1	5886	Hall
34	18	NEWPORT COUNTY	3-1	2-0	4025	Darrell Hall Price
35	25	Scunthorpe United	0-2	0-0	5555	
36	27	GRIMSBY TOWN	0-2	0-0	4961	
37	1 Apr	COLCHESTER UNITED	4-0	3-0	4367	Hall Robson 2 Barker Price
38	3	Gillingham	1-1	1-0	4218	Barker
39	4	WORKINGTON	1-0	0-0	4050	Darrell
40	8	NORTHAMPTON	1-0	1-0	5480	Price
41	15	Southport	4-2	3-0	1713	Price 4
42	19	Cambridge United	5-2	1-1	4248	Hall Robson 2 Barker 2
43	22	DONCASTER ROVERS	2-0	1-0	4727	Turner Robson
44	25	Bury	1-1	0-0	3427	Hall
45	29	Grimsby Town	2-3	2-2	14143	Hall Turpie
46	1 May	READING	3-2	2-1	5749	Darrell Conmy O.G.

Player appearances (shirt numbers; S = substitute)

No	Drewery	Noble	Duncliffe	Oakes	Brookes	Carmichael	Moss	Price	Hall	Conmy	Robson	Darrell	Turner	Iley	Barker	Dighton	Wright	Turpie	Stenson	Kwiatkowski	Russell
1	1	2	3	4	5	6	7	8	9	10	11	S									
2	1	2	3	4	5	6	7	8	9	10	S	11									
3	1	2	3	4	5	6	7	8	9	10	11	S									
4	1	2	3	4	5	6	7	8	9*	10	11	12									
5	1	2	3	4	5	6	7	8	9*	10	11	S									
6	1	2	3	4	5	6	7	8	9	10	11	S									
7	1	2		4	3	6	7	8	9	10	S			11							
8	1	2	3	4		6	7	8	9	11	12		5		10*						
9	1*	2	3	4		6	7	8	9	11	12		5		10						
10	1	2	3	4	11	6		8	9	7	12		5*		10						
11	1	2	3	4		6	12	8	9*	7	11				10		5				
12	1	2	3	4		6		8	9	7	11		S		10		5				
13	1	2	3	4		6	12	8	9	7	11*				10		5				
14	1	2	3	4			S	8	9	7	11	12	5		10		6				
15	1	2	3	4			7	8		10*	11		5		9		6				
16	1	2	3	4				8	9	7	11		5		10		6	S			
17	1	2	3	4				8	9	7	11		5		10		6				
18	1	2	3	4					9*	8	11		5		10		6				
19	1	2	3	4			12	8	9	7*	11		5		10		6				
20	1	2	3	4			7	8	9		11		5				6				
21	1	2	3	4			S	8	9		11	10	5		7		6				
22	1	2	3	4			S	8	9		11	10	5		7		6				
23	1	2	3	4			S	8	9	10	11		5				6				
24	1	2	3	4			7	8			12	S	5		9		6		10		
25	1	2	3	4			12	8	9		11		5		7		6		10*		
26	1	2	3*	4			12	8	9	10	11		5		7		6				
27	1	2*	3*	4			7	8		10	11	12	5		9		6				
28	1	2	3	4			7*	8		10	12		5		9		6				
29	1	2	3	4			7	8		10*	12		5		9		6				
30	1	2	3	4		6	7	8	10		11	S	5		9						
31	1	2	3	4		6			10		11	S	5		8			10			
32	1	2	3	4		6	12	9			11	7	5		8			10			S
33	1	2	3*	4		6		9	10		11	7	5					S			
34	1	2	3	4				9	10		11	6	5		8						7
35	1	2	3	4		6		9	10	S	11		5		8						S
36	1	2	3	4		6		9	10		11		5		8						
37	1	2	3	4		6		9	10		11	S	5		8						
38	1	2	3	4		6		9	10		11	7	5		8						
39	1	2	3			6		9	10		11	7	5		8*					4	
40	1	2	3			6		9	10		11	7	5		8*					4	
41	1	2	3	4		6		9	10		11	7	5		8						
42	1	2	3	4				9	10		11	7	5		8					6	
43	1	2	3	4					10		11	7	5		9			S		6	
44	1	2	3	4		6			10	8	11	7	5		9			S		S	
45	1	2	3	4		6		9	9*	8	11	7	5					10			
46	1	2	3	4		6		9		8	11	7	5					10			12

F.A.Cup

Rnd	Date	Opponent			Att	Scorers	Line-up
1st	20 Nov	Redditch United	1-1	1-0	4500	Price	4 3 2 · 5 · 8 9 7 11 · 5 10 6
1/R	22	REDDITCH UNITED	6-0	4-0	5108	Price Hall 2 Robson Barker 2	4 3 2 · 5 · 8 9 7 11 · 5 10 6
2nd	11 Dec	ENFIELD	4-0	2-0	7702	Price 2 Hall 2	4* 3 2 · 5 · 8 9 7 11 · 5 10 6
3rd	15 Jan	IPSWICH TOWN	0-2	0-1	16970	Conmy	4 3 2 · 5 · 7* 8 10 11 12 · 5 9 6

Football League Cup

Rnd	Date	Opponent			Att	Scorers	Line-up
1st	17 Aug	Charlton Athletic	1-5	1-2	7080	Conmy	1 2 3 4 5 6 7 8 9 10 11 S

Appearances / Goals

League Appearances	45	34	31	44	18	46	17	39	41	28	40	20	35	1	36	1	20	4	2	3	1
League Sub. Appear.					1		9				5	2	6	5			4	5		1	
League Sub. non-Appear.							4				5	2	5	4							1
(3 O.G.) League Goals		2		2				28	5	3	6	9			9	4				5	2
Cup Appearances	5	1	5	5	5	5	2	5		3	5	5	1		4		4	4			
Cup Sub. Appear.							1				1			1							
Cup Sub. non-Appear.		1					2														
Cup Goals								4	4			1	1								2

DIVISION 4

	P	W	D	L	F	A	W	D	L	F	A	Pts
Grimsby T	46	18	3	3	61	26	10	4	9	27	30	63
Southend U	46	18	2	3	56	26	6	10	7	25	29	60
Brentford	46	16	2	5	52	21	8	9	6	24	23	59
Scunthorpe U	46	13	8	2	34	15	9	5	9	22	22	57
Lincoln C	46	17	5	1	46	15	4	9	10	31	44	56
Workington	46	12	9	2	34	7	4	10	9	16	27	51
Southport	46	15	5	3	48	21	3	9	11	18	25	50
Peterboro' U	46	14	6	3	51	24	3	10	10	31	40	50
Bury	46	16	4	3	55	22	3	8	12	18	37	50
Cambridge U	46	11	8	4	38	22	6	6	11	24	38	48
Colchester U	46	13	6	4	38	23	6	4	13	32	46	48
Doncaster R	46	11	8	4	35	24	5	6	12	21	39	46
Gillingham	46	11	5	7	33	24	5	8	10	28	43	45
Newport Co	46	13	5	5	34	20	5	5	15	26	52	44
Exeter C	46	11	5	7	40	30	5	6	12	21	38	43
Reading	46	14	3	6	37	26	3	5	15	19	50	42
Aldershot	46	5	13	5	27	20	4	9	10	21	34	40
Hartlepool	46	14	2	7	39	25	2	5	16	19	44	40
Darlington	46	9	9	5	37	24	5	2	16	27	58	39
Chester	46	10	11	2	34	16	0	7	16	13	40	38
Northampton T	46	8	9	6	43	27	4	4	15	23	52	37
Barrow	46	8	8	7	23	26	5	3	15	17	45	37
Stockport Co	46	7	10	6	33	32	2	4	17	22	55	32
Crewe A	46	9	4	10	27	25	1	5	17	16	44	29

(Back) Brookes, Price, Dighton, Turner, Wright, Drewery, Hall, Oakes.
(Middle) Moss, Noble, Duncliffe, Iley, Turpie, Carmichael, Conmy.
(Front) Robson, Darrell, Garwood, Kwiatkowski.

Season Summary

No giant-killing this season after Posh lose at home to Ipswich. Segregation for 'home' and 'away' fans comes to London Road. A poor run leads to discontent amongst fans with Manager Iley, but a good run in April restores their faith. Posh finish the season in 8th place, and score their most goals since the 1964/65 campaign.

SEASON 1972/73

Football League Division 4

562	Date	Opposition	Res	H.T.	Attend	Goalscorer
1	12 Aug	Stockport County	2-3	1-2	3379	Hall Robson
2	19	SOUTHPORT	0-1	0-0	3978	
3	26	Chester	2-8	1-2	3163	Turner Hall
4	28	NORTHAMPTON TOWN	1-2	0-0	3627	Smith
5	2 Sep	BRADFORD CITY	3-0	1-0	2457	Smith Hall Robson
6	9	Reading	0-2	0-1	3578	
7	16	TORQUAY UNITED	0-1	0-0	2875	
8	19	Newport County	1-1	1-0	3013	Hall
9	23	Cambridge United	1-3	1-1	4378	Oakes D.
10	25	BURY	1-1	1-1	2345	Hall
11	30	LINCOLN CITY	2-2	0-2	4766	Hall 2
12	7 Oct	Barnsley	2-3	2-2	2479	Turner Darrell
13	9	Mansfield Town	2-4	1-1	5379	Park Hall
14	14	DONCASTER ROVERS	3-1	1-0	4134	Smith 2 Robson
15	21	Crewe Alexandra	2-0	2-0	1860	Hall Darrell
16	23	COLCHESTER UNITED	2-2	0-2	5648	Oakes D. Heath
17	28	HEREFORD UNITED	1-1	1-0	6196	Smith
18	4 Nov	Bury	1-3	0-3	2715	Smith
19	11	NEWPORT COUNTY	1-0	0-0	4480	Robson
20	25	HARTLEPOOL	3-0	2-0	4382	Brookes Oakes D. Hall
21	2 Dec	Darlington	2-2	1-2	1343	Heath Robson
22	16	WORKINGTON	2-1	0-0	4929	Turner Hall
23	23	Gillingham	0-2	0-1	2772	
24	26	CAMBRIDGE UNITED	1-1	0-1	7290	Couzens
25	30	Southport	1-2	1-0	3590	Couzens
26	6 Jan	CHESTER	2-2	2-0	3821	Turner Couzens
27	20	Bradford City	4-1	3-1	4203	Hall Couzens 3
28	27	READING	4-2	1-1	5442	Smith 2 Hall Young
29	3 Feb	MANSFIELD TOWN	1-0	0-0	7224	Couzens
30	10	Torquay United	0-1	0-1	2487	
31	12	Exeter City	1-1	0-0	5403	Russell
32	17	STOCKPORT COUNTY	2-3	1-3	5122	Turner Heath
33	23	Workington	2-2	1-2	1256	Young Robson
34	2 Mar	BARNSLEY	6-3	5-3	5083	Turner Couzens Hall 3 Robson
35	9	Doncaster Rovers	1-1	1-0	2633	Couzens
36	17	CREWE ALEXANDRA	4-3	0-2	4875	Heath Hall 3
37	19	ALDERSHOT	1-0	1-0	5982	Freestone
38	24	Hereford United	0-3	0-1	9515	
39	31	Hartlepool	1-0	1-0	2863	Hall
40	7 Apr	DARLINGTON	1-1	1-0	4764	Robson
41	9	Colchester United	0-1	0-0	2437	
42	14	Aldershot	1-2	1-0	5078	Hall
43	20	Lincoln City	0-1	0-1	5231	
44	21	EXETER CITY	1-1	0-1	4593	Turner
45	24	GILLINGHAM	0-1	0-1	4367	
46	28	Northampton Town	3-1	0-0	2441	Couzens Robson O.G.

Player appearance grid (shirt numbers; S = substitute, * = substituted):

#	Drewery	Brookes	Duncliffe	Oakes D.	Turner	Carmichael	Heath	Park	Smith	Hall	Robson	Darrell	Iley	Russell	Moss	Couzens	Young	Bradley	Freestone	Oakes K.	Burton
1	1	2	3	4	5	6	7	8	9	10	11	S									
2	1	2		3	5	6	7	8*	9	10	11	12	12	S							
3	1		3	2	5	6	7*	4	9	10	11		12								
4	1	2	3	4	5	6	7	12	9	10	11	8*									
5	1	2	3	4	5	6	7	8	9	10	11	11		S							
6	1	2	3	4	5	6	7	8	9	10	11	11		S							
7	1	2	3	8	5	4	7	8	9	10	11*	12									
8	1	2	3	8	5	4	7	S	9	9	11	6		12							
9	1	2	3	7*	5	4	8	10		9	11	7*		12							
10	1	2	3	5	5	6	12	10		9	11		4		7*						
11	1	2	3	4	5	6	7	10	9	10	11			8							
12	1	2	3	4	5	6	8	11	9*	10		10	12	S	7						
13	1	2	3	4	5	6	8	8		9	11	4		S	7						
14	1	2		4	5	6	7	8	9	10	11										
15	1	2		4	5	6	7	8	9	10	11	11		S	S						
16	1	2	3	4	5	6	7	8	9	10	11	11*			12						
17	1	2	3	4	5	6	7	8	9	10	11				S						
18	1	2	3	4	5	6	7	8	9	10	11	S			7						
19	1	2	3	4	5	6	7	8	9*	10	11	8		8	12						
20	1	2	3	4	5	6	7	12	9	10	11	8		8	12						
21	1		3	4	5	6	7*	12	11*	10	11*			8		9	12	2			
22	1		3	4	5	6	7*		11*	9	11*			S		8	10	2			
23	1			4	5	6	7			9	11			12		8	10	2			
24	1		3	4	5	6	7		S	9						8	10	2			
25	1		3	4	5	6	7		11	9				S		8	10	2			
26	1		3	4	5	6	7	12	11*	9				12		8	10	2			
27	1		3	4	5*	6	7		11	9						8	10	2			
28	1		3	4	5	6	7		11	9	12					8	10	2	S		
29	1		3	4	5	6	7		11*	9	11					8	10	2			
30	1		3	4	5	6	7			9	11					8	10	2			
31	1		3	4	5	6	7*			9	11	11		12		8	10	2			
32	1		3*	4	5	6	7			9	11	10		12		8	10	2			
33	1		3	4	5	6	7			9	11					8	10	2		S	
34	1		3	4*	5	6	7*			9	11	12				8	10	2			
35	1	2	3*	4	5	6	S			9	11					8	10		12	12	
36	1	2	3	4*	5	6	7			9	11					8	10				12
37	1		3	S	5	6	7			9	11*					8	10	2			4
38	1		3	12	5	6	7			9	11*					8	10	2			4
39	1		3	S	5	6	7			9	11					8	10	2			4
40	1		3	4	5	6	7			9	11			4		8	10*	2		S	
41	1		3	4	5	6	7			9	11					8	10	2		S	
42	1		3	4	5	6	7*			9	11					8	10	2		12	
43	1		3	4	5	6	S			9	11					8	10	2		7	
44	1		3*	4	5	6	7			9	11	12				8	10	2	8*	10	
45	1		3*	4	5	6	7			9	11	12				8	10	2		7	
46	1	3		4	5	6	7			9	11					8	10	2	S	S	

F.A.Cup

1st	18 Nov	NORTHAMPTON TOWN	1-0	0-0	7815	Hall
2nd	9 Dec	Bishop Stortford	2-2	2-0	6000	Couzens Robson
2/R	11	BISHOP STORTFORD	3-1	3-0	8966	Heath Hall Robson
3rd	13 Jan	DERBY COUNTY	0-1	0-1	22000	

F.A.Cup appearances:

1	2	3	4	5	6	10		12	9	11		8	7*
1	2	3	4	5	6	7		12	9	11		8	10
1	2	3	4	5	6	7			9	11	S	8	10
1	2	3	4	5	6	7			9	11	S	8	10
1		3	4	5	6	7		12	9	11*		8	10	2

Football League Cup

1st	16 Aug	Oxford United	0-4	0-0	5049	

Football League Cup appearances:

1	2	3	4	5	6	7	8	9	10	11	S
1	2	3	4	5	6	7	8	9	10	11	S

DIVISION 4

	P	W	D	L	F	A	W	D	L	F	A	Pts
Southport	46	17	4	2	40	19	9	6	8	31	29	62
Hereford U	46	18	4	1	39	12	6	5	10	17	26	58
Cambridge U	46	15	6	2	40	23	5	11	7	27	34	57
Aldershot	46	14	6	3	33	14	8	6	9	27	24	56
Newport Co	46	14	6	3	37	18	8	6	9	27	26	56
Mansfield T	46	15	7	1	52	17	5	11	7	26	34	54
Reading	46	14	7	2	33	7	3	11	9	18	31	52
Exeter C	46	14	8	2	40	18	5	6	12	17	33	50
Gillingham	46	15	4	4	44	20	4	7	12	19	38	49
Lincoln C	46	12	7	4	38	27	4	9	10	26	30	48
Stockport Co	46	14	7	2	38	18	4	5	14	15	35	48
Bury	46	11	7	5	37	19	3	11	9	21	32	46
Workington	46	15	7	1	44	20	2	5	16	15	41	46
Barnsley	46	9	8	6	32	24	5	8	10	26	36	44
Chester	46	11	6	6	40	19	4	9	11	21	33	43
Bradford C	46	12	6	5	42	25	4	5	14	19	40	43
Doncaster R	46	10	8	5	28	19	5	4	14	21	39	42
Torquay U	46	8	10	5	23	17	4	7	12	21	30	41
Peterboro' U	46	10	8	5	42	29	4	5	14	29	47	41
Hartlepool	46	8	10	5	17	15	4	7	12	17	34	41
Crewe A	46	7	8	8	18	23	2	10	11	20	38	36
Colchester U	46	8	8	7	36	28	2	3	18	12	48	31
Northampton T	46	7	6	10	24	30	3	5	15	16	43	31
Darlington	46	5	9	9	28	41	2	6	15	14	44	29

Season appearances:

League Appearances	46	23	45	40	46	46	43	15	22	46	35	12	6	3	24	24	23	2	2	3
League Sub. Appear.				1			1	3			1	4	1	7	2		1	1	2	1
League Sub. non-Appear.				2				2	1			2	7	2				1	3	
League Goals				3	7		4	1	8	21	9		1			10	2	3		1	1
Cup Appearances	5	4	5	5	5	5	5	1	1	5	5		1		3	3	1
Cup Sub. Appear.								2				1		2	
Cup Sub non-Appear.									2						
Cup Goals							1		2	2				1

(Back) Park, Turner, Smith, Russell, Brookes, Dighton, Drewery, Hall, Wade, Freestone, Heath. (Middle) Walker, Noble, D.Oakes, Duncliffe, Carmichael, Iley, Moss, Darrell, Robson, Hails. (Front) K.Oakes, Hill, Marshall, Reedman.

Season Summary

Season starts with acrimony between Supporters' and Football Clubs. A poor start sees the lowest ever League gate attend the first win of the season. Manager Iley resigns and is replaced temporarily by Walker, before Noel Cantwell arrives to take on the job. Violence at London Road for the F.A.Cup clash with Derby. A poor season, with Posh at one time at the foot of the table.

SEASON 1973/74

Football League Division 4

596

#	Date	Opposition	Res	H.T.	Attend	Goalscorer
1	25 Aug	MANSFIELD TOWN	2-1	1-1	7045	Lee Cozens
2	1 Sep	Stockport County	1-1	1-1	2836	Cozens
3	8	SCUNTHORPE UNITED	1-0	0-0	6399	Hill
4	12	Lincoln City	1-1	1-0	5863	Hall
5	15	Bradford City	1-1	1-1	3678	Cozens
6	17	DONCASTER ROVERS	5-1	2-0	6648	Hall 4 Robson
7	22	TORQUAY UNITED	1-1	0-0	7670	Hall
8	29	Reading	1-1	1-0	8228	Llewelyn
9	2 Oct	Doncaster Rovers	1-3	0-1	2383	Cozens
10	6	WORKINGTON	2-0	1-0	6161	Jones Hill
11	13	Brentford	1-0	0-0	6140	Robson
12	20	SWANSEA CITY	3-0	1-0	6686	Cozens Murrey O.G.
13	22	LINCOLN CITY	1-0	0-0	9125	Lee
14	27	Newport County	1-0	0-0	4327	Cozens
15	3 Nov	EXETER CITY	2-0	1-0	9641	Cozens Robson
16	10	Bury	2-0	0-0	5239	Turner Cozens
17	14	Crewe Alexandra	1-2	0-1	1863	Hill
18	17	NORTHAMPTON TOWN	3-0	1-0	10351	Hill 2 Hill
19	1 Dec	HARTLEPOOL	2-0	1-0	7537	Turner Cozens
20	8	Darlington	2-2	2-2	1543	Cozens 2
21	22	READING	2-0	0-0	7815	Walker Robson
22	26	Colchester United	1-1	0-0	7960	Hall
23	29	Scunthorpe United	1-2	0-2	5004	Murrey
24	1 Jan	STOCKPORT COUNTY	3-2	1-1	8272	Jones Cozens Hall
25	12	BRADFORD CITY	1-1	1-0	15461	Robson
26	20	Mansfield Town	1-2	1-0	6913	Llewelyn
27	2 Feb	CHESTER	0-0	0-0	7683	
28	16	BRENTFORD	1-0	1-0	7645	Hill
29	24	Workington	1-4	0-3	1525	Llewelyn
30	2 Mar	COLCHESTER UNITED	2-0	1-0	10714	Cozens Hall
31	9	NEWPORT COUNTY	2-0	2-0	7354	Murrey Hall
32	16	Swansea City	2-0	2-0	2536	Murrey Robson
33	20	Chester	1-2	1-2	1678	Murrey
34	23	BURY	2-2	1-1	8145	Murrey Robson
35	25	ROTHERHAM UNITED	2-0	1-0	7582	Murrey Robson
36	30	Exeter City	2-1	2-0	3592	Walker Cozens
37	3 Apr	Gillingham	0-1	0-0	12297	
38	6	CREWE ALEXANDRA	4-0	2-0	7250	Jones Murrey Cozens Hall
39	13	Northampton Town	1-0	0-0	11378	Murrey
40	15	BARNSLEY	3-0	1-0	10000	Turner O.G. Lewis
41	16	Barnsley	0-0	0-0	4617	
42	20	DARLINGTON	1-0	1-0	9207	Hill
43	27	Hartlepool	1-0	0-0	2291	Robson
44	1 May	GILLINGHAM	4-2	2-1	17569	Lee Turner Cozens 2
45	7	Torquay United	2-1	1-0	2551	Cozens 2
46	11	Rotherham United	1-3	0-1	3100	Lee

Squad shirt numbers are recorded per match in the accompanying grid with player columns (left to right): Drewery, Bradley, Lee, Jones, Turner, Llewelyn, Walker, Cozens, Hall, Hill, Robson, Oakes, Gregory, Carmichael, Murrey, McLachlan, Steele, Phillips, Lewis.

F.A.Cup

Rnd	Date	Opponent	Score	HT	1	2	3												Att	Scorers
1st	24 Nov	Colchester United	3-2	0-1	1	2	3	6	5					4*	9	10	11		12	7	9664	Cozens 2 Murray
2nd	15 Dec	Wycombe Wanderers	3-1	1-1	1	2	3	6	5			4	8	9	10	11	S		3	7	10200	Cozens 2 Hall
3rd	5 Jan	SOUTHEND UNITED	3-1	2-0	1	2	3	6*	5				8	9	10	11			12	7	11684	Cozens Hill Robson
4th	26	LEEDS UNITED	1-4	0-4	1	2	3	6	5				8	9*	10	11			12	7	28000	Cozens

Football League Cup

Rnd	Date	Opponent	Score	HT	1	2	3												Att	Scorers
1st	29 Aug	SCUNTHORPE UNITED	2-2	1-1	1	2	3	6	5		7	8	9	10*	11		4*	12		6339	Lee Robson
1/R	4 Sep	Scunthorpe United	1-2	0-0	1	2	3	6	5		4	8	9	10	11			12	7	4472	Jones

League Appearances	26	36	45	45	44	8		37	46	40	46	46	1	3	9	42		20	1	10
League Sub. Appear.						1							3	9	13			1		
League Sub. non-Appear.				4	2						6	6	6				
League Goals				3	4	3	2	4	19	13	6	9				9			1
Cup Appearances	6	6	6	6	6	2	4	6	6	6	6	6	1	1	5			
Cup Sub. Appear.												1		1	4			
Cup Sub. non-Appear.			1							1						
Cup Goals			1				6	1	1	2			1				

(Left to right) Lee, Walker P., Bradley, Carmichael, Oakes, Hall, Steele, Cozens, Drewery, Llewelyn, Hill, Jones, Turner, Murray, Gregory, Robson.

DIVISION 4

	P	W	D	L	F	A	W	D	L	F	A	Pts
Peterboro' U	46	19	4	0	49	10	8	7	8	26	28	65
Gillingham	46	16	5	2	51	16	9	7	7	39	33	62
Colchester U	46	16	5	2	46	14	6	8	9	22	22	60
Bury	46	18	3	2	51	14	6	8	9	30	35	59
Northampton T	46	14	7	2	39	14	6	11		24	34	53
Reading	46	11	9	3	37	13	5	10	8	21	24	51
Chester	46	13	6	4	31	19	4	9	10	23	36	49
Bradford C	46	14	7	2	45	20	3	7	13	13	32	48
Newport Co	46	13	6	4	39	23	3	8	12	17	42	*45
Exeter C	45	12	5	6	37	20	6	3	13	21	35	†44
Hartlepool	46	11	4	8	29	16	5	8	10	19	31	44
Lincoln C	46	10	8	5	40	30	4	6	13	23	37	44
Barnsley	46	15	5	3	42	16	2	5	16	16	48	44
Swansea C	46	11	6	6	28	15	5	5	13	17	31	43
Rotherham U	46	10	9	4	33	22	5	4	14	23	36	43
Torquay U	46	11	7	5	37	23	2	10	11	15	34	43
Mansfield T	46	13	8	2	47	24	0	9	14	15	45	43
Scunthorpe U	45	12	7	3	33	17	2	5	16	14	47	†42
Brentford	46	9	7	7	31	20	3	9	11	17	30	40
Darlington	46	9	8	6	29	24	4	5	14	11	38	39
Crewe A	46	11	5	7	28	30	3	5	15	15	41	38
Doncaster R	46	10	7	6	32	22	2	4	17	15	58	35
Workington	46	10	8	5	33	26	1	5	17	10	48	35
Stockport Co	46	4	12	7	22	25	3	8	12	22	44	34

Season Summary

Clear-out of players and many new faces. Gates soar as Posh surge to the top of the table after seven consecutive victories. Leeds United end F.A.Cup hopes at London Road. Over 17,000 present for Championship decider with Gillingham. Posh become 4th Division Champions for the second time. Trophy presented at end of season benefit match.

SEASON 1974/75

Football League Division 3

644	Date	Opposition	Res	H.T.	Attend	Goalscorer	Steele	Bradley	Lee	Walker	Turner	Jones	Murrey	Cozens	Hall	Hill	Robson	Gregory	Carmichael	Price P.	Nixon	Galley	Hodson	Oakes	Llewelyn	Price D.	Winfield
1	17 Aug	Huddersfield Town	2-1	0-0	7334	Cozens Hall	1	2	3	4	5	6	7	8	9*	10	11	12									
2	24	BRIGHTON & H.A.	2-0	0-0	9324	Turner Hall	1	2	3	4	5	6	7	8	9	10	11	S									
3	31	Hereford United	0-2	0-1	7315		1	2	3	4	5	6*	7	8	9	10	11		12								
4	7 Sep	WREXHAM	2-1	1-1	7601	Hall Robson	1	2	3	4	5	6	7	8*	9	10	11	12									
5	14	Grimsby Town	2-1	0-0	6379	Turner 2	1	2	3	12	5	6	7	8	9	10	11		4								
6	21	PRESTON NORTH END	0-0	0-0	13120		1	2	3	4	5	6	7	8	9	10	11			S	12						
7	25	HALIFAX TOWN	1-1	1-0	8156	Robson	1	2	3*	4	5		7		9*	10	11	8	6		12						
8	28	Gillingham	1-1	0-0	6635	Walker	1	2		4	5		7			10	11	12	6	9	8						
9	2 Oct	SOUTHEND UNITED	1-0	1-0	8460	Gregory	1	2		4	5	6	3			10	11	12		9	8						
10	5	Charlton Athletic	0-3	0-1	6646		1	2		4	5	6	3			10*	11	8	10	S	7						
11	7	Southend United	2-1	1-1	5730	Lee Robson	1	2	3	4	5	6	7		9		11		10		8						
12	12	WATFORD	1-0	0-0	9747	O.G.	1	2	3	4	5		7			10	11	12	6		8*	9					
13	16	BURY	3-1	2-0	8558	Turner Robson Nixon	1	2	3	4	5		7			10	11	12	6		8	9					
14	19	Plymouth Argyle	0-2	0-1	6843		1	2*		4	5	12	7			10*	11		6		8	9					
15	26	ALDERSHOT	1-1	1-0	8558	Lee	1		3	4	5	12	7			10	11		6		7	9					
16	2 Nov	Crystal Palace	1-1	1-0	18226	Galley	1		3	4	5	6	2			10	11		6		8	9					
17	5	Bury	0-3	0-3	4663		1	2	3	4	5		7	9		10	11		6		8						
18	9	BLACKBURN ROVERS	1-0	1-0	11670	Hill	1	2	3	4	5		7	9		10	11*		6		8						
19	16	Chesterfield	0-2	0-0	5330		1		3	8	5	6	2	9		10*	12	4	6		7						
20	30	PORT VALE	0-2	0-1	7627		1		3	4	5		7	9		10*	11	6	6		10*			2			
21	7 Dec	Walsall	1-0	0-0	4208	Gregory	1	S	3	4	5		7	9		10	11	10	6						2		
22	21	Swindon Town	1-0	1-0	9023	O.G.	1	2	3	4	5	8	7	8		S		10	6		9				11		
23	26	GRIMSBY TOWN	1-3	0-2	10163	Turner	1	2		4	5	3	7	11*		12		10	6		9				6		
24	28	Colchester United	1-4	0-3	7790	Turner	1	2	3	4	5	6	7*	8			12	10	6		9				11		
25	11 Jan	WALSALL	0-0	0-0	8671		1	2	3	4*	5		7			10*	12	8	6		9						
26	18	Port Vale	3-1	1-0	4979	Gregory 2 Nixon	1	2	3	4	5		7			10*	11	10	6		9			12			
27	1 Feb	Blackburn Rovers	1-0	1-0	12323	Lee	1	2	3	4	5		7			S	11	10	6		8				9		
28	8	CRYSTAL PALACE	1-1	0-1	11698	Turner	1	2	3	4	5		7			S	12	10	6		9						
29	22	CHESTERFIELD	0-2	0-1	8599		1	2	3	4	5		7*			11	11	9	6		9			12			
30	1 Mar	HEREFORD UNITED	1-1	0-1	7109	Lee	1	2	3	4	5		S			10	11	10	6		7		8				
31	8	Halifax Town	1-2	1-2	2322	Price D.	1	2	3	4	5		7			S		12	6		9	12					
32	15	GILLINGHAM	0-0	0-0	6389		1	2		4	5		7			S		8	6		11						
33	19	HUDDERSFIELD TOWN	2-1	0-0	4894	Nixon Robson	1	2		4	5		7			S	11	8	6*		10		12			3	
34	22	Wrexham	2-1	0-0	3168	Gregory 2	1	2		4	5		7				11	6*	6		10					3	
35	28	COLCHESTER UNITED	1-0	0-0	7559	Gregory	1	2		4	5		7				11	8	6*		10		12			3	
36	29	SWINDON TOWN	0-0	0-0	7364		1	2		4	5		7				11	8	6		10		S			3	
37	1 Apr	Preston North End	1-1	0-1	6547	Turner	1	2	3*	4	5		7			11	11	8	6		10		9			3	
38	5	Aldershot	0-5	0-3	4141		1	2		4	5		7			9	11	6	6		10		8	12		3	
39	9	Tranmere Rovers	0-1	0-1	1264		1	2		5*	5		7			10	11	8	6*		10		9	9	12	3	
40	12	CHARLTON ATHLETIC	1-1	1-1	7674	Gregory	1	2		4	5		11			10	11	8	6		10		12			3	
41	16	A.F.C. BOURNEMOUTH	3-0	1-0	4580	Nixon 2 Hall	1		2	4*			4		9	10	11	8	6*		7		6			3	
42	19	Watford	3-0	1-0	5788	Robson 3	1			12			2		9	10	11	8			7		4*			3	
43	23	Brighton & H.A.	0-2	0-1	11509		1	2					4		9	10	11	8			7		12			3	
44	26	PLYMOUTH ARGYLE	1-0	1-0	11176	Robson	1	2	3	S			4		9	10	11	8			7		6			3	
45	30	TRANMERE ROVERS	1-2	1-1	5306	Hall	1	2*	3	12			4		9	10	11	8			7		6			3	
46	5 May	A.F.C. Bournemouth	1-2	0-0	4869	Gregory	1	2	3				4		9	10	11	8			7		S			3	

**PETERBOROUGH UNITED
DIVISION 3 (1974-75)**

Back row (left to right) John Musgrave, David Gregory, Peter Price, Keith Oakes, David Llewellyn, Jack Carmichael, Stuart Hodson.
Middle row — Keith Bradley, Jim Hall, Chris Turner, Eric Steele, Alan Welsh, John Watfield, Mick Jones, Freddie Hill.
Sitting — Noel Cantwell (manager), Bert Murray, Paul Walker, John Cozens (captain), Jeff Lee, Tommy Robson, John Barnett son.
In front — Jeff Lissaman, Peter Barnett.

F.A.Cup

						1	2	3	4*	5		7		9	10	11	8	6		12		
1st	23 Nov	WEYMOUTH	0-0	0-0	8984	1	2	3	4*	5		7		9		11	8	6		12		
1/R.	4 Dec	Weymouth	3-3*	1-1	4009	1	2		4	5	6	7			10	11*	8	10		12	3	9
1/2R	9	WEYMOUTH	3-0	0-0	9077	Turner Gregory Llewelyn																
2nd	14	CHARLTON ATHLETIC	3-0	2-0	9642	1	2	3	4	5		7			12	11*	8	2		9	6	9
3rd	4 Jan	TRANMERE ROVERS	1-0	0-0	9962	1	2	3	4	5		7		12	10*	11	8	6		9		
4th	25	Stafford Rangers	2-1	2-1	31160†	1	2	3	4	5		7			10*	11	8	6		9	12	
5th	15 Feb	MIDDLESBROUGH	1-1	1-0	25750	1	2	3	S	5		7			4	11	8	6		9		10
5/R.	18	Middlesbrough	0-2	0-1	34303	1	2*	3	12	5		7			4	11	8	6		9		10

Scorers: Turner Gregory Llewelyn; Turner Gregory 2; Murrey Gregory Nixon; Bradley; Gregory Nixon; Nixon

Football League Cup

						1	2	3	4	5	6	7	8	9	10	11	S
1st	20 Aug	Charlton Athletic	0-4	0-2	5871	1	2	3	4	5	6	7	8	9	10	11	S

* After extra time (2-2 at 90 mins.) † Played at

	46	38	31	38	46	15	45	4	25	27	36	35	33	2	38	7	11	9	3	6	11
League Appearances	46	38	31	38	46	15	45	4	25	27	36	35	33	2	38	7	11	9	3	6	11
League Sub. Appear.			1	3		1			1	2	3	6	2		1	1	7	2	1		
League Sub. non-Appear.	1		1	1	1		1	1	3	2	2	4		2		1	1	2			
(2 O.G.) League Goals	9	8	4	7	8		9		5	1	9	9			5	1			3		1
Cup Appearances		8	8	7	9	2	9	1	2	7	9	8	8		5			3	2	2	
Cup Sub. Appear.									1						3			1			
Cup Sub. non-Appear.	1			1							1	1									
Cup Goals			·		2		1				2	5			3			2	1		

DIVISION 3

	P	W	D	L	F	A	W	D	L	F	A	Pts
Blackburn R	46	15	7	1	40	16	7	9	7	28	29	60
Plymouth A	46	16	5	2	38	19	8	6	9	41	39	59
Charlton A	46	15	5	3	51	29	7	6	10	25	32	55
Swindon T	46	18	3	2	43	17	3	8	12	21	41	53
Crystal P	46	14	8	1	48	22	4	7	12	18	35	51
Port Vale	46	15	6	2	37	19	3	9	11	23	36	51
Peterboro' U	46	10	9	4	24	17	9	3	11	23	36	50
Walsall	46	15	5	5	42	19	3	8	12	21	39	49
Preston NE	46	16	5	2	42	19	3	6	14	21	37	49
Gillingham	46	14	6	3	23	22	3	8	12	22	37	48
Colchester U	46	13	7	3	45	22	4	6	13	25	41	47
Hereford U	46	14	6	3	42	21	2	8	13	22	45	46
Wrexham	46	10	8	5	41	23	5	7	11	24	32	45
Bury	46	13	6	4	38	17	3	6	14	15	33	44
Chesterfield	46	11	7	5	37	25	5	5	13	41	44	
Grimsby T	46	12	8	3	35	19	3	5	15	20	45	43
Halifax T	46	11	10	2	33	20	2	7	14	16	45	43
Southend U	46	11	9	3	42	17	2	7	14	14	34	42
Brighton & HA	46	14	7	2	38	21	2	3	18	18	43	42
Aldershot	46	13	5	5	40	21	1	6	16	13	42	*38
Bournemouth	46	9	6	8	27	25	4	6	13	17	33	38
Tranmere R	46	12	4	7	39	21	2	5	16	16	36	37
Watford	46	9	7	7	30	31	1	10	12	22	44	37
Huddersfield T	46	6	8	9	32	29	2	4	17	15	47	32

Season Summary

Season starts with Texaco Cup matches. Steady start leads to early top of table position. F.A.Cup runs includes defeat of two non-league teams before final exit at Middlesbrough. Bad scenes of violence at Plymouth match. A late surge, but insufficient to earn a second successive promotion.

Football League Division 3

#	Date	Opposition	Res	H.T.	Attend	Goalscorer	Steele	Bradley	Lee	Eustace	Oakes	Murrey	Nixon	Gregory	McCormick	Hughes	Robson	Carmichael	Turner	Cozens	Hodson	Merrick	Telford	Jones	Walker	Rogers	Moss	Heeley
1	16 Aug	WALSALL	0-0	0-0	7174		1	2	3	4*	5	6	7	8	9	10	11	12										
2	23	Shrewsbury Town	1-3	0-1	4473	Nixon	1	2	3	4	6		7	9		11	S	10	5	8					12			
3	30	PORT VALE	0-0	0-0	6065		1	S	3	4	5	2	7	8		10	11	6			9				S			
4	6 Sep	Chesterfield	1-1	0-1	2750	Nixon	1	12	3	4	5	2	7	8		10	11	6			9							
5	13	ALDERSHOT	1-1	0-0	6201	Telford	1		3	4		2	7	8		10	11	6				9*	12		S			
6	20	Chester	1-1	0-1	4063	Robson	1		3		5	2	7	8		4	11	6				9	10*	12				
7	24	WREXHAM	2-0	1-0	5888	Gregory Robson	1		3		5	2	7	8		10	11*	6			12	9		5				
8	27	ROTHERHAM UNITED	1-3	1-0	6543	Telford	1		3	12		2	7*	8		4	11	5				10	9	6				
9	4 Oct	Sheffield Wed.	2-2	1-1	11412	Gregory Jones	1		3			2	7	8		10	11*	6				9	12	5				
10	11	Mansfield Town	1-1	1-0	6983	Turner	1		3	4		2	7	8		10	11	6	9					5				
11	18	BURY	4-0	2-0	7271	Robson 3 Turner	1		3	4		2	7	8		10	11*	6	9					5				
12	21	Preston North End	1-2	0-1	9597	Robson	1		3	4		2	7	8		10	11	6	9					5				
13	25	Hereford United	4-2	1-1	8471	Nixon Gregory Turner 2	1		3	2		4	7	8		10	11	6	9					5				
14	1 Nov	BRIGHTON & H.A.	4-2	1-1	8630	Gregory	1		3	4*		2	7	8		10	11	5	9					6				
15	4	GRIMSBY TOWN	4-2	2-1	7646	Nixon Gregory 3	1		3	4		2	7	8*		10	11	6	S	9				5				
16	8	Crystal Palace	1-1	0-1	19000	Robson	1		3*	4		2	7	8		10	11	6		9				5	12			
17	15	SWINDON TOWN	3-1	3-1	7287	Eustace Robson 2	1	2		4		3	7	8		10	11	6		9				S				
18	29	SOUTHEND UNITED	3-2	1-1	7393	Eustace Nixon Robson	1		3	4		2	7	8		10	11	6		9				12				
19	6 Dec	Halifax Town	1-0	1-0	2289	Murrey	1		3	4		2	7	8*		10	11	6		9				12				
20	20	Gillingham	2-2	1-2	4086	Eustace Robson	1		3	4		2	7	8		10	S	6						9				
21	26	MILLWALL	1-1	1-1	10653	Eustace Robson	1		3	4		2	7	8		10	11	6		9				12				
22	27	Cardiff City	2-5	1-1	16094	Gregory Hughes	1		3	4		2	7*	8		10	11	6		9				S				
23	10 Jan	Port Vale	0-2	0-1	3892		1	2		4*		3	7	8		10	11	6		9					12			
24	14	COLCHESTER UNITED	3-1	1-0	7453	Gregory Hughes Turner	1		12	4		2	7	8		10	S	6	9						3	7		
25	17	CHESTER	3-0	1-0	8674	Robson Cozens O.G.	1		12	4		2	7	8		10	11	6	9		S				3	7		
26	31	PRESTON NORTH END	2-0	1-0	7728	Moss 2	1		2	4	5		7	8		10	11	6	7						3		9	
27	7 Feb	Grimsby Town	1-1	1-1	5482	Hughes	1			4	5	8*	7	8			11	6	7	S				11			10	
28	18	CRYSTAL PALACE	2-0	1-0	13308	Eustace Robson	1		3	4		2	12	8*		12	11	6	7	11					3			
29	21	Swindon Town	3-0	2-0	7477	Eustace Gregory Moss	1		3	4		2	7	8		10	S	6	7					S	3		9	
30	23	Wrexham	0-3	0-1	3640		1	12	3	4		3	7	8		10	11	6						S			9	
31	27	HEREFORD UNITED	0-3	0-2	14106		1	12	3	4		2	7	8		10	11	6	11		2				3	7	9	
32	6 Mar	Brighton & H.A.	0-5	0-2	16398		1	2	3	4		7	12	8		10	11	6	8	4					3	7	9	
33	10	SHEFFIELD WED.	2-2	1-1	8209	Nixon Oakes	1		3	4	5	2	7	8		10*	11	6	5*	7	10				3	9*		
34	13	MANSFIELD TOWN	0-3	0-1	7497		1			4	5	2	7	8		10	12	6	7	7	2				3	9		
35	16	Bury	1-2	0-1	4493	Gregory	1		3					8			12	6		2*			5			11	9	
36	19	Southend United	0-0	0-0	4651		1		3		S			8		10	11	6	9*	2			5		3		9	
37	24	Aldershot	0-1	0-1	3001		1		3					7		10	11	6					5			9	8	
38	27	HALIFAX TOWN	1-0	1-0	4933	Moss	1	3	3				11	8		10	11	6	11		2		5	5	3	9	9	
39	31	GILLINGHAM	1-1	1-1	4594	Cozens	1	3	3					8		10	11*	6	8		4		12	5	3	9	9	
40	3 Apr	Walsall	2-2	1-2	6266	Gregory Hughes	1	2						8		10*	11*	6	7		4		12	5	3	9*	9	
41	6	Rotherham United	1-1	1-0	3872	Moss	1			4				8		10	11	6	7	4*	2		11	5	11	9	9	
42	10	CHESTERFIELD	0-1	0-0	5830		1		4	4				8		10	12	6	7		2*		11	12	12	9	9	
43	16	Colchester United	1-1	0-1	3687	O.G.	1		12*	4			8	7		10	10	6*	8		2		11	11	12	9	9	
44	17	Millwall	0-2	0-2	11377		1		3	4			7	7		10	11	6					11	11	12	9	9	
45	19	CARDIFF CITY	0-0	0-0	6646		1	3	3	2		8	7	8		11	10	6	7	4*			11	11	2	12	9	
46	24	SHREWSBURY TOWN	3-2	3-1	5023	Gregory 2 Moss	1	3	3	4			8	7		10*	10*	6	8	2	2		11	11	3	9	9	12

F.A. Cup

					Scorers
1st	22 Nov	WINSFORD UNITED	4-1	8324	Gregory Nixon Turner Cozens
2nd	13 Dec	Coventry Sporting	4-0	8556	Nixon Hughes Jones O.G.
3rd	1 Jan	Nottm. Forest	0-0	31525	
3/R	7	NOTTM. FOREST	1-0	17866	Nixon
4th	24	Manchester United	1-3	56352	Cozens

Football League Cup

					Scorers
1/1L	20 Aug	Southend United	0-2	4684	
1/2L	27	SOUTHEND UNITED	3-0	4828	Robson Turner Cozens
2nd	10 Sep	BLACKPOOL	2-0	6987	Gregory Robson
3rd	8 Oct	Fulham	1-0	9805	Gregory
4th	11 Nov	Middlesbrough	0-3	17749	

DIVISION 3

	P	W	D	L	F	A	W	D	L	F	A	Pts
Hereford U	46	14	6	3	45	24	12	5	6	41	31	63
Cardiff C	46	14	7	2	38	13	8	6	9	31	35	57
Millwall	46	16	6	1	35	14	4	10	9	19	29	56
Brighton & HA	46	18	3	2	58	15	4	6	13	20	38	53
Crystal P	46	7	12	4	30	20	11	5	7	31	26	53
Wrexham	46	13	6	4	38	21	7	6	10	28	34	52
Walsall	46	11	8	4	43	22	7	6	10	31	39	50
Preston NE	46	15	4	4	45	23	4	6	13	17	34	48
Shrewsbury T	46	14	2	7	36	25	5	8	10	25	34	48
Peterboro' U	46	12	7	4	37	23	7	3	13	22	40	48
Mansfield T	46	8	11	4	31	22	8	4	11	27	30	47
Port Vale	46	11	4	8	33	21	5	6	12	22	33	46
Bury	46	11	7	5	33	16	3	9	11	18	30	44
Chesterfield	46	11	5	7	45	30	6	4	13	24	39	43
Gillingham	46	10	8	5	38	27	6	5	12	20	41	43
Rotherham U	46	11	6	6	35	22	4	6	13	19	43	42
Chester	46	13	7	3	34	19	2	5	16	19	43	42
Grimsby T	46	13	7	3	39	21	3	2	18	23	53	40
Swindon T	46	11	8	4	42	31	5	4	14	20	44	40
Sheffield W	46	12	6	5	34	25	0	10	13	14	34	40
Aldershot	46	10	8	5	34	26	3	5	15	25	49	39
Colchester U	46	9	6	8	27	23	3	8	12	16	38	38
Southend U	46	9	6	7	40	31	3	6	14	25	44	37
Halifax T	46	6	5	12	22	32	5	8	10	19	29	35

Appearance summary

League Appearances	46	9	30	42	9	36	33	46	1	42	39	45	31	21	11	5	3	22	13	1
League Sub. Appear.	3	1	1				2				3	1		1	1		1	5	7	4
League Sub. non-Appear.	2					1				2			1			2	1	5	3	
(2 O.G.) League Goals			5		1	1	6	14		4	13	5	3		2	1		4	2	
Cup Appearances	10	3	7	10	2	10	10	10	1	10	10	9	8	4	1	1		4	2	
Cup Sub. Appear.												1	2		1			1		
Cup Sub. non-Appear.													1	1				2	1	
(1 O.G.) Cup Goals			1			3	3			1	2	2	3	3	1			1		21

Back Row (left to right): Jack Carmichael, Lyndon Hughes, Keith Oakes, Mick Drewery, Eric Steele. Chris Turner, Mick Jones, Stuart Hodson.
Front Row (left to right): Keith Bradley, Jon Nixon, Bert Murray, David Gregory, John Cozens, Peter Eustace, Jeff Lee, Tommy Robson.

Season Summary

Season starts with winning of Tournament in Tunisia. Feature of early season results – draws! Run through to 4th round of League Cup with exit at Middlesborough – again! Forest beaten in F.A.Cup before Posh lose at Old Trafford in 4th round before 56,352.

Football League Division 3

736	Date	Opposition	Res	H.T.	Attend	Goalscorer
1	21 Aug	ROTHERHAM UNITED	0-2	0-1	6247	
2	28	Grimsby Town	2-2	1-1	4057	Gregory Robson
3	4 Sep	YORK CITY	3-0	2-0	6281	Lee Moss O.G.
4	11	Tranmere Rovers	0-2	0-1	2031	
5	14	READING	2-1	0-1	5406	Doyle O.G.
6	18	CRYSTAL PALACE	0-0	0-0	8489	
7	25	Bury	1-4	0-1	4926	Doyle
8	29	SWINDON	1-0	1-0	5783	Turner
9	2 Oct	Chester	1-2	0-1	3614	Turner
10	6	CHESTERFIELD	0-3	0-2	5305	
11	9	MANSFIELD TOWN	2-1	0-0	7031	Turner Nixon
12	12	Preston North End	2-6	1-3	5651	Moss Walker
13	16	Brighton & H.A.	0-1	0-1	18276	
14	23	OXFORD UNITED	2-0	1-0	6111	Doyle O.G.
15	30	Portsmouth	0-0	0-0	8622	
16	2 Nov	Northampton Town	2-2	1-0	7483	Cozens 2
17	6	GILLINGHAM	0-1	0-0	5651	
18	10	Wrexham	0-2	0-1	6258	
19	27	SHEFFIELD WED.	1-2	1-0	8683	Carmichael
20	3 Dec	Walsall	1-1	1-1	3848	Moss
21	27	Reading	0-1	0-1	7264	
22	3 Jan	PORTSMOUTH	4-2	2-0	5424	Cozens 3 Heeley
23	15	PRESTON NORTH END	0-0	0-0	5308	
24	22	Rotherham United	0-0	0-0	6889	
25	29	SHREWSBURY TOWN	2-1	0-1	5541	Carmichael Gregory
26	5 Feb	GRIMSBY TOWN	3-1	1-1	5753	Gregory Oakes Nimmo
27	12	York City	1-2	0-1	3224	Carmichael
28	19	TRANMERE ROVERS	0-0	0-0	4881	
29	26	Crystal Palace	0-0	0-0	16623	
30	5 Mar	BURY	0-1	0-1	4965	
31	7	Port Vale	1-1	1-0	4417	Lee
32	11	CHESTER	3-2	2-2	4781	Nixon Turner 2
33	19	Mansfield Town	1-1	1-0	7728	Gregory
34	22	Gillingham	1-1	1-1	4198	Nixon
35	26	BRIGHTON & H.A.	2-0	0-0	7851	Gregory 2
36	2 Apr	Oxford United	3-2	2-1	3832	Gregory Rogers Cozens
37	9	Swindon Town	4-0	1-0	7394	Doyle Carmichael Heeley Lee
38	12	NORTHAMPTON TOWN	3-1	1-1	8944	Hindley Gregory Cozens
39	16	Chesterfield	0-0	0-0	3350	
40	19	Shrewsbury Town	1-2	1-1	2360	Nixon
41	23	WREXHAM	0-2	0-1	6106	
42	26	LINCOLN CITY	1-2	1-1	4974	Heeley
43	30	Sheffield Wed.	0-4	0-1	8727	
44	4 May	PORT VALE	1-1	1-0	3227	Robson
45	7	WALSALL	3-5	1-3	3933	Doyle Nixon Gregory
46	11	Lincoln City	1-1	0-0	5081	Lee

Player appearances (shirt numbers; * = substitute used, S = substitute):

No	Steele	Hindley	Lee	Doyle	Turner	Carmichael	Parkin	Gregory	Moss	Hodson	Walker	Cozens	Nixon	Oakes	Robson	Hughes	Heeley	Bradford	Waugh	Jeffries	Ross	Nimmo	Rogers	Woof	Granham
1	1	2	3	4	5	6	11	8	9		12	10	7*												
2	1	2	12	4	5	6	7	9			3*	10		8	11										
3	1	2	3	4	5*	6		8	9		12	10		7	11										
4	1	2	3	4	5	6	10	8	9*			12		7	11*										
5	1	2	3	4	5	6		8	9		S	10		7*	11										
6	1	2	3	4	5	6		8	9		2	10		7	11										
7	1	2	3	4	5	6		8	9			10		7*	11	10									
8	1	2	3	4	5	6		8			9	12		S	11*	10	7								
9	1	5	3	4	9	6		8			2			7*	11*	10	7								
10	1	5	2*	4	9	6		8			3			S	11	10	7								
11	1	2	3	4	5	6		8	9				7		11	10		10							
12		2	3	4	5*	6		8*	9		12		7	11				10	1						
13			2	4	5	6		8*	9		3	12	7	11				10	1						
14		2	2	4	5	6		12	9*			8	11	7*	3			10	1						
15		2		4	5	10		9	S			8	11	7*	3		12		1						
16		2		4	5	11		8	12			10	9	3					1						
17		2	2	4	5	3		8	S			10	9	7*	11				1						
18		2	6	4	5	10		9					8		11				1	7					
19		2	3*	4	5	10		12	S			8	7	3	11				1	6					
20		2	3	4	5	7		S	9	11		10	8	7	11				1	6					
21		2	3	4	5	4		9		S		10	8						1	6					
22		2	3	4	5	10		8			9				11		S		1		6				
23		2	3	4	5	10		9				8	S		11		7		1		6				
24		2	3	4	5	10		9					7	S	3				1		6	8	11		
25		2	3	4	5	10		8					7		11		S		1		6	9	11*		
26		2	3	4		10		8			9		7	5	3		12		1		6	9*	11		
27		2	3	4		10		8			8		7	6			S		1		6	9	11		
28	2*	3	3	4		10		8	S			9	7	5	12		S		1		6	5	11	12	
29		3	3	4		10		8			9		7	3	12		S		1		6		11		
30		3	3	4	5	10*		8			9	9	7	7			7		1		6		11	12	
31		2	3	4	5	10		8				9	7	S	4		S		1		6		11	12	
32		2	3	4	6	10					8	9	7	9					1		6		11	9	
33		2	3	4	6	10		8			12	9	7						1		6		11	9*	
34		2	3	4	6	10		8			9		7		12				1		6		11*		
35		2	3	4	6	10		8			9		7						1		6		11		
36		2	3	4	6	10		8			9	9	7*		11		S		1		6		11		
37		2	3	4	6	10		8			8	9	7		12		12		1		6		11		
38		2	3	4	6	10		8			9	9	7	12			12		1		6		11*		
39		2	3	4	6	10		8			9	9	7		12				1		6		11*		
40		2	3	4	6	10		8			9	9	7		11*	11*	12		1		6		11*		
41		2	3	4	6	10		8			9	9	7	S	4		11		1		6				
42		2	3*	4	6	6		8		12			6		3		7		1				11		
43		2	3	4	6	6		8		S			5	5	3		10		1				11	9*	1
44		2	3	4	6	6		8		9*		9	5	5	12		10		1				11		1
45		2	3	4	6	6		8		12		9	5	10	10		3*						11		1
46		2	3	4	6	6		8		S		9	5	10	10		7						11		1

F.A.Cup

	Date	Opponent			Att.	Scorers																					
1st	20 Nov	Tranmere Rovers	4-0	3-0	3431	Carmichael Moss Cozens Robson	2	3	4	5	10		9	8	7	S	11							1	6
2nd	11 Dec	Northwich Victoria	†	1-0	6898	Nixon † (Aban. after 25 mins.)	2	4	5	7	9	S		10	8	3	11							1	6
2nd	14	Northwich Victoria	0-4	0-1	5070		2	4	5	7	9	12	9	10	8	3*	11							1	6

Football League Cup

	Date	Opponent			Att.	Scorers
1/1L	14 Aug	Reading	3-2	0-2	5263	Lee Cozens 2
1/2L	18	READING	0-1	0-0	6286	
1/R.	25	READING	3-1	1-0	5449	Moss 2 Robson
2nd	31	Fulham	1-1	0-1	10222	Doyle
2/R	7 Sep	FULHAM	1-2	0-1	16476	Robson

League Appearances																				
League Sub. Appear.																				
League Sub. non-Appear.																				
League Goals																				
Cup Appearances																				
Cup Sub. Appear.																				
Cup Sub. non-Appear.																				
Cup Goals																				

DIVISION 3

	P	W	D	L	F	A	W	D	L	F	A	Pts
Mansfield T	46	17	6	0	52	13	11	2	10	26	29	64
Brighton & HA	46	19	3	1	63	14	6	6	9	20	26	61
Crystal P	46	17	5	1	46	15	6	8	9	22	25	59
Rotherham U	46	17	9	3	39	30	6	6	11	29	29	59
Wrexham	46	15	6	2	47	22	9	4	10	33	32	58
Preston NE	46	15	4	4	48	21	6	8	9	16	22	54
Bury	46	15	2	6	41	21	6	8	9	23	38	54
Sheffield W	46	15	4	4	39	18	7	5	11	26	37	53
Lincoln C	46	12	9	2	50	30	7	5	11	27	40	47
Shrewsbury T	46	13	7	3	40	21	5	4	14	25	38	45
Swindon T	46	12	6	5	48	33	5	9	11	20	42	45
Gillingham	46	11	8	4	31	21	5	4	14	24	43	44
Chester	46	14	4	5	28	20	4	5	14	20	38	44
Tranmere R	46	10	7	6	31	23	3	10	10	20	30	43
Walsall	46	8	7	8	39	32	5	8	10	18	33	41
Peterboro' U	46	11	4	8	33	28	2	11	10	22	37	41
Oxford U	46	9	8	6	34	29	3	7	13	21	36	39
Chesterfield	46	10	6	7	30	20	4	4	15	26	44	38
Port Vale	46	9	7	7	29	28	2	9	12	18	43	38
Portsmouth	46	8	9	6	28	26	3	5	15	25	44	36
Reading	46	10	5	8	29	24	4	3	16	20	49	35
Northampton T	46	9	4	10	33	29	4	4	15	27	46	34
Grimsby T	46	10	6	7	29	22	2	3	18	16	47	33
York C	46	7	8	8	25	34	3	4	16	25	55	32

(Rear) Walker, Nixon, Hindley, Carmichael, Hughes, Gregory.
(Middle) Barnwell, Cozens, Moss E., Waugh, Steele, Oakes, Doyle, Cantwell
(Front) Rogers, Hodson, Parkin, Turner, Robson, Lee.

Season Summary

A notable draw at Fulham in the League Cup brings the Londoners back to London Road, including George Best. A poor run leads to Manager Cantwell announcing that every League player is up for sale! Posh lose in F.A.Cup by 4-0 at non-League Northwich Victoria. Mark Healey becomes the youngest Posh player to play in League. Cantwell quits at end of season.

SEASON 1977/78

Football League Division 3

762	Date	Opposition	Res	H.T.	Attend	Goalscorer	Anderson	McEwan	Earl	Cliss	Barron	Cozens	Butlin	Robson	Hindley	Heeley	Oakes	Rogers	Hughes	Sargent	Camp	Slough	Ross	Turner	Doyle	Lee	Carmichael	Waugh
1	20 Aug	PORTSMOUTH	0-0	0-0	6099									10	2			11*	10	9	8	7	6	5	4	3	12	1
2	23	Swindon Town	0-2	0-2	7136									11	2					9	8*	7	6	5	4	3	10	1
3	27	Chesterfield	0-2	0-0	4690									11	2		8	S		9		7	6	5	4	3	10	1
4	3 Sep	WREXHAM	2-2	0-1	4874	Turner Robson							8	11	2			7		9*	12		6	5	4	3	S	1
5	10	Lincoln City	1-0	0-0	4698	Butlin							8	11	2		12			9		7	6	5	4	3	10	1
6	13	CARLISLE UNITED	2-1	1-0	4498	Butlin 2						12	8	11*	2					9	12	7	6	5	4	3	10	1
7	17	EXETER CITY	1-1	1-1	5016	Robson					1		8	11	2		12			9*		7	6	5	4	3	10	
8	24	Sheffield Wed.	1-0	0-0	9620	Cozens					1	9	8	11	2*					12		7	6	5	8	3	10	
9	28	Bradford City	1-2	1-1	3217	Butlin					1	9	8	11	2		10			S	9*	7	6	5	9	3	2	
10	1 Oct	WALSALL	0-0	0-0	5389									11	2		10			S		7	6	5	4	3	10	1
11	4	OXFORD UNITED	1-0	1-0	4183	Robson					1	9	8	11	2		3			S		7	6	5	4	10	10	
12	8	Bury	0-0	0-0	5064						1	9	8	11	2					12		7	6	5	4	3	10	
13	15	SHREWSBURY TOWN	2-1	1-0	5563	Robson 2					1	9*	8	11	2					12		7	6	5	4	3	10	
14	22	Port Vale	0-0	0-0	3502					9	1	9*	8	11	2					12		7	6	5	4	3	10	
15	28	Colchester United	0-3	0-2	4827								8	11	2		S					7	6	5	4	3	10	1
16	5 Nov	CAMBRIDGE UNITED	2-0	0-0	7308	Sargent Cliss				9	1		8*	11	2					12		7	6	5	4	3	10	
17	12	Rotherham United	1-0	0-0	4220	Sargent				9*	1		8	11	2					12		7	6	5	4	3	10	
18	19	PLYMOUTH ARGYLE	1-0	1-0	6528	Robson					1			11	2					8		7	6	5	4	3	S	
19	2 Dec	Tranmere Rovers	2-0	0-0	3331	Doyle Turner		10			1		9	11	2					9		7	6	5	4	3	11	
20	10	CHESTER	0-0	0-0	5844			10			1		8	12	2					9		7	6	5	4	3	11*	
21	26	Hereford United	0-0	0-0	5625		9	10			1			S	2							7	6	5	4	3	11*	
22	31	GILLINGHAM	1-1	0-1	10156	Robson	9	10*			1		8	S	2		12					7	6	5	4	3	11	
23	31	PRESTON NORTH END	1-0	0-0	7134	Slough	9	10			1		8*	12	2		12					7	6	5	4	3	11	
24	2 Jan	Cambridge United	0-1	0-0	10998		9	10					8	12	2*		9			8		7	6	5	4	3	11	1
25	14	Portsmouth	2-2	0-2	9569	Turner Anderson	11	8			1			9	2		S	S		9		7	6	5	4	3	10*	
26	4 Feb	LINCOLN CITY	0-1	0-1	5316		11	4	9		1			12			S	S		9		7	6	8	8	3	10*	
27	11	Exeter City	0-1	0-0	4017		11	10			1				2					9		7	4	5	9	3	6	
28	22	SHEFFIELD WED.	2-1	1-0	4252	Anderson Sargent	11	8						12	2		S	S		10	9*	7	6	5	4	8		1
29	25	Walsall	0-1	0-1	5408		11	8							2		12	S		10*		7	6	5	4		9	1
30	4 Mar	BURY	2-1	1-0	4892	Slough Anderson	11	8							2		12	S		10		7	6	5	4		2	1
31	7	Carlisle United	0-0	0-0	4563		11	8									9			9		7	6	5	4		7	1
32	11	Shrewsbury Town	0-0	0-0	2591		11	10						S			12	S				7	6	5	4		7	1
33	14	COLCHESTER UNITED	1-0	0-0	4468	Camp	11	8			1				2		S	S		10*	9	7	6	5	4	S	S	
34	17	PORT VALE	1-1	0-0	4277	Hughes	10	8						7	2		12			3	9	7	6	5	4	S		1
35	25	Gillingham	0-0	0-0	8328		10	8						S	2					3	9*	7	6	5	4	S		1
36	28	HEREFORD UNITED	2-1	1-1	5036	Butlin 2	10	8					9	11	2					3		7	6	5	4	S	S	1
37	1 Apr	Preston North End	1-0	1-0	9695	Robson	10	8					9	11	2					3		7	6	5	4	S	S	1
38	4	BRADFORD CITY	5-0	1-0	6314	Turner McEwan Anderson Robson 2	10	8					9	11	2					3		7*	6	5	4	S	S	1
39	8	ROTHERHAM UNITED	1-0	0-0	7098	Butlin	10	8					12	11	2					3		7	6	5	4	S	S	1
40	11	CHESTERFIELD	2-0	0-0	7309	Robson 2	10	8						11	2					3		7	6	5	4	S	12	1
41	15	Plymouth Argyle	0-1	0-1	5679		10	8						11	2					3		7	6	5	4	S	S	1
42	18	SWINDON TOWN	2-0	1-0	6843	Doyle Anderson	10	8					9	11	2					3		7	6	5	4	S	S	1
43	22	TRANMERE ROVERS	1-0	1-0	8889	Robson	10	8						11	2*					3		7	6	5	4	S	12	1
44	26	Oxford United	3-3	1-3	4652	Turner Slough Robson	10	8						11	2					3		7	6	5	4	S	S	1
45	29	Chester	3-4	1-1	4237	Slough 3	10	8						11	2					3		7	6	5	4	S	S	1
46	1 May	Wrexham	0-0	0-0	20000		10	8					9	11	2					3		7	6	5	4	S	S	1

F.A. Cup

	Date	Opponent	Score	Replay	Att.	Scorers
1st	26 Nov	Barnet	2-1	1-1	5181	Slough Robson
2nd	17 Dec	Gillingham	1-1	0-0	10181	Slough
2/R.	20	GILLINGHAM	2-0	0-0	8542	Carmichael Sargent
3rd	7 Jan	NEWCASTLE UNITED	1-1	1-1	17621	Sargent
3/R.	11	Newcastle United	0-2	0-0	25770	

Football League Cup

	Date	Opponent	Score	Replay	Att.	Scorers
1/1L	13 Aug	BRADFORD CITY	4-1	1-0	3844	Camp 2 Sargent 2
1/2L	17	Bradford City	1-1	1-1	3576	Turner
2nd	30	SCUNTHORPE UNITED	1-1	1-1	3697	Turner
2/R.	6 Sep	Scunthorpe United	1-0	0-0	4564	Slough
3rd	25 Oct	Bolton Wanderers	1-3	0-2	14990	Slough

Appearance / Goals Summary

- League Appearances: 26, 27, 26, 46, 46, 46, 45, 6, 18, 23, 2, 4, 40, 31, 34, 7, 20, 3, 1, 29, 26
- League Sub. Appear.
- League Sub. non-Appear.: 12, 6, 4, 3, 14, 7, 1, 1, 5
- League Goals: 4, 8, 10, 2, 5, 10, 10, 3, 9, 3, 1, 6, 6, 5, 6, 1, 5
- Cup Appearances
- Cup Sub. Appear.
- Cup Sub. non-Appear.
- Cup Goals

DIVISION 3

	P	W	D	L	F	A	W	D	L	F	A	Pts
Wrexham	46	14	8	1	48	19	9	7	7	30	26	61
Cambridge U	46	19	3	1	49	11	4	9	10	23	40	58
Preston NE	46	16	5	2	48	19	4	11	8	15	19	56
Peterboro U	46	15	7	1	32	11	5	9	9	15	22	56
Chester	46	14	8	1	41	24	2	14	7	18	32	54
Walsall	42	12	8	3	35	17	6	9	8	26	33	53
Gillingham	46	11	10	2	36	21	4	10	9	31	39	50
Colchester U	46	10	11	2	36	16	5	7	11	19	28	48
Chesterfield	46	14	6	3	40	16	3	8	12	18	33	48
Swindon T	46	12	7	4	40	22	4	9	10	27	38	48
Shrewsbury T	46	11	7	5	42	23	5	8	10	21	34	47
Tranmere R	46	13	7	3	39	19	3	8	12	18	33	47
Carlisle U	46	10	9	4	32	26	4	10	9	27	33	47
Sheffield W	46	13	7	3	28	14	2	9	12	22	38	46
Bury	46	7	13	3	34	22	6	6	11	28	34	45
Lincoln C	46	10	8	5	35	26	5	7	11	18	35	45
Exeter C	46	11	8	4	30	18	4	6	13	19	41	44
Oxford U	46	11	10	2	38	21	2	4	17	26	46	40
Plymouth A	46	7	8	8	33	28	4	9	10	28	40	39
Rotherham U	46	11	5	7	26	19	2	8	13	25	49	39
Port Vale	46	7	11	5	28	23	1	9	13	18	44	36
Bradford C	46	11	6	6	40	29	1	4	18	16	57	34
Hereford U	46	9	9	5	28	22	0	5	18	6	38	32
Portsmouth	46	4	11	8	31	38	3	6	14	10	37	31

(Back) Camp, Byatt, Slough, Garnham, Waugh, Hindley, Oakes, Winters.
(Middle) Gynn, Cliss, Carmichael, Cozens, Hughes, Nardino, Hails.
(Front) Doyle, Sargent, Ross, Robson, Rogers, Lee, Heeley.

Season Summary

Alan Slough comes to London Road for a £20,000 fee. Mark Healey is dropped from team, goes on trial with Arsenal, and signs for the Gunners for £100,000. Newcastle nearly become the latest giant-killing victim. An exciting season, around the top of the table, ends in disappointment with promotion missed on goal average only.

SEASON 1978/79

Football League Division 3

828	Date	Opposition	Res	H.T.	Attend	Goalscorer
1	19 Aug	SHEFFIELD WED.	2-0	0-0	7468	Slough Robson
2	26	Watford	2-1	0-0	12291	Slough 2
3	2 Sep	TRANMERE ROVERS	1-0	0-0	5229	Butlin
4	8	Chester	1-1	0-0	4506	Slough
5	12	CARLISLE UNITED	0-0	0-0	6283	
6	16	BRENTFORD	3-1	2-1	5881	Doyle McEwen Butlin
7	23	Chesterfield	1-3	1-1	3824	Butlin
8	26	Walsall	1-4	1-2	4835	Robertson
9	30	EXETER CITY	1-1	0-1	6714	Doyle
10	7 Oct	Hull City	1-1	0-0	4531	Styles
11	14	OXFORD UNITED	1-1	1-1	5472	Robson
12	17	Swindon Town	1-3	1-1	4352	McEwen
13	21	GILLINGHAM	1-1	0-1	5001	Butlin
14	28	Swansea City	1-4	1-2	11302	Sargent
15	4 Nov	BURY	2-2	2-0	4780	Doyle Anderson
16	10	Tranmere Rovers	0-1	0-1	2241	
17	14	Plymouth Argyle	2-3	0-2	7398	Cunningham O.G.
18	18	WATFORD	0-1	0-0	8048	
19	6 Dec	SHREWSBURY TOWN	0-2	0-2	3087	
20	9	Blackpool	0-0	0-0	4280	
21	23	Mansfield Town	1-1	0-0	3671	Holman
22	26	LINCOLN CITY	0-1	0-0	4592	
23	30	SOUTHEND UNITED	0-1	0-0	3731	
24	13 Jan	CHESTER	2-1	2-0	4445	Butlin Robson
25	20	Brentford	0-0	0-0	5750	
26	3 Feb	WALSALL	0-3	0-1	4466	
27	10	Exeter City	0-1	0-0	3844	
28	24	Oxford United	2-0	0-0	3842	Cooke O.G.
29	3 Mar	Gillingham	0-1	0-0	6890	
30	10	SWANSEA CITY	2-0	0-0	5550	Guy 2
31	20	Carlisle United	1-4	1-1	4571	Cooke
32	24	PLYMOUTH ARGYLE	2-1	1-1	4039	Cooke Smith
33	27	Sheffield Wed.	0-3	0-1	9868	
34	31	COLCHESTER UNITED	1-2	0-1	3559	Robson
35	7 Apr	Shrewsbury Town	0-2	0-0	5600	
36	14	Lincoln City	1-0	0-0	4610	Sargent
37	16	ROTHERHAM UNITED	1-1	0-1	3807	Cliss
38	17	MANSFIELD TOWN	1-2	0-0	4178	Smith
39	21	Southend United	0-0	0-0	3461	
40	24	SWINDON TOWN	2-1	1-0	4121	Ross Cooke
41	28	BLACKPOOL	1-2	0-0	4004	Gynn
42	1 May	Rotherham United	1-1	0-0	2162	Guy
43	4	Colchester United	2-4	2-1	2692	Cooke Guy
44	8	CHESTERFIELD	0-0	0-0	2338	
45	11	HULL CITY	3-0	3-0	1875	Cliss Gynn Chard
46	19	Bury	0-1	0-0	2298	

Player appearance columns (top to bottom): Chard, Collins, Sharkey, Guy, Smith, Cooke, Gynn, Holman, Cunningham, Sargent, Hindley, Cliss, Byatt, Quow, Robertson, Robson, Anderson, Butlin, McEwen, Slough, Ross, Green, Doyle, Styles, Carmichael, Waugh

F.A.Cup

1st	25 Nov	Southend United	2-3	1-1	6531	Butlin Anderson

Football League Cup

1/1L	12 Aug	Hull City	1-0	1-0	4165	Slough
1/2L	15	HULL CITY	1-2	0-1	4387	Slough
1/R.	22	Hull City	1-0	0-0	4990	Butlin
2nd	29	Middlesbrough	0-0	0-0	12803	
2/R	5 Sep	MIDDLESBROUGH	1-0*	0-0	8093	Robson
3rd	3 Oct	SWINDON TOWN	1-1	1-1	6132	Styles
3/R.	10	Swindon Town	2-0	0-0	7764	Styles Doyle
4th	7 Nov	Brighton & H.A.	0-1	0-1	21421	

* After extra time (0-0 at 90 minutes)

Appearance / Goals summary

	League Appearances	League Sub. Appear.	League Sub. non-Appear.	(2 O.G.) als Cup Appearances	Cup Sub. Appear.	Cup Sub. non-Appear.	Cup Goals
46	46	2		9			
25	25		1	8			2
32	32			9			1
41	41		3	9			
30	30		1	8			
45	45	1	4	9		2	2
10	10		1	6			
33	33	1	2	9	1	2	
30	30		5	8		2	1
23	23	1	1	9			1
29	29	7	4	9			1
12	12	3	1	2		4	
5	5	3	3		1	1	
2	2	1	1				
15	15	4	2	2			
30	30	2		4			
9	9	3	2	2	1	1	
4	4	2	1	1			
9	9	2	1	2			
18	18		5				
15	15	1	2	2			
13	13	2		4			
11	11						
5	5	1	1	1			
5	5	1	1	1			

DIVISION 3

	P	W	D	L	F	A	W	D	L	F	A	Pts
Shrewsbury T	46	14	9	0	36	11	7	10	6	25	30	61
Watford	46	15	5	3	47	22	7	7	36	30		60
Swansea C	46	16	6	1	57	32	6	8	9	26	29	60
Gillingham	46	15	7	1	39	15	6	10	7	27	26	59
Swindon T	46	17	2	4	44	14	8	5	10	30	38	57
Carlisle U	46	11	10	2	31	13	4	12	7	22	29	52
Colchester C	46	13	9	1	35	19	4	8	11	25	36	51
Hull C	46	12	9	2	36	14	7	2	14	30	47	49
Exeter C	46	14	6	3	38	18	3	9	11	23	38	49
Brentford	46	14	4	5	35	19	5	5	13	18	30	47
Oxford U	46	10	8	5	27	20	4	10	9	17	30	46
Blackpool	46	12	5	6	38	19	6	4	13	23	40	45
Southend U	46	11	6	6	30	17	6	10	21	32		45
Sheffield W	46	9	8	6	30	22	8	4	11	18	23	44
Plymouth A	46	11	9	3	40	27	4	5	14	21	41	44
Chester	46	11	9	3	42	21	3	7	13	15	40	44
Rotherham U	46	13	7	3	30	23	4	7	12	19	32	44
Mansfield T	46	7	11	5	30	24	5	8	10	21	28	43
Bury	46	6	11	6	35	32	5	9	9	24	33	42
Chesterfield	46	10	5	8	35	34	3	9	11	16	31	40
Peterboro U	46	8	7	8	26	24	3	7	13	18	39	36
Walsall	46	7	6	10	34	32	6	7	10	22	39	32
Tranmere R	46	4	12	7	26	31	2	4	17	19	47	28
Lincoln C	46	5	7	11	26	38	2	4	17	15	50	25

(Rear) Cooke, McVay, Parkinson, Gwinnett, Waugh, Slough, Slack, Collins.
(Middle) ? , Gale, Anderson, Guy, Chard, Winters, Carmichael, Foster, Barron.
(Front) Cliss, Sharkey, Smith, Lambert, Morris, Quow, Phillips, Doyle, Robson.
(Sitting) Gynn, ? , ,

Season Summary

Chris Turner moves to Luton for a record £115,000 fee. Ambitious Barnwell resigns – disatisfied by Club's lack of ambition and money for players; temporary Manager Hales steps down for same reasons. Peter Morris becomes third Manager of season. Smallest ever home League crowd for last game.

Football League Division 4

674

#	Date	Opposition	Res	H.T.	Attend	Goalscorer
1	18 Aug	Lincoln City	1-0	1-0	4725	Kellock
2	22	TRANMERE ROVERS	1-2	0-0	4878	Lambert
3	25	HALIFAX TOWN	2-1	1-1	4014	Kellock Chard
4	1 Sep	Port Vale	1-0	1-0	2794	Kellock
5	8	York City	2-0	1-0	3102	Robson 2
6	15	CREWE ALEXANDRA	3-0	1-0	4525	Kellock Robson Quow
7	19	ALDERSHOT	1-3	1-1	4449	Kellock
8	22	Northampton Town	0-1	0-1	3678	
9	29	HEREFORD UNITED	2-0	1-0	4051	Kellock Chard
10	6 Oct	HUDDERSFIELD TOWN	1-3	0-2	5183	Kellock
11	8	Tranmere Rovers	0-3	0-2	1907	
12	12	Rochdale	0-0	0-0	1704	
13	20	HARTLEPOOL UNITED	2-0	1-0	3412	Parkinson
14	24	TORQUAY UNITED	2-1	1-1	3130	Parkinson Quow
15	27	Darlington	1-1	0-1	1675	Parkinson
16	30	Aldershot	0-2	0-1	4168	
17	3 Nov	LINCOLN CITY	3-1	2-0	4681	Kellock Parkinson Cliss
18	7	Torquay United	0-2	0-2	3121	
19	9	Doncaster Rovers	1-2	0-2	7447	Foster
20	17	WALSALL	1-3	1-1	4019	Foster
21	1 Dec	A.F.C. Bournemouth	0-0	0-0	3234	
22	8	PORTSMOUTH	0-0	0-0	5371	
23	21	Newport County	1-1	1-1	4653	Kellock
24	26	WIGAN ATHLETIC	1-2	0-1	3312	Quow
25	29	Halifax Town	0-0	0-0	3639	
26	5 Jan	SCUNTHORPE UNITED	3-1	1-0	3014	Carmichael Syrett 2
27	12	Bradford City	1-1	1-1	4629	Kellock
28	21	Stockport County	0-1	0-0	1789	
29	26	PORT VALE	3-0	1-0	3287	Kellock Syrett Cliss
30	1 Feb	Crewe Alexandra	4-1	2-0	2924	Kellock 2 Cliss Syrett
31	9	NORTHAMPTON TOWN	0-0	0-0	4960	
32	16	Hereford United	1-0	1-0	2601	Syrett
33	23	ROCHDALE	2-0	0-0	3796	Phillips Kellock
34	1 Mar	Hartlepool United	2-1	0-1	2856	Kellock Syrett
35	5	YORK CITY	2-1	1-1	3434	Syrett Robson
36	8	DARLINGTON	3-0	2-0	4085	Quow Syrett 2
37	15	Huddersfield Town	0-0	0-0	8172	
38	22	DONCASTER ROVERS	3-2	1-2	4107	Kellock Cliss Syrett
39	29	Walsall	3-2	1-1	5704	Kellock 2 Gynn
40	5 Apr	Wigan Athletic	1-2	0-0	6094	Syrett
41	7	STOCKPORT COUNTY	1-1	1-0	4527	Cliss
42	8	NEWPORT COUNTY	0-1	0-1	5033	
43	12	Scunthorpe United	0-1	0-1	1908	
44	19	A.F.C. BOURNEMOUTH	2-0	1-0	2641	Kellock Lambert
45	26	Portsmouth	0-4	0-2	15095	
46	3 May	BRADFORD CITY	1-0	0-0	5135	Cliss

Appearances / shirt numbers

#	Waugh	Carmichael	Collins	Heppolette	McVay	Foster	Gynn	Kellock	Guy	Parkinson	Lambert	Chard	Robson	Slough	Sharkey	Phillips	Syrett	Smith	Quow	Cliss	Morris	Cassells	Gallagher
1	1	2	3	4	5	6	7	8	9	10*	11	12											
2	1	2	3	4	5	6	7	8	9	10*	11	12											
3	1	2	3	4	5	6	7	8	9	10*	11	12					9*						
4	1	2		4		6	12	8			11	7	10	5		3		5	9				
5	1	2				6	7	8	S		11	4	10			3		5	9				
6	1	2				6	7	8	S		11	4	10			3		5	9*				
7	1	2				6	7	8		12	11*	4	10			3		5	9				
8	1	2				6	7	8	12		11	4	10			3		5	9				
9	1	2		11		6	7	8	9			4	10			3		5	12	S			
10	1	2				6	7	8	9		11	4	10			3*		5	12				
11	1	2			5	6	7	8	12		11	4*	10			3							
12	1	2	3		5	6	7	8	12	11			10				9				4		
13	1	5	3			6	7	8		11		4	10						9				
14	1	5				6	7	8		10		4	11						9				
15	1	5				6	2	8		10		4*	11			3			12	9			
16	1	5			2	6		8		10		S	11			3			7	9			
17	1	5			2	6		8	4	11		S	11			3			7	9			
18	1	5			2	6		8	4			12	11			3			7*	9			
19	1	5		11	2	6	11	8	4			7*	11		4	3				9			
20	1	2	3			6		8	4	10			12		4		11	5	7*	9			
21	1	2				6	11*	8	4			3	S	5	4	3	11	5		9			
22	1	2				6	11*	8	4			S	12	5	4	3	11			9			
23	1	2				6	11	8	4			4*	S	5		3	10		7	9			
24	1	2				6	7*	8	4*				12	5		3	10		11	9			
25	1	2				6		8	4		S		12	5		3	10		7	9			
26	1	2*				6		8	4		12		11	5		3	10		7*	9			
27	1	2				6		8	4				11*	5		3	10		7	9			
28	1	2				6		8	4		12	7*	12	5		3	10		7	9			
29	1	2				6		8*	4				12	5		3	10		7*	9			
30	1	2				6		8	4				S	5		3	10		7	9			
31	1				2	6		8	4		11		12	5		3	10*		7	9			
32	1				2	6	10	8*	4				12	5		3*	10		7	9			
33	1				2	6	11	8*	4*		11		11	5		3	10		7	9			
34	1				3	4	7		8		12		11	5		3	10		7	9			
35	1				3	6	7	8					12	5		3*	10		7*	9			
36	1				3	6	7	8	8				12	5		3	10	S	7	9			
37	1				2	6	7	8	4				11	5		3	10		12	9		11	
38	1				2	6	7	8	4		11*		7	5		3	10		7	9		11	
39	1				2	6	10	8	4	12			11	5		3	10		7*	9		11	
40	1				2	6	11	8	12	11		4*	7	5		3	10*	S	7	9		11	
41	1				2	6		8					12	5		3*	10	5	7	9			
42	1				2	6	7	8		11			12			3	10	5	7	9			
43	1				3	4	7		8	12			9*			2	10	5	7	11			
44	1				2	6	7	8	4		11*		12			3	10	5	7	9		11	
45	1		5		2	6	7	8	12				11	10		3	10	5	4	9*			
46	1		3		2	6	7	S					11	5		5	10		4	9			10

1st	24 Nov	A.F.C. BOURNEMOUTH	1-2	1-2	3777	Kellock

Football League Cup

1/1L	11 Aug	CHARLTON ATHLETIC	3-1	2-0	4140	Kellock 2 Guy
1/2L	14	Charlton Athletic	1-1	0-1	5496	Chard
2nd	29	BLACKPOOL	0-0	0-0	4326	
2/R.	5 Sep	Blackpool	1-0	0-0	5254	Kellock
3rd	26	BRISTOL CITY	1-1	1-0	7067	Parkinson
3/R.	2 Oct	Bristol City	0-4	0-2	9125	

DIVISION 4

	P	W	D	L	F	A	W	D	L	F	A	Pts
Huddersfield T	46	16	5	2	61	18	11	7	5	40	30	66
Walsall	46	16	5	2	47	22	11	9	3	32	24	64
Newport Co	46	16	5	2	43	23	11	2	10	36	28	61
Portsmouth	46	15	5	3	62	23	9	7	7	29	26	60
Bradford C	46	14	6	3	44	14	10	6	7	33	36	60
Wigan A	46	14	8	1	42	26	8	7	8	34	35	55
Lincoln C	46	13	5	5	43	12	9	10	2	30	53	55
Peterboro' U	46	14	8	1	43	12	7	4	12	44	47	52
Torquay U	46	13	7	3	47	25	2	10	11	23	44	47
Aldershot	46	10	7	6	35	23	6	6	11	27	30	45
Bournemouth	46	8	9	6	32	25	9	5	9	20	26	44
Doncaster R	46	11	6	6	37	27	4	8	11	25	36	44
Northampton T	46	14	5	4	33	16	2	7	14	18	50	44
Scunthorpe	46	11	9	3	37	23	4	4	9	10	18	43
Tranmere R	46	10	4	9	37	23	6	14	21	52	43	41
Stockport Co	46	9	9	7	30	31	5	5	13	18	41	40
York C	46	9	6	8	35	34	5	5	13	30	48	39
Halifax T	46	11	9	3	29	20	2	4	17	17	52	39
Hartlepool U	46	10	7	6	36	28	4	4	13	22	36	38
Port Vale	46	8	6	9	34	24	4	6	13	22	46	36
Hereford U	46	8	7	8	22	21	3	7	13	16	31	36
Darlington	46	7	11	5	33	26	2	6	15	17	48	35
Crewe A	46	10	6	7	25	27	1	7	15	10	41	35
Rochdale	46	6	7	10	20	28	1	6	16	13	51	27

League Appearances
League Sub. Appear.
League Sub. non-Appear.
League Goals
Cup Appearances
Cup Sub. Appear.
Cup Sub. non-Appear.
Cup Goals

(Back) Gynn, Chard, Waugh, McVay, Gwinnett, Parkinson, Collins.
(Middle) Bates, Cliss, Lambert, Guy, Heppolette, Smith, Quow, Foster, Barron,
(Front) Sharkey, Kellock, Carmichael, Morris, Phillips, Slough, Robson.

Season Summary

Money is made available, and spent, on new players, but Bob Doyle moves on to Blackpool for £110,000. A 'topsy turvy' season in the League – with a re-built team – ends with a disappointing final 8th place in the division. The Supporters Club are again removed from the 'Posh Club'!

SEASON 1980/81

Football League Division 4

920	Date	Opposition	Res	H.T.	Attend	Goalscorer	Waugh	McVay	Phillips	Robson	Slack	Foster	Quow	Kellock	Cooke	Syrett	Cliss	Gallagher	Hodgson	Lambert	Slough	Guy	Barron	Winters	Gynn	Smith	Collins
1	16 Aug	Lincoln City	1-1	1-1	5131	Cooke	1	2	3		5	6	7	8	9	10	11	S	4								
2	20	HALIFAX TOWN	2-2	0-0	3995	Kellock Cooke	1	2	3		5	6	7	8	9	10*	11	12	4								
3	23	Doncaster Rovers	4-0	1-0	3536	McVay Slack Kellock Syrett	1	2	3		5	6	7	8	9	10	11	S	4								
4	30	BRADFORD CITY	2-2	1-0	4009	Foster Cooke	1	2	3		5	6	7	8	9	10	11		4*	12							
5	5 Sep	Tranmere Rovers	2-1	0-0	1772	Slack Cooke	1	2	3		5	6	7	8	9	10	11*		4	12							
6	13	ROCHDALE	2-2	0-1	3906	Quow Cooke	1	2	3		5	6	7	8	9	10*	12		4	11							
7	15	Southend United	0-1	0-1	5609		1	2	3		5	6	7	8	9	10	11		4	12							
8	20	A.F.C. BOURNEMOUTH	1-0	0-0	3774	Cooke	1	2	3			6	7	8	9	10		12	4	11*	5						
9	27	Torquay United	0-2	0-1	2090		1		3			6	7	8	9	10		12	4	11	5			2			
10	1 Oct	SOUTHEND UNITED	5-2	1-1	4228	Quow Kellock Cooke 2 O.G.		2	3			6	7	8	9	10		11	4	S	5	S	1				
11	4	BURY	2-0	1-0	4080	Syrett 2	1		3			6	7	8	9	10*	12	11	4		5			2			
12	6	Stockport County	4-3	4-2	1794	Kellock Cooke Hodgson Winters	1		3			6	7	8	9	10		11*	4		5	S		2			
13	11	Wigan Athletic	1-1	1-1	4851	Gallagher	1		3			6	7	8	9	10		11	4		5	12		2			
14	18	DARLINGTON	1-0	0-0	4217	Cooke	1		3			6	7	8	9	10		11	4		5	S		2			
15	22	SCUNTHORPE UNITED	0-2	0-0	4282		1		3			6	7	8	9	10		11*	4*		5	12		2			
16	25	Mansfield Town	1-2	1-1	4863	Cooke	1		3			6	7	8	9	10	11		4		5	12		2			
17	28	Wimbledon	1-2	0-0	1901	Quow	1			3		6	7	8	9	10		11*	4		5	S		2			
18	1 Nov	PORT VALE	1-1	1-0	3643	Kellock	1		3		5		7	8	9	10		11*	4*		6			2	12		
19	4	STOCKPORT COUNTY	1-2	1-0	2772	Cliss	1	2	3	S	5		7	8	9	10	11				6				4		
20	8	Aldershot	0-0	0-0	3057		1	2	3		5		7	8	9		11		10		6	S			4		
21	11	Halifax Town	3-2	2-1	1151	Kellock Cooke Gynn	1	2	3	11	5		7	8	9				10		6				4		
22	15	LINCOLN CITY	1-0	1-0	5817	Kellock	1	2	3	11	5		7	8	9		S		10		6				4		
23	6 Dec	HEREFORD UNITED	3-0	0-0	3281	Robson 2 Cooke	1	2	3	11	5		7	8	9*		12		10		6				4		
24	20	Hartlepool United	1-1	0-1	3100	Gynn	1	2	3*	11	5		7	8	9				10		6				4		
25	26	NORTHAMPTON TOWN	3-0	2-0	6265	Robson Kellock Cooke	1	2	3	11	5			8	9		12		10		6	7			4		
26	27	Crewe Alexandra	0-1	0-1	4132		1	2	3	11	5		7*	8	9		12		10		6				4		
27	10 Jan	Scunthorpe United	1-1	1-0	2064	Robson	1	2	3	11*	5			8	9				10		6	7			4		
28	17	YORK CITY	3-0	2-0	3954	Slack Kellock Hodgson	1	2	3	11*	5		7	8	9	S			10		6				4		
29	28	Bradford City	1-1	0-1	3305	Kellock	1	2	3	11	5		7	8	9	12			10*		6				4		
30	31	DONCASTER ROVERS	0-1	0-0	6146		1	2	3	11	5		7	8	9	12			10*		6				4		
31	7 Feb	Rochdale	3-2	0-2	2865	Gynn 2 Quow	1	2	3		5		7	8	9	12			10*		6				4		
32	21	TORQUAY UNITED	1-3	1-2	4172	Cooke	1	2	3	11	5		7	8	9	10	12				6				4		
33	28	A.F.C. Bournemouth	1-4	1-1	5334	Kellock	1	2	3*	11	5		7	8*	9	S	S		10		6				4		
34	4 Mar	WIMBLEDON	1-1	0-0	3201	Cooke	1			3	5		7	8*	9		12		10					2	4	6	
35	7	Bury	1-1	1-0	2522	Syrett	1			3	5		7	8	9	11	S		10					2	4	6	
36	13	WIGAN ATHLETIC	0-0	0-0	3455		1		3	S	5			8	9	11			10			7		2	4	6	
37	18	TRANMERE ROVERS	4-1	3-0	3034	Gynn Slack Kellock 2	1		3		5		7	8	9	11			10					2	4	6	
38	21	Darlington	0-2	0-1	2522		1		3		5		7	8	9	11	S		10					2	4	6	
39	24	York City	2-1	2-1	1726	Cooke 2	1		3		5	6	7	8	9	11	12		10					2	4		
40	28	MANSFIELD TOWN	1-0	1-0	4904	Gynn	1		3		5	6	7	8	9	11	S		10					2	4		
41	4 Apr	Port Vale	1-1	0-0	2982	Cooke	1		3		5	6	7	8	9	11	12		10					2	4		
42	11	ALDERSHOT	0-0	0-0	4783		1		3		5	6	7	8	9	11	S		10					2	4		
43	18	CREWE ALEXANDRA	2-1	1-0	3743	Gynn Cooke	1		3	12	5	6	7	8	9	11*			10					2	4		
44	21	Northampton Town	2-2	0-1	3800	Cooke Foster	1		3		5	6	7	8	9	11*	12		10					2	4		
45	25	HARTLEPOOL UNITED	1-1	0-1	3560	Foster	1		3*		5	6	7	8	9	11	12		10					2	4		
46	2 May	Hereford United	1-1	0-1	2102	Cooke	1			12	5	6	7	8	9	11			10*					2	4		3

F.A.Cup

						1	2	3	11	5	7	8	9	S	10		6	4		
1st	22 Nov	Northampton Town	4-1	2-1	5542	1	2	3	11	5	7	8	9	S	10		6	4	Robson 2 Slack Quow
2nd	13 Dec	Barnet	1-0	1-0	4498	1	2	3	11	5	7	8	9	S	12	10	6	4	Robson
3rd	3 Jan	CHESTERFIELD	1-1	0-0	8631	1	2	3	11	5	7	8	9	S		10	6	7* 4	Cooke
3/R.	6	Chesterfield	2-1	2-1	8216	1	2	3	11	5	7	8	9	S		10	6	4	Cooke 2
4th	24	Notts. County	1-0	0-0	11714	1	2	3	11	5	7	8	9	S		10	6	4	Cooke
5th	14 Feb	MANCHESTER CITY	0-1	0-1	27780	1	2	3*	11	5	7	8	9	12		10	6	4	

Football League Cup

						1	2	3	4	5	6*	7	8	9	10	11	12		
1/1L	9 Aug	FULHAM	3-2	0-1	3662	1	2	3	4	5	6	7*	8	9	10	11	12	Kellock Cooke Syrett
1/2L	12	Fulham	1-1*	0-0	3517	1	2	3	4	5	6	7	8	9	10	11	12	Cooke
2/1L	27	Nottm. Forest	0-3	0-0	16117	1	2	3		5	6	7	8	9	10*	11	12 4	
2/2L	3 Sep	NOTTM. FOREST	1-1	1-1	11503	1	2	3		5	6	7	8	9	10	11*	4 12	Cooke

* After extra time (0-1 at 90 mins).

League Appearances	45	24	41	18	35	25	44	46	30	10	10	44	3	27	1	1	22	28	5	1
League Sub. Appear.				3					3	12	2	2	2	3			1			
League Sub. non-Appear.			1	2					2	6	1	1		7						
League Goals	10	10	1	4	4	3	4	13	4	4		2			1	7		6		
Cup Appearances	10	10	10	8	10	4	9	10	10	4	4	8		6	1					
Cup Sub. Appear.										1	3		1							
Cup Sub. non-Appear.				3					2	2										
Cup Goals				1		1		1	7	1										

DIVISION 4

	P	W	D	L	F	A	W	D	L	F	A	Pts
Southend U	46	19	4	0	47	6	11	3	9	32	25	67
Lincoln C	46	15	7	1	44	11	10	8	5	22	14	65
Doncaster R	46	15	4	4	36	20	7	8	8	23	29	56
Wimbledon	46	15	4	4	42	17	8	5	10	22	29	55
Peterboro' U	46	11	8	4	37	21	6	10	7	31	33	52
Aldershot	46	12	9	2	28	11	6	5	12	15	30	50
Mansfield T	46	13	5	5	36	15	7	4	12	22	29	49
Darlington	46	13	6	4	43	23	6	5	12	22	36	49
Hartlepool U	46	14	3	6	42	22	6	6	11	22	39	49
Northampton T	46	11	7	5	42	26	7	6	10	23	41	49
Wigan A	46	13	4	6	29	16	5	7	11	22	39	47
Bury	46	10	8	5	38	21	7	5	11	17	27	45
Bournemouth	46	9	8	6	30	21	7	5	11	23	36	44
Bradford C	46	9	9	5	30	24	5	7	11	23	36	44
Rochdale	46	11	6	6	33	25	3	9	11	27	45	43
Scunthorpe U	46	8	12	3	40	31	3	8	12	20	38	42
Torquay U	46	13	2	8	38	26	5	3	15	17	37	41
Crewe A	46	10	7	6	28	20	3	7	13	20	41	40
Port Vale	46	10	8	5	40	23	2	7	14	17	47	39
Stockport Co	46	10	5	8	29	25	5	6	15	15	32	39
Tranmere R	46	12	5	6	41	24	1	5	17	18	49	36
Hereford U	46	8	8	7	29	20	3	5	15	9	42	35
Halifax T	46	9	3	11	28	32	2	9	12	16	39	34
York C	46	9	10	2	31	23	2	7	14	16	43	33

(Back) Gallagher, Syrett, Collins, Slack, Phillips, Cliss, Sharkey
(Middle) Winters, Smith, McVay, Waugh, Chard, Heppolette, Foster, Guy,
(Front) Lambert, Gynn, Quow, Morris, Cooke, Kellock, Robson.

Season Summary

A good 2nd leg League Cup tie is played at home to Forest. Nearly 28,000 attend the F.A.Cup 5th round match at London Road versus Manchester City. Despite hovering around the top of the table for much of the season, and 4th with only 6 games left, promotion is again missed (by 3 points). Robbie Cooke scores 29 League goals.

SEASON 1981/82

Football League Division 4

966	Date	Opposition	Res	H.T.	Attend	Goalscorer	Smelt	Winters	Collins	Gynn	Slack	Rodaway	Quow	Kellock	Cooke	Hodgson	Massey	Chard	Clarke	Butler	Smith T.	Freeman	Syrett	Cliss	Phillips	Smith B.	Barnard	Rayment
1	29 Aug	MANSFIELD TOWN	1–0	0–0	4310	Kellock	1	2	3	4	5	6	7	8	9	10*	11	12										
2	5 Sep	Halifax Town	1–1	0–0	1809	Cooke	1	2	3	4	5	6	7	8	9	10		12	11*									
3	12	ROCHDALE	5–1	2–1	3768	Slack Quow Cooke 3	1	2	3	4	5	6	7	8	9		S	10	11									
4	18	Stockport County	0–3	0–1	2382		1	2	3	4	5	6	7	8	9		12	10	11*									
5	22	Hull City	1–1	0–1	3713	Cooke	1		3	4		6	7	8	9	10	11	S		2	5							
6	26	CREWE ALEXANDRA	3–0	2–0	3775	Kellock Cooke Hodgson			3	4		6	7	8	9	10	11	S		2	5	1						
7	3 Oct	Darlington	0–0	0–0	1628				3	4		6	7	8	9	10	11*	12		2	5	1						
8	10	Hartlepool United	1–0	0–0	2450	Kellock			3	4		6	7*	8	9	10		12		2	5	1	11					
9	17	A.F.C. BOURNEMOUTH	1–0	1–0	4673	Cooke			3	4		6	7	8	9	10	11	S		2	5	1						
10	19	Port Vale	3–1	1–1	2884	Cooke Massey Chard			3	4		6	7*	8	9	10	11	12		2	5	1						
11	24	YORK CITY	0–1	0–0	4220				3	4		6		8	9	10	11*	7		2	5	1		12				
12	28	HEREFORD UNITED	3–1	1–1	3040	Collins Kellock Syrett			3	4		6		8	9	10		S		2	5	1	7	11				
13	31	Scunthorpe United	1–0	0–0	2004	Syrett			3	4		6		8	9	10	S	11		2	5	1	7					
14	4 Nov	ALDERSHOT	7–1	2–1	3781	Gynn Cooke Massey2 Smith T. Syrett 2			3	4		6		8	9	10	12	11*		2	5	1	7					
15	7	BLACKPOOL	3–1	2–0	5442	Kellock Hodgson Syrett			3	4		6		8	9	10	11	S		2	5	1	7					
16	14	Bury	1–3	1–2	6426	Kellock			3	4		6		8	9	10	11	S		2	5	1	7					
17	28	NORTHAMPTON TOWN	1–0	1–0	5293	Kellock			3	4				8	9	10	12	11		2	5	1	7*		6			
18	5 Dec	Bradford City	0–2	0–2	4875				3	4				8	9	10	12	11		2	5	1	7		6*			
19	19 Jan	Wigan Athletic	0–5	0–2	4111				3	4		6		8	9	10	12	11*		2	5	1	7					
20	23	Mansfield Town	2–1	2–0	3242	Gynn Syrett			3	4		6		8	9	10	11*	12		2	5	1	7					
21	26	HALIFAX TOWN	0–0	0–0	3016				3	4		6		8	9	10	11*	7	12	2	5	1						
22	30	STOCKPORT COUNTY	2–0	1–0	3525	Cooke Clarke			3	4		6		8	9	10*	11	12	7	2	5	1						
23	6 Feb	Rochdale	1–1	0–1	1241	Cooke			3	4		6		8	9	10	11*	12	7	2	5	1						
24	10	HULL CITY	3–0	1–0	3161	Cooke Chard Clarke			3	4		6		8	9	10		11	7	2	5	1	S					
25	13	DARLINGTON	3–1	1–1	3702	Cooke 2 Clarke			3	4		6		8	9	10		11	7	2	5	1	S					
26	19	Crewe Alexandra	1–0	1–0	1628	Chard			3	4		6		8	9	10		11	7	2	5	1	S					
27	23	Tranmere Rovers	2–1	1–1	1185	Cooke 2			3	4		6		8	9	10		11	7	2	5	1	S					
28	27	HARTLEPOOL UNITED	4–4	3–4	4610	Gynn Cooke 3			3	4		6		8	9			11	7	2	5	1	S			10		
29	6 Mar	A.F.C. Bournemouth	1–1	0–0	7351	Cooke			3	4		6		8	9			11	7	2	5	1	S			10		
30	10	PORT VALE	1–0	0–0	4151	Cooke			3	4		6		8	9	12		11	7	2	5	1				10*		
31	13	York City	3–4	2–2	2178	Cooke Clarke Syrett			3	4		6			9	8		11	12	2	5	1	7			10*		
32	16	Aldershot	1–0	1–0	1453	Gynn				4		6			9	8		11	12	2	5	1	7		3	10*		
33	20	SCUNTHORPE UNITED	2–1	1–0	4785	Gynn Hodgson				4		6		8	9	10		11	7	2	5	1	S		3			
34	24	TORQUAY UNITED	1–0	1–0	4045	Smith T.				4		6		8	9	10		11	7*	2	5	1	12		3			
35	27	Blackpool	2–2	1–0	2855	Cooke Kellock				4		6		8	9	10		11	7	2	5	1			3		S	
36	3 Apr	BURY	1–0	1–0	4931	Phillips				4		6		8	9	10		11	7	2	5	1			3		S	
37	10	Torquay United	2–1	1–0	1989	Gynn Kellock				4		6		8	9	10		11*	7	2	5	1			3		12	
38	13	COLCHESTER UNITED	2–2	0–0	5402	Smith T. Kellock				4		6		8	9	10		11	7	2	5	1			3		S	
39	17	BRADFORD CITY	2–0	1–0	6765	Phillips Cooke				4		6		8	9	10		11	7	2	5	1			3		S	
40	21	SHEFFIELD UNITED	0–4	0–3	13439					4		6		8	9	10		11	7	2	5	1			3*		12	
41	24	Northampton Town	0–1	0–1	4975					4		6		8	9	10*		11	12	2	5	1	7		3			
42	27	Colchester United	1–1	0–1	2212	Syrett				4		6		8	9	10		11		2	5	1	7		3		S	
43	1 May	WIGAN ATHLETIC	0–3	0–2	6229					4		6		8	9	10		11	12	2*	5	1	7		3			
44	5	Hereford United	1–2	1–1	2357	Kellock		2	10	4	5	6		8	9			11				1	7*		3		12	
45	8	Sheffield United	0–4	0–0	23923			2	10	4	5				9			S	7			1		11	6		8	3
46	15	TRANMERE ROVERS	1–2	0–2	1897	Slack		2	10	4	5			8	9			11*	7			1		12	6			3

F.A.Cup

1st	21 Nov	Halifax Town	3-0	0-0	2614	Cooke 2 Syrett
2nd	2 Jan	WALSALL	2-1	1-0	5421	Cooke Chard
3rd	6	BRISTOL CITY	0-1	0-0	6811	

Football League Cup

1/1L	2 Sep	BARNSLEY	2-3	1-2	4608	Slack Cooke
1/2L	15	Barnsley	0-6	0-4	11198	

Appearances

League Appearances	5	7	34	46	7	42	10	43	46	38	13	31	22	39	39	41	16	2	17	5	1	2
League Sub. Appear.									1		5	8	5				1	2				3
League Sub. non-Appear.										2	7					7						5
League Goals		1	6	2		1		11	24	3	3	4		3	3	8	3		2			
Cup Appearances	2	2	5	5	2	4	2	5	5	3	1	4	2	3	3	3	3	1	1			
Cup Sub. Appear.										1	1											
Cup Sub. non-Appear.								4			2						1					
Cup Goals			1									1										

(Top) Cliss, Shelton, Syrett, Gwinnett, Waugh, Smith, Phillips, Quow.
(2nd Row) Harvey (Physio), Gale, Chapman, Slack, Gallagher, Collins, Winters, Hodgson, Butler (Coach)
(3rd Row) Gynn, Cooke, Massey, Morris (Manager), Clarke, Chard, Kellock, Rodaway.
(Bottom) Rayment, Dixon, Smitheringale, Scarff (Youth Devt.), Ippolito, Wilson, Sutton.

DIVISION 4

	P	W	D	L	F	A	W	D	L	F	A	Pts
Sheffield U	46	15	8	0	53	15	12	7	4	41	26	96
Bradford C	46	14	7	2	52	23	12	6	5	36	22	91
Wigan A	46	17	5	1	47	18	9	8	6	33	28	91
Bournemouth	46	12	10	1	37	15	11	9	3	25	15	88
Peterboro U	46	16	3	4	46	22	8	7	8	25	35	82
Colchester U	46	12	6	5	47	23	8	6	9	35	34	72
Port Vale	46	9	12	2	26	17	9	4	10	30	32	70
Hull C	46	14	3	6	36	23	5	9	9	34	38	69
Bury	46	13	7	3	53	26	6	4	10	27	33	68
Hereford U	46	10	9	4	36	25	7	7	8	23	31	67
Tranmere R	46	7	9	7	27	25	7	9	7	24	31	60
Blackpool	46	11	5	7	40	26	4	8	11	26	34	58
Darlington	46	10	5	8	36	28	5	8	10	25	34	58
Hartlepool U	46	9	9	6	36	34	4	8	11	34	50	55
Torquay U	46	9	8	6	30	25	5	5	13	17	34	55
Aldershot	46	8	7	8	34	29	5	8	10	23	39	54
York C	46	9	5	9	45	37	5	5	13	24	54	50
Stockport Co	46	10	5	8	34	28	2	13	8	14	39	49
Halifax T	46	6	11	6	28	30	3	11	9	23	42	49
Mansfield T	46	8	6	9	39	35	4	4	14	24	47	47*
Rochdale	46	8	6	9	39	39	5	4	14	24	40	46
Northampton	46	9	5	9	32	27	2	4	17	25	57	42
Scunthorpe U	46	9	5	9	32	35	2	6	15	17	44	42
Crewe A	46	6	3	6	14	19	3	3	10	52	27	27

Season Summary

Tommy Robson is released, after 13 years at London Road. 'Sodastream' become Club's first major sponsor. Rumours of a new stadium come to nothing. After victory at Tranmere, Posh lie 2nd in League, but momentum not maintained, and promotion missed. Top of table clash at home to Sheffield United attracts 13,439.

SEASON 1982/83

Football League Division 4

1012	Date		Opposition	Res	H.T.	Attend	Goalscorer	Seaman	Winters	Collins	Gynn	Firm	Rodaway	Slack	Benjamin	Cooke	Linton	Chard	Imlach	Clarke	Rayment	Sutton	Cliss	Quow	Small	Carmichael	Ippolitto	Naylor	Mercer
1	28 Aug		Stockport County	1-1	0-1	2003	Benjamin	1	2	3	4	5	6	7	8	9	10	11	S	S									
2	4 Sep		HARTLEPOOL UNITED	2-1	1-1	3499	Winters Linton	1	2	3	4	5	6	7	10	9	8	11	11	S									
3	8		WIMBLEDON	0-3	0-1	3458		1		3	4	5	6	7	10	9	8	11	12		2*								
4	11		Aldershot	0-2	0-1	1691		1	2	3	4		6	7	10	9	8	11	12	7		5*							
5	18		BURY	1-1	1-0	2826	Gynn	1	2	3	4	5	6	S	10	9	8	11	7										
6	25		York City	1-1	0-1	1872	Cooke	1		3	4	5	6	7	10	9	8	11*			2		12						
7	27		Mansfield Town	0-0	0-0	2414		1		3	4	5	6	7	10	9	8	11			2			S					
8	2 Oct		BRISTOL CITY	3-0	2-0	2739	Gynn 2 Benjamin	1	2	3	4	5	6	7	10	9	8*	11						12					
9	9		SCUNTHORPE UNITED	0-1	0-1	3075		1	2	3	4	5	6	7*	10	9	12	11	8*					2		8			
10	16		Tranmere Rovers	0-1	0-1	1086		1	2	3	4	5	6		10	9	7	11	7							8	9			
11	20		Chester	1-1	0-1	1401	Gynn	1	2	3	4	5	6		10	9	9	11	9	S	7			S		8				
12	23		TORQUAY UNITED	1-3	0-3	2869	Clarke	1		12	4	5	6		10	9	9	11*	3	7				2		8				
13	30		Northampton Town	0-0	0-0	3284		1		9	4	5		6	10*	9		11	3	7	2					8	12			
14	3 Nov		HALIFAX TOWN	2-1	1-0	2038	Firm Small	1		9	4	5		6	10	9		11*	3	7	2					8	12			
15	6		Hull City	1-4	1-2	5535	Clarke	1		12	4	5		6	10	9	S	11	3	7	2			S		8*	9			
16	13		ROCHDALE	1-0	1-0	2245	Cooke	1	2	3	4	5	8	6	10	9	4	11		7				S						
17	27		PORT VALE	0-0	0-0	3043		1	2	3	4*	5	8	6	10	9		11		7					12					
18	4 Dec		Swindon Town	0-1	0-0	3961		1	2	3	4	5	8	6	10*	9		12		7					11					
19	27		COLCHESTER UNITED	2-1	1-1	4235	Winters Firm	1	2	3	4	5	8	6	10*	9		12		7					11					
20	28		Crewe Alexandra	2-0	2-0	1631	Gynn 2 Clarke	1	2	3	4	5	8	6	10	9*		12		7					11					
21	1 Jan		HEREFORD UNITED	4-0	1-0	3543	Gynn 2 Firm Cooke	1	2	3	4	5	8	6	10	9	S	S		7					11					
22	3		Blackpool	3-0	1-0	2388	Gynn Cooke Clarke	1	2	3	4	5	8	6	10	9	12	11*		7	2			S	11					
23	12		Hartlepool United	0-0	0-0	1161		1		3		5		6	10	9	8	11		7					11					
24	15		STOCKPORT COUNTY	1-0	1-0	2911	Benjamin	1		3		5	8	6	10	9	4	8	11	7	2			S						
25	22		Wimbledon	1-2	1-1	2119	Quow	1		3	4	5	8	6	10	9		8		7	2				11					
26	29		ALDERSHOT	0-0	0-0	2841		1		3	4	5	5	6	10	9	5	8		7	S				11					
27	5 Feb		YORK CITY	2-2	1-1	2652	Gynn Cooke	1		3	4	5	8	6	10	9	8	12		7	S				11*					
28	12		Bristol City	0-1	0-1	3959		1	2	3	4	5	8	6	10	9	S	11		7	2				11					
29	16		CHESTER	0-1	0-1	1661		1	2	3	4	5	8	6	10	9	11	11		7	2				11					
30	26		TRANMERE ROVERS	3-0	1-0	2045	Gynn Clarke Ippolitto		2	3	4	5	8	6	10	9	12	9*		7								S		
31	1 Mar		Halifax Town	2-1	1-1	2002	Ippolitto 2		2	3	4	5	8	6	10	9	S	9		7	S			2				11	1	
32	5		Torquay United	1-2	0-1	1537	O.G.		2	3	4	5	8	6	10	9	8	9		7								11	1	
33	12		NORTHAMPTON TOWN	2-0	0-0	3778	Gynn Clarke			3	4	5	5	6	10	9	8	9		7	S						2	11	1	
34	19		HULL CITY	1-1	0-0	3805	Gynn			3	4	5	5	6	10	9	8	9		7	S						2	11*	1	
35	26		Rochdale	1-1	0-0	1560	Chard			3	4	5	5	6	10	9	9	11		7							2		1	
36	1 Apr		Colchester United	0-1	0-1	3759			2	3	4	5	8	6	10	9	11	9*		7	S						12		1	
37	2		CREWE ALEXANDRA	2-1	0-1	2490	Clarke Chard		2	11	4	5	8	6	10	9	11	9		7							3		1	
38	9		SWINDON TOWN	4-3	4-1	2522	Gynn Slack Clarke Chard	1	2	3	4	5	5	6	10	9		9	S	7	S									
39	16		Bury	0-1	0-1	2761		1	2	3	4	5	5	6	10	9	8	9		7	S									
40	23		DARLINGTON	1-1	0-0	2185	Linton	1	2	3	4	5	5	6	10	9	11	9		7	S							11		
41	26		Scunthorpe United	0-3	0-0	3211		1	2	3	4	5	5	6	10	9	S	9		7	11						2	11		
42	29		Port Vale	1-2	1-2	5375	Gynn	1	2	3	4	5	5	6	10	9	S	9		7	11									
43	4 May		BLACKPOOL	3-1	3-1	1636	Gynn Benjamin Chard	1	2	3	4	5	4*	5	6	10	9	S	9		7	11						12		
44	7		MANSFIELD TOWN	3-2	1-0	2209	Gynn Clarke Rayment	1	2	3			4*	5	8	6	10	12	9		7	11								
45	14		Hereford United	1-0	0-0	2075	Rayment	1	S	3		4		8	5	10	6	9	4	3	7	11					5	6	11	2
46	17		Darlington	3-4	2-1	1002	Benjamin 2 Linton	1		4		5		5	6	10	6	6	3	7	11					S	S	S	2

F.A.Cup

1st	20 Nov	Chesterfield	2-2	1-1	2965	Gynn Clarke
1/R.	24	CHESTERFIELD	2-1	1-1	3185	Gynn Cooke
2nd	11 Dec	DONCASTER ROVERS	5-2	2-1	4012	Gynn Cooke 2 Clarke Quow
3rd	8 Jan	Luton Town	0-3	0-2	11151	

Football League Cup

1/1L	31 Aug	Darlington	2-0	1-0	2436	Gynn Cooke
1/2L	15 Sep	DARLINGTON	4-2	4-1	2117	Benjamin Cooke 2 Imlach
2/1L	6 Oct	CRYSTAL PALACE	0-2	0-1	3798	
2/2L	26	Crystal Palace	1-2	1-2	4502	Clarke

Appearance record labels:

- League Appearances
- League Sub. Appear.
- League Sub. non-Appear.
- (1 O.G.) League Goals
- Cup Appearances
- Cup Sub. Appear.
- Cup Sub. non-Appear.
- Cup Goals

DIVISION 4

	P	W	D	L	F	A	W	D	L	F	A	Pts
Wimbledon	46	17	4	2	57	23	12	7	4	39	22	98
Hull C	46	14	8	1	48	14	11	7	5	27	20	90
Port Vale	46	15	4	4	37	16	11	6	6	30	18	88
Scunthorpe U	46	13	7	3	41	17	10	7	6	25	23	83
Bury	46	15	4	4	43	20	8	8	7	31	26	81
Colchester U	46	17	5	1	51	19	7	4	12	24	36	81
York C	46	18	4	1	59	19	4	9	10	20	39	79
Swindon T	46	14	3	6	45	27	5	8	10	16	27	68
Peterboro' U	46	13	6	4	38	23	6	7	10	20	29	64
Mansfield T	46	11	6	6	32	26	5	7	11	29	44	61
Halifax T	46	9	8	6	31	23	7	4	12	28	43	60
Torquay U	46	12	3	8	38	30	5	4	14	18	35	58
Chester	46	8	6	9	28	24	7	5	11	27	36	56
Bristol C	46	10	8	5	32	25	3	9	11	27	45	56
Northampton T	46	10	8	5	43	29	4	4	15	22	46	54
Stockport	46	11	8	4	41	31	3	4	16	19	48	54
Darlington	46	8	5	10	27	30	5	8	10	34	41	52
Aldershot	46	11	5	7	40	35	1	10	12	21	47	51
Tranmere R	46	8	7	8	30	29	5	6	13	19	42	50
Rochdale	46	11	4	8	38	25	0	8	15	17	48	49
Blackpool	46	10	8	5	32	23	4	6	13	22	51	49
Hartlepool U	46	11	5	7	30	24	2	4	17	16	52	48
Crewe A	46	9	6	9	35	32	2	3	18	18	39	41
Hereford U	46	8	6	9	19	23	3	2	18	23	56	41

POSH 1982/83

Back row (from left): Richard Sutton, David Harrison, John Winters, Colin Clarke, David Seaman, Ian Benjamin, Steve Murphy, Mike Lyon, Mario Ippolito, Paddy Rayment, Tony Cliss, Mike Imlach, Trevor Slack, Neil Firm, Steve Collins, Ivor Linton, Steve Mercer. front: Robbie Cooke, Phil Chard, Bill Harvey, Martin Wilkinson, Billy Rodaway, Trevor and Micky Gynn.

Season Summary

Financial restraints cause unrest, and lead to departure of Manager Morris. Billy Kellock moves to Luton for £30,000, and goalkeeper Davis Seaman signs for Posh for a small fee. Two Peterborough players are sent off in the season's first league match. More rows between the Supporters' and Football Clubs!

SEASON 1983/84

Football League Division 4

1056	Date	Opposition	Res	H.T.	Attend	Goalscorer	Seaman	Chard	Imlach	Benjamin	Wile	Slack	Beech	Pike	Clarke	Quow	Buchanan	Rayment	Hankin	Linton	Firm	Tydeman	Ippolitto	Waddle	Holmes	Zenchuk	Worrall	Kelly	Allen
1	27 Aug	HARTLEPOOL UNITED	3-1	2-0	3213	Benjamin Buchanan Clarke	1	2	3	4	5	6	7	8	9*	10	11	12											
2	3 Sep	Wrexham	2-2	1-1	1680	Clarke 2	1	2	3	4	5	6	7	8	9	10	11	S											
3	6	York City	0-2	0-0	3709		1	2*	3	4	5	6	7	8	9	10	11	12											
4	10	TORQUAY UNITED	5-0	3-0	3135	Chard Clarke Hankin 2 O.G.	1	2	3	S	5	6	4*	8	11	10	7		9										
5	17	Hereford United	1-2	0-2	3172	Slack	1	2	3	12	5	6	4	8	11	10	7		9										
6	24	MANSFIELD TOWN	3-0	2-0	3490	Chard Buchanan 2	1	2	3	4	5	6		8	11	10	7		9										
7	28	CREWE ALEXANDRA	1-0	1-0	3783	Benjamin	1	2	3	4	5	6		8	11	10*	7	12	9										
8	8 Oct	DONCASTER ROVERS	1-1	0-1	4400	Pike	1	2	3	4	5	6		8	11	10	7	12	9										
9	15	Halifax Town	1-2	0-1	1079	Benjamin	1	2	3	4	5	6		8	11		7		9*	10	S								
10	18	Rochdale	1-2	0-1	1299	Hankin	1	2	3	4	5	6		8	11		7		9	10	12								
11	22	TRANMERE ROVERS	2-0	1-0	3311	Pike Hankin	1	2	3	4	5	6		8	11		7		9			10	S						
12	29	Bristol City	1-0	0-0	7380	Buchanan	1	2	3	4	5	6			11*		7		9			8		10					
13	2 Nov	READING	3-3	2-2	4073	Chard Imlach Waddle	1	2	3	4	5	6			11		7		9			8		10*					
14	5	Aldershot	2-3	1-2	1856	Clarke Quow	1	2	3	4	5	6			11	10	7					8		9					
15	12	CHESTERFIELD	2-0	1-0	3607	Quow Waddle	1	2	3	4	5	6			11	10	7					8		9					
16	26	STOCKPORT COUNTY	2-0	1-0	3240	Hankin 2	1	2	3	4	5	6			11	10	7		9			8		12					
17	29	Bury	2-2	1-1	2013	Chard Waddle	1	2	3	4	5	6			11	10	7					8		9					
18	3 Dec	Blackpool	2-1	1-0	4439	Benjamin Quow	1	2	3	4	5	6			11	10	7		12			8		9					
19	17	Chester City	1-1	0-1	1191	Chard	1	2	3	4	5	6	7*		S	10			9			8							
20	26	COLCHESTER UNITED	2-0	0-0	6527	Beech Waddle	1	2	3	4	5	6	7*		12	10			9			8		11					
21	27	Northampton Town	1-2	0-2	6464	Waddle	1	2	3	4	5	6	7*		10*	10			9			8		11					
22	31	SWINDON TOWN	1-1	1-0	4140	Slack	1	2	3	S	5	6	4			10			9		5	8		11					
23	2 Jan	Darlington	0-1	0-1	1471			2	12		5	6	4			10	10		9		5	8*		11		1			
24	7	WREXHAM	0-1	0-1	3277		1	2	12	12	5		4	7		10			9		6	8*		11	3				
25	21	HEREFORD UNITED	1-1	0-1	2559	Benjamin	1	2	12	9	5		4	7*	10						6	8		11	3				
26	28	Torquay United	0-1	0-0	1461		1	2	7	9	5	8	4		10*						6			11	3				
27	4 Feb	BURY	2-1	1-0	2507	Benjamin 2	1	2	7	11	5	8	4	S	10						6	12		11	3				
28	11	Mansfield Town	0-0	0-0	2179		1		7		5	8	4		10*						6			11	3		12		
29	15	Reading	1-1	1-1	2996	Waddle	1	2	3	7	5		4*	12			9				6	8		11	3		12		
30	18	BRISTOL CITY	4-1	1-1	3356	Hankin Waddle 2 Worrall	1	2	3	7	5		4	S			9				6	8		10	3		11		
31	24	Tranmere Rovers	0-0	0-0	1763		1	2	3	7	5		4	S			9				6	8		10	3		11		
32	3 Mar	ROCHDALE	2-0	0-0	2835	Wile O.G.	1	2	3	7	5		4	2			12				6	8		10*	3		11		
33	7	ALDERSHOT	1-2	0-0	3568	Wile	1	2	3	7	5	5	4		12						6	8		10*	3		11		
34	10	Chesterfield	0-1	0-1	2853		1	2	3	7		5	4		10						6	8*		10*	3		11		
35	17	Doncaster Rovers	1-1	1-0	3672	Chard	1	2	3	7		5	4	S	10						6	8		11	3		11		
36	24	HALIFAX TOWN	4-0	1-0	2304	Benjamin Worrall Chard Kelly	1	2	3*	7		5	4		12						6	8		9*	6		11		
37	27	Hartlepool United	1-1	1-1	1689	Kelly	1	2	3	7		5	4	8							6			11	3		11		
38	1 Apr	YORK CITY	0-2	0-0	5216		1	2			8	5	4					12	12		6			9	3		11		10
39	7	Crewe Alexandra	1-0	1-0	2024	Beech	1		2			5	4	7				2	S		6	8		9	3		11		10
40	14	BLACKPOOL	4-0	1-0	2921	Beech Waddle Kelly 2	1	2	2			5	4*	7				2	12		6	8		9*	3		11		10
41	21	Colchester United	1-1	0-1	1746	Holmes	1					5	4	7	12			2			6	8		9	3		11		10
42	24	NORTHAMPTON TOWN	6-0	3-0	3481	Waddle 2 Rayment Holmes	1					5	4	7	12			2			6	8		9	3		11		10*
43	27	Stockport County	1-4	0-3	1753	Waddle	1					5	4	7	12			2			6	8		9	3*		11		10
44	5 May	DARLINGTON	2-2	0-1	1925	Slack Quow	1		12			5	4	7	3			2			6	8*		9			11		10
45	7	Swindon Town	0-2	0-1	1876		1			S		5	4	7	8			2			6			9			11		10
46	12	CHESTER CITY	1-0	0-0	1679	Kelly	1		3	12		5	4	7	9*			2			6			9*			11		10

F.A.Cup

						1	2	3	7	5	6	4	11*	10	12		8	9
1st	19 Nov	Oxford United	0-2	0-1	6343												8	9

Football League Cup

						1	2	3	4	5	6	7	8	9	10	11*	12		8	9
1/1L	30 Aug	Crystal Palace	0-3	0-1	3975	1	2	3	4	5	6	7	8	9	10	11*	12			
1/2L	14 Sep	CRYSTAL PALACE	3-0*	2-0	3504	1	2	3	12	5	6	4	8	11	10	7	9*	Clarke Quow Hankin	9*	7
2/1L	5 Oct	Stoke City	0-0	0-0	11085	1	2	3	4	5	6	8	11	7	9	10*	12		9	10*	12
2/2L	26	STOKE CITY	1-2	0-1	9898	1	2	3	4	5	6	8	11	7*	9	10		Chard	9	10	12

* After extra time (3-0 score at 90 mins.) Match won 4-2 on penalties

Associate Members Cup

						2	3		5			7*	9	10*	8	12		24	3		29		33		11		14	18	11
1st	21 Feb	Wrexham	2-3†	1-0	1018	Pike Quow																							1

† After extra time (2-2 score at 90 mins.)

	45	38	29	31	32	39	38	28	17	9	24	13	8	25	3	24	5	29	33	20	11	14	18	11
League Appearances	45	38	29	31	32	39	38	28	17	9	24	13	8	25	3	24	5	29	33	20	11	14	18	11
League Sub. Appear.			3	3				7	1	4	3	5	5	2		1				1				1
League Sub. non-Appear.				4			5				1	1	2	1	1	1			1			1		
(2 O.G.) League Goals	7		1	8	2	3	3		5		4	1		3	2	1		1	12	2		1	7	
Cup Appearances	5	6	6	4	5	6	4	6	5		4	5			3	2		1	1	1				
Cup Sub. Appear.				1							1		2			1								
Cup Sub. non-Appear.												1		1										
Cup Goals	1							1	1	2														

DIVISION 4

	P	W	D	L	F	A	W	D	L	F	A	Pts
York C	46	18	4	1	58	11	13	4	6	38	23	101
Doncaster R	46	15	6	2	46	22	9	7	7	36	32	85
Reading	46	17	6	0	51	14	5	10	8	33	42	82
Bristol C	46	18	3	2	51	17	6	9	19	27		82
Aldershot	46	14	6	3	49	29	8	3	12	27	40	75
Blackpool	46	15	4	4	47	19	6	5	12	23	33	72
Peterboro' U	46	15	5	3	52	16	3	9	11	20	32	68
Colchester U	46	14	7	2	45	14	3	9	11	24	39	67
Torquay U	46	13	7	3	32	18	5	6	12	27	46	67
Tranmere R	46	11	5	7	33	26	6	10	7	20	27	66
Hereford U	46	11	6	6	31	21	5	9	9	23	32	63
Stockport Co	46	12	5	6	34	25	5	6	12	26	39	62
Chesterfield	46	10	11	2	34	24	5	4	14	25	37	60
Darlington	46	13	4	6	31	19	4	4	15	18	31	59
Bury	46	9	7	7	34	32	6	7	10	27	32	59
Crewe A	46	10	8	5	35	27	4	6	13	24	41	59
Swindon T	46	11	7	5	34	23	4	6	13	24	33	58
Northampton T	46	10	8	5	32	32	6	3	14	21	46	53
Mansfield T	46	9	7	7	44	27	4	6	13	22	43	52
Wrexham	46	9	7	7	34	33	4	9	10	25	41	48
Halifax T	46	11	6	6	36	25	1	6	16	19	64	48
Rochdale	46	8	9	6	35	31	3	7	13	16	47	49
Hartlepool U	46	8	8	8	31	28	3	2	18	16	57	40
Chester C	46	7	5	11	23	35	0	8	15	22	47	34

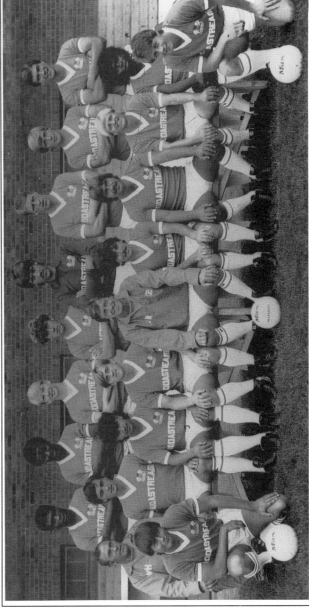

(Back) Linton, Benjamin, ? , Rayment, Seamen, Firm, Clarke, Slack.
(Front)Harvey, Chard, Ippolito, Imlach, Wile, Gynn, Winters, Beech, Quow. (Kneeling)Pike, Buchanon.

Season Summary

New Manager John Wile suffers from continual financial restraints. Micky Gynn moves to Coventry for £60,000. Posh beat Palace in Milk Cup 2nd leg penalty shoot-out after losing 1st leg 3-0. First Sunday match played. Early promotion hopes fade in second half of season with final 7th placing.

SEASON 1984/85

Football League Division 4

1106	Date	Opposition	Res	H.T.	Attend	Goalscorer
1	25 Aug	TRANMERE ROVERS	1-0	0-0	3045	Holmes
2	1 Sep	Hereford United	0-1	0-1	2728	
3	8	MANSFIELD TOWN	1-0	0-0	3502	Kelly
4	15	Wrexham	3-1	2-0	1704	Wile Kelly Quow
5	18	Aldershot	0-0	0-0	2318	
6	22	HARTLEPOOL UNITED	3-1	0-0	3491	Beech Johnson Klug
7	29	Torquay United	0-0	0-0	1271	
8	3 Oct	SCUNTHORPE UNITED	3-1	2-1	3620	Kelly 2 Worrall
9	7	Swindon	1-1	1-1	4010	Slack
10	13	STOCKPORT COUNTY	3-1	1-1	3739	Johnson Klug Worrall
11	20	Rochdale	1-2	1-2	1169	Cassidy
12	24	HALIFAX TOWN	2-0	2-0	3770	Kelly Cassidy
13	27	Port Vale	1-3	1-1	3943	Cassidy
14	3 Nov	CREWE ALEXANDRA	2-1	1-1	3682	Slack
15	7	BLACKPOOL	2-0	1-0	4296	Worrall Cassidy
16	10	Southend United	1-2	0-1	1779	Cassidy
17	24	DARLINGTON	1-1	1-0	5341	Worrall
18	1 Dec	Colchester United	1-3	1-3	2070	Kelly
19	15	Exeter City	1-0	1-0	3012	Beech
20	19	BURY	1-4	1-2	3836	Worrall
21	26	Northampton Town	3-0	0-0	4350	Kelly Worrall Shepherd
22	29	Chesterfield	0-2	0-1	4045	
23	1 Jan	CHESTER CITY	3-1	1-1	3799	Kelly 2 Shepherd
24	5	Tranmere Rovers	0-4	0-1	1511	
25	12	HEREFORD UNITED	1-1	0-1	3709	Johnson
26	26	WREXHAM	2-1	1-0	3091	Shepherd 2
27	2 Feb	TORQUAY UNITED	1-0	0-0	3168	Shepherd
28	9	Hartlepool United	3-0	0-0	1060	Kelly 2 Hankin
29	12	Scunthorpe United	1-2	0-2	1219	Worrall
30	23	Crewe Alexandra	1-2	0-1	1735	Cassidy
31	2 Mar	PORT VALE	0-0	0-0	2668	
32	5	Halifax Town	0-0	0-0	1071	
33	9	ROCHDALE	1-1	0-1	2495	Pike
34	16	Stockport County	1-1	1-0	1340	Worrall
35	23	SWINDON TOWN	0-1	0-1	2329	
36	27	Mansfield Town	0-0	0-0	1945	
37	30	Blackpool	2-4	1-2	3809	Pike Shepherd
38	2 Apr	NORTHAMPTON TOWN	0-0	0-0	2482	
39	5	Chester City	3-1	1-1	2020	Pike Shepherd Worrall
40	13	SOUTHEND UNITED	1-4	0-2	2095	Cassidy
41	17	ALDERSHOT	1-2	0-0	1467	Johnson
42	20	Darlington	1-2	1-1	3795	Slack
43	27	COLCHESTER UNITED	0-1	0-1	1684	
44	4 May	EXETER CITY	0-0	0-0	1464	
45	6	CHESTERFIELD	0-0	0-0	3692	
46	11	Bury	1-1	1-1	2986	Pike

Appearances / team line-ups

#	Seaman	Chard	Pike	Beech	Wile	Holmes	Johnson	Klug	Kelly	Quow	Worrall	Cassidy	Rayment	Waddle	Slack	Turner	Parr	Shepherd	Firm	La Ronde	Martin	Hankin	Lowther	Reilly	O'Keefe	Wilkins
1	1	2	3	4	5	6	7	8	9	10	11	S														
2	1	2	3		5	6	7*	8	9	10	11	4	12													
3	1	2	3	S	5	6	7	8	9	10	11	4		6	6	1	1									
4	1	2	3	S	5	6	7	8	9	10	11	4			6	1	1									
5	1	2	3	S	5	6	7	8	9	10	11	4			6	1	1									
6	1	2	3	12	5	6	7	8	9	10	11	4*			6	1	1									
7	1	2	3	4	5	6	7	8	9	10	11	S			6	1	1									
8	1	2	3	4	5	6	7	8	9	10	11	S			6	1	1									
9	1	2	3	4	5		7	8	9	10	11			S	6	1	1									
10	1	2	3	4*	5	7	7	8	9	10	11			12	6	1	1									
11	1	2	3	S	5	7	7	8	9	10	11	4			6	1	1									
12	1	2	3	S	5	7	7	8	9	10	11	4			6	1	1									
13	1	2	3	12	5	7	7	8	9	10*	11	4			6	1	1									
14	1	2	3	10	5	7	7	8	9		11	4		S	6	1	1									
15	1	2	3	4	5	S	7	8	9		11	10		S	6	1	1					S				
16	1	2	3	4	5		7	8	9		11	10*			6	1	1					12				
17	1	2	3	4	5		7	8	9		11	10			6	1	1									
18	1	2	3	4	5	S		8	9	10	11	S			6	1	1									
19	1	2	3	4	5			8	S	10	11			9	6	1	1	7								
20	1	2	3	4	5			8	12	10*	11			9	6	1	1	7								
21	1		3	4	S	2		8	7		11	10			6	1	1	9	5							
22	1		3	4	S	2		8	7		11	10			6	1	1	9	5							
23	1		3	4		2		8	7		11	10*		S	6	1	1	9	5							
24	1		3	4	5	4*	7	8	12		11				6	1	1	9	5	2						
25	1		3		5	S	7	8		10	11	10*			6	1	1	7		2	4	9				
26	1		3		5	12	S	8		10	11	10			6	1	1	7			4*	9				
27	1		3		5				12	10	11	10			6	1	1	7		2	4*	9	2			
28	1		3		5		8	8	12	10	11				6	1	1	7		2	S	9*				
29	1		3		5		8	4	4	10	11				6	1	1	7		2	4	9				
30	8		3		5		12	8	12		11	10					1	7	6	2	4	9				
31	8		3	3	5			8	12	8*	11	10				1	1	7	6	2	4	9				
32			3	4	5			9	S		11	10				1	1	7		2	4	9				
33			3	4	5		12	8	9	2	11*	10			6	1	1	7			4					
34			3	2	5		S	8	9	5	11	10			6	1	1	7			4					
35			3		5	7	12	8	S	4	11	10		S	6	1	1	7	2*	2	4					
36			3		5	7*		8	S	2	11	10			6	1	1	7			4			S		
37			3		5*			8	12	2	11	10			6	1	1	7			4			12		
38	8		3		5	8	S	8	S	2	11	10			6	1	1	7		2	4					
39	8		3		5	7	12		9*	2	11	10			6	1	1	7			4					
40	8		3		5	7	S		S	2	11	10			9	1	1	7	5		4					
41	10		3		5	7*	8	12	S	2	11	10		S	6	1	1	7			4					
42	8		3		5		7*	8	12	2	11	10			6	1	1	7			4					
43	8	8	3		5*	6	S		9	2	11	4				1	1	7								
44	8	10	3		5	4	12		9*	2	11	S			6	1	1	7		2					12	
45	8	8	3		5		9	10	S	2	11	S			6	1	1	7								
46	8	10	3		5	4	8	10	9	2	11	7*			6	1	1	7							12	12

F.A.Cup

	Date	Opponent	Score	HT	Att	Scorers													
1st	17 Nov	Cambridge United	2-0	1-0	5641	Kelly 2	2	3	4	5	11	7	8	9	S	10		6	1
2nd	8 Dec	Dagenham	0-1	0-0	3302		2	3	4	5	7	8	9	10	11	S		6	1

Football League Cup

	Date	Opponent	Score	HT	Att	Scorers													
1/1L	28 Aug	Sheffield United	0-1	0-1	7451		1	2	3	4	5	6	7	8	9	10	11	S	
1/2L	5 Sep	SHEFFIELD UNITED	2-2*	2-0	4362	Kelly Cassidy	1	2	3	4	5	6*	7	8	9	10	11	4	12

* After extra time (2-1 at 90 minutes)

Freight Rover Trophy

	Date	Opponent	Score	HT	Att	Scorers													
1/1L	23 Jan	CAMBRIDGE UNITED	2-1	2-0	2095	Slack Quow	3			5	4	S	S	8	10	11	S	31	6	1
1/2L	5 Feb	Cambridge United	0-2	0-0	1740		3			6	S	S	7	10	11	S			8

DIVISION 4

	P	W	D	L	F	A	W	D	L	F	A	Pts
Chesterfield	46	16	6	1	40	13	10	7	6	24	22	91
Blackpool	46	16	7	1	42	15	9	7	7	31	24	86
Darlington	46	16	4	3	41	22	8	9	6	25	27	85
Bury	46	15	6	2	46	20	9	6	8	30	30	84
Hereford U	46	16	2	5	38	21	6	9	8	27	26	77
Tranmere R	46	17	1	5	50	21	7	2	14	33	45	75
Colchester U	46	13	7	3	49	29	7	7	9	38	36	74
Swindon T	46	16	4	3	42	21	5	5	13	20	37	72
Scunthorpe U	46	14	6	3	61	33	5	8	10	22	39	71
Crewe A	46	10	7	6	32	28	8	5	10	33	41	66
Peterboro U	46	11	5	7	29	21	5	7	11	25	32	62
Port Vale	46	11	8	4	39	24	3	10	10	22	35	60
Aldershot	46	11	6	6	33	20	6	2	15	23	43	59
Mansfield T	46	10	8	5	25	15	3	10	10	16	23	57
Wrexham	46	10	6	7	39	27	5	6	12	24	42	54
Chester C	46	11	3	9	35	30	4	6	13	25	42	54
Rochdale	46	8	7	8	33	30	5	7	11	22	39	53
Exeter C	46	9	7	7	30	27	4	7	12	27	52	53
Hartlepool U	46	10	6	7	34	29	4	4	15	24	49	52
Southend U	46	8	8	7	30	34	5	3	15	28	49	50
Halifax T	46	9	3	11	26	32	6	2	15	16	37	50
Stockport C	46	11	5	7	40	26	2	4	18	18	53	47
Northampton T	46	10	1	12	32	42	4	4	15	21	42	47
Torquay U	46	5	11	7	18	24	4	3	16	20	39	41

Appearances

League Appearances	8	25	45	20	41	13	26	39	33	35	46	31	2	41	38	8	27	8	8	13	6
League Sub. Appear.			2			4	4		7	1	1	1	1		1					1	1
League Sub. non-Appear.				4	2	2	3		3	1	5		4							1	1
League Goals	1		4	2	1	1	4	2	11	1	9	7		3			3				
Cup Appearances	2	4	6	3	5	6	3	5	5	5	5	2		3	4		1	1		1	2	2
Cup Sub. Appear.							2			2	1	1	3		1						
Cup Sub. non-Appear.				3					3	1		1	1								
Cup Goals																	5		1		

(Back – Youth team). (Middle) Holmes, Chard, Waddle, Firm, Seamen, Hankin, Slack, Klug, Harvey. (Front) Kelly, Beech, Worrall, Rayment, Wile, Cassidy, Johnson, Pike, Quow. (Sitting – Apprentices)

Season Summary

A good start lifts Posh to 4th in table. Under-21 International squad player Seaman leaves for £100,000 fee. Posh lose in F.A.Cup at non-League Dagenham – a match marred by fighting and a collapsed wall. Ray Hankin is sacked after his fifth sending-off. Final disappointing mid-table placing in League.

SEASON 1985/86

Football League Division 4

1150

#	Date	Opposition	Res	H.T.	Attend	Goalscorer
1	17 Aug	Preston North End	4-2	2-1	3177	Gallagher 2 Worrall 2
2	24	CHESTER CITY	3-0	0-0	2667	Pike 2 Kowalski
3	27	Orient	2-2	1-2	2577	Holmes Worrall
4	31	SCUNTHORPE UNITED	1-0	1-0	2928	Fuccillo
5	7 Sep	Rochdale	1-2	0-2	2600	Gallagher
6	14	SWINDON TOWN	3-0	2-0	2946	Holmes Gallagher 2
7	18	TORQUAY UNITED	2-0	1-0	3432	Quow Kowalski
8	21	Hereford United	1-2	0-2	3261	Holmes
9	28	BURNLEY	0-0	0-0	3700	
10	1 Oct	Tranmere Rovers	1-0*	1-0	1406	Kowalski (* Abandoned after 57 mins.)
11	5	Hartlepool United	1-2	1-1	2584	Gallagher
12	12	NORTHAMPTON TOWN	0-5	0-2	3866	
13	18	Stockport County	2-2	1-0	1634	Gallagher Shepherd
14	23	CREWE ALEXANDRA	0-0	0-0	2670	
15	26	Cambridge United	1-3	0-0	3234	Holmes
16	29	Tranmere Rovers	0-7	0-1	1318	
17	2 Nov	EXETER CITY	1-1	1-0	2200	Rees
18	6	WREXHAM	1-1	1-0	1948	Rees
19	9	Halifax Town	1-1	1-0	1007	Worrall
20	23	PORT VALE	1-0	0-0	2852	Worrall
21	30	Aldershot	0-1	0-1	1375	
22	14 Dec	MANSFIELD TOWN	4-2	2-1	3128	Kelly Cassidy 2 Slack
23	21	Chester City	1-2	0-1	2331	Gallagher
24	28	ORIENT	2-2	0-0	3238	Gallagher Kelly
25	1 Jan	SOUTHEND UNITED	1-1	0-0	3104	Kelly
26	11	Scunthorpe United	0-2	0-2	1842	
27	18	PRESTON NORTH END	1-1	0-1	2711	Shepherd
28	4 Feb	Crewe Alexandra	1-1	1-1	1009	Shepherd
29	1 Mar	Burnley	1-1	1-0	2686	Slack
30	5	TRANMERE ROVERS	0-1	0-1	1512	
31	8	HARTLEPOOL UNITED	3-1	1-0	2361	Slack Shepherd Gallagher
32	11	Torquay United	0-2	0-1	1243	
33	15	Northampton Town	2-2	0-2	3332	Slack Kelly
34	19	Exeter City	0-1	0-0	1460	
35	22	CAMBRIDGE UNITED	0-2	0-2	2894	
36	26	HEREFORD UNITED	0-0	0-0	1560	
37	29	Southend United	1-0	0-0	1687	Gallagher
38	31	COLCHESTER UNITED	1-2	1-1	2316	Fuccillo
39	5 Apr	Wrexham	1-0	0-0	1138	Shepherd
40	8	STOCKPORT COUNTY	2-0	2-0	1610	Kowalski Shepherd
41	12	HALIFAX TOWN	1-1	1-1	2260	Slack
42	15	Swindon Town	0-3	0-1	6426	
43	19	Port Vale	0-2	0-1	3765	
44	22	Colchester United	0-5	0-1	1863	
45	26	ALDERSHOT	3-0	2-0	1942	Fuccillo Gallagher O.G.
46	3 May	Mansfield Town	1-0	1-0	3008	Quow
47	7	ROCHDALE	1-1	1-0	1592	Quow

Player appearance grid (shirt numbers by match), columns:
Brown, Moules, Bryant, Parslow, Nuttall, Cavener, McManus, Astbury, Collins, Gage, Rees, McClure, Corder, Shepherd, Johnson, Slack, Whymark, O'Keefe, Cassidy, Worrall, Kelly, Gallagher, Fuccillo, Kowalski, Holmes, Wile, Quow, Pike, Paris, Turner

F.A.Cup

	Date	Opponent	FT	HT	Att	Scorers
1st	16 Nov	BISHOP Stortford	2-2	2-2	1981	Worrall O.G.
1/R.	20	BISHOP STORTFORD	3-1	2-1	2778	Kowalski Galagher Cassidy
2nd	7 Dec	BATH CITY	1-0	0-0	3388	Gallagher
3rd	4 Jan	LEEDS UNITED	1-0	0-0	10137	Shepherd
4th	25	CARLISLE UNITED	1-0	1-0	8311	Shepherd
5th	15 Feb	BRIGHTON & H.A.	2-2	2-2	15812	Kelly Shepherd
5/R.	3 Mar	Brighton & H.A.	0-1	0-0	19010	

Football League Cup

	Date	Opponent	FT	HT	Att	Scorers
1/1L	21 Aug	NORTHAMPTON TOWN	0-0	0-0	3117	
1/2L	3 Sep	Northampton Town	0-2	0-0	2464	

Freight Rover Trophy

	Date	Opponent	FT	HT	Att	Scorers
Prel.	21 Jan	Cambridge United	1-4	1-0	2253	Gallagher
Prel.	17 Apr	ALDERSHOT	2-0	1-0	279	Kelly Johnson

Appearance summary categories:

- League Appearances
- League Sub. Appear.
- League Sub. non-Appear.
- (1 O.G.) League Goals
- Cup Appearances
- Cup Sub. Appear.
- Cup Sub. non-Appear.
- (1 O.G.) Cup Goals

DIVISION 4

	P	W	D	L	F	A	W	D	L	F	A	Pts
Swindon T	46	20	2	1	52	19	12	4	7	30	24	102
Chester C	46	15	5	3	44	16	8	10	5	39	34	84
Mansfield T	46	13	8	2	43	17	10	4	9	31	30	81
Port Vale	46	13	9	1	42	11	8	7	8	25	26	79
Orient	46	11	6	6	39	21	9	6	8	40	43	72
Colchester U	46	12	6	5	51	22	7	7	9	37	41	70
Hartlepool U	46	15	6	2	41	20	5	4	14	27	47	70
Northampton T	46	9	7	7	44	29	9	3	11	35	29	64
Southend U	46	12	6	5	35	29	6	6	11	26	40	64
Hereford U	46	14	6	3	43	27	5	6	12	26	40	64
Stockport U	46	15	6	2	55	30	3	4	16	19	43	64
Crewe A	46	9	9	5	35	28	8	4	11	28	43	64
Wrexham	46	10	6	7	35	26	8	3	12	19	35	63
Burnley	46	11	5	7	34	24	6	4	13	34	56	60
Scunthorpe U	46	11	7	5	33	30	5	8	10	25	35	59
Aldershot	46	12	6	5	45	25	5	6	12	21	49	58
Peterboro' U	46	9	11	3	31	19	4	6	13	21	45	56
Rochdale	46	12	7	4	41	29	2	6	15	16	48	55
Tranmere R	46	9	11	3	46	41	6	4	15	28	32	54
Halifax T	46	10	8	5	27	25	4	4	15	25	44	54
Exeter C	46	10	4	9	26	25	3	11	9	21	34	54
Cambridge U	46	12	2	9	45	38	3	7	13	20	42	54
Preston NE	46	6	7	4	12	32	4	6	13	22	48	43
Torquay U	46	8	5	10	29	32	1	5	17	14	56	37

(Back) Harvey, Cassidy, Slack, Shepherd, Astbury, Turner, Gage, Paris, Collins, Wile.
(Front) O'Keefe, Worrall, Gallagher, Johnson, Quow, Pike, Fucillo, Kowalski.

Season Summary

Posh Chairman announces that Club is up for sale! Early season injury crisis. Controversial 'derby' match at London Road with Northampton ends in 5-0 defeat. Leeds beaten in F.A.Cup. Poor away form contributes to 8th from bottom final placing in table.

SEASON 1986/87

Football League Division 4

1196		Date	Opposition	Res	H.T.	Attend	Beasley	Paris	Collins	Gunn	Price	Gage	Nightingale	Fuccillo	Lawrence	Shepherd	Luke	Christie	Gregory	Gallagher	Doyle	Nuttell	Butterworth	Wile	Shoemake	Moulds	Doig	Phillips	Kelly	Smeulders	Crichton	Carr	Fife	Goalscorer
1		23 Aug	SOUTHEND UNITED	2-0	1-0	3548	1	2	3	4	5	6	7	8	9	10	11	S																Lawrence Shepherd
2		30	Orient	0-1	0-1	2471	1	2	3	4	5	6	7*	8	9	10		12	11															
3		6 Sep	ALDERSHOT	1-1	0-0	2797	1	2	3	4	5	6		8	9	10	11*	7	12	10															Gregory
4		14	Northampton Town	1-2	0-2	5517	1	2	3	4		6	11	8	9			7	12	10*	5														Gregory
5		20	CREWE ALEXANDRA	1-2	0-1	2406	1	2	3	4	5	6	11	8	9			7	10	12	8*														Gunn
6		27	Colchester United	3-1	1-0	2343	1			3	5	6	2		9			7	7	10	4	11													Gunn Lawrence Gregory
7		1 Oct	CARDIFF CITY	1-2	1-1	2558		12		3	5	6	2	8*	9	11			7	10	4	11													Lawrence
8		4	Hereford United	0-2	0-2	2104		2	12	3	5	6		8	9				7	10*	4	11			1		11								
9		11	ROCHDALE	1-1	0-1	2289	1	2	9	3	5*	6	2	8					7	10	4				1		11								Gunn
10		14	Wrexham	3-4	0-4	2400		9	3	4		6*	2	8					7	10	4	12			1		11			8					Nightingale Gregory Gallagher
11		18	Hartlepool United	2-1	0-1	1753		5	S			6	11	8					7	10	5	9			1		11								Gunn O.G.
12		22	SWANSEA CITY	1-1	0-1	2301		10		3	5	6	2	8	9				7	12	4	9*			1		11								Gallagher
13		25	LINCOLN CITY	0-1	0-0	2364		7	3		5	6	2*	8					12	10	4				1		11								
14		1 Nov	Burnley	0-0	0-0	2229		7	3		5	6	2	8	9				10	S	4				1		11								
15		5	TRANMERE ROVERS	2-1	1-0	1812		7	3	4	5	6	2	8*	9			12	10	9	4				1		11								Lawrence Gregory
16		8	Exeter City	1-1	0-1	2701		7	3	4	5	6	2		9			11	10	S	5				1		11								Phillips
17		22	Cambridge United	1-1	0-1	3498		2	3	4	5	6	8				S		7	9	11				1					10					Gregory
18		29	PRESTON NORTH END	2-1	0-0	3462		2	3	4	5	6	8				11*		7	9	12				1					10					Luke Phillips
19		13 Dec	HALIFAX TOWN	2-0	1-0	3135		2	3	8	5	6	4				7	11*		9				1					10	12					Luke 2
20		26	SCUNTHORPE UNITED	1-1	1-1	4267		2	3	8	5	6	4				7	11*		9				1					10	12					Luke
21		27	Stockport County	1-3	0-1	2120		2	3	8	5	6	4				7			9		S		1					10	11					Phillips
22		1 Jan	Wolverhampton W.	3-0	1-0	4399		2	3	S	5	6	4	8			7			9				1					10	11					Luke Gallagher Phillips
23		4	CAMBRIDGE UNITED	2-1	0-1	4713		2	3	S	5	6	4	8			7			9				1					10	11					Luke Kelly
24		10	Southend United	2-2	1-1	2605		2	3	S	5	6	4	8			7			9				1					10	11					Nightingale Gallagher
25		17	ORIENT	0-1	0-0	3513		2*	3	12	5	6	4	8			7			9				1					10	11		1			
26		24	Aldershot	1-1	0-1	2093		2	3		5	6	4	8			7			9	S			1					10	11					Phillips
27		31	NORTHAMPTON TOWN	1-0	0-0	7911		2	3*		5	6	4	8			7		12	9				1					10	11					
28		7 Feb	WREXHAM	0-0	0-0	2935		2		3	5	6	4	8					7	9	S			1					10	11					
29		14	Crewe Alexandra	3-1	3-0	1169		2		3	5	6	4	8					12	9*				1					10	11					Gallagher Phillips Kelly
30		21	COLCHESTER UNITED	2-0	2-0	3474		2		3	5	6	4*	8					S	9				1					10	11					Gallagher Phillips
31		28	Cardiff City	1-0	1-0	2620		2		3	5	6	4	8					12	9				1					10	11					Luke
32		4 Mar	BURNLEY	1-1	1-0	4304		2		3	5	6	4	8					12	9				1					10*	11					Gallagher
33		8	Lincoln City	2-1	0-1	3304		2		3	5	6	4	8			7		S	9				1					10	11					Luke Phillips
34		14	HARTLEPOOL UNITED	3-1	2-0	4116		2		3	5	6	4	8*			7		12	9				1					10	11					Luke Phillips Kelly
35		17	Swansea City	1-0	1-0	4168		2		3	5	6	4	8			7		S	9				1					10	11					Luke
36		21	Rochdale	2-3	1-0	2170		2		3	5	6	4*	8			7		12	9				1					10	11					Gregory 2
37		28	HEREFORD UNITED	2-1	1-1	4110		2		3	5	6	4	8*			7		S	9				1					10*	11					Gunn Gage
38		31	Torquay United	0-1	0-1	1279		2		3	5	6	4	8			7		12	9				1					10	11					
39		4 Apr	EXETER CITY	2-2	1-2	3583		2		3	5	6	4	8			7		12	9*				1					10	11					Phillips 2
40		11	Tranmere Rovers	1-1	0-1	1379		2		3	5	6	4*	8			7		S	9				1					10	11					Kelly
41		18	WOLVERHAMPTON W.	1-1	0-1	9547		2		3	5	6	4*	8			7		12	9				1					10	11					
42		20	Scunthorpe United	0-2	0-2	2470		2		3	5	6	4				7		12	9				1					10*	11					
43		25	TORQUAY UNITED	2-1	1-0	3083		2	4	3	5	6		8			8		7	9*	12				1					10	11					Gunn 2
44		2 May	Preston North End	0-0	0-0	7919		2	4	3	5	6		8			7		12	9*									10	11		1				
45		4	STOCKPORT COUNTY	0-0	0-0	2968		2	4	3	5	6		8			7		12	9*									10	11		1		8*		
46		9	Halifax Town	0-1	0-1	1004		2	4	3	5	6					7			9			12						10	11		1	8*	10		

| 1st | 16 Nov | Northampton Town | 0-3 | 0-1 | 9114 | |

| 7 | 3 | 4 | 5 | 6 | 2 | 9* | 8 | 9 | 10* | 11" | 12 | 13 | | 1 | 8 |

Football League Cup

1/1L	26 Aug	Colchester United	0-0	0-0	1551	
1/2L	3 Sep	COLCHESTER UNITED	2-0	0-0	2698	Luke O.G.
2/1L	24	NORWICH CITY	0-0	0-0	6956	
2/2L	8 Oct	Norwich City	0-1	0-0	10027	

1	2	3	4	5	6	7	8	9	10*	11"	12	13			
1	2	3	4	5	6	S	8	9	10*	11	7	12			
1	2		4	5	6	11	8		7	10	3*	12	S		
	11	3	4	5	6	2	8		7	10	9	S			

Sherpa Van Trophy

| Prel. | 25 Nov | Colchester United | 1-2 | 0-1 | 1404 | Phillips |
| Prel. | 3 Dec | ALDERSHOT | 3-3 | 1-0 | 1168 | Nightingale Gregory Doyle |

| 2 | 3 | 10 | 5 | 6 | 4 | | 12 | | 7 | 9 | 11* | S | | | 8 |
| 2 | 3 | 8 | 6 | 5 | 4 | | 7* | | 12 | 11 | 9 | 14 | | | 10" |

	League Appearances	7	43	26	38	42	46	40	37	12	3	30	6	16	38	13	5		34		7	30	26	1	4	1	1
	League Sub. Appear.		2	1	1							2	2	15	2	2	1					2					
	League Sub. non-Appear.			3						1		1	1	5	2	2	1				11						
	(1 O.G.) League Goals				7		1	2	4	10			8	8	8							11		4				
	Cup Appearances	3	7	6	7	6	4	4	4	3	2	5	2	4	4	4			4			3					
	Cup Sub. Appear.									1		2	1		1	2	2										
	Cup Sub. non-Appear.		6	7	6						1						2										
	(1 O.G.) Cup Goals			1		1		1			1			1			2						1				

DIVISION 4

	P	W	D	L	F	A	W	D	L	F	A	Pts
Northampton T	46	20	2	1	56	20	10	7	6	47	33	99
Preston NE	46	16	4	3	36	18	10	8	5	36	29	90
Southend U	46	14	4	5	43	27	11	1	11	25	28	80
Wolves	46	12	3	8	36	24	12	4	7	33	26	79
Colchester U	46	15	3	5	41	20	6	4	13	23	36	70
Aldershot	46	13	5	5	40	22	7	5	11	24	35	70
Orient	46	15	2	6	40	25	5	7	11	24	36	69
Scunthorpe U	46	15	3	5	52	27	3	9	11	21	30	66
Wrexham	46	8	13	2	38	24	7	7	9	28	29	65
Peterboro' U	46	10	7	6	29	21	7	9	7	32	27	65
Cambridge U	46	12	6	5	37	23	5	5	13	23	39	62
Swansea C	46	13	3	7	21	4	8	11	25	40	62	
Cardiff C	46	6	12	5	24	18	9	4	10	24	32	61
Exeter C	46	11	10	2	37	17	0	13	10	16	32	56
Halifax T	46	12	5	6	35	13	5	5	13	27	42	55
Hereford U	46	10	6	7	33	23	4	5	14	27	38	53
Crewe A	46	8	9	6	38	35	5	5	13	32	37	53
Hartlepool U	46	6	11	6	24	30	5	7	11	20	35	51
Stockport Co	46	9	6	8	25	27	4	6	13	15	42	51
Tranmere R	46	6	10	7	32	27	5	7	11	22	35	50
Rochdale	46	8	7	8	31	30	3	9	11	23	43	50
Burnley	46	9	7	7	31	35	3	6	14	22	39	49
Torquay U	46	8	8	7	28	29	2	10	11	28	43	48
Lincoln C	46	8	7	8	30	27	4	5	14	15	38	48

(Back) Doyle, Luke, Paris, Price, Gallagher, Christie, Gunn, Shepherd.
(2nd Row) D.Poole, Fucillo, Harvey, Gage, ?, Beasley, Shoemake, Lawrence, Nightingale, ?, Blades, Robson.
(3rd Row and sitting at front in White tops – Apprentices)

Season Summary

Large turnaround in the playing staff, nine new players, and later Boardroom changes. London Road to stage Under-21 England International. Poor start, near bottom of League, Club £400,000 in debt. Shareholders demand resignation of Manager Wile – sacked after Burnley match. Noel Cantwell returns as Manager, to much acclaim. Talk of selling Ground is unpopular with fans.

SEASON 1987/88

Football League Division 4

#	Date	Opposition	Res	H.T.	Attend	Goalscorer	Neenan	Paris	Gunn	Gooding	Pollard	Price	Kelly	Phillips	Riley	Halsall	Luke	Collins	Lawrence	Nightingale	Butterworth	Carr	Nuttell	Shoemake	White	Kerr	Benning	Corner	Fife	Philpott	Genovese
1	15 Aug	CARLISLE UNITED	1-0	1-0	3849	Gooding	1	2	3	4	5	6	7	8	9	10	11	S	S												
2	22	Rochdale	1-1	1-1	1808	Riley	1	2	3	4	5	6	7	8	9	10	11	S	14	12											
3	29	CAMBRIDGE UNITED	1-0	0-0	4623	Phillips	1	2	3	4	5	6	7	8	9	10	11	S	S		7*										
4	31	Bolton Wanderers	0-2	0-1	3746		1	2	3	4		6	7	8	9	10	11"				7*										
5	5 Sep	DARLINGTON	1-2	1-2	3200	Riley	1	2	3	4	5	6	7	8*	9	10	11	S	12	14	7										
6	12	Colchester United	1-4	0-1	1164	Lawrence	1	2	3	4	5	6	7	8	9	10	11	S	7				S								
7	16	WOLVERHAMPTON W.	1-1	0-1	3089	Gooding	1	2	3	4	5	6*	7		9	10	11	8	7	12		6*	S								
8	19	WREXHAM	1-1	1-0	2805	Lawrence	1	2	3	4	5	6	7		9	10	11*	8	7	12		7	S								
9	26	Leyton Orient	0-2	0-0	3426			2	3	4	5	6	7		9	10	11*	8	7	12		7	S	1							
10	30	Hereford United	1-0	1-0	2010	Paris	1	2	3	4	5	6	7		9	10	11	8	7	12		10"	S								
11	3 Oct	SCUNTHORPE UNITED	1-1	1-0	3616	Gooding	1	2	3	4	5	6	7		10	10	11	8	9	12		12	S								
12	10	Stockport County	1-0	0-0	1594	Lawrence	1	2	3	4	5	6	7		10	10	11	8	9	14		10	S								
13	17	CARDIFF CITY	4-3	1-2	3473	Gooding Luke 2 Lawrence	1	2	3	4	5"	6				8	7	11	9	14		12	10*								
14	21	NEWPORT COUNTY	3-0	2-0	3165	Gooding 3	1	2	3	4		6				8	7	11	5	5		10	S								
15	24	Halifax Town	0-0	0-0	1615		1	2	3	4		6				8	7	11	5	5		10	S								
16	31	TORQUAY UNITED	0-2	0-0	3866		1	2*	3	4		6		12		8	7	11	5	5	14	10"									
17	7 Nov	HARTLEPOOL UNITED	0-1	0-1	3232	Halsall	1	2	3	4		6	10*			8	7	11	9	S	12	5									
18	21	Swansea City	1-2	1-1	4033	Paris Gooding 2 Kelly Collins	1	2*	5	4		6	14			8	11	3*	9	10	12	7"									
19	28	BURNLEY	5-0	3-0	3523	Luke	1	2	5	4		6	7	S		8	11	3	9	10	S	S			9	10					
20	12 Dec	Scarborough	1-1	0-1	2525	Luke	1	2	5			6	12	S		8	11	3	9	4		7"			9	10					
21	18	CREWE ALEXANDRA	0-4	0-3	2836		1	2	5	4		6*	S			8	11	3*	9*	12		7"			10	7	S				
22	26	LEYTON ORIENT	1-2	0-1	4493	Gooding	1	2	5	4		6*	12			8	11	3	9	4					10	7					
23	28	Tranmere Rovers	1-3	0-1	3193	Halsall	1	2	5			6	S			8	11	3	S	6			14		10	7	S				
24	1 Jan	Cambridge United	3-1	2-0	3975	Halsall Luke O.G.	1	2	5	4		6	S			8	11	3	S	7					9	10					
25	2	COLCHESTER UNITED	2-0	0-0	3665	Luke White	1	2	5	4		6	S			8	11	3		7					9	10					
26	9	ROCHDALE	1-1	1-1	3213	White	1	2	5	4		6		S		8	11	3		7		10			9	10	S				
27	16	Wrexham	1-3	0-1	1506	Kerr	1	2	5	4		6				8	11	3		7					9	10					
28	30	BOLTON WANDERERS	0-4	0-2	3485		1	2*	5	4		6				8	11	3		7		12	S		9	10					
29	13 Feb	TRANMERE ROVERS	2-1	1-1	2230	White Kelly	1	2	6	4		5	12			8	11*	3		7		14	S	1	9"						
30	20	Carlisle United	2-0	2-0	2026	Gooding White	1	2	6	4		5	10			8	11*	3		7		S	S	1	9						
31	24	HEREFORD UNITED	1-2	1-0	2065	Gooding	1	2	6	4		6	10*			8	11"	3		7	12	14	S	1	9						
32	27	Scunthorpe United	0-5	0-1	3378		1	2	6	4		6	10*			8"	11	3*		7	11	12	S	1	9						
33	4 Mar	Carlisle United	0-0	0-0	4172		1	2	5	4		5				8	11	3		7	11	12	10		9						
34	9	Exeter City	1-0	0-0	1584	Gooding	1	2	5	4		5	9			8		3		7	11	S	S					3	S		
35	12	STOCKPORT COUNTY	0-0	0-0	2193		1	2	5	4		5	10			8				7	14	S	9"				9"	5	12		
36	15	Darlington	1-2	0-0	1816	Gooding	1	2	10	4		6	12			8				7	14	9	9					5			
37	19	Torquay United	0-0	0-0	2544		1	2	5	4		6	12	9		8	11	3		7		S	8*					10			
38	22	Wolverhampton W.	1-0	0-0	8049	Gooding	1	2	5	4		6	12	9		8	11*	3		7		12	S					10			
39	26	HALIFAX TOWN	1-0	1-0	2308	Gooding	1	2	5	4		6	12	9		8"	11	3*		7		14	S					10			
40	2 Apr	Hartlepool United	1-0	1-0	2315	Phillips	1	2	5	4		6	12	9		8	11	3		7		12	S					10			
41	4	SWANSEA CITY	0-1	0-0	3360		1	2	5	4		6	S	9*		8*	11"	3		7		12	S					10		12	
42	9	Newport County	4-0	1-0	988	Nightingale Phillips 3	1	2	5	4		6	10	9		8	11	3		7		14	14					10			
43	12	EXETER CITY	2-1	1-0	2278	Gooding 2	1	2	5	4		6	12	9		8	11*	3		7	12	S	S				3	10			10
44	30	Burnley	2-1	0-1	6305	Halsall Luke	1	2	6	4		5	12	9		8	7	3		7	12	S					4*				
45	2 May	SCARBOROUGH	0-0	0-0	3244		1	2	6	4		5	12	9		8	11	3		7	10	S	S				4*				10
46	7	Crewe Alexandra	1-0	1-0	1533	Luke	1	2	5	4		6	12	9		8	11	3		7	10	S	S								S

F.A.Cup

Rd	Date	Opponent	Score	HT	Att	Scorers
1st	14 Nov	CARDIFF CITY	2-1	1-1	4342	Gooding 2
2nd	5 Dec	SUTTON UNITED	1-3	1-2	4723	Lawrence

Line-ups:
1st	1	2	5	4	6	12	S	8	9	6	3	9	10	7*
2nd	1	2	5	4	6	7"	10	8	11	6	3*	9	4	12	14

Football League Cup

Rd	Date	Opponent	Score	HT	Att	Scorers
1/1L	18 Aug	Chesterfield	1-2	1-1	1938	Kelly
1/2L	26	CHESTERFIELD	2-0	1-0	2994	Gunn O.G.
2/1L	22 Sep	PLYMOUTH ARGYLE	4-1	3-0	3843	Gooding Riley Halsall Lawrence
2/2L	6 Oct	Plymouth Argyle	1-1	0-0	5549	Gooding
2nd	28	READING	0-0	0-0	6285	
3/R	4 Nov	Reading	0-1	0-1	6000	

Line-ups:
1/1L	1	2	3	4	5	6	7	8	9	10	11	8	9	3	6	5	8	6	S	S
1/2L	1	2	3	4	5	6	7	8	9	10	11	8	9	3	6	7	5	5	S	S
2/1L	1	2	3	4	5	6			9	10	11	8	7	S	9	S			S	1
2/2L	1	2	3	4	5	6		10		8	7	11	9	S	9				S	
2nd	1	2	3	4	5	6	S		8	7	11	9	5	10		3	3		S	10
3/R	1	2	3	4	6	14	10"	8	7	11	9	5*	12		3	4	1			12

Sherpa Van Trophy

Rd	Date	Opponent	Score	HT	Att	Scorers
Prel.	13 Oct	Colchester United	2-3	0-2	912	Gooding Nuttell
Prel.	1 Dec	CAMBRIDGE UNITED	3-0	1-0	1247	Luke Nuttell O.G.
1st	19 Jan	Walsall	2-1	0-0	2894	Gooding Carr
2nd	9 Feb	Wolverhampton W.	0-4	0-1	6155	

Line-ups:
Prel.	1	2	3	4	6	5	7	8	8	7*	11	9"	5	14	12	12	10		1
Prel.	1	2	6	8	5	7	10		11	3	4	12	S	9			1	1
1st	2	5	4	6*	9		8	11	S	7	12		10		1
2nd	2	5	4	6	14		8	11	3	7*	10"	9		12	1

Appearance Summary

League Appearances	40	46	46	44	12	44	10	16	12	45	43	39	16	31	6	8	6	6	14	10	2	9
League Sub. Appear.						2	8	2			4	5	7	4	5	5	5	5	10	2	1	1
League Sub. non-Appear.			2	18		8	2		2	4	1	4	4	3	7	17			4		2	1
(1 O.G.) League Goals	9	12	12	11	4	12	4	6	4	11	12	10	7	8		3	3	3	4	1		
Cup Appearances							3								1	4	1		1			
Cup Sub. Appear.			1	6		1		2		1	1		2	3	2	2	1	2				
Cup Sub. non-Appear.											1		2	2	1	2					
(2 O.G.) Cup Goals																						

DIVISION 4

	P	W	D	L	F	A	W	D	L	F	A	Pts
Wolves	46	15	3	5	47	19	12	6	5	35	24	90
Cardiff C	46	15	6	2	39	14	9	7	7	27	27	85
Bolton W	46	16	5	2	42	12	7	6	10	24	30	78
Scunthorpe U	46	14	5	4	42	20	6	12	5	34	31	77
Torquay U	46	10	6	7	34	16	11	7	5	32	25	77
Swansea C	46	9	7	7	35	28	11	3	9	27	28	70
Peterboro' U	46	10	5	8	28	26	10	5	8	24	27	70
Leyton Orient	46	13	4	6	55	27	6	8	9	30	36	69
Colchester U	46	10	5	8	23	22	9	5	9	24	29	67
Burnley	46	12	5	6	31	22	8	2	13	26	40	67
Wrexham	46	13	3	7	46	26	7	3	13	23	32	66
Scarborough	46	12	8	3	38	19	5	6	12	18	29	65
Darlington	46	13	6	4	39	25	5	5	13	32	44	65
Tranmere R*	46	14	2	7	43	20	5	7	11	18	33	64
Cambridge U	46	10	6	7	32	24	6	7	10	18	28	61
Hartlepool U	46	9	7	7	25	25	6	7	10	25	32	59
Crewe A	46	7	11	5	25	19	6	8	9	32	34	58
Halifax T†	46	11	5	7	37	25	3	7	13	17	34	55
Hereford U	46	8	7	8	25	27	6	5	12	16	32	54
Stockport Co	46	7	7	9	26	26	5	8	10	18	32	51
Rochdale	46	5	9	9	28	34	6	6	11	19	42	48
Exeter C	46	6	8	9	33	29	3	7	13	20	39	46
Carlisle U	46	9	5	9	38	33	3	3	17	19	53	44
Newport Co	46	4	5	14	19	36	2	2	19	16	69	25

Season Summary

Money raised for buying players from fund-raising schemes. City Council reject suggestion to sell Ground and re-locate Club. Administrators take over in October. Chairman Kendrick followed by rest of Board resign. On brink of disaster. Lose at home to non-League Sutton in F.A.Cup.

(Back) Gooding, Carr, Gunn, Nightingale, Halsall, Luke.
(Middle) Jones, Pollard, Shoemake, Nuttell, Neenan, Lawrence, Harvey.
(Front) Paris, Riley, Price, Cantwell, Collins, Kelly, Phillips.

SEASON 1988/89

Football League Division 4

Match results

No.	Date	Opposition	Res	H.T.	Attend	Goalscorer
1	27 Aug	Carlisle United	2-2	1-1	2650	Gooding 2
2	3 Sep	SCARBOROUGH	1-4	1-1	3956	Gooding
3	10	Darlington	2-2	1-1	1521	Cusack 2
4	17	LINCOLN CITY	1-1	0-0	4256	Genovese
5	19	Tranmere Rovers	0-1	0-1	2597	
6	24	YORK CITY	0-1	0-0	2756	
7	1 Oct	Wrexham	1-1	1-0	1826	Cusack
8	5	STOCKPORT COUNTY	1-0	1-0	2572	Goldsmith
9	8	Grimsby Town	0-0	0-0	2822	
10	15	BURNLEY	3-0	1-0	5023	Oakes Cusack Goldsmith
11	22	HEREFORD UNITED	2-1	1-0	3460	Cusack Longhurst
12	25	Halifax Town	0-5	0-0	2248	
13	29	SCUNTHORPE UNITED	1-2	1-1	3532	Luke
14	5 Nov	Leyton Orient	2-1	1-0	3695	Collins Longhurst
15	9	HARTLEPOOL UNITED	0-1	0-0	3148	
16	12	Doncaster Rovers	3-2	1-0	2224	Cusack Gunn 2
17	25	Crewe Alexandra	1-1	0-1	2646	Cusack
18	3 Dec	ROCHDALE	1-0	0-0	3273	Oakes
19	17	EXETER CITY	0-1	0-0	3149	
20	26	Colchester United	2-1	1-0	2828	McElhinney Gunn
21	31	Torquay United	0-1	0-0	2877	
22	3 Jan	CAMBRIDGE UNITED	1-5	1-3	4622	Swindlehurst
23	7	ROTHERHAM UNITED	0-3	0-0	3368	
24	14	Scarborough	1-2	0-0	2279	Cusack
25	21	CARLISLE UNITED	1-4	0-2	2537	Halsall
26	28	Lincoln City	1-1	0-0	4150	Goldsmith
27	4 Feb	TRANMERE ROVERS	1-1	0-0	2744	Oakes
28	11	York City	1-5	0-2	2438	Walsh
29	25	Burnley	1-1	0-0	6848	Gunn
30	1 Mar	HALIFAX TOWN	2-1	0-0	2159	Oakes Cusack
31	4	Hereford United	0-4	0-0	2094	
32	11	LEYTON ORIENT	0-1	0-0	3306	
33	14	Scunthorpe United	0-3	0-1	3983	
34	18	DARLINGTON	1-1	1-0	2484	Longhurst
35	25	Cambridge United	1-2	0-0	4215	Goldsmith
36	27	COLCHESTER UNITED	3-0	1-0	3529	Longhurst 2 O.G.
37	1 Apr	Exeter City	1-3	0-2	2522	Oakes
38	4	Rotherham United	1-1	0-0	4762	Goldsmith
39	8	TORQUAY UNITED	3-1	1-0	2614	Longhurst 2 Sterling
40	15	WREXHAM	1-0	1-0	3067	Cusack
41	21	Stockport County	2-1	2-0	2091	Gunn Luke
42	25	GRIMSBY TOWN	1-2	1-0	2937	Osbourne
43	29	CREWE ALEXANDRA	3-2	1-1	3546	Gunn Luke Sterling
44	1 May	Hartlepool United	1-2	0-0	1643	Gunn
45	6	Rochdale	0-0	0-0	1430	
46	13	DONCASTER ROVERS	2-0	1-0	2984	Goldsmith Sterling

Player appearance / squad-number grid (by match number 1–46)

Player	Shirt numbers used across matches (m1 → m46)
Harle	4 (m36–39), 4 (m43–45), 4* (m46)
Sterling	7 (m36–46)
Osborne	S (m35), 12 (m36,37), S (m38), 12 (m39,40), S (m41), 12 (m42), 11 (m43,44), 11* (m45), 12 (m46)
Walsh	4 (m27,28), 11 (m29–31)
Pollard	S (m25,26), 6" (m27,28), 5 (m29–35)
Swindlehurst	9 (m21–23), 9" (m24)
Butterworth	14 (m19), 4 (m25,26), 12 (m28), 4 (m29–31), 4* (m32), S (m33–35)
Carr	S (m14), S (m17), 12 (m18)
Crichton	1 (m14–19), 1 (m22–46)
Philpott	S (m18), 7" (m19), 12 (m20), S (m21), S (m24), 14 (m32)
Longhurst	10 (m9–14), 14 (m15), 12 (m16), 10* (m17), 10 (m18–21), 10* (m22), 10" (m23), 10 (m24–29), 10* (m30), 10 (m31–36), 10* (m37), 10 (m38–46)
Madrick	12 (m4,5), 7 (m6), 10* (m7), 10 (m8), 7 (m13), S (m14), 14 (m15), 12 (m16,17), S (m18), 12 (m19), S (m20,21)
Andrews	S (m1–3), 7 (m4,5), S (m6), 7 (m7–18), S (m19–21), 7 (m22), 2 (m23), 7 (m24), 5 (m25), 7* (m26), 7 (m27), 5 (m28), 7 (m29–33), 7* (m34), 6 (m38,39), 4* (m40), 5 (m43), 5* (m44), 6 (m45,46)
Goldsmith	S (m1), 12 (m2,3), 11 (m4–21), 11" (m22,23), 14 (m24,25), 11 (m26–28), S (m29–31), 11" (m32,33), 11 (m34–36), 11" (m37), 11 (m38), 11" (m39,40), 11 (m41,42), 12 (m43,44), 6 (m45), 11* (m46)
Luke	11 (m1–3), 4 (m4–25), 7 (m26,27), 2 (m28–46)
Gunn	10 (m1–3), 3 (m4,5), 10 (m6), 3 (m7–25), 2 (m26), 5 (m27,28), 3 (m29–46)
Cusack	9 (m1–46, occasional 9* m36,39)
Halsall	8 (m1–46; 8* m19,26)
Genovese	7 (m1,2), 7" (m3), 10* (m4,5), S (m6), 12 (m7), S (m8), 10 (m24), 12 (m25), S (m26,27), 14 (m28), 12 (m29), S (m30), 14 (m31), 4 (m32), 14 (m33), S (m34–46)
Oakes	6 (m1–46, mostly)
McElhinney	5 (m1–6), 5* (m17,18,19), 5* (m24), S (m34), 5 (m36,37), 5 (m39), 5* (m42), 5 (m45,46)
Gooding	4 (m1–3)
Collins	3 (m1–3), S (m4,5), 3 (m6), 14 (m7), 12 (m8), 2 (m9), S (m10–12), 12 (m13), 2 (m14), 2* (m15), 2 (m16–21), 11 (m23), 3 (m25,26), 3 (m27), 3* (m28), 11 (m33), 4 (m34,36), 8 (m38,40), 12 (m43), 4 (m45,46)
Langan	2 (m1–6), 2* (m7,8), 2 (m9–11), 2* (m12), 12" (m14,15), 4 (m19), 7 (m20–23), 2 (m24)
Neenan	1 (m1–13), 1 (m20,21)

F.A.Cup

							2	5	6	4	3	8	9	11	7	S	10	1	S
1st	19 Nov	Gillingham	3-3	1-0	4509	Longhurst 3	2	5	6	4	3	8	9	11	7	S	10	1	S
1/R.	23	GILLINGHAM	1-0*	0-0	4494	O.G. *(After extra time. 0-0 at 90 min)	2	5	6	4	3	8	9	11	7	S	10	1	S
2nd	10 Dec	Brentford	0-0	0-0	5608		2	5	6	4	3	8	9	11	7*	S	10	12	1
2/R.	14	BRENTFORD	2-3	1-1	5605	Halsall Cusack	7	2	5	6	4	3	8	9	11	7	S	10	S	1

(Football League) Littlewoods Cup

							2	3	4	5	6	7	8	9	10	11	7	S	10	1	S
1/1L	31 Aug	West Bromwich A.	3-0	1-0	4264	Oakes Genoveve Cusack	2	3	4	5	6	7	8	9	10	11	S	S
1/2L	7 Sep	WEST BROMWICH A.	0-2	0-2	4216		2	3	4	5	6	7	8	9	10	11	S	S
2/1L	27	LEEDS UNITED	1-2	1-2	4979	Goldsmith	2	14	5"	6	12	8	9	3	4	11	10*	10
2/2L	12 Oct	Leeds United	1-3	0-1	8894	Gunn	2	5	6	8	9	3	4	11	7	S	10	S

Sherpa Van Trophy

							4	2	6	8	3	11	7	S	10	12	1	5*
Prel.	29 Nov	Cambridge United	2-2	2-0	1296	Oakes Longhurst	4	2	6	8	3	11	7	S	10	12	1
Prel.	21 Dec	NOTHAMPTON TOWN	0-2	0-1	1754		2	5	6	8	9	3	4	11	7*	S	10	12	1	5*

Appearances Summary

League Appearances	15	18	28	3	33	41	42	44	46	45	34	33	3	37	1	31				3	6	3	12	7
League Sub. Appear.		1	6				8				6	5	2		1		2	2	3		6
League Sub. non-Appear.			5	1		16					4	5	11		4		2	2		1	1	3
(1 O.G.) League Goals			1	3	1	5		10	7	3	6			7				1	1	
Cup Appearances	4	5	9	2	9	10	2	10	10	9	8	7	1	7			6		1
Cup Sub. Appear.							1											3
Cup Sub. non-Appear.			1			2		1	2		2	2	7	4	2		2		2
(1 O.G.) Cup Goals						2	1	1	2		1								2

DIVISION 4

	P	W	D	L	F	A	W	D	L	F	A	Pts
Rotherham U	46	13	6	4	44	18	9	10		32	17	82
Tranmere R	46	13	6	2	34	13	6	11	6	28	30	80
Crewe A	46	13	7	3	42	24	8	6	9	25	24	78
Scunthorpe U	46	11	9	3	40	22	10	5		37	35	77
Scarborough	46	12	7	4	33	23	9	7		34	39	77
Leyton Orient	46	16	2	5	61	19	6	5		25	31	75
Wrexham	46	12	7	4	44	28	7	7		33	35	71
Cambridge U	46	12	7	4	36	37	7		13	25	34	68
Grimsby T	46	11	9	3	33	18	6	6	11	32	41	66
Lincoln C	46	12	6	5	39	26	6	4	13	25	34	64
York C	46	10	8	5	43	27	7	5	11	19	36	64
Carlisle U	46	14	4	5	46	23	4	2	17	19	45	60
Exeter C	46	9	6	8	26	25	8	9		27	27	60
Torquay U	46	15	2	6	32	23	2	6	15	13	37	59
Hereford U	46	11	8	4	40	27	3	8	12	26	45	58
Burnley	46	12	6	5	35	20	2	7	14	17	41	55
Peterboro' U	46	10	3	10	29	32	4	9	10	23	42	54
Rochdale	46	10	3	2	26	13	4	16	24	56	53
Hartlepool U	46	10	6	7	33	33	4	4	15	17	45	52
Stockport Co	46	8	10	5	31	20	2	3	16	23	32	51
Halifax T	46	10	7	6	42	27	3	4	16	27	48	50
Colchester U	46	9	6	8	35	30	4	7	12	25	48	50
Doncaster R	46	9	6	8	32	32	4	4	15	17	46	49
Darlington	46	3	12	8	28	38	5	6	12	25	38	42

(Back) Nuttell, Fife, Oakes, Cusack, Pollard, Luke.

(Middle) Harvey, Goldsmith, Sanderson, Andrews, Neenan, Carr, Butterworth, Philpott, Robson.

(Front) Gunn, Collins, Gooding, Jones, Halsall, Genovese, Langan.

Season Summary

John Devaney saves Posh – wipes out debts and takes over as Chairman. £400,000 made available to invest in team. Fans and Club are optimistic, but yet another indifferent season, with Posh often hovering near the bottom of the League.

SEASON 1989/90

Football League Division 4

#	Date	Opposition	Res	H.T.	Attend	Goalscorer
1	19 Aug	MAIDSTONE UNITED	1-0	0-0	6522	Halsall
2	26	York City	0-1	0-0	2569	
3	2 Sep	ALDERSHOT	1-1	1-1	3787	Robinson
4	9	Doncaster Rovers	3-0	1-0	2327	Luke Halsall Richards
5	16	SCUNTHORPE UNITED	1-1	0-1	4350	Richards
6	23	Hartlepool United	2-2	0-1	1703	Halsall Butterworth
7	27	Lincoln City	0-1	0-0	6106	
8	30	GILLINGHAM	1-1	0-0	4199	Graham
9	7 Oct	EXETER CITY	4-3	2-1	3831	Sterling Harle Graham O.G.
10	14	Rochdale	2-1	0-0	1767	Luke Culpin
11	17	Burnley	2-1	1-0	7187	Luke 2
12	21	STOCKPORT COUNTY	2-0	1-0	4804	Halsall 2
13	28	Colchester United	1-0	0-0	3460	Osborne
14	1 Nov	GRIMSBY TOWN	1-1	0-1	6827	Robinson
15	4	Southend United	0-0	0-0	4894	
16	11	HEREFORD UNITED	1-1	0-0	4983	Osborne
17	25	TORQUAY UNITED	1-1	0-0	4175	Richards
18	2 Dec	Carlisle United	0-0	0-0	4608	
19	17	Cambridge United	2-3	0-2	4811	Halsall Osborne
20	26	CHESTERFIELD	1-1	0-0	5422	Osborne
21	30	SCARBOROUGH	1-2	0-2	4153	Richards
22	1 Jan	Halifax Town	2-2	1-0	1578	Butterworth Harle
23	6	Wrexham	1-2	0-0	1937	Osborne
24	13	YORK CITY	1-1	0-1	3678	Richards
25	20	Maidstone United	1-1	1-0	2707	Hine
26	27	DONCASTER ROVERS	2-1	1-0	4080	Oakes Sterling
27	7 Feb	HARTLEPOOL UNITED	0-2	0-1	2813	
28	10	Scunthorpe United	0-0	0-0	3188	
29	17	CARLISLE UNITED	3-0	1-0	4088	Hine Jepson O.G.
30	24	Torquay United	1-2	0-1	2467	Robinson
31	27	Aldershot	1-0	0-0	1138	Hine
32	3 Mar	WREXHAM	3-1	2-1	3990	Jepson Riley Culpin
33	6	Gillingham	0-0	0-0	4301	
34	13	LINCOLN CITY	1-0	0-0	6204	Jepson
35	17	Exeter City	0-2	0-1	4676	
36	21	ROCHDALE	3-0	1-0	3445	Hine Jepson O.G.
37	24	BURNLEY	4-1	2-0	3841	Halsall Robinson Jepson Riley
38	30	Stockport County	0-0	0-0	3651	
39	7 Apr	COLCHESTER UNITED	1-0	1-0	4025	Sterling
40	10	Grimsby Town	2-1	2-0	8123	Halsall Riley
41	14	HALIFAX TOWN	3-0	2-0	4570	Halsall Jepson Riley
42	16	Chesterfield	1-1	0-1	5696	Riley
43	21	CAMBRIDGE UNITED	1-2	0-1	9257	Luke
44	25	Scarborough	1-2	0-1	1838	Sterling
45	28	Hereford United	2-1	0-1	2276	Halsall Hine
46	5 May	SOUTHEND UNITED	1-2	0-2	7958	Halsall

F.A.Cup

	Date	Opponent	Score	H/A																	Scorer
1st	18 Nov	HAYES	1-1	1-0	1	2	3	4	5	7	12	14	10	9*	11	6	1	8"			Sterling
1/R.	21	Hayes	1-0	1-0	1	2	3	4	5	7	10	9	12	11	6	S	8*				Robinson
2nd	9 Dec	Swansea City	1-3	0-1	1	2	3	4	5	7	10*	9	12	8	11	6*	14				Andrews

Attendances: 5172, 4524, 4175

Football League Cup

	Date	Opponent	Score	H/A																Scorers
1/1L	23 Aug	ALDERSHOT	2-0	2-0	1	2	3	4	5	6	7	8	9*	10	11	12	S			Sterling Richards
1/2L	29	Aldershot	2-6*	0-1	1	2	3	4	5	6	7	8	9	10	11	12	S	2 S	S	Halsall Richards

*After extra time (2-4 at 90 mins.)

Attendances: 3397, 1507

Leyland Daf Cup

	Date	Opponent	Score	H/A															Scorers
Prel.	8 Nov	FULHAM	1-0	0-0	1	2	3*	5	7	4	9	14	6	11	1	10	8"		Andrews
Prel.	12 Dec	Notts. County	2-2	1-1	1	2	3	4	5	7	9	10*	14	6	11"	12	6	8	Luke Harle
1st	10 Jan	HERFORD UNITED	0-1	0-0	1	2	12	4	5	3*	7	9	10"	12	6	11	6	14	8

Attendances: 1939, 1616, 1824

League Appearances	24	43	40	46	45	27	46	10	16	14	5	12	9	29	34	16	1	14	9	6	22	18	6	15
League Sub. Appear.			2			2		4	4	7	1	21	10		1			1	3				1	1
League Sub. non-Appear.			2			1			1	1	1	5	4	1				8	2				2	2
(2 O.G.) League Goals		5		11	4	1	4	2	5		5		2					2	2		4	5		5
Cup Appearances	6	7	7	7	8	3	8	5	6	5	2	4	6	4	2	2		2	3		1			
Cup Sub. Appear.			1					1	1	1	4							1	1					
Cup Sub. non-Appear.		1		1	1		2		2				2		1	1		1						
Cup Goals																								1

DIVISION 4

	P	W	D	L	F	A	W	D	L	F	A	Pts
Exeter C	46	20	3	0	50	14	8	2	13	33	34	89
Grimsby T	46	14	4	5	41	20	8	6	9	29	27	79
Southend U	46	15	3	5	35	14	6	10	26	34	75
Stockport Co	46	13	6	4	45	27	8	5	10	23	35	74
Maidstone U	46	13	6	4	45	49	8	4	11	28	40	73
Cambridge U	46	14	4	5	49	21	8	3	12	26	31	73
Chesterfield	46	12	6	5	30	10	7	5	11	22	31	71
Carlisle U	46	15	4	4	38	20	6	4	13	23	40	71
Peterboro' U	46	10	8	5	35	23	7	7	9	24	23	68
Lincoln C	46	11	6	6	30	27	7	8	8	18	21	68
Scunthorpe U	46	9	9	5	42	25	8	6	9	27	29	66
Rochdale	46	11	4	8	28	23	9	2	12	24	32	66
York C	46	10	5	8	29	24	6	11	6	26	29	64
Gillingham	46	9	6	8	28	21	8	3	12	18	27	62
Torquay U	46	12	2	9	33	29	3	10	10	20	37	57
Burnley	46	9	6	8	28	21	4	11	8	26	37	56
Hereford U	46	7	12	4	31	32	8	4	11	26	37	56
Scarborough	46	10	5	8	35	28	6	5	13	25	45	55
Hartlepool U	46	12	4	7	45	33	6	1	14	21	55	55
Doncaster R	46	7	7	9	29	29	7	2	14	24	31	51
Wrexham	46	7	9	7	28	28	5	4	14	23	39	51
Aldershot	46	8	7	8	28	26	4	7	12	21	43	50
Halifax T	46	5	9	9	31	29	7	4	12	26	36	49
Colchester U	46	9	3	11	26	25	2	7	14	22	50	43

Peterborough United 1989-90: Back row (from left) — Robert Atkin, Steve Osborne, Dave Robinson, Keith Oakes, Adrian Speedie, Gary Andrews, Shaun Wills. Middle row — Worrell Sterling, Noel Luke, Gerry McElhinney, Paul Crichton, Tony Godden, Carl Richards, Milton Graham, Craig Goldsmith. Front row — David Longhurst, David Harle, Mick Halsall, Garry Andrews, Robert Sullivan, Phil Crosby.

Season Summary

Over £¼ million spent on players. First game versus newly promoted Maidstone United. Manager Jones departs after indifferent start – Devaney appoints replacement – Mark Lawrenson. Only narrowly beat Hayes in F.A.Cup. Bitter disappointment as even a play-off place is not obtained.

SEASON 1990/91

Football League Division 4

1380	Date	Opposition	Res	H.T.	Attend	Goalscorer
1	25 Aug	Wrexham	0-0	0-0	2863	
2	1 Sep	CARLISLE UNITED	1-1	1-1	3675	Bremner
3	8	Scunthorpe United	1-1	0-1	3028	Russell
4	15	WALSALL	0-0	0-0	4099	
5	18	HALIFAX TOWN	2-0	1-0	3082	Culpin Russell
6	22	Northampton Town	2-1	2-0	5573	Culpin Russell
7	29	TORQUAY UNITED	1-2	1-0	3960	Culpin
8	2 Oct	Darlington	1-0	0-0	3748	Culpin
9	6	Stockport County	1-2	1-1	2974	Luke
10	13	LINCOLN CITY	2-0	1-0	4766	Sterling Culpin
11	20	BURNLEY	3-2	3-2	5102	Luke Berry Culpin
12	23	Hartlepool United	0-2	0-2	2190	
13	27	Cardiff City	1-1	0-1	2940	Hine
14	3 Nov	CHESTERFIELD	2-1	0-0	4225	Berry Hine
15	10	DONCASTER ROVERS	1-1	0-0	4691	Bremner
16	24	Hereford United	0-0	0-0	2148	
17	1 Dec	Maidstone United	0-2	0-3	1920	
18	15	YORK CITY	2-0	0-0	3335	Sterling Culpin
19	21	SCARBOROUGH	2-0	0-0	3233	Riley Culpin
20	26	Blackpool	1-1	1-1	3658	Culpin
21	29	Aldershot	0-5	0-3	2363	
22	1 Jan	ROCHDALE	1-1	1-0	3687	Sterling
23	12	Carlisle United	2-3	1-1	2744	Sterling 2
24	19	WREXHAM	2-2	0-0	3208	Sterling 2
25	26	Walsall	1-0	0-0	4438	O.G.
26	1 Feb	Halifax Town	1-1	0-1	1133	Riley
27	5	NORTHAMPTON TOWN	1-0	0-0	5932	Halsall
28	22	Doncaster Rovers	2-0	0-0	2995	Halsall Osbourne
29	26	Gillingham	3-2	0-1	3088	Halsall Riley 2
30	2 Mar	MAIDSTONE UNITED	2-0	1-0	4623	Oakes Riley
31	9	York City	4-0	3-0	2511	Hine Riley 2 Robinson D.J.
32	12	DARLINGTON	2-2	2-0	8362	Riley Robinson D.J.
33	15	Torquay United	0-0	0-0	2800	
34	19	Lincoln City	2-0	1-0	5524	Riley Robinson D.J.
35	23	STOCKPORT COUNTY	0-0	0-0	7047	
36	30	BLACKPOOL	2-0	1-0	7721	Berry Gavin
37	3 Apr	Scarborough	1-3	1-3	2141	Gavin
38	6	ALDERSHOT	3-2	2-1	5543	Oakes Gavin Cooper
39	13	Rochdale	3-0	1-0	2384	Halsall 2 Gavin
40	16	GILLINGHAM	2-0	1-0	5831	Sterling Gavin
41	20	Burnley	1-4	1-4	10018	Oakes
42	23	SCUNTHORPE UNITED	0-0	0-0	5774	
43	27	HARTLEPOOL UNITED	1-1	0-0	7636	Berry
44	4 May	CARDIFF CITY	3-0	1-0	6642	Culpin Bremner Robinson D.
45	7	HEREFORD UNITED	3-0	2-0	7433	Sterling Berry Gavin
46	11	Chesterfield	2-2	2-2	8837	Berry Robinson D.

Player appearance grid (players listed as rows, matches 1–46 as columns): Pope, Cooper, Costello, Charlery, Gavin, Morgan, Robinson D.J., Danzey, Clayton, Bradshaw, Russell, Hine, Hill, McInerney, Watkins, McElhinney, Herbert, Culpin, Osbourne, Butterworth, Riley, Bremner, Oakes, Sterling, Berry, Robonson I., Halsall, Crosby, Luke, Dearden.

(Back) Luke, Butterworth, Watkins, Bremner, Hine, Crosby, Graham.
(Mid.) Robinson, Culpin, Oakes, Bradshaw, Berry, Osborne, McElhinney.
(Front) Harvey, Riley, Lawrenson, Halsall, Booth, Clarke, Sterling.

Season Summary

Success at last! Posh soon get amongst promotion contenders. Former striker Longhurst dies during match. F.A.Cup match on Wycombe's new Ground. Chris Turner becomes new Manager. Great scenes after draw at Chesterfield in last match gets promotion. Six new players signed.

SEASON 1991/92

Football League Division 3

Player appearance / line-up grid. Column headers (players, by shirt number) read left-to-right across the grid:
Barber (1), White (2), Butterworth (3), Halsall (4), Robinson D. (5), Walsh (6), Sterling (7), Ebdon (8), Gavin (9), Riley (10), Kimble (11), Luke (12), McInerney (14), Cooper G., Turner, Charlery, Costello, Culpin, Johnson, Howarth, Robinson R., Adcock, O'Connor, Barnes, Curtis, Cooper S., Salmon, Bennett, Edwards.

No.	Date	Opposition	Res	H.T.	Attend	Goalscorer
1	17 Aug	PRESTON NORTH END	1-0	0-0	6036	Riley
2	24	Hull City	2-1	0-0	4806	Kimble McInerney
3	31	STOKE CITY	1-1	1-1	7174	Kimble
4	3 Sep	Bury	0-3	0-2	2240	
5	7	WIGAN ATHLETIC	0-0	0-0	4488	
6	14	Birmingham City	1-1	0-0	9408	O.G.
7	17	West Brom. Albion	0-4	0-2	10037	
8	21	EXETER CITY	1-1	1-0	4249	Halsall
9	28	Swansea City	0-1	0-1	2685	
10	5 Oct	LEYTON ORIENT	0-2	0-1	4291	
11	12	Brentford	1-2	0-1	7705	Culpin
12	19	Reading	1-1	1-0	2954	Charlery
13	26	HARTLEPOOL UNITED	3-2	2-0	3385	Riley 2 Charlery
14	2 Nov	Shrewsbury Town	0-2	0-0	1866	
15	5	CHESTER CITY	2-0	2-0	2810	Charlery 2
16	9	BRADFORD CITY	2-1	1-0	9224	Sterling Riley
17	23	Darlington	2-1	0-1	2815	Riley Charlery
18	30	TORQUAY UNITED	1-1	0-0	4007	Culpin
19	14 Dec	Stockport County	0-3	0-1	2768	
20	20	HULL CITY	3-0	2-0	7904	Robinson D. Riley Charlery
21	26	Stoke City	3-3	2-2	14733	Halsall Robinson D. Sterling
22	28	Preston North End	1-1	1-0	5200	Charlery
23	1 Jan	BURY	0-0	0-0	5567	
24	11	FULHAM	4-1	1-0	4975	Sterling Ebdon Adcock 2
25	18	Huddersfield Town	0-0	0-0	8763	
26	1 Feb	READING	5-3	2-2	3792	Halsall 2 Charlery Kimble O.G.
27	8	Hartlepool United	1-0	0-0	2481	Charlery
28	15	STOCKPORT COUNTY	3-2	1-1	5301	Adcock 2 Cooper G.
29	22	Fulham	1-0	1-0	5233	Adcock
30	29	BOLTON WANDERERS	1-0	0-0	6270	Adcock
31	4 Mar	HUDDERSFIELD TOWN	2-0	1-0	6257	Barnes Riley
32	7	A.F.C. Bournemouth	2-1	1-1	5379	Barnes Riley
33	10	Chester City	4-2	1-0	1063	Adcock Cooper G. 2 Barnes
34	14	SHREWSBURY TOWN	1-0	1-0	7377	Halsall
35	21	Bradford City	1-2	0-2	6896	Riley
36	24	Bolton Wanderers	1-2	1-2	5421	Charlery
37	28	DARLINGTON	1-1	1-1	5218	Robinson D.
38	31	BIRMINGHAM CITY	2-3	1-1	12081	Barnes 2
39	3 Apr	Wigan Athletic	0-3	0-1	2485	
40	8	A.F.C. BOURNEMOUTH	2-0	2-0	4910	Charlery Cooper G.
41	11	WEST BROM. ALBION	1-0	1-0	9040	
42	18	Exeter City	2-2	1-1	3057	Charlery Butterworth
43	21	SWANSEA CITY	3-1	1-0	5526	Sterling Charlery Kimble
44	25	Leyton Orient	2-1	0-1	5996	Ebdon Charlery
45	28	Torquay United	2-2	1-1	1934	Charlery 2
46	2 May	BRENTFORD	0-1	0-1	14539	

Line-ups (shirt number — player; * / " denote grid annotations, S = substitute)

No.	Team
1	1 Barber, 2 White, 3 Butterworth, 4 Halsall, 5 Robinson D., 6 Walsh, 7* Sterling, 8 Ebdon, 9* Gavin, 10 Riley, 11 Kimble, 12 Luke, 14 McInerney
2	1 Barber, 2 White, 3 Butterworth, 4 Halsall, 5 Robinson D., 6 Walsh, 7 Sterling, 8 Ebdon, 9 Gavin, 10* Riley, 11 Kimble, 12 McInerney
3	1 Barber, 2 White, 3 Butterworth, 4 Halsall, 5 Robinson D., 6 Walsh, 7 Luke, 8 Ebdon, 9 Gavin, 10* Riley, 11* Kimble, 12 McInerney, 14 Sterling, S Turner
4	1 Barber, 2 White, 3 Butterworth, 4 Halsall, 5 Robinson D., 6 Walsh, 7 Luke, 8* Ebdon, 9 Gavin, 10* Riley, 11 Kimble, 12 McInerney, 14 Sterling
5	1 Barber, 3 Butterworth, 4 Halsall, 5 Robinson D., 6 Walsh, 7 Sterling, 8 Cooper G., 9* Charlery, 11 Kimble, 12 Costello, S White
6	1 Barber, 3 Butterworth, 4 Halsall, 5 Robinson D., 6 Walsh, 7 Sterling, 8 Cooper G., 9 Gavin, 10 McInerney, 11 Kimble, S Charlery
7	1 Barber, 3 Butterworth, 4 Halsall, 5 Robinson D., 6 Walsh, 7 Sterling, 8 Cooper G., 9 Gavin, 10 McInerney, 11* Kimble, 12 White, 14 Charlery, 12 Ebdon
8	1 Barber, 3 Butterworth, 4 Halsall, 5 Robinson D., 6 Walsh, 7 Sterling, 8* Cooper G., 9 Gavin, 10 Charlery, 10* McInerney, 11" Kimble
9	1 Barber, 3 Butterworth, 4 Halsall, 5 Robinson D., 6 Walsh, 7 Sterling, 8 Cooper G., 9 Gavin, 10 Charlery, 11 Kimble, 14 McInerney, S White
10	1 Barber, 3 Butterworth, 4 Halsall, 5 Robinson D., 6 Walsh, 7 Sterling, 8* Cooper G., 10" Charlery, 11 Kimble, 12 McInerney/Ebdon
11	1 Barber, 2 Luke, 3 Butterworth, 4 Halsall, 5 Robinson D., 6 Walsh, 7 Sterling, 8* Cooper G., 9 Riley, 10 Charlery, 11 Kimble, 14 Culpin, 14 McInerney
12	1 Barber, 2 Luke, 4 Halsall, 5 Howarth, 6 Walsh, 7 Sterling, 8 Cooper G., 9* Riley, 10 Charlery, 11 Kimble, 12 Culpin, 3 Johnson, S Butterworth, S White
13	1 Barber, 2 Luke, 4 Halsall, 5 Howarth, 6 Walsh, 7* Sterling, 8 Cooper G., 9 Riley, 10 Charlery, 11 Kimble, 3 Johnson, 12 Ebdon, 2 Butterworth, S White
14	1 Barber, 2 Luke, 4 Halsall, 6 Walsh, 7 Sterling, 8 Cooper G., 9 Riley, 10 Charlery, 11 Kimble, 3 Johnson, 14 Culpin, 12 Butterworth, 8* White
15	1 Barber, 2 Luke, 4 Halsall, 5 Robinson D., 6 Walsh, 7* Sterling, 8* Cooper G., 9 Riley, 10 Charlery, 11* Kimble, 3 Johnson, 12 Culpin
16	1 Barber, 2 Luke, 4 Halsall, 5 Robinson D., 6 Walsh, 7 Sterling, 8* Cooper G., 9 Riley, 10 Charlery, 11" Kimble, 3 Johnson, S Culpin, S Gavin, 11 Butterworth
17	1 Barber, 2 Luke, 4 Halsall, 5 Robinson D., 6 Walsh, 7 Sterling, 8 Cooper G., 9 Riley, 10 Charlery, 11 Kimble, 3 Johnson, S Butterworth
18	1 Barber, 2 Luke, 4 Halsall, 5 Robinson D., 6 Walsh, 7 Sterling, 8 Cooper G., 9 Riley, 10 Charlery, 11* Kimble, 3" Johnson, 12 Culpin, 12 Robinson R., S Butterworth
19	1 Barber, 2 Luke, 4 Halsall, 5 Robinson D., 6 Walsh, 7 Sterling, 8 Cooper G., 9* Riley, 10 Charlery, 11 Kimble, 3 Johnson, 14 Culpin
20	1 Barber, 2 Luke, 4 Halsall, 5 Robinson D., 6 Walsh, 7 Sterling, 8* Cooper G., 9 Riley, 10 Charlery, 11 Kimble, 3" Johnson, 12 Ebdon, 12 Robinson R., S Culpin
21	1 Barber, 2 Luke, 4 Halsall, 5 Robinson D., 6 Walsh, 7 Sterling, 8 Cooper G., 9 Riley, 10 Charlery, 11* Kimble, 3" Johnson, 14 Culpin, 12 Robinson R.
22	1 Barber, 2 Luke, 4 Halsall, 5 Robinson D., 6 Walsh, 7* Sterling, 8 Cooper G., 9 Riley, 10 Charlery, 11 Kimble, 3 Johnson, 12 Gavin, 12 Robinson R., S Culpin
23	1 Barber, 2 Luke, 4 Halsall, 5 Robinson D., 6 Walsh, 7 Sterling, 8 Ebdon, 9* Riley, 10 Charlery, 11* Kimble, 3 Robinson R., 12 Adcock, S Johnson
24	1 Barber, 2 Luke, 4 Halsall, 5 Robinson D., 6 Walsh, 7 Sterling, 8 Ebdon, 9 Adcock, 10 Charlery, 11 Kimble, 3 Robinson R., 12 White, S Riley
25	1 Barber, 2 Luke, 4 Halsall, 5 Robinson D., 6 Walsh, 7 Sterling, 8 Ebdon, 9 Adcock, 10 Charlery, 11 Kimble, 3 Robinson R., S White
26	1 Barber, 2 Luke, 4 Halsall, 5 Robinson D., 6 Walsh, 7 Sterling, 8 Cooper G., 9 Adcock, 10 Charlery, 11* Kimble, 3 Robinson R., S White
27	1 Barber, 2 Luke, 4 Halsall, 5 Robinson D., 6 Walsh, 7 Sterling, 8 Cooper G., 9 Adcock, 10 Charlery, 11 Kimble, 3 Robinson R., S White
28	1 Barber, 2 Luke, 4 Halsall, 5 Robinson D., 6 Walsh, 7 Sterling, 8 Cooper G., 9 Adcock, 10 Charlery, 11* Barnes, 3 Robinson R., S White
29	1 Barber, 2 Luke, 4 Halsall, 5 Robinson D., 6 Walsh, 7 Sterling, 8 Cooper G., 9 Adcock, 11 Barnes, 3 Robinson R., S Costello, S White
30	1 Barber, 2 Luke, 4 Halsall, 5 Robinson D., 6 Walsh, 7 Sterling, 8 Cooper G., 9 Adcock, 10 Riley, 11 Barnes, 3 Robinson R., S Costello, S White
31	1 Barber, 2 Luke, 4 Halsall, 5 Robinson D., 6 Walsh, 7 Sterling, 8 Cooper G., 9 Adcock, 10 Riley, 11 Barnes, 3 Robinson R., S Costello
32	2 Luke, 4 Halsall, 5 Robinson D., 6 Walsh, 7 Sterling, 8 Cooper G., 9 Adcock, 10 Riley, 11 Barnes, 3 Robinson R., 14 White
33	2 Luke, 4 Halsall, 5 Robinson D., 6 Walsh, 7 Sterling, 8 Cooper G., 9 Adcock, 10* Riley, 11 Barnes, 3 Robinson R., S Charlery
34	2 Luke, 4 Halsall, 5 Robinson D., 6 Walsh, 7 Sterling, 8 Cooper G., 9 Adcock, 10* Riley, 11 Barnes, 3 Robinson R., 12 Charlery, 14 Howarth/Butterworth
35	2 Luke, 4 Halsall, 5 Robinson D., 6 Walsh, 7 Sterling, 9 Adcock, 10* Riley, 11 Barnes, 3" Robinson R., 12 Charlery
36	2 Luke, 4 Halsall, 5 Robinson D., 6 Walsh, 7 Sterling, 8* Cooper G., 9 Adcock, 10 Charlery, 11* Barnes, 3 Robinson R., 12 Cooper S., 14 Riley, S Salmon
37	2 Luke, 4 Halsall, 5 Robinson D., 7 Sterling, 8 Cooper G., 9 Adcock, 10 Charlery, 11* Barnes, 3 Robinson R., 10* Cooper S., S Salmon
38	2 Luke, 4 Halsall, 5 Robinson D., 6 Walsh, 7 Sterling, 8 Cooper G., 9 Adcock, 12 Charlery, 11* Barnes, 3 Robinson R., 10 Cooper S.
39	2 Luke, 4 Halsall, 5 Robinson D., 6 Walsh, 7 Sterling, 8 Cooper G., 9 Adcock, 12 Charlery, 11* Barnes, 3 Robinson R., 14 Cooper S.
40	1 Salmon, 2 Luke, 4 Halsall, 5 Robinson D., 6 Walsh, 7 Sterling, 8 Cooper G., 9* Adcock, 10* Charlery, 11* Barnes, 3 Robinson R., 12 Riley, 14 Howarth, 14 Cooper S., 1 Bennett?
41	1 Salmon, 2 Luke, 4 Halsall, 5 Robinson D., 6 Walsh, 7 Sterling, 8 Cooper G., 9* Adcock, 10 Charlery, 11 Barnes, 3* Robinson R., 12 Riley, 5 Howarth, 14 Cooper S.
42	1 Salmon, 2 Luke, 4 White, 5 Robinson D., 6 Walsh, 7 Sterling, 8 Ebdon, 9* Adcock, 10 Charlery, 11" Barnes, 3* Robinson R., 12 Riley, 4 Butterworth
43	1 Salmon, 4 Halsall, 5 Robinson D., 7 Sterling, 8 Ebdon, 9* Adcock, 10 Charlery, 11 Kimble, 3* Robinson R., 12 Cooper S.
44	1 Salmon, 2 Luke, 4 Halsall, 5 Robinson D., 6 Howarth, 7 Sterling, 8 Ebdon, 9* Adcock, 10 Charlery, 11* Kimble, 3 Robinson R., 12 Cooper S.
45	1 Salmon, 2 Luke, 4 Halsall, 5 Robinson D., 6 Howarth, 7 Sterling, 8 Ebdon, 9* Adcock, 10 Charlery, 11 Kimble, 3 Robinson R., 12 Cooper S.
46	1 Salmon, 2 Luke, 4 Halsall, 5 Robinson D., 6 Howarth, 7 Sterling, 8 Ebdon, 9* Adcock, 10 Charlery, 11* Kimble, 3 Robinson R., 12 Cooper S.

F.A.Cup

1st	16 Nov	HARLOW TOWN	7-0	6-0	4341	Halsall Ster'g Riley Cooper G.2 Charley Culpin
2nd	7 Dec	READING	0-0	0-0	5328	
2/R.	17	Reading	0-1	0-0	4373	

Rumblelows (Football League) Cup

1/1L	20 Aug	ALDERSHOT	3-1	1-0	2731	Gavin 3
1/2L	27	Aldershot	2-1	1-0	1601	Halsall Gavin
2/1L	24 Sep	Wimbledon	2-1	2-1	2081	Sterling Charley
2/2L	8 Oct	WIMBLEDON	2-2	1-0	5939	Riley Kimble
3rd	29	NEWCASTLE UNITED	1-0	0-0	10382	Charley
4th	3 Dec	LIVERPOOL	1-0	1-0	14114	Kimble
5th	8 Jan	MIDDLESBROUGH	0-0	0-0	15302	
5/R.	12 Feb	Middlesbrough	0-1	0-0	21073	

Autoglass Trophy

Prel.	22 Oct	WREXHAM	2-0	0-0	1085	Charley Howarth
Prel.	14 Jan	Mansfield Town	1-2*	1-2	1771	Sterling (Abandoned 69 mins.)
Prel.	4 Feb	Mansfield Town	3-0	2-0	2578	Sterling Gavin O.G.
1st	18	SHREWSBURY TOWN	1-0	0-0	2049	Costello
2nd	25	EXETER CITY	1-0	0-0	2321	Charley
3rd	17 Mar	WREXHAM	3-1	2-0	3929	Charley Costello Riley
S/F 1 L	6 Apr	Stoke City	3-3	1-2	14355	Halsall Charley O.G.
S/F 2 L	15	STOKE CITY	0-1	0-0	12214	

Third Division Play-Offs

S/F 1L	11 May	HUDDERSFIELD TOWN	2-2	0-1	11751	Halsall Charley
S/F 2L	14	Huddersfield Town	2-1	0-1	16167	Sterling Cooper S.
Final*	24	Stockport County	2-1	0-0	35087	Charley 2

* Played at Wembley Stadium

Appearances Legend

- League Appearances † 42
- League Sub. Appear. †
- League Sub. non-Appear.
- (2 O.G.) League Goals
- Cup Appearances 16
- Cup Sub. Appear.
- Cup Sub. non-Appear.
- (2 O.G.) Cup Goals
- † Includes play-off matches.

Season Summary

The best season ever!! Early F.A.Cup exit, but Posh reach semi-finals of Rumbelow's (League) Cup, including victories over Wimbledon, Newcastle and Liverpool, plus reach Southern Final of Autoglass Trophy. Promotion to re-numbered 'First Division' following exciting play-off victory over Stockport County at Wembley Stadium.

League Table

	P	W	D	L	F	A	Pts
Brentford	46	25	7	14	81	55	82
Birmingham	46	23	12	11	80	51	81
Huddersfield	46	22	12	12	59	38	78
Stoke	46	21	14	11	69	49	77
Stockport	46	22	10	14	75	51	76
Posh	46	20	14	12	65	54	74
WBA	46	19	14	13	64	49	71
Bournemouth	46	19	14	13	58	58	71
Fulham	46	19	13	14	52	48	70
Orient	46	18	11	17	52	52	65
Hartlepool	46	18	11	17	57	65	65
Reading	46	16	13	17	59	59	59
Bolton	46	17	17	19	57	59	59
Hull	46	14	17	15	56	56	59
Wigan	46	15	19	19	54	59	58
Bradford	46	15	14	17	62	59	58
Preston	46	15	12	19	61	72	57
Chester	46	14	14	18	56	72	57
Swansea	46	14	17	18	55	65	53
Exeter	46	14	11	21	57	80	51
Bury	46	13	12	21	55	74	47
Shrewsbury	46	13	12	23	53	68	47
Torquay	46	13	8	25	42	63	47
Darlington	46	10	7	29	56	90	37

The Promotion Squad
1991/92 season

(Top) Halsall, Kimble, Butterworth, Barber, Charlery, Turner, Culpin, Pope.
(Middle) Harvey, Costello, Swales, Robinson D., Bennett, Welsh, Gavin, Curtis, White, Oakes.
(Bottom) Ebdon, McInerney, Sterling, Fuccillo, Turner, McElhinney, Luke, Riley, Cooper.

ADVANCED SUBSCRIBERS

Mick Groom

Pat Groom

Pete McCray – Canberra, Australia

Helen Hollington

Lynn Sexton

John Motson

Andrew Hart Loyal Supporter in Plymouth

Graham Spackman

John A. Harris

David Keats Thornton Heath

Derek Hyde

Donald Ashwood

Chris Harte

B.H. Standish

Mr. L. Burgess

Geoffrey Wright

Raymond Shaw

Duncan Watt

P.H. Whitehead

Mr. Harry Kay

J. Ringrose

Fred Lee, Plymouth Argyle

Jonathan Hall

Steve Emms

W.D. Phillips

K.P. Wood

Richard Wells

A.H. Atkins – Canada

Brian Tabner

Bill and Sheila Evans

Martin Simons – Belgium

John Treleven

David Jowett

A & J A Waterman

Charles B. Ducker

Arch Woodard

Mr. P. Keane

Willy Østby (Norway)

British Non League Programme Club

To Tim a True Posh Fan

Martyn Wilcockson

M. Payne

For David Downs and Marion Peer

David Gale. Thanks for the memories

J. Reed

Miss K. Lanman

Ian John Boyden

Eric Trundle & Roy Trundle

Colin Cameron

Geoff Allman

Michael Campbell

John J. Byrne, Barrhead, Glasgow

Dave Smith

Andrew Treherne

Leslie Rice

Lars–Olof Wendler – Sweden

Gareth Anderson

Pete Day

Thanks,Pete,Journo II Chris Turner–Chris Long

Romford – Daft about Posh Facts

H. Peters – Holland

Mr. L.A. Zammit

Ray Hopkins – Bradford City Fan

Christer Svensson – Sweden

Francis Devine, Dublin

Fiachra O'Duibhinn, Dublin

Phil loves Lisa forever

P. Baxter

Paul Matthews, Aylesbury

Adrian Randall

Peter

Jonny Stokkeland – Norway

Moira and Fred Furness, North Shields

Sean Woodward, Now Then, St. Neots.

Ian Naylor

Robert Craig

Paul Turner from Paston

Lee Wood & Paul Wood

Ian Pearson

To Steven All My Love Pauline

Paul Kidston

Trond Isaksen – Norway

Robert Lilliman

Patrick, Miriam and Danny Knight

David Lumb

Terry Frost

David Ingleby

Stephen Kieran Byrne

Cyril Hurry

Roy Hurry

David Hurry

Christopher Hooker, Ajax, Ontario, Canada

Donald Maddams

Simon and Denise Fitch

Adrian Durham – Exiled but Loyal

Nigel Earth

Steven Earth

Peter Frankland of Oldham

Roger Wash

For Geoff, a Dream Fulfilled

Bob Coull

Michael McConkey, Luton

Michael Pell – Thurlby

Tony, Merry Xmas love Tina & Babe

Alan Hindley

John Hann, Helensburgh

Chris & Rosemary Smalley, Gt. Yarmouth

David G. Smith, Methwold,Norfolk

Mr. R. Betts

Jason R. Edwards 25-12-92

Catherine & Posh, I Love You!

K.W.G. Mayes

Paul Snape

Ray Bickel

David Earnshaw, Belper, Derbyshire

P.R. Rowe

R.H. White

Peter Cogle Aberdeen

Graham Cornish

Dougie Stitcher Posh's Greatest Fan

Mr. R. Winterbone

Herbert & Mary Jackson

Lawrence Batterham

Kevin L. Martin

Bryn Brothers

Julian Barrasso 165 Oundle Road, Woodston

Lets Beat Those Cambridge B****s, Turner '92

Stuart Maloney Wishes Posh Good Luck

Brian Dennis

Felicitations-Bill Mckee-Hull, Quebec, Canada

Nigel Rose, The Holy Grail

Neil Ellis Melton Mowbray

John & Linda Hurrey

Paul Heanes

Alan Heanes

Phil – 20th Anniversary 14/10/72 Doncaster R.

Miss Karen Sanderson, Oadby, Leics.

For Billy Walker, True Posh Fan.

Richard Bedford of Benwick

David Parnell

Sue & Dave Hennis, Bayswater, London

Wembley May 92, Colin Jennings

Dave Skerritt

Wembley 1992, The Dream Came True

Stephen Burges

Andy & Jo Barks

Malcolm John Walker

Phillip Sibley

Patrick John Baylis

Wappie is Dutch is Posh

Jeremy Manners

Nigel Cowling

Jonathan Dickens

ADVANCED SUBSCRIBERS

Chris, Richard, Timothy & Nicholas Sheppard

Philip Harburn, Allen Road, Peterborough

R.W. Hunter - Rowe

To Stephen Ivill love from Catherine

Paul J. Desborough

Dennis & John Ludman

Steven Wickens

Super Posh - Ian & Jack Gow

Craig Skinner the Dream Comes True

Ian, Lynn, Gavin & Jonathan Slater

Jon Happy Christmas 1992 love Gill

Ian Thomas Ratcliffe

Tony Self, regular from 1945!

Michael Barry Collins

John Pickard

Gollings - Posh through and through

Matthew Ray Empingham, Rutland, Christmas 1992

Neil Ellis Melton Mowbray

'What A Year!' Happy 40th Angus

Trafford James

Jack & June Beeby

Remember The "Seven".

David & Jane James

Mr. Anthony William Groom

Andrew Dembicki A True Posh Supporter

David Thompson Class one Referee, Stamford

Matthew Allen Chatteris, Cambs.

Toby & Daniel Wood, Glebe Road

Paul Brookbanks

To Peter from Mum, Happy Christmas

1st Goalkeeper for the Club 1934

Chris Stallebross

Steve Lane

Mr. R.N. Griffin

Mr. R.N. Griffin

To A Successful Future - Robert Redhead

Dave Reed - The No.1 Posh Fan

Graham Watson

"Emery was the Greatest" - Bob Rawlings

To Dad from Jim and Loraine

Happy Christmas Ken, up the Posh

Mike, Diana, Ceri & Amber Stokes

Timothy Davison

Chris Richards

Gill, Peter & Neil Williams

To Jim from Loraine

To Daddy love Rachel & Jamie

John Connolly

Stephen & Joanne Thorpe

Julian Summers

Justin Bentley

Terence John Rawlings 'Bayview' Ufford, Stamford

Mark Walter - Posh forever

Michael Sulch

Simon Paul Bosett No. 1 Posh Fan

Joe Rollings

Darren Butcher A Loyal Posh Supporter

Ian J. Behagg

Arthur White - loyal supporter of Posh

Kevin William Veale

James Way, Swavesey

Stephen Way, Bluntisham

Thanks for all my many memories

Tony, Karl, Mark: Holly Bush

Lee for Xmas 1992

R.D.F. at Orient, make some noise

Andrew Turner

Simon,Jonathan & Matthew Hobbs-Good Luck

Best Wishes Posh, David Laud & Family

Dad for your Ruby Wedding

R. Aucott

S.C. Regan

Wayne Mark Daly - aged 13

Sorry Susan, more boring football, Ian.

Claret & Amber, Blue & White

Graham Haynes

Martin Dexter

V. King

Christine Malinowski Posh's most loyal fan

Rodney D. Crabb

Christmas '92 love from Mum & Dad

Andrew Dexter

Supporter since 1946 - Geoff Dexter

A. Sulch

For the one I love, Amanda

Chris Hornby - keep going - King's Lynn

Colin Day - keep going Brotherhoods!

Mark Tyler

Barry Watson

To David love from Gran - Christmas 1992

To Matthew love from Nan - Christmas 1992

Thanks Dad for that spare ticket - Yvonne

Trevor Pearson - a Lifelong Posh Supporter

Kevin, Simon & Robert Green - Nov. 1992

"Knotty Was There - Where Were You?"

A. Loades

Happy Christmas - Mr. Northfield

Andrew Mash

From John, Jean, Stuart & Paul Marlow

C. Bland

Rob Jex

Grant Saunders, Well Done Posh

Harry Sykes

To My Husband J.Morris, Xmas 1992

Proud Posh Supporter-Paul Starr, Wellingboro'

John F. Pope

Good Luck to Posh in 1992/93

A Posh Birthday Arnold Maddams - love Pete

Up the Posh - Pete Maddams

Mr. C. Hallam

Douglas Lamming

Simon Hull

Margaret Headland

Stephen Baxter

Mr.Peter J.C.Lane & Mrs.Sandee Lane

Happy Christmas Paul from Barbara 1992

Tim, Happy Xmas 1992, Denise, Mike & Emily

Keith Smith

Mike McCarthy

Andrew Anderson

Paul Dennis - No more Shandy Drinking

Mark Swann - "Halsall, You've Done Nothing!"

Never mind Clapton, Turner is God

This Book Belongs to Glyn Vaughan

Alan Davies

Mum, Merry Christmas Love Joanna

Mr. Peter Wintersgill

Miss B.C. Atkinson

David, Charmaine & Katie Miami Green

Alan Platt

To Dad Love Carly & Gary

D.S. Allen

G.E. Ward

P.A. Mason

True Supporters Trevor & Rita Clarke

D.S. Allen

Happy Christmas - David Fitzjohn

Michael Jones

Mrs. L.S. Ross

Mrs. L.S. Ross

Adrian Stratton

Christopher Stratton

Sharon Broughton

Stephanie Bentley - Dedicated Posh Fan

Stephen Bruster A London Road Faithful

Mark Asplen

Mr. David Marzy

Arran Matthews